OXFORD
TWENTY-FIRST CENTURY
APPROACHES TO LITERATURE

OXFORD
TWENTY-FIRST CENTURY
APPROACHES TO LITERATURE

Archives
Power, Truth, and Fiction

Edited by
ANDREW PRESCOTT
AND
ALISON WIGGINS

Great Clarendon Street, Oxford, OX2 6DP,
United Kingdom

Oxford University Press is a department of the University of Oxford.
It furthers the University's objective of excellence in research, scholarship,
and education by publishing worldwide. Oxford is a registered trade mark of
Oxford University Press in the UK and in certain other countries

© The several contributors 2023

The moral rights of the authors have been asserted

All rights reserved. No part of this publication may be reproduced, stored in
a retrieval system, or transmitted, in any form or by any means, without the
prior permission in writing of Oxford University Press, or as expressly permitted
by law, by licence or under terms agreed with the appropriate reprographics
rights organization. Enquiries concerning reproduction outside the scope of the
above should be sent to the Rights Department, Oxford University Press, at the
address above

Chapter 23, 'Accidentally on Purpose: Denying Any Responsibility for the
Accidental Archive' is available online and distributed under the terms of a Creative
Commons Attribution – Non Commercial – No Derivatives 4.0 International
licence (CC BY-NC-ND 4.0), a copy of which is available at
http://creativecommons.org/licenses/by-nc-nd/4.0/.

You must not circulate this work in any other form
and you must impose this same condition on any acquirer

Published in the United States of America by Oxford University Press
198 Madison Avenue, New York, NY 10016, United States of America

British Library Cataloguing in Publication Data

Data available

Library of Congress Control Number: 2023942442

ISBN 9780198829324

Pod

Links to third party websites are provided by Oxford in good faith and
for information only. Oxford disclaims any responsibility for the materials
contained in any third party website referenced in this work.

ACKNOWLEDGEMENTS

Most of all, we are grateful to the volume's contributors whose willingness to collaborate has made this venture a reality and whose care, generosity, and insights have opened up the volume's possibilities. In addition, we acknowledge and thank the following. The UK Arts and Humanities Research Council funded two symposia at the University of Glasgow in 2018, during the early stages of scoping the volume. Paul Strohm, as series editor, has offered encouragement and advice from the start, and David Thomas and Victoria Van Hyning have been there at crucial points for very helpful conversations. The initial proposal and complete volume draft were read by anonymous peer reviewers whose depth of attention and astute analyses benefitted the book throughout. The editorial team at OUP have supported production at every step. Colleagues at the University of Glasgow have provided a community and an enriching environment for these conversations.

CONTENTS

List of Illustrations	x
Notes on Editorial Policy	xiv
Abbreviations	xvi
Notes on Contributors	xx
CAROLYN STEEDMAN *Foreword*	xxviii

ANDREW PRESCOTT AND ALISON WIGGINS Introduction   1

Part I CONCEPTIONS

1 MICHELLE CASWELL 'The Archive' is Not an Archives: Acknowledging the Intellectual Contributions of Archival Studies   21

2 LOUISE CRAVEN Where and What Are the Boundaries of the Archive?   37

3 HARIZ HALILOVICH AND ANNE J. GILLILAND Digitality and the Reconfigured Global Archive(s) of Forced Migration   53

4 JAMES LOWRY The Record as Command   69

5 ANDREW HOSKINS New Memory and the Archive   87

6 NIAMH MOORE Response to 'Conceptions'   100

Part II FRAMEWORKS

7 ANDREW PRESCOTT Appraisal and Original Order: The Power Structures of the Archive   107

8 ANNA SEXTON Archival Education and Professionalism   121

9 LISA GITELMAN Metadata   134

viii CONTENTS

10 RUTH AHNERT AND SEBASTIAN E. AHNERT Networks — 145

11 MICHAEL MOSS AND DAVID THOMAS Authenticating and Evaluating Evidence — 160

12 VICTORIA VAN HYNING AND HEATHER WOLFE More Content, Less Context: Rethinking Access — 174

13 JANET FOSTER Response to 'Frameworks' — 192

Part III MATERIALITIES

14 ALISON WIGGINS The Materiality of Written Textual Forms — 197

15 SIMON POPPLE Sound and Vision: The Audio-Visual Archive — 215

16 CATHERINE RICHARDSON Doors into the Archives: Material Objects and Document Collections — 233

17 JANE BIRKIN Archives, Art, and the Performativity of Practice — 251

18 EIRINI GOUDAROULI Digital Innovation and Archival Thinking — 267

19 LAURA MANDELL Response to 'Materialities' — 282

Part IV ENCOUNTERS AND EVOLUTION

20 ERIC KETELAAR The Agency of Archivers — 287

21 PAUL LIHOMA State Power and the Shaping of Archives in Malawi — 296

22 PAUL STROHM Archival Impulses and the Gunpowder Plot — 310

23 NADINE AKKERMAN AND PETE LANGMAN Accidentally on Purpose: Denying Any Responsibility for the Accidental Archive — 323

24 JULIE A. FISHER Response to 'Encounters and Evolution' — 337

Part V NARRATORS

25 KARINA BERAS AND JARRETT MARTIN DRAKE From Repositories of Failure to Archives of Abolition — 343

26 RACHEL DOUGLAS Writer–Editors Making the Haitian and Caribbean Archives Talk — 359

27 SYLVIA FEDERICO Finding Women in the Archives of 1381 — 375

28 NORMA CLARKE On Family History and Archives — 386

29 RUTH MACLENNAN An Artist Unpacks the Archives — 397

30 ALAN STEWART Response to 'Narrators' — 420

CONTENTS   ix

Part VI   ERASURES AND EXCLUSION

31 LAE'L HUGHES-WATKINS   America's Scrapbook: A Reckoning in the
Archives   425

32 REBECCA KAHN   Irreconcilable Archives: Queer Collections and the
Truth and Reconciliation Commission   437

33 REBECCA ABBY WHITING   Destruction and Displacement:
The 2003 War and the Struggle for Iraq's Records   455

34 EDWINA ASHIE-NIKOI, EMMANUEL ADJEI, AND MUSAH ADAMS
Of Bonfires, Mindsets, and Policies: The Multi-Causal Matrix
of Silence in Ghanaian Public Archives   471

35 KIRSTEN WELD   Response to 'Erasures and Exclusion'   489

VERNE HARRIS Afterword   492
Index   494

LIST OF ILLUSTRATIONS

6.1. Dorothy Berry, 'I feel like the Archives Sheriff', Twitter, 5 January 2021.   101

7.1. The original passenger lists in The National Archives (BT 26) were used to reimagine artistically the destroyed Windrush landing cards. These recreated cards were used for the exhibition *Windrush: Arrivals 1948*, undertaken by Goldsmiths, University of London, in 2019, co-curated by John Price and Will Cenci, relocated to City Hall and Lewisham Shopping Centre the same year: www.gold.ac.uk/windrush. The passenger information in the recreated cards was historically correct although their visual appearance was based on earlier iterations, given that the original cards had been destroyed. Photo: John Price.   111

7.2. Visitors looking at the 1,027 recreated individual landing cards, each representing a passenger who arrived on the MV *Empire Windrush* at Tilbury docks on 22 June 1948. Photo: by John Price showing the 2019 Goldsmiths historically contextualized art installation, *Windrush: Arrivals 1948*.   112

7.3. Records Continuum Model.   115

10.1. Nodes and edges in an undirected network.   146

10.2. Nodes and edges in a directed network.   148

10.3. An illustration of betweenness centrality.   152

10.4. Bipartite network of archives and correspondents.   157

10.5. Projected networks of archives and correspondents.   158

12.1. 'Library of Time', created by Jer Thorp, 2018, as part of 'Serendipity Engine' for the Library of Congress at https://labs.loc.gov/work/experiments/innovator-in-residence-jer-thorp/. Screenshot taken 26 January 2022, 10:41:50am, Eastern Time, from https://library-of-time.glitch.me/.   187

14.1. King James VI to his mother Mary, Queen of Scots, 29 January 1581. The inside of the letter, The National Archives, SP 53/11 f. 44r (reproduced with permission).   202

LIST OF ILLUSTRATIONS   xi

14.2. King James VI to his mother Mary, Queen of Scots, 29 January 1581. The outside address and endorsement of the letter. The National Archives, SP 53/11 f. 44v (reproduced with permission).   203

15.1. Title page of the Atlas Group Archive from https://commons.wikimedia. org/wiki/File:Online_archive_of_The_Atlas_Group.png accessed 14 February 2022. CC BY-SA 4.0.   219

15.2. Michael C. Coldwell, Cross Templar Street, 1901–2017. From *The Remote Viewer* exhibition at the Brotherton Gallery, Leeds, 5 October 2018. Reproduced courtesy of the author. Created using archival materials courtesy of University of Leeds Special Collections (photographs of properties situated in the Quarry Hill unhealthy area, taken December 1900 and January 1901).   224

15.3. Archives+ at Manchester Central Library front entrance; image reproduced by permission.   226

15.4. 'Comforting' archival media supports © Simon Popple 2022.   229

16.1. Dr John Bargrave's cabinet of curiosities, Canterbury Cathedral Archives and Library (reproduced with permission).   234

16.2. A page from Bargrave's travel journal, CCA-U11/8, showing the town of Sancerre (reproduced with permission).   237

16.3. John Evelyn's cabinet on a stand, 1652, John Hammond / Museum of the Home: 46/1979.   238

16.4. Cupboard doors from the Exchequer of Receipt, TNA E 409 (reproduced with permission).   241

16.5. Corporation cupboard of boxes, Shakespeare Birthplace Trust, STRST: SBT L513 (1594 002). CC-BY-NC-ND © Shakespeare Birthplace Trust.   244

16.6. Outside Studios' 2012 rebuild of Roald Dahl's writing hut for the Roald Dahl Museum and Story Centre, Great Missenden; image reproduced by permission.   245

16.7. Photograph of Francis Bacon's Studio by Perry Ogden. Collection & image © Hugh Lane Gallery, Dublin © The Estate of Francis Bacon. All rights reserved/DACS 2023.   247

17.1. Still from *El Rastro* at 0'25" © Jane Birkin 2014.   253

17.2. Still from *El Rastro* at 2'27" © Jane Birkin 2014.   255

17.3. Still from *El Rastro* at 4'41" © Jane Birkin 2014.   259

17.4. Still from *El Rastro* at 5'08" © Jane Birkin 2014.   262

17.5. Still from *El Rastro* at 9'17" © Jane Birkin 2014.   264

26.1. Triangulation: Working Definition. After Susan Greenberg, *A Poetics of Editing* (London: Palgrave Macmillan, 2018), 19.   359

26.2. The triangle of the transatlantic slave trade.   360

26.3. Franckétienne, *L'Oiseau schizophone* (Paris: Jean-Michel Place, 1998), 386.   365

xii LIST OF ILLUSTRATIONS

26.4. Kamau Brathwaite, 'Dream Haiti', in *DS (2): dreamstories* (New York: New Directions, 2007), 195. — 366

29.1. *Memory Retrieval Systems* poster, designed by Kapitza 2001 © Ruth Maclennan. — 398

29.2. *The Gatekeepers*, single channel video, 14'34", 2001 (installation view, Lewis Glucksman Gallery, 2014) © Ruth Maclennan. — 399

29.3. *Calling all workers*, single channel video, 10'52", 2004, video still © Ruth Maclennan. — 400

29.4. *Dialogue #3 (That's not for me to say)*, single channel video, 11'58", 2002, video still © Ruth Maclennan. — 401

29.5a. and 29.5b. Photograph from Beatrice and Sydney Webb Archive and National Institute for Industrial Psychology Archives, London School of Economics (reproduced with permission). — 402

29.6. *Calling all workers*, single channel video, 10'52", 2004 © Ruth Maclennan. — 403

29.7. *We Saw It—Like a Flash*, single channel video projection, 46'52", 2003–2005 (footage ©BBC). — 404

29.8. *Satellite Contact*, with Uriel Orlow, synchronized two channel video projection 1h 3'39" © Ruth Maclennan and Uriel Orlow. — 405

29.9. *Capital*, single channel video, 16'54", 2007 production still © Ruth Maclennan. — 406

29.10. *Re: the Archive, the Image, and the Very Dead Sheep*, with Uriel Orlow London: Double Agents, 2004 © Ruth Maclennan and Uriel Orlow. — 407

29.11. *Archway Polytechnic in a Suitcase*, installation view in the exhibition, *The Eagle Document*, Stephen Lawrence Gallery, University of Greenwich, 2009 © Ruth Maclennan. — 408

29.12. *Dialogue #5 (What is your problem?)*, four channel video installation and performance, 23', photo by Rowan Durrant 2009–2010 © Ruth Maclennan. — 409

29.13. *Unpacking Archway Polytechnic in a Suitcase*, performance, *The Eagle Document* symposium, Stephen Lawrence Gallery, University of Greenwich, 2009 © Ruth Maclennan. — 409

29.14. *Hide*, twelve-hour live online video broadcast, production photograph © Anna Hart, 2010 © Ruth Maclennan. — 410

29.15. *Valley of Castles*, single channel video, projection, 19'26", 2007 production photograph © Alexander Ugay © Ruth Maclennan. — 411

29.16. *Valley of Castles*, video still from eagle camera © Ruth Maclennan. — 412

29.17. *Anarcadia*, single channel HD video, projection, 35', 2010–2011 video still © Ruth Maclennan. — 413

29.18. *Capture* synchronized two channel video projection, 3'16", 2007 © Ruth Maclennan. — 413

29.19. *The Railway Workers*, series of framed anonymous photographs from
the Documentary Film and Audio Archive of Kazakhstan, 1939–1961
(reproduced with permission). 414

29.20. *The Faces They Have Vanished*, wall text, installation at Institute of
Contemporary Interdisciplinary Arts (ICIA), University of Bath, 2013
© Ruth Maclennan. 415

29.21. *Call of North*, single channel HD video, 25', 2015 video still © Ruth
Maclennan. 416

NOTES ON EDITORIAL POLICY

Further Reading

Each chapter in this volume is followed by a list of Further Reading that selects some of the key works in the field while avoiding too much repetition between chapters or across in the whole volume. Taking the lead from Michelle Caswell's opening call to reach across disciplines, the Further Reading aims to achieve a balance between publications by archive professionals and those from other fields, such as literary critics, historians, artists, and social scientists. We hope that these references will help researchers from a range of disciplinary backgrounds to weave into the own publications references to research by archive professionals and vice versa.

Transcriptions

Transcriptions from historical primary sources are lightly modernized in so far as the use of u/v and i/j is normalized to follow modern conventions. Abbreviations are expanded. In other respects, the spelling and punctuation follow the original source texts.

Volume Structure

The chapters in this volume are organized within six sections: Conceptions, Frameworks, Materialities, Encounters and Evolution, Narrators, and Erasures and Exclusion. These topics enact an approach to the archive that is thematic and where the emphasis is upon the archive's fluidity and plurality (rather than organizing the volume by, say, historical period, discipline, profession, genre, or media). Each section is curated to include a range of perspectives that reflect current critical themes and concerns. The 'Response' in each section draws out and highlights key themes from the chapters and sets these in the context of the respondent's own distinct position, or in the light of broader theoretical frames, thereby offering readers another entry point into the ongoing debates and unsettled matters that are threaded throughout the volume. This book in no way attempts to offer a flat map or an evenly narrated story of the archive. Its polyphony acknowledges the existence today of the archival multiverse and of the shimmering, endlessly evolving, multifaceted nature of the archive.

ABBREVIATIONS

A2A	Access to Archives programme [UK]
ACARM	Association of Commonwealth Archivists and Records Managers
ACM	Association for Computing Machinery
AHRC	Arts and Humanities Research Council [UK]
AI	Artificial Intelligence
ANC	African National Congress
ANSI	American National Standards Institute
ARA	Archives and Records Association UK and Ireland
AV	Audio-Visual
BRCC	Ba'th Regional Command Collection
CAS	Computational Archival Science
CCA	Canterbury Cathedral Archives
CC0	Creative Commons Zero Licence
CPA	Coalition Provisional Authority
CT	Computerized Tomography
DACS	Describing Archives: A Content Standard
DAMS	Digital Asset Management Systems
DC	District Commissioner
DCDC	Discovering Collections, Discovering Communities [Conference]
dLOC	Digital Library of the Caribbean
DTD	Document Type Description
DVD	Digital Versatile Disc
EAD	Encoded Archival Description
EMLO	Early Modern Letters Online
EMMO	Early Modern Manuscripts Online
EVA	Ethyl Vinyl Acetate

GALA	Gay and Lesbian Memory in Action
GBC	Ghana Broadcasting Corporation
GDPR	General Data Protection Regulation
GFIC	Ghana Film Industry Corporation
GLOW	Gay and Lesbian Organization of the Witwatersrand
GNA	Ghana News Agency
HD	High Definition
HMC	Historical Manuscripts Commission [UK]
HTML	HyperText Markup Language
HTR	Handwritten Text Recognition
HRW	Human Rights Watch
ICA	International Council on Archives
ICE	United States Immigration and Customs Enforcement
ICIA	Institute of Contemporary Interdisciplinary Arts
IIIF	International Image Interoperability Framework
IIRIRA	Illegal Immigration Reform and Immigration Responsibility Act [US]
IDP	Immigration Defense Project
IFLA	International Federation of Library Associations
IJA	Iraqi Jewish Archive
INLA	Iraq National Library and Archive
IRCA	Immigration Reform and Control Act [US]
IRMT	International Records Management Trust
IRO	Independent Research Organization [UK]
ISAD-G	International Standard Archival Description (General)
ISD	Information Services Department [Ghana]
ISO	International Organization for Standardization
JISC	Joint Information Systems Committee
LAGO	Lesbians and Gays Against Oppression
LGBTQI	Lesbian, Gay, Bisexual, Transgender, Queer and Intersex
LIS	Library & Information Studies
LOC	Library of Congress
LOCKSS	Lots of Copies Keep Stuff Safe
MARC	Machine-Readable Cataloguing Record
MCP	Malawi Congress Party
MERL	Museum of English Rural Life
MLIS	Master of Library & Information Science
MRI	Magnetic Resonance Imaging
MSD	Management Services Division

MUFC	Mandela United Football Club
NAG	National Archives of Ghana
NAM	National Archives of Malawi
NARA	National Archives and Records Administration [US]
NCGLE	National Coalition for Gay and Lesbian Equality
NCT	National Compensation Tribunal
NGO	Non-governmental Organisation
NRA	National Register of Archives [UK]
NSA	National Security Agency [US]
NSF	National Science Foundation [US]
NYIC	New York Immigration Coalition
OCLC	Online Computer Library Center
OCR	Optical Character Recognition
OED	Oxford English Dictionary
OLGA	Organization of Gay and Lesbian Activists
OPC	Office of the President and Cabinet [Malawi]
PCPA	Permanent Committee on Public Archives [Ghana]
PDF	Portable Document Format
PIP	Particular Instance Paper
PLO	People's Land Organization
PRAAD	Public Records and Archives Administration Department [Ghana]
PRO	Public Record Office [UK]
PAO	Public Archives Ordinance
PNDC	Provisional National Defence Council [Ghana]
QR code	Quick Response Code
RFID	Radio-frequency Identification
RLUK	Research Libraries UK
RTI	Reflectance Transformation Imaging
SAA	Society of American Archivists
SALSA	Spanish and Latino Student Association
SBT	Shakespeare Birthplace Trust
SGML	Standard Generalized Markup Language
SPIRES	Stanford Physics Information Retrieval System
SPO	State Papers Online
STAND	Student Activism Now Documented
STEM	Science, Technology, Engineering, and Mathematics
STOP	StoryTelling & Organizing Project
TAVP	Texas After Violence Project

TEI	Text Encoding Initiative
TGIJP	Transgender, Gender Variant, and Intersex Justice Project
TK	Traditional Knowledge
TNA	The National Archives [UK]
TRC	Truth and Reconciliation Commission
URI	Uniform Resource Identifier
USG	United States Government
VHS	Video Home System
VIAF	Virtual International Authority File
W3C	World Wide Web Consortium
WMD	Weapons of Mass Destruction
WWW	World Wide Web
XML	Extensible Markup Language
XRF	X-ray Fluorescence

NOTES ON CONTRIBUTORS

Musah Adams, PhD, is Senior Lecturer in the Department of Information Studies, University of Ghana. He is the former president of the Archivists and Records Management Association of Ghana. Before joining the University of Ghana in 2002, he worked as a records officer in a commercial bank for eighteen years. His recent publications include *Information Studies in Ghana: A Reader* (2017; with A. Alemna, P. Dadziem, and E. Adjei) and articles on health information behaviour of graduate students and records management and football administration in Ghana.

Emmanuel Adjei, PhD, is Associate Professor in the Department of Information Studies, University of Ghana where he has been a faculty member since 2000. He was educated at the University of Ghana and UCL. His publications include *Freedom of Information: Implications for Records Management in Ghana* (with L. Woode, 2011) and *Information Studies in Ghana: A Reader* (with A. Alemna, P. Dadzie, and M. Adams, 2017). He has also published a wide range of articles on records management in Ghana, with a particular emphasis on medical recordkeeping.

Ruth Ahnert is Professor of Literary History and Digital Humanities at Queen Mary University of London. She is the author of *The Rise of Prison Literature in the Sixteenth Century* (2013), editor of a special edition of *Renaissance Studies* entitled *Re-Forming the Psalms in Tudor England* (2015), and co-author (with Sebastian Ahnert, Catherine Coleman, and Scott Weingart) of *The Network Turn: Changing Perspectives in the Humanities* (2020). She is Principal Investigator on the AHRC-funded project *Living with Machines*, Co-Investigator on the AHRC-funded project *Networking Archives*, and co-editor (with Elaine Treharne) of the book series Stanford Text Technologies.

Sebastian E. Ahnert is a University Lecturer at the University of Cambridge, in the Department of Chemical Engineering and Biotechnology. His research interests lie on the interface between theoretical physics and biology, with a focus on algorithmic complexity and network analysis. He has published over sixty articles in a number of journals, including Science, Nature, Cell, PNAS, Royal Society Interface, and English Literary History, and has just published a monograph with Ruth Ahnert, entitled *Tudor Networks of Power*.

NOTES ON CONTRIBUTORS xxi

Nadine Akkerman, PhD, FRHistS is Professor of Early Modern Literature and Culture at the Centre for Arts in Society at Leiden University. Her book *Invisible Agents: Women and Espionage in Seventeenth-Century Britain* won the Society for the Study of Early Modern Women and Gender prize for the best book published on women and gender, 2018. She has edited the Correspondence of Elizabeth Stuart, Queen of Bohemia, and written a biography of Elizabeth (2021). She a currently leading a large-scale European Research Council Consolidator Grant on early modern manuscript culture and mediated authorship.

Edwina Ashie-Nikoi, PhD, is Lecturer in the Department of Information Studies, University of Ghana and affiliated with the University of Ghana's Institute of African Studies. With a background in African Diaspora history, she is interested in how culture and history are traditionally remembered, documented, and represented in African/diasporan cultural systems. She is on the advisory council of the Archivists and Records Management Association of Ghana and recently assisted with the establishment of Ghana's first community archives.

Karina Beras is a PhD student in anthropology at Cornell University and studied previously at the University of Michigan and Cornell University. Her research interests are centred around migration, citizenship, kinship, and identity; specifically, how the construction of kinship and its role in identity formation are based on cultural contexts and can be informed by notions of citizenship and the state. Prior to her doctoral studies, Karina served in various student services roles at Barnard College and Swarthmore College.

Jane Birkin is an artist, designer, and scholar. She is a Research Fellow at Winchester School of Art, University of Southampton, and has worked in archives for many years. In her art practice she works with description techniques that define and manage the photographic image, acting as a platform for exploring time and temporal progression. She has exhibited and performed widely and has written extensively on photography and archive and her monograph *Archive, Photography and the Language of Administration* was published in 2021.

Michelle Caswell, PhD, is Professor of Archival Studies in the Department of Information Studies at the University of California Los Angeles (UCLA) and the co-founder of the South Asian American Digital Archive (www.saada.org), an online repository that documents and provides access to the diverse stories of South Asian Americans. She is the author of *Archiving the Unspeakable: Silence, Memory and the Photographic Record in Cambodia* (2014), as well as *Urgent Archives: Enacting Liberatory Memory Work* (2021).

Norma Clarke is Emeritus Professor of English Literature and Creative Writing at Kingston University. Her books include *Dr Johnson's Women, The Rise and Fall of the Woman of Letters, Queen of the Wits: A Life of Laetitia Pilkington,* and *Brothers of the Quill: Oliver Goldsmith in Grub Street.* She reviews regularly for the *TLS* and other literary journals and has published five novels for children. She is currently at work on a sequel to *Not Speaking.*

Louise Craven is currently a freelance archives researcher and volunteer archivist. She was Head of Cataloguing at the National Archives of England and Wales (TNA), and worked previously for the Historical Manuscript Commission and the Greater London Record Office, now the London Metropolitan Archives. She edited *What Are Archives? Cultural and Theoretical Perspectives: A Reader* (2008). She has published a number of journal articles and book chapters on archival subjects.

Rachel Douglas is Reader in French and Comparative Literature at the University of Glasgow. Her work focuses on Caribbean literature and film in French and English with a special focus on Haiti and its writers. Her most recent monograph, *Making the Black Jacobins: C. L. R. James and the Drama of History*, is published by Duke University Press, 2019. Other work includes *Frankétienne and Rewriting: A Work in Progress* (2009), the first single-author monograph on Haiti's leading writer and visual artist.

Jarrett Martin Drake is a doctoral student in anthropology at Harvard University, where he engages in a variety of archival, educational, and organizing projects that pertain to prison abolition. Prior to Harvard, he was the Digital Archivist at Princeton University as well as an advisory archivist for *A People's Archives of Police Violence in Cleveland*. During Drake's time at Princeton, he volunteered as an instructor in the New Jersey Scholarship and Transformative Education in Prisons (NJ-STEP) Consortium through the Princeton Prison Teaching Initiative, teaching preparatory writing and introductory college composition.

Sylvia Federico is Professor of English at Bates College. Her publications include *New Troy: Fantasies of Empire in the Late Middle Ages* (2003) and (edited with Elizabeth Scala) *The Post-Historical Middle Ages* (2009). Her most recent book, *The Classicist Writings of Thomas Walsingham: 'Worldly Cares' at St Albans Abbey* (2016), considers Thomas Walsingham as a major overlooked contemporary of Chaucer. She has also recently published an article discussing the 1381 rebels' use of the English road system as part of their discourse of resistance.

Julie A. Fisher is an educator and historian of early America. Currently at the National Historical Publications and Records Commission of the US National Archives, she has previously worked with the Yale Indian Papers Project, the National Park Service, the American Philosophical Society, and Bard High School early College in Washington, DC. She is the co-author of *Ninigret, Sachem of the Niantics and Narragansetts: Diplomacy, War and the Balance of Power in Seventeenth-Century New England and Indian Country*.

Janet Foster is a professionally qualified archivist with extensive experience of a variety of specialist repositories, including St Bartholomew's Hospital London. Since 1990 she has been self employed as a consultant, providing advice to a range of organizations from learned societies to community history groups. She is one of the directors of the Archive-Skills Consultancy, an archives and records management consultancy involving project work and the delivery of Basic Archives Skills Training courses. Her publications include *British Archives: A Guide to Archives Resources in the United Kingdom* (4th ed., 2002), jointly edited with Julia Sheppard.

Anne J. Gilliland is Associate Dean for Information Studies and a Professor in the School of Education & Information Studies at the University of California, Los Angeles, where she directs the specialization in Archival Studies. She also directs the UCLA Center for Information as Evidence. Her many publications include *Research in the Archival Multiverse* (edited with S. McKemmish and A. Lau, 2016) and *Conceptualizing 21st Century Archives* (2014). She is a Fellow of the Society of American Archivists and recipient of numerous awards and honorary appointments in archival and information studies.

Lisa Gitelman is Professor of English and media studies at New York University. Her most recent book is entitled *Paper Knowledge: Towards a Media History of Documents* (2014), and she has an edited collection, *'Raw Data' Is an Oxymoron* (2013). Previous works include *Always Already New: Media, History and the Data Culture* (2006). Among her many awards and honours are Jay and Deborah Last Fellowship, American Antiquarian Society; Senior Scholar in Residence, Center for Cultural Analysis, Rutgers University; Leslie Center Humanities Institute Fellow, Dartmouth College; and Fellow, University of Iowa Obermann Center for Advanced Study.

Eirini Goudarouli, PhD, is Head of Digital Research Programmes at The National Archives (TNA), UK, leading a team that conducts and enables interdisciplinary digital research. She has a background in the history of science, digital scholarship, and archival research. Before joining TNA, she was a researcher at the University of Warwick and at Birkbeck, London, a visiting scholar at the Universities of Cambridge and Helsinki, and spent over five years working with the historical and digital collections at the University of Athens.

Hariz Halilovich, PhD—an award-winning social anthropologist and author—is Professor and Australian Research Council Future Fellow at the Social and Global Studies Centre, RMIT University, Melbourne. As an anthropologist specializing in multi-sited, visual and digital ethnography, he has researched how displaced people use narratives and digital technologies to build life stories about place, migration, and communal identity. Much of his work has an applied focus, and he has conducted research on migration and human rights-related issues for a range of non-governmental and governmental bodies, including the Minister for Immigration and Citizenship (Australia) and Minister for Human Rights and Refugees (Bosnia-Herzegovina).

Andrew Hoskins is Interdisciplinary Professor in the College of Social Sciences at the University of Glasgow, UK. He researches and writes on the relationship between media, war, remembering, and forgetting. He is founding Co-Editor-in-Chief of the new journal of *Memory, Mind & Media;* founding Editor-in-Chief of the journal *Memory Studies*; and founding Co-Editor of the Palgrave Macmillan Memory Studies book series. His books include: *Risk and Hyperconnectivity: Media and Memories of Neoliberalism* (with John Tulloch, 2016) and *Radical War: Data, Attention & Control in the Twenty-First Century* (with Matthew Ford, 2022).

Lae'l Hughes-Watkins is the University Archivist for the University of Maryland. From 2013 to 2018 she served as the University Archivist at Kent State University. She is the founder of Project STAND, a centralized digital space documenting collections emphasizing student activism in marginalized communities which recently received a $750,000 Mellon grant in collaboration with Robert Woodruff Library at Atlanta University Center Consortium and the University of Maryland. She is a 2019 Mover and Shaker, and a 2018–2019 Academic Research Library Leadership Career Development Fellow.

Rebecca Kahn is a postdoctoral researcher at the University of Vienna and an associated researcher at the Alexander von Humboldt Institute for Internet and Society in Berlin. Her work focusses on the use of linked open data for digital cultural heritage collections and the epistemic changes that take place in museum and archive collections as they are digitized. She completed her PhD in Digital Humanities at King's College, London, in 2016.

Eric Ketelaar is Emeritus Professor at the University of Amsterdam. From 1997 to 2009 he was Professor of Archivistics in the Department of Media Studies of the Faculty of Humanities of the University of Amsterdam. As an honorary fellow of his former department he continues his research which is concerned mainly with the social and cultural contexts of record creation and use. He was General State Archivist (National Archivist) of The Netherlands from 1989 to 1997. From 1992 to 2002 he held the part-time chair of archivistics in the Department of History of the University of Leiden. He recently published *Archiving People. A Social History of Dutch Archives.*

Pete Langman, PhD, is an independent scholar, author, and editor. He has published widely on cricket, Parkinson's Disease, music, and history and philosophy of science. Editor of *Negotiating the Jacobean Printed Book* (2011), Pete is also the author of *Slender Threads: A Young Person's Guide to Parkinson's Disease* (2013), and *The Country House Cricketer* (2015). As for fiction, his first novel is *Killing Beauties: The Chronicle of Susan Hyde* (2020).

Paul Lihoma is Director of the National Archives of Malawi. He was (2017–2019) president of the Eastern and Southern Africa Regional Branch of the International Council on Archives (ESARBICA) and an executive board member of ICA. He served as an International Panel member of the British Library's Endangered Archives Programme (2008–2014). He obtained both his Master of Science in Information Management & Preservation (Archives & Records Management) degree and PhD degree in Information Science from the University of Glasgow.

James Lowry is Assistant Professor at the Graduate School of Library and Information Studies, Queens College, City University of New York, and founder and director of the Archival Technologies Lab. James is an Honorary Research Fellow and former co-director of the Liverpool University Centre for Archive Studies. He has a PhD from University College London, and a background in state archives and records management. His current projects include *Displacements and Diasporas*, exploring the technical and theoretical problems connected with disputes and claims over displaced archives. James is convenor of *Archival Discourses*, the International Intellectual History of Archival Studies research network, and editor of the *Routledge Studies in Archives* book series.

Ruth Maclennan is an artist. Her work includes films, multi-channel moving image installations, photographs, performances, writing, and interdisciplinary curatorial projects. Ruth's recent films and photographs explore how the climate emergency has irrevocably transformed ways of understanding landscape and place—both for their inhabitants, and as representation. *Cloudberries, Call of North,* and *Hero City* filmed in the Russian Arctic premiered at the London Film Festival. She exhibits internationally in exhibitions and film festivals, and since April 2020 has contributed to www.crownproject.art. She also teaches artists' moving image at Central Saint Martins and lectures internationally. She has a PhD from the RCA and is Institute Associate at The Scott Polar Research Institute. LUX Artists' Moving Image distributes her films https://lux.org.uk/artist/ruth-maclennan.

Laura Mandell is Director of the Center of Digital Humanities Research and Professor of English at Texas A&M University. She is the author of *Breaking the Book: Print Humanities in the Digital Age* (2015), *Misogynous Economies: The Business of Literature in Eighteenth-Century Britain* (1999), and numerous articles primarily about eighteenth-century women writers. She is Project Director of the Poetess Archive, an online scholarly edition and database of women poets, 1750–1900 (www.poetessarchive.org), Acquisitions Editor of 18thConnect (www.18thConnect.org), and Director of ARC (www.ar-c.org), the Advanced Research Consortium overseeing NINES, 18thConnect, and MESA.

Niamh Moore is Senior Lecturer in the School of Social and Political Science, University of Edinburgh, Scotland, with a background in interdisciplinary feminist studies. She published, with Andrea Salter, Liz Stanley, and Maria Tamboukou, *The Archive Project: Archival Research in the Social Sciences* (2016). Niamh's research includes work on ecofeminist activism (*The Changing Nature of Ecofeminism: Telling Stories from Clayoquot Sound*, 2015), the archiving and re-use of data, and community-based participatory research, including with community food growing projects.

Michael Moss (died 9 February 2021) was Emeritus Professor, Department of Computer and Information Sciences, Northumbria University. From 1970 to 1974, he was Registrar of the National Register of Archives (Scotland) Western Survey, where he rescued many endangered business archives. From 1974 to 2001 he was University Archivist at the University of Glasgow, with responsibility for the university's own records and one of the largest collections of business records in Europe. He was appointed a research professor in Archival Studies at the University of Glasgow in 2001 and directed the successful Information Management and Preservation MSc programme. He was a prolific historian writing on a wide range of subjects from the history of whisky to archival practice.

Simon Popple is Senior Lecturer in Photography and Digital Culture at the School of Media and Communication, University of Leeds. His research interests are focused on archival practices and the roles communities and institutions can play in developing open and collaborative archive spaces using digital and co-produced tools. He is particularly interested in the relationships between archives, their users, and the potential of digital co-production and creativity.

Andrew Prescott is Professor of Digital Humanities at the University of Glasgow and AHRC Theme Leader Fellow for Digital Transformations. He was formerly a Curator of Manuscripts at the British Library, where he was the principal British Library contact for the *Electronic Beowulf* project. He has also worked at the University of Sheffield, University of Wales Lampeter, and King's College London.

Catherine Richardson is Professor of Early Modern Studies and Director of the Institute of Cultural and Creative Industries at the University of Kent. She writes about early modern material culture, for instance in *Domestic Life and Domestic Tragedy in Early Modern England* (2006), *Shakespeare and Material Culture* (2011), and, with Tara Hamling, *A Day at Home in Early Modern England, The Materiality of Domestic Life, 1500–1700* (2016). She has edited *Clothing Culture 1350–1650* (2004), (with Hamling) *Everyday Objects: Medieval and Early Modern Material Culture* (2010) and *The Routledge Handbook of Material Culture in Early Modern Europe* (2016, with Gaimster), is currently editing *Arden of Faversham*, and is PI on the AHRC project 'The Cultural Lives of the Middling Sort': https://research.kent.ac.uk/middling-culture/.

Anna Sexton is Lecturer in Archives & Records in the Department of Information Studies at University College London, and is an archivist whose interests include research use of government administrative data, participatory archive practice, community-based research, record access and rights issues, archival ethics, and new thinking around digital records and computational methods. Anna holds a PhD and MA in Archives and Records Management from UCL, and has twenty years of experience working across the archive sector and academia, most recently as Head of Research at The National Archives. Anna is also the current Deputy Director for Collaborations and Partnerships for the London Arts and Humanities Partnership (LAHP) AHRC Doctoral Training Partnership.

Alan Stewart is Professor of English and Comparative Literature at Columbia University and International Director of the Centre for Editing Lives and Letters in London. His publications include, most recently, *Shakespeare's Letters* (2008) and *The Oxford History of Life-Writing*, volume 2, *Early Modern* (2018). Joint Director of the Oxford Francis Bacon, he is the editor of volume 1, Bacon's *Early Writings 1584-1596*, and is now editing volume 2, *Late Elizabethan Writings 1596–1602*.

Paul Strohm has taught at Columbia University and, previously, the University of Oxford and Indiana University. His first book was *Social Chaucer* (Harvard, 1989), followed by other books concerning medieval literature in its historical setting. Most recently, he has published *Conscience: A Very Short Introduction* (Oxford, 2011) and *The Poet's Tale* (Profile, 2015).

David Thomas is currently a visiting professor in the iSchool at Northumbria University. Until 2013 he was Director of Technology at the UK National Archives where he was responsible for the acquisition and preservation of digital records and websites from government departments, including the development of preservation systems. His recent publications include two books edited with Michael Moss, *Do Archives Have Value?* (2019) and *Archival Silences: Missing, Lost and Uncreated Archives* (2021). Other publications include *Beggars, Cheats and Forgers: A History of Frauds Through the Ages* (2014) and *The Silence of the Archive* (with Simon Fowler and Valerie Johnson, 2017).

Victoria Van Hyning is Assistant Professor of Library Innovation in the College of Information Studies, University of Maryland. She has created several cultural heritage crowdsourcing projects, and developed new approaches to text transcription. At Zooniverse.org from 2014 to 2018, she led the development of *AnnoTate*, *Shakespeare's World*, and other projects, and served as Humanities Principal Investigator, while holding a British Academy Postdoctoral Fellowship. She worked at the Library of Congress from 2018 to 2020 to create *By the People*, a crowdsourcing project. Her monograph *Convent Autobiography: Early Modern English Nuns in Exile* (2019) explores how nuns expressed themselves within the constraints of monasticism.

Kirsten Weld, a scholar of political conflict and social movements in twentieth-century Latin America, is Professor of History at Harvard University. Her first book, *Paper Cadavers: The Archives of Dictatorship in Guatemala* (Duke University Press, 2014), received the 2015 WOLA-Duke Human Rights Book Award and the 2016 Best Book Prize from the Recent History and Memory Section of the Latin American Studies Association; a Spanish edition was published by Guatemala's Association for the Advancement of the Social Sciences (AVANCSO) in 2017. She is currently writing a history of the impact and legacies of the Spanish Civil War in Latin America, to be published by Harvard University Press.

Rebecca Abby Whiting completed her PhD in History and Information Studies at the University of Glasgow in 2021, considering archives displaced during the Gulf Wars. Her research centres archives as sites of political struggle through which domestic and international politics, socioeconomic and culture structures can be traced. Her academic background is in Middle East Studies, Philosophy, and Middle East Politics. She has also worked in journalism and the humanitarian sector, primarily in Lebanon.

Alison Wiggins is Reader in English Language and Manuscripts at the University of Glasgow. She was AHRC Leadership Fellow for *Archives and Writing Lives* and PI for the AHRC *Letters of Bess of Hardwick Project*. She formerly worked at the AHRC Centre for Editing Lives and Letters, University of London, and has collaborated on projects with the National Trust, Chatsworth House Archive, The National Archives, The Bodleian Library, and National Library of Scotland.

Heather Wolfe is Curator of Manuscripts and Associate Librarian at the Folger Shakespeare Library. Her book *Elizabeth Cary, Lady Falkland: Life and Letters* (2000) received the first annual Josephine Roberts Scholarly Edition Award from the Society for the Study of Early Modern Women. 'The Material Culture of Record-Keeping in Early Modern England', co-written with Peter Stallybrass, received the 2019 Archival History Article Award from the Society of American Archivists. She is currently working on various manuscript transcription crowdsourcing projects and on early modern European writing paper, and has published widely on text technologies in early modern England. She has a PhD in English Literature from the University of Cambridge and an MLIS from University of California, Los Angeles.

FOREWORD

CAROLYN STEEDMAN

The invitation to write a foreword to this volume was first made by the editors, Andrew Prescott and Alison Wiggins, at a conference about the truth of archives way back in 2017, in pre-pandemic days when you could travel to archives and record offices, and to conferences about them. This is written in May 2022, so I could get back to the places where I have spent so much of my life, but it's the train, the cheap hotel, that gives me pause, not the safe harbour of the (usually, in the UK) 1960s brick building on the outskirts of some county town or other. This dating is related to law: 'a local authority may do all such things as appear to it necessary or expedient for enabling adequate use to be made of records under its control' (10 & 11 Eliz. II c.52). In the UK, counties, boroughs, and metropolitan authorities are obliged to preserve their records, but not obliged to make them available to the public (though all do). Their foundational collections are administrative and legal: parish records, containing the narratives of so many lost lives, are there because the parish was a fundamental unit of civil and ecclesiastical government for more than a thousand years. This legislative factor may produce a high-handed sense of ownership in some historian users: these are our records; I have a right to see them! Late twentieth-century legislation interpellated users as citizens: a 2000 Act (47 Eliz. II c.36) created a 'right of access' to information held by public authorities. But really, there had never been any point to feeling outrage in the search room. If you could work your way through the card or online catalogue and fill in your call slip correctly, you could lay your hands on the records. The law—what it permits, what it obfuscates, what it denies—is the overarching, often unspoken, story of the thirty-five contributions to this book.

'Story' probably is the right word for all the things that get written out of the archives, and all the chapters in this volume show the making and unmaking of stories from the archives in a wide variety of national contexts. And stories were what Alison and Andrew told me about at that conference. I'd refused to present a paper though I'd hoped the organizers would have me in the audience. I pleaded ignorance of 'the archival turn'—I didn't know why it happened, or what it was—I hadn't done any reading on the *the archive* (a happy formulation of this book) since the year 2000. Yes, I knew that I'd written a book that had 'archive' in the title, but that was only because the US publishers believed that if I published it as *Dust* (as it was in the UK) it would end up in the good housekeeping section of bookstores. They subtitled it *The Archive and Cultural History*. How could readers not believe it was about archives? Well; it was, a bit. It conducted a brisk survey of Jacques Derrida's philosophy of the archives, and I emoted along with Jules Michelet's nineteenth-century poeticized agony of the Archives Nationales, but only, really, to get me to the topic in hand, which was the writing of history: History as the Story of the Dust, of that which cannot go away, or be dispersed. Anyway, I do think that my summary of Derrida's 1992 *Mal d'archive* has been useful to a couple of generations of college students in the US wanting a reasonably accurate crib; no one (in either the US or the UK) ever mentions the 'History' or the 'Dust', in commentary, reference, or footnote.

In 2017, at that conference, Alison and Andrew both discussed the fictions of the archive, as they tell readers here, in their Introduction. I was working with legal records at the time (for what became *History and the Law. A Love Story*), records of the grinding displacement of so many lives under the English Poor Law, Old and New. We were talking about settlement, I think, the requirement that a poor person demonstrate their right to relief and aid in a particular place, and about the peculiar narrative form of the statements, caught sometimes in a magistrate's notebook, or in the papers sent to the high court of King's Bench when a decision by one set of county magistrates against another's was disputed (this was what was at stake: which property owners should bear the burden of the poor out of the rates they paid?). Andrew and Alison both suggested paying attention to legal and administrative records as text, asking about the magistrate's clerk who transcribed them (rarely the magistrate). In medieval times—and just as likely in the eighteenth century—their concern was to ensure conformity with the correct legal form; sometimes they would take short cuts and even invent details. Administrative documents preserved in record offices tell stories which are shaped by their institutional and governmental context; they are as deceptive and full of invention as more self-consciously literary works. Historians need to know about this textual world where practices and assumptions were very different to our own.

When someone tells you something new and true, it's always as if you've always known it. I had littered my writing about the English poor with caveats for over thirty years: when Nottinghamshire parents were recorded as saying to a local magistrate in 1788, that they were 'poor and impotent and not able to provide for themselves and their children a Boy and a Girl', this was probably not what they actually said, wrote I. It was a legal statement of their narrative; it was the form of language to be used on a warrant or a summons—as it was when in 1775, Mary

Hardy complained that 'her Husband beats abuses her and her child without cause or provocation and contrary to Law', or in 1779, when Ann Stevenson of Barton in Fabris said that John Stevenson had 'assaulted her and kicked her over her instep without cause or provocation and contrary Law'. The idea that you read these statements as you might a literary text, was exhilarating, allowed you wonder about the incantatory 'contrary to Law', and what ascribing law-knowledge to the poor might mean.

Who said it? Was it said at all? What will you write out of the lies, the omissions, the misattributions, the ignorance, the wide, empty spaces in the archives? What will you make out of the labours and stories of others, dead and gone? Not just a question for historians, but for all those who use the words of others 'true' or not, to make something of their own, as the contributors to this volume illustrate in many different ways. Ownership hovers here. Now that the extraordinary survey offered by the wide range of international contributors to the present volume of the truth and power at work in the making of many archives is in place, 'whose?'—whose words, experience, history—is the next big question to ask.

INTRODUCTION

ANDREW PRESCOTT AND ALISON WIGGINS

This chapter introduces the material forms, social functions, and symbolic conceptualization of the archive as set out by the contributors to *Archives: Power, Truth, and Fiction*. The first section of this introductory chapter, 'The Ubiquitous Archive', highlights the vibrancy and urgency of the field and the problems of defining the archive, its structure and content, its metaphorical and material meanings. It emphasizes the need for radically interdisciplinary and cross-cultural approaches, reflected in the way in which this volume reaches across and encourages dialogue between archive professionals and users who include creative practitioners, academic historians, literary critics, theorists, community groups, individual members of the public, governments, businesses, and digital developers, from different locations, institutionally and globally. The next two sections of this introductory chapter consider the themes that are highlighted in the title of this volume. In 'Power and the Archive' we explain the well-known paradox whereby the archive can be both a means of oppression and of empowerment and outline how contributors to this volume engage with the enmeshment of archives with power. The content, structure, and nature of archives has been shaped by shifting social and political agendas, and this section reviews the assumptions that underpinned the emergence of Western archival theory in the nineteenth century. In 'Truth and Fiction in the Archive' we explain how awareness of the constructedness of archival truths has been exhibited through a series of 'archival turns' that date back over a century, each of which has challenged and redefined conceptions of the role and purpose of archives. We outline how contributors to this volume discuss the unstable dynamics between truth and fiction, which are directly tied to the legal function of archives as sources of evidentiary proof as well as to the evolving nature of archives, especially in contexts of changing digital technology. There follows, in 'Navigating This Book', an overview of the six-part structure of this volume which has been designed to draw threads through the uneven and shifting multiverse of archives, where time and space are not linear or stable. We would emphasize that this volume is in no sense aiming or claiming to map the field, rather its intensions are to unsettle, encourage debate, and draw out issues generated by the dynamism and perpetual motion of the archive. A 'Coda' considers an archival icon, The Domesday Book, as a microcosm for the volume's concerns with the archive as both monumental symbol and as a continually evolving network of meanings activated and animated by social contexts of use. Gargantuan in scale and conception yet never sufficient or complete, the archive can be on the one hand a space for empowerment and expression and on the other an instrument of constraint and repression, and plays a central role in how societies define their values and ethics. The way in which the archive is structured, made available, and developed can potentially help create a more socially just, fair, and equitable world.

The Ubiquitous Archive

Archives have never been more complex, expansive, or ubiquitous. As Louise Craven observes in her chapter on archival boundaries, archives are now everywhere and belong to every person and every kind of organization wishing to store data. The archive embraces every conceivable artefact and cultural record. There are archives of film, image, sound, web pages, computer programs, games, scents, seeds, and genomes. Consequently almost every imaginable medium can be seen as archival. Catherine Richardson shows how such material objects as cabinets and doors have archival properties, while Edwina Ashie-Nikoi, Emmanuel Adjei, and Musah Adams remind us of the importance of oral tradition, ritual, and dance in the archives of Ghana. As the scope of the archive has expanded, it has ceased to be primarily about the past and is increasingly preoccupied by contemporary experience, as can be seen from the proliferation of online archives on subjects ranging from queer zines to sport.

The chapters in this volume, while they resist the temptation to press for definitions, help articulate and navigate this burgeoning and evolving field of the archive. They illustrate the heterogeneous, fluid, and multi-faceted character of the archive today—reinforced by the short responses at the end of each section of the book that further illustrate the multivocality of approaches to the archive. As the metaphor of 'the archive' has become more pervasive, there are various ways to conceptualize the archive to reflect dynamics of power and authority within society. The Victorian founders of Western archive administration imposed a rigid legalistic view of the archive as restricted to official documents produced by governments and other corporate bodies. This belief in the probity of the official record reflected a colonialist mindset. It is a conceptualization that contrasts with those presented here in this volume, where archives are repeatedly decoupled from nation and territory through processes that include displacement, global migrations, and digitization. As many of the chapters in this volume show, by expanding our view of what an archive can be, we are engaging in a conscious act of decolonization (or anti-racism) offering suppressed and forgotten voices a means of being heard again.

These chapters illustrate time and time again how the imposition of arbitrary definitions of the archive can result in the exclusion of particular groups and narratives. Yet, in seeking to widen the scope of discussion, there is a risk that the archive can become a loosely applied metaphor of limited analytical value. It might be felt that, as references to the archive have become more prominent in intellectual discourse, the view of what an archive is and how it should be read has become more unstable and unsettled. Nevertheless, at the same time, there is an imposing international infrastructure regulating archives, with an International Council of Archives (ICA) which in 2011 partnered with UNESCO to issue a Universal Declaration on Archives.[1] ICA is the custodian of such standards for the processing and cataloguing of archives as ISAD-G (General International Standard Archival Description).[2] These bodies feed into other international standards, such as ISO 15,489, a standard for the creation, capture, and management of records,[3] which play an increasingly important part in dealing with the challenges posed by the growth of born-digital records discussed in the chapter by Eirini Goudarouli. The national bodies that are represented on the ICA are largely responsible for defining the professional training given to archivists.[4] Anna Sexton, in her chapter on archival education and professionalism, discusses the challenge involved in conveying the key messages of the canonical texts of Western archives management while at the same time engaging future archivists with increasingly pluralistic and fluid notions of an archival multiverse.

The definitions of archives offered by bodies such as the ICA remain rooted in traditional Western conceptions of the archive.[5] While the ICA recognizes that archives come in a wide variety of formats and are held by many different institutions and individuals, nevertheless they stress that archives are 'contemporary records created by individuals and organisations as they go about their business'. Such records are assumed 'to provide a direct window into past events' and the ICA stresses the key requirements of authenticity (the record is what it claims to be); reliability (an accurate representation of the event); integrity (the archive should be complete); and accessibility and usability. These professional concerns still represent the canonical view of the archive, regardless of more expansive views expressed in this volume. In such cases as the Gunpowder Archive or the archives from Malawi and Ghana (examined here in the chapters by Paul Strohm, Paul Lihoma, and Ashie-Nikoi, Adjei, and Adams), the need to respect such precepts as original order, integrity, and reliability is essential to ensure that archives perform their social and legal function of offering proof. Yet there is a potential tension between the approaches of professional bodies, essential to promoting transparency and accountability, and the more eclectic and opportunistic approaches evident in

Ruth Maclennan's discussion of her photographic work, or the necessarily subjective approaches considered by Norma Clarke in researching the history of her family.

Michelle Caswell forcefully reminds us, in her chapter, how professionally oriented discussion of archive theory is often ignored by academic commentators. This volume is designed to break out of the professional and academic silos within which discussion of archives has been all too often constrained. Reaching across disciplinary boundaries is important because, as Eric Ketelaar explains in his chapter, we have become aware of the range of 'archivers' involved in creating, making accessible, and using archives. Ketelaar describes this range of archivers, who include 'authors, clerks, registrars, antiquarians, record managers, keepers, website builders, genealogists'. Each of these archivers remakes and opens up the archive in different ways in a never-ending process. It is a reality very different to that of the detached and submissive archivist described as the ideal model custodian by such early theorists as Sir Hilary Jenkinson. Rather than passively accepting whatever records bureaucrats should pass on, these archivers increasingly engage in active intervention to protect and make available records which serve social justice and good governance.

As the boundaries of the archive continue to expand, there is a risk that the archive becomes a shorthand for all institutions of cultural memory, eliding museums, galleries, libraries, and archives under problematically unspecific and vague umbrella terms such as 'cultural heritage', despite their distinct professional, theoretical, and institutional identities. These difficulties are exacerbated by the way in which management structures of bodies like local councils or university professional services tend to group archives, libraries, and museums into integrated managerial units. The interaction between heritage professions is further complicated by the increasing awareness of the role memory plays in cultural formation, as Andrew Hoskins discusses in his chapter on memory and media decay. Nevertheless, distinctive features of archival practice such as appraisal and original order retain their importance, as Andrew Prescott discusses. The nature of the professional training offered to archivists will, as Sexton highlights, play a key role in defining the future scope of the field.

These issues of disciplinary and professional boundaries are further complicated by the growth in machine-readable records. The digitization of manuscript and printed resources already blurs users' awareness of the distinctions between archive, library, and museum resources. Goudarouli shows how, as records become increasingly born-digital, completely new approaches will be required. While the idea of organic accretion might be an appropriate way of describing a medieval or early modern archive, the management of born-digital records is more of a continuum of assessment and review. One characteristic of work with archives is the issue of dealing with information at enormous scales, which will become even more pressing with the explosion in born-digital records. Management of these may increasingly require the use of AI, which may raise concerns about power and agency in the archive to even greater pitches.

Power and the Archive

Many chapters in this book are suffused with anxiety about the way in which archives are enmeshed with the exercise of power. Lihoma describes how colonizers in Malawi used written documents to seize land and extort taxes, while after independence the emergence of dictatorial rule was facilitated by the manipulation of official documents and archives. Likewise Dei Ashie-Nikoi, Adjei, and Adams report how, in Ghana, the coup against Kwame Nkrumah in 1966 was marked by a bonfire of his papers and books stored in the Presidential Palace. In Ghana, these losses are not only documentary. The loss by fire of the Ghana Broadcasting Corporation's rich Film and Video archive in 1989 was due to wider policy and preservation failures that also led to gaps and losses in government archives and other multimedia resources. For North America, Lae'l Hughes Watkins and Karina Beras and Jarrett Martin Drake document ways in which archives have excluded the Black voice and actively support racist legal systems and immigration policies. The chapters by Jane Birkin, James Lowry, and Beras and Drake each remind us of the role of the archive in the use of photographs by police for racial and criminal profiling. James Lowry memorably explores how the record can be viewed as command.

The role of archives in power structures mean that they are prone to seizure and destruction. Rebecca Abby Whiting's chapter shows how various actors struggled to secure the records and archives of the Iraqi government after the 2003 invasion. Andrew Prescott discusses the destruction of the landing cards of West Indian immigrants to the UK and shows how changes in immigration policy resulted in the loss of records vital to proving the British citizenship of the Windrush Generation. Rebecca Kahn shows how queer narratives do not necessarily find their place even in the South African Truth and Reconciliation process. One of the most dramatic and notorious illustrations of bureaucratic sanitization of archives are the UK migrated archives, which are discussed by a number of contributors to this volume including Lihoma, Ketelaar, and Beras and Drake. In 2011, during legal action by participants in the Mau Mau rising in Kenya, it was revealed that, as Britain's African colonies gained independence, files relating to these colonies thought to contain information embarrassing to Britain were either destroyed or returned to London. Lihoma discusses the effect of this sequestration and destruction on the National Archives of Malawi, and similar gaps occur in the archives of other British African colonies. Some 20,000 files relating to these colonies were held by the Foreign and Commonwealth Office in a secret store. They were only finally transferred to The National Archives, where they are now FCO 141, after legal opinions had been obtained. At the time of writing, The National Archives has temporarily withdrawn access to these archives because evidence was found that the records had been treated in the past with insecticide and might pose health risks to those handling them.[6] The sad story of the migrated archives is bound up with the power dynamics of late colonialism. The selection of archival material for return to Britain was undertaken by white officials as a means of maintaining colonial-era hierarches after independence. Moreover, the existence of these files was what has been described as a racialized secret—thousands of people knew about their existence and occasionally researchers were allowed to see them, but almost all these people were white.[7]

The preoccupation with power evident in recent writing on archives contrasts with the views of late-nineteenth and twentieth-century European archival theorists. These theorists forged the Western story of the origins of the archive in a move that disregarded millennia of knowledge systems held by indigenous cultures and memory retrieval systems that had long been in place globally.[8] Their outlook reflected the positivist views of Victorian historians who saw administrative documents as providing more objective evidence than literary reports in chronicles, pamphlets, and newspapers. Influenced by the fields of science and experimentation, they evoked the metaphor of 'archives as laboratories' for the distillation of facts. The *Manual for the Description and Arrangement of Archives* compiled in 1898 for the Royal Society of Archivists in the Netherlands by Samuel Muller, Johan Feith, and Robert Fruin seems surprisingly rigid and excluding today.[9] It insisted that archives comprised the written documents produced by an administrative body and intended to remain in the custody of that body. Documents and manuscripts not generated by the administrative process that created the archive should be removed from it and placed elsewhere, since they interfered with good order in the repository and were an embarrassment to the archivist. Under no circumstances should the needs of future researchers be taken into account.

Such views were echoed by other commentators such as Sir Hilary Jenkinson of the Public Record Office in London who in 1922 published an influential *Manual of Archive Administration*.[10] For Jenkinson, archives were documents which formed part of an official transaction. He insisted on the importance of official custody, and denied full archive value to collections like the charters and state papers in repositories like the British Library because they had been violently torn from their original context. For Jenkinson, it was up to the administrators who created the documents to decide what should be preserved; the role of the archivist was to preserve whatever the administrators passed on. Jenkinson's views were criticized by Theodore Schellenberg of the US National Archives because of his failure to come to terms with the explosion in the number of records produced by modern bureaucracy.[11] Schellenberg argued that effective management of modern papers required active intervention by archivists and that the needs of future historians should be considered. While Schellenberg allowed the archivist more freedom of action than Jenkinson, nevertheless he felt that the archivist's loyalty was primarily towards the government or corporation that they worked for.

For the authors of these manuals that were foundational for the modern Western archive (the Dutch manual, Jenkinson, and Schellenberg), it was axiomatic that public officials could be trusted to produce full and accurate records. In an age of dodgy dossiers, deleted WhatsApp messages, and fake news, this assumption now seems impossibly naive.[12] Nevertheless, these manuals introduced concepts which remain fundamental to archival practice. Most important was the understanding that, in the words of the Dutch Manual, 'an archival collection is an organic whole, a living organism, which grows, takes shape and undergoes changes in accordance with fixed rules'.[13] The structure of the archive should reflect the organization of the administrative body which created it. From these precepts flow two key principles of modern archival practice: the importance of preserving the structure of *fonds* or record groups (*respect des fonds*) and the need for archival arrangement to reflect original order. If these principles are not observed, there is a risk of the loss of contextual information about the record and the administration which produced it.

So long as the archivist is regarded as a passive custodian of records shaped by the state or other corporations, there is a risk that the archivist could be complicit in oppressive or illegal acts. This risk became a reality in apartheid South Africa from the late 1980s, as officials covered their tracks by the unauthorized destruction of public records and refused to transfer records to the archives.[14] These issues by no means vanished with the collapse of the apartheid regime, as Kahn's chapter on the Truth and Reconciliation Commission shows. Verne Harris describes how 34 boxes of testimony given to the Truth and Reconciliation Commission including an account of the assassination of the Black activist Dulcie September were effectively removed from public access by transfer to South Africa's National Intelligence Agency in 1999.[15] Harris resorted to what he calls 'banditry' to facilitate litigation to secure access to this material so that it remained in the public domain. Banditry is far removed from the detachment of the idealized image of the archivist in the early handbooks of archive administration. Many of the authors in the present volume see themselves as activists using archives to hold governments and officials to account and using archives to promote the voices of the marginal, excluded, and forgotten. Hariz Hallovich and Anne J. Gilliland describe archives representing the collective memories of refugees in the Bosnian War of 1992–1995. Rachel Douglas shows how writers in Haiti have reinvented processes of editing and recording to preserve collective memories.

These approaches can be viewed in their larger context as part of a series of shifts that date back at least to the early twentieth century with the Black Archival Turn, whereby the archive itself has become the subject of scrutiny.[16] Subsequent archival turns during the twentieth century brought feminist, queer, indigenous, and alternative archives into focus as community groups took control of their own historical narratives and created their own archives. There is a persistent tendency, in the scholarship, to refer to a single 'archival turn' typically attributed to the influence of Jacques Derrida and Michel Foucault in the 1980s and 1990s.[17] While the attribution is a misnomer, the discussions by these exceptional thinkers brought the archive more into mainstream view and continue to exercise a profound influence on the field.[18] For Derrida, the effectiveness of a democracy is measured by the social functioning of its archive and he famously commented that: 'There is no political power without control of the archive, if not memory.'[19] In this context, it is insufficient to examine individual documents in isolation. In understanding the political, administrative, and cultural pressures that shape documents, it is essential to examine critically the structure of the archive as a whole. The focus of the most prominent twenty-first century 'archival turn' was announced by Ann Laura Stoler in 2009, who illustrated the richness of considering 'the archive as subject' by showing how the structures of the Dutch colonial archive revealed the Dutch colonial mindset.[20] The chapters in the present volume and the responses to each section reflect the energy unleashed by the debates around the past decade's 'archival turn', which is by no means restricted to the kind of 'top down' analysis exemplified by Stoler. The contributors to the present volume explore many examples of high-impact community collections that range from queer archives in South Africa, to refugee archives in the Balkans, to the Atlas group archive exploring the Lebanese civil war discussed by Simon Popple. Such community collections blur the traditional distinctions between archive and collection, print and manuscript, official and personal.

The result, we might propose here, is a 'dirty archive', generating a form of dirty history which rejects the emphasis on rational meanings and higher purposes and instead focuses on the excluded and oppressed. It echoes the disruptiveness and deliberate quirkiness of queer methodology. It is informed by anthropological concepts of dirt as matter out of place, and is influenced by histories of reading that focus on textual reception as a form of production.[21] Such approaches which are well known to literary criticism and book history have relocated the locus of meaning more equitably towards reader, user, or receiver of texts, exploring the social life of texts and seeing critics travelling through the soiled margins of texts seeking signs of use. It offers a way to return the human back to the archive: to move away from notions that archives offer an objective view of reality or uncomplicated reflections of 'what really happened'. It is to emphasize the value of reading along and against the grain of the archive, of observing the spaces and interstices, and of getting beyond tilted collections by making new knowledge. It further involves enriching the archive through permissive inclusions and methods of networking and encoding that are critically alert to the central role of the archive in the functioning of a just and fair society.

Truth and Fiction in the Archive

It is now thirty-five years since Natalie Zemon Davis published her epoch-making study *Fiction in the Archives* that discussed the elaborate stories proffered by those seeking royal pardons for homicide in sixteenth-century France and linked those stories to fictionalized narrative stereotypes.[22] As discussed in the previous section, European Victorian historians regarded archives as vast fact quarries offering an objective form of evidence because documents were generated by official transactions.[23] But, as Zemon Davis demonstrated, administrative requirements distort the narratives in documents such as pardons so they are just as subject to representational frameworks and a repertoire of linguistic patterns and conventions as any other form of discourse. No record will offer a direct mirror of reality or a complete account of an event; every text is a representation bounded by linguistic, cultural, and material forms. Archival documents such as coroners' inquests or witness examinations have their own strict textual requirements, which are as rigid and potentially distorting as literary genres. Speaking from a different perspective, even such a conservative historian and archivist as Roy Hunnisett of the Public Record Office in London came to the conclusion, after a lifetime's study of legal records, that many are a 'haphazard mixture of fact, fiction, and error.'[24]

Users of archives have long recognized that information in them cannot be taken at face value. The chapter by Michael Moss and David Thomas unpicks the methods and processes involved in authenticating and evaluating evidence. They describe how legal forms such as common recoveries include fictitious litigants and actions which can easily deceive the unwary, as they track the long history of John Doe and Jane Roe. Such deceptions are not restricted to archaic forms of record: Moss and Thomas note how a major problem for the enquiry into the disaster at the Hillsborough Stadium in 1989 was the unreliability of notes and statements made by the police. Archivists understand how bureaucratic requirements shape the contents of records and can be read both along and against the grain to take account of these distorting factors. Factual accuracy is rarely a 'yes' or 'no' but a matter of context and form of expression; nevertheless, as Moss and Thomas remind us, archives have a fiduciary role. The chief executive of a corporation will want to know whether or not it legally owns a particular property, and the title deeds held by the archives will be vital in establishing the company's title to the property. To know whether one country is obliged to assist another in time of war, leaders will look to the treaties held in archives. Although the texts and material format of title deeds and treaties have a long and fascinating history, this will not be of any interest to a prime minister or chief executive demanding information. They expect the archivist or records manager to provide authoritative answers, which can be backed up in court with evidence if necessary.

The legal truth of archives—their fitness to stand up as evidence in a court of law—relates profoundly to our increasing awareness of how archives can be manipulated, invented, destroyed, or simply not kept by those in power. It is true that the structure of an archive can exclude and erase. But if archives are to hold those in power to account and be a key instrument of democratic accountability, then society and the public must feel and believe that those archives are reliable and trustworthy, and this inherently involves the use of some kind of measure of the extent to which documents are true. At the time of writing, these issues have been brought into sharp focus by the efforts of the US National Archives and Records Administration to recover classified documents relating to Donald Trump's Presidency from his residence at Mar y Lago.[25] Nobody would want courts to accept doubtful or untrustworthy documents. These issues are likely to become more pressing as we increasingly confront the explosion in born-digital records. To deal with the vast quantities of born-digital records, we will probably have to rely on non-human mediation, including the use of artificial intelligence, in such key areas of archival access as metadata and appraisal, as Lisa Gitelman, Goudarouli, and Prescott describe. As we increasingly use auto-matically created visualizations and quantitative analyses, how can we be sure that they are not biased or distorted? There are a number of ways in which the chapters in this volume respond to these concerns and problems, and do so in ways that move the debate on well beyond Zemon Davis and connect with archives today.

One answer to these dilemmas, which emerges from the examples discussed in this volume, is to expand the range of materials and documents in the archive. The growth of community archives described by Kahn, Popple, and other authors here acts as a counterweight by constantly expanding the range of voices represented in archives. Ruth and Sebastian Ahnert show the potential of social network analysis for creating richer and more detailed views of the relationships between people documented in archives. By developing a fuller understanding of the ways in which archives document networks, we can also better understand how the archive relates to the wider community. As archivists increasingly become activists they bring a wider range of material into the archive that assists in understanding how evidence is shaped. Lowry, inspired by Rancière, argues for a radical remaking of the way records are made and data collected, so as to counter state surveillance, 'unleashing new possibilities for participation, information symmetry and ultimately power' (82).

Although the need for the archive to provide reliable evidence to serve key corpo-rate functions will always be there, there is increasingly greater awareness that the archive serves a much wider range of cultural functions. The burgeoning dialogue between archives and the creative practice of artists, musicians, and writers has been one of the most lively and exciting areas of archive work in recent years. Archives can be sources of tales and creative inspiration beyond supporting documentary-based historical studies. Maclennan describes how archives have been an integral part of her creative practice as a filmmaker and Clarke describes how researching a family history is crafting a story. Douglas describes how the experiences of Haiti are forging new intersections between writers and editors, where archival silences become a space for new forms of knowledge. This interaction with creative practice is itself generating new perspectives on the archive, as can be seen from Jenny Sharpe's recent *Immaterial Archives: An African Diaspora Poetics of Loss* which discusses how the way in which Caribbean artists and writers introduce into the archive such intangible phenomena as affects, spirits, and dreams that capture cultural memories of the African diaspora.[26]

Another answer to concerns over the interrelation of truth and trust comes in the calls in this volume for renewed focus on archival materiality. The vast scale of the material archive shapes all of our engagements with it. It is difficult to deny the reality or significance of kilometres of shelving, so many that The National Archives of England and Wales must make use of salt mines as additional storage. Engagement with materiality is vital in helping us to understand how the contents of archives were shaped and fashioned. In the case of the story told by Nadine Akkerman and Pete Langman, of the recovery of texts from a trunk retrieved from a seventeenth-century shipwreck, this engagement with materialities can yield new accidental archives. The chapter by Alison Wiggins calls for greater scrutiny of materiality that is inclusive of archival and digital infrastructures and of performativity. These responses are part of a larger tendency, across this volume, towards unlayering user-created meanings from the archive, adding new ones, and finding archives taking shape in the process. They are a reminder of the intensity, complexity, and multisensory experience of working with archives, and the inevitable interpretative impact of archival displacements and remediations.

In understanding the dynamic between truth and fiction in the archive, it is necessary to examine with greater precision the ways in which archives are read and used. As Stuart Hall reminds us,

> An archive may be largely about 'the past' but it is always 're-read' in the light of the present and the future ... Archives are not inert historical collections. They always stand in an active, dialogic, relation to the questions which the present puts to the past; and the present always puts its questions differently from one generation to another.[27]

In exploring the archive, we are constantly struck by sudden flashes of recognition, of present and past parallels, which change and fluctuate, reinventing the archive for us as we read it. We never explore the archive alone; hints, suggestions, and advice from archivists, senior academics, other researchers, friends and colleagues are vital in guiding our path through the archive. Sylvia Federico describes how important friendly advice and help was to her in making sense of the records of a medieval popular uprising. The way in which readers and users engage with the archive is being changed by technology, and Victoria Van Hyning and Heather Wolfe describe how citizen science methods build new communities around the archive. It is another way that the community of what Ketelaar calls 'archivers' can be expanded. As Lowry discusses, by expanding the range of voices, readers, and stories encompassed by the archive, we can help counteract the archive's inherent tendency to be an instrument of power and instead use it to promote social justice.

Navigating This Book

This book is deliberately designed so as not to privilege any particular period, discipline, or form of archival practice. It presents a series of case studies which place archivists, curators, users of archives, theorists, and literary, historical and other scholars in dialogue. The structure is envisaged as fusing both current literary and historical interest in the conception and performance of the archive together with debates among archival practitioners as to the process by which the archive is created and managed. The book attempts to echo and reflect the multivocality of what is commonly described as the archival multiverse. In order to provide a variety of perspectives, an important feature of the book are the short responses at the end of each section. These allow the presentation of alternative perspectives on the themes of the book, so that we can hear (for example) how a working archivist in an underfunded repository might react to some of the larger theoretical concerns raised in the book. At the end of the volume, one of the most influential current archival practitioners and theorists, Verne Harris, provides us with an afterword which is a trumpet call to further thought and action.

Section I, 'Conceptions', problematizes the boundary and character of the archive, reflecting how our understanding of the range of archival material has recently been widened in response to increased awareness of the colonial and Western power dynamics which traditionally shaped the archive. The incorporation in the archive of oral and non-written traditions associated with such groups as children, women, refugees, and indigenous peoples, has disrupted these traditional power dynamics. Increased automation both reinforces and shifts these power structures. As we see the archive as, in Foucault's formulation, 'the mass of things spoken in a culture, preserved, valorized, re-used, repeated and transformed',[28] its intersection with other cultural heritage institutions such as libraries, museums, and galleries and with the study of cultural perceptions of memory becomes more complex.

Section II, 'Frameworks', looks at the institutional structures which shape the archive and is the section which most extensively discusses archival practice and theory. The process of creating the record is of course inherent to the archive, and is assuming greater prominence with the increasing importance of automated records. But it is the process of appraisal which is the most distinctive and controversial aspect of the archivists' work. This is the process of deciding which records are kept—which for some modern government departments might be as little as 4 per cent of the records created. As a result, one of the most characteristic features of the archivists' work is the controlled destruction of documents. In this context, how do we evaluate the evidential value of the surviving records. How far does the metadata of cataloguing exemplify or obscure the archive? Can new approaches such as the study of networks generate more inclusive perspectives? For most users, the main conception of the archive is through the store and the search room, with archivist acting as a gatekeeper. The training of the archivist is key to access to archives. Enlightened archivists can exploit the opportunities offered by new technologies to engage new communities of volunteers in opening up the archive and enhancing access.

Section III, 'Materialities', attends to the characteristic genres of the archive. It draws out the extraordinary range and extent of the textual and material forms encompassed by the metaphor of the archive. Likewise, the distinctive textual forms gathered within archives (charters, letters, accounts, depositions) may represent characteristic expressions of the archiving impulse, but do they retain their distinctiveness as genres when set beside sound, film, or digital records? The role of sound, film, and photographic archives is vital, since their development was one of the first trends to fracture and blur conventional understanding of the archive. More recent archives have extended the metaphor to include material culture and artworks. The archiving of the web and the need to address born-digital records extends these issues further. As our understanding of the diverse material character of the archive expands, so likewise the performativity of engagement with the archive becomes more wide-ranging and varied.

Sections IV and V, 'Narrators' and 'Encounters and Evolution', show how the archive is shaped by a range of different creators, curators, and users. Current changes in views of the nature of the archive are driven not only by changing views of government and business but also by the increasing role of communities in generating their own archives. However, the shifts in the expressions of social and cultural identity in the archive are also driven by changes in the archival profession itself, by shifts in academic practice, and by the rise of major new groups of users such as family historians.

Section VI, 'Erasures and Exclusions' confronts most directly the questions about truth and power which suffuse the entire volume. This section looks at fictional and rhetorical textual strategies of the archive, but also provides a counterpart to this textual analysis by examining the role of the archive in the Truth and Reconciliation work of countries such as South Africa. It has been claimed that authenticity is central to the work of the archivist, but how does this claim impact on scholarly views of the deceptiveness of text and the necessity of selectivity? This section also confronts directly the tension between the archive as an instrument of power and the way in which it is a vehicle for recovering excluded and marginal communities. Above all, the silences of the archive may be eloquent, as the rewriting activity of Haiti demonstrates.

Coda: An Archival Icon

The noisy, crammed and anxious space of the archival multiverse, crowded with ghosts of the past, explored in this volume, may seem far removed from traditional notions of the quiet, ordered, and trustworthy record office searchroom. It may seem surprising to find the archivist not as a detached and passive custodian but as a fighter for social justice. But these dynamics have been at play in the archive for centuries, and can be found in the most traditional and venerable archival artefacts.

The cover of this book shows how the Chapter House of Westminster Abbey, a masterpiece of gothic architecture, was used by the English government in the early nineteenth century for the storage of legal and other records. Among the records kept in the Chapter House from the late eighteenth century was the Domesday Book, the massive survey of medieval England compiled between 1085 and 1087 for William the Conqueror.[29] Domesday is considered the oldest English public record, because it has not left official custody in over 900 years. Already by the twelfth century, it was viewed as an instrument of power and oppression. The English population christened it Domesday because, like the day of judgement, there was no appeal against it. Domesday, with its venerable history of official custody and its reputation for providing authoritative information, in many ways epitomizes the traditional image of the Western archival record. As the book against which there was no appeal, Domesday demonstrates the intimate connection between recordkeeping and political power.

Yet Domesday Book was also a means of liberation as well as oppression. In the fourteenth century, the belief circulated that if a town or village was mentioned in Domesday Book, tenants could resist attempts by landlords to impose new rents and services. The quantity of litigation based on Domesday Book reached such a pitch in 1376 that it seemed almost like an uprising, a 'great rumour'.[30] This litigation was generally unsuccessful, but the double-edged nature of Domesday Book had been revealed. It was not simply an instrument to serve the landed elites, but could also be an instrument of social justice. One troubled monk wrote that memoranda such as Domesday Book 'should not be let fall into the hands of unbelievers, lest something sinister should come of it to the prejudice of our church'.[31] Nor is Domesday such a stable and enduring artefact as it might seem. In its earliest form, it comprised two volumes. Following various rebindings, it is now in five parts. Domesday is a working document and many clerks, editors, curators, photographers, and researchers have left their traces on the document, ranging from marginal annotations to folio numbers, so that one is constantly aware of their ghostly presence. Information in Domesday is summarized from other documents, so that Domesday itself forms part of a network linked to a variety of 'Domesday satellites'. The more we examine Domesday Book, the more it appears as a complex multi-dimensional object which is constantly remade as it has been re-formed materially and taken on new functions for readers with different uses. For the Victorians, Domesday was an emblem of the stability and endurance of the English state and actively used in their nation building. But today, as the data in Domesday Book is migrated, rearranged, and linked to other manuscripts, it illustrates how archives are open-ended, dynamic, and heterogeneous. It is this exciting, fluid, and fissiparous world of the archives that is the subject of this volume.

FURTHER READING

Jaimie Baro, *The Archive Effect: Found Footage and the Audio-Visual Experience of History* (London: Routledge, 2014)

Jeannette A. Bastian and Andrew Flinn, *Community Archives, Community Spaces: Heritage, Memory and Identity* (London: Facet, 2019)

Francis X. Blouin and William G. Rosenberg, eds, *Archives, Documentation, and Institutions of Social Memory: Essays from the Sawyer Seminar* (Ann Arbor: University of Michigan Press, 2005)

Caroline Brown, ed., *Archival Futures* (London: Facet, 2018)

Michelle Caswell, *Urgent Archives: Embracing Liberatory Memory Work* (Abingdon: Routledge, 2021)

Liesbeth Corens, Kate Peters, and Alexandra Walsham, *Archives & Information in the Early Modern World* (Oxford: Oxford University Press, 2018)

Louise Craven, ed., *What Are Archives?* (Aldershot: Ashgate, 2008)

Natalie Zemon Davis, *Fiction in the Archives: Pardon Tales and their Tellers in Sixteenth-Century France* (Stanford: Stanford University Press, 1987)

Arlette Farge, *The Allure of the Archives*, trans. Thomas Scott-Railton (New Haven: Yale University Press, 2013)

Anne J. Gilliland, Sue McKemmish, and Andrew J. Lau, eds, *Research in the Archival Multiverse* (Clayton: Monash University Press, 2016)

Stuart Hall, 'Constituting an Archive', *Third Text* 15 (2001), 89–92

Verne Harris, *Archives and Justice* (Chicago: Society of American Archivists, 2007)

Verne Harris, *Ghosts of Archive: Deconstructive Intersectionality and Praxis* (Abingdon: Routledge, 2021)

Eric Ketelaar, 'Tacit Narratives: The Meanings of Archives', *Archival Science* 1 (2001), 131–141

Eric Ketelaar, 'Archival Temples, Archival Prisons: Modes of Power and Protection', *Archival Science* 2 (2002): 221–238

Eric Ketelaar, 'Cultivating Archives: Meanings and Identities', *Archival Science* 12 (2012): 19–33

Jenny Kidd, *Museums in the New Mediascape* (London: Routledge, 2017)

Jason Lustig, 'Epistemologies of the Archive: Toward a Critique of Archival Reason', *Archival Science* 20 (2020): 65–89

Achille Mbembe, 'The Power of the Archives and its Limits', in Carolyn Hamilton, Verne Harris, Michèle Pickover, Graeme Reid, Jane Taylor, and Razia Saleh, eds, *Refiguring the Archive* (Cape Town: David Phillip/Kluwer, 2002), 19–27

Sue McKemmish, 'Are Records Ever Actual?', in Sue McKemmish and Michael Piggott, eds, *The Records Continuum: Ian McLean and Australian Archives: First Fifty Years* (Clayton: Ancora Press in association with Australian Archives, 1994), 187–203

Susan L. Mizruchi, ed. *Libraries and Archives in the Digital Age* (London: Palgrave Macmillan, 2020)

Niamh Moore, Andrea Salter, Liz Stanley, and Mara Tamboukou, eds, *The Archive Project: Archival Research in the Social Sciences* (London: Routledge, 2017)

Michael Moss and David Thomas, eds, *Archival Silences: Missing, Lost and Uncreated Archives* (Abingdon: Routledge, 2021)

Tom Nesmith, Greg Bak, and Joan M. Schwartz, eds, *All Shook Up: The Archival Legacy of Terry Cook* (Chicago: Society of American Archivists and Association of Canadian Archivists, 2020)

Carolyn Steedman, *Dust* (Manchester: Manchester University Press, 2001)

Hugh A. Taylor, *Imagining Archives: Essays and Reflections*, Terry Cook and George Dodds, eds (Lanham and Oxford: Scarecrow Press, 2003)

David Thomas, Simon Fowler, and Val Johnson, *Silence of the Archive* (London: Facet, 2017)

NOTES

1. www.ica.org/en/universal-declaration-archives.
2. www.ica.org/en/isadg-general-international-standard-archival-description-second-edition.
3. www.iso.org/standard/62542.html.
4. For example: www.archives.org.uk/a-career-in-recordkeeping; www2.archivists.org/prof-education/graduate. For international programmes being developed by the ICA, see www.ica.org/en/our-professional-programme.
5. 'What Are Archives?': www.ica.org/en/what-archive. Discussed by Sexton in Chapter 8. A helpful summary is provided by J. Lustig, 'Epistemologies of the Archive: Toward a Critique of Archival Reason', *Archival Science* 20 (2020), 65–89; doi:10.1007/s10502-019-09313-z.
6. Reference at https://cdn.nationalarchives.gov.uk/documents/background-temporary-withdrawal-fco-141.pdf.
7. On the migrated archives, see now T. Livesey, 'Open Secrets: the British "Migrated Archives", Colonial History and Postcolonial History', *History Workshop Journal* 93 (2022), 2–20; doi:10.1093/hwj/dbac002.
8. See for example relevant chapters in *Research in the Archival Multiverse*, ed. A. J. Gilliland, S. McKemmish, and A. J. Lau (Clayton: Monash University Publishing, 2017), 2–15, 31–73, 96–121, 433–455; S. Vermeersch, 'Archival Practice in Pre-Modern Korea; Record Keeping as Archive and Historiography', *Journal of Korean Studies* 24 (2019), 201–223; doi:10.1215/07311613-7,686,562.
9. S. Muller, J. A. Feith, and R. Fruin, trans. A. H. Leavitt, *Manual for the Arrangement and Description of Archives* (Chicago: Society of American Archivists, 2003). This is a translation of the second edition and has an extended introduction by P. Horsmann, E. Ketelaar, T. Thomason, and M. R. Barritt. See also E. Ketelaar, 'Archival Theory and the Dutch Manual', *Archivaria* 41 (1996), 31–40.

10. H. Jenkinson, *A Manual of Archive Administration*, 2nd ed. (London: Percy Lund, Humphries, 1966).

11. T. R. Schellenberg, *Modern Archives: Principles and Techniques* (Chicago: Society of American Archivists, 2003). See also R. Stapleton, 'Jenkinson and Schellenberg: A Comparison', *Archivaria* 17 (1983), 75–85.

12. On 'dodgy dossiers' see further M. Moss, 'The Hutton Inquiry, the President of Nigeria and What the Butler Hoped to See', *English Historical Review* 120 (2005), 578–592; doi:10.1093/ehr/cei121.

13. Muller, Feith, and Fruin, *Manual*, 19.

14. 'The systematic destruction undertaken by the apartheid state in its last days had been an endeavour to cover its tracks—a systemic amnesia falling into the category of what Ricoeur would call "destructive forgetting"': V. Harris, *Ghosts of Archive: Deconstructive Intersectionality and Praxis* (Abingdon: Routledge, 2021), 22.

15. Harris, *Ghosts of Archive*, 7–8.

16. M. M. Castromán Soto, 'Schomburg's Black Archival Turn: "Racial Integrity" and "The Negro Digs Up His Past"', *African American Review* 54 (2021), 73–90.

17. Lustig, 'Epistemologies of the Archive', 82–83; A. L. Stoler, *Along the Archival Grain: Epistemic Anxieties and Colonial Common Sense* (Princeton, NJ: Princeton University Press, 2009), 44.

18. Lustig, 'Epistemologies of the Archive', 68–70; 82–83.

19. J. Derrida, *Archive Fever: A Freudian Impression*, trans. E. Prenowitz (Chicago: University of Chicago, 1996), 2.

20. Stoler, *Along the Archival Grain*.

21. M. Douglas, *Purity and Danger* (Routledge & Kegan Paul, 1966); W. H. Sherman, *Used Books: Marking Readers in Renaissance England* (Philadelphia: University of Pennsylvania Press, 2007); A. Gillespie and D. Lynch, *The Unfinished Book*, Oxford Twenty-First Century Approaches to Literature (Oxford: Oxford University Press, 2020); E. Treharne, *Perceptions of Medieval Manuscripts: The Phenomenal Book* (Oxford: Oxford University Press, 2021).

22. N. Z. Davis, *Fiction in the Archives: Pardon Tales and Their Tellers in Sixteenth-Century France* (Stanford: Stanford University Press, 1987).

23. J. Arnold, *History: A Very Short Introduction* (Oxford: Oxford University Press, 2000), 35–58; C. Steedman, *Dust* (Manchester: Manchester University Press, 2001). 66–88; J. Tollebeek, '"Turn'd to Dust and Tears": Revisiting the Archive', *History and Theory* 43 (2004), 237–248.

24. R. F. Hunnisett, 'The Reliability of Inquisitions as Historical Evidence', in *The Study of Medieval Records: Essays in Honour of Kathleen Major* ed. D. A. Bullough and R. L. Storey (Oxford: Clarendon Press, 1971), 227.

25. The difficulty in retrieving records from President Trump is not unprecedented— a former secretary of President Franklin D. Roosevelt tried to sell some of his papers: www.washingtonian.com/2022/08/10/why-is-the-national-archives-pursuing-trumps-records-a-former-official-explains/.

26. J. Sharpe, *Immaterial Archives: An African Diaspora Poetics of Loss* (Evanston: Northwestern University Press, 2020).

27. S. Hall, 'Constituting an Archive', *Third Text* 15 (2001), 92.

28. L. Lawlor and J. Nale, eds, *The Cambridge Foucault Lexicon* (Cambridge: Cambridge University Press, 2014), 20.

29. E. Hallam, *Domesday Book Through Nine Centuries* (London: Thames and Hudson, 1986).
30. R. Faith, 'The "Great Rumour" of 1377 and Peasant Ideology', in R. H. Hilton and T. H. Aston, eds, *The English Rising of 1381* (Cambridge: Cambridge University Press, 1984), 43–73.
31. V. H. Galbraith, *Studies in the Public Records* (London: Thomas Nelson, 1948), 116.

PART I

CONCEPTIONS

PART I

CONCEPTIONS

CHAPTER 1

'THE ARCHIVE' IS NOT AN ARCHIVES

Acknowledging the Intellectual Contributions of Archival Studies

MICHELLE CASWELL

Two Parallel Tracks

We do not all mean the same thing when we talk about 'archive'.[1] For humanities scholars, 'the archive' denotes a hypothetical wonderland, the 'first law of what can be said', the system that governs the appearance of statements as unique events', according to Foucault, or a curious materialization of the death drive and pleasure principle according to Derrida.[2] For archival studies scholars and practising archivists, archives—emphasis on the 's'—are collections of records, the institutions that steward them, the places where they are physically located, and the processes that designated them 'archival'.[3] These archives, material and immaterial, analogue and digital (which, from an archival studies perspective, is just another form of the material), are *'actually existing archives'*.[4]

The two discussions—of 'the archive' by humanities scholars, and of archives by archival studies scholars (located in library and information studies departments and schools of information)—are happening on parallel tracks in which scholars in both disciplines are largely not taking part in the same conversations, not speaking the same conceptual languages, and not benefiting from each other's insights. Since Derrida's *Archive Fever* hit the presses in 1995, tomes of humanities scholarship have been dedicated to critiquing 'the archive'. 'The archive' has been deconstructed, decolonized, and queered by scholars in fields as wide-ranging as English, anthropology, cultural studies, and gender and ethnic studies. Yet almost none of the humanistic enquiry at 'the archival turn' (even that which addresses 'actually existing archives') has acknowledged the intellectual contribution of archival studies as a field of theory and praxis in its own right, nor is this humanities scholarship in conversation with ideas, debates, and lineages in archival studies. In essence, humanities scholarship is suffering from a failure of interdisciplinarity when it comes to archives.[5]

This chapter both explores why there has been such a failure of interdisciplinarity and proposes concrete solutions for bridging this intellectually unsustainable divide. First, I will provide a brief overview of the concepts that have defined and preoccupied archival studies in its recent history, rendering the field visible in the face of its erasure. Next, I will provide examples of humanities scholarship on 'the archive' that fails to acknowledge archival studies scholarship. I argue that the refusal of humanities scholars to engage with scholarship in archival studies is a gendered and classed failure in which humanities scholars—even those whose work focuses on gender and class—have been blind to the intellectual contributions and labour of a field that has been construed as predominantly female, professional (that is, not academic), *and* service-oriented, and as such, unworthy of engagement. Finally, I will advocate for overcoming this divide through workshops, collaborative scholarship, and co-taught courses that create dialogue between humanities scholars, archival studies scholars, and professional archivists.

Archival Studies: A Very Brief Intellectual History

Archival studies is a subfield of information studies dedicated to understanding the nature, management, and uses of records. Also known as 'archival science' by its more social science-oriented proponents and 'archivistics' by some of its European scholars, archival studies is deliberately chosen here as a larger umbrella term that broadly encompasses the cultural, social, political, technical, and scientific aspects of the study of archives. It is a field defined by its object of study, rather than its methodology, so that it includes a wide range of methods from the scientific, the social scientific, and the humanistic.[6] This section will briefly outline the intellectual lineage of archival studies in the dominant English-speaking Western paradigm, situating the field within the disciplines of history, library science, and more recently, information studies. Next, this section will describe some of the key conceptual preoccupations of the field, namely conceptions of record, provenance, value, and representation. Although it is impossible to summarize the intellectual contribution of an entire field in just a few pages, this section will underscore the theoretical basis for archival studies, hoping to put to rest any lingering misconceptions that archival studies is narrowly confined to the realm of practice.

Although some version of archival thinking and practice (broadly defined) has been present in every human society, the dominant Western English-speaking archival studies tradition traces its lineage to two major publications: the 1898 *Manual for the Arrangement and Description of Archives* (known fondly as 'The Dutch Manual') by Samuel Muller, Johan Adriaan Feith, and Robert Fruin (later translated into English), which introduced foundational organizational principles such as original order and *respect des fonds*; and the 1922 *A Manual for Archive Administration* by Sir Hilary Jenkinson, which posited the importance of provenance over content.[7] In the American context, T. R. Schellenberg's 1956 *Modern Archives: Principles and Techniques* first detailed how such European concepts were adapted to the US National Archives, and provided guidance for the practice of appraisal based on what Schellenberg termed informational and evidential value. Much of the dominant archival studies tradition arose from a government records context, which assumed both that records were created by public agencies in accordance with fulfilling their core missions and that archivists have an ethical obligation to make records publicly accessible to hold government officials accountable.[8] While such principles remain foundational, they have resulted in a rather myopic development in archival theory that is only now stretching beyond government records to incorporate personal manuscript collections, community memory formations, and more pluralist conceptions of what records are.

As the field emerged, so to did the need for professional training programmes. Until the 1980s, American archivists were trained primarily in history departments, and underwent a brief three-course sequence on archival studies that included a practicum. But over the next two decades, archival education became not only more rigorous and robust, but shifted largely from the purview of history departments to that of library science programmes.[9] By the early 2000s, archival studies emerged as a full-grown field within the discipline of information studies (formerly known as library and information science), with all the signs thereof: several peer-reviewed archival studies academic journals; doctoral students and PhD-holding faculty with ambitious research agendas; and, by 2009, the creation of academic venues to discuss archival studies research such as the yearly Archival Education and Research Institute (as opposed to purely professional venues like the Society of American Archivists Annual Meeting).[10] Today, more than a dozen archival studies programmes within (what are known as) iSchools (or schools of information)[11] train not only Masters of Library and Information Studies (MLIS) students who will pursue professional practice as archivists, but doctoral students whose research explores the social, cultural, political, personal, and scientific aspects of records and archives. This is to stress that, while there is certainly a body of literature focused on professional practice, archival *theory* remains an important aspect of archival studies. Although it is impossible to summarize an entire field in a few pages, what follows is an analysis of a few key archival concepts that preoccupy researchers in the field, offered in the hopes of enticing readers more thoroughly to explore the presented concepts (and others) in archival studies literature.

The 'record' is *the* foundational concept in archival studies. Records, according to the prevailing definition in archival studies given by Geoffrey Yeo, are 'persistent representations of activities, created by participants or observers of those activities or by their authorized proxies'.[12] While records contain information, they are distinct from other forms of documents in that they may also serve as evidence of action. While not using the word 'evidence', per se, Yeo's definition implicitly distinguishes records from information objects (such as published books) that are not necessarily related to nor are products of activities (other than the act of writing itself). Jonathan Furner further clarifies that records are not evidence in and of themselves but are defined by their potentiality; they are *capable* of serving as evidence in support of claims about the past by a wide range of users.[13] Archivist Brien Brothman convincingly argues in the postmodern vein that notions of records and evidence are cleaved by a sense of temporality that cannot be fixed, regardless of archivists' best efforts. In this light, evidence is always contextual, always *of* something *for* someone, Brothman argues.[14]

Pluralist and deconstructionist archival theorists have challenged these dominant evidence-based definitions of records. Indigenous Australian scholar Shannon Faulkhead, for example, offers a pluralist view of records as 'any account, regardless of form, that preserves memory or knowledge of facts and events. A record can be a document, an individual's memory, an image, or a recording. It can also be an actual person, a community, or the land itself'.[15] For Faulkhead, the defining characteristic of a record is not its ability to serve as evidence, but as a springboard for memory. Shifting the focus from record-ness to archive-ness, deconstructionist archival theorist Verne Harris highlights the importance of archival labour in making something 'archival'. He writes, '"archives" is defined by three fundamental movements or attributes: one, a trace on, or in, a surface; two, a surface with the quality of exteriority, and: three, an act of deeming such a trace to be worthy of protection, preservation, and the other interventions which we call archival'.[16]

The records continuum model, first developed in Australia by Frank Upward and Sue McKemmish, provides a comprehensive understanding of records and archives rooted in archival studies thinking.[17] The continuum proposes a multidimensional model of concentric circles through which records are *created* as the byproduct of activity, *captured* as evidence (disembedded from their creation and extracted into systems that allow them to be used), *organized* into personal or institutional archives as memory (migrated into systems which allow their use across an organization), and *pluralized* as collective memory (migrated into systems which allow their use across society).[18] The continuum model is characterized by the dynamic and transformative nature of records and recordkeeping within multiple and interacting dimensions such that, 'while a record's content and structure can be seen as fixed, in terms of its contextualization, a record is "always in a process of becoming"'.[19] In this view, the archives is not a stable entity to be tapped for facts, but rather, a constantly shifting process of re-contextualization.

While not a continuum theorist per se, Dutch archivist Eric Ketelaar sees records as dynamic objects in motion, continually shifting with each new use and contextualization. He traces the changing ways in which records are used to construct meaning and posits that records are 'activated' with each use. For Ketelaar, such activations then become part of the records' 'semantic genealogy', influencing all future activations of the record, such that 'we can no longer read the record as our predecessors have read that record'.[20] In this light, the use of records fundamentally changes them, becoming part of their provenance.

Provenance is another key theoretical concept in archival studies. Through provenance, archival studies insists on the importance of the context of the record. Within the mainstream Western archival tradition, provenance has been defined as 'the origin or source of something' or 'information regarding the origins, custody, and ownership of an item or collection'.[21] The principle of provenance traditionally prescribes both that records made by different creators be kept separately and that their original order is maintained. However, this dominant traditional conception of provenance has been challenged on several fronts within archival studies over the past two decades. New re-conceptions of provenance view it not merely as an 'organizing principle' or a 'physical and intellectual construct' but a 'socio-historical context', in the words of Jennifer Douglas.[22] Tom Nesmith, for example, defines provenance as 'the social and technical processes of the records' inscription, transmission, contextualization, and interpretation, which account for its existence, characteristics, and continuing history'.[23] In this new re-conceptualization, provenance is an ever-changing, infinitely evolving process of recontextualization, encompassing not only the initial creators of the records, but the subjects of the records themselves; the archivists who acquired, described, and digitized them (among other interventions); and the users who constantly reinterpret them. Similarly, Laura Millar, influenced by the broader conceptualization of provenance in museum studies, posits that archival conceptions of provenance should include: creator history or 'the story of who created, accumulated, and used the records over time'; records history or 'the story of the physical management and movement of the records over time'; and custodial history, 'the explanation of the transfer of ownership ... and the subsequent care of those records'.[24] In this estimation, archivists and users are active participants in the provenance of records, and are therefore important stakeholders in their custody, mediation, and uses. Provenance is not only about the past, but the future of the records as well; this approach to provenance includes all possible potential activations in its scope.

Furthermore, some of these recent reinterpretations open provenance up to broader community-based configurations. Joel Wurl, for example, has posited that ethnicity, rather than origin in an organization or governmental agency, can form a meaningful basis on which to trace provenance.[25] Similarly, Jeannette Bastian has urged archivists to expand the scope of provenance to include subjects of records and not just their creators—an arrangement that, in Bastian's case study, balances custody of colonial records between postcolonial nations and their former colonial rulers.[26] Bastian also argues that all of these stakeholders become part of a 'community of records'.[27] In Bastian's expansive interpretation, provenance becomes a tool for community inclusion, rather than one of limitation, for hearing the voices of those previously silenced, rather than amplifying the voices of the powerful.

In some cases, these reinterpretations of provenance collapse previous distinctions between the creator and subject of records, so that both become co-creators of the record. Central to this discussion is the definition not just of provenance, but of creatorship. Recently, a host of Australian archival theorists, influenced by Indigenous Australian philosophies, have posited that, not only should records' subjects be included in provenance, but that the subjects of records themselves should be seen as co-creators. Writing about the records of Australian colonization, theorist Chris Hurley has described a 'parallel provenance', that is, two differing claims to the origins of records—one provenance tracing records back to the colonizers who created the records, and one provenance tracing the records back to the colonized subjects of them, resulting from diverging conceptions of creatorship.[28] Building on Hurley's work, Livia Iacovino advocates for a participant model of provenance, whereby all participants in the creation of records are deemed co-creators, and as such enter into a relationship marked by a series of rights and responsibilities.[29] In this conception, not only should provenance be expanded to include the society from which the records emerge(d), but the notion of creatorship is expanded to include the subjects of records.

Value is another core archival studies concept.[30] Contrary to popular misconceptions, archivists do not keep everything. Instead, they make appraisal decisions based on a careful evaluation of records. Here, value refers not to the monetary value of records, but their value in attesting to the events from which they emerged, their value in representing some important aspect of the past, and, in some strands of archival thinking, their value for present and future users. Appraisal is the process by which archivists determine the enduring value of records offered to a repository. Selection is the process by which archivists pick which records to keep based on the value determined during appraisal. Value is not an objective quality that exists outside of context, but rather is inextricably linked to the mission and policies of the particular archival repository for which the archivist works, the training and philosophy of the archivist and the repository, the political, historical, and cultural milieu in which the archivist works, and the archivist's professional ethics and personal values. Like 'evidence', 'value' always exists *for* someone in a particular place at a particular time. Through the determination of value made during the appraisal process, archivists decide which materials to keep and which will be gone forever. This assignation of value is perhaps the greatest expression of archival power and expertise, through which archivists act as gatekeepers to the past.

Representation is another foundational archival concept. More commonly known as archival description, representation is the process by which archivists produce descriptive metadata, or data about the data stored in collections. This descriptive metadata then 'allow[s] users to locate, distinguish, and select materials on the basis of the material's subjects'.[31] Descriptive metadata can then be used to formulate a finding aid, which is a description of an archival collection used by researchers to gain access to collections, or to create a catalogue record in a database, which can also be used by researchers to access collections. Archivists might also create many other descriptive tools, such as inventories, abstracts, guides, and accession records, all of which detail the context and content of the records in a particular collection. Through representation, archivists name the subject of their collections, creating access points that can aid (or prevent) users from finding collections, bringing certain aspects of collections to the fore (or obscure them through omission), and gaining physical and intellectual control over collections.

The term 'representation' is used here rather than the more narrow term 'description' in order to highlight that this process is a 'fluid, evolving, and socially constructed practice', in the words of Elizabeth Yakel.[32] It is up to the archivist to describe what she thinks is important about an object, and in so doing, to provide a particular narrative about it. Furthermore, as Wendy Duff and Verne Harris argue, 'description is always story-telling—intertwining facts with narratives, observation with interpretation'.[33] How archivists represent records determines how researchers may access them, and subsequently, which records they use.

Theorists in the traditional dominant strand of Western archival thinking, like Sir Hilary Jenkinson, denied archivists an active role in description, claiming that archivists were impartial mediators between the record and its description. However, over the past twenty years, archival studies scholars influenced by deconstructionist thinkers have questioned the notion of the archivist as neutral describer; for them, archival description is a contested act through which power is exercised.[34] This exercise of power may operate overtly when the archivist has an obvious political agenda, but it always operates subconsciously, given that all archivists bring assumptions, identities, and experiences to the task of description. Wendy Duff and Verne Harris, for example, have called on archivists to deconstruct the process of archival description, asserting that all representations are incomplete.[35] Duff and Harris propose 'liberatory' descriptive practices that acknowledge the role of the archivist in the representation, allow for input from diverse constituents, and destabilize the view that its categories are natural. In this light, archival representation should be an ongoing collaborative process that welcomes diverse input, not an end-product (such as a finding aid) that presents an authoritative or definitive voice.

This chapter has now provided a brief overview of ongoing theoretical discussions concerning four foundational concepts in archival studies: record, provenance, value, and representation. It will now address how and why such theoretical concerns have been ignored by humanities scholarship on the 'the archive'.

Gender, Class, and Intellectual Disrespect:
A Familiar Disappointment

Like many of my colleagues in archival studies, I eagerly purchase books that have the word 'archive' in the title: Diana Taylor's *The Archive and the Repertoire*; Carolyn Steedman's *Dust: The Archive and Cultural History*; Ann Cvetkovich's *An Archive of Feelings*; Ann Laura Stoler's *Along the Archival Grain: Epistemic Anxieties and Colonial Common Sense*; and the edited volume *Archive Stories: Facts, Fictions, and the Writing of History*, edited by Antoinette Burton to name just a few.[36] I shuffle immediately to the bibliography to see who is cited. Time and time again, I experience the same disappointment. No Verne Harris cited. No Terry Cook. No Sue McKemmish. No Anne Gilliland. Even the best humanities work that acknowledges archival labour, such as Kate Eichhorn's *The Archival Turn in Feminism: Outrage in Order* (which, to its credit, even briefly addresses the de-skilling of librarians and archivists), largely ignores archival studies scholarship.[37] Why?

This omission is not the result of chance, but, I contend, is a result of the construction of archival labour as a feminine service industry and archival studies (if it is ever even acknowledged as existing) as imparting merely practical how-to skills.[38] There seems to be little understanding in the humanities that professional archivists have masters degrees, that archival standards and best practices are culturally constructed artifacts, and that behind every act of archival practice is at least a century-old theoretical conversation. Like so many other feminized professions—education and nursing are prime examples—archivists have been relegated to the realm of practice, their work deskilled, their labour devalued, their expertise unacknowledged.

Archivists themselves are partially to blame for constructing their own feminized service roles as 'handmaidens to historians'. As archival scholar Terry Cook wrote:

> Until the 1980s, archivists ... often described themselves—proudly—as 'the handmaidens of historians'. In retrospect, that phrase is astonishing for its servility and its gender connotations. Until recently, women remained largely invisible in social and historical memory, relegated as the silent and usually unrecognized supporters of male accomplishment; so too, archivists have remained invisible in the construction of social memory, their role also poorly articulated and rarely appreciated. I might go further to say that just as patriarchy required women to be subservient, invisible handmaidens to male power, historians and other users of archives require archivists to be neutral, invisible, silent handmaidens of historical research.[39]

Thankfully, the past decade of archival studies scholarship has put to rest any lingering illusions of neutrality and instead, archival studies scholars and archivists have embraced their active—and political—role as shapers of history.[40] Humanities scholarship, as a whole, lags behind in realizing the influence of archival labour, and when archival labour is recognized, vocabulary for archival functions such as appraisal and representation are absent.[41] This gap in vocabulary limits humanities scholars because they are unable to address the specificities of archival interventions and to communicate meaningfully with archivists and archival studies scholars.[42]

When archivists are acknowledged, they are seen as mindless bureaucrats who hinder rather than aid access to records. For example, in a piece that recognizes how archivists shape history by allowing or denying access to records, historian Durba Ghosh refers to archivists as 'beadle[s]' and as 'archive dwellers', rather than highly skilled professionally-trained experts.[43] In that same volume, communications scholar Craig Robertson describes being denied access to Passport Office records at The National Archives and Records Administration and launches a diatribe against a particular archivist who he sees as an instrument of secrecy, power, and control.[44] He writes, 'The staff here, like all workers in documentary archives, knows the power of the printed and written word. They recognize the need to police the documents that enter and leave an archive, and to control them once they have been admitted.'[45] While I have no doubt that some archivists inhibit access to collections, Robertson downgrades professional archivists to 'workers' and seems astonished that someone whom he perceives to be lower on the totem pole might dictate the conditions under which he is allowed to work. Then, despite his entreaty that 'scholars who use archives need to critically analyze not only documents but also the institutions that house them', he does not cite any archival studies scholars, despite decades of archival scholarship that does just that.[46]

The gendered and classed nature of this disregard is particularly unsettling in the case of humanities scholarship that explicitly addresses issues of gender and class. Indeed, a well-known humanities scholar recently repeated the humanities-has-theory, archives-have-practice trope and told me that there is so much in common between our fields because when her graduates fail to get tenure-track jobs as academics they can always become archivists! As if being an archivist was a fallback career that did not require its own postgraduate-level education and training. As if every act of practice was not laden with theory. As if archival studies could not offer its own important intellectual contribution.

I tell this anecdote to show that there is a huge knowledge gap about the existence, nature, and contributions of archival studies to humanistic inquiry about 'the archive'. It is important to stress here the systemic nature of this divide; it is not an issue of a single scholar's ignorance, but a failure across the humanities. I can think of no other field whose erasure in this way would be acceptable, let alone the norm. It is impossible, for example, to think of humanities scholarship that engages the law without citing legal scholarship, or medical anthropology that does not take seriously the existence and knowledge base of doctors, even while remaining critical of that knowledge base.[47] The failure is not that humanities scholars do not take professional knowledge seriously, it is that they only acknowledge the existence of *certain* professional knowledges; not coincidentally, those professions that have been predominantly male and well-paid are the most respected and legitimized. While it is difficult to find evidence of an erasure, let alone the gendered and classed nature of such erasure (something with which many humanities scholars of 'the archive' will agree), I argue that this erasure can be attributed to the fact that archival studies as a field has been feminized and relegated to the realm of 'mere' service-oriented practice rather than engaged with as a serious intellectual project.[48]

Ways Forward

Although this analysis has painted a rather bleak picture, there are ways that we can heal this rift. For their part, archival studies scholars have to do more to articulate the existence and value of their perspectives to humanities scholars. Given that this chapter is aimed at a humanities audience, I will focus my recommendations on concrete actions that humanities scholars can take to learn about archival studies perspectives and engage archival studies scholars as intellectual equals. These recommendations centre around three key actions: read and cite archival studies scholarship; organize and participate in joint conferences and reading groups between archival studies and humanities scholars; and jointly teach doctoral seminars about differing approaches to archive(s) as a pedagogical strategy. Through each of these recommendations, I assert that interdisciplinarity is a two-way street; humanities scholars must acknowledge and engage archival studies scholarship, just as archival studies scholars have engaged and should continue to engage more deeply with the humanities. Such engagement with archival studies will only deepen humanities scholarship, as humanities learn more about the theory and processes that inform archival labour.

As a unique area of inquiry, archival studies has a well-developed body of published scholarship. Humanities scholars can begin to engage archival studies by reading archival studies journals. *Archival Science* is the top-ranked international journal in the field, publishing scholarship that is often theoretical in nature. Recent themed issues—on topics as diverse as archives and human rights, activist archives, and affect—draw on interdisciplinary scholarship from fields like anthropology, law, gender studies, and ethnic studies. The Australian journal *Archives and Manuscripts* publishes a wide range of scholarship with a particular emphasis on records continuum theory and Indigenous perspectives on the rights and responsibilities associated with records and their archivization. For a window into the rich Canadian lineage of archival thinking (the birthplace of concepts like macroappraisal and functional analysis), the Association of Canadian Archivists publishes *Archivaria*, a journal that spans both the theoretical and practical aspects of archival studies. The Society of American Archivists' journal *The American Archivist* focuses on practical concerns, often reporting on research anchored in social science methods to study the appraisal, description, and use of archives.

The UK and Ireland Archives and Records Association publishes *Archives and Records*, which has featured articles on personal archives, community archives, and artists' collections.

Edited volumes also provide fertile terrain. *Currents of Archival Thinking* (edited by Terry Eastwood and Heather MacNeil) provides a basic overview of core values and principles in the field, while the comprehensive *Research in the Archival Multiverse* (edited by Anne Gilliland, Sue McKemmish, and Andrew J. Lau) details dozens of archival studies approaches—ranging from the humanistic to the scientific—to answering research questions.[49] Increasingly, archival studies scholars are publishing sole-authored book-length manuscripts as well. *Archives and Justice: A South African Perspective* by Verne Harris, *Ephemeral Material: Queering the Archive* by Alana Kumbier, and *Conceptualizing 21st-Century Archives* by Anne Gilliland all exemplify the (too often untapped) potential of archival studies to engage wider and more diverse audiences.[50] At the risk of being self-promoting, my own book *Archiving the Unspeakable: Silence, Memory and the Photographic Record in Cambodia* introduces records continuum theory to a general humanities audience and anchors its discussion of Khmer Rouge era mug shots to archival studies interpretations of provenance.[51] It is one of the first books in archival studies published by a mainstream university press and geared towards in interdisciplinary audience (in this case scholars of human rights and Southeast Asian studies). Becoming familiar with archival studies literature is an important first step. Engaging with the ideas contained in them and acknowledging their intellectual merit by citing them is the necessary next step. Citation is a political act that legitimates intellectual lineages.[52]

Creating and supporting joint venues to present research, exchange perspectives, and hosting and taking workshops is another key step. It is not uncommon to see listings for humanities conferences on 'the archive' that do not feature a single archival studies scholar or practising archivist. This rift is untenable and easily remedied. Talk to each other. Reach out across departments to ask questions. Seek out and value each other's opinions. Invite archival studies scholars to present research at humanities conferences. Respect them as thinkers and not just as technicians. Locally, humanities scholars can reach out across the divide to archival studies scholars and archivists at their universities to form informal interdisciplinary reading clusters and research groups that address issues of archive(s). For example, archivists, faculty, and graduate students at the University of Texas at Austin formed the Archives and Human Rights Working Group at the Rapoport Center for Human Rights and Justice on campus.[53] In another example, together with historian Geoffrey Robinson, I co-founded a human rights archives working group at UCLA that hosted an interdisciplinary symposium, 'The Antonym of Remembering', in October 2013. The symposium brought together archival studies scholars, practising archivists, historians, anthropologists, legal scholars, and activists to talk about intersections and divergences in approaches to archives documenting human rights abuse and resulted in a special double issue of the journal *Archival Science*.[54] The perspectives of each field were strengthened by this exchange.

Finally, train doctoral students to think interdisciplinarily by offering seminars jointly taught by humanities and archival studies scholars. Lay bare the differences between the approaches. Be honest about incommensurability and point out areas where more intellectual work is needed. Such seminars would teach humanities doctoral students to appreciate archival thinking and practice and teach archival studies students how humanities scholars view archive(s) and what they expect from them as users and theorists. These seminars may be difficult to co-teach, but the pedagogical potential is immense. At UCLA, archival studies scholar Anne Gilliland and anthropologist Hariz Halilovich (visiting from Monash University) co-taught a graduate seminar called 'Migrating Memories: Archives, Diasporas and Human Rights', which was listed in the Department of Information Studies, but drew students from Chicana/o studies, gender studies, history, and anthropology. As a result, there has been more interest in taking additional archival studies courses among graduate students in the humanities. This model is easily replicable at other universities and could lead to a generational shift in humanities scholars' understanding of archival theory and practice.

Conclusion: Healing the Rift

This chapter has described some of the intellectual concerns of archival studies, delineated the intellectual rift between archival studies scholarship and humanities scholarship about 'the archive', and proposed a few concrete steps we can take to heal this rift. Archival studies scholars and practising archivists are more than willing to meet humanities scholars halfway, but there has to be a willingness to engage and a baseline of respect in interdisciplinary exchange that is currently lacking. Humanities scholars can begin to demonstrate respect for archival studies by reading its literature, engaging its scholars in dialogue, and co-teaching seminars with archival studies scholars. Throughout, it is key that humanities scholars acknowledge the existence of archival studies as a legitimate academic field rather than just a prescription for practice. This chapter, I hope, will spark such a mutually respectful interdisciplinary exchange.

FURTHER READING

Michelle Caswell, *Archiving the Unspeakable: Silence, Memory and the Photographic Record in Cambodia* (Madison: University of Wisconsin Press, 2014)

Anne J. Gilliland, *Conceptualizing 21st-Century Archives* (Chicago: Society of American Archivists, 2014)

Jacinta Kelly, 'Of Archives and Architecture: Domestication, Digital Collections, and the Poetry of Mina Loy', *Australian Feminist Studies* 32.91–92 (2017): 171–185

Alana Kumbier, *Ephemeral Material: Queering the Archive* (Sacramento: Litwin Books, 2014)

Jessica Lapp, '"Handmaidens of History" Speculating on the Feminization of Archival Work', *Archival Science* 19.3 (2019): 215–234

Sue McKemmish, Michael Pigott, Barbara Reed, and Frank Upward, eds, *Archives: Record-keeping in Society* (Wagga Wagga: Centre for Information Studies, Charles Sturt University, 2005)

NOTES

1. This chapter originally appeared as: M. Caswell, '"The Archive" Is Not an Archives: On Acknowledging the Intellectual Contributions of Archival Studies', *Reconstruction: Studies in Contemporary Culture* 16.1 (2016) (special issue 'Archives on Fire', edited by S. Howard), previously at: http://reconstruction.eserver.org/Issues/161/Caswell.shtml, also at https://escholarship.org/uc/item/7bn4v1fk. After writing and titling this article, I was made aware of Jessa Lingel's short but spot-on blog post, which makes similar observations, 'This Is Not An Archive', November 2013, http://jessalingel.tumblr.com/post/66108958850/this-is-not-an-archive.

2. M. Foucault, *Archaeology of Knowledge and The Discourse on Language*, trans. A. M. Sheridan Smith (New York: Pantheon Books, 1972), p. 129; J. Derrida, *Archive Fever: A Freudian Impression*, trans. E. Prenowitz (Chicago: University of Chicago Press, 1996).

3. For a more detailed discussion of the differences between the use of 'archive' in humanities scholarship and 'archives' in archival studies scholarship, see the introduction to A. Kumbier, *Ephemeral Material: Queering the Archive* (Sacramento: Litwin Books, 2014), 1–35; T. Cook, 'The Archive(s) Is A Foreign Country: Historians, Archivists, and the Changing Archival Landscape', *American Archivist* 74 (2011), 600–632; and Lingel, 'This Is Not an Archive'.

4. A. Cvetkovich, *An Archive of Feelings* (Durham: Duke, 2003), 268. To complicate matters, archival studies is not interested *only* in 'actually existing archives', but rather, in 'imaginary records' as well, but read through an archival studies lens, that is, demonstrating concern about archival concepts such as record, evidence, etc., as later addressed. See M. Caswell and A. J. Gilliland, 'Dead Perpetrators, Imagined Documents, Emergent Evidence and False Promises: Deconstructing an Archival Paradox', *International Journal of Human Rights* 19.5 (2015), 615–627, and A. J. Gilliland and M. Caswell, 'Records and Their Imaginaries: Imagining the Impossible, Making Possible the Imagined', *Archival Science* 16.1 (2015), 53–75.

5. The converse can also be said about archival studies, but to a much lesser extent, as archival studies scholars routinely draws from fields like philosophy, history, anthropology, memory studies, and cultural studies. For example, while an article by T. Jacobsen, R. Punzalan, and M. Hedstrom called on archival studies scholars to expand their citation pools, the accompanying citation analysis showed that archival scholars routinely cite J. Derrida, M. Halbwachs, D. Lowenthal, and A. L. Stoler on collective memory. See:

T. Jacobsen, R. Punzalan, and M. Hedstrom, 'Invoking "Collective Memory": Mapping the Emergence of a Concept in Archival Science', *Archival Science* 13 (2013), 217–251.

6. For a comprehensive demonstration of the range of archival studies methods, see: A. J. Gilliland, S. McKemmish, and A. J. Lau, eds, *Research in the Archival Multiverse* (Melbourne: Monash University Press, 2016).

7. For a detailed bibliographic essay on the history of the dominant archival studies tradition, see: J. M. O'Toole and R. J. Cox, *Understanding Archives and Manuscripts* (Chicago: Society of American Archivists, 2006). Two edited volumes also serve as compilations of important American archival studies thinking: M. Daniels and T. Walch, eds, *A Modern Archives Reader: Basic Readings on Archival Theory and Practice* (Washington, DC: National Archives and Records Administration, 1984); and R. C. Jimerson, ed., *American Archival Studies: Readings in Theory and Practice* (Chicago: Society of American Archivists, 2000).

8. For a more detailed history of how the contemporary archival profession emerged out of the conflicting strands of the public records tradition and more humanistic manuscripts tradition, see L. Gilliland-Swetland, 'The Provenance of a Profession: The Permanence of the Public Archives and Historical Manuscripts Traditions in American Archival History', *American Archivist* 54 (1991), 160–175.

9. This shift is not entirely complete. As Richard Cox notes, between 1970 and 2000, 30 archival studies faculty joined LIS programmes, while 15 joined history departments. R. Cox, 'Graduate Archival Education in the United States: A Personal Reflection about Its Past and Future', *Journal of Contemporary Archival Studies* 2 (2015): http://elischolar.library.yale.edu/cgi/viewcontent.cgi?article=1008&context=jcas.

10. 'Archival Education and Research Institute', http://aeri.website/.

11. 'iSchools', http://ischools.org.

12. G. Yeo, 'Concepts of Record (1): Evidence, Information, and Persistent Representation', *American Archivist* 70 (2007), 334.

13. J. Furner, 'Conceptual Analysis: A Method for Understanding Information as Evidence, and Evidence as Information', *Archival Science* 4 (2004), 233–265.

14. B. Brothman, 'Afterglow: Conceptions of Record and Evidence in Archival Discourse', *Archival Science* 2 (2002), 311–342.

15. S. Faulkhead, 'Connecting through Records: Narratives of Koorie Victoria', *Archives and Manuscripts* 37.2 (2010), 60–88.

16. V. Harris, 'Genres of the Trace: Memory, Archives, and Trouble', *Archives and Manuscripts* 40.3 (2012), 150.

17. The continuum model represents a radical shift from the previously predominant records life cycle model, which sees archival deposit as the final resting place for inactive records.

18. F. Upward, 'Modelling the Continuum as Paradigm Shift in Recordkeeping and Archiving Processes and Beyond', *Records Management Journal* (December 2000): unpaginated.

19. Upward, 'Modelling', 335.

20. E. Ketelaar, 'Tacit Narratives: The Meaning of Archives', *Archival Science* 1.2 (2001), 138.

21. Society of American Archivists, 'Provenance', *Dictionary of Archives Terminology*, http://dictionary.archivists.org/entry/provenance.html.

22. J. Douglas, 'Origins: Evolving Ideas about the Principle of Provenance', in T. Eastwood and H. MacNeil, eds, *Currents of Archival Thinking* (Santa Barbara, CA: Libraries Unlimited, 2010), 24.

23. T. Nesmith, 'Still Fuzzy but More Accurate: Some Thoughts on the "Ghosts" of Archival Theory', *Archivaria* 47 (1999), 146.

24. L. Millar, 'The Death of the Fonds and the Resurrection of Provenance: Archival Context in Space and Time', *Archivaria* 53 (2002), 12–13.

25. J. Wurl, 'Ethnicity as Provenance: In Search of Values and Principles Documenting the Immigrant Experience', *Archival Issues* 29.1 (2005).

26. J. Bastian, *Owning Memory: How a Caribbean Community Lost Its Archives and Found Its History* (Westport, CT: Libraries Unlimited, 2003).

27. Bastian, *Owning Memory*, 5.

28. Hurley defines parallel provenance as 'the coterminous generation of the same thing in the same way at the same time'. However, I would add that in many contentious examples, particularly those involving disputes over the physical custody of records, the provenance is not parallel, but on a collision course. C. Hurley, 'Parallel Provenance', www.infotech.monash.edu.au/research/groups/rcrg/publications/parallel-provenance-combined.pdf, 10. See also: C. Hurley, 'Parallel Provenance: What If Anything Is Archival Description?', *Archives and Manuscripts* 33.1 (2005), 110–145.

29. L. Iacovino, 'Rethinking Archival, Ethical and Legal Frameworks for Records of Indigenous Australian Communities: A Participant Relationship Model of Rights and Responsibilities', *Archival Science* 10 (2010), 353–372.

30. For an excellent, more detailed overview of the concept of value in archival studies, see C. Trace, 'On or Off the Record? Notions of Value in the Archive', in Eastwood and MacNeil, *Currents in Archival Thinking*, 47–68.

31. Society of American Archivists, 'Descriptive Metadata', 2010.

32. E. Yakel, 'Archival Representation', *Archival Science* 3 (2003), 2.

33. W. Duff and V. Harris, 'Stories and Names: Archival Description as Narrating Records and Constructing Meanings', *Archival Science* 2 (2002), 263–285 (276).

34. T. Cook, 'Fashionable Nonsense or Professional Rebirth: Postmodernism and the Practice of Archives', *Archivaria* 51 (Spring 2001), 14–35; Duff and Harris, 'Stories and Names'.

35. Duff and Harris, 'Stories and Names', 275.

36. This list includes books on 'actually existing archives' and on 'the archive' in the broader humanistic understanding. D. Taylor, *The Archive and the Repertoire* (Durham: Duke, 2003); C. Steedman, *Dust: The Archive and Cultural History* (New Brunswick: Rutgers, 2002); A. Cvetkovich's *An Archive of Feelings* (Durham: Duke, 2003); A. L. Stoler, *Along the Archival Grain: Epistemic Anxieties and Colonial Common Sense* (Princeton: Princeton University Press, 2009); A. Burton, ed., *Archive Stories: Facts, Fictions, and the Writing of History* (Durham: Duke University Press, 2005).

37. K. Eichorn, *The Archival Turn in Feminism: Outrage in Order* (Philadelphia: Temple University Press, 2013).

38. The archival profession in the US is in majority female, with 65% of respondents reporting as women in a recent professional survey conducted by the Society of American Archivists. Society of American Archivists, A*Census (2006): www2.archivists.org/sites/all/files/ACENSUS-Final.pdf.

39. T. Cook, 'Remembering the Future: Appraisal of Records and the Role of Archives in Constructing Social Memory', *Archives, Documentation, and Institutions of Social Memory: Essays from the Sawyer Seminar* (Ann Arbor, University of Michigan, 2006), 170.

40. V. Harris, *Archives and Justice: A South African Perspective* (Chicago, Society of American Archivists, 2006).

41. For a classic example of this, see M.-R. Trouillot, *Silencing the Past: Power and the Production of History* (Boston: Beacon Press, 1995). Trouillot is oblivious to the archival function of appraisal, though he is acutely aware that not all records make it into archives.

42. For another illustration of this gap, see A. Arondekar et al. 'Queering Archives: A Roundtable Discussion', *Radical History Review* Special Issue on 'Queering Archives: Intimate Traces', 122 (2015), 211–231. This conversation would read as largely unintelligible to the majority of archival studies scholars and archivists, even to the more theoretically-oriented among them.

43. D. Ghosh, 'National Narratives and the Politics of Miscegenation', in Burton, *Archive Stories*, 41; 32.

44. C. Robertson, 'Mechanisms of Exclusion', in Burton, *Archive Stories*, 76.

45. Robertson, 'Mechanisms of Exclusion', 68.

46. Robertson, 'Mechanisms of Exclusion', 77. He bases his analysis on the work of Allan Sekula, a photographer and art critic who, while having much to say about archives and much to offer archival theory, is not trained as an archival studies scholar.

47. Terry Cook makes a similar claim about nursing and engineering. See Cook, 'The Archive(s) is a Foreign Country', 614.

48. The feminization of the field as a whole occurs despite a preponderance of unhelpful male archivists described in humanities scholarship.

49. Eastwood and MacNeil, *Currents in Archival Thinking*; Gilliland, McKemmish, and Lau, *Research in the Archival Multiverse*.

50. Harris, *Archives and Justice*; Kumbier, *Ephemeral Material*; A. J. Gilliland, *Conceptualizing 21st-Century Archives* (Chicago: Society of American Archivists, 2014).

51. M. Caswell, *Archiving the Unspeakable: Silence, Memory and the Photographic Record in Cambodia* (Madison: University of Wisconsin Press, 2014).

52. S. Ahmed, 'Making Feminist Points', 11 September 2013: feministkilljoys.com/2013/09/11/making-feminist-points/.

53. For more information, see: www.utexas.edu/law/centers/humanrights/faculty/working-groups.php.

54. For more information on the symposium, see: UCLA Human Rights Archives Working Group, accessed 7 December 2015, https://uclahumanrightsarchives.wordpress.com/. See also 'Special Double Issue on Archives and Human Rights', *Archival Science* 14.3–4 (2014).

CHAPTER 2

WHERE AND WHAT ARE THE BOUNDARIES OF THE ARCHIVE?

LOUISE CRAVEN

In the past few decades the world of archives has been transformed. In England, archives reflecting the world of the rich and powerful, the government, the landed, and the legal have been held on vellum, parchment, and paper since the twelfth century. Over the centuries, the records of colonial administrations and the growing bureaucracy of state, together with personal papers and the records of large private bodies have swelled the holdings of formal documents. Yet the means of storing and preserving records changed little until the late twentieth century. Over the last two decades, however, archives have shifted to reflect the world of which they are part and, in doing so, have changed radically in content and in format. Archives now belong to everyone and to every type of organization wishing to store data. They are notable by their bulk and they are held in an international dynamic digital environment. The means by which they have done this is, of course, the technological infrastructure of the internet. Now the media specialist, Gabriella Giannachi,[1] urges us to map the everyday and archive everything; in this new world then, where do the boundaries of the archive lie?

This chapter is an attempt to answer this question. In doing so, the issues surrounding automation and digitization and how they have changed the ways in which archives are made available will be discussed, the relationship between archives, museums, and libraries, and the potential of new audiences will be considered and the power of the archive and the roles of truth and fiction in archives will be given new focus. Now the archive touches everyone and we will look briefly at some of the groups and institutions so affected. Firstly, though, we need to examine those changes in society and in the use of language, where the spread of the archive first became apparent.

Society

The digital revolution of the late twentieth and early twenty-first century changed society irrevocably. Firstly, the means of communication between people was transformed, by email, then by smartphones, then by social media. William Merrin comments that at this point, *people themselves* became part of the internet, 'a node in the communication network; liking, tweeting, adding, video-ing, all at once'.[2] An abundance of information became available. The impact on politics and economics was and remains seismic. Economically, the World Wide Web became a symbol of global capitalism and in time it transformed our buying habits and our high streets. Politically, digitization proved to be a huge democratic force, opening politics and political activity to many who previously had been resigned to having no voice. The internet, and more specifically social media, gave power to the people in a way perhaps never anticipated. The freedom to speak out became part of popular culture. While, on one hand digitization was the great leveller, on the other, it ushered in the post-truth era with its characteristic qualities of emotion, personal belief, changeability, pragmatic truth, and alternative facts.

Language

Over the years spanning the late twentieth century into the twenty-first, the usage and meaning of the words 'archive' and 'archives' have changed. Whether to use the singular or plural forms of the noun has long been contentious in the archive community, but now the words have much greater currency and are used interchangeably. Moreover, the verb 'to archive' has acquired a general usage. The term used to refer to the formal process by which some records, those thought to have historical significance, were selected from much larger collections of administrative records by a process termed 'appraisal', and then permanently preserved in the archive; now, thanks to the digital revolution everybody can archive and everybody can have an archive. The terms have been adopted by any individual, group, organization, or business who wishes to store and retain evidence of the past and present for future use. Of this huge diversity, there are now roughly three types of archive: firstly, historical and governmental archives; secondly a large and heterogeneous group we might call 'diverse or alternative archives', which includes everything from community archives to political websites; and thirdly, huge administrative datasets primarily of corporate origin. Unlike historical archives, both diverse archives and administrative datasets are unlikely to have been appraised, may not grant public access, and may contain anything from financial accounts, records of business meetings, day-to-day routines, criminal activities, and encrypted security records, to diaries, personal stories, poetry, streamed music, photographs, performance art, or simple emails. By their size and number these new archives have overshadowed the scale of historical archives and have adopted its terminology. For many, a business necessity, for others, archiving has become a cultural activity. The boundary of the archive is clearly fluid in language and has moved into many other activities of life.

The Historical Archive

What happened in the historical archive in response to the technological changes of the digital revolution? In the UK, France, Germany, the USA, and Canada, plans for addressing electronic and then digital archives began in the 1990s with electronic archive catalogues. Boosted by the technological advances then achieved and by international standards aimed at easing the exchange of information, official archives with an internet presence grew rapidly. Now, in 2023, The International Council on Archives (ICA) boasts well over 2000 institutional members in 200 countries and territories, and the boundaries of historical and governmental archives stretch from Fiji to Lithuania, from Australia to Iceland.

In the archive itself, some extremely significant historical documents—Magna Carta, American Declaration of Independence, for example—were available in digital format from the British Library and the United States' Library of Congress from the 1990s, but it was not until some years later that archives began to make digital documents more systematically available. This gap can be explained to great extent by size and funding, but also, some would argue, by curatorial attitudes and outlook which began to change significantly in leading archive institutions in the later nineties. Family history enthusiasts wasted no time in exploiting these developments by vastly increasing the number of visitors to the archive. Then the worldwide online archive began to develop. Blogs and websites appeared and, in short order, users began to curate their own material. At the same time, the digital camera, used freely in the record office, 'set records and documents free to have new independent lives'.[3] New networks arose. As Wolfgang Ernst commented, 'dynamically generated information is now the signature of the internet'.[4] Within a decade, technological advance would lead to declining numbers of visitors to the physical archive, but not yet. All this change and innovation not only signified new audiences and new activities but also a shifting outlook on the part of archive management. Historical archives no longer reflected solely the nation state, or the dominant social and political stratum, or the imperialist and colonial past, but also came to reflect social and cultural diversity within the wider society, with record-collecting policies which embraced that change.

During the first decade of this century, much research on historical archives focussed on participation based on users' own experience, as Alexandra Eveleigh explains in her thesis 'Crowding Out the Archivist?' begun in 2009.[5] And it was the appearance of blogs, personal archive material, and participatory information which together signalled a real shift in the traditional archival paradigm which had long stressed the singular importance of the creator of the archival document and which privileged bureaucratic contexts and custody. In 1996, Australian archivist Sue McKemmish had demonstrated that a record could be as much about *content* as about the creator in her article 'Evidence of Me'.[6] This marked a real turning point in archivists' thinking about the subjectivity and objectivity of the record, but it was clear from the popularity of participatory and experiential material, that it was now the user, as much as the archivist, who determined what was and what was not historical archival material. Moreover, it does not appear that the evidentiality of the document is diminished through digitization. Walter Benjamin said that the 'aura' of an original work of art was lost in reproduction[7] and this may also be true of an historical document, but it does not appear to be the case here as many users simply print out the digital copy and use it as the original. And though there are legal restrictions remaining on the use of copies,[8] those who seek their own or their family's history through the records tend to regard the digitized document as evidence in their quest. Clearly, the boundaries to the archive have shifted in an epistemological sense in terms of the philosophical and the subjective and in a personal sense in terms of ownership and identity.

New focus on participatory archive material throws the old questions around truth and fiction into new light. In the actual and the virtual archive there are truths, fictions, lies, and falsehoods; how do you know what is true and what is not? Natalie Zemon Davis has demonstrated how the narratives constructed from royal letters of pardon and remission in sixteenth-century France are full of fictional qualities, that is to say 'the extent to which their authors shape the events of a crime into a story'.[9] How, you might say, do these letters of pardon differ from defendants' depositions in court at the English Assizes? Here the clerk writes down what he hears as he hears it: it is not a story, not fiction. But the doubt might remain. Some records are thought to be more reliable than others: financial transactions and land conveyances fall into this category, whereas correspondence and minutes of meetings do not. All historical documents need to be approached with the utmost caution and it is only with a rigorously critical eye and a weighing of the evidence that some attempt to find out what actually happened can be made. Both truths and falsehoods in the archive may be constructed from narrative which enables the researcher to piece together a story arising from the records. But is it true or false?

From a different perspective, whilst the boundaries to the archive are open and spreading, it is to be noted that there are threats to the historical archive in both its analogue and digital form. Security, privacy, closure, and confidentiality may be seen in this light. More practically, the condition of records is a definite threat. Deterioration through age and usage may endanger the record and language, religion, and culture, can inhibit understanding, but these latter can be overcome. Destruction however, cannot. This can take the form of appraisal which prevents records from entering the archive. Though less operative in the digital world, appraisal severely restricts what *can* enter the archive. In the United States only between

2 and 5 per cent of administrative records find their way into the National Archive and Records Administration (NARA) and in the UK a similar amount is taken into The National Archives (TNA), which means that all remaining records are destroyed. More worryingly, the difficulty and cost of answering many Freedom of Information requests are leading some archivists and record managers to consider the wholesale destruction of records to avoid these problems. Destruction may also take the form of political oppression as we have seen in so many regimes from the Soviet Union to South Africa to Bosnia and Syria. All forms of destruction bring silences to the archive. Silences also pertain from agreements *not* to document proceedings, as for example, in the Suez Crisis or in Tony Blair's government, which distort the recording of government or administration. Silence also emanates from the owners of those huge social media records and corporate datasets that are private and therefore unknown. Silences often tell us more about the originating source than we might expect, but all this serves to remind us that what we can glean from the archive is only ever a partial and fragmentary picture of what might have been. Security, destruction, and silence limit the boundaries of the historical archive and its counterparts in the wider world.

Different Kinds of Archives

Recent decades have witnessed an explosion of community archives, independent archives, alternative archives, counter archives, and identity archives—which taken together might be called 'diverse archives'. These archives can represent all manner of social and geographical communities, lesbian, gay, and transgender organizations, minority groups, local historical societies, religious groups, political archives, and environmental organizations of all kinds. Community archives did of course exist well before the digital revolution, but it has been internet technology and social media which has spurred this recent surge. Andrew Flynn talks of community archives reflecting 'grass roots', making history from below accessible to everybody for whom 'control and ownership are essential'.[10] Community archives can provide spaces crucial to record the voices of people not otherwise heard, and they are, by definition political, for as Rebecka Sheffield points out, 'the very act of taking control of one's own documentary heritage is political'.[11] In the UK, community archives have gained significant support from both TNA and the Archives and Records Association (ARC) and in Canada, First Nations and Indigenous Heritage Groups are part of Library and Archives Canada's official collection. Community archives can also give counter space for support to other minority groups. The Interference Archive in Brooklyn is one such, which reflects the grassroots activities of documenting, recording, and exploring its opposition to the speed and immediacy of today's world, whilst at the same time providing space on its website for diverse social movements from Europe, Latin America, and China as well as the USA.[12]

Recently, community archives have been joined by autonomous archives—promoting specific social or political acts—by participatory archives, and by Do-It-Yourself (DIY) archives, which reflect an individual's or a group's interest. An archive which seems to cross the divide between community, autonomous, and DIY archive is that of the Birmingham Centre for Contemporary Cultural Studies (BCCCS) at the city's University. The archive was opened in 2013, some years after the acrimonious relationship between the Centre and the University administration, which ended in the closure of the Centre in 2002. The archive's stated aim was to document the material history of the Centre and to ensure that the achievements and insights of cultural studies were appropriately recognized.[13] In Wakefield, a craft collective of silversmiths, potters, bookbinders, and ceramicists has created an archive for storage, discussion, and reference of art-work, and in Bristol, *Yellow Feather* provides a site for street art with archives for storage and reference.[14] These DIY archives echo those active on the international scene. Also to be mentioned in the context of diverse and independent archives are the archives of those bodies which use the Web in a dynamic way, to organize political events. Of alt-right, hard-left, and anarchist tendencies, the activities of these groups are orchestrated by social media, their records are encrypted to avoid detection, and their archives are hidden from view. Unlike many diverse archives, the archives of these bodies may be temporary and their internet presence short lived.

Overall, it is clear that diverse archives will continue to flourish in future years. Given today's environment, the support forthcoming from professionals, and the ease of use of social media, they are highly likely to thrive: the boundaries of these archives will surge well into the future.

Archives, Museums, and Libraries

It might be thought that the way to counteract declining attendance in archive buildings which are expensive to maintain would be for archives to join with other institutions in the heritage business to offset costs and attract new audiences. There are however, many reasons why this is not done as a matter of course: funds, location, and professional values seem to be the main barriers.[15] The theoretical aspect of joint ventures was addressed by Geoffrey Yeo in 2008. He noted that some items—a painting, a photograph, a report, for example—transcend the boundaries between archive, museum, and library categories, and suggested that we move towards cross-domain standards to facilitate the access to such material. In the future, user expectations and the digital revolution would make it increasingly difficult to justify the separate maintenance of 'silos' of resources.[16] A similar trend towards education that treats libraries, archives, and museums as one cultural entity is emerging in library and information schools in Canada and the US. Additionally, professional moves to bring archives, libraries, and museums together to the user have been successful in Australia and in the US: in 2011, the National Library of Australia unveiled the Trove system which provides a search engine bringing together newspapers, archives, and manuscripts and in 2016 the Digital Public Library of America presented a similar service. In Britain, both TNA and Research Libraries UK (RLUK) are exploring similar possibilities.

More recently, a proposal for widening the scope of archives in another direction has come from Andrew Prescott. In a lecture in November 2018, he suggested that a *human body* could be regarded as an archival artefact if the body is preserved in a museum and when other sources, for example, letters and papers about the individual exist.[17] Other archives are moving to share archive, museum, and artistic materials to a different end. In Haiku Adventure for example, Ceci Williams and James Morgan use the collection of Ukiyo-e archives of Japanese woodblock prints at the William Morris Gallery in Walthamstow to explore the intersection between traditional woodblock art and the craft of video games. Their exhibition is aimed at the Indie and Gaming scenes, but it also aims to engage audiences which perhaps do not traditionally go to art galleries and archives.[18] As enterprising in a quite different way, are the curators of the Whitechapel Gallery, hosting The Imaginary Archive, who ask the public about planned exhibitions, which in fact have never seen the light of day. This question, prompted by an archive gallery exhibition, presents sculptors' models, photographs of artworks on show, and correspondence concerning unrealized projects, about which the curator asks: 'With the passage of time, can archive materials such as sketches and letters, make unrealized projects as tangible as those that really happened?'[19] Our consciousness is being explored here. Clearly, historical archives are moving towards collaborative work with other professions, and all are seeking to push the boundaries of the archive to new and unexpected places.

Individual Archive Researchers

What then of the individuals working on archival material, where do the boundaries of the archive lie for them? Let's look at someone with a personal archive, at a PhD student, and at a genealogist to see what all the technological, philosophical, and ontological changes have meant for them. For the individual with a personal archive, the Cloud seems to offer a limitless boundary to the storage of such data as it does for digital photographs in the .jpeg format. Alternatively, MyKive at the University of Illinois will copy, preserve, and manage personal archives, as will Facebook, Twitter, and WhatsApp. Elsewhere, the student working for a PhD is now able to get many of the sources, reference works, articles, and some of the theses immediately online, available at their desktop. Whilst this greatly reduces the time to be spent on these sources, the amount of material now available on any scholarly topic is much greater than it ever was and that amount increases daily. Additionally, participatory archives, blogs, and other sources of archive material hugely increase the amount of information to be studied, checked, and analysed. Meanwhile, genealogists now find a great deal of material online and can order digitized copies of many significant documents. They also benefit from participatory archives, blogs, and social media sites and from family history society meetings on Zoom; from here, the genealogist may create a website, which in turn becomes a site for others to read. Self-curation adds greatly to the material available online, which both student and genealogist need to check. All seem happy with the spreading technology and philosophy of the archive.

Professional Archivists

Despite this huge proliferation in the variety of new archives, professional archivists the world over remain mainly concerned with issues arising from their domestic context. Debates about the changes to archival principles and practice brought by the digital revolution are still unresolved and questions of original order, provenance, and description dominate. Arguments about appraisal, about what is evidential or enduring and what is not, continue. In the printed world, archivists are engaged in wider debates: for example, about social justice (should our energies be directed here or should we concentrate on the real issues of bulk, records management and Freedom of Information?); about fake news (to collect or not?); and about community archives (can we learn from their aims and practices, and should we?). Practical and theoretical issues as ever intertwine. Archivists have been interested in archival theory from the days of Jenkinson and Schellenberg, but really only at a theoretical level. By and large, apart from recent writings which we shall come to, interest in archival theory has tended to focus archivists inward, onto their own issues, rather than outward.

Perhaps surprisingly, it was a philosopher and sociologist, not an archivist, who was to make the greatest contribution to archival theory in the last 30 years. In *Archive Fever,* published in 1995, Jacques Derrida, stressed the authority and power of the archive: 'There is no power without the archive, if not of memory' and he affirmed its political function: access to the open archive is, 'the essential criterion of democracy'.[20] It was not expected that someone from outside the realm of archives would contribute so major a work, and it took professional archivists some time to respond. The main archival contributors—Brien Brothman, Terry Cook, Verne Harris, Randall Jimerson, Sue McKemmish, Tom Nesmith, and Sarah Tyacke—responded to Derrida at a time when ideas in post-modernist thinking had also raised wider issues of meaning, interpretation, communication, and the relevance of written documents. In consequence, reaction was diverse, some exploring power and social memory, some adhering fully to notions of the post-modern linguistic turn, others more cautiously looking at what this could mean for the archive and the records it contained. Discussion of related issues continued into the new millennium. Overall however, publications from archivists over these years served to obscure what was actually being said about archives elsewhere, and elided a number of issues about archives which were emerging in different academic disciplines.

By contrast, over the last three years there have been huge new departures in archival thinking. Four collections of essays by professional archivists question the epistemological basis of the old archival paradigm, raise fundamental practical and theoretical issues and bring new issues to archives. These are *Currents of Archival Thinking,* edited by Heather MacNeil and Terry Eastwood (2017); *Silence of the Archive,* edited by David Thomas, Stephen Fowler, and Val Johnson (2017); *Archival Futures,* edited by Caroline Brown (2018); and *Do Archives Have Value?,* edited by Michael Moss and David Thomas (2019). As the titles indicate, archivists have moved a long way from debates about shelving and the life cycle of a record. From the four collections, then, certain specific issues stand out and illustrate the transformations in outlook. These are: archives in the future and the problems inherent in online digital collections; the silence of the archive in the past and, perhaps more ominously, the impact of destruction in the future; the difficulties of archival research in the post-truth world; and a new and wide perspective of the value of archives in various countries in an economic, cultural, and evidential context. We are encouraged to ask—perhaps for the first time—what is *not* in the archive and why, and we are also treated to thoughts on the role of archives in social justice, new views of the activities of users, and a radical take on community archives. Most significant of all, however, is the revelation of the existential shift which has already taken place in archives. In their essay in *Archival Futures,* Michael Moss and David Thomas comment that the archive world has changed irrevocably, for *the internet* is now, by default, *the archive* and, by providing information of and for everyone, the internet has prevented the historical archive from any longer privileging information.[21] New ideas indeed.

Whilst these critical views come from the most prominent archival theorists on the international scene, they do not seem to be typical of most archivists. The old problem which Hugh Taylor identified about social and cultural changes in communication having made a profound impact on civilization, but being ignored by archivists, still rings true. Though it is extremely difficult to assess the views of working archivists, it seems as though many assume that, despite the huge changes made by the digital revolution, archives will stay much the same as they always have been. The burning questions of the day about the future of the archive and of the profession are not addressed. Notions that the role which *society plays in archives* should be considered, or that content should be widened further to include more than support of community archives, or that the social dislocations in society might be helped by archive policies, are rarely countenanced. Moreover, current contributions about archives from academics in other fields, which we are about to come to, have generated little response from archivists. Wolfgang Ernst commented: 'Never has the concept of the archive as a research space or object of cultural theory been so salient as today',[22] but many archivists do not seem to have noticed. Whilst archives are growing and networking in a way that cannot have been imagined some years ago, it seems that many professional archivists will be sidelined unless they too embrace the archive whose boundaries are fluid, social, and political, evolving, and inclusive.

Other Academic Disciplines

Before the onset of the digital, the archive was being discussed by academics in philosophy, language, anthropology, and psychology as an item within the human memory and as a place where the important documents of a culture could be kept. This latter view had emerged from Foucault's *Archaeology of Knowledge*;[23] the former stemmed from discussions of classical interpretations of memory and from Freudian psychoanalysis. Later, Derrida's *Archive Fever* gave new momentum to these debates and widened the field to include academics from sociology, political science, literary criticism, cognitive sciences, and media studies. Among the many subjects arising here, memory, time, and narrative are notable, as are a number of new approaches to the whole topic of archives.

The appearance of the journal *Memory Studies* in 2008 and the development of memory as a burgeoning field of interdisciplinary research in academic institutions worldwide gave archives a new relevance. Archivists have of course written about memory, about the collective memory emerging from the archives, but it was the media theorist Wolfgang Ernst and then the sociologist Andrew Hoskins who gave us a totally different understanding of memory, time, the digital, and the archives. In 2002, Ernst wrote of 'inverted time in the archive' and later, in 2013, Hoskins' article 'The End of Decay Time' appeared.[24] This captured the moment when the digital revolution enabled the new archive, no longer subject to the ravages of rot and decay, to bring the past into being in the present and the future.[25] Of course, the notion that the digital has brought with it changes to time is not new, as Tom Stoppard, Terry Pratchett, and *Dr Who* well attest, but further studies which have influenced our thinking on the transformation brought by the digital were to follow. In 2009, the political analyst Viktor Mayer-Shönberger explained that nothing is forgotten in the digital world as a record of every event is retained *for ever* in the digital archive—a global retention that can affect our grasp of chronology and our ability to remember things.[26] Later, the cultural theorist Mark Fisher noted that this jumbling up of time, this bringing the past into the present, reduced the experience of today's world to a feeling that 'there is no present to grasp and articulate anymore'.[27] Popular readership, global networking, and social media gave common currency to these analyses of the social, cultural, and psychological impact of the digital.

Memory and narrative have long been considered fruitful areas of research, attracting academics from diverse fields. In 2007, the developmental psychologist Katharine Nelson defined narrative as the structural glue 'which ties the who, what, where, when, and why together',[28] and in the following year, psychologist Robyn Fivish considered how individual lives are constructed in family narratives.[29] However, it is really as an adjunct to memory that the importance of narrative in the archive comes into its own. In *Beyond the Archive: Memory, Narrative, and the Autobiographical Process*, the philosopher Jens Brockmeier suggests that narrative is fundamental to autobiographical memory.[30]

In 2016, *The Archive Project: Archival Research in the Social Sciences,* looked at the archival turn in quite another way. From the standpoint of empirical sociology, Niamh Moore, Andrea Salter, Liz Stanley, and Maria Tamboukou asked: what is an archive? how does it come into existence? what are the ways to analyse the traces of the past, and what changes has the digital made to research?[31] New questions for historical archivists. With a similar approach, media sociologist Debra Ramsay examined and analysed archival interfaces (specifically that at TNA) in terms of how and what information was made available and how the changing shifting interface met user expectations. She concluded that far from being a neutral functioning search engine, the interface 'is a liminal state, that extends and delimits our pathways to the past; one that plays a pivotal role in the process of memory making and its relationship to individual, organization, and State'.[32]

Another wholly different view of archives has emerged from the media expert Gabriella Giannachi in *Archive Everything*. Giannachi comments that over the centuries, archives have moved from storing information and knowledge to *transmitting* information in the digital world. In previous decades, novels, film, and television boosted the role of archives within our cultural imagination and now, more significantly, new archives are developing—Giannachi's 'archives 3.0' and '4.0'. In this new world, artists, critics, curators, and performance artists have developed a new 'generative' role for the archive in which the user plays a productive part in the development of the archive. This new archive enables users to experience the archive and to interact with it.[33] This is an archive of the future, not of the past: no longer objective in any sense, but entirely subjective, creative, and imaginary.

It is evident that over the past two decades, publications from colleagues in diverse disciplines outside archives have brought fresh, exciting, and thought-provoking ideas to consideration of the topic; clearly the boundaries of the archive have widened here and show no sign of diminishing.

History

What then of the discipline of history, long considered complementary to historical archives? How are historians affected by the spreading boundaries of the archive? A divide between archivists and historians developing from the later 1960s is discussed by archivist Francis Blouin and historian W.G. Rosenberg in *Processing the Past*, published in 2011. They see the divide as having developed from the rise of records management and the technological needs of archivists on the one hand, and the post-modernist concerns of historians on the other.[34] However, Blouin and Rosenberg may have been overtaken by events, for at much the same time as they were writing about the impact of the division, historians *working with* archivists began to utilize the advantages presented by digital technology to develop ambitious and hugely successful new projects. London Lives, Crime, Poverty, and Social Policy in the eighteenth century for example, brings together historical research methodology with archival search guides to produce fifteen datasets from eight archives giving access to 3.35 million names. From 2017, the Machine Reading the Archive project at Cambridge has enabled historians and archivists to work together on text mining techniques. Clearly, the digital revolution has moved historians at the cutting edge of their profession into closer involvement with forward-looking archivists to achieve new research and new history.

At the same time, historians of literature have been using the techniques of the digital to enable extraordinary discoveries concerning the text of medieval and Renaissance documents. It appears that the boundaries of the archive, in this context, lie not entirely in the words on the page which can be *read* but in the writing on the page that the naked eye *cannot see*. In the past, marginalia and marks of ownership have, in many cases, been ignored by historians of reading, largely because of convention but also and more obviously, because they could not *see* them. Now, the digital environment enables readers to scrutinize previously unseeable text and images as well as marginalia and graffiti. Examples of this research have mostly been carried out in leading manuscript libraries and not in archives,[35] and they have revealed much about the society and culture in which they were created. Most illuminatingly, Bridget Whearty explains that she has used digital techniques to examine the manuscripts of Sir Thomas Hoccleve (1368–1426), and has used the information found in marginal drawings and graffiti therein to elucidate the working conditions of fourteenth-century scribes.[36] She shows that the physical demands complained of then were similar to those experienced by data assistants working for Google today. Perhaps in the future, new historical studies in the archive will arise from the graffiti and marginalia of archival documents with similarly startling results. We are used to multiple readings of a text: perhaps now we should investigate multiple *writings*.

Future Technology

In the end, we are all part of the internet, the new information landscape, and this is where the future of the archive lies. Yet the future here is not quite as clear as we might have thought: as we know, obsolescence, changing file formats, and data vulnerability haunt the digital world. A solution to this ever-changing, endlessly reconfiguring digital world is offered by a new technology, blockchain technology, which works through a distributed network of blocks of data which can be chained together and verified by a consensus algorithm and in this way can become permanent and unchangeable. For historical archives the transference from current technology to blockchain has the promise of avoiding obsolescence and preserving accuracy, but it throws up all the old questions of authenticity, originality, and integrity of historical records, along with some new ones surrounding contextual information that may be detached from records on blockchain. Moreover, as Luciana Duranti points out, it is not simply these questions that need to be addressed but also, and perhaps more substantively, those timeless ones about evidence and 'truth'. In the time of post-truth and fake news, archivists and record managers need to consider whether there are global values that dictate the acceptance or rejection of sources of evidence.[37] Philosophical and epistemological issues aside, a straightforward structural problem remains: the networked structure of blockchain technology does not lend itself to historical archive data, which tends to be organized in hierarchical fashion. For many other types of archives, similar problems loom. Much work then needs to be done to enable archivists and record managers to adopt blockchain technology. Vicki Lemieux explains that blockchain might be applicable to historical archives and to records management, but that its application is a non-trivial task requiring archivists and record managers to collaborate with computer scientists over some years. Moreover, for this to work, archivists and record managers need to change their way of thinking:[38] Lemieux is not alone in calling for change; Terry Eastwood, Michael Moss, Tim Gollins, David Thomas, and Luciana Duranti do likewise.[39] Hopefully, the findings of a research cluster at the University of British Columbia and a research project already underway at TNA, which enables archives to register hashes of documents on a permissioned blockchain, will lead the way in terms both of digital discovery and changes to the profession's approach.[40] On the whole, though, it has to be said that neither Luciana Duranti nor Vicki Lemieux are sanguine about archivists' ability to address post-truth on the one hand, or the new technological infrastructure on the other. Are we facing a situation where historical archivists themselves might limit the further spreading of the archive? Let's hope not.

What then can be said in conclusion to this chapter on the boundaries of the archive? The digital revolution and the way archives have developed and can be accessed have generated a shift—epistemological, philosophical, and ontological—which has unlocked archives from their historical context and enabled the boundaries of the archive to spread throughout the everyday world. Archives are now more powerful than ever. As archives have moved from paper to bytes, from the historical to the global, they have shifted from the official to the personal, from the objective to the subjective, into human consciousness, into the creative and the imaginary.

I leave the last words here to Gabriella Giannachi, for whom the boundaries of the archive have extended to include all of us: we are the archive. 'We embody the archive...' she says, 'but in embodying the archive we inhabit our past and adventure into our future.'[41]

FURTHER READING

Jens Brockmeier, *Beyond the Archive: Memory, Narrative and the Autobiographical Process* (Oxford: Oxford University Press, 2015)

Wolfgang Ernst, *Stirrings in the Archive: Order from Disorder*, trans. Adam Siegel (Lanham: Rowman and Littlefield, 2015)

Gabrielle Giannachi, *Archive Everything: Mapping the Everyday* (Cambridge, MA: MIT Press, 2016)

Viktor Mayer-Schönberger, *Delete: The Virtue of Forgetting in the Digital Age* (Princeton, NJ: Princeton University Press, 2009)

Michael Moss and David Thomas, eds, *Do Archives Have Value?* (London: Facet, 2019)

Bridget Whearty, *Digital Codicology: Medieval Books and Modern Labor* (Palo Alto: Stanford University Press, 2022)

NOTES

1. G. Giannachi, *Archive Everything: Mapping the Everyday* (Cambridge, MA: MIT Press, 2016).
2. W. Merrin, *Media Studies 2.0* (London and New York: Routledge, 2014), 9.
3. D. Thomas, *Silence of the Archive* (London: Facet, 2017), 90.
4. W. Ernst, *Stirrings in the Archive: Order from Disorder*, trans. A. Siegel (Lanham Maryland: Rowman & Littlefield, 2015), 93.
5. A. Eveleigh, 'Participatory Archives', in H. MacNeil and T. Eastwood, eds, *Currents of Archival Thinking* (Santa Barbara, California: Libraries Unlimited, 2017), 299–326.
6. S. McKemmish, 'Evidence of Me!', *Australian Library Journal* 45.3 (1996), 174–187.
7. W. Benjamin, *The Work of Art in the Age of Mechanical Reproduction*, trans. J. A. Underwood (London: Penguin, 2008), 7.
8. 'Digital Files and Records and their Legal Admissibility in the UK', AMAGNO, https://amagno.co.uk/digitalfilesandrecords/20713 [accessed 10 January 2019].
9. N. Z. Davis, *Fiction in the Archives: Pardon Tales and Their Tellers in Sixteenth-Century France* (Stanford: Stanford University Press, 1987).
10. A. Flinn, M. Stevens, and E. Shepherd, 'Whose Memories, Whose Archives?', *Archival Science* 9.1 (2009), 71–86 (73).
11. R. Sheffield, 'Community Archives', in MacNeil and Eastwood, *Currents of Archival Thinking*, 369.
12. 'About the Interference Archive', https://interferencearchive.org [accessed 7 November 2018].
13. M. Hilton, 'Cultural Studies in the Archive: The Birmingham Centre for Contemporary Cultural Studies', *Cultural Studies* 27.5 (2013), 664–666.

14. Wakefield Axis web, www.axisweb.org/archive/news-and-views/in-focus/craft-collectives [accessed 15 December 2018]; Bristol Street art, http://yellowfeatherblog.com/beautiful-bristol-street-art [accessed 16 December 2018].

15. J. A. Bastian, 'GLAMS, LAMS and Archival Perspectives', in MacNeil and Eastwood, *Currents of Archival Thinking*, 335, 345.

16. G. Yeo, 'Concepts of Record (2): Prototypes and Boundary Objects', *American Archivist* 71.1 (2008), 118–142.

17. A. Prescott, 'Working with Archives' (lecture given at the *Working with Archives symposium*, University of Glasgow, 10 November 2018).

18 'Haiku Adventure: The Craft of Games', William Morris Gallery, https://www.wmgallery.org.uk/whats-on/exhibitions-43/haiku-adventure and see also https://www.digitalartsonline.co.uk/features/printing/from-haiku-to-hokusai-how-a-new-puzzle-game-was-inspired-by-ancient-japanese-art/.

19. 'The Imaginary Archive', Whitechapel Gallery, www.whitechapelgallery.org/events/imaginary-archive/.

20. J. Derrida, *Archive Fever*, trans. E. Prenowitz (Chicago: Johns Hopkins University Press, 1995), 4 n. 1.

21. M. Moss and D. Thomas, 'The Accidental Archive', in Caroline Brown ed., *Archival Futures* (Edinburgh: Facet, 2018), 117–136 (132).

22. Ernst, *Stirrings in the Archive*, 29.

23. M. Foucault, *The Archaeology of Knowledge*, trans. A. M. Sheridan Smith. (London: Routledge, 2002), 144–145.

24. Ernst, *Stirrings in the Archive*, Chapter 10; A. Hoskins, 'The End of Decay Time', *Memory Studies* 6.4 (2013), 387–388.

25. See Chapter 5, Hoskins, 'Memory Beyond Media Decay',

26. V. Mayer-Schönberger, *Delete: The Virtue of Forgetting in the Digital Age* (Princeton, NJ: Princeton University Press, 2009), 1–16 (169).

27. M. Fisher, *Ghosts of My Life: Writings on Depression, Hauntology and Lost Futures* (Winchester: Zero Books, 2014), 9.

28. K. Nelson, 'Developing Past and Future Selves for Time Travel Narratives', *Behavioural and Brain Sciences*, 30.3 (2007), 327–328 (327).

29. R. Fivush, 'Remembering and Reminiscing: How Individual Lives are Constructed in Family Narratives', *Memory Studies* 1.1 (2008), 49–58.

30. J. Brockmeier, *Beyond the Archive: Memory, Narrative and the Autobiographical Process* (Oxford: Oxford University Press, 2015), ix.

31. N. Moore, A. Salter, L. Stanley, and M. Tamboukou, eds, *The Archive Project* (London: Routledge, 2016), Prologue, 3.

32. D. Ramsay, 'Tensions in the Interface', in Andrew Hoskins, ed., *Digital Memory Studies* (London: Routledge, 2018), 280–302.

33. Giannachi, *Archive Everything*, 16.

34. F. X. Blouin and W. G. Rosenberg, *Processing the Past: Contesting Authority in History and the Archives* (Oxford: Oxford University Press, 2011).

35. J. Scott-Warren, 'Reading Graffiti in the Early Modern Book', *Huntingdon Library Quarterly* 73.3 (2010), 363–381; E. Treharne, 'Fleshing out the Text: The Transcendent Manuscript in the Digital Age', *Postmedieval*, 4.4 (2013), 465–478.

36. B. Whearty, *Digitial Codicology: Medieval Books and Modern Labor* (Palo Alto: Stanford University Press, 2022).

37. L. Duranti, 'Whose Truth? Records and Archives as Evidence in the Era of Post-Truth and Disinformation', in Brown, *Archival Futures*, 26.

38. V. Lemieux, 'The Future of Archives as Networked, Decentralized, Autonomous, and Global', in Brown, *Archival Futures,* 33–34.

39. MacNeil and Eastwood, *Currents of Archival Thinking*, 21; M. Moss and T. J. Gollins, 'Our Digital Legacy: An Archival Perspective', *Journal of Contemporary Archival Studies* 4, Article 3 (2017), 1–29 (5); Thomas, *Silence of the Archive*, 95; Duranti in Brown, *Archival Futures*, 26.

40. Blockchain Research Cluster at UDC, https://blockchain.ubc [accessed 15 January 2019]; TNA UK leads the project *Archangel* in partnership with the University of Surrey and the UK Data Institute.

41. Giannachi, *Archive Everything*, 187.

CHAPTER 3

DIGITALITY AND THE RECONFIGURED GLOBAL ARCHIVE(S) OF FORCED MIGRATION

HARIZ HALILOVICH AND ANNE J. GILLILAND

Movement and dispersion have always been a part of the archival as well as the human experience. Recent work on displacement and diasporas by anthropologists and archival studies scholars has highlighted the interdependencies between movement and archives.[1] Literally, archives move as people carry them, or carry them away, through either migration or conquest.[2] Figuratively, archives are creatures of the imagination and emotion, moving and transporting their users to other times, places, and ways of being; protecting or dashing the longings and impossibilities of alternative outcomes and realities.[3] Practically, however, the trajectories, experiences, and affects, as well as the enduring interpersonal connections and effects of the movement of humans until recently were poorly captured and surfaced in the archival record. This was especially the case with involuntary movement, where those who were fleeing or forced to leave their homes were able or allowed at best to bring with them only the few personal and community documents they could carry or conceal. Remaining connected with loved ones, sharing experiences, and documenting journeys were often impossible, and those who were displaced and resettled often later stayed silent, shrouded in sadness, or perhaps out of continuing fear of persecution, and a desire not to project what they had experienced onto their descendants. But this situation has changed considerably as a consequence of the intersections between two of the most powerful global phenomena of the past three decades—pervasive digitality, and unprecedented and shocking levels of displacement and mass migration.

Today displaced and migrating people virtually preserve, create, move, and disseminate digital materials that can serve, in the midst of the most difficult of circumstances, as compelling additional evidence and counter-narratives to those created by the burgeoning bureaucratic recordkeeping of governments, NGOs, and other organizations that are involved with mass migration. These organizations today are deploying state-of-the-art processes for tracking and documenting displaced and migrating individuals, including datafying their identities by means of biometric markers, DNA, facial recognition, and other bio-based mechanisms. At the same time, the individuals themselves have turned to technologies and applications that are freely accessible to them in order to meet their human and social needs, to document their journeys, and, as necessary, to resist undue authority and memory erasure and instead present and preserve their own accounts of events.

Together these phenomena have led to the creation of whole new and often unexpected forms of and uses for archives that document displacement and migration. The immediate and longer-term social and affective dimensions of such movement have also become a focus of archives. 'Archives' as classically understood encompass not only materials, but also processes and place. Archives that document forced displacement or diasporas include the materials and processes of bureaucracy; the memory-keeping of local communities in each country or jurisdiction from which migrants originate or through which they pass or eventually settle; and the documentation, communications, and resistance strategies of migrants themselves. Each of these results in different archival content and archival formations. Each grows and evolves across time and space, and the affect associated with them changes with every encounter, addition, or experience. In McKemmish's words, archives are 'always becoming'.[4] When we contemplate these many archival formations in totality, and their meaning, causality, and import, we might talk of them collectively as a societal Archive of forced migration and diaspora. That Archive currently largely remains an intangible entity, notwithstanding that it is critically interrogated by scholars for what it says about historical and continuing power dynamics and injustices. And even as professional archivists are increasingly deploying digitization, digital description and artificial intelligence to piece together individual archives and other traces of displacement and migration in order to make underlying networks and patterns visible, digitality itself is reconfiguring the very nature and behaviours of the Archive, and of diasporic archives across the globe, in unprecedented ways.

In recent years the concepts of the Archive and archives have undergone significant epistemological and ontological changes and re-interpretations within many fields. While these changes cannot be solely attributed to new digital technologies and affordances, the latter have certainly been a critical enabler in the so-called 'archival turn'.[5] These changes have been foremost the result of socio-political developments that have linked and reciprocally enmeshed local and global like never before. As displaced populations move, transit, and eventually settle elsewhere in diaspora, previously locally situated communities, practices, and stories have literally gone global. In some instances, the actual (geographical) locale might be completely replaced by a globally dispersed translocal and virtual network made up of people originating in or relating to a specific place, region, or country. Many of these people—consciously or unconsciously—are attempting to document, preserve, or recover their memories, experiences, communities, and cultures. This is especially true for millions of refugees fleeing violence, wars, and genocides for whom mobile technologies, free internet accounts, and social media facilitate connectivity and encourage self-documentation and sharing of experiences.

This chapter draws upon the authors' fieldwork to tell the stories and contemplate the reconfigured nature, possibilities, and affects of such global archives for those who have been displaced or who are in diaspora. We approach the idea of global archives from the perspective of the personal, the family, and the community, particularly looking at how archives emerge and change as we move away—in space, time, and across generations—from the original events that led to displacement and diaspora, and as new technologies for documenting, storytelling, preserving, and accessing become available. We investigate how the collective memory of those events shifts and is transmitted through narratives via evolving technologies such as video postcards, social media, and mobile phones. Focusing on Bosnians around the world who were displaced by the wars that marked the collapse of the former Yugoslavia, and looking from the vantage point of twenty-five years or more later, we illustrate the changing ways in which memories and archives of displacement are made, remade, repurposed, and reclaimed.

Bosnian Displacement and the Reconfigured Global Archive

Current media reports on the Syrian refugee crisis in many ways resemble accounts of the plight of the Bosnian refugees more than two decades ago.[6] At the time, millions of ordinary people from across Bosnia-Herzegovina fled their homes looking for safety in European countries such as Austria, Germany, and Sweden as well as beyond Europe. While many of them believed that their displacement was of a temporary nature until the situation in their homeland calmed down, the longer they stayed in the countries of their temporary refuge, the more their return became less certain.[7] Over the last two-and-a-half decades, 'former' Bosnian refugees have become a distinct transnational migrant community, representing one of the largest and globally most widespread migrant groups to have come from the former Yugoslavia.[8] In addition to their embodied interactions, their collective identities and memories as members of the global Bosnian diaspora—and as communities of people coming from and living in very particular localities—have been increasingly mediated, performed and sustained through the internet and mobile technologies. However, unlike refugee groups today, who use mobile technologies to organize, track, and record their flight while it is still in progress, Bosnian refugees came in contact with these technologies much later in their 'refugee cycle', i.e. only after they settled in their respective countries of refuge or immigration.[9] Consequently, due to a very broad dispersion of refugees from Bosnia, involving at least three continents—Europe, Northern America, and Australia—the utility of emerging popular information and communication technologies was discovered and the technologies adopted at a very fast pace and high rate across a broad spectrum of different generations. These technologies as well as social media continue to play important roles in how the Bosnian diaspora operates on a day-to-day basis.

By adopting the internet as their preferred medium of communication and reconnection with the members of their pre-war local communities, many of the refugee groups from Bosnia-Herzegovina have been able to reclaim their local identities and memories by creating vibrant translocal 'cyber villages' as alternatives to the spaces and communities from which they were displaced.[10] Indeed some of the places destroyed during the Bosnian War now only exist in cyberspace and as a part of the digitally mediated social relations of those who identify with the lost places. Usually starting as an individual exchange of scanned photographs, documents, and other records between people coming from the same place, many such grassroots initiatives have grown into sophisticated portals and online repositories of documents, images, and stories about these communities' 'former' local places—in other words, into organically and participatorily created, and geographically distributed global archives about very specific local places that today may no longer have any physical existence.

Historical Background

The 1990s will be widely remembered as a decade of rapid globalization in which digital technologies radically reshaped the way we interact, work, trade, access, and disseminate information, and even how we think about our personal and collective selves. While some saw the last decade of the twentieth century as the start of the end of history as we knew it,[11] others talked about a new era marked by a compression of time and space in which the world would become a global village.[12] However, for many people from villages and towns across Bosnia-Herzegovina—and for others from the region now known as the Former Yugoslavia—the 1990s came foremost to symbolize a decade of violence, social fragmentation, and displacement.[13] In addition to immense personal tragedies involving loss of human life and property, for many ordinary Bosnians the tragic events of the 1990s have also become emblematic with the loss of their place-based political and social identities, and certainties.

As it was widely reported at the time, the 1992–1995 Bosnian War created the largest refugee crisis in Europe since World War Two.[14] While close to a million Bosnian citizens were turned into internally displaced persons, a further 1.5 million became refugees and asylum seekers, predominantly in Scandinavia and other Western European countries, and later on in the USA, Canada, and Australia.[15] Their lives were irreversibly changed not by the digital revolution of the mid to late 1990s that was inspired by the founding of the World Wide Web Consortium in late 1994, and which their tragedy just slightly preceded, but by becoming refugees, immigrants, and members of the Bosnian worldwide diaspora. The 3G cellular network that would for the first time support fast internet connections and smartphone applications was not implemented until 2001, but it was rapidly adopted by users around the world, and by 2005 it was supporting widespread social media use. As such, digital developments have become almost universally accessible, including by those who are currently displaced or fleeing conflicts. They have also had—and continue to have—a significant impact on the Bosnian diaspora in terms of supporting them in recreating, reimagining, and reimaging their shattered social worlds.

Bosnia, along with Rwanda, might have even tainted optimistic depictions of the 1990s as the decade that began the global digital revolution, since this decade will also be remembered for the mass violence against 'ethnic others' at a scale that had not been seen since World War Two.[16] Violence in Bosnia culminated in the 1995 Srebrenica genocide in which more than 8000 Bosniak men and boys were executed by Serb forces.[17] This episode as well as the 'ethnic cleansing' campaigns of the towns and villages in eastern, northern, and western Bosnia-Herzegovina, in which more than 100,000 people perished and close to 40,000 were declared missing, continue to shape the memories and identities of many now fractured Bosnian families and communities in both Bosnia-Herzegovina and its worldwide diaspora.[18]

Over the last several years, we have explored memories and narratives of flight and displacement among the families and communities in Bosnia and in the diaspora—in Australia, the USA, Sweden, and Austria. In particular, we have been interested in the fragmented historical knowledge that exists in personal archives, creative and cultural practices, and local memories, or what Michel Foucault termed 'popular memory', the memory of those who do not have access to publishing houses, movie studios, and political and cultural institutions.[19] Such fragmented knowledge and memories often get lost in or purposely excluded from the 'bigger' narratives that are officially sanctioned as historical knowledge and supported by the contents of official archives and other formal memory institutions. This has been the case in many places in Bosnia, especially those in the part of the country that has become known as Republika Srpska, for example, the towns of Prijedor, Foča, Višegrad, and Zvornik. The reason for the exclusion is that these popular memories tell a different story from that which has become the official nationalist discourse in these places. As such they act as alternative truths and 'counter-memories', forms of resistance from below to the memory making and unmaking projects from above.[20]

VHS Records: Video Postcards from the Past

Parallel to what was officially recorded and reported by local and international professional journalists—including some of the most prominent international veteran war reporters such as Martin Bell, Christiane Amanpour, and Ed Vulliamy—ordinary people were creating their own visual records about life during the war. Filmed mostly on VHS home cameras by video amateurs, they became a widely popular mode of creating and communicating 'war video postcards' or 'video letters'. These were smuggled out of besieged cities and towns to relatives and friends who fled abroad or were internally displaced in other parts of the war-torn country. The flow of VHS tapes was actually two-way: from and into the besieged Bosnian towns and cities. Most had very personal content directed to the intended recipients, providing them with details about everyday life and sending greetings and good wishes. For many people, the tapes were the only way to see and hear their loved ones after their separation by the war. Watching these tapes more than twenty-five years later provides an historical account of everyday life within these families separated. However, as with the censored Red Cross messages that came out of the war-torn country, the videos were also subject to security censorship and as such would require 'decoding' by an insider in order to convey their full meaning today. Nonetheless, the affective dimension of the content of the tapes is captured in simple but profound ways.

> I'd love to greet my son Amar and to tell him that I love him ... that I think of you every day and night. Study hard over there [in Germany] and listen to your mother. The war will soon be over and we will be together.
> (VHS recording, Srebrenica 1994)

> This is where the shell hit our apartment building. Neighbour Meho was killed. We were hiding in the basement. Thanks for the parcel you sent. It means a lot that you are thinking of us. We miss you.
> (VHS recording, Sarajevo 1993)

Many refugees outside the country sent video letters to Bosnia:

> We are well and you don't need to worry about us at all. The kids go to school, it's a Bosnian school but they are learning Danish fast.
> (Copenhagen, refugee centre Flotila Europa, 1992)

These extracts come from numerous VHS tapes that were recorded and sent to relatives. While many of the surviving tapes form a part of private and family archives, increasingly they are being digitized and uploaded on YouTube.

Flotel Europa

Vladimir Tomić's story, captured on VHS, is representative of many of the tapes we have watched in the homes of the survivors, especially those living in what has become known as the Bosnian diaspora. Rather than keeping it as part of his home video archive, or sharing it via YouTube with others, Vladimir has done something remarkably different; he has turned them into a film.

Vladimir was a twelve-year-old boy living in Sarajevo when the war started. For various reasons, his father, grandparents, and other family members remained in the city during the lengthy siege, while Vladimir, his mother, and older brother sought refuge in Denmark, where he still lives today. Upon reaching Copenhagen, the displaced family of three was put up on a hotel ship, along with a thousand other refugees from the region; all living together in close quarters on the Flotel Europa; all of them supposing their stay there would be temporary until more permanent housing was found.

Twenty years on, in an attempt to build an archive of home VHS recordings—of which, it has been discovered, there are hundreds upon hundreds of hours—a call was put out for people to send copies of any tapes they still possessed from during the war. One of the people who had such material is a man who features in Tomić's debut feature film, *Flotel Europa*. Since the phone connection to Bosnia often did not work, Rusmir, an accountant from Sarajevo and a refugee on the Flotel Europa bought a VHS camera with which he started documenting life on the boat, sending these video letters to family and friends. At the same time, television news from home was transmitted fairly consistently to the ship's TV room, where people sat for hours, helplessly watching on TV what was happening in their homeland. Using the archival VHS footage Tomić constructed a narrative, which he then turned into a documentary film. The resulting film, *Flotel Europa* was initially screened in front of an international audience at the 2015 Berlinale film festival and thereafter at many other film festivals across Europe and Northern America. Described as being on the edge of the real and the imagined, the film represents much more than a straightforward documentary—meanings change, multiply, fragment, and diversify into many refractions of a long-ago event, embedded in the memory, and perpetually living outside the confines of time.[21]

The personal VHS tapes are especially important for learning about life in besieged outlying towns such as Srebrenica, where hardly any TV crew ventured during the four years of conflict. While being quite rare and remaining in private hands, these tapes provide exceptional insights into life under siege in the UN safe area before it was overrun by the Serb forces in July 1995. Notwithstanding the technical and ethical challenges involved in obtaining and examining these visual records, for ethnographers, historians, and archival scholars they represent a unique source documenting the life, pain, longing, and hope of the people in the UN safe area—before it was erased in the genocide.

Srebrenica on VHS

Ibro Zahirović and Velid Delić used their home VHS camera to create video post-cards from besieged Srebrenica. These videos were mainly intended to deliver family news from the besieged enclave to relatives in refugee camps across Europe. But Ibro and Velid also filmed ordinary and not so ordinary events during the four years of siege, including some scenes of the fall of Srebrenica in July 1995. Unlike Velid, who perished in the ensuing genocide, Ibro survived the Serb-forced March of Death from Srebrenica to Tuzla. He carried some of the video tapes with him while others were left in Srebrenica or lost during the escape. He also kept recording the Srebrenica exodus for as long as the battery on his camera lasted. For years, his video tapes have been the only material possessions remaining from his previous life. Together with the tapes that Velid filmed and smuggled out of Srebrenica to his family and friends, Ibro's possessions represent a unique video archive of Srebrenica and its people before and during the genocide. It took almost two decades for Ibro to consolidate his personal collection and to start digitizing it. In 2015, Bosnian television BHTV ran a two-series documentary based on his VHS tapes. Similarly, in July 2017, *BIRN* published the article 'Video Messages from the Dead of Srebrenica' featuring several of Velid's videos.[22] To many survivors now dispersed as far away as Australia, the USA, and Scandinavia, these videos literally brought belated messages from their perished relatives.

Scorpions Video

It was not only the professional journalists, propagandists and ordinary people who made the videos of war, perpetrators also used cameras to record their crimes. One such 'home video' of the Serbian Special Police Unit, 'Scorpions', executing Bosniak civilians from Srebrenica in July 1995 has become widely known.

In May 2005, televisions across the world were yet again broadcasting atrocities from Bosnia. This time it was not a real-time broadcast but rather the broadcasting of a previously recorded video record of a war crime. What was shown was close–up footage of the execution of six civilians from Srebrenica ten years earlier. Their hands were tied behind their backs, they looked exhausted and one of them, a man wearing a blue shirt, asked the executioners, the Serb soldiers, if he could get some water before they killed him. The request was denied with laughter and abuse by the captors, who continued filming. For the Salkić family, Bosnian refugees who settled in Melbourne's suburb of St Albans, these disturbing scenes watched on the evening news on the Australian public television broadcaster could only be compared with the surrealism of a bad nightmare. In the bruised man dressed in a blue shirt cap-tured on the hand–held camera, they recognized their missing father and husband, Sidik. At the other end of the world, in Bosnia, Nura Alispahić was watching the same video on the Bosnian state television in her temporary refugee accommodation near Tuzla. Seeing the video, she instantly recognized her sixteen-year-old son Azmir. 'I saw him. He was second in the row. They were pushing him. He turns, and I see him—and it was my Azmir. Then they shoot him. He falls.' After ten years, Sidik and Azmir were gunned down in front of a global audience of TV viewers that included their loved ones. While the video message took ten years to reach the unintended audience, it provided a record of a war crime that was subsequently used as evidence in the International Criminal Tribunal for the Former Yugoslavia prosecutions of several perpetrators. The footage was added to the immense, and itself unanticipatedly generated, multimedia archive of evidence introduced in the Hague prosecutions of accused war criminals from both the former Yugoslavia and Rwanda (www.irmct.org/en/archives). The archive, retained by what is now known as The Mechanism, also includes video and transcripts of courtroom proceedings; the testimonies of eyewitnesses, experts, and the accused; documents; photographs; satellite images; forensic evidence and many other artifacts. Beyond its value as evidence, it is an archive of affect—very much connected to living and intergenerational memory with a continuing emotional resonance for and connection to Bosnian communities worldwide. The Salkić and Alispahić families keep rewinding these video images both in their reality and imagination. Like many other survivors, they have their own memorials and archives including material evidence that the lives they once had really existed. And along with the photographs in their living room of Sidik, an ambulance driver, and Azmir, a schoolboy, they too retain a copy of the awful video clip, which now serves a memorializing function.

The videos and other visual records of the war tell stories that are often beyond the capacity of words to describe. There remain also many untold stories about those who affectively engage with the images of the people, places, and events captured in such videos. The post-war identities of survivors are based on memories of and narratives about the war that are continually being constructed and reconstructed from both directions—from above and from below, often intertwining and blurring this distinction. At times, even the memories of survivors who witnessed the events first-hand have been altered as they internalize memories that were recorded by officials and others and then played and replayed on television.

While from today's perspective the VHS recordings represent a crude predecessor to the immediacy and intimacy of digital videos that can be recorded and instantaneously uploaded onto the Web and widely disseminated via smartphones and communications and social media such as Skype, Viber, or FaceTime, or Facebook and Instagram, these wartime tapes that often contain the images of persons who perished after they were recorded became a treasured part of private/family archives, amid other personal historical artifacts of the war. In addition to their personal and sentimental value, these superseded visual media constitute valuable documentation of the affective impact of the 'everyday war' on ordinary people between 1992 and 1995. Using the affordances of the Web to move this valuable knowledge about the war from personal and family archives into the public domain would obviously be highly desired by researchers. However, there are several technological, ethical, and logistical challenges to doing so. How may archivists even learn of the existence of these fragile media, and beyond that, how should they preserve, digitize, store, and interpret them in ways that are directed by the families themselves and that remain responsive to the sensitivities and desires of changing generations?

Photographs and Smartphone Memories

As the above example illustrates, video and other documentation created during the war in Bosnia may not only capture some of the last moments of loved ones or places, and thus support the memories and identities of survivors, but also may provide critical evidence in later prosecution of those responsible. The same is the case for personal materials that were created before the war. Among the many cruel legacies for survivors of genocides, violent conflicts, and persecution, however, is how few, if any, of these personal documents may survive, the resulting loss of personal, family and community memory, and the long-term consequences of that loss. Photographs, letters, video, and sound recordings are often erased together with the individuals and locations that held them. Or they may be scattered, abandoned, or removed from displaced people as they seek refuge away from their homes. These materials serve both as memory vessels and important legal evidence of people and places that have been erased through conflict, and in the case of Bosnia, deliberate 'ethnic cleansing'. Today this collective archive, while still fragmented, is being mobilized by current refugees as well as those from prior displacement crises through smartphones and social media. These devices and channels have become vehicles for individually and collectively creating, capturing, and sharing firsthand accounts and experiences of human rights abuses and humanitarian plight. Some of these are organized endeavours, such as the street video witnessing and verification of human rights abuses occurring in the conflict in Syria by The Syrian Archive or the Amnesty International-supported Quipu Project that is building a collective memory archive of phoned-in firsthand accounts of forced government sterilization of indigenous Peruvians in the 1990s. But mostly this digitally enabled agency, sometimes radical and resistant, sometimes simply resilient and resourceful is more individual, uncoordinated, and immediate in its purpose. We might think, for example, of the articles and book written by Kurdish-Iranian journalist Behrouz Boochani solely through WhatsApp messages to his translator and publisher, documenting his life in Manus Island, the Australian offshore holding facility for asylum seekers.[23]

Ivy Kaplan, writing in October 2018 in *The Globe Post* about the use of smartphones by refugees, notes some of the tensions between what the phones contribute in terms of memory and evidence to the personal and the official archive through the content they carry, create, and share:

> Because of their ability to take and store photos and videos, the smartphones and SIM cards of refugees often contain both positive memories, as well as documentary evidence of the conflict and torture they have experienced. Upon arrival in their new host-countries, these images become key in confirming their status as refugees through their archived digital passage to Europe and in remembering their past life before it was uprooted.[24]

Because the Bosnian War occurred prior to the digital revolution and the widespread availability of smartphones, few personal or family photographs survived.[25] It is hard to underestimate the importance and affect of surviving photographs for refugee memory over time, and what it means to those in diaspora when someone provides a digitized copy of a photograph of a familiar person, group, or place on a digital portal or social media site. Ever since the early days of photography we have come to rely on the image captured through a photograph, a video, or even a newsreel, as an augmentation, a surrogate, and a prompter for our own memories of the people and places that they capture. This is especially so with those that provide us with the last look backwards to where we are leaving, or what may be the last look toward us by our loved ones. In their absence, memories become reified and overlaid with imaginings of what life might have been.

Ana and her family were displaced multiple times during her high school years because of the wars in Bosnia and Croatia in the early 1990s. They fled first from their home in Bosnia and then were displaced twice from locations where they were resettled across the border in Croatia because of further inter-ethnic conflict. One day, some ten years later, while we were having lunch together in their small top floor apartment in Zadar, Croatia, looking out over the Adriatic, her husband nudged her—'show Anne your photographs'. Ana got up from the table to get them for us to look at. 'She has three', he said. 'Two here on the cabinet and one beside the bed'. They were photographs of her as a child on her own and with her parents and grandparents—of the kind that many families would typically display in their home. Her archive of childhood images had been reduced to these three photographs, and the remembrances and conjurings that they triggered for her. She had once gone back to the houses where these photographs were taken but found strangers living there, and she said it distorted the memories she associated with the images. That she *and* her husband could specify the exact location in the apartment and the contents of each photograph underscored the import of these photographs in both their lives today. Each image was the physical embodiment of and testifier to its own story of displacement and survival. Mementoes of individual moments extracted out of a childhood presumably full of such moments and freeze framed, the photographs had taken on additional value because of their rarity, never to exist as just three among many such images. They were more than aide-memoires, they were invocations of memories of everything that had transpired since the photographs were taken. At the same time they also conjured imaginings of a different adulthood that might have been, thus encapsulating and traversing an entire life both real and imagined and not simply capturing a single moment as they represented on their face. The nudge from her husband encapsulated something else as well—the understandings that had developed between her and him about her past and the way that it inhabited their relationship. He himself was a Croatian who had not experienced displacement, but he negotiated the memories and trauma of his wife's experiences on a daily basis.

Affective attachment to photographs, and identifying them with past life is not unique to Ana's experience. In the absence of other contextual reminders, photography becomes evidence of something that really happened, something that exists as part of human experience. As such, photography serves both as memory and archive of reality.[26] For people like Ana and her husband, the family photographs evoke the imaginary connection between them and their family members across time and space, allowing them to 'touch the past'[27] and providing them with a platform from whence to create their oral history, their own 'archives in formation'. In the process they reclaim their own past as well as situate themselves in the present. Thus, as researchers—as Dever et al. insist—'we must consider photographs and ephemera as examples of archival artifacts that "tell" stories, convey narratives and shape how we think about our subjects'.[28] Photographs may also assume other social lives and purposes beyond immediate family members, and become familiar images in the most unfamiliar settings, as, for instance, Caswell has described in the case of the use and (re)purposing of the mug shots of the victims of the Khmer Rouge atrocities.[29] Photographs of genocide victims thus serve multiple roles: as archival evidence of the crime, as a record of someone's existence, as memorials to the victim(s), and as images that any person can adopt in their very personal narrative of a particular event. In fact, as illustrated by the examples described in this chapter, the social life of records, images, and video clips can be as unpredictable and novel as the life of any living person.

Smartphones, social media, Web portals, and other technologies are helping earlier diasporas such as the Bosnians to recover and share memories and surviving photographs. They are also helping those who are newly displaced to copy and transport materials from their prior lives. Despite much recent hype, however, smartphones in particular, have not diminished the traumas and dangers of displacement or secured the archives for the future, rather they have dramatically changed their dynamics. New fears and forms of loss have replaced some of those of the past. Although the smartphone and the applications and media it accesses provide some measures against complete loss of photographs and other documentation, the information, images, voices, and memories they hold may be at risk in new ways—they can be hacked into, taken away, exposed to the public, and destroyed through the vulnerability of a single device if its contents have not been copied or shared elsewhere. An important consideration also is that this digital archive of displacement and the unique traces it contains may be subject to lack of trust and repudiation, when presented as legal evidence, because of the very affordances of the technologies being used, and the precarity surrounding their creation and preservation.

The Private Archive

Finally, we should remember that there is almost always one other kind of personal archive—the private, intimate one made up of what a person keeps closest: objects, letters/messages and secrets—that may be shared much later, or never. Over time, all kinds of diasporic archives become harder to 'read' as we lose those who recognize the faces in the photographs and videos; who can decode the messages hidden in those videos or in letters; who, more literally, can understand and read the language being used; or who can tell us why an item was kept or recount the story of how it survived the traumas of forced displacement. As the example of families in the Armenian diaspora poignantly illustrates, the absence of surviving documentation, the inter-generational silences, and the loss of knowledge of language and script in time can make these private archives especially unreadable and proliferate the trauma of genocide and the obliteration of identity across successive generations. Such trauma is only multiplied when coupled with continuing inaccessibility of official records held by a hostile state, and lack of knowledge of the fate of those who disappeared.

New technologies are playing a role here too. Children and grandchildren who grew up in the countries where their families eventually settled and who have no firsthand experience of displacement increasingly seek to address the silences and lack of knowledge about historical homelands by turning to new digital tools to recover the experiences and understand the lives of previous generations as well as something of their own identity in relation to the place of origin of their family. They may try to interview older family members using their mobile phones, although memories are recounted and shared with others, not on demand, but when the moment is right, and thus often still go unrecorded. They attempt to collect, decipher, and digitally preserve and share surviving family documents; and they scour new digital access services offered by archivists and corporate entities such as Ancestry.com for any traces of their family members in the archives and libraries of other countries. Nevertheless, we would be remiss not also to underscore what the absence or unavailability of archives means for those in diaspora around the globe. In the face of the refusal or incapacity of many state archives in countries of displacement to make their records available to those in diaspora, the excruciating absence or paucity of documentation—photographs, letters, recordings—reverberates over and over again.

By focusing on the Bosnian refugees and genocide survivors of the 1990s, the aim of this chapter has been to demonstrate how different forms of personal, private, and intimate archives become vessels of stories, memories, and identities, as well as evidence, of displacement and diaspora, transcending time, space, and generations—even reconnecting the dead with the living in many unexpected ways. From an affective and metaphorical perspective, the stories shared in this chapter help us to understand how the personal and community archives of forced displacement are continuously shaped and reshaped according to important recurring themes such as fracture and fragmentation, longings and imaginings, recovery and repair, identity construction and transmission, and generational change. Facilitated by pervasive digitality, even the most private archives' creation, preservation, and sharing are taking place within an increasingly accessible global Archive of displacement and of diaspora. This is not simply a matter of deployment of available evolving technologies, but also of the creative uses and workarounds being made by those who have been forcibly displaced. These deployments were never envisaged by the creators of the technologies and applications but they promise, finally, to help in surviving, recovering from, and building understanding of the traumas of forced displacement through the creation of that global Archive.

FURTHER READING

Maryanne Dever, Sally Newman, and Anne Vickery, 'The Intimate Archive: Journeys through Private Papers', *Archives and Manuscripts* 38.1 (2010), 94–137

Anne J. Gilliland, 'Moving Past: Probing the Agency and Affect of Recordkeeping in Individual and Community Lives in Post-Conflict Croatia', *Archival Science* 14 (2014), 249–274

Anne J. Gilliland and Michelle Caswell, 'Records and their Imaginaries: Imaging the Impossible, Making Possible the Imagined', *Archival Science* 16 (2016), 53–75

Hariz Halilovich, 'Reclaiming Erased Lives: Archives, Records and Memories in Post-War Bosnia and the Bosnian Diaspora', *Archival Science* 14 (2014), 231–247

Hariz Halilovich, 'Re-imaging and Re-imagining the Past after "Memoricide": Intimate Archives as Inscribed Memories of the Missing', *Archival Science* 16 (2016), 77–92

James Lowry, ed., *Displaced Archives* (Abingdon: Routledge, 2017)

NOTES

1. J. Lowry, ed., *Displaced Archives* (Routledge: Abingdon, 2017).
2. P. Ricardo, 'Archival Diasporas: A Framework for Understanding the Complexities and Challenges of Dispersed Photographic Collections', *The American Archivist* 77.2 (2014), 326–349; A. J. Gilliland and H. Halilovich, 'Migrating Memories: Transdisciplinary Pedagogical Approaches to Teaching about Diasporic Memory, Identity and Human Rights in Archival Studies', *Archival Science* 17.1 (2017), 79–96.

3. A. J. Gilliland and M. Caswell, 'Records and Their Imaginaries: Imagining the Impossible, Making Possible the Imagined', *Archival Science* 16 (2015); doi:10.1007/s10502-015-9259-z.

4. S. McKemmish, 'Are Records Ever Actual?', in S. McKemmish and M. Piggot, eds, *The Records Continuum: Ian Maclean and Australian Archives First Fifty Years* (Clayton: Ancora Press in association with Australian Archives, 1994), 200.

5. C. Simon, 'Introduction: Following the Archival Turn', *Visual Resources* 18.2 (2002), 101–107; E. Ketelaar, 'Archival Turns and Returns', in A. J. Gilliland, S. McKemmish, and A. J. Lau, *Research in the Archival Multiverse* (Clayton: Monash University Press, 2017), 228–268.

6. M. Valenta, J. Jakobsen, D. Župarić-Iljić, and H. Halilovich, 'Syrian Refugee Migration, Transitions in Migrant Statuses and Future Scenarios of Syrian Mobility', *Refugee Survey Quarterly* 39.2 (2020), 153–176; doi:10.1093/rsq/hdaa002.

7. H. Halilovich, 'Bosnian Austrians: Accidental Migrants in Trans-local and Cyber Spaces', *Journal of Refugee Studies* 26.4 (2013), 524–540.

8. M. Valenta and S. P. Ramet, eds, *Bosnian Diaspora: Integration in Transnational Communities* (Farnham: Ashgate, 2011).

9. H. Halilovich and N. Efendić, 'From Refugees to Trans-local Entrepreneurs: Crossing the Borders between Formal Institutions and Informal Practices in Bosnia and Herzegovina', *Journal of Refugee Studies*, 34.1 (2019), 663–680; doi:10.1093/jrs/fey066; S. M. Holmes and H. Castañeda, 'Representing the "European Refugee Crisis" in Germany and Beyond: Deservingness and Difference, Life and Death', *American Ethnologist* 43.1 (2016), 12–24.

10. Halilovich, 'Bosnian Austrians'.

11. F. Fukuyama, *The End of History and the Last Man* (New York: Simon and Shuster, 1992).

12. D. Harvey, *The Condition of Postmodernity: An Enquiry into the Origins of Cultural Change* (Oxford: Blackwell, 1990).

13. H. Halilovich, 'Re-imaging and Re-imagining the Past after "Memoricide": Intimate Archives as Inscribed Memories of the Missing', *Archival Science* 16.1 (2016), 77–92.

14. K. Zitnanova, *Refugee Protection and International Migration in the Western Balkans* (UNHCR Bureau for Europe, 2014).

15. Ministry for Human Rights and Refugees of Bosnia-Herzegovina—MHRR BiH, *Pregled stanja bosanskohercegovačkog iseljeništva* (Sarajevo: BiH Government, 2018).

16. T. Cushman, 'Anthropology and Genocide in the Balkans: An Analysis of Conceptual Practices of Power', *Anthropological Theory* 4.1 (2004), 5–28; doi:10.1177/1463499604040845.

17. L. J. Nettelfield and S. Wagner, *Srebrenica in the Aftermath of Genocide* (Cambridge: Cambridge University Press, 2014).

18. Research and Documentation Centre—RDC, *Human Losses in Bosnia and Herzegovina 1991–1995* (Sarajevo: RDC, 2007).

19. 'Film and Popular Memory: An Interview with Michel Foucault', *Radical Philosophy* 11 (1975), 24–29.

20. H. Halilovich, 'Reclaiming Erased Lives: Archives, Records and Memories in Post-War Bosnia and the Bosnian Diaspora', *Archival Science* 14.3–4 (2014), 231–247.

21. P. Cohn, 'Videos Home: How VHS Found Footage Became a Ground-breaking Film about Bosnian Refugees', *The Calvert Journal* 22.10 (August 2015).

22. I. Spaic, 'Video Messages from the Dead of Srebrenica', *BIRN* (10 July 2017) https://balkaninsight.com/2017/07/10/video-messages-from-the-dead-of-srebrenica-07-07-2017/.

23. B. Boochani, trans O. Tofighian, *No Friend but the Mountains: Writing from Manus Prison* (Sydney: Macmillan, 2018).

24. I. Kaplan, 'How Smartphones and Social Media have Revolutionized Refugee Migration', *The Globe Post*, 19 October 2018, https://theglobepost.com/2018/10/19/refugees-social-media/.

25. H. Halilovich, 'The Outsider', in V. Colic-Peisker and P. Waxman, eds, *Homeland Wanted: Interdisciplinary Perspectives on Refugee Resettlement in the West* (New York: Nova Science Publishers, 2005), 209–239.

26. Halilovi, 'Reclaiming'.

27. C. Mavor, *Pleasures Taken: Performances of Sexuality and Loss in Victorian Photographs* (Durham and London: Duke University Press, 1995), 33.

28. M. Dever, S. Newman, and A. Vickery, 'The Intimate Archive: Journeys through Private Papers', *Archives and Manuscripts* 38.1 (2010), 94–137 (127).

29. M. Caswell, *Archiving the Unspeakable: Silence, Memory, and the Photographic Record in Cambodia* (Madison: University of Wisconsin Press, 2014).

CHAPTER 4

THE RECORD AS COMMAND

JAMES LOWRY

First, the cord of the harpedonaptes *marks out a field and with its flexibility surrounds it: can anything be defined without it? To this object, second, it attaches the subject, as if to its knowledge or to its property. And third, it informs others, contractually, of the situation produced by the enclosure: can there be collective forms of behaviour without this? These practices concern, respectively, form, energy, and information; they are, if you will, conceptual, material, and judicial; geometric, physical, and legal. Bonds of knowledge, of power, and of complexity. All in all, its triple tress links me to forms, to things, and to others, and thus initiates me into abstraction, the world, and society. Through its channel pass information, forces, and laws.*[1]

Michel Serres, *The Natural Contract*

Commands

'Mangia!' ('Eat!')

This command, given by the Duke (Paolo Bonacelli) to the unnamed victim played by Renata Moar in Pier Paolo Pasolini's last film, *Salo; or the 120 Days of Sodom*, takes place in a discrete moment that crystallizes the political analogy of Pasolini's masterpiece: it is a command to engage in coprophagia.[2,3] In the instant of the Duke's command, there is nothing outside of the command—a pronouncement of law; an expression of *imperium*. Moar's character seems to have no recourse beyond the supremacy of the *signori* who, as in Sade's original text, represent total authority.[4] Resistance to the command would criminalize her in the regime of their unbridled sovereign power.

The moment of the Duke's command is made discrete by the silences before and after the command, and by the cinematography, which uses long shots that put the viewer at a distance and works with the mise-en-scène, with the actors arranged at the edge of the room, to position the viewer as a spectator and an accomplice in the abuse. As Christopher Roberts wrote, 'even as the film tempts many critics to adopt the perspective of the censor, it also imposes upon the viewers the perspective of the *signori*.'[5] This complicity on the part of the spectator takes on new meaning in view of the film's sociopolitical setting. In transposing Sade's scenario to the Repubblica Sociale Italiana, the final iteration of Mussolini's fascist State, Pasolini signalled fascism's requirement for compliant bodies. Roberts has suggested that Pasolini meant to extend this analogy to the entire history of sociopolitical organization, and film studies scholar Naomi Greene attests to this intention, writing that the 'obsession with precise formulas and bureaucratic regulations that characterizes his libertines represented, [Pasolini] declared, the strategies embraced by all power in its pure arbitrariness, that is, its own anarchy'.[6] Through this arbitrariness, between the force of the command and the space within which it is enacted, Pasolini makes a statement about how participation and regularization co-constitute and maintain power.

Mangia! Jussi Parikka has asserted that 'all acts of language are acts of power: attempts to draw territories, define borders, impose operations'.[7] If the command, a directive according to John Searle's classifications of illocutionary speech acts, is a performative utterance, if it changes reality, then answering back is also a performative utterance.[8] Cornelia Vismann and JoAnne Yates have both observed that feedback enables management and control,[9] which cannot be exercised by a one-way flow of commands. This return of information creates a kind of call and response between *signori* and *victimmi* that defines the character of power in the State. At scale, the body politic also responds to commands: its responses have been called the 'general will'. The philosopher Michel Serres considers the exile of Anaxagoras of Clazomenae from Athens as an illustration of how the general will binds subjects together:

> By what right, then, does some citizen criticize Anaxagoras? By this fundamental legal right that founds the existence of the city and that is sometimes called the social contract. If, because you're observing the planets, you lose interest in your country, then you break the contract that unites us, and thus society must logically exclude you, condemn you at least to exile and at most to death.[10]

Serres observes that in order to be general, the general will must be all-encompassing, and that when one opts out, one is in effect pronouncing one's own sentence: 'The contract', he writes, 'in its logic, knows no mercy'.[11] In this way, the general will binds or excludes subjects. For political philosopher Jacques Rancière, this social bond is maintained by an 'endless manufacture of acquiescence'.[12] To do anything but acquiesce is to risk moving from juridical personhood into bare life. Command, compliance, revolt, silence, refusal, rejection of or inclusion in the general will; these are all operations of information exchange.

The Record as Command

Inasmuch as a command is performative according to speech act theory, recording a command is performative. Michel Foucault's notion of disciplinary writing—that individuals can be bound up in a 'network of writing'—constitutes a tool for the government of subjects.[13] Records may be written commands. Vismann has elaborated a theory of the record where every 'file note indirectly contains a command. Reporting the execution of an order triggers the next one.'[14] In his study of bureaucracy in Pakistan, Matthew Hull wrote that the file 'is a technology for materially enacting an authoritative decision, for making a decision out of various utterances and actions'[15] and Akhil Gupta's study of bureaucracy's structural violence in India foregrounds the performativity of writing which 'is itself a form of action and is perhaps the most important of bureaucratic activities'.[16]

The writing down of the command and other speech acts also confers authority on the speech, as Hull suggested when he wrote that 'the requests, complaints, decisions, understandings, permissions, evasions, and refusals ... eventually must find their way onto the paper of files to have a life beyond talk'.[17] This idea that writing, and particularly bureaucratic writing, makes speech actionable in a substantive way was also expressed by Vismann when she wrote that within the 'imagined chain of replacements for the spoken language, *supplements* [after Derrida], files are the closest to the presence of speech' and that files 'compensate for the transitoriness of speech but without abandoning presence'.[18] Such references to 'presence' suggest the representational potency of the file. The file bears the marks of authority; stamps, signatures, and seals. It is through these diplomatic symbols of power that power can be represented beyond its immediate presence, and it is no longer necessary for the institution or personification of power to be present at the site of the command's execution. Power could emanate from 'institutions beyond the immediate experience and comprehension of the individual subject'.[19] Record-making makes this possible.

Documents have long been used to communicate directives to subjects at a distance, but they were also increasingly used to identify individual subjects. A relationship developed between the physical body and its documentation, further fleshing out the juridical person found in traces across records of their activities and interactions with the State. In addition to the subject's inscription in registers, licenses, certificates and dossiers, documentation of the person in the form of identification documents allowed the individual to be a data point within a documentary regime that mirrored and enacted a government of physical entities (bodies, goods, records, territories). This relationship became symbiotic, and the physical body became readable in a formal sense: 'The body "documented" identity such that information was always co-present with the appearance of a person'.[20] Identification documents such as passports moved with physical persons, or as Craig Robertson puts it, passports and visas 'not only controlled the flow of information by stopping the movement of "knowledgeable" bodies, they also facilitated governing over distance by making knowledge mobile; the passport contained information for officials to read'.[21]

These moves to codify the physical body in documents are the roots of biometrics, and today biometric technologies are perfecting the documentation and interpretation of irises, ears, gaits, typing styles, odours, and voices. This is the datafication of the human body, and relates to the notion developed in surveillance studies, of the 'data double', which Kevin Haggerty and Richard Ericson explain as a 'distinctively hybrid composition' that is 'broken down by being abstracted from its territorial setting. It is then reassembled in different settings through a series of data flows. The result is a decorporealized body, a "data double" of pure virtuality'.[22] This data double appears in records as the object of control. In a sense, information is essential to constituting the juridical body—the person who exists before the law must first exist in documentation. As Judith Butler wrote:

> Constituted as a social phenomenon in the public sphere, my body is and is not mine. Given over from the start to the world of others, it bears their imprint, is formed within the crucible of social life; only later, if at all, do I lay claim to my body as my own.[23]

In the modern State, the physical person is constituted as a juridical person through documentation created with and by others. Once the data double exists within a documentary regime, a regime of disciplinary writing, a degree of systemic control is established. And here we have not yet fully reckoned with what Tonia Sutherland has called the 'carceral archive'.[24]

When every site, person and activity can be conceived of as a data point, element or set, governance becomes datafied and information becomes the primary apparatus of power to an extent that exceeds the written orders of kings (after Vismann) or the information gathering of the colonial, totalitarian, and neoliberal regimes of the modern period. Safiya Umoja Noble and Sarah T. Roberts' study of the Janus-like surveillance potential of wearables is a powerful illustration of control's voraciousness for data. As they say:

> The ubiquity of making the previously mundane and anonymous experience of living in public spaces is increasingly being diminished through multiple modes of surveillance, facilitated by Internet-based reproduction and dissemination.[25]

Data for governance requires ongoing acquisition, or as Lisa Gitelman has written:

> Filling in and filing away are the ways that bureaucracies collect and connect; like the micrologics of enclosure and attachment, they are part of a repertoire of techniques through which bureaucracies come to know.[26]

As ways of knowing, official records connote the values of the cultures and systems within which they circulate, as vividly illustrated by Jacqueline Wernimont's study of mortality bills and 'colonial quantum media'; the choices in enumeration and presentation tell us who was deemed worth counting, and how they were classified in the official mind.[27] Thomas Richards has described the connection between government and knowledge acquisition in the context of British imperialism, writing that much 'Victorian thought participated in ... imagining a kind of complete documentary knowledge of human life that would exist solely for the state'.[28] Imperial governance is only possible through the acquisition of information, which requires the ongoing transmission of data across physical territories.

The materiality of records participates in the broader materiality of the State, as Jack Goody made clear when he wrote that in

> the vast majority of regimes, ancient or modern, whether capitalist or socialist, the postal service is organized by, and in an important sense on behalf of, the state, carrying its paperwork by priority and without payment. Right at the beginning such a system involved the upkeep of roads and canals so that deliveries could be effected in reasonable time.[29]

Today, this connection between the physical infrastructure of the State and its ability to transmit commands in writing has a digital counterpart that arguably extends the reach of authority, but records, whether made on physical or digital carriers, operate as commands only insofar as they bear the marks of authority. This has led to a centuries long discourse on authenticity and documentary evidence.[30]

Establishing and maintaining authenticity in records is the province of recordkeeping. Vismann observes that the law 'operates not *in mundo* but in the medium of literality; it believes only what is written—more precisely, what it has itself written down'.[31] This is the function that the registry, the records store room, and the archive perform for the law; they not only house the records, but attempt to assign authenticity so that the records can serve as evidence that can be relied upon by the organs of the State. Recordkeeping consolidates power *in* records, ensuring they are 'value-laden instruments of power'.[32]

As power could be projected over time and space through official documentation, chains formed. Thinking about the verification of personal identities, Robertson notes that 'documents verified documents, and the authority of the state remained to some extent continuous'.[33] The interrelated processes and documents of government form links that theoretically return eventually to authority. The file or record is a sign of an absent referent (State authority), removed in two senses: by physical space and by a sequence of processes. A similar notion of records standing in for authority is drawn out of Sigmund Freud's work by Jacques Derrida when he describes the 'topology of archives' as 'what ought to exclude or forbid the return to the origin'.[34]

So the record stands in for the original thing; it is a representation of power. Records, while supplements, also constitute power. Files, Ilana Feldman says, 'can be authoritative and can impart authority to the government that does the filing without conferring legitimacy on that government'.[35] Feldman argues that the functioning of a system of bureaucratic writing, form filling and filing creates a sense of authority and binds subjects in that cycle of command and compliance required by power: 'Under conditions where government was tenuous and lacked a stable ground, it was the repetitions of filing procedures, the accumulation of documents, and the habits of civil servants that produced the conditions of possibility for authority.'[36] Feldman takes the notion of the filing system standing in for power and suggests that, in the case of Gaza's bureaucracy, people 'were asked to participate in its workings. It was, again, authority (of bureaucracy itself) rather than legitimacy (of the regime) that bureaucratic repetition promoted.'[37] As well as representing power, then, these disciplinary writings can help to manufacture authority for political regimes or the machineries of government that surround them, much as the formulas of officialdom do at Salo.

Records and files may eventually become archives of the State that also have roles in creating power relations. Kirsten Weld has articulated the paradox of the State archive that appears neutral but is shaped through sequences of systems, practices, and choices:

> The Enlightenment notions undergirding the concept of state archives, as both *a part of* and *apart from* modern societies, represent these institutions as neutral storehouses of foundational documents. In practice, however, the politics of how archives are compiled, created, and opened are intimately tied to the politics and practices of governance, and are themselves historical in a way that transcends the content written on their documents' pages.[38]

Weld was right that archivists are aware of the complex ways in which archives represent and perform power; this is apparent in the archival studies literature. A full analysis of the treatment of power in the archival literature is impossible in one essay, but even a cursory look at the literature would show an accelerating move away from the illusions of and aspirations to neutrality characteristic of archival thinking in the late nineteenth and twentieth centuries, towards acknowledgements of, responsibility for, and now use of archival power. In 2002, Joan Schwartz and Terry Cook edited a two-part series of special issues of *Archival Science* on the theme of archives and power, and a number of articles in these two issues are now recognized as important works in archival theory. In the first of the series, Verne Harris argued that 'the archival record is at once expression and instrument of power.'[39] On the role of the archive in the power dynamics of apartheid South Africa, he wrote that by 'their silences and their narratives of power, their constructions of experience, apartheid's memory institutions legitimized apartheid rule.'[40] In the second issue, Eric Ketelaar's 'Archival Temples, Archival Prisons: Modes of Power and Protection' used Foulcauldian concepts to elaborate the panoptical and knowledge creating power of archives as institutions that exclude and control.[41]

More recently, much work in the burgeoning area of critical archival studies is concerned with overturning dominant power structures enacted through archives.[42] Such work frequently recognizes that the kind of power described in this chapter is only one of many types of power, that archives can be sites for 'liberatory memory work', can act against 'symbolic annihilation', and hold affective power.[43] This work has engaged indigenous knowledge, feminist, queer, and critical race theories and other work in the humanities to advance archival theory and practice. Other archival theorists and practitioners have been using the concept of 'rights in records'—that records' subjects may be co-creators and have rights in records, including State records—to redress power asymmetries embedded and enacted through records and recordkeeping. Examples include the Refugee Rights in Records and Setting the Record Straight for the Rights of the Child projects.[44] These projects engage directly with bureaucracies and their making and use of records.

From the inscription of the record to its circulation through offices, hands, screens, archives, incinerators, etc., the bureaucrat is present. If Vismann is right that a letter 'is nothing but a transmittable order', how is the order, the command, transmitted from the site of power, and how is proof of its execution returned? It is through the apparatus of bureaucracy.

Bureaucracy as Apparatus

Bureaucracy is the apparatus through which the State exercises power, and its materiel is information. Kregg Hetherington's study of 'guerilla auditing'—the use of records and archives by Paraguayan tenant farmers to defend their rights—showed that 'at its core, the state functions through the creation, circulation, and endless interpretation of documents' and that for the farmers, 'documents do not store information so much as make it possible, and state power is therefore not about seeing or inscribing so much as it is about controlling who reads what and under what circumstances'.[45] Though Hetherington downplays the importance of inscription somewhat in this statement, his suggestion that documents make information possible underscores the generative quality of bureaucratic writing. Such writing is central to the bureaucratic project, as Hull posits:

> From the official bureaucratic point of view, a person who is an agent but not an author, who causes things to happen without writing or being written about, is improper at best, corrupt at worst.[46]

It is the role of the bureaucrat to write. The State:

> acts through its civil servants and thus ideally through every citizen. As if it were a supersubject composed of subjects, the state is credited with all its administrative operations and utterances. Once civil servants embody the state, there is no administrative act, no matter how trivial, that does not carry the sovereignty of the entire state with it.[47]

What Vismann describes here is an amorphous entity; beyond the 'supersubject composed of subjects', she alludes to administrative practices that evoke a whole set of contingent systems, actors and actions, a *dispositif*,

> a thoroughly heterogeneous ensemble consisting of discourses, institutions, architectural forms, regulatory decisions, laws, administrative measures, scientific statements, philosophical, moral and philanthropic propositions... The apparatus itself is the system of relations that can be established between these elements.[48]

This complex apparatus is a writing machine.

Gupta noted that one of the 'most striking aspects about references typically made of the state ... is the unitary character of the object being described'.[49] Gupta's call for closer studies of bureaucracy's heterogeneity recognizes that the State is, as Vismann says, a supersubject, and one that incorporates, quite literally, (its) subjects. The *dispositif* that is bureaucracy operates 'ideally through every citizen',[50] and according to Matteo Pasquinelli, 'bureaucracy descends into the bodies of the workers' so that it is difficult to establish the boundaries of bureaucracy.[51] As theories of the firm suggest,

> it makes little or no sense to try to distinguish those things that are 'inside' the [organization] from those things that are 'outside' of it. There is in a very real sense only a multitude of complex relationships (i.e., contracts) between the legal fiction [the organization] and the owners of labor, material and capital inputs and the consumers of output.[52]

The subject's engagement with a particular office or service is the means through which they are entangled in a relationship with bureaucracy, becoming part of the system of relations. Gupta has observed this characteristic: 'the boundary between state and society may actually be constructed through the everyday practices of state offices and representations created by officials'.[53] These everyday practices, engagements, and transactions with subjects, establish or reinforce the social relationship, so that each person is brought into the power relation by 'signing', tacitly or actually, any number of documents that bind them with the State. Ordinary office work comes to produce the right to rule. Returning to Feldman's study, these mundane activities can constitute the authority bureaucrats come to wield. This assigns power in a way that Judith Butler shows to be problematic for those excluded from the social contract. Writing about the Guantanamo Bay detention camps, Butler says:

> Those who decide on whether someone will be detained, and continue to be detained, are government officials, not elected ones, and not members of the judiciary. They are, rather, part of the apparatus of governmentality; their decision, the power they wield to 'deem' someone dangerous and constitute them effectively as such, is a sovereign power, a ghostly and forceful resurgence of sovereignty in the midst of governmentality.[54]

Sovereign power, then, is diffused through bureaucracies. When the boundaries of bureaucracy are porous, and individuals move into positions of power and back out as subjects, often constituted as both, where are the limits of power, and how should the subject know how to navigate them? Entanglements with these complex apparatuses are exercises of power that require participation. Vismann observed that 'outgoing and incoming writs were collected in such a way as to make up a file. Accordingly, the monological rule changed and became—for all its asymmetry—dialogical.'[55] Hull expressed this idea when he wrote that 'Governing paper is central to governing the city. And paper is also the means by which residents acquiesce to, contest, or use this governance.'[56] This dialogical rule is the written rendering of the command and compliance embodied in the coprophagia at Salo. Bureaucracy depends on information exchange because the management of people is done by proxy through information about them.[57] Some have even suggested that this information becomes embedded in people and objects. Pasquinelli sees a close interdependency between bureaucracy and information in Romano Alquati's study of the Olivetti factory, which produced typewriters and mainframe computers. According to Pasquinelli, Alquati observed 'control information' used to monitor processes and 'valorising information', 'the flow running upstream and feeding the circuits of the whole factory. Such valorizing information is continuously absorbed by machinery and finally condenses into products.'[58]

This embedded or embodied nature of information *in* subjects binds or connects subjects into supersubjects. The ability of information to connect and bind has been observed in numerous studies of bureaucracy. For instance, Hull has shown how the circulation of files acts to draw people into matters across hierarchies, organizations, or across the porous State/civil society divide:[59] 'A property document and a government file may inhabit the same world of bureaucratic inscription, but they circulate differently and gather around themselves different people and things.'[60] Records bind people to each other, to institutions and to obligations. Once records (as evidence of subject–State interactions) accrue, they stand between the seat of power and the governed body. The archive not only contains evidence, but, as a corpus of records, is itself evidence of the tacit acceptance of the social contract, because the records are, as Vismann argues, dialogical. It no longer matters if the founding compact is lost to memory, because a series of *supplements* (the archives) has been created.

Bureaucracy needs the participation of the body politic; the body must respond to commands. Engaging in the dialogue, writing back, is the act of acquiescence that power needs. If the State is constituted through writing,[61] the 'wheels of government grind to a halt without a file'[62] and documents 'embodied and congealed state power'[63] but these are dialogical products, what are the political implications of not writing back?

From Records-as-Command to Data-as-Command

Information systems unify information about subjects and in so doing, bind subjects more closely to the State as they become more and more richly documented. Similarly, it could be argued that the proliferation of civic technologies reposition political subjects as prosumers more closely tied to the State by the data they feed into these technologies. Finn Brunton and Helen Nissenbaum see a general trend that is driven by information technologies and directly relates to the individual's place and participation in the social contract, enjoyment of rights, etc.:

> Things we once thought were private—if we thought of that at all—become open, visible, and meaningful to new technologies... There is a constantly advancing front of transition from meaningless to meaningful—from minor life events to things that can change our taxes, our insurance rates, our access to capital, our freedom to move, or whether we are placed on a list.[64]

New technologies and the emergence of this big data environment allow the regime of documentary writing to take on more granularity, with more data points, more richly documented persons and actions, and discrete information exchanges opened up to comparison and reconciliation, and it becomes possible to speak of 'data as command'. Today, data-as-command goes beyond the dialogical collection of information: technology, psychology, decision sciences, behavioural economics and marketing have converged around the collection, aggregation and repurposing of data about individuals and their preferences that is volunteered by them to different and seemingly unconnected systems.[65]

As datafication continues, who and what will be data points to be individualized and massed together? Robertson observed that digital verification (of identities) has 'moved the claimed authority of identification closer to that of a "mechanical objectivity", if not a scientific objectivity, as proponents claim that the assessment of individuals is less necessary'.[66] Ruha Benjamin's work reveals the personal and social consequences that can follow, exposing this supposed mechanical objectivity as 'the employment of new technologies that reflect and reproduce existing inequities but that are promoted and perceived as more objective or progressive than the discriminatory systems of a previous era'.[67] This is often unknown or poorly understood by the 'data subjects'. How should the subject respond? As suggested earlier in this chapter, the refusal to write back is an act that propels the subject into bare life, an exclusion zone outside of Athens, beyond the law and outside of juridical personhood.

In *On the Shores of Politics*, Rancière wrote:

> Exhibition in place of appearance, exhaustive counting in place of imparity, consensus in place of grievance—such are the commanding features of the current correction of

democracy, a correction which thinks of itself as the end of politics but which might better be called post-democracy.[68]

Against this, Rancière has outlined a revitalization of the adversarial aspect of democracy. He observes moments of 'impertinent dialectic'[69] when a 'community of equals' forms through the assertion of rights, by answering back, though not necessarily according to the forms and structures of bureaucracy, that is, not in its own terms, but through different means, more direct and public. The impertinent dialectic is, inter alia, a technique of *dissensus*, which Rancière says is not a 'conflict of interests, opinions or values; it is a division inserted in "common sense": a dispute over what is given and about the frame within which we see something as given'.[70] The impertinent dialectic is not possible without a change in the power dynamic that currently operates through bureaucracy and the record, and increasingly through data, which are both sites of dissensus even as they figure in dissensual renegotiations of power.

Every way in which we interact with government through information is, then, deeply political. If information is the materiel of bureaucracy, the information we supply contributes to the acquisition of knowledge/power and the feedback required of commands, the qualities of that information bear directly on the operations of the machinery of government. Hetherington observed that when 'guerilla auditors encounter documents, they unleash undisciplined interpretations and hence novel possibilities into the situations that the documents purport to describe'.[71] Documents are 'sites of possibility', 'not a store of information as a static thing but as a tool for making it as a political effect'.[72] What are the radical uses of government records?

Rita Raley has claimed that for 'every system of disciplinary power ... there is a "countervailing" response from those in precarious, subordinate, or marginal positions....'[73] If the exchange of information is the essence of the State-subject power relation, the way the subject treats information, both as its writer and its reader, is political and essential to any impertinent dialectic. Alexei Monroe wrote that 'no matter how discrete, fixed, or closed a regime / system / machine appears to be, it always contains within its coding possibilities of escape, supersession, obsolescence, disintegration, or mutation'.[74] When the regime, system or machine is bureaucracy, records are foremost among those possibilities.

Records Systems as Sites of Dissensus

In a datafied world, Rancière's impertinent dialectic will necessarily be acted out in examinations and critiques of data and records, as well as within the systems that manage data and records. Information systems are therefore sites where power and control operate, and though power asymmetries can be reinforced or designed into systems these systems can also be made into sites of dissensus. We must see design justice in information systems, including systems of record-making and archiving.[75] System design should allow us to answer back. However, recalling Feldman's observation that 'Filing delimits both the terrain of possibility and modes of objection,'[76] there is a risk that participation becomes endorsement, and that such close engagement with systems would enact the *dispositif* of bureaucracy 'through every citizen.'[77] The co-option of the citizen-bureaucrat as a quality controller for government information, enriching and improving the databanks of the State, is one possible outcome of participatory systems, and one which is under-acknowledged in the participatory archives literature.[78] Is our enrichment of data in fact Alquati's valorizing information: is it 'feeding the circuits of the whole factory'?[79] Participatory systems can only become dissensual systems through a critical engagement with them. Not only do users need to be critical of the data they are seeing, but critical of the systems that collect and present that data, as Safiya Noble has so powerfully shown in *Algorithms of Oppression*.[80]

Are co-created or participatory information systems enabling engagement to be a form of control by more fully forming data doubles? Srikant Sarangi and Stefaan Slemrouck argue that the management of people is done through the management of information: the more fully formed the data double, the more knowable and manageable the person.[81] One could swap 'body' for 'data double' in Butler's statement: 'Constituted as a social phenomenon in the public sphere, my [data double] is and is not mine.'[82] Furthermore, opening up information systems as forums for debate turns them into possible sites of dissensus that, like the streets, may be policed, curfewed, and closed down. The State's (increasingly privatized and enclosed) monopoly on 'legitimate force' lies behind the information system as it does behind the political system.

The Dissensual Archive

Acquiescence and complicity are terms that often bear negative connotations, but like 'bureaucracy', they can only be positive or negative in particular instances and from particular perspectives. Whatever their character, acquiescence and complicity in the context of the social contract require performative utterances, which, in the modern State, take the forms of record- and data-as-command. It is this performative documentation that makes the physical person into a juridical person, inside the regime of law and rights. This documentation is not fixed, but accrues and moves around its subject as the subject acts. The record- and data-as-command are forms of disciplinary writing that allow power to operate at a distance and designate as unique and controllable people, actions, places, relationships, etc. to make of everything a data point. They are performative in an immediate and localized sense of making things happen in the world, and in a broader political sense of manufacturing power that looks general.

Records as deployed by bureaucracies can manufacture power in two distinct ways. Firstly, as Feldman has shown, they, and the processes they animate, engage subjects in relationships that channel discourses and actions in controlled ways, so that governance is done regardless of the validity or strength of the legal or popular basis of authority. Secondly, as is widely recognized in the literature but perhaps best explicated by Richards and Wernimont, records contain the information required as a knowledge base for governments. Record-making and recordkeeping allow data to be collected, aggregated, analysed, and used in various ways by governments to such an extent that to be outside of this regime of documentation is to be outside of the social contract, that is, to leave behind juridical personhood and approach bare life. But to the law, and anyone who wishes to operate within it, these records must be authentic, and this has been a major concern of recordkeeping over time.

Bureaucracies are multivalent, porous *dispositifs*, supersubjects, endlessly extensible through control information and valorizing information. Even individual instances of bureaucracies cannot be characterized definitively, since their priorities and modes of operation are always in flux as a result of their supersubject nature. Butler has illustrated the negative aspect of this phenomenon, where appointed officers take positions of power that can have direct and damaging consequences for the lives of others. In other instances, bureaucracies are functional, benevolent, even radically progressive, but always bringing control to relationships, persons, and territories through the materiality of records and data, which give form to voice.

The individual body and the body politic are juridical entities only through records. Juridical personhood and its attendant rights and duties are created through documentation, and as legal and political systems have become more complex, the documentation of the person and their rights and duties has become richer, technologies of record-making and recordkeeping responding to the informational needs of power and opening up new possibilities for control in a recursive cycle of development. Open government data, big data, biometrics, surveillance and counterveillance technologies, all reveal the recent acceleration of the historical process of the datafication of persons. This is only an extension of past inscriptive practices: 'The examination that places individuals in a field of surveillance also situates them in a network of writing; it engages them in a whole mass of documents that capture and fix them.'[83] As information technologies have developed, this kind of documentation has become more thorough and more easily aggregated—'the ability to collect and use this information has been constrained because traditionally it has been recorded on paper and stored by a large number of State and local governments'—but now it is set free through datafication.[84] The increasing richness of the data available from records, government, and other systems, and the new data that can be created by their combination and comparison, together with the data individuals push into the public sphere through online content creation—the richness of this data is widely recognized by data subjects, businesses and governments alike. This richness means that our data doubles are taking shape more clearly, particularly where there are moves to aggregate, share and combine datasets. When the individual and public space are both datafied, a control environment is established; one that is asymmetrical. The power dynamic that operates through the record-as-command comes to operate through data-as-command, which is more granular and blurs the already fuzzy boundaries between subjects and supersubjects, bureaucracies and polities.

Power's need for data is consistent: the panoptical impulse of current State dataveillance has a parallel with the archival impulse of imperialism, for instance. One response to this is dissensus, Rancière's idea of a radical remaking of democracy via an impertinent dialectic. According to Rancière, political subjects are 'not social groups but forms of inscription that (ac)count for the unaccounted'[85] and 'rights are inscriptions, a writing of the community as free and equal ... the Rights of Man are the rights of those who make something of that inscription, deciding not only to "use" their rights but also to build cases to verify the power of the inscription'[86] These inscriptions—social groups, rights—in fact, all data points in the State—might be re-inscribed in different ways and places. How disciplinary writing in general and records in particular are used, abandoned or rethought under an impertinent dialectic remains to be seen.

Anaxagoras of Clazomenae cannot opt out of the general will in Athens and live, and maybe Raley is right that opting out is not an option for us: 'should we not also be able to opt out of ... the whole system of "cybernetic capitalism" itself? But it is arguably the case that exit in the form of forgetting or genuine anonymity is no longer possible, that disappearance itself has disappeared'.[87] Notwithstanding the attempt of the General Data Protection Regulations to inaugurate a 'right to be forgotten', opting out of 'cybernetic capitalism' or in any case out of the datafied environment is to move outside of the social.

As Rancière observes, the strength of our rights 'lies in the back-and-forth movement between the initial inscription of the right and the dissensual stage on which it is put to the test'.[88] Following the ideas of the record- and data-as-command, information systems, including record-making systems and archives, can be seen as such dissensual stages. An impertinent dialectic is possible through data, records, and archives, exploding the formal dialogue of the file, unleashing new possibilities for community, information symmetry, and ultimately power.

FURTHER READING

Amelia Acker and Mitch Chaiet, 'The Weaponization of Web Archives: Data Craft and COVID-19 Publics', *The Harvard Kennedy School (HKS) Misinformation Review* 1.3 (2020) https://misinforeview.hks.harvard.edu/article/the-weaponization-of-web-archives-data-craft-and-covid-19-publics/

Marika Cifor, Patricia Garcia, T. L. Cowan, Jasmine Rault, Tonia Sutherland, Anita Say Chan, Jennifer Rode, Anna Lauren Hoffmann, Niloufar Salehi, and Lisa Nakamura, *Feminist Data Manifest-No* (2019) www.manifestno.com

Jamila J. Ghaddar, '*Total Archives* for Land, Law and Sovereignty in Settler Canada', *Archival Science* 21 (2020), 59–82; doi:10.1007/s10502-020-09353-w

Jamie A. Lee, 'In Critical Condition: (Un)Becoming Bodies in Archival Acts of Truth-Telling', *Archivaria* 88 (2019) https://archivaria.ca/index.php/archivaria/article/view/13703

Tonia Sutherland, 'Making a Killing: On Race, Ritual and (Re)Membering in Digital Culture', *Preservation, Digital Technology and Culture* 46.1 (2017); doi:10.1515/pdtc-2017-0025

Stacy Wood, 'The Paradox of Police Data', *KULA: Knowledge Creation, Dissemination, and Preservation Studies* 2.1 (2018); doi:10.5334/kula.34

NOTES

1. M. Serres, *The Natural Contract* (Ann Arbor: University of Michigan Press, 1995), 107.
2. In this chapter I want to consider power in records before they become archives, to show how they are imbued with and imbue power from their creation. Some of their power as archives follows from this intrinsic power. I will look particularly at State records, and in the absence of a critical records management literature, I draw mostly on writing about records from studies of bureaucracy in anthropology, sociology, etc.; what Stacy Wood has termed 'critical bureaucracy studies'. Even as these studies have typically ignored or been unaware of archival studies work (see Chapter 1 by Michelle Caswell), they are useful sources for the study of records and power in pre-archival settings.
3. P. P. Pasolini, *Salò o Le 120 giornate di Sodoma* (London: British Film Institute, 1975). The significance of this moment in the film was pointed out to me by Patricia MacCormack.
4. D. A. F. Sade, *The 120 Days of Sodom* (London: Arrow Books, 1990).
5. C. Roberts, 'The Theatrical Satanism of Self-Awareness Itself: Religion, Art and Anarchy in Pasolini's Salò', *Angelaki* 15.1 (2010), 29–43.
6. N. Greene, 'Salo: The Refusal to Consume', in P. Rumble and B. Testa, eds, *Pier Paolo Pasolini: Contemporary Perspectives* (Toronto: University of Toronto Press, 1994), 232–242.
7. J. Parikka, *Digital Contagions: A Media Archaeology of Computer Viruses* (Oxford: Peter Lang Publishing, 2007), 139.
8. J. Searle, 'A Taxonomy of Illocutionary Acts', *Language, Mind and Knowledge* 7 (1975), 344–369.
9. C. Vismann, *Files: Law and Media Technology*, trans by G. Winthrop-Young (Stanford: Stanford University Press, 2008), 95. See also J. Yates, *Control through Communication: The Rise of System in American Management* (Baltimore: Johns Hopkins University Press, 1993), xvii–xv.
10. Serres, *The Natural Contract*, 67.
11. Serres, *The Natural Contract*, 67.
12. J. Rancière, *On the Shores of Politics* (London; New York: Verso Books, 2007), 83.

13. M. Foucault, *Discipline and Punish: The Birth of the Prison*, trans. by A. Sheridan, 2nd ed. (New York: Vintage Books, 1995), 190.
14. Vismann, *Files,* 8.
15. M. Hull, *Government of Paper: The Materiality of Bureaucracy in Urban Pakistan* (Berkeley: University of California Press, 2012), 127.
16. A. Gupta, *Red Tape: Bureaucracy, Structural Violence, and Poverty in India* (Durham: Duke University Press, 2012), 188.
17. Hull, *Government of Paper*, 113.
18. Vismann, *Files,* 8–9.
19. J. Sconce, 'On the Origins of the Origins of the Influencing Machine', in E. Huhtamo and J. Parikka, eds, *Media Archaeology: Approaches, Applications, and Implications* (Berkeley: University of California Press, 2011), 82.
20. C. Robertson, *The Passport in America: The History of a Document* (Oxford: Oxford University Press, 2010), 183.
21. Robertson, *The Passport*, 188.
22. K. Haggerty and R. Ericson, 'The Surveillant Assemblage', *British Journal of Sociology* 51.4 (2000), 611.
23. J. Butler, *Precarious Life: The Powers of Mourning and Violence* (London and New York: Verso Books, 2004), 82.
24. T. Sutherland, 'The Carceral Archive: Documentary Records, Narrative Construction, and Predictive Risk Assessment', *Journal of Cultural Analytics* 1.1 (2019); doi:10.22148/16.037.
25. S. U. Noble and S. T. Roberts, 'Through Google-Colored Glass(es): Design, Emotion, Class, and Wearables as Commodity and Control', *Media Studies Publications* 13 (2016), 7.
26. L. Gitelman, *Paper Knowledge: Toward a Media History of Documents* (Durham: Duke University Press, 2014), 32.
27. J. Wernimont, *Numbered Lives: Life and Death in Quantum Media* (Cambridge, MA: MIT Press, 2018), 52.
28. T. Richards, *The Imperial Archive: Knowledge and the Fantasy of Empire* (London; New York: Verso, 1993), 74.
29. J. Goody, *The Logic of Writing and the Organization of Society* (Cambridge: Cambridge University Press, 1986), 96.
30. See for example L. Duranti, *Diplomatics: New Uses for an Old Science* (Lanham: Scarecrow Press, 1998) and R. Head, 'Documents, Archives and Proof around 1700', *The Historical Journal* 56.4 (2013).
31. Vismann, *Files,* 56.
32. Terry Cook and J. M. Schwartz, 'Archives, Records, and Power: From (Postmodern) Theory to (Archival) Performance', *Archival Science* 2.3 (2002), 178.
33. Cook and Schwartz, 'Archives, Records, and Power', 212.
34. J. Derrida, *Archive Fever: A Freudian Impression* (Chicago: University of Chicago Press, 1998), 92.
35. I. Feldman, *Governing Gaza: Bureaucracy, Authority, and the Work of Rule, 1917–1967* (Durham: Duke University Press, 2008), 32.
36. Feldman, *Governing Gaza*, 3.
37. Foldman, *Governing Gaza*, 16.

38. K. Weld, *Paper Cadavers: The Archives of Dictatorship in Guatemala* (Durham: Duke University Press, 2014), 13.
39. V. Harris, 'The Archival Sliver: Power, Memory, and Archives in South Africa', *Archival Science* 2.1 (2002), 84.
40. Harris, 'The Archival Sliver', 69.
41. E. Ketelaar, 'Archival Temples, Archival Prisons: Modes of Power and Protection', *Archival Science* 2.2 (2002).
42. M. Caswell, R. Punzalan, and T. K. Sangwand, 'Critical Archival Studies: An Introduction', *Journal of Critical Library and Information Studies* (2017); doi:10.24242/jclis.v1i2.50.
43. 'Liberatory memory work' was coined by C. Gould and V. Harris in 'Memory for Justice: A Nelson Mandela Foundation Provocation' (2014). The concept has been developed in the work of Jarrett Martin Drake and Michelle Caswell. See, for examples: Jarrett Martin Drake, 'Liberatory Archives: Towards Belonging and Believing', *On Archivy* (2016) https://medium.com/on-archivy and Michelle Caswell, *Urgent Archives: Enacting Liberatory Memory Work* (London: Routledge, 2021). On symbolic annihilation in archives, see Michelle Caswell, 'Seeing Yourself in History: Community Archives and the Fight against Symbolic Annihilation', *The Public Historian* 36.4 (2014), 26–37. On affect in archival studies, see M. Cifor, 'Affecting Relations: Introducing Affect Studies to Archival Discourse', *Archival Science* 16.1 (2016), 7–31.
44. UCLA Center for Information as Evidence 2018. https://informationasevidence.org/refugee-rights-in-records and Setting the Record Straight for the Rights of the Child Initiative 2017 https://rights-records.it.monash.edu/.
45. K. Hetherington, *Guerrilla Auditors: The Politics of Transparency in Neoliberal Paraguay* (Durham: Duke University Press, 2011), 151.
46. Hull, *Government of Paper*, 130.
47. Vismann, *Files*, 110.
48. M. Foucault, *Power/Knowledge: Selected Interviews and Other Writings, 1972–1977*, trans. by C. Gordon, L. Marshall, J. Mepham, and K. Soper (New York: Pantheon Books, 1980), 194.
49. Gupta, *Red Tape*, 44.
50. Vismann, *Files,* 110.
51. M. Pasquinelli, 'To Anticipate and Accelerate: Italian Operaismo and Reading Marx's Notion of the Organic Composition of Capital', *Rethinking Marxism* 26.2 (2014), 183.
52. M. C. Jensen and W. H. Meckling, 'Theory of the Firm: Managerial Behavior, Agency Costs and Ownership Structure', *Journal of Financial Economics* 3.4 (1976), 311.
53. Gupta, *Red Tape*, 55.
54. Butler, *Precarious Life*, 59.
55. Vismann, *Files,* 95.
56. Hull, *Government of Paper*, 1.
57. S. Sarangi and S. Slembrouck, *Language, Bureaucracy, and Social Control* (New York: Routledge, 2014).
58. Pasquinelli, 'To Anticipate and Accelerate', 183.
59. Hull, *Government of Paper*, 18.
60. Hull, *Government of Paper*, 20.
61. Gupta, *Red Tape*, 143.

62. Gupta, *Red Tape*, 146.

63. Gupta, *Red Tape*, 208.

64. F. Brunton and H. Nissenbaum, *Obfuscation: A User's Guide for Privacy and Protest* (Cambridge, MA: MIT Press, 2015), 50.

65. For instance, in 2013 M. Kosinski, D. Stillwell, and T. Graepel showed the accuracy with which sexual orientation, race, and political allegiances can be predicted from an analysis of a data subject's Facebook 'likes'; 'Private Traits and Attributes are Predictable from Digital Records of Human Behavior', *Proceedings of the National Academy of Sciences* 110.15 (2013), 5802–5805. In 2000, the economist Joseph E. Stiglitz, proposing some lines of enquiry for the field of information economics, predicted: 'Some [of the advances] will entail an integration of economics with other social sciences—with psychology, on, for instance, how individuals process information, form expectations, and select among possible signals; and with sociology, on, for instance, the creation of social knowledge and signaling conventions'; 'The Contributions of the Economics of Information to Twentieth Century Economics', *The Quarterly Journal of Economics* 115.4 (2000), 1471.

66. Robertson, *The Passport in America*, 249.

67. R. Benjamin, *Race after Technology* (Cambridge: Polity Press, 2019), 6

68. Rancière, *On the Shores of Politics*, 98.

69. Rancière, *On the Shores of Politics*, 91.

70. J. Rancière, *Dissensus: On Politics and Aesthetics* (London: Bloomsbury, 2010), 77.

71. Hetherington, *Guerrilla Auditors*, 9.

72. Hetherington, *Guerrilla Auditors*, 166.

73. R. Raley, 'Dataveillance and Countervailance', in L. Gitelman, ed., *Raw Data is an Oxymoron* (Cambridge, MA: MIT Press, 2013), 131.

74. Alexei Monroe, *Interrogation Machine: Laibach and NSK* (Cambridge: MIT Press, 2005), 8.

75. S. Costanza-Chock, *Design Justice: Community-Led Practices to Build the Worlds We Need* (Cambridge, MA: MIT Press, 2020).

76. Feldman, *Governing Gaza*, 32.

77. Vismann, *Files*, 110.

78. For instance, in E. Benoit and A. Eveleigh, 'Defining and Framing Participatory Archives in Archival Science', in E. Benoit and A. Eveleigh, eds, *Participatory Archives: Theory and Practice* (London: Facet Publishing, 2019), 1–13.

79. Pasquinelli, 'To Anticipate and Accelerate', 183.

80. S. U. Noble, *Algorithms of Oppression: How Search Engines Reinforce Racism* (New York: New York University Press, 2018).

81. Sarangi and Slembrouck, *Language, Bureaucracy, and Social Control.*

82. Butler, *Precarious Life*, 82.

83. Foucault, *Discipline and Punish*, 189.

84. A. Roberts, *Blacked Out: Government Secrecy in the Information Age* (New York: Cambridge University Press, 2008), 208.

85. Rancière, *On the Shores of Politics*, 43.

86. Rancière, *On the Shores of Politics*, 76.

87. Raley, 'Dataveillance', 130.

88. Raley, 'Dataveillance', 81.

CHAPTER 5

NEW MEMORY AND THE ARCHIVE

ANDREW HOSKINS

New Memory and the Archive

Memory has broken out of the traditional archive, the organization, and the self, and diffused through a hyperconnectivity between brains, bodies, and personal and public lives. Once the reassuring and reliable repository, offering a secure place for the past's protection from loss, theft, and erasure, today, the archive has been infiltrated and ransacked by the digital arbiters of how societies remember and forget. Google and Facebook are surely the supreme organizations of anti-memory, monetizing the voluntary uploading of the everyday on an unimaginable scale, presiding over an astonishing archive that has eclipsed all other modes of memory's externalization.

The 'connective turn'[1]—the sudden abundance, pervasiveness, and immediacy of digital media, communication networks, and archives, muddies provenance, accountabilities, and potential redress for versions of the past that have been hacked, manipulated, and reconfigured for a range of ends. In these circumstances, the archive, its owners, and its hackers, have shaped a new form of memory, one perpetually in motion, made through their arresting of everyday communications. From the mundane through to the exceptional, most human communications have to travel through the infrastructural and algorithmic net (the ultimate capture metaphor), scattering their traces. This *new memory*[2] is forged through the incoming stream of the uploading of everything, continually making and remaking a trail of the becoming of a new kind of past of self and society. And then we can ask when memory becomes entangled with data, is it inevitably lost to human imagination and navigation in what are fast becoming post-human trajectories of the past?

Just a note on this idea of 'new memory'. It is intended to highlight that remembering is a process that inevitably is shaped in and through the present. Memory is continually awake to today's shifting personal, social, and political needs and adapts accordingly. It has little relationship to accuracy or truth, in that it is subject to both the vagaries of human forgetting and human motivation for surviving and thriving, and for both maintaining and transforming self and group identity. But new memory also signals that the value afforded to remembering and forgetting also changes over time. We are certainly at least in some parts of the world living through a period of successive 'booms' in memory when there is a more intensive turn to as well as a turn on the past. And new memory also highlights that at least part of the present day shift in what memory is and what memory does is shaped through the technologies and media of the day. This in turn directly shapes what it is possible or not to remember in future times.

However, the evolution of the accounting of the relationship between media and memory, is clouded with long standing belief as to external (to the mind and body) technologies strengthening and enhancing what is ultimately highly fragile human memory. Successive media ecologies of writing, print, and the electronic have transformed human cognition and the capacity, control, and power to remember. Similarly, the idea of the archive has long been seen as the supreme medium, as the external and institutional basis for the remembering of societies at different stages of development across history, and as an ultimate storage medium and metaphor of memory.

At least with the advent of digital and networked archives, the main subject of this chapter, there is more of an emergent focus on the dysfunctions of the media of memory. But the main challenge to grasping the relationship between media and memory, is in the persistence of the very terms just used! This problem is underpinned by the overwhelming public, political, and scholarly attention afforded to remembering not being matched by a concern with forgetting.[3] Although there are some influential typologies of forgetting in social anthropology[4] and cultural studies[5] these have not rebalanced the wider focus of the field of Memory Studies at least, from remembering to forgetting. In psychology, there are established theories of human forgetting building on Ebbinghaus' work from 1885, including the commonly considered ideas of 'decay' and 'interference'.[6] But the social sciences and humanities do not have such developed trajectories of work on forgetting. What would our view and understanding of archives be if we approached them primarily in terms of forgetting, rather than remembering? This chapter at least, 'decay' is offered as one mode of illuminating the dissipating and degrading effects of media and other external forms on which human memory has been seen to be reliant or dependent.

By way of an overview of work that does recognize the limits of memory, and of archives, we can see that its principal traditional constraints were time, and space, respectively. Understanding of the temporal limits of memory have been influenced by the work of the sociologist Maurice Halbwachs, most often associated with the notion of 'collective memory'. Halbwachs argues, 'Our hold on the past … never exceeds a certain boundary, which itself shifts as the groups to which we belong enter a new phase of their existence. It is as if the memory needed to be unburdened of the growing mass of events that it must retain.'[7] Here then is the formula of the critical mass of the group needed to sustain living memory and the functional accounting of forgetting, as something normal and necessary.

Also influential, is Jan Assmann's distinction between 'communicative' and 'cultural' memory.[8] The former—communicative—invokes a limited temporal horizon of memory (around eighty years or three or four generations) whereas the latter—cultural—'has its fixed point; its horizon does not change with the passing of time'[9] and:

> comprises that body of reusable texts, images, and rituals specific to each society in each epoch, whose 'cultivation' serves to stabilize and convey that society's self-image.[10]

In other words, outside of and beyond living human memory there exists a more durable past, or even what John Urry calls 'glacial time'[11] which offers a continuity of existence, embedded in more tangible and fixed modes of space and place (often seen as books, traditional monuments, museums, and so on).

And relatedly the archive is conceived of in terms of the limitations of storage and access space. And it is often presumed that digital content is unencumbered by such constraints. So, today the archive is transformed, networked, connected, liberated from the constraints of 'archival space' suddenly riding the fluidities of 'archival time'.[12] Thus, for Ernst, 'the emphasis in the digital archive shifts to regeneration, (co-)produced by online users for their own needs'.[13] Or, to echo Halbwachs, whereas he saw the group as sustaining collective memory, dependent on the connectivity of the living, today it is the archive that comes alive in its fostering of a new multitude of memory.[14]

But changes in what are set out below as shifts in 'decay time'[15] dissolve communicative and cultural memory distinctions. Or, rather, communicational media and the archive—the modus operandi of cultural memory studies—have converged and collapsed.

Another example is the photograph. The ontology of this medium, often taken as a supreme index of cultural memory with scarcity value by virtue of its susceptibility to highly tangible and visible decay, has been transformed in its digital becoming. Ritchin considers that:

> The photograph's documentary status has been altered, in part, by its transformation from a physical object derived from chemical processes to an expression of digital code. Rather than being viewed as the result of a recording process ... the ephemeral and easily malleable online photograph ... can be increasingly considered an expression of a particular point of view, a commentary on events that is more akin to writing than it is a definitive rendering.[16]

Under these circumstances media that once helped 'stabilize and convey that society's self-image' in Assmann's terms are suddenly made fluid and susceptible to rapid contagion, mutation, and indeed, oblivion. This spread of vulnerabilities is hardly the basis for a common, collective, or cultural perpetuation or conversely delimitation of memory.

At another level, transformations in the media management conventions of the individual and group render uncertain the generational limits of remembering. For example, the advent of the highly mobile and pervasive digital camera, and its merging with the mobile phone and computer—the smartphone—challenges the traditional preservative function of the family photograph. Instead, as Rasmussen argues, the post-scarcity culture of photography:

> is becoming individualized, unstable, and subject to impulsive treatment. These photographs loosen up the traditional image of the family as a highly integrated group, and present it as a group of connected individuals.[17]

Similarly, as Baruch Gottlieb observes: 'With the preponderance of today's digital media technology in every hand from young to old, even every family event is dissected into numerous points-of-view facets.'[18] This is the emergent memory of the multitude, increasingly hostaged to the spreadability of their media. The duration of different types of memory is thus much less fixed by generations or by 'reusable' 'texts, images, and rituals' in Jan Assmann's terms,[19] but rather is bound up in the vagaries of digital hyperconnectivity. Again, the communicative and the cultural have collapsed in the digital archive.

The discussion that follows asks if the once healthy dissipation of memory through media decay and degeneration is arrested by the digital networked archives that envelop and entangle the everyday. What kind of memory is made or lost through an archive whose principal curator is the algorithm?

Media Decay and Scarcity

The passing of the present into the past was once shaped through familiar decay. Media rotted, yellowed, faded, and flickered, becoming inevitably obscure and obsolete. And the places of its collection, the archive, concentrated emissions of volatile organic compounds: the fusty smell of a second-hand bookstore or library was a mark of age which accompanied the visible signs of use and decay. And the analogue recording and storage media, dominant for much of the twentieth century—magnetic tape, film, vinyl records—stretched and scratched and wore thin through their machinic capture and replay.

You can see, smell and taste nostalgia, in monochrome or the sepia hues of 1970s television, in organic archival decomposition, and in Proust's madeleine. This is the very essence of remembering: representing and re-imagining earlier times, events, and experiences, from a previous point on the continuum of chronological or clock time, from a past that is over. This is sometimes aided with the retention and preservation of media and objects deemed of personal and public worth. The chronological certainty of the inexorable passage of time fits with the everyday but misleading notion of a once-complete-past that somehow drains away under the dual pressures of the failings of the mind and the relentless distancing of time between now and previous moments, events, experiences.

In physical machinic ecologies, it was the finitude of media forms that signalled the past's decline, buffering a proper distance between then and now, offering a vision of the dissipating memory of a given society. This distance was mediated through the scarcity (and sometimes fragility) that comes with machinic and artefactual decay, degradation, and loss. The result was familiar deterioration. The classic marker of modern decay time is in the physicality of the photograph, inexorably displaying and authenticating signs of its age, of its past; it fades, it folds, it yellows.

I have a memory of going into a local shop as a child—perhaps in the early 1970s—with a green-tinted film lining the window to protect the clothing stock from the bleaching of the sun. I wonder why you don't see that anymore. Is it that modern fabrics and fixtures are more sunlight-resistant, or that all the shops are safely ensconced away from the sun in the caverns of malls, or that the faded and torn and worn add as well as subtract value? Does decay time come in and out of fashion?

What can be said is that decay time is linked to a culture of scarcity. This is a simple equation of the passage of decay time accumulating a value of sorts to the past and making it worthy of excavation, representation, remembrance. And it is odd then that perhaps the peak of a kind of electronic collective memorial power of the late twentieth century was the mass availability and use of the audio and video cassette recorder. Odd, that is, that this period, when the electronic media of deterioration, of decay time, were in full sway, is associated with the contemporary or 'second' 'memory boom',[20] the archival tendencies of which were driven by the principles of scarcity and the bounding of space.

This second memory boom was principally driven by two components: the influence of a new will to remember and the technologies that gave the remembrances their form. Pierre Nora articulates a tension or at least a separation of the two in this assessment:

> No society has ever produced archives as deliberately as our own, not only by volume, not only by new technical means of reproduction and preservation, but also by its superstitious esteem, by its veneration of the trace.[21]

And to reiterate, the electronic media of this day, in their fairly rapid decay time, were hardly a sound basis for any kind of usable archival future.

And the media of publication and of broadcast of much of the twentieth century, and that of the twenty-first, was fundamentally anti-archival. In fact there is a double scarcity to much of the broadcast era's media. Firstly, the norm was of non-documentation, much of the everyday was not routinely or systematically 'published', recorded or disseminated in an indiscriminate and continuous fashion; and, secondly, there was limited routine or systematic or accidental archiving, even of texts such as television programmes broadcast to audiences of millions. Prior to the 'connective turn' then, there is no default media trace of time but rather a default of media decay.

And today, one response to the diminishment of decay time under the conditions of hyperconnectivity is its re-imagination or re-creation as a sign of age, scarcity, and thus value. So, scarcity value is returned as a marker of past, of heritage, of history, rendered visible through the preservation and even the restoration of the signs of decay of an object or place that make it authentically of and from that time, that event, that catastrophe. For example, the stately home Calke Abbey in Derbyshire in the UK, is preserved at the critical moment of its demise: 1985. The Assistant House Manager of Calke, Yanni Simpson explains: 'Anything that fell before 1985 is historic and it can stay, anything after that which probably created by visitors and our building works has to go. So we've got a nice sort of line of what becomes historic dirt and what becomes dust.'[22]

Occasionally, we learn of scarcity past's sudden rediscovery (although there is increasingly less to find which makes each revelation more significant): the unearthing of the unexpected, hidden in the attic space (often the preserve of a generation) and once discarded with its future value then unknowable. For example, in 2002 the historian Peter Worden found 800 nitrate film reels of footage shot by the commercial filmmakers Sagar Mitchell and James Kenyon depicting early twentieth-century British life. Uncovered in a derelict shop in Blackburn, Lancashire, the unstable cellulose nitrate film was preserved and remediated in a number of forms.[23] Pushed through the digital sausage machine, fascinating glimpses of Edwardian and early Victorian life are made viewable for twenty-first-century TV, DVD, and YouTube audiences.

For instance, *The Lost World of Mitchell and Kenyon* first broadcast on the BBC in 2005 conjoins the restored footage with the living testimony of the descendants of those depicted as they watch their previous generations anew: faded personal stories given new public audio-visual form through being authenticated with the witnessing of living memory.

In some ways there is little remarkable about this story (other than the sheer chance finding and recognition of scarcity's past). It appears indicative of the selective restorative process through which societies generate their history: rediscovery plus translation (and remediation) through the representational, archival, and circulatory technologies, discourses, and witnesses of the day. But today the digital haphazardly annexes the past and what is left of scarcity culture uncovered is soon converted into post-scarcity, remade in today's media ecology.

The legacy of the second memory boom is an era characterized by patchy and irregular recording and retention, and is in a number of ways defined by scarcity culture and by forgetting. For example, think of the telephone conversations and the momentous decisions reached or failed to be reached, personally, politically, culturally, of which there was no record made, lost to human memory.

A great deal of early radio and also television programming was broadcast live without even broadcasters recording their output, and viewers did not have the technological means. Even later, many of the institutional recordings made were recorded over or simply wiped.

And, even with the advent of the audiotape and videocassette recorder (VCR), systematic recording and archiving by individual viewers was hardly connected, shared, or distributed: the recorded memory of broadcast media, despite all the claims as to its magical 'collective memory' effects, has no 'centre'. This point is well made with an exception.

The acclaimed British comic Bob Monkhouse obsessively recorded television programmes on multiple VCRs in his house and it was not until some time after his death (in 2003) that the true scarcity value of his collection was revealed: a treasure trove of film and TV programmes believed to be lost. He was amongst the first to own a VCR (as early as 1966[24]). But a comprehensive record of this age would have required thousands if not millions of Monkhouses. This example also points to the patchiness and inaccessibility of big media's own archives of the day, for those growing up in a 1970s British family with a single television set with three channels. Today, the former (single-medium household) is a rarity, and the latter (a containment of television to the channels BBC1, BBC2, and ITV) an impossibility; seemingly unlimited choice is not a genie that can be put back in the bottle. And to have missed a television or radio programme in that decade, the chance of being able to get hold of it post-broadcast were miniscule. Even the great institutional archives of broadcasting corporations routinely wiped tapes for their re-use given their cost and a great deal of broadcast output was live and ultimately not even recorded, let alone archived.

Occasionally the finding of a 'lost' tape in a private collection makes the news. For example, two missing 1960s *Dr Who* episodes were rediscovered in 2011 and promoted via an annual British Film Institute event 'Missing Believed Wiped' devoted to screening re-discovered UK television footage previously 'wiped'[25] (including footage from the Monkhouse archive, above). So, the history of the media of memory of the second memory boom only patchily survives today with consequences for the personal and the public record.

Another example is the former Liverpool and Hamburg striker Kevin Keegan who reflects on the incomplete televisual record of the highlights of his footballing career of the 1970s and 1980s:

When I was playing, there were only three games on *Match of the Day* each week, so only 65 of my 100 goals have been filmed. The other 35 are lost for ever. Today all goals are filmed. You'll never see some of the best things I ever did.[26]

So, scarcity culture marks a time in which despite all of memory's previously acclaimed fixities and externalisations (from the oral to the image, from writing to Gutenberg, and from the artefactual to the electronic) the past was still a place of patchy storage and also of steady decay, degradation, and loss. So, the rather random memory of media interleaves with an inevitable and inexorable diminishment of past experience as memory.

But today, the very relationship between the passage of time, decay, and scarcity, has been smashed and reconstituted by the digital archive. We will now turn to explore the nature and the prospects for memory remade in these times.

The Inverted Archive

In writing of the digital archive's shaping and scattering of past-present-future, as communication, as occurring on-the-fly, I am drawn to the influential work in the psychology of memory of Frederic Bartlett.[27] For Bartlett, the central process of individual remembering is how the past is introduced into the present to 'reactivate' consciousness. Thus:

> Remembering is not the re-excitation of innumerable fixed, lifeless, and fragmentary traces. It is an imaginative reconstruction, or construction, built out of the relation of our attitude towards a whole active mass of organized past reactions or experience.[28]

This reactivation also held for group or social, as well as individual, forms of remembering, in that memory is a continual representing, reassessing, and remaking of the past to make it relevant to ongoing personal, social, and political concerns. This is the popular and lived active model of memory, seen as dynamic, imaginative, directed, and shaped in and from the present.

However, in the digital archive, the matter of the 'whole active mass of organized past reactions or experience' in Bartlett's terms, becomes hijacked by largely invisible agents under cover of the apparent liveliness of all our digital practices. The linking, liking, editing, posting, deleting, snapping, and sharing digital multitude, certainly feel as though they are in control. And yet, it is algorithms that are the new invisible arbiters of what is retained and found, lost and unremembered. And this is occurring at an astonishing scale. For instance, YouTube claims to have over one billion users with over a billion hours of video watched on its platform every day.[29] But YouTube's awesome power is not so much as repository, but rather as recommender. Its Chief Product Officer claims that it is the site's video-recommendation algorithm that is responsible for 70 per cent of its views.[30] In other words, users' clicks and views determine what they are prompted to watch next; their past behaviour informs machinic predictions of what to present them with in order to hold their attention.

Here then, the digital flips the Bartlett inspired functional accounting of the relationship of the past to the present, to a state in which algorithmic selection by and from the archive in effect monetizes if not weaponizes the 'mass of organized past reactions or experience'. The past is caught up in this algorithmic narrowing of information, knowledge and life. And there is important work that illuminates how the algorithmic mediation of the social internet is hacked and exploited for inciting violence, for disrupting elections, and for information warfare.[31] But what is the archival and the memorial difference here to the workings of earlier media ecologies?

As suggested, above, a paradox of the second memory boom of the late twentieth century is that it propelled the virtue of remembering into an era whose technological mechanisms and capacity of holding its past seemed to have delivered memory unlimited, negating the need for human remembering. And yet, the ever more pervasive and affordable electronic media of the day offered a perversely shaky basis for any kind of robust archival future. But at least there was a continuity in the assured decay time of this media. Media have long kept memory in-check and held the past at some distance through their own in-built modes of decay.

In this way media have been an essential component of the forgetting of any given group. The decay time of media helped prevent the past from getting out of control, from accumulating beyond any one society's capacity to manage, make sense of, and use it. In as much as we can speak of a 'usable' past, one that is functional in the processing and coping with the uncertainties of the incoming present, today its usefulness is under serious strain.

The contemporary phenomenon of digital and political polarization is shaping an alienation from the past, a form of social forgetting. This seems an odd outcome given that the key criteria for algorithmic selection and curation is popularity—the links, likes, recommendations of a seething digital multitude. But this is what I call a 'sharing without sharing', how individuals and groups feel *active* in an array of connective practices such as posting, linking, liking, recording, swiping, scrolling, forwarding, etc, digital media content, and yet are barely conscious of the algorithms that underpin and shape these practices. And it is algorithms that value sharing, perversely limit the range of content that can be shared.

Molly Sauter for example, identifies three 'memory systems' of predictive text, 'reminiscence databases' such as Facebook Memories or Timehop that represent images or events that it determines are significant from your social media timeline, and 'data doppelgangers', ads targeted at users on the basis of what they have looked at or purchased before.[32] And the core strategy of these models, Sauter neatly suggests is: 'Those whose past is legible will be exhorted to repeat it'.[33] The apparent free for all and pervasiveness of data about the self then is like we are living in an age of the inverted archive. No longer located in place and time, the archive has been turned inside out, it follows us, it consumes us, it remakes us.

And given that repetition and rehearsal are so key to individual remembering, whether at the auto/biographical level of the individual smartphone, or on the scale of the billions of videos replaying on YouTube, digital media are paradoxically narrowing the past. And thus, it is important not to mistake the seeming availability of everything presented through online search, for accessibility.

The Datafication of the Mundane

The fundamentally archival incoming present is where the ease and the compulsion of connectivity, the recording of everything, and the entanglement of the network ego, engenders the fetishization of total memory (through life-tracking and life-journaling), and which feeds the myth of the digital as a reality of one's past. This gives digital life the character of something easy to control, of being harnesseable through a suite of apps and programs as with the appearance of something easily erasable. Thus, as Floridi argues: '"undo" facilities may have formatted our expectations about how much it is actually reversible in real life'.[34] And Bratton argues: '"new content", like the billions of images uploaded to Facebook or its Instagram, are already archived, socialized, and disseminated in near real-time. For such services, the archive is the primary channel of communication; the index is the medium of the message.'[35] It is no wonder then that basic everyday communication through messaging apps, texts, tweets, and emails, have become part of a new battleground of privacy: of ownership and control over one's digital trails, a new kind of haunting, of not being forgotten.

The principal change is the digital convergence of communication and archive, entangling human and machinic memory, into new in/visible relations. Users may feel empowered through seizing hold of mass culture online as a 'rogue archive',[36] through curating, ordering, tagging and sharing, and remaking the past anew. This archive appears effortless, in its interfaces, searchability, connectivity, and mass volume, all a click away. And yet, this is a perfect disguise; the affordance of individual control is by far the best cover for the wholesale capture of attention, a fundamental distraction of a generation of 'archive me'. Distraction, that is from the fall of the concept of the archive in the public sense, in ironically the most public of its form in history. Rather, the data that fills the public, is in fact private, it is proprietary data. But what feeds the convergence of communication and archive, is the truly epochal transformation, which is the existence of multiple forms of information about individuals. And it is precisely the addictive frenzy of 'The world's first ever public, live, collective, open-ended writing project'[37] that produces that most valuable of digital commodity—data.

The more the invisible the technology the more of the mundane seems to be captured, recorded, stored, and shared. But these are quite benign descriptions.

The mundane is also systematically tracked, harvested, aggregated through what I call the datafication of the mundane. This is how the self is reduced to a series of datapoints—an item of information about you and where you are and what you are doing—part of a new accountability of the digital self.

Memory is 'mediatized' through a compulsion of recording and connectivity, a sharing without sharing, that opens up the potential of information about the self to linger, to haunt, and to emerge into the public at unpredictable times. So memory here is tied in some ways to the relative finitude or openness of media forms.

But the datafication of the mundane raises the prospect of a radically new memory. That is, of a memory of self that did not previously exist. This is something I call the 'unremembered self'. The individual has become networked, but also archived, searchable, and ultimately accountable for every communication, every message, every personal or social act requiring media. Our basic everyday communicational acts are archival, we scatter digital traces of ourselves just through being social, through working, or even by doing nothing, information pours out of our smartphones as we sleep. So, whereas media audiences had collective anonymity in their media consumption of the twentieth century, in today's digital media ecology, it is users that are made personally accountable. And the prospects for aspects of your life, acts, traces, emerging at unpredictable times in the future are massively increased. So we all are burdened by a new unwieldy and uncontrollable, memory in the world.

So, the transformation of the inverted archive is both how and what of data of the self can be discovered, aggregated, and predicted, and also the how and what of data about the world that the self can and cannot find. Thus the inverted archive is unique in that it is confrontational, and as Weinberger puts it, 'Filters no longer filter out. They filter *forward*, bringing their results to the front.'[38]

In sum, the inverted archive arrives after a shift from a relatively steady but fairly predictable decay time of media forms and of the historical record—in effect a kind of forgetting, to a point today where there is much less certainty about the finitude of the digital record, in terms of its ownership, control, potential for both mass circulation and virality, and its capacity for 'emergence', as well as for its obsolescence. The paradox of this situation, of a new set of risks around not being forgotten, is that at the same time, the complexity and volume of digital records makes it impossible to make sense of, to manage, or to use for memory. The inverted archive can thus be seen as both nowhere and everywhere, risky and worthless to remembering.

FURTHER READING

Geoffrey C. Bowker, *Memory Practices in the Sciences* (Cambridge, MA: MIT Press, 2006)

Terry Cook, 'Evidence, Memory, Identity, and Community: Four Shifting Archival Paradigms', *Archival Science* 13 (2013), 95–120

Wolfgang Ernst, *Digital Memory and the Archive*, ed. Jussi Parikka (Minneapolis: University of Minnesota Press, 2013)

Andrew Hoskins, 'The End of Decay Time', *Memory Studies* 6.4 (2013), 387–389

Andrew Hoskins ed., *Digital Memory Studies: Media Pasts in Transition* (London and New York: Routledge, 2017)

Jay Winter, *War Beyond Words: Languages of Remembrance from the Great War to the Present* (Cambridge: Cambridge University Press, 2017)

NOTES

1. A. Hoskins, 'Media, Memory, Metaphor: Remembering and The Connective Turn', *Parallax* 17.4 (2011), 19–31; A. Hoskins, 'The Restless Past: An Introduction to Digital Memory and Media', in A. Hoskins, *Digital Memory Studies: Media Pasts in Transition* (London and New York: Routledge, 2018), 1–24.
2. A. Hoskins, 'New Memory: Mediating History', *The Historical Journal of Film, Radio and Television* 21.4 (2001), 191–211; Hoskins, 'The Restless Past'.
3. I develop this observation and possible responses to it in a forthcoming work: A. Hoskins, *Breaking the Past*.
4. P. Connerton, 'Seven Types of Forgetting', *Memory Studies* 1.1 (2008), 59–71.
5. A. Assmann, 'Forms of Forgetting', Public Lecture, 1 October 2014; https://h401.org/2014/10/forms-of-forgetting/.
6. M. T. Dewar et al., 'Forgetting Due to Retroactive Interference: A Fusion of Müller and Pilzecker's (1900) Early Insights into Everyday Forgetting and Recent Research on Anterograde Amnesia', *Cortex* 43.7 (2007), 616–634.
7. M. Halbwachs, *The Collective Memory*, trans. F. J. Ditter Jr and V. Yazdi Ditter (London: Harper & Row. 1980), 120.
8. J. Assmann, 'Collective Memory and Cultural Identity', *New German Critique* 65 (1995), 125–133.
9. Assmann, 'Collective Memory', 129.
10. Assmann, 'Collective Memory', 132.
11. J. Urry, 'Time, Leisure and Social Identity', *Time and Society* 3.2 (1995), 131–149.
12. W. Ernst, 'The Archive as Metaphor', *Open* 7 (2004), 46–53.
13. Ernst, *Digital Memory*, 95.
14. A. Hoskins, 'Memory of the Multitude', in Hoskins, *Digital Memory Studies*, 85–109.
15. A. Hoskins, 'The End of Decay Time', *Memory Studies* 6.4 (2013), 387–389.
16. F. Ritchin, *Bending the Frame: Photojournalism, Documentary, and the Citizen* (New York: Aperture, 2013), 10.
17. R. Terje, 'Devices of Memory and Forgetting: A Media-Centred Perspective on the "Present Past"', in E. Rossaak, ed., *The Archive in Motion: New Conceptions of the Archive in Contemporary Thought and New Media Practices* (Oslo: Novus Press, 2010), 121.
18. B. Gottlieb, *Gratitude for Technology: Mimeography & Navigable Narrative for the Manifestation of the Human Origins of Things in the Work of Digital Media* (New York: Atropos Press, 2009), 78.
19. Assmann, 'Collective Memory.'
20. J. Winter, *Remembering War: The Great War between Memory and History in the Twentieth Century* (New Haven: Yale University Press, 2006); J. Winter, *War beyond Words: Languages of Remembrance from the Great War to the Present* (Cambridge: Cambridge University Press, 2017).

21. P. Nora, 'Between Memory and History: *Les Lieux de Mémoire*', trans by Marc Roudebush, *Representations* 26 (1989), 7–25.
22. Speaking on 'Heritage! The Battle for Britain's Past', Episode 3: 'Broken Propylaeums', first broadcast 21 March 2013, BBC Four, UK.
23. The complex process of preservation of this film stock is detailed here: www.bfi.org.uk/features/mk/preservation.html.
24. The Secret Life of Bob Monkhouse: www.youtube.com/watch?v=tooDIHN6o2o& feature=related.
25. www.bbc.co.uk/news/entertainment-arts-16,136,521.
26. Kevin Keegan interviewed by Stuart Jeffries in *The Guardian*, 25 June 2011, 38.
27. F. C. Bartlett, *Remembering: A Study in Experimental and Social Psychology* (Cambridge: Cambridge University Press, 1932).
28. Bartlett, *Remembering*, 213.
29. www.youtube.com/about/press.
30. www.cnet.com/news/youtube-ces-2018-neal-mohan.
31. R. DiResta, 'Free Speech Is Not the Same as Free Reach', *Wired*, 30 August 2018: www.wired.com/story/free-speech-is-not-the-same-as-free-reach.
32. M. Sauter, 'Instant Recall. How Do We Remember when Apps Never Forget?', *Real Life*, 27 June 2017, https://reallifemag.com/instant-recall.
33. Sauter, 'Instant Recall'.
34. F. Luciano, 'Google's Privacy Ethics Tour of Europe: A Complex Balancing Act', *The Guardian*, 16 September 2014: www.theguardian.com/technology/2014/sep/16/googles-european-privacy-ethics-tour.
35. B. H. Bratton, *The Stack. On Software and Sovereignty* (Cambridge, MA: MIT Press, 2015), 125–126.
36. A. De Kosnik, *Rogue Archives: Digital Cultural Memory and Media Fandom* (Cambridge, MA: MIT Press, 2016).
37. R. Seymore, 'The Machine Always Wins: What Drives Our Addiction to Social Media', *The Guardian*, 23 August 2019: www.theguardian.com/technology/2019/aug/23/social-media-addiction-gambling.
38. D. Weinberger, *Too Big to Know* (New York: Basic Books, 2011), 11.

CHAPTER 6

RESPONSE TO 'CONCEPTIONS'

NIAMH MOORE

This section on 'Conceptions', which is the first in *Archives: Power, Truth, and Fiction*, opens with Michelle Caswell's call for more cross-fertilization between archivists and humanities academics. It enacts an important response to that appeal, offering as it does a site where archivists and academics (not a mutually exclusive category in any case) are put into conversation. What new archive is being born out of the ongoing fertile and furious engagement with the archive, what archival turn comes next, and how will the archive continue to turn?

Caswell's searing call to account of humanities academics who rhapsodize about 'the archive', while failing to cite any of the rich, vibrant, and lively archival tradition and archival theory—or are perhaps unaware of its existence—may yet help enact the archival turn that she so desires but has not yet witnessed. Hers is a frustration shared by many and underlined, for example, by Dorothy Berry from the Houghton Library at Harvard, who tweeted that she feels like the 'archives sheriff' whenever she reviews texts on archives by historians or digital humanists who fail to cite any archive scholars (Berry 2021).[1]

Just to note, here, that there is no need for an archives sheriff for this collection. Similarly, Arike Oke, while Managing Director of the Black Cultural Archives (UK), evocatively described the experience of being perceived by researchers as being merely the person who delivers boxes from the archive, a kind of Amazon delivery for research materials (which speaks to the—gendered and other—labour conditions of archiving that Caswell also signals).[2] Berry's tweet also suggests that #archivestwitter might actually be one of the more important impacts of the internet on archiving, offering an opportunity for archivists to escape the black box of the archive into a digital counterpublic where archivists can speak back to researchers who may remain ignorant of archival expertise.

This opening section promises new understandings of archives—archives, as well as archivists, are allowed to escape the black box. Here, Louise Craven's chapter comprehensively sets the scene for the radical changes in archiving in the last few decades. As Craven documents, archives now appear everywhere in the most

Figure 6.1 Dorothy Berry, 'I feel like the Archives Sheriff', Twitter, 5 January 2021.

unexpected places, and are produced even in the process of movement, as Hariz Halilovich and Anne Gilliland recount. They demonstrate how pervasive digitality, mass migration, and displacement meet, though turning to visual records in the form of VHS tapes made by refugees and survivors of the Bosnian war of 1992–1995. These visual postcards, made throughout the war and after, circulated both in Bosnia and abroad and maintained connections between diasporic and home communities. This almost accidental, distributed archive emerged in the connections made as videos were digitized and transformed from private archives to circulate on YouTube as a global archive of everyday life in difficult times. In their recognition that 'movement and dispersion have always been a part of the archival as well as the human experience', they show how people can carry and create archives as they move, and how pervasive digitality has facilitated the connection of otherwise disparate fragments in ways which would once have been almost impossible in the context of forced migrations.

Andrew Hoskins' chapter picks up on Halilovich and Gilliland's recognition of the surprising generativity of fragments, particularly once connected through the affordances of digital platforms. For Hoskins, digitization matters because it can shift attention from scarcity to abundance. This productive troubling of assumptions of scarcity or abundance also brings to mind Saidiya Hartman's ongoing archival work, which traverses the limits of both the *dearth* of archives of Black experiences of transatlantic slavery and the *profusion* of data about Black lives to be found in the social surveys of the early-twentieth-century US, in which Black lives appear only as social problems. In *Wayward Lives, Beautiful Experiments*, Hartman sutures together archival fragments from a hundred years or so ago to conjure 'an archive of the exorbitant, a dream book for existing otherwise', in her re-imagination of the lives of black working-class girls in New York and Chicago.[3] Her contribution offers a generative reimagination of the common concern, that Craven articulates, that what we can glean from the archive is only ever a partial and fragmentary picture of what might have been.

These unconventional archives—accidental archives of diasporas sutured together through the emergence of digital platforms and the imagined lives of black girls—serve as examples of the developments that Craven notes; it is not only the boundaries of the (physical site of the) archive that are being remade, but further that the boundaries of archival *practice* are being re-configured. What Craven articulates as 'diverse archives', such as the development of DIY archival practices, provide a site for articulating identities and politics, as well as involving a resourceful reimagining of archival practices. Terry Cook's article on four paradigms of the archive is worth invoking here.[4] He did not identify the digital archive as one of his paradigms but rather, for him, it is community archiving that define innovative developments. His is an account of archives that is not overdetermined or overawed by the huge reach of digital corporations, but rather he brings into communication the affordances of digital technologies with community archiving and the participatory practices which open up the democratization of the archive.

Yet even when we return to the more recognizable territory of state archives, and the bureaucracy of government, our grasp of the archive is being remade. James Lowry's chapter does crucial work to extend understanding of the power of records beyond recognition of the lack of neutrality or objectivity of the archive. He draws on critical bureaucracy studies to clarify the power of state archives, showing how records begin to act on the world even before they enter any archive. He approaches state records as written commands functioning as performative utterances that we cannot avoid or evade, and which enrol us in responding to the demand, generating data, and enabling 'the acquisition of information' that governance relies on. The archive, as the formal site of recordkeeping, acts to assign authenticity to the record, ensuring the record's status as an instrument of power, and illuminating how bureaucracy is the apparatus of state power in consolidating the force of records. Datafication of subjects only intensifies the regimes of information exchange and the possibilities of accumulating information on subjects from seemingly disparate systems, enacting a shift from records as demand to data as demand.

This section, 'Conceptions', signals birth and rebirth, a thinking and rethinking of archives. What is clear already is that there will be no faithful child of archival fathers, but something more generative is already emerging from the diffractive frictions of archives, archivists, academics, disciplines, communities, and technologies, where taking 'archive as subject' signals not just an archival turn, but rather that archiving is in perpetual movement.

NOTES

1. D. Berry, 'I feel like the archives sheriff ...' [Online] Twitter, 5 January 2021; https://twitter.com/dorothyjberry/status/1346597981886283782 (accessed 18 December 2021).
2. A. Oke, 'The Civic Archivist', filmed November 2020 at *London School of Economics Library* [Online]. London. Video, 1:14:39; www.lse.ac.uk/library/events/general/the-civic-archivist (accessed 18 December 2021).
3. S. Hartman, *Wayward Lives, Beautiful Experiments* (London: Serpent's Tail, 2019), xvii.
4. T. Cook, 'Evidence, Memory, Identity, and Community: Four Shifting Archival Paradigms', *Archival Science* 13.2 (2013), 95–120.

PART II

FRAMEWORKS

CHAPTER 7

APPRAISAL AND ORIGINAL ORDER

The Power Structures of the Archive

ANDREW PRESCOTT

It might seem that one symptom of archive fever is an obsession with preserving traces of the past, with keeping every scrap of paper and vellum. The proliferation of specialist archives and libraries could suggest that collecting fever is a disease of modern society. But the archive is as much about controlled destruction as it is about collecting. The vast quantities of documents and data generated by such corporate bodies as governments, commercial companies, and educational institutions cannot possibly be retained, otherwise the world would drown in an ocean of records. In order to ensure that documents can be safely stored, easily located, and authenticated in a cost effective manner, it is necessary that archivists and record managers design systems that identify which documents should be retained and provide procedures for the destruction of redundant documents.

This process is known as appraisal. It is the most important responsibility of all those involved in the management of archives. Archivists and record managers have developed systems to ensure that appraisal is undertaken in a transparent and rational fashion. The process of appraisal is governed by international standards such as ISO 15,489-1:2016 for records management and ISO/TR 21,946: 2018 specifically on appraisal. Nevertheless, the extent of destruction is still little appreciated by archive users. In Britain, it has been estimated that 98 per cent of modern government papers never reach The National Archives. In 1989, the Home Office produced files occupying some 1379 feet of shelving. The files eventually transferred to The National Archives occupied only 35 feet of shelving, or about 3 per cent of the whole.[1] Because the destruction of records is a routine part of archives management, appraisal provides a cloak by which tyrannical regimes can conceal their crimes.

The apartheid regime in South Africa engaged in mass sanitization of The National Archives of South Africa to protect the guilty and avoid retribution.

Writers on archives frequently express astonishment at their vast size and the way in which researchers can immerse themselves in the endless *fonds*. But the process of appraisal means that what survives is only ever a fragment or, in the words of Verne Harris, 'a sliver of a sliver of a sliver'.[2] The growth of modern bureaucracies and now the explosion of born-digital records makes the process of appraisal both more pressing and much more complex. Moreover, appraisal is not only an issue confined to the management of modern documents. The Victorian archivists who established the first modern archive offices were just as bewildered by the immense scale of medieval and early modern archives and engaged in reckless and imprudent rationalization and destruction of medieval archives.

The decision to destroy a document is the most important and difficult confronting anyone charged with the management of records. It is in the process of appraisal that the archivist exercises power and the archives become an active instrument of power. This has been eloquently expressed by the Canadian archivist Terry Cook:

> In appraisal, archivists (along with record creators and managers) decide for society who in future will be heard and who will not. With remembering comes forgetting. In appraisal we archivists are cocreating the archives. We are making history. We are exercising power over memory. And as we include, we also overwhelmingly exclude.[3]

This chapter will explore the relationship between appraisal and power. It will consider how the criteria for appraisal are bound up with the power structures of the institutions which generated the archives. This is inextricably linked with the way in which archives are processed and documented. In order to understand the institutional context of archival documents, it is vital that the original file and document series structures are retained—a fundamental principle enshrined in the watchwords *respect des fonds* which feature prominently in international manuals of archival practice. But by enshrining bureaucratic power structures in the arrangement and cataloguing of the archive, there is a risk that our historical understanding remains trapped within the confines of historical power structures and that stories of the poor, disadvantaged, and marginal in the archive disappear from sight. Appraisal and original order represent two pillars by which traditional archives reinforce and encapsulate existing power structures in society.

A dramatic illustration of ways in which the disposal of archives can devastate the lives of ordinary citizens was the Windrush scandal in Britain. The Windrush generation, named after the ship which brought one of the first large groups of Caribbean people to Britain in 1948, are those who arrived in the UK from Caribbean countries between 1948 and 1973. Because the Caribbean was part of the British Empire, these people were automatically British citizens and free permanently to live and work in the UK. Changes in legislation gradually circumscribed this right to settle.

Moreover, the onus came to be placed on the migrant, rather than the government, to establish that they had a right to live in the UK.

From 2010, the Conservative Home Secretary Theresa May sought to reduce immigration by creating a 'hostile environment' for illegal immigrants. In many everyday situations such as applying for jobs, medical treatment, government benefits, rental accommodation, and mortgages, it was necessary to provide documentary proof of the right to live and work in the UK. Many of the Windrush generation did not have such proof although they had lived in Britain for decades. A former cook in the House of Commons who had come to Britain in 1968 at the age of ten and never held a British passport was sent to an immigration removal centre for deportation to Jamaica. A man who had worked in Britain for forty-four years as a mechanic was denied cancer treatment because he could not show he was in the country legally. Another victim, who had lived in Britain since he was six, decided to visit Jamaica for his fiftieth birthday. He was told he could not return to Britain on his Jamaican passport. He lived in bedsits and hostels in Jamaica for nearly two years until his case was resolved, but on his return to Britain he was told he owed £4,500 for unpaid rent and council tax and was evicted and has been homeless ever since.

By 2017, it became apparent that hundreds of black Britons has been wrongly detained, deported, and denied legal rights. Theresa May, by then Prime Minister, apologized and the Home Secretary Amber Rudd resigned. Particular concern centred around the onerous demands for documentation proving the right to live in the UK. Whistle blowers in the Home Office revealed that the Home Office had an archive of landing cards or registration slips which recorded when individuals had landed in the UK and the name of the ship. This was vital evidence in proving when a member of the Windrush generation had arrived in the UK and whether they had residence rights. In 2009, as part of an office move, it was decided that these landing cards should be disposed of. Some officials protested that they still used these records:

'You can't do that—we still use those files', one of his colleagues was saying. 'You can't destroy them.'

'They were very angry. Some of them had worked in the Department for twenty years. They were astonished that the papers were going to be destroyed', Martin told me later.

The manager just shrugged. 'I'm not doing it. I've just been told it is happening. I've got no say in it.'

'What happens if there is case of dispute?' Martin asked. He said he was told that the vast majority of people named in the cards were in their seventies and eighties, that most of the cases would have been resolved, the remainder must be very small in number and that the office did 'not have the resources to keep them'. He remembers protesting, 'Even if half the people are dead, they are historical records'. His manager responded that the cards were 'redundant'.[4]

The landing cards were destroyed sometime in 2010. As the hostile environment began to bite, Home Office officials noticed an increase in requests for information held by the Home Office recording when an individual had arrived in the UK. The Home Office did not reveal that this information had been destroyed, but sent out a standard reply that it held no such data. When eventually news of the destruction of the landing cards leaked out, Freedom of Information requests were submitted to get more information about their disposal. One response claimed, unconvincingly, that the cards had been destroyed in order to ensure compliance with data protection legislation and that they had no bearing on immigration decisions.[5] Another saw the disposal as a routine piece of records management: 'Any Windrush papers would have been destroyed in line with the retention and disposal periods set for the wider record collections in which they were located.'[6]

The Windrush scandal was due to many causes, including the complex and changing legislative framework, poor management in the Home Office, the effect of outsourcing, and racist assumptions in many government agencies. Nevertheless, the destruction of the landing cards symbolized the thoughtless and inhuman treatment of the Windrush generation. The management of public records such as these is governed by the 1958 Public Records Act, as amended by the 1967 Public Records Act, the 2000 Freedom of Information Act, and the 2010 Constitutional Reform and Governance Act. Civil service departments appoint a Departmental Records Officer who is the primary point of contact with The National Archives. This official decides which records should be kept and supervises the reviews controlling the transfer of records to The National Archives. The current record collecting policy of The National Archives gives priority for preservation to documents recording policy decisions by government.[7] There is a strong bias in favour of keeping records illustrating the institutional development of government. While The National Archives current policy allows for the preservation of 'case files, datasets, and other records which contain extensive information about the lives of individuals or groups, organizations, and places, which contribute substantially to public knowledge and understanding of the people and communities of the UK',[8] which could apply to the Windrush landing cards, on the other hand the policy also states that large-scale records posing storage problems may be destroyed. Difficult decisions can be referred to the Advisory Council on National Archives and Records, but the case of the Windrush landing cards was never referred to the Advisory Council and the decision on destruction was made by local Home Office officials.[9]

The Windrush case illustrates the potential pitfalls and shortcomings of the appraisal process. It is not clear whether appropriate procedures were followed. The quantities of documents involved were vast: files were brought back from storage piled four feet high. At one point, a manager discovered a forgotten room full of files whose origin and purpose had been forgotten. It was all immensely confusing:

If you were a British citizen, the Home Office would not keep a file on you, because this system was only there for keeping records of immigrants. As Windrush-generation people were effectively moved from being seen as citizens to being classified as migrants, they were forced to make applications to regularize their status; these applications could have been helped by accessing their Home Office files, only most of them discovered they had no Home Office files because the Home Office had never viewed them as migrants who needed files.[10]

Expert advice was lacking, and, as soon as the scandal came to light, it emerged that the inward passenger lists deposited by the Board of Trade in The National Archives (BT 26) record the arrival of most of the Windrush generation (see Figure 7.1 and 7.2).[11]

The Windrush case was not the first time that concern had been expressed that the record management processes of the UK government encouraged the destruction of material of historical importance. Paul Rock, David Downes, and Tim Newburn, in writing the official history of criminal justice in Britain, found that,

Figure 7.1 The original passenger lists in The National Archives (BT 26) were used to reimagine artistically the destroyed Windrush landing cards. These recreated cards were used for the exhibition *Windrush: Arrivals 1948*, undertaken by Goldsmiths, University of London, in 2019, co-curated by John Price and Will Cenci, relocated to City Hall and Lewisham Shopping Centre the same year: www.gold.ac.uk/windrush. The passenger information in the recreated cards was historically correct although their visual appearance was based on earlier iterations, given that the original cards had been destroyed. Photo: John Price.

Figure 7.2 Visitors looking at the 1,027 recreated individual landing cards, each representing a passenger who arrived on the MV *Empire Windrush* at Tilbury docks on 22 June 1948. Photo: by John Price showing the 2019 Goldsmiths historically contextualized art installation, *Windrush: Arrivals 1948*.

while papers of Royal Commissions and interdepartmental committees were meticulously preserved, the documents illustrating why Royal Commissions had been set up and recording government reaction to their findings had not been preserved. There were no papers relating to the decision to establish the Wolfenden Committee on Homosexual Offences and Prostitution in 1954 and none on what the government made of it. The false confessions extracted by police for the murder of the trans woman Maxwell Confait in 1974 had led to a Royal Commission on Criminal Procedure, but key Home Office files relating to decisions of this case had not been retained.[12]

In the UK, early appraisal theory was deeply influenced by the writings of Sir Hilary Jenkinson, who published a *Manual of Archive Administration* in 1922. Jenkinson argued that it is impossible to anticipate what the historian of the future might find useful. He felt that the most objective procedure was for administrators themselves to identify what documents were vital to reconstruct why a decision had been made. The role of the archivist, in Jenkinson's view, was simply to preserve and make available the documents selected by the government. In the light of events such as the Windrush scandal and the sequestration and uncontrolled destruction by the UK government of British colonial archives, this now appears very naive. Michelle Caswell and Anna Sexton in their chapters discuss the criticisms of Jenkinson's approach, which have become widespread in recent years. By contrast, in the United States, Theodore Schellenberg argued that the overwhelming mass of modern records meant that the archivist had actively to intervene in selecting material for future preservation. He put these views into action in the National Archives and Records Administration, destroying old records and introducing new methodologies for selecting records for preservation.

However, the Royal Commission on Public Records in the UK under Sir James Grigg whose report formed the basis of the 1958 Public Records Act seem to have been preoccupied with saving space and stemming the 'dreadful flood of documents'.[13] While they found Jenkinson's 1922 *Manual* interesting in its approach, Jenkinson was excluded from the Commission. Contact was made with Schellenberg, whose influence was reflected in the establishment of a Public Records Department which provided archival guidance to civil service departments on retention policy. The 1958 Act, as amended by subsequent legislation, created a system whereby files are reviewed by departments after closure and destroyed if they had no administrative value. After thirty years (now twenty), the files are then subject to a second review to see if they have historical value. If the file survived second review, it would be transferred to The National Archives. If files contain sensitive information, such as personal data or information relating to national security, they may be closed for extended periods. In all this, the constant refrain was disposal and saving space. The term used for identifying redundant documents, 'weeding', was telling. A report in *The Times* in 1975 showed a group of weeders merrily throwing records into wastepaper bins and quoted a senior weeder as saying: 'These are the happiest days of our life ... We spent 40 years writing these documents and now we are throwing them away.'[14]

The system established by the Grigg report was particularly suspicious of the retention of records of routine transactions with individual citizens, such as the Windrush landing cards ('Particular Instance Papers' or PIPS, to give them their technical name), because of their large size. Archivists themselves are also perhaps suspicious of Particular Instance Papers because they eat up space and cataloguing resources and are thought mainly of value to family historians. In the 1960s and early 1970s, there was a 'long and confused debate' about the lists of crews of merchant vessels submitted to the Registrar General of Shipping.[15] These were considered too large for transfer to the UK National Archives and it was proposed to retain only a 10 per cent sample of lists from 1860. The loss of so much genealogical and other information created an outcry, particularly in North America. The outcome was very messy: all records before 1860 were transferred to the UK National Archives; one 10 per cent sample of all lists from 1861 to the present day was held by the UK National Archives; another 10 per cent sample was transferred to the National Maritime Museum in London; the remainder was acquired by the National Memorial University Newfoundland, with the exception of a few lists acquired by local record offices. Sampling of this sort has also been used in the past on many other records such as war pension records and supplementary benefit claims.[16] Sampling is unhelpful since it is the individual details that researchers want to see. Already by the 1970s, it was evident that name-rich material like the crew lists is suitable for searching by computer and in recent years a consolidated online index to the crew lists from 1863 to 1913 has been created by volunteers (www.crewlist.org.uk).

'Particular Instance Papers' may assume unlikely forms. As part of his theatrical censorship duties, the Lord Chamberlain retained copies of the scripts of plays licenced for performance. Plays licensed between 1824 and 1904 were sent to The National Archives, which returned them to St James's Palace as unwanted in 1923. The plays for 1824 to 1851 were then transferred as a gift to the British Library in 1932. The remaining nineteenth-century plays were given to the British Library in 1953, although it took the Library nine years to find the space to accommodate them.[17] The difficulties of appraisal can even be evident with audio-visual archives. The costs of storing television programmes, particularly in the early days of videotape, were very high. The BBC prioritized the preservation of videotape of events deemed to be of historical importance, such as election coverage, and wiped entertainment programmes such as television plays by Alan Bennett or Dennis Potter or comedy shows like *Dad's Army* and Peter Cook and Dudley Moore's *Not Only But Also*, which are perhaps more significant cultural documents.[18]

It should not be assumed that appraisal decisions, good or bad, are only of relevance to modern records. As medieval and early modern records were transferred to newly created record offices in the nineteenth century, they were subject to appraisal processes which nowadays appear very crude. The records of the Tudor Exchequer of the Receipt had been dumped in a basement in Somerset House where they were in very poor condition. The civil servant responsible was reluctant to go to the trouble of transferring them to the newly created Public Record Office and sold the documents by the pound to a fishmonger. Very soon, the fishmonger's customers noticed that their fish was wrapped in vellum bearing signatures of Henry VIII and Queen Elizabeth, leading to a scandal and a public inquiry.[19]

Even when documents were transferred to the newly created archives, they were not safe. The voluminous file series of medieval and early modern law courts were transferred to the new Public Record Office in Chancery Lane where they remained in sacks. It was assumed that the files did not add much to the information in the plea rolls. On this basis, many seventeenth- and eighteenth-century files were destroyed without examination.[20] When the surviving files afterwards came to be examined, it was found that they contained working documents from which the plea rolls were compiled and are rich in further administrative and contextual information. It is difficult now to gauge how much was lost as a consequence of the nineteenth-century destruction schedules.

With the advent of born-digital records, completely different approaches to appraisal are required. While storage costs are an issue with digital records, other matters are more pressing. It is necessary regularly to ensure that born-digital records can still be read. They have to be kept in forms which facilitate public access. Born-digital records often contain large amounts of personal and other sensitive data, so sensitivity reviews are more pressing and difficult. With paper files, once and for all reviews make sense; with digital files it is necessary to undertake continuous review processes. This has led to the development of a records continuum model, which envisages the management of records as a continuous circular process of creation, organization, and review (see Figure 7.3).

The requirements of managing born-digital records as well as concerns to create more transparent forms of appraisal mean that increasingly records managers focus on evaluating the corporate structures which generate records rather than on simple questions of disposal and retention. The latest version of ISO 15,489 describes appraisal as 'the process of evaluating business activities to determine which records need to be created and captured and how long the records need to be kept'. In the past, the focus of the archivist was on looking after the records of the past; today,

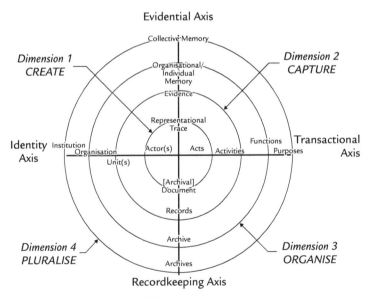

Figure 7.3 Records Continuum Model.

there is a stronger emphasis on reviewing the systems which create the records, an approach described as post-custodial. While this wider perspective has its benefits, it nevertheless runs the same sort of risk as the older approach of Sir Hilary Jenkinson, namely that the archive becomes a testimony of the power structure of the institution which created it.

The huge growth of interest in community archives recording the voices of for example ethnic and indigenous groups, different genders, or LGBTQIA+ people reflects the increasing concern that conventional corporate professionally administered archives exclude the voices of these groups. These excluded groups naturally seek to record and preserve their own history. It is striking what strong support has emerged for the growth of community archives in the archives community in recent years. Indeed, increasingly many archivists see themselves as activists ensuring that forgotten and marginal voices find their place in the historical record, as can be seen from the work of the Activist Archivists in recording the Occupy movement or the creation of 'rebel archives' of those Mexican and Indigenous communities in the Inland Empire area of Southern California described by Genevieve Carpio.[21]

It is also important to remember that records management and appraisal are a major dividing line between corporate archives and Special Collections holdings in institutions such as the British Library. The bulk of acquisitions by institutions such as the British Library are made by purchase, often in sale rooms, or by donation. The process of selection in such collections thus occurs at the point at which it is decided to purchase one particular manuscript, and not another, or when a donation is accepted or not. This means that the holdings of institutions such as the British Library can be very haphazard in character, as the plums have been pulled out of various archival pies over the years.

Another major difference between corporate archives and library Special Collections is the emphasis in the management of corporate archives on original order. Acquisitions by Special Collections such the British Library's Manuscripts Collections are added to continuous numerical collections such as the Additional Manuscripts and the Additional Charters, even when the manuscripts represent the distinct archive of a family, company, or estate. It can be difficult to locate and reconstruct these remnants of archives within the artificial sequences used in somewhere like the British Library. Within a corporate archive such as the UK National Archives, the primary concern is usually to ensure that the arrangement of the archives preserves the file structures used by the administrative units which generated the archive.[22] This principle of original order or *respect des fonds* has been a fundamental principle of the management of archives ever since the publication of the *Dutch Manual for the Arrangement and Description of Archives* in 1898. It is enshrined in the relevant international standards for the cataloguing and processing of archives such as the *General International Standard Archival Description* (ISAD-G) promulgated by the International Council on Archives.

The idea of original order emphasizes the organic nature of the archive. An influential illustration of this are the records of the exchequer in England. The core series of exchequer accounts, the Pipe Rolls, date back to at least 1130. During the twelfth century, a copy of the pipe rolls known as the Chancellors Rolls began to be kept. Informal memoranda kept by officials attending the exchequer coalesced into two series of Memoranda Rolls in the thirteenth century. Further series such as the Issue Rolls and the Receipt Rolls emerged. By following the evolution and development of these record classes, we learn a great deal about the evolution of the exchequer and government finance. Any attempt to 'rationalize' the arrangement of these documents, as happened in the nineteenth century with petitions to the medieval parliament, destroys information about the interrelationship of documents which is fundamental not only to understanding the document itself but also the history of the department which created it.

The preservation of original order is just as important with documents produced by modern government as it is with the medieval exchequer. The docketing, registration, and filing of all documents received by government departments has been fundamental to British government procedure since the sixteenth century and such business-like procedures were vital to the growth of the British Empire. Sir Christopher Foster recalled of his early days as a civil servant in the 1960s:

> Underpinning their knowledge of their jobs was an exhaustive, but marvellous, filing system. Everything was written down. Almost every meeting discussed a paper, which was revised as it rose through the hierarchy towards the minister or was sent down again by her. (There was no problem identifying who suggested, and who authorized, every change to a paper, as there was to the 2002 Iraq dossier.) Every meeting, every lunch, was minuted.[23]

The structure of this filing system says a lot about how government functioned, and it is for this reason that archivists seek to retain, and even sometimes reconstruct, this original order.

Unlike a library, which imposes an arbitrary classification, an archive reproduces the administrative structure of the organization which creates it. In order to find your way around a corporate archive, you need first to understand the history of the administration which created it. This means that catalogue information for corporate archives looks very different to that for Special Collections in libraries. In a library, we expect that a catalogue entry for a twelfth-century manuscript includes such information as date and localization of script, decoration, ruling, provenance, and so on. If we turn however to one of the most important surviving series of English twelfth-century records, the Pipe Rolls, we find that the description consists of a very lengthy narrative account of the administrative context and development of the pipe rolls, but that for each individual manuscript, we are given only the archive reference and the dates covered by the record. This reflects the fact that, in order to locate material in a corporate archive, we need to understand the way the administration functioned and use this to anticipate where information will occur, rather than relying on searching overly detailed catalogues. This insistence on original order is another way in which the archive can be seen as reinforcing existing power structures. Because the structure of the archive reflects the bureaucracy which produces it, we inevitably view records through the eyes of the governments and other corporate bodies which produced them.

How far will all this change as the archive increasingly becomes born-digital? Current thinking about appraisal is still rooted in the paper age, in managing and controlling those tottering towers of files that so overwhelmed the Home Office officials involved in the Windrush scandal. Digital systems produce information on a vastly larger scale than hitherto, but it is arguably easier and cheaper to store and retrieve large-scale digital archives than unwieldy physical indexes such as the Windrush landing cards. However, digital archives pose greater challenges in terms of safeguarding sensitive and personal information and in long-term maintenance. As was pointed out at the time of the Windrush scandal, digital storage offers the prospect of retaining those pesky Particular Instance Papers and using them for new types of academic study.[24]

Approaches to appraisal have been shaped by the constraints of storing, organizing, and retrieving the vast quantities of vellum and paper produced by large governments and corporations. The process of appraisal all too often reflects institutional and academic biases but, as the Windrush scandal made clear, general public awareness of the scale of appraisal and its impact on the historical record is limited. As archives increasingly become born-digital, new approaches to appraisal will be required in response to the opportunities offered by larger and cheaper storage and retrieval on the one hand and new anxieties about privacy and security on the other. This offers the opportunity for a renewed dialogue between record creators, record managers, record users, and the wider public as to what records are kept and why. As the Windrush scandal amply illustrates, appraisal is too important to be left to bureaucrats and archivists alone.

FURTHER READING

Terry Cook, '"We Are What We Keep: We Keep What We Are": Archival Appraisal Past, Present and Future', *Journal of the Society of Archivists* 32.2 (2011), 173–189

Richard J. Cox, *No Innocent Deposits: Forming Archives by Rethinking Appraisal* (Lanham and Oxford: Scarecrow Press, 2004)

Verne Harris, 'The Archival Sliver: Power, Memory and Archives in South Africa', *Archival Science* 2 (2002), 63–86

Juan Ilerbaig, 'Archives as Sediments: Metaphors of Deposition and Archival Thinking', *Archival Science* 21 (2021), 83–95

Sue McKemmish, 'Placing Records Continuum Theory and Practice', *Archival Science* 1 (2001), 333–359

Paul Rock, '"The Dreadful Flood of Documents": The 1958 Public Record Act and its Aftermath. Part 1: The Genesis of the Act', *Archives* 51.132-3 (2016), 48–69; 'Part 2: After Effects', *Archives* 52.134 (2017), 26–50

NOTES

1. P. Rock, '"The Dreadful Flood of Documents": The 1958 Public Record Act and Its Aftermath Part 2: After-effects', *Archives* 52.134 (2017), 45–47.
2. V. Harris, 'The Archival Sliver: Power, Memory, and Archives in South Africa', *Archival Science* 2 (2002), 84.
3. T. Cook, review of Richard J. Cox, 'No Innocent Deposits: Forming Archives by Rethinking Appraisal', *The American Archivist* 68.1 (2005), 165.
4. A. Gentleman, *The Windrush Betrayal: Exposing the Hostile Environment* (London: Guardian Faber, 2020), 149.
5. Gentleman, *Windrush Betrayal*, 154.
6. www.whatdotheyknow.com/request/478,977.
7. Available at: https://cdn.nationalarchives.gov.uk/documents/information-management/records-collection-policy.pdf.
8. Records Collection Policy 3.1.3.
9. www.whatdotheyknow.com/request/windrush_landing_cards_retention.
10. Gentleman, *The Windrush Betrayal*, 148–149.
11. 'National Archives Records Back Case for Windrush Migrants', *Financial Times*, 20 April 2018.
12. P. Rock, 'A Brief History of Record Management at The National Archives', *Legal Information Management* 16 (2016), 60.
13. In moving the second reading of the Public Records Act in 1958, Sir Harry Hylton-Foster declared: 'I shudder to think of what it must have looked like to those working in the [Public Record] Office—a dreadful flood of documents descending upon those scholarly and not underburdened civil servants who give such admirable public service'; Rock, '"The Dreadful Flood of Documents"', Part 2, 68.
14. P. Hennessy, 'Life with the Weeders, Who Throw Out Our Unwanted Secrets', *The Times*, 12 July 1975, 12.
15. K. Matthews, 'Crew Lists, Agreements, and Official Logs of the British Empire 1863–1913', *Business History* 16.1 (1974), 78–80.
16. D. Thomas, V. Johnson, and S. Fowler, *The Silence of the Archive* (London: Facet, 2017), 20–21.
17. K. Johnson, 'Gems from the Lord Chamberlain's Coal Cellars? An Informal Account of the Genesis, Progress, and Results of the Buried Treasures Project', *Nineteenth-Century Theatre and Film* 36.2 (2009), 2–5.
18. D. Fiddy, *Missing Believed Wiped: Searching for the Lost Treasures of British Television* (London: British Film Institute, 2001).

19. A. Prescott, 'Administrative Records and the Scribal Achievement of Medieval England', in A. S. G. Edwards and O. da Rold, eds, *English Manuscripts Before 1400*, English Manuscript Studies 17 (London: The British Library 2012), 173–176.

20. C. A. F. Meekings, 'King's Bench Files' in J. H. Baker, ed., *Legal Records and the Historian*, (London: Royal Historical Society, 1978), 97–127; Euan Roger and Andrew Prescott, 'The Archival Iceberg: New Sources for Literary Life-Records', *Chaucer Review* 57.4 (2022), 494–522.

21. Activist Archivists, 'Why Archive?': https://activistarchivists.wordpress.com/2012/10/19/why-archive-2 and Howard Besser, 'Archiving Media from the Occupy Movement: Methods for Archives Trying to Manage Large Amounts of User-Generated Audiovisual Media' (2012): http://besser.tsoa.nyu.edu/howard/Papers/besser-girona-occupy-paper.pdf; G. Carpio, 'Tales from the Rebel Archive: History as Subversive Practice at California's Margins', *Southern California Quarterly* 102 (2020), 57–79.

22. Although it should be noted that the late nineteenth-century enthusiasm for rationalizing the archive led to the creation of 'artificial classes' in the UK National Archives such as the SC and LR series which do not respect the principal of *respect des fonds*.

23. M. Moss and D. Thomas, 'How the File Was Invented', *Administory* 4 (2019), 30.

24. A. Boyd, M. Woollard, J. Macleod, and A. Park, 'The Destruction of the "Windrush" Disembarkation Cards: A Lost Opportunity and the (Re)Emergence of Data Protection Regulation as a Threat to Longitudinal Research', *Wellcome Open Research* 3 (2018), 112; doi:10.12688/wellcomeopenres.14796.1.

CHAPTER 8

ARCHIVAL EDUCATION AND PROFESSIONALISM

ANNA SEXTON

Writing in 2016 from within a South African context on decolonizing the curriculum, Lesley Le Grange seeks to problematize dominant views on what a 'curriculum' is and does, drawing on Madeleine Grumet's 1981 article 'Pedagogy for Patriarchy' to suggest that a curriculum is 'the stories that we tell students about their past, present and future'. This chapter [1] seeks to take Le Grange's problematization as a starting point for considering how, in the context of professional archival and recordkeeping education in the United Kingdom, we have told a particular story around the establishment of theory.[2]

Within this story, the figures of several foundational fathers loom large. Foremost of these is Sir Hilary Jenkinson, who joined the Public Record Office as a civil servant in 1906, and who eventually rose to became Deputy Keeper from 1947 to 1954. Amongst many things, Jenkinson was a central advocate in distinguishing the career of the archivist from that of a librarian, through the establishment of an archival professional qualification route, and when a course in Archive Administration was first introduced in 1947, it was Jenkinson who gave the inaugural address. Despite being first published in 1922, Jenkinson's *A Manual of Archive Administration* is still upheld as a beacon in the story of the development of archival professional practice.

On the postgraduate Archive and Records Management course in the Department of Information Studies, where I now teach, the conceptual framework through which Jenkinson underpins his codification of archive management is often challenged, critiqued, and reimagined from a variety of perspectives from within our programme. Nevertheless, up until now, Jenkinson's mindset has formed the central anchor point, and has been used as a means to lock in and ground our students in their understandings of archival theory's past, present, and future. Jenkinson had a variety of strands within his framing of archive management and these are picked up, and to a greater or less extent, unpicked within our teaching. These include: the impartiality of the record, and the sanctity of the evidence it contains; the organic nature of the accumulation of archival records and the importance of not disrupting the organic relationships between records through archival processes; the importance of the impartiality of the archivist as a 'selfless devotee of truth'; the first duties of the archivist being towards preservation (the physical and moral defence of the record) as opposed to access; the inter-relatedness of archive records and the importance of preserving this inter-relatedness (provenance and respect for original order); and the importance of establishing a chain of custody around archival records to ensure authenticity and enable the record to act as evidence. These have become key conceptual underpinnings which we encourage our students to interrogate, asking them to establish for themselves a position on the currency and relevance of Jenkinson's concepts and values to their own future practice.

Other foundational fathers join the story that we tell. From North America, Theodore Roosevelt Schellenberg, becomes an important counterpoint to Jenkinson. We focus on the publication of *Modern Archives: Principles and Techniques* in 1956, in which he allows for intervention by the archivist in the process of selecting records for permanent preservation. His criticism of Jenkinson as an 'old fossil' is brought to the fore, and his value system for selecting records becomes a significant anchor point in our introductions around archival appraisal. From Europe, the Dutch trio of Muller, Feith, and Fruin are introduced through a focus on what we call their 'Dutch manual' of 1898, particularly in relation to its codification of provenance as a key archival concept, alongside that of original order.

In this way, the 'Holy Trinity' of our teaching around the origins of archival theory is formed. We offer our students these foundational roots, highlighting concepts such as impartiality, authenticity, and provenance as key essential building blocks, before we begin to take them on a journey around how these concepts have evolved, and what other concepts sit alongside them, both historically and in the present. Our intention, in taking this teaching pathway, has been to tell the story of archival theory as the profession in the UK has come to know it, whilst allowing our students to dig into the story and the concepts that underpin it—either to uphold those concepts, or reimagine them for the present day, or entirely reject and dig away from them as they themselves choose. In doing so, we have perhaps been operating in the spirit of Ridener's framing of the contemporary archival paradigm and his statement that:

> The contemporary archival paradigm is one that [informed by critical thinking] is historically orientated and engaged with questioning many, if not all, concepts and values that may have been taken for granted in past archival theories and paradigms, includes questioning core concepts to better understand archival theory as a whole.[3]

Some may suggest that our teaching method is a legitimate and useful one. As educators, we introduce some anchor points that have been important building blocks in professional practice, and we give an indication of our own individual perspectives on these concepts, then step back to offer counterpoints and alternatives, giving students the intellectual freedom to define their own position and stance. However, there is a need to reflect critically on the implications and impacts of the way we teach the archival theory origin story.

Le Grange draws on a broad range of curriculum scholars to draw attention to the difference between curriculum *as* 'planned', so our intentions as archival educators, and the curriculum *as* 'lived' by both educators and students.[4] Placing attention on the experience of our teaching; should make us pause to consider critically our foundational framing, with its emphasis on western, white male forefathers, and the ways in which it might be a relatively comfortable and comforting story for some, and an alienating and unsettling story for others. Le Grange also draws out the difference between the explicit, hidden, and null curriculum:

> The explicit curriculum is what students are provided with such as module frameworks, prescribed readings, assessments guidelines, etc. The hidden curriculum is what students learn about the dominant culture of a university and what values it reproduces. The null curriculum is what universities leave out—what is not taught and learned in a university.[5]

This chapter will seek to set out some of the ways in which our teaching around impartiality, as a key concepts unfolds, including some of the alternative perspectives that we introduce, before returning to the challenges posed by Le Grange around the lived experience of our curriculum and its hidden and null aspects.

A Re-examination of Impartiality and How We Teach It

Turning to an examination of impartiality, I will start by returning to Jenkinson, for whom the impartiality of the archival record was pre-determined by the borders that he placed around his definition of archival records. For Jenkinson, the archival record was a particular type of document, preserved by its creator, who was by necessity an official in an administrative system, as first-hand evidence of a given official transaction. For Jenkinson, such records were written in the interests of serving their official function, as opposed to being written knowingly by their creator in the interest of posterity. Under these conditions, Jenkinson argued that such records are unquestionably impartial carriers of truth:

> They are simply written memorials, authenticated by the fact of their official preservation, of events which actually occurred, and of which they themselves formed a part.[6]

This impartiality of the archival record is linked to the impartiality of the Archivist, who must not interfere in the natural processes of records creation and accumulation and the passing of selected records to the archive for permanent preservation, and who must offer no opinion on the contents of the record, but must instead make:

> [His] Creed ... the Sanctity of Evidence ... his Part ... the Conservation of every Scrap of Evidence attaching to the Documents committed to his charge ... his Aim ... to provide, without prejudice or afterthought, for all who honestly wish to know the Means of Knowledge[7]

Within Jenkinson's notion of impartiality, we find that the neutrality of both record and archivist is seen as both possible and necessary, and that the passivity of the archivist is viewed as an essential building block of an impartial archival process.

In our classes, we offer students some contextual framing to enable them to assess Jenkinson's principles and their ongoing relevance or otherwise. In particular, we link Jenkinson's thinking to positivist philosophy and related ideas around the assertion of facts that stand as objective truths when logically constructed. The central idea within positivist thought that such 'facts' can and do remain value-free is opened up for critique, and students are made aware of how fact-based empiricism has, over the course of the twentieth century, been widely discredited from within the academy.

We also demonstrate how Jenkinson's position on impartiality of both the record and the archivist, and the connected notion of objective truth, has been challenged and overturned by a significant number of prominent thinkers within the archival field. We focus on Howard Zinn, and his 1970 Society of American Archivists speech which was later published in 1977, where he articulates how through their passivity, archivists align and reproduce existing power structures, favouring the history of the rich over the poor, and the powerful over the powerless and how, in the light of this, archivists must both acknowledge and own the politics of their craft:

> The archivist, in subtle ways, tends to perpetuate the political and economic status quo simply by going about his ordinary business. His supposed neutrality is, in other words, a fake. If so, the rebellion of the archivist against his normal role is not, as so many scholars fear, the politicizing of a neutral craft, but the humanizing of an inevitably political craft.[8]

Gerald Ham becomes another focal point in our story, in his echoes of Zinn's sentiments around how the archivist's 'passivity and perceptions produce a biased and distorted record'.[9] We also draw attention to Ham's call for 'active archivists' who are willing proactively to intervene in filling the gaps and silences in the archival record, and willing to move to the archival edge to see the kind of histories that 'you can't see from the centre'.[10] We also draw heavily on the Canadian Terry Cook who in an influential analysis of archival ideas since 1898, traces the Western professional canon to argue that 'all acts of societal remembering' are not value-free or objectively positioned but are 'culturally bound and have momentous implications',[11] highlighting how traditional archival institutions act as agents for legitimizing power, and in turn have a history of marginalizing those without power. Cook's debunking of the myth of impartiality is continued throughout his writing, including a piece written with Joan Schwartz examining the concept of archival power, which states that:

> Archival practice perpetuates the central professional myth of the past century that the archivist is (or should strive to be) an objective, neutral, passive (if not impotent then self-restrained) keeper of truth.[12]

Cook and Schwartz go on to trouble how the refusal to acknowledge the archivist's active role in shaping the archive has had implications not just for archivists but also archive scholars who have not fully recognized 'the heavy layers of intervention and meaning coded into the archives by their creators and by archivists long before any box is opened in the search room'.[13]

From these strands of discourse, we also seek to enable our students to trace how, over the last decade, a variety of contemporary thinkers from divergent perspectives, with many writers pushing against the notion that archival records, archival institutions and archivists can ever claim neutral ground, expanding into new areas of archival theory as a result.

However we also seek to show how, alongside these threads, Jenkinson inspired notions of impartiality which are still perpetuated within our discourse and persist within the professional mindset. One strand of continuing assertion has come to the fore in the wake of what is felt by some to be a new era of disinformation. Archival thinkers such as Luciana Duranti, have recently argued that practices of disinformation are acknowledged to be ancient in their origins whilst suggesting that:

> What has changed in the digital age is the prevalence of a continuous connectivity, that lets falsehoods (be they by mistake or by design) circulate at rates unimaginable only a few decades ago, as well as the pervasiveness of distribution channels, that tend to sidetrack traditional institutions—such as archives, libraries, and museums—in favor of a populism where reputation as a trusted source no longer carries much, if any, weight.[14]

In the wake of fake news, and deepfakes, and the telling of outright lies by public figures, Duranti argues not for a straightforward return to Jenkinson's concepts, but certainly a re-imagining of them, particularly his notion of the 'sanctity of evidence' that he suggests impartiality allows for. The impetus behind this return has been to establish how archivists can act in defence of, not necessarily truth (or at least not truth in a positivist sense), but of the provision of adequate contextual framing around the record to enable judgements to be made on the integrity, accuracy, reliability, and authenticity of the record and its informational content.

Duranti argues forcefully that archivists have a role in enabling society to assess the 'truth value of a particular claim or set of claims' existing with the record.[15] For Duranti, this role could be realized as the profession moves forward, through the adept use of technological tools that can aid in the assessment of the record's 'evidential capacity', and in establishing 'the traceability of data back to their record sources', and in enabling an 'evaluation of the reliability and authenticity of donated materials'.[16]

There is an acknowledgement within Duranti's position that 'truth-value' varies between and across different socio-political environments, and this acknowledgement carries through into her suggestion that it is 'important to develop models for handling different kinds of sources of truth'.[17] Her vision is for archivists to be central players in 'fostering a meta-literacy that would take people beyond digital literacy (i.e. knowing how to search and find information) to understanding how to evaluate and assess sources of evidence'.[18] However, in acknowledging that methods for asserting and assessing truth can vary, Duranti chooses not to foreclose the possibility of establishing global values for the acceptance or rejection of sources of evidence, nor does she engage deeply with the problematics associated with digital tools as non-neutral agents of power, or apply this problematic to archivists and their archival institutions.

The result, therefore, certainly feels like Jenkinson reimagined for the digital age. Although it is acknowledged that different pockets of society may assess truth-claims differently, the relative impartiality of the archival institution is untroubled within the suggestion that archivists can be central agents in establishing which sources of information the public can rely on and trust. Both the potential benefits of this argument (establishing conditions for verifying truth-claims to aid the detection of fraudulence, deception, and lies), and the potential negative consequences of this argument (reinforcing dominant truth-values and delegitimizing sources that align to divergent means of establishing the veracity of an information source) are presented to our students. We also acknowledge that there are degrees of difference within the teaching team in regards to the extent to which we personally align or seek to trouble the Jenkinsonian threads running through these strands of 'post-truth' archival discourse.

Another strand of contention around impartiality is introduced through Ann Gilliland's writing on neutrality, social justice, and the obligations of archival education and educators in the twenty-first century. Gilliland draws out how neutrality (as a synonym for impartiality) has remained as a central underpinning concept within international and national professional codes of ethics for archivists, and how this sits in tension with other statements within these codes which appear to encourage archivists to act on instances of social injustice.[19]

Within our teaching, a particular focus is also given to the 2013 debate within *The American Archivist* instigated by Mark Greene who sought to offer a critique on the idea that social justice should be seen as an archival imperative.[20] We encourage our students to read the article from Randall Jimerson that acted as an invited response in the same issue,[21] and the letter to the editor from Michelle Caswell.[22] We pick up in our teaching on how impartiality, neutrality, and objectivity and their relation to passivity are framed differently by Greene and Jimerson. Highlighting, for example, that Greene claims it is possible to be an 'active archivist' who proactively seeks to diversify collections whilst at the same time remaining politically neutral. Whilst, Jimerson argues that objectivity in the sense of stepping back from your subjectivity has potential relevance to the archivist's role, but neutrality is impossible within an active archival stance. We also use Caswell's comments on how Greene limits his discussion of social justice predominately to the work of a handful of white male archival thinkers to encourage students to think about how the power dynamics of our foundational father figures within the professional canon are replicated and reinforced in ongoing debates within archival studies. In surfacing Greene's article and the ensuing debate, we not only seek to add to their knowledge of different perspectives around key concepts but we also seek to get our students to engage critically with 'how power animates the politics of whose voices get legitimated and whose get silenced'[23] within professional and academic archival discourse.

That question of silencing is one that we should, as educators, turn back on ourselves and our pedagogy, to examine critically our role in amplifying particular voices in the debate around impartiality whilst leaving other voices with less visibility and less of a chance of being heard by our students.

Writing in *The American Archivist* in 2015, Mario Ramirez critically examines Greene's 2013 article as 'emblematic of the pervasive, yet unconscious, privileging of whiteness in the profession'.[24] He demonstrates how Greene's assertion of neutrality is tied into 'prevailing notions of whiteness as the "neutral" ground upon which racial difference and exclusion are determined'.[25]

Ramirez interrogates Greene's distinction between the diversification of archival holdings (seen by Greene as a worthy endeavour) and social justice demands focused on political attempts to change structural inequalities. He highlights how, although Greene recognizes 'archival power' and the importance of establishing an advocacy agenda for the profession, he remains critical of moving the boundaries of engagement too far. Ramirez goes on to suggest that:

> By restricting diversity solely to this gesture [diversifying archival holdings], and shunning its more challenging permutations (i.e., critiques of racism, sexism, homophobia, etc.), Greene inadvertently contributes to policing the boundaries of difference and the corralling of its ramifications for personal and institutional change. In other words, diversity is allowed to thrive only if it refrains from challenging the ability of whiteness to control it. Once it rebels and dares to open the Pandora's box of structural inequalities and problematic power dynamics, it is wholly unwelcome.[26]

I have had cause to reflect personally on the fact that although Ramirez's article appears on our reading list for our main archival theory module, the premise of his arguments that centre on the link between Greene's notion of neutrality and the pervasiveness of white privilege within our profession is a part of the discourse that has not been particularly amplified and centred within our teaching. What causes me to reflect further is that Ramirez links the issue of whiteness as a dominating force within our professional discourse back to the formation of a white Eurocentric professional canon. Drawing on Honma, Ramirez asks:

> If the epistemological tradition ... only allows for the formation of white Eurocentric knowledge to emerge as the legitimate form of knowledge that shapes and informs the discipline then can we really get at the heart of the reproduction of whiteness and the power of white privilege in the discipline?[27]

Writing on 'reclaiming history' in relation to the professional archival canon, Hannah Ishmael juxtaposes the archival thinking and contextual positioning of Sir Hilary Jenkinson with his focus on impartiality and authenticity as key archival concepts, as codified in *A Manual of Archive Administration*, with that of Arthur Schomburg who focused on recovery and transformation as key archival concepts as outlined in *The Negro Digs Up His Past*.[28] In doing so Ishmael argues that 'as a Black man, the significance of Schomburg's work has been obscured through the historic construction of race and power', the political ramifications of which flow through and within 'the focus on neutrality and objectivity' that forms the heart of the professional archival canon.

In highlighting Schomburg as a notable figure, born just eight years before Jenkinson, yet left out in the cold of how the story of the early development of archival theory is told, Ishmael draws concrete attention to divergent archival traditions that remain unseen from within the construction of the professional canon. This points us towards how continuing oppression and marginalization resonates outwards from how we, as archival educators, have reflected and reinforced the origin story of archival theory. Ishmael also highlights the importance of committing to a full and nuanced contextual reading of the figures we choose to centralize, as a precursor to a fuller and more critically engaged understanding of the meaning and ramifications of their writing. Ishmael draws attention to the importance of situating Jenkinson within a broader dialogue of colonialism and Empire because 'thinking about archival development as part of global discourses tied to history and the effects of colonialism helps to highlight and re-centre the development of professional practice as one that has many strands'.[29]

Ishmael's article 'retethers Jenkinson to a specific context and world view—one that is suffused by his position as a civil servant—at the heart of colonial administration' in which 'notions of rationality and objectivity are racialized and constructed within a framework of whiteness (and masculinity) and an assumed natural order'.[30] Furthermore, Ishmael's article bridges an important gap for those of us who have been immersed in the existing professional canon, in situating Schomburg as part of a divergent archival tradition, and by placing his work in the broader context of the pan African movement, Ishmael provides us with the means to dig into divergent traditions, and origin stories around the archive. In following

Ishmael's trajectory we can see how Schomburg's emphasis on 'recovery' and 'transformation' link to contemporary understandings around historical trauma and reparative histories resonating in and around the work of Black British activists and archivists. Drawing on Bergin and Rupprecht, Ishmael surfaces how trauma can act as:

> A contemporary structure of feeling, which functions as a cultural dominant within which the reparative organizes modes of remembrance in relation to inherited experience. It structures cultural memory around guilt, loss and pain by producing divisive and fragmented conditions that work to legitimize, privatize and contain that structure of feeling within a redemptive narrative of 'working through'. Yet reparative history is about more than contemplating injury or apportioning blame. It is about agency, and it can be wedded to a form of memory energized by the emancipatory activism, solidarity and political struggles of the past.[31]

This trajectory from Schomburg's conceptual foundations around recovery and transformation through to the rich and complex understandings around trauma and repair that resonate into and through contemporary Black archival spaces is a trajectory that has not had the visibility that it deserves within professional archival education.

Time to Shift Our Ground?

It would be fair to say that across our postgraduate course in Archives and Records Management we have found ways to link the foundational story as we have told it to a variety of perspectives sitting around archive and recordkeeping theory and practice. There are many moments within the programme when we offer perspectives that disrupt, challenge, and outright reject the Jenkinson mindset, particularly as we explore social justice as an archival and recordkeeping imperative, and in our unpacking of independent, community, activist, DIY, and participatory approaches to recordkeeping and archive practice.

We also frequently use the concept of the archival multiverse, as first developed by the Archival Education and Research Institute, and later picked up on by Gilliland, McKemmish, and Lau,[32] as a frame for our students to consider pluralistic approaches to archives and the multiplicity of perspectives and positions that co-exist within recordkeeping theory and practice. We also explicitly seek to surface and confront the structural and systemic inequalities that are embedded within recordkeeping practice and the profession, particularly as we talk through issues of professional identity, and as we ask the students to analyse recordkeeping infrastructures, systems, and networks.

However, I seek now to return to Le Grange's provocations on the curriculum and the need to trouble the 'truths' we are privileging still, through the origin story that we tell with its focus on Jenkinson and his concept of impartiality as a central bedrock and anchoring point. I want to ask, what is the lived experience of our teaching and how hospitable is it for our whole student body to have a Eurocentric, white, male story prevailing as our backbone? What trajectories and threads of archival thinking and practice remain invisible, delegitimized, and unseen from within our central core?

I would argue, in line with Ramirez and drawing on his thinking, that impartiality (and its synonym neutrality) is a problematic concept for us as archival educators to focus on as an anchor point. Unintentionally or otherwise, centring the concept of 'impartiality' acts as a form of protectionism and reinforcement over its terms. Even as we challenge and disrupt, the continual return to 'impartiality' as a concept to revolve around gives it a particular form of agency; an active quality in the here and now that serves to cement its continuing hold. It has been widely argued that impartiality as a professional value leads to the replication of power imbalances, and the maintenance of systems and structures of privilege and dominance, so I believe we have to consider how we can lessen its foothold as we work with our students to form their professional mindset. Educating, like archiving, is not a neutral process, it is an inevitably political craft, and our choice of anchor points have profound consequences in shaping the mindset and approach of the students that leave our programme. I would argue then, that it is time to consider a shifting of the archival ground around which we centre our students.

Yet of course this is a complicated assertion, which demands careful attention and unpicking. I believe we must attempt to shift the ground and de-centre our previous anchoring points, whilst still acknowledging and introducing our students to the past, as constructed by the Western archival tradition that has shaped the profession. Whilst we must critique and decentre from within our ongoing construction of the professional canon, this is not the same as denial and erasure of the narratives, perspectives, and positions that have made the profession what it is today.

An ongoing return to the origin story therefore retains relevance in enabling a tracing of the intellectual threads that have fed into how the field is structured, and is vital in contextualizing why particular methods and practice prevail still. In an essay first written in 2016, revised as for this volume as Chapter 1, Caswell has also demonstrated how the intellectual contributions of archival studies as a branch within the information science discipline, have been discounted and silenced in humanities discourse around the archive, where 'the archive' is decoupled from concrete instances of collections, archivists, and archiving activities, approached instead from an abstracted, metaphorical starting point which largely ignores archival studies, archival practice, and archival scholarship. Caswell introduces the notion that archival labour has been seen as a feminine service industry that has resulted in archival studies being barely acknowledged, either in a practical or theoretical sense, but particularly as a source of theoretical insight around the archive.

I believe therefore, that as we move forward with our teaching we must unpick, critique, and decentre the origin story as we have told it, whilst still advocating for the vital contribution that our field's theoretical discourse makes to understanding 'the archive'. We must advocate that whilst this discourse may be rooted in the concrete reality of recordkeeping and archiving, as active, complex, and messy tasks, the intellectual discussion around records and archives, that is rooted in this work, is equal in depth and rigour to any humanities-based counterpart. I believe therefore, that the required change in the stance we need to take as archives and records management educators, is to open our eyes to a wider variety of rich and divergent threads existing beyond the Western origin story, that are equally rooted in archiving as an active task, and equally rich in accompanying theoretical discourse. These need to become visible and welcome as central anchoring points within our MA in Archives and Records Management programme.

If we can lean in to knowledges about records and archives that are built from the reality of practice, but that currently sit outside of the traditional origin story, and commit to a process of self-education as we do so, and if we can build mutually beneficial relationships with individuals that can inject perspectives and lived experiences around managing records and archives that is different to our own into our teaching, and if we can also look at the potential to diversify our core teaching staff, then I believe we will be moving towards an enrichment of the student experience within a more hospitable and inclusive approach. Ultimately, we must more fully embrace the concept of the multiverse around the record, *living* it through our teaching to enable different archival knowledges, and their origin stories to co-exist, without privileging the one that sits within the existing teaching staff's immediate comfort zone. We must also balance enabling our students to be anchored in a way that resonates with their sense of self and their cultural background whilst encouraging them to see beyond their own positioning to understand the positioning of others. Adopting Caswell and Cifor's thinking around radical empathy has resonance here, to embed the spirit of empathy towards others as an attitude that flows within our teaching approach.[33]

A dismantling of the ways in which we as archives and records management educators are reinforcing oppression and marginalization through our teaching practice is, of course, also about more than shifting the conceptual underpinnings of our programme. I have focused on unpicking impartiality and its problematics as a way in to thinking about the content that we teach to our students, but if we think about the curriculum as a 'lived experience' as meant by Le Grange, it means also reimagining how we deliver that content, and who the students get to see at the front of the classroom. There is therefore much to do, over the next few years, to shift the ground from which we teach to be a more pluralistic, welcoming, hospitable space for introducing ways of thinking and knowing about records and archives, that are rich, multi-stranded, complex, and diverse yet ultimately rooted in the common ground of being connected to the actual doing.

FURTHER READING

Michelle Caswell and Marika Cifor, 'From Human Rights to Feminist Ethics: Radical Empathy in the Archives', *Archivaria* 81 (2016), 23–43

J. J. Ghaddar and Michelle Caswell, '"To Go Beyond": Towards a Decolonial Archival Praxis', *Archives and Museum Informatics* 19.2 (2019), 71–85

Hannah Ishmael, 'Reclaiming History: Arthur Schomburg', *Archives and Manuscripts* 46 (2019), 269–288

Lesley Le Grange, 'Decolonising the University Curriculum', *South African Journal of Higher Education* 30.2 (2016), 1–12

Mario Ramirez, 'Being Assumed Not to Be: A Critique of Whiteness as an Archival Imperative', *The American Archivist* 78 (2015), 339–346

Elizabeth Shepherd, *Archives and Archivists in 20th Century England* (Abingdon: Routledge, 2016)

NOTES

1. Throughout this chapter I deliberately included lengthy quotations from cited sources as a means of enabling the introduction of different voices into the text on their own terms.
2. My knowledge of professional archives and records management education in the United Kingdom has a localized context as it has been built up from my long-standing association with the MA in Archives and Records Management at UCL. I was a student on the course myself in 2000–2001; then became a sessional lecturer and tutor between 2013 and 2016 whilst conducting doctoral research in the Department; and I have now become a permanent lecturer on the programme, joining at the mid-point of the 2018–2019 academic year. Whilst my experiential knowledge of how professional education in the recordkeeping field is delivered is limited to the teaching on the UCL programme, I would contend that these issues of framing of the foundational story are not UCL's alone but exist across many of the archives and records management postgraduate programmes that are currently accredited by the Archives & Records Association.
3. J. Ridener, *From Polders to Postmodernism: A Concise History of Archival Theory* (Duluth, MN: Litwin Books, 2009), 11.
4. L. Le Grange, 'Decolonising the University Curriculum', *South African Journal of Higher Education* 30.2 (2016), 1–12.
5. L. Le Grange, 'Decolonising the University Curriculum', 7.
6. H. Jenkinson, *A Manual of Archive Administration, New and Revised Version* (London: Percy Lund, Humphries and Co Ltd, 1937), 4.
7. H. Jenkinson, 'British Archives and The War', *The American Archivist* 7.1 (1944), 16.
8. H. Zinn, 'Secrecy, Archives, and the Public Interest', *The Midwestern Archivist* 2.2 (1977), 20.
9. G. Ham, 'The Archival Edge', *The American Archivist* (January 1975), 5.
10. Ham, 'The Archival Edge', 13.
11. T. Cook, 'What Is Past is Prologue: The History of Archival Ideas since 1898 and the Future Paradigm Shift', *Archivaria* 43 (1997), 18.

12. T. Cook and J. Schwartz, 'Archives, Records, and Power: The Making of Modern Memory', *Archival Science* 2.1–2 (2002), 5.
13. Cook and Schwartz, 'Archives, Records and Power', 6.
14. Luciana Duranti, 'Whose Truth? Records and Archives as Evidence in the Era of Post-Truth and Disinformation', in Caroline Brown, ed., *Archival Futures* (London: Facet, 2018), 19–32.
15. Duranti, 'Whose Truth?'.
16. Duranti, 'Whose Truth?'.
17. Duranti, 'Whose Truth?'.
18. Duranti, 'Whose Truth?'.
19. A. J. Gilliland, 'Neturality, Social Justice, and the Obligations of Archival Education and Educators in the Twenty-First Century', *Archival Science* 11.3 (2011), 193–209.
20. M. Greene, 'A Critique of Social Justice as an Archival Imperative: What Is It We're Doing that's All That Important?', *The American Archivist* 76.2 (2013), 302–334.
21. R. Jimerson, 'Archivists and Social Responsibility: A Response to Mark Greene', *The American Archivist* 76.2 (2013), 335–345.
22. M. Caswell, 'Not Just between Us: A Riposte to Mark Greene. Letter to the Editor', *The American Archivist* 76.2 (2013), 605–608.
23. Caswell, 'Not Just between Us', 606.
24. M. Ramirez, 'Being Assumed Not to Be: A Critique of Whiteness as an Archival Imperative', *The American Archivist* 78.2 (2015), 339–346.
25. Ramirez, 'Being Assumed Not to be', 340.
26. Ramirez, 'Being Assumed Not to be', 345.
27. Ramirez, 'Being Assumed Not to be', 343.
28. H. Ishmael, 'Reclaiming History: Arthur Schomburg', *Archives & Manuscripts* 46.3 (2019), 269–288.
29. Ishmael, 'Reclaiming History', 270.
30. Ishmael, 'Reclaiming History', 271.
31. Ishmael, 'Reclaiming History', 279.
32. A. J.Gilliland, S. McKemmish, and A. J. Lau, eds, *Research in the Archival Multiverse* (Clayton: Monash University Press, 2016).
33. M. Caswell and M. Cifor, 'From Human Rights to Feminist Ethics: Radical Empathy in the Archives', *Archivaria* 81 (2016), 23–43.

CHAPTER 9

METADATA

LISA GITELMAN

When leaker-whistleblower Edward Snowden revealed the extent of domestic surveillance by the United States National Security Agency (NSA) in 2013, then Attorney General Eric Holder tried to reassure people that the NSA was only collecting metadata. Spies weren't listening to your phone calls; they were only tracking who called whom, when, and where: metadata. The 'It's-just-metadata' defence suggested that the government was hoping it could deflect concern: a mere technicality; metadata, there's nothing to worry about here. If we can take this episode as an index, then metadata is both a ubiquitous condition of modern life—a fact of our highly mediated existence—and a recondite matter of concern. The NSA wouldn't want metadata, after all, if metadata didn't offer a potential means to discover things—call them 'security issues'—that government analysts imagine that they want to know.[1]

This chapter unpacks a little of the history and a few implications of the metadata concept. Beginning with the computational contexts within which the term *metadata* was initially deployed, it addresses ways that the idea may have achieved its belated power within the so-called archival turn and identifies its continued currency as something of a stalking horse (by other lights a fig leaf) for algorithmic culture. More broadly, if the notion of the archive can point us towards questions of power, truth, and fiction—as this volume both assumes and elaborates—then the concept of metadata stands to call our attention to matters of control. While suggesting the fantasy of a total description or a total ontology of information resources, the metadata concept helps to support a particular epistemic frame—vernacular, trenchant, inescapable—in which finding ostensibly equals knowing and in which data remains defined largely by those with power. Like networks and algorithms, then, we should probably all understand something about metadata, at least in a general way.

The year 1968 is remembered for many things and not for metadata, but that's when the word *metadata* was first coined according to the Oxford English Dictionary. The OED is convincing because its lexicographers cite computer scientist

Philip Bagley defining 'what we might term a "metadata element"'. Metadata, he proposes, is simply 'data "about"' other data. These meta-elements can be used descriptively to specify the domain of possible values for data, for instance, or administratively to limit the conditions of access to data.[2] Wikipedians—as of this writing—have located the first use of *meta data* (two words) a year earlier and in reference to a subject-heading scheme devised by MIT researchers applying computer systems to library resource management.[3] For his part, Bagley had been part of the first generation to conceive of digital systems for information retrieval (he wrote a Masters thesis on the subject at MIT back in 1951), and that was the broad context within which the metadata concept would eventually flourish. The word *database* (or *data base* or *data-base*) apparently hails from 1955 and competed with the term *databank* (or *data bank*) in the 1960s and 70s. The Cold War was on and computers had begun to shed some of their specific military associations and emerge with evident commercial potential as systems for what was already called enterprise management. That is, digital computers were increasingly adopted for the storage and retrieval of information by large-scale institutions: corporations, government agencies, hospitals, and universities.

Today metadata still jibe with Bagley's definition. There are descriptive metadata and administrative metadata. There are also use metadata, like the Who, When, and Where regarding telephone calls that remain of such interest to the NSA, or the many factors Netflix assigns to the data it collects about each of our video streaming habits. Most metadata get pretty technical, like the standards-based specifications baked into digital files that help to make them usable as such. That's an example of metadata embedded in or attached to the resource to which they refer. So a commercial DVD contains permissions metadata that make it playable within only one industry-defined region of the globe, for instance, and electronic texts contain structural metadata—markup and markup schema—that help to determine the way they are displayed onscreen. Metadata can also exist external to the resources they describe, the way library catalogue data and metadata describe an item on the shelf in the collections, for instance, or the way an inventory database describes an item on the shelf in a warehouse. In these last cases the external data and metadata still need to point unambiguously to the resource being described, and those resources need to have unambiguous locations. This sort of addressing is frequently done via some sort of labelling scheme, and today labels are likely to include a barcode, QR code, or RFID tag.

Despite its present utility, uptake of Bagley's coinage was slow. Even as the history of the modern database unfolded in the 1970s—the relational model, the query language—*metadata* was rarely in evidence explicitly as such. Judging at least from a 1975 paper delivered at the first annual International Conference on Very Large Databases, the term still needed definition (if not re-coining) and the concept still needed promotion among colleagues. A team from the Stanford Public Information Retrieval System (SPIRES, a recasting of the Stanford Physics Information

System) emphasized 'the role of metadata: schemae that describe the physical or logical mapping of databases [and] are themselves records in the databank'. Other papers delivered at the conference also touch upon data description, data definition, and schema, but never use the term *metadata*, which remained rare. The Stanford group credited 'the metadata concept' with the adaptability of its campus-wide information system. That's what they had come to talk about.[4] SPIRES was already being used to provide access to library catalogue information and a robust directory of research, while its use for student services (records regarding everything from admissions, registrations, fees, grades, and housing to student demographics) was actively under development. SPIRES had originally been conceived at SLAC, the Stanford Linear Accelerator Center, as a resource management system for particle physics. (SLAC would later be an early adopter of the World Wide Web, which was invented at another research campus for high-energy physics, Europe's CERN, in 1990–1991.)

One textbook on the *Fundamentals of Data Base Systems* still found it necessary in 1977 to explain '*metadata* (that is, data about data)' while rehearsing its importance, and plenty of other textbooks from the same period don't use the word at all.[5] This was the extended moment of metafiction (a minor literary movement christened by William Gass in 1970), of *Metahistory* (Hayden White's important title of 1973), and Donald Knuth's Metafont (a computer language for typography, 1979), but the term *metadata* largely lay fallow, it would seem, as if waiting for the sociotechnical conditions of its broader utility. Those conditions would begin to emerge gradually around 1990 in an extended moment that is identifiable in retrospect as the moment of the World Wide Web. This is not to say that the WWW itself initiated a broader concern for metadata—later HTML 2.0 (1995) did contain at <META> tag—but rather that the conditions which helped to make the WWW both thinkable and then so massively successful helped to underwrite the metadata concept and encourage its eventual (or at least its potential) familiarity. There are two things worth noting here. First, this was a moment of 'worldwide' aspirations (as opposed to campus-wide or nationwide), evident in the conception of WWW and other efforts of the period, like the Unicode Consortium's worldwide encoding strategies.[6] Second, this was a moment for focus not just on data per se but also on documents and thus on markup. The WWW arrived on the heels of SGML, the Standard Generalized Markup Language (ISO standard 8879, published in 1986). The hypertext markup language of the web, HTML, would be defined within SGML.

I have called it the moment of the WWW, but we might also think of it as the dawning age of the world template.[7] Like the history of databases, the history of markup awaits the attentions of future cultural and intellectual historians.[8] Though print production long involved the 'marking up' of copy, early SGML users traced their own history back to efforts in the late 1960s among those involved specifically with the electronic publication and the 'interchange' of digital documents. With so many different computer systems, techniques, and applications in competition with one another and under development, generic coding strategies seemed crucial for interoperability. By the late 1970s an ANSI (American National Standards Institute) group was looking at the problem, and the discussion soon shifted to ISO. The ISO standard 8879 of 1986 'never describes SGML as a meta-language, but' the description certainly seemed apt.[9] SGML offered a powerful 'new dimension' for publishing.[10] Like the extensible markup language that followed (XML), it offered a way to describe the structure of electronic texts apart from their contents and thereby to support portability across different word processing and publication systems as well as their availability to sophisticated data retrieval systems.

In 1990–1991 while Timothy Berners-Lee and colleagues at CERN were using SGML to create descriptors for electronic pages in a worldwide web of information (that is, webpages), specialists elsewhere were working with digital texts, and the general public would soon begin to take notice. In the United States, the executive branch of government had started using an electronic records system for communication back in 1985, and as President Ronald Reagan was leaving office in 1989, journalist turned archivist Scott Armstrong and others sued to prevent the destruction of the electronic records. The government tried to substitute printouts instead of electronic files, and consensus emerged within the archival community that paper or microform copies 'would be acceptable only if all the associated data about the record [were preserved], *including data known only to the system*'.[11] (The case was complicated; a younger attorney Eric Holder would help to argue the government's case on appeal. We can guess that he was learning how to say 'It's just metadata' in an exculpatory tone.) This description begs the word *metadata*, which first appeared in the pages of the journal *The American Archivist* in 1992. The term clearly gained traction throughout the 1990s. In 1995 the National Center for Super Computing Applications (which had just released its Mosaic web browser two years earlier) hosted a workshop with library cataloguing giant OCLC 'to advance the state of art in the development of resource description (or metadata) records' for resources on the WWW.[12] That parenthetical clarification suggests that Bagley's term was still coming into its own, almost thirty years after it had been coined. The workshop was held in Dublin, Ohio, and it would lay the groundwork for a descriptive metadata schema known today as the Dublin Core.

When you first learn a new word you sometimes see and hear it everywhere, an illusion called the Baader-Meinhof phenomenon. So the word *metadata* must have seemed to crop up at every turn in certain circles and after a certain point in the mid- or late-1990s. The increasing frequency and broad utility of its usage were not just an illusion however. Rather, like Cinderella's glass slipper after the ball, the word *metadata* was a shoe that almost miraculously seemed to fit hitherto neglected feet. Metadata itself was not new, clearly, but now it was being named. Unlike a glass slipper, its fit would prove flexible, suitable for a range of different feet. In fact, some of the things that seemed newly nameable as metadata had existed long before the term itself was even coined. Library cataloguing rubrics offer a case in point. Libraries have had cataloguing systems since Antiquity, yet only recently has the term *metadata* become necessary to their description, and no one would think of defining metadata today without using libraries (as I have above) as an exemplary context. International efforts at machine-readable cataloging (MARC for short) for libraries began back in the 1960s and aimed at creating an electronic format consisting of data (author's name, title, etc.) along with '*content designators* (tags, indicators, and subfield codes)' helpful in characterizing data elements, plus an overall '*structure*, or "empty container"'.[13] This description ('content designators' plus 'structure') again begs the word *metadata*. In short, MARC and related efforts helped to introduce one key setting in which the metadata concept has come into its own and flourished.

I am suggesting that after its early coinage(s) and long years of virtual neglect, a confluence of forces and events belatedly helped to garner *metadata* the power that it has today. Whatever their specific character, these forces and events involved the history of databases and of data systems for document retrieval, including the history of online library catalogues and standards relevant to electronic publication and document interchange. Corollary to these developments were the professionalization of related domains of inquiry, cooperation within and among relevant communities of practice, as well as lessons broadly learned by users—all of us— as the WWW became a massively shared electronic resource, an infinity of pages and portal to diverse applications and the data they aggregate, analyse, and allow us to access. Above all and finally thanks to Google, we learned to search. Professional archivists meanwhile, once leery of the standards process and reluctant to embrace library-derived solutions, came to see the benefits of coordinated efforts to catalogue archival collections and promote online access to the finding aids that describe the scope and content of collections.[14] As they watched the 'archival turn' play out culturally—indexed perhaps most of all by the galloping and imprecise use of the term *archive* by non-specialists—professional archivists worked to develop Encoded Archival Description (EAD), a markup standard for archival finding aids.[15] When the journal *Archival Science* started publishing in 2001, its third issue was devoted entirely to the subject of metadata.

It would seem that the concept of metadata arose only after data themselves became digitally incarnate, objects of electronic entry, storage, analysis, and retrieval. Metadata tell us something about digital data then, even though the term *metadata* is sometimes used (metaphorically it may be) in reference to analogue phenomena. This is true at a literal level—metadata describe data within digital systems—and I would argue that it is true at a more abstract level too. Like stopping to ponder the ways that '"raw data" is an oxymoron' or 'how we became our data',[16] pausing to think about metadata stands to tell us something about the ever more data-intensive, algorithmic culture that we have come to inhabit.[17] One thing it could tell us—to put this tendentiously—is that we should consider how or whether the archival turn in the humanities might be an epiphenomenon related to the age of the world template.

Taking a long view, intellectual historian Daniel Rosenberg has explained the ways that data are fundamentally rhetorical and must thus be distinguished from facts, which are by contrast ontological. (Rhetoric is the ancient art of persuasion; ontology is a philosophical inquiry into being, a question of what *is*.) 'Facts are facts', we say. Facts are by definition inherently true. Unlike facts, data can be good, bad, or just okay. Data can be complete or incomplete, relevant or irrelevant for the purposes you intend. 'Data are just data', we might as well say. The point is that data *as such* are neither inherently true nor false but are rather used as givens in making arguments: they are rhetorical, forming the basis for making claims that can prove more or less persuasive.[18] That's why the word *database* contains the *base*, the basis of argument, and why it is so satisfying that the term *databank* never won out, at least not in English. (Check Google's Ngram Viewer, and you'll see that— for whatever reason—it never really stood a chance.) Tables, charts, graphs, and other visualizations amplify this rhetorical quality of data, as data get represented in specific contexts. If data can be good, bad, or just okay, then any representation of that data can in turn be good or not, well designed or junky. This means that bad data can be visualized seductively, in an effort to obfuscate or mislead perhaps, while sometimes really good datasets fall flat purely because of the way they are graphically mobilized.

As 'data "about" other data' (per Bagley) metadata share the rhetorical character of data. Metadata can be better or worse, useful or not. But metadata also help to manage the rhetorical character of data by insinuating an ontological premise. That is, metadata form part of the way we all keep forgetting to notice that data aren't facts.

Metadata mostly work behind the scenes. They aren't for our direct consumption but rather form an infrastructural condition of the ways we use (search, manipulate) data electronically. Think of the technical specifications baked into an image file, the markup tags and strategies that format a text on screen, or the MARC tags that allow you to locate a particular author's publications in a library catalogue. We could find and examine all of these metadata and oodles more if we went looking, but these metadata are not really there for us at all, at least not directly; they are there for the relevant systems, applications, and algorithms that help us deal with (search, manipulate) the data that they describe. And behind the scenes metadata operate in a declarative mode, making statements about data: this image file is x; this segment of text is y; this publication is authored by z. Some statements are readily traceable to human actors, like the cataloguer behind a MARC record, but plenty of statements are not. They are statements made by hardware and software that have been engineered to make statements (generate metadata) in the regular course of being used. Either way, the behind-the-scenes work of making declarative statements like these is based on pre-arranged parameters—more metadata—that have been developed to define the kinds of statements that can be made and the form they take.

Today's information and computer scientists actually refer to some of these pre-arrangements as ontologies, and while I won't go into detail, it is worth noting a few basic ways that metadata work effectively to define what *is*. One relevant device is the controlled vocabulary. You might construct a biometric database, for instance, in which one field, like eye colour, has only a very limited, tightly controlled set of possibilities. Eye colour, you stipulate, can only be brown or blue. Your controlled vocabulary—metadata—defines the universe of data according to these two terms, such that the statement 'this person's eye colour is x' can only have one of two values for x. Some might quibble with your decision, but your metadata formats eye-colour *data* in a precise way.[19] Eyes themselves might actually come in blue-green or grey, in other words, but eye-colour data only has two possible values in your particular universe. Some controlled vocabularies are tiny, like this, while others are gigantic. The US National Library of Medicine, for instance, maintains a controlled vocabulary of medical subjects, of which 'eye colour' is one. Medical subject data are necessarily legion, and eye colour is one accepted value in this domain. Users searching the medical literature may occasionally puzzle over subject designations—'How do I find y?'—but metadata make subject data functional by controlling what those data can be.

Text encoding too has involved techniques of control amid ongoing efforts by communities of practice to create and adapt markup strategies to account both structurally and functionally for a huge range of textual components across different kinds of texts. Archivists worked for years, for instance, to develop a Document Type Definition (DTD) for finding aids, a metadata schema in XML that would define all of the necessary tags and options for encoding this diverse and idiosyncratic genre. This was the process of developing Encoded Archival Description, but it was also in another sense an extended inquiry regarding archival finding aids and what a finding aid fundamentally *is*, an inquiry not without implications perhaps for the question of what an archive itself entails. In literary studies Jerome McGann and his colleagues at the University of Virginia worked for years to develop a DTD for romantic poetry, a metadata schema in SGML and then XML that would define all of the necessary tags and options for encoding literature. This was the process of developing projects like the Rossetti Archive (rossettiarchive.org), but it was also in another sense an extended inquiry regarding what the literary fundamentally *is*. Likewise, groups of scholars working to create metadata standards for electronic texts in the humanities (of which the Text Encoding Initiative or TEI is paramount) have been engaged both implicitly and explicitly in protracted, illuminating wrangles over the question, 'What is text?' and it has certainly proved easier in the long run (although hardly easy at all) to answer this question for texts we understand as informational than it has for texts that are literary or otherwise works of imagination.[20]

To be clear, I am not venturing the useless proposition that metadata are somehow bad. I am pointing instead to the necessary work they do and the analytic project entailed. Data are powerful—available for analysis and thus the basis for claims—because metadata define, delimit, and describe what data are. Some metadata schemes do this well, some poorly. Metadata are an occasion to think critically about the data we preserve and the phenomena to which those data refer. They are an occasion to think critically about what data are actually for and who might have access. While this is true of metadata generally, it is clearest in relation to descriptive metadata within the sphere of cultural heritage—archives, libraries, and museums—and so I conclude with two very brief examples from that domain.

First, in 2005 book artist and scholar Johanna Drucker addressed her fellow book artists, proposing that they develop 'what librarians refer to as "meta-data"— the information about the information in a record'.[21] Her aim was a DTD for artists' books, and her rationale was both practical and provocative. The book is an underappreciated artistic medium, she observed, and the book arts lack an established canon or a critical, descriptive vocabulary that might support the work of collectors, museum registrars, library cataloguers, curators, scholars, and the art world generally. Having a DTD would offer a measure of control, while *creating* a DTD would involve a productive, collaborative process of critical self-reflection in which book artists could articulate for themselves the shared parameters of their art form. Drucker's proposal sparked outrage. That the project had clear evaluative implications—it would require/allow the description of especially successful and therefore valuable artists' books—did not help, but mostly there was sustained hostility to the idea that a template, any template, could capture the past, present, and future diversity of book art. For Drucker, who of course understands artistic practice, this was missing the point. Not a perfect analogy, but consider if literary authors refused to have their books cataloged because leery of catalogue templates.

Second, Local Contexts (localcontexts.org) is a project initiated by Jane Anderson and Kim Christen 'to support Native, First Nations, Aboriginal, Metis, Inuit and Indigenous communities in the management of their intellectual property and cultural heritage specifically within the digital environment'. Working with indigenous communities, Local Contexts has designed a group of Traditional Knowledge Labels or TK Labels, which allow community members to participate in the identification and interpretation of cultural materials that form part of catalogued cultural heritage collections around the world. Used typically in collaborations between cultural heritage institutions and indigenous communities—for instance, the US Library of Congress and the Passamaquoddy people in the area now called Maine— the TK Labels can help educate non-community members about the significance of traditional materials by supplementing and annotating existing metadata, which might otherwise frame traditional knowledge based entirely on Western assumptions of authorship, ownership, and provenance. The labels can clarify custodial relationships, for instance, or identify any number of community-specific functions and restrictions that pertain to objects collected and described. Indigenous communities in this way become agents of collections management, and their perspectives help identify what relevant cultural materials in fact are, even apart from the discussions about the repatriation of materials or their digital surrogates that identification enables.

A tempest among book artists and a strategy toward decolonizing archival and museum collections are hardly comparable, yet both examples help to index the role that metadata can play as community-based standards. The alternatives to a community orientation are many and can be less appealing. What I have here called the belatedness of metadata is another way to mark the extended processes by which the human and nonhuman have been remade over the last half-century or so in the contexts of digital systems. In the broadest possible terms, rhetoric and ontology have become as confused and entangled as knowledge and information. If today's algorithms are black boxes—industry secrets, technically sophisticated and forever changing ('optimizing')—then metadata might be seen as unnoticed occasions or missed opportunities. Thinking about metadata means thinking about templates and the conditions of their present and necessary ubiquity. The description of data isn't just about description or about data, after all; it's about sovereignty, dignity, privacy, equity, and the many human virtues we ignore at our peril.

FURTHER READING

Ruth Ahnert and Sebastian E. Ahnert, 'Metadata, Surveillance and the Tudor State', *History Workshop Journal* 87 (2019), 27–51

Richard Gartner, *Metadata: Shaping Knowledge from Antiquity to the Semantic Web* (Cham: Springer, 2016)

Lisa Gitelman, ed., ' *Raw Data' Is an Oxymoron* (Cambridge, MA: MIT Press, 2013)

Safiya Umoja Noble, *Algorithms of Oppression: How Search Engines Reinforce Racism* (New York: New York University Press, 2018)

Jeffrey Pomerantz, *Metadata* (Cambridge, MA: MIT Press, 2018)

NOTES

1. For a recent example attuned to past and present see R. Ahnert and S. E. Ahnert, 'Metadata, Surveillance and the Tudor State', *History Workshop Journal* 87 (2019), 27–51; doi:10.1093/hwj/dby033.

2. OED; see also 'Philip R. Bagley (1927-2011)' http://stevenbagley.net/blog/philip-r-bagley.html, 29 May 2017. The report was published by the University City Science Center and sponsored by the Air Force Office of Scientific Research; see https://apps.dtic.mil/sti/pdfs/AD0680815.pdf. The description of a 'metadata element' is on p. 26. An earlier paper by Bagley on 'Principles and Problems of a Universal Computer-Oriented Language' flirted with 'metalinguistic descriptions'; *Computer Journal* 4.4

(1962), 305–312. See C. P. Bourne and T. B. Hahn, *A History of Online Information Services, 1963–1976* (Cambridge, MA: MIT Press, 2003), 2. Bagley's MA thesis was about searching magnetic tape.

3. S. D. McIntosh and D. M. Griffel, 'ADMINS: for computer based library management' (Cambridge, MA: MIT, Centre for International Studies, 1967); http://hdl.handle.net/1721.1/85122. ADMINS was a system being devised with NSF support to handle large social science data sets compiled from multiple sources.

4. J. R. Schroeder, et al., 'Stanford's Generalized Database System', *ACM VLDB '75: Proceedings of the 1st International Conference on Very Large Data Bases September 1975*, 120–143; doi:10.1145/1282480.1282488.

5. S. M. Deen, 'Features and Requirements', in *Fundamentals of Data Base Systems*, Macmillan Computer Science Series (London: Palgrave, 1977), 61–88 (78); doi:10.1007/978-1-349-15843-0_4.

6. Unicode Consortium, *The Unicode Standard: Worldwide Character Encoding, Version 1.0* (Reading, MA: Addison-Wesley, 1990).

7. My echo of Martin Heidegger's 'age of the world picture' is intentional; see R. Chow, *The Age of the World Target: Self-Referentiality in War, Theory, and Comparative Work* (Durham, NC: Duke University Press, 2006), 12.

8. Here's one good account: A. H. Renear, 'Text Encoding', in S. Schreibman, R. Siemens, and J. Unsworth, eds, *A Companion to Digital Humanities* (New York: Wiley, 2004), 218–239; doi:10.1002/9780470999875.ch17.

9. C. F. Goldfarb, *The SGML Handbook*, ed. Y. Rubinski (Oxford: Oxford University Press 1990), p. xi. This is from Rubinski's foreword (pp. ix–xi). Goldfarb's Handbook contains a 'Brief History of the Development of SGML', 567–570. See also E. van Herwijnen, *Practical SGML* (Dordrech, Netherlands: Kluwer, 1990).

10. The phrase is used both by Rubinsky (p. x) and by van Herwijnen (p. ix). The latter was at CERN.

11. D. Bearman, 'The Implications of "Armstrong v. Executive of the President" for the Archival Management of Electronic Records', *The American Archivist* 56.4 (1993), 674–689 (682, emphasis added). See *Armstrong v. EOP Appeal: Brief of Appellees* (1993) published by *Public Citizen*, www.citizen.org/article/brief-appellees-preservation-electronic-mail-and-wp-records-1993 (accessed September 2018; no longer available at this url, but accessible via the Internet Archive Wayback Machine).

12. Quoted in J. Pomerantz, *Metadata* (Cambridge, MA: The MIT Press, 2015), 67.

13. H. D. Avram, *MARC: Its History and Implications* (Washington, DC: Library of Congress, 1975), 7; emphasis original. Avram calls MARC 'an assemblage of formats, publications, procedures, people, standards, codes, programs, systems, equipment, etc., that has evolved over the years stimulating the development of library automation and information networks' (31).

14. See '"NISTF II" and EAD: The Evolution of Archival Description', *The American Archivist* 60.3 (Summer 1997), 284–296. This whole issue is on EAD.

15. On *archive* used by non-specialists see M. Manoff, 'Theories of the Archive from across the Disciplines', *Portal: Libraries and the Academy* 4 (January 2004), 9–25.

16. The phrase is from G. C. Bowker, *Memory Practices in the Sciences* (Cambridge, MA: The MIT Press, 2005), 184; see also L. Gitelman, ed., *'Raw Data' Is an Oxymoron* (Cambridge, MA: The MIT Press, 2013) and C. Koopman, *How We Became Our Data: A Genealogy of the Informational Person* (Chicago: University of Chicago Press, 2019).

17. See for instance F. Pasquale, *The Black Box Society: The Secret Algorithms that Control Money and Information* (Cambridge, MA: Harvard University Press, 2015); articles in the special issue on algorithms, *Science, Technology, & Human Values* 41.1 (2016); and S. U. Noble, *Algorithms of Oppression: How Search Engines Reinforce Racism* (New York: New York University Press, 2018).
18. See D. Rosenberg, 'Data before the Fact', in Gitelman *'Raw Data'*, 15–40.
19. The attention of Koopman, *How We Become Our Data*, 12, to 'formatting' and 'fastening' is instructive here (12).
20. See for example A. Renear, S. DeRose, et al., 'What is Text, Really?', *Journal of Computing in Higher Education* 1.2 (1990); and J. McGann, *Radiant Textuality: Literature after the World Wide Web* (New York: Palgrave, 2001), Chapter 5.
21. (9) *The Bonefolder* 1.2 (2005), 3–15 (9); available at archive.org.

CHAPTER 10

NETWORKS

RUTH AHNERT AND SEBASTIAN E. AHNERT

What have networks to do with the archive? They seem at first glance to be conceptually incompatible. The archive is 'a place in which public records or other important historic documents are kept': as such it is a bounded concept, an enclosed or walled space, containing a finite collection of documents (archive, *n.*1, OED). Networks, by contrast, embody a different metaphorical world. The earliest known use of the word network appears in William Tyndale's 1530 translation of the Pentateuch: 'And he made a brasen gredyren of networke'.[1] In this context the words describe a physical work, a gridiron ('gredyren') or frame of parallel bars or beams, crossed or interlaced in the fashion of a net. The component words—'net' and 'work'—are from common Germanic stock. What the word 'net' and the compound 'network' have in common is that they evoke a regular, systematic, and repeated pattern of threads. As people recognized these patterns in both natural and artificial systems, the word 'network' was used to describe systems of interconnection in general, without necessarily requiring a physical substrate. The word further expanded to describe not simply the pattern, but the system it scaffolded. Thus, networks extended from fabrics, to rivers, to railroads, to friendships. By contrast to the archive, then, the metaphor of the network is not bounded, but connective and fibrous.

The contention of this chapter, however, is that networks in fact provide a powerful lens for accessing information about the contents and makeup of archives, and that the seeming incompatibility is due to an analogue mindset about what the archive or archives are. The concept of the network, as we are most accustomed to encountering it today, is inherently tied up with the digital. Online social networking platforms and the World Wide Web have encouraged us to understand our connected world in terms of networks. Networks are also an area of research in their own right. 'Network science' or 'quantitative network analysis' is an interdisciplinary field of study that emerged in the wake of a series of key publications in the 1990s and early 2000s by scholars such as Albert-László Barabási, Reka Albert, Duncan J. Watts, and Steven Strogatz. These scientists showed that a huge variety of real-world networks—such as, for example, neural networks, transport networks, biological regulatory networks, and social networks—share an underlying order and follow simple laws, which means that they can therefore be analysed using the same mathematical tools and models. These publications build on work from various different disciplines, including sociology, mathematics, and physics, which stretches back several decades. In the last decade these approaches have increasingly gained traction as a way of analysing cultural artefacts and phenomena.

In the field of network analysis there is a particular terminology used to describe the network. Entities are described as nodes (or sometimes vertices), and the connections between them are edges (or sometimes arcs).

This very abstract framework allows us to consider many different systems as networks: the nodes might be members of the music industry and edges represent collaborations between them; the nodes might be websites and the edges hyperlinks between them; the nodes might be species of animals and the edges denote who eats whom in that food ecosystem. But how does this apply to the archive? What are the nodes, and what are the edges?

To answer this, we need to think of the way that documents are catalogued as creating layers of data and metadata. This mode of thought is already familiar to the archivists who have laboriously catalogued holdings, and put in place the intellectual and technical infrastructures to support digitization. Cataloguing is an intellectual process that creates a new stratum of information for users, which in the digital world we would call metadata (a set of data that describes and gives information about other data). The mantra of archivists and librarians has been 'no digitization without metadata'.[2] The making of digital archives creates various

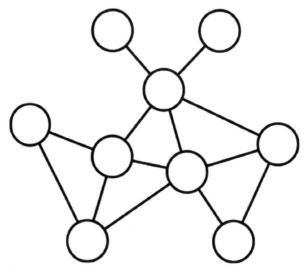

Figure 10.1 Nodes and edges in an undirected network.

additional layers of metadata that stack up one upon the other, as the original material document not only needs to be described, but the digital surrogate too. To give a sense of the scale of the task, The National Archives have created a taxonomy of seven types of metadata including: legacy metadata, primary metadata, secondary metadata, supplementary metadata, derived metadata, control metadata, and 'Meta' metadata.[3] The generation of all these layers of information creates a massive amount of work, but also renders the work accessible and navigable in new ways.

This labour, however, often remains invisible to users who encounter digitized archives through the interfaces that have been for designed for public or academic access. Many interfaces seem to imagine and prescribe a certain kind of use. It is one that assumes—and, in most cases, probably rightly—that users will access the data held therein in much the same way that people use analogue archives: by surfing through the documents as we would leaf through pages (the 'Browse' function), or by calling up specific letters or texts already identified (the 'Search' function). But, as Jo Fox observed at the 2019 Gerald Aylmer Seminar, 'we cannot presume that analogue thinking will suffice'. The analogue thinking offered by existing interfaces allows users only to scratch the surface of what is possible with the wealth of data and metadata that is lying beneath. However, if we break the data free of the interfaces a whole new way of accessing the archives—and therefore a whole new way of thinking—is made possible. Scholars in the humanities are increasingly realizing that computational approaches allow the data underlying digital archives to be analysed at scale. Such approaches have been described variously as 'distant reading', 'macroanalysis', and 'cultural analytics'. Regardless of the name, the concept is the same: rather than trying to read all the material, we can use computational models to aggregate and analyse it. Network analysis provides one way of doing this. Instead of browsing and searching the data, we can instead network the data.

Network analysis is particularly useful for navigating archives of certain kinds. One of the most obvious to conceptualize, and indeed to operationalize, are archives of letters. Letters are particularly amenable to network analysis because they are relational, designed to transfer information from sender to recipient. Their value in understanding historical communication in particular is vital: Gary Schneider has described Renaissance letters as 'sociotexts': as 'crucial material bearers of social connection, instruments by which social ties were initiated, negotiated, and consolidated'.[4] Letters were the method by which people sought patronage, garnered favour, and engineered their social mobility; they were a means of communicating alliance, fidelity, and homage; and they could be used 'as testimonies, as material evidence of social connectedness'. In the past, however, that freighted sense of connectedness that these documents evoke was something that existed in the imagination or had to be pieced together manually: literally drawing connections between these individual documents. This is possible with a handful of documents, or even a couple of hundred. However, when we get to the scale of thousands of letters, the task is beyond the capacity of imagination or the power of pencil and paper. In the digital era, there is an alternative: by leveraging the metadata of these letters, we can (relatively) quickly network that information, turning senders and recipients into nodes, and inferring edges between those nodes where a letter was sent.

The resulting network is one that is both 'directed' and 'weighted'. What we mean by that is that an edge can encode the direction in which a letter was sent. The edge can also be imbued with a weight, expressing the number of times a letter passed between those two people.

From this information we can begin to generate some statistics that describe the distribution of correspondence across all the people in the network. For example for any node, we can tell how much incoming correspondence a given person received ('in-strength'), how many letters they sent ('out-strength'), the number of unique people that write to them ('in-degree'), or the number of people they wrote to ('out-degree'). For each of those statistics we can give information about where that person ranks in the network as a whole: for example, they have the eighth highest in-degree and are therefore in the top 1 per cent for that measure. This concise set of statistics can provide a basic connectivity profile of every correspondent in the network.

But what does this process—getting from a collection of documents to a measurable network—look like in practice? Our book *Tudor Networks of Power* provides an extended example, focussing on letters held in the State Papers archive. The State Papers constitute the working papers of the monarch's principal secretary (equivalent to the modern Secretary of State), comprising heterogeneous materials which

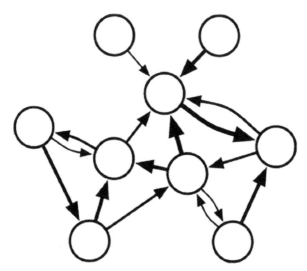

Figure 10.2 Nodes and edges in a directed network.

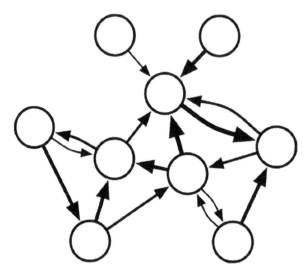

include letters, papers, reports, memoranda, treatises, grants, commissions, state trials, treaties, and ambassadors' reports. Upon entering the hands of the monarch's principal secretary, these documents were regarded as his personal papers, meaning that they were often subsequently incorporated into that individual's own private archives. For this reason the state papers were scattered across numerous locations and collections, and others were lost. Whilst much of the surviving material was subsequently requisitioned by the State Papers Office, and later incorporated into the Public Record Office (now part of The National Archives), many of the State Papers still reside elsewhere, most notably within the Lansdowne, Harleian, and Cottonian collections of the British Library and those at Hatfield House. State Papers Online (SPO), an online repository launched by the company Gale Cengage in 2008, reunites many of these documents in a virtual environment, linking high-quality digital surrogates of the manuscripts to their fully text-searchable Calendars (a series of chronologically arranged catalogues, begun in 1825), which provide detailed summaries of the documents' contents. Most important, SPO provides metadata for each document, which in the case of the letters contains valuable relational information, including: name of sender, name of recipient, date of composition (where given), place of writing (where given), unique document identifiers, and a content description. This metadata is our starting point for constructing a network. Our work therefore stands on the shoulders of work by archivists over several generations, who organized and catalogued these documents, creating information structures which formed the basis of the metadata fields created by SPO.

To turn the data from SPO into a letter network, however, we needed to get below the interface. Gale Cengage kindly sent us the underlying data as XML files, on two hard drives. (This kind of access to pay-walled repositories like SPO has been facilitated in the United Kingdom by the 'text and data mining copyright exception', which enables researchers to make copies of copyright material for computational analysis as long as they have a personal or institutional subscription.) From these XML files, we separated the letters from other kinds of document by extracting all records that had an entry in both the 'author' and 'recipient' fields. While these metadata fields made the correspondence relationships contained in SPO readily available, their contents only became useful for computational analysis after an extensive data-cleaning process. In particular, the author and recipient fields needed thorough disambiguation and de-duplication, for a number of reasons: variant spellings of early modern names; letters addressed to a titular office rather than a named individual (e.g. the Archbishop of Canterbury); changing office-holders; changing titles over a person's lifetime as they accrued honours and offices; and women's names changing due to marriage. Furthermore Tudor families were often unimaginative in their naming practices. Just a handful of men's and women's names dominated, with some recurring over several generations of one family. Simply put: single people could be referred to by multiple different names; and single names or titles could refer to multiple people. The complexity of the sender and recipient metadata fields meant that although we initially extracted 37,101 unique name entities, there were in fact only 20,560 unique correspondents. This cleaning process took eighteen months to complete (nine months of them full-time).

Once an authoritative list of persons has been established, it is then comparatively easy to render that list of persons and their communications as a network. There are a plethora of tools and methods available, that range from out-of-the-box software for visualization and analysis, such as Palladio, Cytoscape, Gephi, NodeGoat, NodeXL, and Linkurious, to libraries of code for studying networks and graphs, such as the NetworkX library available for researchers versed in the coding language Python (each with dedicated tutorials that can easily be discovered via resources such as *The Programming Historian*, programminghistorian.org). The former provide a relatively easy entry point, although only Palladio was designed specifically with humanities researchers in mind, whereas the other software has a steeper learning curve. With the exception of Palladio, which focuses on visualization, these tools combine visualization capabilities with some quantitative measures. By comparison, NetworkX (which we used on our project) requires more advanced programming skills but also allows the analysis to be customized to a much greater extent, and can deal in quantities of data that render visualization difficult or obscure.

So what is the point of leveraging network analysis? What can it tell us about the archive that we did not already know? Beginning with the low-hanging fruit: we can count for the first time the attributes of the communication network archived in the State Papers. We now know that there are 20,560 nodes (the correspondents) and 36,687 edges (epistolary relationships marked by one or more letters). We know that the person in Henry VIII's reign with the highest 'degree' (calculated as the total of the in-degree and out-degree, outlined above) is Thomas Cromwell, the principal secretary to Henry VIII, Lord Privy Seal and Chancellor of the Exchequer, with a degree of 2,149. It is a rough way of understanding the number of people with whom Cromwell corresponded. By comparison, 3,937 people corresponding in Henry's reign have only one in-going or out-going connection. That is 68 per cent of the total correspondents dating from that reign. And that proportion remains remarkably constant over the Tudor period: in Edward VI's reign 68.8 per cent of people correspond with only one person, in Mary's that is 67.4 per cent, and in Elizabeth's 66 per cent.

These statistical insights are the beginning of a new way of viewing and accessing the archive. For example, we can look at the above statistics to conceptualize the State Papers in two separate ways. The first, and the more standard way of considering this archive, as a record of the government's purview, is supported by the statistical dominance of figures like Cromwell. As the Principal Secretary to Henry, Cromwell was one of the very figures who created this archive through his personal and professional recordkeeping, and allows us to reconstruct his administrative reach, and the extent of the information he marshalled through these administrative structures. But looking at the statistics another way, we can see the extent to which Cromwell is an outlier. Rather, the truly dominant category of correspondents, are those who only have one connection. These one-time correspondents comprise many different kinds of people, from minor administrators to petitioners writing to the Principal Secretary, seeking favour or aid of some kind. The latter are implicated in this network merely because they want something from the government. They are structurally peripheral to the network: we might think of these 13,729 correspondents (across the whole Tudor period), as forming a giant fringe around the edge of the network. Network analysis provides a way of asking the data to show us all the people who constitute this giant fringe by returning a list of all these one-time correspondents. This allows us to harness the archive to tell different kinds of stories, about ordinary people in the sixteenth century and the things that concerned them: their legal standing, their property, income, or freedom. In fact, their pleading letters may be the only evidence that they ever lived, apart perhaps from entries of their births, marriages, and deaths in a parish register. It also helps to remind us that histories most often reconstructed through the study of the State Papers represent less than 10 per cent of all the people implicated in this archive. Network analysis can therefore have a powerful democratizing influence, allowing us to uncover the histories of people at the peripheries of the government's purview, and thereby inverting the usual ways in which the archive is used.

This starts to show how the network provides another kind of lens through which we can view the data, an alternative to the search or browse. But network analysis could also be regarded as a search function that is applied to a different dimension of the data: rather than looking for a known person, or predefined word, we are instead looking for a defined network attribute or set of attributes. The degree statistic discussed above is the most basic of these. There are also more complex algorithms that help us uncover more subtle things about connectivity in the archive. One algorithm we have harnessed to good effect in a number of studies is the measure of 'betweenness centrality'. For any two nodes in a network (in the case of an epistolary networks, people), there is a shortest path between them, and betweenness tells us how many of these shortest paths go through a given node. In other words, it shows us how central a particular node is to the network's organization, and how important it is in connecting other nodes. It is a therefore a useful indicator of the infrastructural significance of a given node for the movement of information. We can see in the following diagram that the only way for information to pass from node A to node B is via node C. For this reason, node C would have the highest betweenness score.

So what can this help us see? In the State Papers archive betweenness highlights diplomats because they create bridges in the network, uniting otherwise separate communities, and spanning geographical divides (what Roland Burt has described as 'structural holes' in a network).[5] The reasons for that are obvious: the very nature

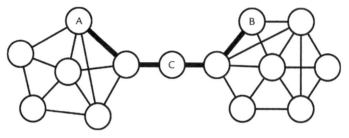

Figure 10.3 An illustration of betweenness centrality.

of the diplomatic commission is to maintain channels of two-way communication between foreign states and sovereign entities, overcoming structural holes—not only geographic distance, but also lacunae in information. Diplomats, then, are bridges. But what is the point of identifying diplomats using fancy algorithms when there are useful resources like Gary M. Bell's *A Handlist of British Diplomatic Representatives: 1509–1688*? Its use is not so much the identification per se; rather its utility is in showing us how particular societal or governmental roles link to certain epistolary behaviours (or profiles). And this prevents us from categorizing people simply in terms of their job titles, but instead allows us to think of the kinds of people that might share epistolary profiles. For example, in the Henrician period there were fewer career diplomats, and church leaders were often sent on embassies. Their diplomacy rather than their official title is what we can discover by using this measure. And the similarity of their epistolary behaviours to other correspondents can help to illustrate how different Principal Secretaries gathered and marshalled intelligence over the Tudor period, supplementing the reports offered by official ambassadors with information from a whole tranche of ad hoc 'intelligencers', from soldiers, to merchants, and travelling scholars.

We can also enact more advanced structural searches by layering up different algorithms. For example, if we look for individuals with a combination of high betweenness and relatively low degree in the final three decades of the sixteenth century, we get a set of results that include a high proportion of Catholic conspirators, double agents, and spies. The reasons for this are partially to do with the behaviours of these individuals: they are creating bridges between communities that are not only separate but actively opposed, and are therefore the only point of contact between them. The other reason derives from the making of the archive. The reason the correspondence of these individuals exists in this archive at all is because of the seizure of their letters, either by the covert and targeted interception of particular letters, or the wholesale requisitioning of personal archives. What this example shows is that network analysis of an archive cannot recapture the social networks that produced it, but only the collection rationales, and the vicissitudes of time, that determined its final shape.

All archives have rationales and biases of collection, and so network analysis must first use measures to identify those, before examining the underlying data in more interesting ways. For example, our earlier work on an underground community of Protestants writing in the Catholic reign of Mary uses an archive that was collected to celebrate the lives and martyrdoms of the so-called Marian martyrs: a number of prominent Protestant leaders who were executed during Mary's reign for their religious dissidence. Many of these men wrote to their co-religionists from prison, as well as penning theological tracts, which were collected and subsequently entered Emmanuel College Library and the British Library. Almost all measurements we applied to this network showed the martyrs (whose lives were documented in Foxe's *Book of Martyrs*) to be central to its organization. That is because their celebration is the rationale behind the archive. However, by looking at the people mentioned within the letters in addition to the senders and recipients we can begin to recover the makeup of the wider community. By then analysing this enriched network we discovered that individuals with low degree, high betweenness, and high eigenvector centrality (a prestige measure closely related to Google's PageRank algorithm), a category of people emerge as significant to the network's infrastructure. These are a group of women who financially supported the martyrs, and letter couriers. A structural bias in an archive's formation therefore need not act as an impediment to retrieving figures whose lives and letters might have previously been overlooked, we just need to think carefully about the best ways to reveal them algorithmically.

But there is a kind of letter archive that is much less suited, in its standard form at least, to network analysis. These are the 'archives' that are built around a single historical figure. They may have originally begun as the private papers of that individual. Or it may be a virtual archive in the sense that that individual's epistolary oeuvre is in fact scattered across multiple archives and only reunited through an editorial act, through the production of an edited collection or online edition of letters. The task of reuniting these scattered letters can become the life work of a given scholar (or, in some cases, whole communities of scholars). We might describe this kind of network as an ego network, in that it is focused around one central node. But it is not a true ego network by the definition used in social network analysis. In that context, an ego-network is one that consists of a focal node ('ego') and the nodes to whom the ego is directly connected (these are called 'alters'), plus the ties or edges among the alters. Of course, the networks we have in edited collections of correspondence contain much less data because we lack those connections or edges between the alters. Without those edges between alters there are very few quantitative measures that can be derived. All we can count are: the degree of the ego (i.e. how many unique correspondents s/he has), because the degree of all other nodes would be one; the ego's in- and out-degree (the total number of people s/he writes to, or receives letters from); and the strength or weight of the edges the ego shares with their alters (i.e. how many letters passed along those edges in each direction).

Other algorithms return banal results: if we calculated the betweenness of the nodes in such a network, everyone except the ego would have a betweenness score of zero.

The limits of network analysis for these kinds of archives present us with a challenge to find another way of networking them. What does that mean? A less ambitious answer would be to pull metadata from other archives to fill in the edges between alters in a given ego network. The more ambitious answer would be to attempt to connect up all the metadata that has been created by archives and editorial projects to create one giant communication network, or meta-archive. This is the idea behind the Semantic Web project. The Semantic Web is an extension of the World Wide Web through standards proposed by the World Wide Web Consortium (W3C) to promote common data formats and exchange protocols on the web. The aim is to allow data to be shared and reused across application, enterprise, and community boundaries. Underpinning the vision of the Semantic Web are the principles of 'linked data' (a term coined by Tim Berners-Lee), the first principle being to use Unique Resource Identifiers (URIs): a string of characters that unambiguously identifies a particular resource. In the context of letters in archives we might think of a letter author or recipient as an entity that requires a URI so that it is referred to by the same unique string in each separate archive's database. The result is that separate archives become hyperlinked by the authors and recipients they have in common.

Such a vision reverses the process of fragmentation of epistolary networks across the manifold archival holdings in which the constituent letters came to rest. However, its feasibility is subject to the same challenges that have been identified in the project of the Semantic Web, specifically, the difficulties in setting it up and a lack of general-purpose usefulness that prevents the required effort from being invested. However, there are reasons to be hopeful. For one, archivists and librarians were thinking about solutions to the problem of data silos long before the World Wide Web existed. Since the early 1960s, libraries have agreed upon the MARC standard for the arrangement of their data which can be used to exchange, use, and interpret bibliographic and authority information between libraries, thus enhancing interoperability between them. The established nature of these systems means that libraries and archives are well placed to engage with and further the principles of the linked data movement. Work is being done to identify the specific MARC fields that are capable of hosting linked data information.[6] Perhaps more importantly, we do not have to wait for the whole system to be worked out before we can begin the networking process. By beginning work on a circumscribed set of data, we can begin to understand the complexities and to develop solutions. This was the principle behind another of our projects Networking Archives (a collaboration with the Cultures of Knowledge project in Oxford), which built on Early Modern Letters Online (EMLO) as a prototype of the meta-archive, linking multiple archives and collections. The project successfully united EMLO's union catalogue, which brought together letter metadata from almost 150 catalogues, with the epistolary data extracted from the State Papers in our previous project, Tudor Networks of Power. To this was added a third dataset: the records of letters in the Stuart State Papers. Together this created a consolidated meta-archive of c.450,000 letter records and provided the materials for an analysis of how 'intelligence' was gathered and transmitted in the early modern period, in the service both of consolidating of state authority and open intellectual exchange within the international 'republic of letters'.

The benefit of using EMLO as the site for this effort is that the resource has many of the kinds of ego network described above. Already, thanks to the efforts of the EMLO team who have carefully built this resource catalogue by catalogue over the last decade, the alters in those various ego networks have begun to accrue edges between them, making paths between epistolary worlds. By then layering this data with a different kind of archive like the State Papers, we were able to map a very different kind of network, we can begin to gain a fuller understanding of how different communities interacted and how information moved. While we are confident that bringing together this combination of archives and catalogues will continue to yield considerable new insights, this is only the beginning. By creating a critical mass of metadata for almost half a million letters in one meta-archive, we hope to create such a centre of gravity that it necessarily pulls in others' efforts. We want to create a resource of such a scale and value that it makes sense for other scholars working on analogue or digital editions to ensure that their metadata fields are also recorded in EMLO, both in order to expand their network datasets, and to drive traffic from EMLO to the original 'homes' of that metadata. While editorial projects, online editions, and institution-specific digitization projects are the way that additional data and metadata on letters and other archival holdings will become available to users for analysis, we would like EMLO to become a model for how we can create meta-archives—not just for letters but all manner of archival holdings—that function as data brokers between various libraries, museums, archives, other open access digitization projects, and commercial data providers. We hope to demonstrate the importance of such provision by driving up access to the constituent documents, and showing how they allow us to craft broader and more ambitious research questions.

While the project is relatively tractable compared to the implementation of a fully functional Semantic Web, the process of networking these resources into a single meta-archive presents considerable challenges. The most notable is tied up with the process of disambiguation and de-duplication already mentioned above. Establishing whether a given name label refers to the same historical person as another name label is one thing in a single archive, but determining those across multiple archives is an even greater challenge. It is easier to be confident when dealing with figures of historical significance, such as, for example, William Cecil, Lord Burghley. Once it has been ascertained two or more labels or URIs refer to the same historical figure, once simply needs to enable reconciliation by adding a link to the URI used for that individual in the other archives and projects. However, you can make this process easier by adding linked data even before you think about marshalling multiple archives. For this reason the data cleaning tool we developed (which is a work space for assisted manual data cleaning) contains a field for entering links to biographical URIs, so that we can easily retrace our identification process, and also enable automatic reconciliation with projects using those same standard URIs. In this case, we use Wikidata, Oxford Dictionary of National Biography, and VIAF. Once these links are in place they provide a very basic way of future-proofing one's research. By entering linked data into a dataset or database it can subsequently be connected to other resources, and used for purposes that the original researcher might not have imagined.

Where linked data does not exist (which applies to approximately 80 per cent of individuals in the Tudor State Papers correspondence) there are further challenges to discovering whether, for example, two people with the same names and approximate floriate dates appearing in different archives might in fact be the same person. Tools that generate suggestions for likely matches have been developed to address this challenge. EMLO uses 'Recon', a multipurpose tool for semi-automatic matching of records developed by Eetu Mäkelä.[7] However, verifying these suggestions still requires expert users, and therefore a significant amount of labour. The reality is that the full networking of an archive will also require people to join forces when contributing labour and expertise, and that it may also take time, multiple iterations, and careful thought on how to deal with incomplete data.

The use of linked data to connect archival holdings can be generalized to other kinds of documents besides correspondence, as letters are not the only kinds of documents that testify to relationships between historical persons. Recent scholarship on the history of print is beginning to leverage network analysis to understand the significance of the dense networks of people involved in bringing texts to press. A number of scholars have harnessed the data fields found on title pages, which are also often documented in catalogue entries, to understand the relationships between authors, translators, editors, printers, dedicatees, etc.[8] Most work in this area undertaken so far has limited itself to printed books (in itself a mammoth task). However, if we want to expand our ambition, there is no reason why we could not think about establishing edges or connections between document types. For example, if we think about a figure who has generated his own social-network-inspired project (Six Degrees of Francis Bacon), we might begin with the evidence of Francis Bacon's political epistolary activity documented in the State Papers to produce a network of his correspondents, before layering up data about his intellectual network through his literary activity: for example, using the information from the first edition of his famous *Essayes* in 1597, we can add a connections to John Windet and Humfrey Hooper (the former printed the book on behalf of the latter) and his brother Anthony Bacon (to whom he dedicated the book).

However, one of the side-effects of the approaches described in the previous four paragraphs is the erasure of the archive. What we are describing for the EMLO meta-archive is a pieced-together communication network unbounded by archival walls. But by creating those hyperlinks between archival holdings, the history of how those individual letters came to reside in particular collections necessarily recedes from view. Depending on the research question, that might not be a problem. But if our interest is in the archives themselves, how can we factor this into a networked approach? One answer to this is the framework provided by bi-partite or multi-partite networks. Bipartite networks are a particular class of networks, whose nodes are divided into two sets X and Y, and only connections between two nodes in different sets are allowed. A toy example may be a useful way to think about this. For example, if we think of archives as being one kind of node, and the authors and recipients of letters held within those archives as another node type, we could create a bipartite network linking correspondents (node type one) with the archives they are contained within (node type two):

From this network we can then begin to ask questions, such as: which correspondents appear together in such archives? Which correspondents are most popular for inclusion in archives? How closely are archives related to one other in terms of the overlap in their holdings? We can answer these questions more simply by turning the bipartite network into a weighted network of archives or of correspondents by performing what is known as a 'one-mode projection'. This means that the ensuing network contains nodes of only one of either of the two sets. So if we created a one-mode projection of the archives, the resulting network would have the archives as nodes, and those nodes would share edges if they have correspondents in common. The edge between them would carry a weight telling us how many correspondents they have in common. Conversely, we could produce a one-mode connection of correspondents. Instead of creating edges by considering the letters that passed between them, we would create edges between them if they co-occur

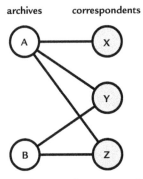

Figure 10.4 Bipartite network of archives and correspondents.

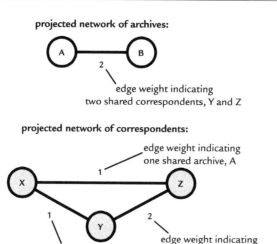

Figure 10.5 Projected networks of archives and correspondents.

in the same archive, and the edge weight would tell us in how many archives they co-occur.

So, in our toy network illustrating this, correspondent X appears in archive A, and correspondents Y and Z appear in both archives A and B, so the bipartite network has connections A-X, A-Y, A-Z, B-Y, and B-Z. As we can see, the projected networks look much simpler. The projected network of archives has a connection A–B with weight 2, since A and B share two correspondents, Y and Z. In the inverse-view of the same bipartite network, the projected network of correspondents has links between X and Y, and X and Z of weight 1 (since they share archive A) and between Y and Z of weight 2 (since they share archives A and B).

This kind of approach can tell us very different things about the history of an archive, or of the process by which a given author's oeuvre might have been dispersed across separate archives. It can help us think about the kinds of cultural narratives and literary histories that have been developed in the past because of the accidents and design of archival co-location. As far as we know, a bipartite network analysis of archives has not yet been undertaken, but we can see how by breaking open the bounded concept of the analogue archive in favour a networked vision we can overcome the current confines of our physical access to available knowledge and at the same time create a map of this new realm.

FURTHER READING

Ruth Ahnert and Sebastian E. Ahnert, 'Protestant Letter Networks in the Reign of Mary I: A Quantitative Approach', *English Literary History* 82.1 (2018), 1–33

Ruth Ahnert and Sebastian E. Ahnert, *Tudor Networks of Power* (Oxford: Oxford University Press, 2023).

Ruth Ahnert, Sebastian E. Ahnert, Nicole Coleman, and Scott Weingart, *The Network Turn* (Cambridge: Cambridge University Press, 2020)

Tom Brughams, Anna Collar, and Fiona Coward, eds, *The Connected Past: Challenges to Network Studies in Archaeology and* History (Oxford: Oxford University Press, 2016)

Shawn Graham, Ian Milligan, and Scott Weingart, *Exploring Big Historical Data: The Historian's Macroscope* (London: Imperial College Press, 2015)

Yann Ryan and Sebastian E. Ahnert, 'The Measure of the Archive: The Robustness of Network Analysis in Early Modern Correspondence', *Journal of Cultural Analytics* 7 (2021), 57–88

Yann Ryan, Sebastian E. Ahnert, and Ruth Ahnert, 'Networking Archives: Quantitative History and the Contingent Archive', *Proceedings of the Workshop on Computational Humanities Research* (CHR 2020), http://ceur-ws.org/Vol-2723/

NOTES

1. W. Tyndale, *Biblia: The Bible* (Cologne?, 1535; STC 2063), f. lxx^v.
2. A. Prochaska, 'Digital Special Collections: The Big Picture', *RBM: A Journal of Rare Books, Manuscripts, and Cultural Heritage* 10.1 (2009), 13–24.
3. M. Hillyard, 'Digital Archiving: the Seven Pillars of Metadata': https://blog.nationalarchives.gov.uk/blog/digital-archiving-seven-pillars-metadata/.
4. G. Schneider, *The Culture of Epistolarity: Vernacular Letters and Letter Writing in Early Modern England, 1500–1700* (Newark: University of Delaware Press, 2005), 27.
5. R. S. Burt, *Structural Holes: The Social Structure of Competition* (Cambridge, MA: Harvard University Press, 1992).
6. I. Papadakis, K. Kyprianos, and M. Stefanidakis, 'Linked Data URIs and Libraries: The Story So Far', *D-Lib Magazine* 21 (2015).
7. E. Hyvoönen, R. Ahnert, S. E. Ahnert, J. Tuominen, E. Maökelaö, M. Lewis, and G. Filarski, 'Reconciling Metadata', in H. Hotson and T. Wallnig, eds, *Reassembling the Republic of Letters in the Digital Age* (Göttingen University Press, 2019), 223–236.
8. See for example, D. M. Brown, A. Soto-Corominas, and J. L. Suárez, 'The Preliminaries Project: Geography, Networks, and Publication in the Spanish Golden Age', *Digital Scholarship in the Humanities* 32 (2017), 709–732; doi:10.1093/llc/fqw036.

CHAPTER 11

AUTHENTICATING AND EVALUATING EVIDENCE

MICHAEL MOSS AND DAVID THOMAS

Users of archives are suspended between the monster Scylla and the whirlpool Charybdis; they have to deal with records which appear valid, but whose information is obscure or inaccurate, if not fake. Like Odysseus, users have to negotiate carefully between the two perils, identifying what is true without being swallowed up in a whirlpool of falsehoods.

We contend that archives operate in two truth spaces: the mundane and the imaginal. Archives can fulfil their mundane administrative functions and meet all possible tests of authenticity but remain full of half truths, distortions, and lies.

There are four categories of false information: the first is where a genuine administrative transaction is being recorded, but where the information contained in the record is false. The second concerns records where the truth or meaning of the informational content cannot be determined. The third is where false information is deliberately introduced into an archive and the final one is plain forgeries.

The Truth Claims of Archives

Ours is far from a conventional view of archives. Despite the blandishment of the post modernists, the leaders of the archival profession and some historians have made quite elaborate claims for the evidential value of archives. We will assess these claims both in the analogue world and the digital and will demonstrate that they are problematic.

Archives only became essential to historians with the development of the German school of history in the nineteenth century and even then access could be problematic. This school, often referred to as the scientific or documentary method, has dominated British, European, and North American historiography ever since. It is frequently associated with Leopold von Ranke and is an approach to history that relies on the systematic examination of all available documentation. Unlike the antiquarians who preceded it, scientific history relied not on chronicles and earlier published works, but on close reading of archives. In 1886, Lord Acton wrote a review article on the German school of historians in the first issue of the *English Historical Review*. It discussed the German 'scientific' approach to history, and described the work of the Frankfurt librarian, Johann Böhmer:

> For the centuries to which he confined himself, from the eighth to the fourteenth, he made it a precept that truth dwells in documents, and not in chronicles or lives. The author of a state paper knows what he is doing; the author of a book does not. In one case history is told by those who make it; in the other, by those who hear of it from other people. The chronicle is a mixture of memory, imagination, and design. The charter is reality itself.[1]

This type of history was made possible by the establishment of national and state archives. In his inaugural lecture at Cambridge in 1895, Lord Acton said:

> We are still at the beginning of the documentary age, which will tend to make history independent of historians, to develop learning at the expense of writing, and to accomplish a revolution in other sciences as well.[2]

Acton himself did not make elaborate truth claims for archives. This was partly because Acton was much less concerned with the outcomes of historical research than with the process. He famously preferred solidity of criticism to the plenitude of erudition.[3] It was also, as he explained in his article in the *English Historical Review*, because the nineteenth century had been plagued with historical forgeries. As Acton pointed out, 'Prince Eugene should be well known to us through his autobiography, the collection of six hundred of his letters, and the "Life" by Kausler. But the letters are forged, the "Life" is founded upon them, so is the autobiography by the Prince de Ligne.'[4] Even the great Ranke was taken in by a forged document concerning the Juliers succession of 1609.

The centrality of the archive to the work of historians was emphasized by Carolyn Steedman:

> the religious and state archives of Europe and North America and their more local records of government and administration were (and still are) evoked in order to describe what it is a historian does and what it is she writes out of that activity, whenever the historical profession is presented to its outsiders or its apprentices.[5]

The US National Archives and Records Administration says in its mission statement:

> Our Mission is to provide public access to Federal Government records in our custody and control. Public access to government records strengthens democracy by allowing Americans to claim their rights of citizenship, hold their government accountable, and understand their history so they can participate more effectively in their government

... We will be known for cutting-edge access to extraordinary volumes of government information and unprecedented engagement to bring greater meaning to the American experience.[6]

The United Kingdom professional body, the Archives and Records Association, says in its code of ethics:

The primary duty of members is to preserve and protect the integrity of documents in records and archives in the public interest, in order to ensure that they continue to provide reliable evidence of past actions.[7]

In more recent years, such views have come under attack from some archivists who have claimed that, by selecting records for preservation, archivists were manufacturing history. In 2007, Terry Cook wrote 'We literally are creating archives. We are deciding what is remembered and what is forgotten, who in society is visible and who remains invisible, who has a voice and who does not.'[8]

More recently, the failure of governments and other creating bodies to preserve material of historical significance and the huge number of records which have been closed on the grounds of privacy or state security has come under renewed attack. These restrictions have a long history. In 1616, Sir Thomas Wilson, the joint keeper of the State Papers, explained to James I how he had been instructed by the Lord Chamberlain that:

I shold lett noe man see any thing in the office of your Majesty's Papers, unless I had first a warrant from Your Majesty himself, which comandement I have strictly observed, unless it were to Mr Secretary, or such others of your Majesty's Privy Counsell.[9]

These restrictions remained in place until the 1850s. In 1775, the Prime Minister Lord North had to seek the permission of George III before he was allowed free access to the State Papers.[10] This restrictive outlook influenced recordkeeping elsewhere. In 1849 J. D. Cunningham, an officer in the political department of the East India Company, was sent back to his regiment for quoting official documents in his history of the Sikhs and Anglo-Sikh relations. As a result of the Cunningham case, the archives of the Raj were closed to researchers.[11]

Despite this, huge efforts have been and continue to be made by archivists to guarantee the validity of their holdings and, in order to achieve this end, everything from the science of diplomatics to blockchain are being called into service. Such ventures are pointless because archival truth is complex, subtle, and requires the exercise of careful analysis if we are to begin to make sense of it.

Some writers have a different slant on archives, seeing them as not just the product of administrative processes, but as also having a literary character. Andrew Prescott said: 'For all their difficulties and deceptions, the stories in medieval archives are a form of historical literature which enable us to explore people and places who are often absent from other medieval texts.'[12] Holger Schott Syme took the literary allusion further when he reminded us that many documents, notably witness statements in court, had the characteristic of play-scripts. These statements were taken by commissioners but were not presented as written evidence. Instead, they were read out—performed—by the court clerk. This performance could take the court a long way from the written document. In 1615, at the trial of Anne Turner, who was accused of murdering the poet Sir Thomas Overbury, the clerk read out a parchment containing magic spells which had been found in the rooms of the physician and astrologer Simon Forman. By doing so, he was performing an act of conjuration. Lord Chief Justice Coke expressed the hope that reading out the document would not conjure the devil, but as it was read, there was a great cracking noise from the staging in the court room and panic ensued.[13]

Archival Fictions

Many records in England are the product of legal fictions which arose because litigants wanted a remedy which did not meet the current forms of actions or where those were expensive. Judges wanted a tentative change in the law without dismantling existing rules or procedures, or wanted to do justice to claimants who, for want of evidence, could not prove certain facts. Some fictions were small scale and made it possible for justice to be done expeditiously. In 1773, in the case of Fabrigas, a native of Minorca who had fallen foul of the governor, Lord Mansfield concluded that Fabrigas would not obtain justice unless his case was heard in London and took the unusual step of deciding that, for the purpose of the action, Minorca was in London.[14]

A rather more serious example is the development from the reign of Elizabeth I onwards, of the action for ejectment.[15] This was concerned with disputes over the ownership of land, in particular where one party believed that another party had unjustly occupied property. Under Henry II a new form of action, novel disseisin had developed to deal with such cases, but this fell out of favour because it was slow, required precise adherence to procedures and favoured the defendant who could endlessly delay actions.

Leaseholders had a much simpler remedy—the action for ejectment. This was a development of the medieval action for trespass *vi et armis* which was a remedy for forcible wrongs done against the king's peace and which had been developed to deal with intrusions on leasehold property. From the late years of Queen Mary I's reign, it was gradually adapted so that it could be used to try the title to freeholds that critically came to have voting rights. The procedure was for the claimant to grant a lease to a second party (the lessor) who would then enter into the land and was possessed of it until another party, the casual ejector, entered with force and arms and ejected him. The casual ejector wrote to the real defendant urging him to appear in court and be substituted as defendant, otherwise the casual ejector would suffer judgement against him and the defendant would be turned out of possession. This procedure allowed the court to try the ownership of the property.

The action for ejectment became increasingly fictional as time went on. During Elizabeth's reign, there was a real lease to a real lessor and the casual ejector too was real. But the need for a real ejection was abandoned. Between 1650 and 1657, the lease became fictionalized. It was no longer necessary to seal a lease, merely to issue a declaration that a lease had been made and about, the same time, it was agreed that the casual ejector could be a fictional person. By the time of the Glorious Revolution, the action of ejectment had reached its full fictional form. There was no lease and no ejection and both the lessor and the casual ejector were fictional characters with names like Thrustout, Goodtitle, and Makepeace and, from 1771, John Doe.

Ejectments are true accounts of an administrative function—litigation to establish the ownership of a piece of property. However they are also untrue since the whole process was fictitious, the lease, the ouster, Thrustout, Goodright, and John Doe and others did not exist. Large numbers of such cases took place in the seventeenth, eighteenth, and early nineteenth centuries. Their records can be found at The National Archives amongst the files of King's Bench and Exchequer, as well as in local archives. John Doe is mentioned in 1,200 reports of ejectment actions in the published law reports.

One of the most common fictions that can be very misleading is to be found in company accounts on the asset side of the balance sheet in the term 'reserves'.[16] Unless reserves are supported by readily realizable securities, they provide little or no help in a crisis. More often than not they comprise shares in related companies or lumpy assets or just goodwill. Fixed assets can also be misleading if they have not been adequately depreciated or under-represent the underlying true value. As is now well known since the 2008 banking crisis, not all debt is represented on the balance sheet. This was especially true of bills of exchange, the principal method of finance until well in to the twentieth century. Indeed during the French wars government bills became a form of currency. For the unwary they can be very confusing and are little understood even though references in archives are ubiquitous.

Bills of exchange or promissory notes have a long history and were a simple way of securitizing debt without incurring a charge on any asset. In the United Kingdom their use was codified in legislation in 1882, which included the definition that all students of banking learned by heart—'an unconditional order in writing addressed by one person to another, signed by the person or company giving it, requiring the person or company to whom it is addressed to pay on demand or at fixed or determinable future time a sum certain in money to, or to the order of, a specified person or company, or to bearer'.[17] In other words it is a binding promise to pay for a good or service at a future date. Bills were usually payable in three to six months, but could be renewed if a trade transaction had not been completed or, as Adam Smith emphasized in relation to the failure of the Ayr Bank in 1772, used fraudulently to fund capital projects.[18]

The political economist Walter Bagehot observed in his essay of 1873 on Lombard Street, the financial heart of the City of London: 'English trade is carried on upon borrowed capital to an extent of which few foreigners have an idea.' He added: 'In every district small traders have arisen, who "discount their bills" largely, and with the capital so borrowed harass and press upon, if they do not eradicate the old capitalists.'[19] He went on to explain how by resorting to bill finance a merchant could make a much better return than by relying solely on their own capital. Bills and other credit instruments depended entirely on trust between the two parties, they could be endorsed by third parties who guaranteed to meet any payment if the acceptor failed to honour the obligation to pay. The novels of Anthony Trollope are full of references to the folly of endorsing fraudulent bills. In *Framley Parsonage*— published in 1861, the Reverend Mark Robarts finds himself liable for £400–£500 through endorsing a bill unwittingly:

> This was terrible to be borne. He had heard much lately which had frightened and scared him, but nothing so terrible as this; nothing which so stunned him, or conveyed to his mind so frightful a reality of misery and ruin.[20]

Such literature as exists tends to focus on such fraudulent use of bills, for example so-called 'pig on bacon' bills where no goods or services changed hands, but the bills were discounted by unsuspecting brokers. When the leather merchants Streatfield, Laurence & Mortimer failed in 1860 with debts of over £3 million as a result of the fraudulent use of bills, it brought down thirty other leather companies.[21]

Records Whose Truth Cannot Be Determined

There are many records whose truth cannot be determined, often because they contain personal statements whose background or validity cannot be assessed. Pleas of insanity in murder cases are a good example. Before the 1957 Homicide Act which introduced a distinction between capital murders (where the death penalty was mandatory) and non-capital murders, the only defence available to defendants who admitted having killed intentionally was insanity. Juries could find a defendant guilty but insane and so not liable to be sentenced to death.[22]

Large numbers of people pleaded insanity before 1957. In the period 1909 to 1949, of 3,130 people committed for trial for murder, 798 were found guilty but insane, while another 477 were found to be insane before the trial and a further 48 were certified insane after conviction and sentencing.[23] It is impossible to know how many of these pleas were accepted by juries not because the convicted murderers were insane, but because they believed that a particular murderer should not hang. Certainly there was some belief that the plea of insanity was used very widely, an editorial in *The Times* of 1920 said that it 'has become common form in the case for the defence'.[24] Some commentators have argued that, anecdotally at least, accomplices and young people were more likely to have pleas of insanity accepted and thus be spared the noose, while the opposite applied to those who killed with guns or poison, who murdered policemen or who were born overseas.

Another example of the difficulty of assessing the truth claims of archives comes from the *Lettres de Cachet* from the Bastille in the eighteenth century. A selection of these was edited by Arlette Farge and Michel Foucault.[25] These letters were a product of the French absolute monarchy. They were the result of an administrative process which allowed poorer families to deal with disputes by making a complaint to the head of the Paris police, the Lieutenant General. Wives could complain about their husbands and husbands about their wives. Parents could complain against their children. The Lieutenant General would investigate and make a report to the king and council. If they approved, the Lieutenant General could order the person concerned to be imprisoned.

The issues which were complained about included drunkenness, debauchery, vagabondage (wandering from town to town), domestic violence, and theft of family property. The mechanism was used if families could not use the justice system because it was too uncertain, costly, or shameful. While the petitions had to conform to rigid rules about process and begin and end with elaborate paragraphs, the details of the petitions themselves are very much written in the authentic voices of the petitioners with their misspelling and abandonment of grammar. The petitioner had to pay the cost of the imprisonment, except in a few cases when parents asked that their children be sent to the French penal colonies known as the Islands—at this time referring to such islands in the French West Indies as Martinique, Guadalope, and Tortuga, places from which few returned.[26] Sometimes the petitioners submitted a second petition asking that their relative be released, or that they remain in prison.

In 1758, Nicolas Chapuis, a wigmaker petitioned that his son Nicolas be imprisoned and sent to the Islands because of his libertinage. The father's motive appears to be that he was concerned that his son would be convicted of some crime and executed. Further evidence was given to show that the son had behaved violently and provoked fights. The son was imprisoned in the cells of the Hopital Bicêtre. However, he then decided to join a regiment and his father petitioned for him to be released in order that he could enlist. He was not tall enough to join the regiment and instead took up with a married woman and behaved scandalously. His father then petitioned that he be reimprisoned until he could be sent to the colonies.[27]

This case (and many others like it) encapsulate the dilemma of the archive user. The records provide us with information about the charges which were brought and the investigations carried out. In some cases there is also evidence from neighbours, priests, and others, and we sometimes learn what was the opinion of the Lieutenant General. However, they do not tell us anything of the realities of the situation or the real lives of the people involved. We are not told very much about the bad behaviour of Chapuis fils (apparently to spare the blushes of his mother). What we do know is that the father was anxious to present himself as having tried to give his son a good upbringing and that he was concerned that his son would bring dishonour on his family. We do not know the inwardness of the relationship between Chapuis père and Chapuis fils. Did the father really understand the implication of sending his son to the Islands—by doing so, he was in effect asking for a death sentence on the young man. The horror of such confinement is amply illustrated by the Dreyfus case.

As Farge and Foucault comment:

> Presented in this manner, private life allowed itself to be seen, visited, rifled through, and yet it never showed its true face with any certainty. It stepped forward in disguise, cloaked in many colours by those who would defend it and those who would blacken it. It will not unmask itself to our overly curious and often distorted prying. At the end of the story we will never know who these people screaming out of torment and asking for love truly were ... What is left is the visible, the words written, the investigations undertaken, the letters sent.[28]

False Information

Our third category is where false information is introduced into archives, either deliberately or accidentally. In 1989 there was a crush at the Hillsborough Football Ground in Sheffield before a match between Liverpool and Nottingham Forest and ninety six people were killed. Following the disaster, the police present at the ground made written reports of the disaster. These reports were typed up and were used in evidence to two public inquiries. However, subsequent investigations revealed that the typed transcripts were not accurate copies of the written notes. The South Yorkshire police and their lawyers had toned down the remarks to remove anything critical of senior officers or which suggested that they had lost control of the situation. Here again we have an example of a record having an administrative truth. These were records of the South Yorkshire police and were presented in evidence to public inquiries. However, they are not valid, since they are not a true reflection of the views of police officers.[29]

Forgeries

Forgeries are another example of where records live mainly in the fictional realm. Forgeries have lived alongside genuine documents as long as records of administrative processes have been created. T. F. Tout, the medieval administrative historian, described how Crowland Abbey's records were burned in a fire in 1091. In 1115, the abbot sent for Orderic Vitalis the chronicler to record what was known of the abbey's history. Orderic recorded the existence of two charters which are now known as forgeries, one by Ethelbald, king of the Mercians, giving lands to Guthlac. The problem was this was sealed with a seal—but documents were not sealed in Ethelbald's time. Worse, Guthlac was dead when the charter was issued.[30]

Forgeries are largely part of the imaginal realm, but like the *Lettres de Cachet*, while they do not contain the truth, they do provide us with some information. As Anthony Grafton noted, the German scholar of Gnosticism, Richard August Reitzenstein was one of the earliest writers to point out that forgeries need subtle analysis rather than sarcastic dismissal.[31] The Crowland forgeries tell us nothing about lay patronage of religious houses in the Anglo Saxon period. They do tell us something about early medieval attitudes to forgery and false information. As Tout pointed out, the punishment of forgers could be quite lenient until as late as the reign of Elizabeth I when the law was tightened up.[32]

The other feature of forgeries is that they mess with time. In the paper world, events and the documents recording them have a fixed place in chronology. Forgeries lack this temporality because many survive for long periods, sometimes after they had been discredited. The longest surviving forgeries may be the false epistles of the Sicilian tyrant Phalaris (~570–554 BCE). These were faked between the second and fourth centuries, criticized in the seventeenth, defended by Sir William Temple in 1690, and finally proved to be false by Richard Bentley in 1699.[33]

Even material which should have been decently buried decades ago achieves a new life on the internet. The Protocols of the Elders of Zion were a wholly invented account of a meeting of Jewish leaders in the 1890s where they discussed plans for Jewish world domination. There was no such meeting and hence there could have been no minutes. They were published in Russia in 1903 and were probably written by a Russian anti-semite, possibly with the support of the head of the Russian secret service in Paris.[34] In 1921, Philip Graves, the correspondent of *The Times* in Constantinople recognized that the Protocols were a crude plagiarism of Maurice Joly's *Dialogue aux enfers entre Machiavel et Montesquieu*, a dialogue of the dead which Joly used as an attack on the ambitions of Napoleon III. Graves then published three articles in *The Times* which should have sunk the Protocols.[35]

But they survived. They were accepted as true by Adolf Hitler and taught in German schools in the Nazi era. Before the internet, the Protocols found new fame in the pseudohistorical work *The Holy Blood and the Holy Grail* in which the authors argued (on the basis of further forged documents in the Bibliothèque Nationale de France) that the text had nothing to do with Judaism or an international Jewish conspiracy but was rather masonic in origin and was a product of the Priory of Zion, a mysterious organization established to secure the revival of the Merovingian dynasty.[36] A Google search for the Protocols of the Elders of Zion will reveal a vast amount of material. The first five returns to our search for 'Protocols Zion' brought up two websites which said they were true, two that they were false, and a link to Amazon.

Proofs of Authenticity

Generations of archivists from Jenkinson onwards have put forward three proofs of the authenticity of archives: provenance, diplomatics, and technology. It is argued that records are valid if they can be shown to have come from a valid official resource (provenance) and if they are written in the proper form for an authentic document of that period, including language, style, and layout (diplomatics). Finally, they must be created using the appropriate technologies of their day: ink, paper, or digital.

These tests are not designed to determine the validity of the information contained in records, merely whether the records themselves are valid. In the case of ejectment, the provenance of the records are entirely valid—they are records of the English courts and their history can be traced with confidence from their creation to their current resting place in The National Archives at Kew and elsewhere. Equally, there is nothing wrong with their diplomatics—they are recorded in legal Latin and later English, on rolls, and are in the same form for hundreds of years. In terms of technology, they are unimpeachable, written in iron gall ink on parchment and enrolled in the same rolls as other legal business. But, of course, this proof of their authenticity does not guarantee the quality of the information they contain; they were fictional actions and the parties mentioned in them—were entirely fictitious.

The *Lettres de Cachet* are quite genuine records, but they do not let us learn the truth about either the motives of the complainants or the behaviour of those complained against.

The Hillsborough police statements are equally valid as records—they were created by the South Yorkshire Police, overseen by their lawyers and transferred to the archives. It was only the fact of there being two copies of the statements, an 'original' and an 'approved' that cast doubts on their truthfulness.

A range of technological tests can be applied to detect the existence of forgeries. Martin Allen, in *Hidden Agenda: How the Duke of Windsor Betrayed the Allies*, suggests that the Duke had betrayed Britain by providing Hitler with details of the French defences, thus facilitating the Nazi invasion of 1940.[37] It was partly based on a letter from the Duke of Windsor to Adolf Hitler which Albert Speer had given to Allen's father. The letter contained veiled references to a tour of the French front line which Windsor had just made and urged Hitler to pay full attention to the information which an intermediary bringing the letter had memorized. It also implied that the Duke would be willing to resume the throne when Britain had made a peace treaty with Germany.

This is sensational stuff. However, the letter was examined by three experts who said it was a forgery. There were discrepancies between the handwriting of the Duke and that of the letter; it contained at least 50 'pen lifts', a sure sign of someone trying to imitate the handwriting of another person and the paper seemed to have been baked to give it the impression of age.[38]

Apart from the application of scientific tests in some limited cases, there are two ways to determine the truthfulness of documents. The first way is to compare the information in the document with external sources and this is where the internet and social media offer huge advantages. Traditionally, historians have used records to evaluate sources such as chronicles. The early years of the reign of Henry VII of England were traditionally only known from chronicle sources but these were partial and provided little information on crucial aspects of Henry's life, partly because Henry did not encourage speculation about his claim to the throne, the disappearances of Edward V and his brother, and the events of his time in France. The increased availability of archival sources over the past 180 years has meant that a revised history of Henry's reign is possible.[39]

In the digital era, however, the increased availability of internet-based resources, including social media (the modern equivalent of chronicles) has turned the world upside down and it is now possible to use this as a way of criticizing and validating archives. Let us take the example of warfare. Traditionally, information about warfare was controlled by governments. Information was recorded in official files and in broadcasts by embedded (and inevitably sympathetic) journalists, but things have changed. William Merrin explained how, in 1996, the US had decided that in future, they would dominate warfare not only on the battlefield, but would also control all information about the progress of the war. However,

> Web 2.0 blew this policy apart. Instead of a future of reduced information and tightly-controlled, on-message broadcasters, the explosion of popular online platforms for 'user-generated content', cheap internet connections and public Wi-Fi, and multimedia phones (and eventually smartphones), combined with a remarkable cultural revolution in the use of digital technologies and the way we lived our life through them with ourselves at the centre of our own 'me-dia' worlds, to create a perfect storm that swept aside government messages, military control and even the centrality and dominance of broadcast-era media themselves. It meant there was now no way to stop the creation and sharing of information from and about the battlefield.[40]

Merrin goes on to say that some of the information produced by citizen journalists and others is unreliable. Nevertheless, it is now possible to triangulate official government accounts against the social media records of the event.

The second approach to determine whether the content of a document is genuine is to apply the scholarly tests which have been developed by classicists and biblical scholars since the sixteenth century and which are as relevant in the digital era as they were when applied to the second century Epistles of Phalaris. One of the great literary forgeries of the eighteenth century was the *De Situ Britanniae*, a description of Roman Britain which had allegedly been written by a medieval monk, Richard of Cirencester who, apparently, had access to lost original sources, as well as some previously unknown itineraries. It was forged by a young Englishman, Charles Bertram who lived in Copenhagen and was published by the antiquarian

William Stukeley in 1757. It was considered genuine by many people until 1869 when the Cambridge classics scholar John B. Mayor investigated the text.[41] His work should probably be compulsory reading for anyone trying to understand how to determine the authenticity of information contained in a document, since he applies virtually every tool available. He had access to another text by Richard of Cirencester, and was able to show that the two were not written in the same style or used the same sources. He attacked the language of the *De Situ*; for example the author used *Murum Hadrianum* for Hadrian's wall when the correct Latin would be *Vallum Hadriani*. He was able to show that the forgery was derived from published sources; for example the forger copied an error from Camden's *Britannia*; Camden used *Thetis* as opposed to the correct form *Tethys*, while the map which accompanied the text was copied from one published in 1618. Above all, he pointed out the anachronisms in Bertram's work. As he explained, eighteenth century Latin texts might be addressed to *candido et benevolo lectori;* medieval ones never were.

To a large extent what we are doing is restating the views of Lord Acton. Acton saw history not as a product with a final conclusion, but a process of criticism and evaluation which requires everything, including the authenticity of documents, to be continually evaluated. This has resonance with archival scholars, such as Eric Ketelaar, who consider all evidence to be in a state of becoming, as circumstances change and new facts emerge.

As we explained earlier, although Acton helped set the course of British history on a scientific, archive-based path, he did not place much weight on authenticity. He saw history as an intellectual discipline which challenged its practitioners to develop critical skills. For him, history was a process, not an outcome. Rooted in the German philosophical tradition as he was, he realized the dangers of determinism in the German historical school. As he said:

> For our purpose, the main thing to learn is not the art of accumulating material, but the sublimer art of investigating it, of discerning truth from falsehood and certainty from doubt. It is by solidity of criticism more than by the plenitude of erudition, that the study of history strengthens, and straightens, and extends the mind.[42]

FURTHER READING

John Emerich Edward Dalberg-Acton, Lord Acton, 'The German Schools of History', *English Historical Review* 1 (1886), 7–42

C. S. L. Davies, 'Information, Disinformation and Political Knowledge under Henry VII and Early Henry VIII', *Historical Research* 85 (2012), 228–253

Arlette Farge and Michel Foucault, *Disorderly Families: Infamous Letters from the Bastille Archives*, ed. Nancy Luxon, trans. Thomas Scott-Railton (Minneapolis: University of Minnesota Press, 2014)

Andrew Prescott, 'Tall Tales from the Archive', in Jennifer Jahner, Emily Steiner, and Elizabeth M. Tyler, eds, *Medieval Historical Writing: Britain and Ireland 500–1500* (Cambridge: Cambridge University Press, 2019), 356–369

Holger Schotte Syme, 'Becoming Speech: Voicing the Text in Early Modern English Courtrooms and Theatres', *Compar(a)ison: An International Journal of Comparative Literature* 1 (2003), 107–124

David Thomas, *Beggars, Cheats and Forgers. A History of Frauds Throughout the Ages* (Barnsley: Pen and Sword Books, 2014)

NOTES

1. Lord Acton, 'German Schools of History', *English Historical Review* 1 (1886), 28–29.
2. Lord Acton, *Lectures on Modern History*, ed. J. N. Figges and R. V. Laurence (London: Macmillan 1907), 7.
3. Acton, *Lectures*, 15.
4. Action, 'German Schools of History', 21.
5. C. Steedman, *Dust* (Manchester: Manchester University Press, 2001), x.
6. National Archives and Records Administration, *Mission, Vision and Values*, www.archives.gov/about/info/mission.
7. Archives and Records Association, Code of Ethics www.archives.org.uk/images/ARA_Documents/ARA_Code_Of_Ethics.pdf.
8. T. Cook, 'Remembering the Future: Appraisal of Records and the Role of Archives in Constructing Social Memory', in F. X. Blouin and W. G. Rosenburg, eds, *Archives, Documentation and Institutions of Social Memory: Essays from the Sawyer Seminar* (Ann Arbor: University of Michigan Press, 2007), 169.
9. The National Archives, SP 14/86, f. 6 (4 Jan. 1616). Gale No. MC4323785179.
10. *30th Annual Report of the Deputy Keeper of Public Records* (London: HMSO, 1869), Appendix, 267, No. 389.
11. S. Bhattacharya, *Archiving the British Raj* (New Delhi: Oxford University Press, 2019), 2.
12. A. Prescott, 'Tall Tales from the Archive', in J. Jahner, E. Steiner, and E. M. Tyler, eds, *Medieval Historical Writing: Britain and Ireland, 500–1500* (Cambridge: Cambridge University Press, 2019), 369.
13. H. S. Syme, 'Becoming Speech: Voicing the Text in Early Modern English Courtrooms and Theatres', *Compar(A)ison* 1 (2003), 115–117.
14. F. Schauer, 'Legal Fictions Revisited', in M. Del Mar and W. Twining, eds, *Legal Fictions in Theory and Practice* (London: Springer, 2015), 122.
15. P. Sparkes, 'Ejectment: Three Births and a Funeral', in Del Mar and Twining, *Legal Fictions*, 275–291.
16. M. Moss, 'The Lost Art of Bill Finance—The Case of William Denny & Brothers of Dumbarton, Shipbuilders', in M. Lescure and M. Moss, eds, *Aspects of Corporate Finance: Inter-firm Lending: Explorations from a Modern European Perspective* (Paris: Institut de la gestion publique et du développement économique, 2019), 105–121, available at: https://books.openedition.org/igpde/6031; S. Nishimura, *The Decline of Inland Bills of Exchange in the London Money Market 1855–1913* (Cambridge: University Press, 1971).

17. Bills of Exchange Act 1882: 45–46 Vict. c. 1.
18. H. Rockoff, 'Parallel Journeys: Adam Smith and Milton Friedman on the Regulation of Banking', in B. Pasanek and S. Polillo, eds, *Beyond Liquidity: The Metaphor of Money in Financial Crisis* ([Abingdon]: Routledge, 2013), 24–52.
19. W. Bagehot, *Lombard Street: A Description of the Money Market* (London: Henry S. King, 1873). 8.
20. A. Trollope, *Framley Parsonage* (London: Smith, Elder, 1861), vol. 2, 47.
21. *The Economist*, 7 July 1860, 15.
22. C. L. Evans, 'At Her Majesty's Pleasure: Criminal Insanity in 19th-Century Britain', *History Compass* 14.10 (Oct 2016), 470–479.
23. *Royal Commission on Capital Punishment 1949–53. Report*, 300–301.
24. *The Times*, 20 April 1920, 15.
25. A. Farge and M. Foucault, *Disorderly Families: Infamous Letters from the Bastille Archives*, ed. N. Luxon, trans. T. Scott-Railton (Minneapolis: University of Minnesota Press, 2016).
26. Farge and Foucault, *Disorderly Families*, 302.
27. Farge and Foucault, *Disorderly Families*, 242–243.
28. Farge and Foucault, *Disorderly Families*, 41–42.
29. It was found that 164 witness statements had been altered. Of these, 116 had material removed which was critical of South Yorkshire Police: S. Tyacke, 'Trusting the Records: The Hillsborough Football Disaster 1989 and the Work of the Independent Panel 2010–12', in M. Moss and D. Thomas, eds, *Do Archives Have Value?* (London: Facet, 2019), 67; Phil Scraton, 'The Legacy of Hillsborough: Liberating Truth, Challenging Power', *Race & Class* 55.2 (2013), 21–22.
30. T. F. Tout, 'Mediaeval Forgers and Forgeries' in *The Collected Papers of Thomas Frederick Tout*, vol. 3 (Manchester: Manchester University Press, 1934), 129–135.
31. A. Grafton, *Forgers and Critics: Creativity and Duplicity in Western Scholarship* (Princeton: Princeton University Press, 1990), 83.
32. Tout, 'Mediaeval Forgers', 121.
33. Grafton, *Forgers and Critics*, 72–74.
34. M. Hagemeister, 'The Protocols of the Elders of Zion: Between History and Fiction', *New German Critique* 103 (Winter 2008), 83–95.
35. *The Times*, 16, 17, and 18 August 1921. Graves's articles were reprinted as *The Truth about the Protocols: a Literary Forgery* (London: The Times, 1921).
36. M. Baigent, R. Leigh, and H. Lincoln, *The Holy Blood and the Holy Grail* (London: Cape, 1982).
37. M. Allen, *Hidden Agenda: How the Duke of Windsor Betrayed the Allies* (London: Macmillan, 2000).
38. *Sunday Times*, 3 July 2005, 15.
39. C. S. L. Davies, 'Information, Disinformation and Political Knowledge under Henry VII and Early Henry VIII', *Historical Research* 85 (2012), 228–253.
40. W. Merrin, *Digital War: A Critical Introduction* (Abingdon: Routledge, 2019), 195–196.
41. J. B. Mayor, *Ricardi de Cirencestria, Speculum Historiale de Gestis Regum Angliae*, vol. 2, *Chronicles and Memorials of Great Britain and Ireland during the Middle Ages* (London: Longman, Roberts and Green, 1869).
42. Acton, *Lectures*, 15.

CHAPTER 12

MORE CONTENT, LESS CONTEXT

Rethinking Access

VICTORIA VAN HYNING AND HEATHER WOLFE

Let's face it. Almost all archival research begins with a Google search. Searchers sometimes do not even know that they are engaging in archival research. They are looking for information about an ancestor, or a geographic location, or an historic event, and they end up emailing an archivist for the first time in their lives because their search took them to a finding aid that includes their search term. Their query is abstract, since they are unsure what, exactly, the archive holds, but could we please send them a scan of the relevant document? These are the comparatively lucky cases where an archive has made just enough information available to be discoverable to a search engine.

This is not the type of search query or information-seeking behaviour archivists had in mind when finding aids emerged as the primary access tool in North America in the nineteenth and twentieth centuries. Finding aids provide an overall roadmap for an archival collection, reflecting the administrative organizations of the agencies and individuals that created it, and a scope and content note which describes it as a whole. By nature finding aids do not aspire to granularity, and thus the experience of searching a finding aid is very different from searching the archive that it describes. As discussed elsewhere in this volume, finding aids and published calendars are the biased products of the archivists who create them and can never serve as digital surrogates of the original items. While the richly detailed published calendars of the Public Records Office and the Historical Manuscripts Commission in the United Kingdom are a notable exception to the parameters of the typical finding aid or inventory,[1] they paraphrase or describe the manuscripts of elite men (and some elite women), and often omit references to domestic issues or to marginalized members of their households. This sort of incidental detail was not deemed worthy of research at the time of their publication.

Despite the transformative potential of Encoded Archival Description to enhance the usability of finding aids, the transition to digital finding aids has not been smooth, reproducing and amplifying the shortcomings of their paper-based predecessors. Finding aids encoded in EAD are based in a hierarchical framework that goes from the general to the specific, with containers, folders, and subfolders representing both intellectual and physical units. EAD provides online access, but, as Rachel Walton notes, 'significant room remains for improvement for online finding aids, especially in the realms of usability, navigation, and user interface design'.[2] The transition from analogue to digital finding aid is not dissimilar to the transition from manuscript codex to printed book; that is, when you scale up a format so that many more people may use it, you discover that many key attributes or guiding principles no longer make sense.

The International Council on Archives' (ISAD-G) definition for finding aids is singularly focused on *control*: 'The broadest term to cover any description or means of reference made or received by an archives service in the course of establishing administrative or intellectual control over archival material.' Recent trends in archival selection, archival inclusivity, archival activism, and the exponential growth of born-digital archives and digital surrogates, should encourage us to think differently about whether control is the best word to describe the purpose of a finding aid, and consider whether the definition should be more user-centric than archivist-centric. In fact, should the finding aid as a concept and tool still be the primary form of access, or do we need a new model that reflects the needs of new and future researchers? The statement of principles in the most recent version of *Describing Archives: A Content Standard* (DACS), suggests that the tide is turning. Three of the eleven guiding principles in DACS are now focused on access by users: 'Users are the fundamental reason for archival description', 'Archival description is accessible', and 'Archival description should be easy to use, re-use, and share.'[3]

As Anne Gilliland observes:

> in recent years there has been increasing criticism that collection-level, hierarchical metadata as exemplified in archival finding aids, while valuable for retaining context and original order, represents an oversimplified view of the actual complexities of records-creation processes and provenance, privileges the scholarly user of the archive (and those who are familiar with the structure and function of archival finding aids) while leaving the non-expert user baffled, and unnecessarily perpetuates a paper-based descriptive paradigm.[4]

In a recent article detailing the fraught history of finding aids and decades of effort to agree upon and implement new archival practices, Gregory Wiedeman similarly notes that 'finding aids continue to marginalize the delivery of content' and were originally intended to be 'a creative solution to the problem of tremendous scale' at The National Archives and Records Administration of the USA, in a staffing environment that 'would always fall short of fulfilling [the] nearly unlimited mission' of archivists.[5] They were a temporary measure to secure patrimonial heritage and provide archival control over collections through a logical structure that reflected the way in which they were created. They were not intended, really, to be what end users would consult. How can we accommodate the information-seeking behaviour of current and future searchers without abandoning the importance of context for interpretation and archival custodianship? How can we make archives accessible in meaningful ways to searchers of many kinds?

This chapter advocates for a fundamental shift in the way archivists spend their time and limited resources on providing access to collections—away from creating finding aids, and towards community engagement, crowdsourcing, co-creation, and the use of different data structures and tools to provide access. Our focus is narrow for the purposes of this thought experiment and because of our areas of expertise: access to handwritten archives in North America and the United Kingdom that are usually described in EAD finding aids (XML documents created using the Encoded Archival Description standard). Our proposal is based on the premise that we want to create the deepest and most unbiased level of access and findability to archives online for the greatest number of people, while cognizant of the limited resources and staffing of most archival repositories. We urge readers to trust their potential audiences a little bit more and focus on giving them access to full text content rather than aggregate level structured data, and to include audiences in the process of content creation. Said simply, we advocate for more content, less context.[6]

This chapter only considers a very narrow sliver of the concept of 'access'. It is meant to spark a discussion among archivists and end users about what sort of data we should be creating in order to make our handwritten collections available to the widest possible user base. Access can be hampered by many things which are not discussed here: privacy, data protection, copyright, Freedom of Information laws, donor restrictions, preservation issues, proprietary databases and paywalls, the lack of appropriate tools and support for people with visual, hearing, cognitive or motor impairments (some archives provide assistive study rooms and tools), accommodation of service animals, and the record's stage in its life cycle. We hope that future scholarship and discourse within the profession and among users will more fully articulate *what* we make available, *how* we make it available, and *who* has access to it.

Digitization as Access?

Creating digital surrogates of archival items is a significant part of the solution to widening access, but digitization is insufficient in itself, because most images of documents are not machine readable or legible to most content management systems, or web searches without the addition of metadata, tags, or transcriptions. Murtha Baca's observations typify a now widely held view in the field of archival practice and cultural heritage preservation more broadly: 'the mere act of creating digital copies of collection materials does not make those materials findable, understandable, or utilizable to our ever-expanding audience of online users. But digitization combined with the creation of carefully crafted metadata can significantly enhance end-user access—and our users are the primary reason we create digital resources.'[7] However, 'carefully crafted metadata' don't go far enough, and will not pull in wider audiences, because the sort of metadata archivists create does not anticipate the search strategies of most users, whose first point of entry for research is an internet keyword search and whose expectation is that if something isn't online, it probably doesn't exist.

This gap between traditional archival arrangement and enhancement and user search behaviour is exacerbated by modern technologies, but stems from the fundamentally different organizing paradigms of archives and libraries, and the ways in which most people are taught to seek out information. Archival description follows the evidentiary paradigm ('ofness') while printed books and library materials are arranged and described according to an informational paradigm ('aboutness'). Archives are arranged by creator (an institution, department, or individual), and according to the hierarchical and organizational structures under which they were created—the *fonds*, subgroups, series, subseries, file unit, item—to achieve administrative and intellectual control over the evidentiary aspects of the archive. Yet archives are often mined by researchers for their 'aboutness' rather than their 'ofness'. Studies such as one by Hensley, Murphy, and Swain (2014) indicate that without special training (and even with special training), researchers' unfamiliarity with archival theory and standards for description limits their ability to discover and use archives.[8] As Wiedeman writes: 'Archivists cannot educate the entire world to look for scope and content notes [archival metadata] to guide them through collections, but they can work to present this information in ways explicit and familiar to uninitiated users.'[9] We must meet users where they are and provide interfaces and structures that are intuitive from a user perspective, silently bridging the gap between traditional archival practice and evolving user behaviour. While digitization of archival materials and digital preservation protocols almost universally reproduce the ofness paradigm, in order to tie new digital surrogates to their analogue originals and finding aids, there is greater value to a greater number and diversity of users when digital objects are presented in ways that meet users' aboutness-driven research behaviour. This includes making images, audio, and video surrogates available, along with transcriptions and plain language tags that more readily anticipate users' search needs. We need to adopt practices that reflect the multiplicity and diversity of archival collections, as well as their users.

User-Generated Content: A Case Study

We have each worked on a variety of projects and methods that fundamentally aim to widen access to archives by increasing the amount and availability of aboutness to users through search engines and online archival repositories. We are driven by a shared goal of creating more machine-readable transcriptions from digitized images (including audio and video materials). We are early modernists deeply committed to the recovery of lesser-known authors such as women, people of colour, and religious minorities, and most of our projects focus on manuscript and some print materials that have not been traditionally the focus of detailed archival description and finding aids—materials more often categorized as 'miscellaneous', rather than the central focus of a collection, and lightly, if at all, described. These materials have generally not been digitized and run through Optical Character Recognition (OCR) or hand keyed as part of Google Books, Internet Archive, Hathi Trust, Early English Books Online, or Eighteenth Century Collections Online resources. We have worked individually, together, and with a wide variety of people, including web developers, data scientists in the public and private sectors, astronomers, cultural heritage specialists including archivists, librarians, and curators, educators and students from the humanities and sciences, and countless (sometimes anonymous) online volunteers, to further our goals in five key areas:

1. Increasing the amount and diversity of materials that are digitized by cultural heritage institutions.

2. Making a case for the value and utility of user-generated content—such as digital images, machine-readable transcriptions, and tags—and the need for institutions to gather, preserve, and share these.

3. Engaging broad non-specialist audiences through online crowdsourcing projects that enable people to discover and explore historical context while creating new data, such as transcriptions and descriptive tags.

4. Teaching palaeography to students, educators, and non-specialists, in order to help people access, read, and utilize original sources in their research, whether that's a local or family history, work of fiction, student essay, blog post, doctoral thesis, article, edition, or book.

5. Democratizing access to handwritten documents within a search environment that has a strong print bias and creating a search experience that places a high value on serendipitous discovery.

In 2013 the Folger Library was awarded a three year grant from the Institute of Museum and Library Services to build Early Modern Manuscripts Online (EMMO), a portal to enable full text search in modern and early modern English of transcribed manuscripts in the Folger's collections. Most early modern English manuscripts are written in 'secretary hand', a script with letter forms that are very different from modern cursive letter forms, which typically requires in-person specialized training to gain proficiency. The original plan was for Heather and her colleagues to use an in-house transcription platform, Dromio, to engage paleography students, researchers, and grant-funded staff to create transcriptions for EMMO, which would then live alongside archival description, metadata, and document images. Dromio was originally developed as a pedagogical tool by Heather and Michael Poston in 2006, but as more and more researchers asked if they could use it as a transcription-hosting site, its functionality evolved and it became a workhorse for EMMO.

The ideals and ambitions of the EMMO project resonated with Victoria, who saw an opportunity to involve a wider community in the process of transcription and archival exploration—not just students and scholars, but enthusiastic amateurs as well. In 2013 Victoria approached Heather, and Zooniverse.org, an academic crowdsourcing group at the University of Oxford, Department of Astrophysics, to propose that Folger repurpose some of the EMMO grant money to create a crowdsourcing project on the Zooniverse platform. This led to her appointment as a digital humanities postdoctoral fellow with Zooniverse, and a partnership between Folger, Zooniverse, and the Oxford English Dictionary to build Shakespeare's World (shakespearesworld.org).[10] This project invited volunteers to create transcriptions of early modern letters, recipe books, and early newsletters, which were automatically scanned by the site for new words and variants for the OED.

At the time Zooniverse hosted more than fifty projects in the sciences and a few in the humanities, including Operation War Diary, which was devoted to partial transcription and metadata extraction about life on the front in the First World War from British and Irish military unit diaries. The platform boasted over half a million registered users, few of whom had subject expertise in the early modern period. We saw this as a chance to reach new users who were probably unlike Folger's existing base, and for Zooniverse to experiment with full text transcription, rather than metadata extraction. Like Dromio, the Zooniverse system we developed for Shakespeare's World, and a sister project called AnnoTate (with Tate Britain), enables multiple people to independently transcribe documents, and for the research team to use a variety of algorithms including clustering, genetic sequencing, and other approaches, to compare and aggregate the transcriptions as a form of quality control. This method now underpins all text transcription projects on the free Zooniverse Project Builder site where anyone can create their own project (zooniverse.org/lab). We designed Shakespeare's World so that Zooniverse volunteers could transcribe as little as a word or line on a page. We hypothesized that this granular approach would encourage non-specialist volunteers to give early modern transcription a try and know that, even if they couldn't transcribe a whole page, they were still making a meaningful contribution by transcribing whatever they could read.

The granular approach paid off in this respect: eighteen months into the project, 40 per cent of all transcriptions had been completed by users who did thirty-nine or fewer lines of transcription, and while a superuser group of seventeen people did emerge, consisting of volunteers who did more than 500 transcriptions each, they contributed only 24 per cent of transcriptions overall. This is markedly different from other projects, notably Transcribe Bentham at University College London, whose team have been exemplary in publishing information about their project over the years. In 2014 project leaders Tim Causer and Melissa Terras wrote that:

> The great majority of the work [of transcriptions completed between 2010 and 2013] has been carried out by a core of 17 'Super Transcribers' [who contribute 1000+ transcribed and TEI encoded pages]. These expert volunteers sustain the project [...] However, heavy reliance upon Super Transcribers does leave *Transcribe Bentham* in a precarious position: if one or more ceased participating, then the transcription rate would decrease precipitously.[11]

Shakespeare's World attracted 3,926 registered volunteers, and an unknown number of anonymous participants, who transcribed 11,490 digital images of single and double-page openings over a period of nearly four years, before we put the project on hiatus in October 2019, in order to process the resulting data and for the Folger team to focus on their efforts to publish it. Roughly 19,000 additional transcriptions have been produced in Dromio between 2014 and 2020, by hundreds of Folger docents, staff, palaeography students, pedagogical partners, transcribathon participants, and volunteers, several hailing from Shakespeare's World after 2019.[12] So far, over 15,500 transcriptions of single and double-page openings from the combined pool of over 30,000, have been vetted and are now full text searchable on the Folger's digital image platform (luna.folger.edu) as of October 2023. A smaller subset are available as diplomatic, semi-diplomatic, and normalized transcriptions (to enable modern and early modern word search), and as downloadable TEI-P4 compliant XML files, within the EMMO platform (emmo.folger.edu).

Volunteer Motivation, Skill, Dedication

Many registered volunteers not only transcribed, but participated on Talk, the Zooniverse discussion forum, where they raised questions and concerns that helped us refine and improve the project; alerted OED editors to potential antedatings of words, alternative spellings, and new usages; directed researchers to relevant source documents for their work through the use of agreed-upon hashtags; found mistakes in Folger finding aids which were corrected immediately; assisted each other in answering palaeographical questions; wrote blog posts; created glossaries; and let their curiosity lead them down fascinating rabbit holes; to name just a few activities. Volunteer and early modernist Dr Elisabeth Chaghafi, @mutabilitie on the Zooniverse platform, uncovered a nearly 200-year antedating of the phrase 'white lie' and a constellation of earlier uses of 'partner', in the sense of life partner, that pipped Milton's usage in *Paradise Lost* by ninety years. Chaghafi uncovered numerous instances of 'partner' in the family letters of Anne Broughton (née Bagot) and her husband Richard, not only as a term of endearment for one another, but also as they wrote about one another to Anne's father, Richard Bagot. Chaghafi's findings exemplify the sort of evidence of women's contributions to the development of English language that we were hoping to uncover for the OED, by inviting people to transcribe non-canonical early modern documents, and explicitly inviting them to tag pages written by women using the hashtag #womanwriter.

Public engagement requires the creation of context, but typically this context and sense-making takes a radically different form from the finding aid and may be more closely aligned with the norms of LibGuides, a content management system used within the library sector to create context for general audiences, classroom use, as well as for specialists. Finding aids, and underlying descriptive metadata, if they exist, can serve as part of the context in crowdsourcing projects, but the dearth of item-level description typically makes them of limited utility to volunteers. Crowdsourcing can therefore be framed as an exploration, a call to volunteers to help an institution or community of scholars discover what the archives are about.

Period- or subject-specific scaffolding and resources are probably more valuable to the general volunteer than traditional archival description detailing the relationship of documents within a hierarchy. The Shakespeare's World team created contextual scaffolding geared towards non-specialists, including glossaries of place names, numerical and financial terms and notation, transcription conventions, sample alphabets, and new functionality to allow people to snip and save parts of manuscripts to create their own palaeography cheat sheets. We spent countless hours blogging, emailing, tweeting, and speaking with volunteers via Talk, to answer volunteers' questions and provide context on a case-by-case basis—essentially performing reference work through these means. The best crowdsourcing—the kind that sets out to create community amongst volunteers and lasting connections between them and the organization, in addition to creating meaningful data—requires a significant investment of time in these activities, also known as 'community management'. These activities are often little different from the reference work archivists and librarians already perform, and can have value across numerous collections. Generally speaking, these investments of time, energy, and resources pay off in myriad ways, typically by producing data on a larger scale than is possible for core staff within the typical institution, by prompting staff to create evergreen scaffolding to aid users in understanding collections, and also in creating long-term relationships between new users and the host institution. The Shakespeare's World project created a bond and sense of purpose between the Folger's metadata and cataloging staff, volunteers, and researchers, in addition to improving the quality of the Folger's descriptive cataloging and creating the content that will lead to increased access and discoverability by traditional and unanticipated users.

Folger and Zooniverse are hardly alone in conducting this sort of reference work and forging these kinds of connections. Many national libraries, archives, college and university archives, genealogy groups, and many others now conduct some form of crowdsourcing. The Library of Congress By the People crowdsourced transcription and tagging project (which Victoria worked to establish with a group of archivists, technologists, and innovators in 2018–2020) attracted many volunteers eager to make non-machine-readable documents accessible to full text search and to people using screen readers. Most volunteers had no prior transcription experience. Henry Rosenberg came to the project in retirement looking for a way to volunteer and give back to society. In just 22 months he transcribed over 15,000 pages, edited thousands of others, and encouraged countless fellow volunteers by answering their questions, helping them parse handwriting, and navigate the By the People site. Henry was interviewed for a blog post about his experience in August 2020. When asked 'prior to becoming a volunteer, what relevant skills did you have?' he replied:

> None. Frankly, I am a terrible typist. I had never done anything like this before. When I started I had a lot of trouble reading Mary Church Terrell's handwriting and it took a few weeks before I began to get the nuances of her script.[13]

Henry only learned about Terrell's many contributions to the Civil Rights movement through this project, including her work to found the National Association of Colored Women and the National Association for the Advancement of Colored People—'I learned so much about prejudice and the fight for civil rights. She was a remarkable woman.' He put the time into learning to read her nineteenth-century script and conduct additional research about her life. His journey into the virtual archive is not uncommon.

It might surprise readers to learn that inviting volunteers to transcribe old documents written in unfamiliar scripts could result in quality data. We are happy to say that in addition to the benefits of engaging with volunteers via Talk and other means, the overall quality of Shakespeare's World transcriptions seems to be very high (though we are still processing and assessing the data). This has led us and the Zooniverse team more widely to question the value of requiring multiple independent volunteers to transcribe documents, and then aggregating these texts into a single reading. Zooniverse has since developed another multi-transcriber line-by-line transcription method in which volunteers can see what other people have transcribed and either accept it or edit it.[14]

Both Zooniverse methods differ from most other crowdsourced transcription projects, which invite volunteers to transcribe and edit one another's work in an 'open' system, where registered users or those with a special editor designation can revise transcriptions. Examples of 'open' systems include Transcribe Bentham, the Smithsonian Transcription Center, By the People, and countless projects on the From the Page platform. From the Page is a subscription product that allows organizations and individuals to create their own projects. It is a good fit for most scholars and institutions seeking to engage volunteers with transcription and linked data.[15] It was built with the needs of cultural heritage institutions in mind and has the most fluid integrations between archival and digital asset management systems, as well as automated OCR for modern printed documents, and integrations with the International Image Interoperability Framework (IIIF) and the Internet Archive. In the spirit of experimentation and in an effort to speed up the pace at which we create content for 'full-text finding aids', our institutions began on new From the Page projects in 2020 (Heather at the Folger, Victoria at the University of Maryland, College of Information Studies and the David C. Driskell Center). The lessons we have learned through Shakespeare's World and By the People will guide our community engagement, scaffolding, and our search for alternatives to the traditional finding aid.

Similar to the participatory archives movement, crowdsourcing represents a potentially transformative shift in *how* access to archival material is created, and *who* creates it. We can up-end the power structure of the archivist disseminating partial information to others through privileged access to collection material, and work together to create an open and transparent framework for accessing material at all stages. Archivists and volunteers become partners in a collaborative effort to unlock the text of digitized manuscripts and make it freely discoverable to anyone with an internet connection. Learning and discovery flow in multiple directions, between the archival repository and its often new content contributors, who have a wide range of motives for participating, and of course between volunteers. Individuals who may never have previously engaged in a cultural institution's programming or visited it in person are now co-creators of content that help the institution to reach even more people like them.[16]

Outcomes and Future Directions

In terms of early modern English archival material, the addition of hundreds of thousands of newly discoverable words that record the experiences and voices of women and non-canonical, non-elite, and marginalized people, contributes to a reassessment of long-held assumptions about literacy, domestic arrangements, social networks, and self-determination. The integration of crowdsourced transcriptions into the underlying metadata of digital images has greatly increased the utility and searchability of Folger manuscripts. In the four and a half years since the Folger quietly launched the 'Manuscripts Transcription' collection in our digital image database, there were over 150,000 page views, or roughly 2,800 views per month, with a marked increase in usage during the pandemic. We expect these numbers to get higher as we publicize their availability.

Many cultural heritage organizations do not have an established practice of storing and displaying transcriptions—crowdsourced or otherwise—alongside digital surrogates within their content management system. Not all archival systems support page level description and often limit the number of characters in fields where one might conceivably try to wedge this sort of data. Each institution engaged in crowdsourcing so far has elected to use a proprietary tool or software, cobble together an in-house solution, work with their content management system provider to make changes to existing tools, or has not yet found or implemented a solution. According to a 2020 study of From the Page users, by Allyssa Guzman et al., fourteen out of twenty-seven surveyed users (mostly archives and other cultural heritage organizations) incorporate transcriptions into DAMS 'as part of a digital object or record' while others only make content available upon request.[17] Archivists can have the highest impact on the discoverability of their collections by integrating transcription and scanning opportunities into their workflows, and advocating for a digital asset management system that displays transcriptions alongside images and metadata as a matter of course.

Data Reuse

The vetted Folger data have contributed to the development of a commercial application that may have wider implications for the archival profession, and the dream of making the aboutness of all primary materials searchable. In 2018, Adam Matthew Digital (a SAGE Publishing Company, working in partnership with an unnamed deep learning research group in Europe) used transcriptions from EMMO and Shakespeare's World to train a machine-learning system to create on-the-fly Handwritten Text Recognition (HTR) of digitized documents. HTR, as well as OCR and transcripts of audio and video files, underpin the search capabilities of Quartex, their digital asset management system. The Quartex platform can automatically generate and display editable transcriptions of digitized manuscripts, making all digitized archival material fully searchable. Other organizations and consortia have developed cheaper and more equitable access to HTR and scanning tools, including Transkribus, an AI-powered platform for the automated recognition, transcription, and searching of historical documents funded initially by grants and now by institutional and individual memberships.[18] Transkribus represents progress towards a future where digitized print, handwritten, and audio texts can be searched synchronously and cross-institutionally. Emerging machine-learning approaches like OpenAI's large language model have also transformed automated transcription capabilities. The dream of this kind of functionality within search engines is far more appealing, and is, as Victoria has discussed elsewhere, a hitherto unrealized goal of Google Books.[19]

We hope it is not long before these kinds of search capabilities are normative, and that rates of accuracy continue to improve, though if the last fifty years of machine learning and text recognition research are anything to go by, the goal may be elusive for some time yet. But even in their current form, these functionalities broadly meet current user expectations, give the widest scope to the most diverse range of voices represented in the archive, and go a long way to transforming archival practice. The promises of HTR beg two questions: What room will there be for volunteers if transcription and tagging become obsolete? Why should archivists embrace community engagement and crowdsourcing if or when that happens?

Because cursive handwriting provides enough unique and insurmountable challenges for even the most powerful artificial intelligence—inconsistent patterns of joining letters together, abbreviations, deletions, interlineal insertions, writing along both horizontal and vertical edges, non-standardized spelling, and messiness to the point of illegibility, for example—HTR will never fully replace the need for archivists and volunteers to create transcriptions, or at least improve and correct them generated through artificial intelligence. The need for the Handwritten Text Recognition equivalent of OCR-correction projects, like TROVE Australia, may well prove endless, but we anticipate that the perennial need for digitization and the generally limited funds for this activity might be the next significant area to benefit from volunteer effort, and a shift to a more community-driven form of archival practice.

The National Archives' Innovation Hub in Washington, DC offers an example of scalable and sustainable citizen scanning and metadata creation. In the Innovation Hub's 'scanning room', volunteer researchers use scanning equipment, free of charge, to digitize selected records. They can keep a copy of their scans, and NARA adds their copies to the online catalogue as well. Since the scanning project began in July 2015, volunteers have scanned nearly 600,000 pages of records, making files available to people who would not otherwise be able to access them. Led by Catherine Brandsen, the project takes into consideration limited staff resources by continually fine-tuning the workflows for quality control, image post-processing, technical support, and community management. Volunteers and staff use a Google form to collect metadata, which feeds into a spreadsheet where the raw information is formatted. Scanning takes place on flatbed and overhead scanners with pre-settings that, according to Brandsen, 'hit the sweet spot between producing a good-quality scan and scanning quickly enough'. Initially, The National Archives accepted that they will not meet the highest standards of digitization and designated the images as 'access scans' rather than preservation copies.[20] However, NARA adopted a new digitization policy in 2019 designed to improve image quality for digitization projects across the agency, including citizen scanning. The images and metadata are checked by archivists and then uploaded to their catalogue, with a turnaround time of four to ten weeks. Brandsen notes that many volunteers scan documents that are related to their ancestors or to their military regiments, while others work on any project or set of documents that is readily available. This work also provides digitized records for Citizen Archivist, NARA's crowdsourced transcription programme that allows volunteers to transcribe and tag any digitized NRA record directly in the online catalogue. In August 2020 volunteers hit an important milestone of enhancing a million pages of records with tags or transcriptions.

Many researchers now spend their time taking photos in reading rooms, creating personal digital archives for deeper study at home. One Folger researcher reported taking 17,000 across three institutions in a single year. Likewise, most archivists' cell phones are overflowing with hundreds, if not thousands, of quick and dirty reference images taken either for in-house use or to respond to reference questions. The Folger recently launched the 'Folger Reference Image Collection' as a way to share these 'access' images more widely, releasing the first batch of 2,663 images taken by reference staff in September 2020. The goal is to provide an easy upload form for researchers to add their images, which can then be linked to item-level metadata and made accessible in our digital image database. This provides another route for aggregating images and making them available for transcription. The images have a CCO 1.0 Universal Public Domain Dedication License, which means they can be freely copied, modified, and distributed for both non-commercial and commercial purposes, all without asking permission. We believe that staff and user-generated content, generous licensing, and ongoing crowdsourcing efforts will combine to enhance the utility of Folger's collections, and a diversification of the user base.

Future Possibilities

Crowdsourced transcription and scanning projects are scalable and sustainable ways for organizations to keep up with the demands for access to digitized and full text searchable documents. Our experiences working with both in-person and distributed online crowdsourcing projects has taught us that creating better access to archives is not just about improving online finding aids and connecting users to the documents they need. Creating better access is also about inviting others into the process of content creation, opening up our reading rooms virtually and inviting volunteers to connect with archivists, librarians, catalogers, researchers, and other collaborators all over the world, on their own time and at their own pace. The prospect of empowering volunteers to collaborate directly with archival repositories, to use the transcriptions to undertake their own research or community projects, and the prospect of institutions supporting new and innovative uses of collections by scholarly and non scholarly users, must be at the heart of our work to revamp archival practice. The collaborative creation of 'full text finding aids' would not only provide content to traditional finding aid users, and the users we describe at the start of this chapter, but also create endless opportunities for serendipitous discoveries and new avenues for social network analysis and computational corpus linguistics projects, as well as for any number of unanticipated uses. We must respond to changes in user behaviour with changes in our own behaviour, creating and democratizing access through the use of open source and community-driven software and systems that allow our images and transcriptions to be easily shareable, downloadable, and interoperable.

Innovative projects spearheaded by the Library of Congress Labs team, such as the year-long innovator in residence program established in 2017, exemplify the benefits of loosening archival control, providing more granular access to archival material, and encouraging the use of archival data and metadata to non-traditional modes of research, discovery, and play. During his residency web developer and hip hop artist Brian Foo (2019–2020) created 'Citizen DJ', a tool that enables anyone with a robust internet connection to explore historic LOC sound recordings and mix their own hip hop tracks.[21] This tool facilitates both search and creation. Foo has produced an album titled 'Some Tracks from the Stacks' based on the 'Inventing Entertainment: The Early Motion Pictures and Sound Recordings of the Edison Companies' [collection], a set of materials curated by the Library, featuring digital copies of early sound recordings from Edison Diamond Discs published between 1912 and 1929.[22] Data Artist Jer Thorp (2017–2018) created a number of tools for serendipitous exploration, including 'Library of Time', a virtual clock that tells time by displaying snippets of library description from the LOC's Prints and Photographs Division collections.

The numerals of each hour, minute, and second are hyperlinked and lead directly to an image and its online catalogue record. As the seconds tick past they turn grey, move down, and then off the screen. Tantalizing fragments of description tick along—each new second, a new link, a new possibility, and potentially a missed opportunity if you don't click fast enough. The passage of time and the serendipity and urgency of discovery are made real in ways that simply browsing through a finding aid or catalogue cannot achieve. Thorp and LOC staff hope that tools like

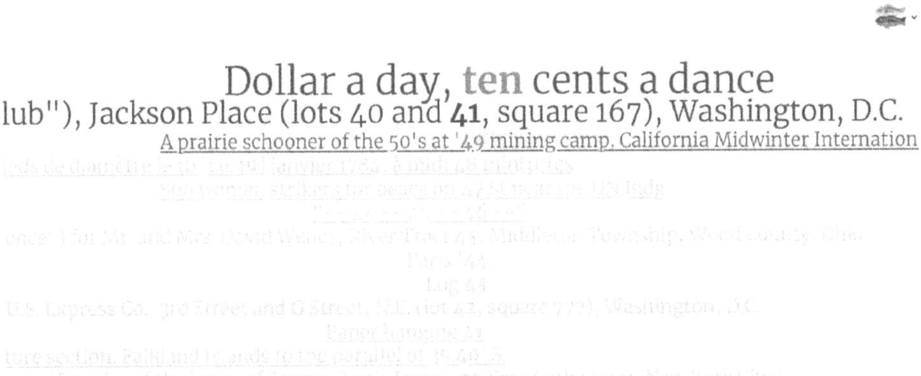

Figure 12.1 'Library of Time', created by Jer Thorp, 2018, as part of 'Serendipity Engine' for the Library of Congress at https://labs.loc.gov/work/experiments/innovator-in-residence-jer-thorp/. Screenshot taken 26 January 2022, 10:41:50am, Eastern Time, from https://library-of-time.glitch.me/.

this will meet the search needs and curiosity of users who do not have a specific research question or deep familiarity with finding aids and other archival practices. Curiosity and serendipity, rather than familiarity with archival norms, are the gateways to content discovery. Traditional library and archival context and digital surrogates made these projects possible, but imagine what users could do with 'full text finding aids', that unlock access to the full content of the original sources, and make them legible to search engines. Imagine how much more diverse our user base might be if we were willing and able to pursue partnerships like these, along with more collaborative approaches for generating and sharing archival data.

The institutions, projects, and platforms we have mentioned so far are not alone in their efforts to dramatically widen access to archives and cultural heritage by changing and challenging the paradigms of description and digitization norms, search architecture, and research methods. Crowdsourcing is one part of a larger movement to create access to, and connections between, collections around the world in exciting and innovative ways that engage new audiences in unexpected ways. For example, Europeana unites and preserves user-generated digital surrogates and metadata alongside institutional collections and systems from across Europe, and the Time Machine consortium project, which shares many of the same institutional partners as Europeana, has the additional aim of creating collections as data—large reusable datasets of various kinds of media and metadata that can be approached at scale. Future projects could include ones similar to those undertaken by LOC innovators in residence or, to give a simpler example, looking at the frequency and distribution of a word or phrase across an entire corpus of searchable text, rather than looking for individual instances of the word or phrase in individual texts. Investigating language usage at scale can help us understand bigger questions about the evolution or function of language over time. Living with Machines, a collaboration between the Alan Turing Institute, the British Library and the Universities of Cambridge, East Anglia, Exeter, and Queen Mary University of London, brings together humanities scholars, STEM researchers, and cultural heritage professionals to study the historical and cultural impacts of the first industrial revolution, by harnessing 'the combined power of massive digitized historical collections and computational analytical tools to examine the ways in which technology altered the very fabric of human existence on a hitherto unprecedented scale'. Their use of archival and library collections at scale, and their interdisciplinary work will culminate in 'a bold proposal for a new research paradigm'.[23] Each of these projects exemplify the benefits of scale, digitization, public engagement, and interdisciplinarity in different ways. They invite us to think big about our shared cultural heritage, our users, and the ongoing work of making the past viscerally and digitally present, and serviceable for future uses and needs. Archival practice can and must prioritize creating machine-readable open content at scale: volunteer effort, diverse perspectives, and a greater emphasis on content over context will best serve users now and in future.

ACKNOWLEDGEMENT

We would like to thank Julie A. Fisher for providing useful feedback on this chapter.

FURTHER READING

Murtha Baca, ed., *Introduction to Metadata* (Los Angeles: Getty Publications, 2016; 3rd edn); www.getty.edu/publications/intrometadata

Samantha Blickhan, Coleman Krawczyk, Daniel Hanson, Amy Boyer, Andrea Simenstad, and Victoria Van Hyning, 'Individual vs. Collaborative Methods of Crowdsourced Transcription', *Journal of Data Mining and Digital Humanities*, Special Issue on Collecting, Preserving, and Disseminating Endangered Cultural Heritage for New Understandings through Multilingual Approaches (2019); doi:10.46298/jdmdh.5759

Katherine Crowe, Katrina Fenlon, Hannah Frisch, Diana Marsh, and Victoria Van Hyning, 'Inviting and Honouring User-contributed Content', in Mark A. Matienzo and Dinah Handel, eds, *The Lighting the Way Handbook: Case Studies, Guidelines, and Emergent Futures for Archival Discovery and Delivery* (Stanford, CA: Sanford Universities Libraries, 2021), 115–131; doi:10.25740/gg453cv6438

Jennifer Douglas, 'Towards More Honest Description', *The American Archivist* 79 (2016), 26–55

Mark Greene and Dennis Meissner, 'More Product, Less Process. Revamping Traditional Archival Processing', *The American Archivist* 68 (2005), 208–263

Trevor Owens, *The Theory and Craft of Digital Preservation* (Baltimore: Johns Hopkins University Press, 2018)

Mia Ridge, ed., *Crowdsourcing Our Cultural Heritage* (Farnham: Ashgate, 2014)

Victoria Van Hyning, 'Harnessing Crowdsourcing for Scholarly and GLAM Purposes', *Literature Compass* 16.3-4 (2019); doi:10.1111/lic3.12507

NOTES

1. The Royal Commission on Historical Manuscripts (HMC) was established in 1869 to document the location of records and papers in private hands, chiefly Great Britain's aristocratic families. It published surveys and calendars of non-official records of institutions and families; that is, all the papers outside of the jurisdiction of the Public Record Office (PRO) which 'tend to the elucidation of History, and the illustration of Constitutional Law, Science and Literature'. Beginning in 1945, HMC oversaw the development of the National Register of Archives (NRA). In 2003, the HMC merged with the PRO to form The National Archives (TNA). TNA's catalogue, Discovery, includes records from NRA, Access to Archives (A2A), ARCHON (a directory of archives) and the Manorial Documents Register and contains over 32 million descriptions.

2. R. Walton, 'Looking for Answers: A Usability Study of Online Finding Aid Navigation', *The American Archivist* 80.1 (2017), 30–52 (31). Also of interest is V. Addonizio, 'The Evolution of the Finding Aid', ArchivesSpace webinar 16 May 2018; https://archivesspace.org/archives/291.

3. Technical Subcommittee on DACS, SAA, 'Statement of Principles', *Describing Archives: A Content Standard*, Version 2019.0.3, https://saa-ts-github.io/dacs/04_statement_of_principles.html.
4. A. J. Gilliland, 'Introduction to Metadata: Setting the Stage', in M. Baca, ed., *Introduction to Metadata*, 3rd ed. (Los Angeles: Getty Publications, 2016), unpaginated; www.getty.edu/publications/intrometadata/setting-the-stage.
5. G. Wiedeman, 'The Historical Hazards of Finding Aids', *The American Archivist* 82.2 (2019), 381-420 (383, 387); doi:10.17723/aarc-82-02-20. Also of interest is *Making Archival and Special Collections More Accessible* (Dublin, Ohio: OCLC Research, 2015): www.oclc.org/content/dam/research/publications/2015/; oclcresearch-making-special-collections-accessible-2015.pdf. This freely available compilation of previously published essays includes several that are particularly relevant to our discussion, e.g., J. M. Dooley, M. O'Hara Conway, M. Proffitt, and J. Schaffner.
6. Here we echo M. Greene and D. Meissner, 'More Product, Less Process: Revamping Traditional Archival Processing', in *The American Archivist* 68.2 (2005), 208–263; doi:10.17723/aarc.68.2.c741823776k65863.
7. M. Baca, 'Introduction', in Baca, ed., *Introduction to Metadata*, unpaginated; www.getty.edu/publications/intrometadata/introduction/.
8. M. K. Hensley, B. Murphy, E. D. Swain, 'Analyzing Archival Intelligence: A Collaboration between Library Instruction and Archives', *Communications in Information Literacy* 8.1 (2014), 96–114; doi:10.15760/comminfolit.2014.8.1.155.
9. Wiedeman, 'The Historical Hazards', 405.
10. The project is currently on hiatus, but its vibrant volunteer and research process are visible online via the Talk discussion board and placeholder project page located at this link www.zooniverse.org/projects/zooniverse/shakespeares-world.
11. T. Causer and M. Terras, '"Many Hands Make Light Work. Many Hands Together Make Merry Work": Transcribe Bentham and Crowdsourcing Manuscript Transcription', in M. Ridge, ed., *Crowdsourcing our Cultural Heritage* (Farnham: Ashgate, 2014), 57–88 (73).
12. On a different scale altogether, between June 2013 and December 2019, the Smithsonian Transcription Center had 13,890 digital volunteers and 496,300 pages transcribed, including creating 130,755 catalog records that were previously unavailable to the public; https://si-siris.blogspot.com/2019/12/the-smithsonians-journey-of_17.html. L. Parilla and M. Ferriter, 'Social Media and Crowdsourced Transcription of Historical Materials at the Smithsonian Institution: Methods for Strengthening Community Engagement and Its Tie to Transcription Output', *The American Archivist* 79.2 (2016), 438–460.
13. S. Schireson and H. Rosenberg, 'Volunteer Vignette: Transcribe Without Fear, Don't Be Intimidated!', *The Signal Blog*, Library of Congress (1 October 2020), https://blogs.loc.gov/thesignal/2020/10/volunteer-vignette-henry.
14. S. Blickhan, C. Krawczyk, D. Hanson, A. Boyer, A. Simenstad, and V. Van Hyning, 'Individual vs. Collaborative Methods of Crowdsourced Transcription', *Journal of Data Mining and Digital Humanities*, Special Issue on Collecting, Preserving, and Disseminating Endangered Cultural Heritage for New Understandings through Multilingual Approaches (2019); doi:10.46298/jdmdh.5759.
15. Further discussion of linked data and archives can be found here: OCLC Research Archives and Special Collections Linked Data Review Group, *Archives and Special*

Collections Linked Data: Navigating between Notes and Nodes (Dublin, Ohio: 2020); doi:10.25333/4gtz-zd88.

16. T. Owens, 'Making Crowdsourcing Compatible with the Missions and Values of Cultural Heritage Organizations', in Ridge, ed., *Crowdsourcing*, 269–280. Also of interest by the same author: 'Archives as a Service: From Archivist as Producer and Provider to Archivist as Facilitator and Enabler', in C. Weideman and M. A. Caldera, eds, *Archival Values: Essays in Honor of Mark A. Greene* (Chicago: Society of American Archivists, 2019); doi:10.31229/osf.io/6m4ue.

17. A. Guzman, A. A. Palacios, and J. O. Baco, 'FromThePage Collection Owner User Study Report', *Enabling and Reusing Multilingual Citizen Contributions in the Archival Record—NEH Grant Documentation* (Austin, TX: University of Texas at Austin, 15 September, 2020); https://repositories.lib.utexas.edu/handle/2152/82841. From the Page, crowdsourced transcription site, https://fromthepage.com.

18. Transkribus https://readcoop.eu/transkribus/, platform for the automated recognition, transcription and searching of historical documents.

19. V. Van Hyning, 'Harnessing Crowdsourcing for Scholarly and GLAM Purposes', *Literature Compass*, 16.3–4 (2019); doi:10.1111/lic3.12507.

20. Private email, Catherine Bransden to Heather Wolfe, 27 April 2020, with attached document, 'Innovation Hub Scanning Room—How It Works'.

21. B. Foo, *Citizen DJ* (May 2020); https://labs.loc.gov/work/experiments/citizen-dj.

22. B. Foo, 'Some Tracks from the Stacks' (September 2020); https://soundcloud.com/functionfoo/sets/some-tracks-from-the-stacks.

23. https://livingwithmachines.ac.uk/about.

CHAPTER 13

RESPONSE TO 'FRAMEWORKS'

JANET FOSTER

In this response to the second section of *Archives: Power, Truth, and Fiction*, on 'Frameworks', I bring my perspective as a freelance archivist and provider of training in archives and records management in the UK and beyond. Often my project work deals with archives and records for organizations and individuals who have little prior understanding of what archivists do. To assist in explaining the work that archivists need to undertake, I present archival activities as inter-connected and co-dependent struts in a framework. The chapters in this section similarly illustrate the structures within which archivists and record managers operate to fulfil the functions of assessing, collecting, preserving, and providing access to the archives in their care. Some of the long-established concepts and procedures espoused as fundamental to the archival profession are here questioned, highlighting how these ways of working can result in archives that reflect only the historically dominant power structures of White, male, Eurocentric archives.

These chapters offer suggestions to develop our professional work in the context of breaking free from old ideas so that archives can document, and encourage, the involvement of all communities. This is already happening in some areas of archival activity with the growth of community archives. Anna Sexton shows how UK archival educators are broadening their approach beyond the exclusivity of the Western story to provide a more inclusive and culturally diverse space for aspiring archivists. In this response, I will briefly reflect on the practical implications of taking up the ideas and opportunities flagged in these chapters, particularly from the perspective of smaller less well-resourced repositories.

Many of the chapters in this section have a national focus and privilege national examples. Appraisal is a fundamental activity because there are not, and never will be, the resources to keep every record created. The examples of appraisal decisions given by Andrew Prescott highlight decisions made at national level dictated by storage space restrictions and political reasons. However, for smaller organizations, the resources and expertise available to support appraisal work may be limited. Prescott's suggestion that there could be greater collaboration in appraisal involving users and the general public aligns with current innovations in archive work, particularly as born-digital records reduce the storage imperative and increase access possibilities, although how this can be achieved more widely remains to be seen.

The examples given by Michael Moss and David Thomas in 'Authenticating and Evaluating Evidence' show that the widely used archival test for the authenticity of a record—a valid creator, format, language, and technology for the period—does not necessarily validate the content. Many robust examples are given to support this thesis but all are drawn from official records with a national focus which may give a skewed impression. Local history examples can help counter this impression, for example lease and release conveyances where the lease is essentially a fictional document which can be misleading if separated from its associated release. We must also remember that forgeries survive even when recognized as such because they make a good story. When I was archivist at St Bartholomew's Hospital everyone knew that Rahere's foundation charter was a forgery, but I was always asked to include it in exhibitions.

Metadata is a relatively new term for archivists, as Lisa Gitelman acknowledges. It only gained currency in the 1990s because the archival profession in general was resistant to the notion of standardization necessary for archival finding aids to be machine-readable. This is no longer the case because archivists have embraced metadata as a way of ensuring users can get the most from on-line querying of finding aids. It is done by adding key words and including, in traditional catalogues of cultural heritage collections, metadata relevant to and produced by different communities. Ruth and Sebastian Ahnert, however, contend that such archive description still often reflects 'analogue thinking' and show how network analysis can allow us to dive deeper than browsing. Their work, when applied to dispersed collections and used to foreground people on the margins, is exciting. However, again resource issues loom. It is clear that network analysis requires financial, IT, and human resources as well as collaborative arrangements that may be unattainable for any but the larger national and international repositories.

How far can crowdsourcing provide a solution to these resource constraints? Victoria Van Hyning and Heather Wolfe reflect the growing trend to harness the knowledge and effort of archive users in expanding the content of descriptions. This form of detailed description can contrast with those created by archivists that are structured to reflect context. Van Hyning and Wolfe suggest that using context as a framework for descriptions limits the ability to provide wider access to archives because it is not understood by users. My ideal would be 'more content in context' because context is essential to understand the structure and nature of the archive. The citizen science project described by them not only provides richer information about the content of the material but also has benefits in creating palaeographical skills for the volunteers. However, once again there is a large resource implication in managing the project and checking the volunteers' work and this may prevent less well-resourced repositories from taking advantage of crowdsourcing on this scale.

While these chapters on Frameworks provide a basis for wider understanding of the work that archivists do, the constraints of working in smaller archives with limited resources—perhaps the typical situation for most archivists—are absent here, given that the focus is on activities within national or other well-resourced institutions. While archivists perform vital work in employing the professional tools to preserve and make heritage accessible, too often they are asked to do so on a shoestring within services which are given a low priority for resources.

PART III

MATERIALITIES

CHAPTER 14

THE MATERIALITY OF WRITTEN TEXTUAL FORMS

ALISON WIGGINS

To study materiality is a corrective to any notion of written texts as static containers of inert information. Materialities remind us that a single piece of writing can have multiple functions and uses. The functions of a text are dependent upon and are activated by material processes that include collection, storage, reading, annotation, and, more recently, encoding, tagging, linking, and algorithmic searching. This chapter considers the meanings of materiality and how written textual forms have been harnessed and handled by recent archival research projects. The materiality of texts can be conceptualized as *distributed*, *formal*, *forensic*, and *performative*, and as both analogue and digital. Materiality is never stable or fixed, but is remade each time a text is used, read, photographed, searched for, visualized, or encoded. Archival texts are not there only to be mined for factual nuggets about dates and dynasties, or to serve up memorable quotations to attach to larger narratives. They have value for the information carried in the forms of their collection contexts, reception histories, formal features, and in their paper, ink, and bindings, about the economics of labour, knowledge networks, intelligence exchange, and patterns of trade. Every written textual object has at least two stories: the story told by the informational content of the words on the page, and the story about where, when, how, and by whom it was produced and received. These parallel stories of production and reception can be excavated from a written text's materiality to draw out new insights and alternative narratives that may be otherwise hidden. As we look to archival futures, we will require a model of written textual forms that emphasizes the layered archaeology of materiality, that considers the blurred boundary of the linguistic and material, that leans towards performativity, and that encompasses both analogue and digital. Such a model will allow us to generate more precise critical frameworks and more imaginative responses to their potential. Before moving on to consider these points, it is necessary to offer some definitions and to draw distinctions between writing, language, text, and materiality.

Concepts and Definitions: Writing, Language, Text, Materiality

Writing is not language, it is a representation of language. This distinction, between writing (which is scripted characters) and language (which is the communication system of a community), has direct implications for the operations of the archive, where conventionally writing is dominant. The dominance of the written archive in our own time is known from cases of claims for land rights by indigenous communities in Canada and Australia, where Western styles of recording history have worked against oral evidence. The difference between oral and written records encompasses a form of bias that still holds when oral accounts become fixed to other media, given that the assessments of reliability and authenticity demanded for written records may not be appropriate for records that capture oral forms.[1] The situation is further complicated by digitization, where Western forms likewise dominate. It is true that some minority languages have been bolstered by digital technologies, but the Web does not provide digital space or visibility for writing in every language. We do not yet have Unicode allocations for all the world's languages, minority and indigenous languages being the least well represented. Although one third of the world's languages are used in Africa, only a small proportion of these are digitally treatable.[2] Endangered and under-resourced languages must jostle for digital territory alongside other languages and compete with saleable emojis.[3] The land-grab for digital textual terrain means that text encoding has the potential not only to reflect but to amplify existing power structures. Ultimately, languages represented by written scripts that cannot be made digital are at risk of archival marginalization or annihilation.

The materiality of writing must be distinguished not only from language, but also from text. Text (in reference to writing) refers to visual and linguistic rhetorical conventions that are themselves imbricated with materiality.[4] Generic conventions, patterned formulae, procedural terms, and fixed phrases are the warp and weft of textual discourses and they are shaped and structured by the affordances of material forms, given that written texts can appear on an enormous variety of surfaces. We might think of analogue substrates used to transmit text made from skin, rags, wood, bark, wax, or clay fashioned into rolls, sheets, slips, chits, bills, codices, or tablets. In addition are myriad cultural objects that have functioned as carriers of text, from bones, knives, cups, combs, tapestries, and sewing samplers, to prison walls, pin badges, and protest banners, each bearing verses, messages, logos, slogans, inscriptions, or other forms of text that we find held in memory repositories. These objects require us to engage with questions around where the boundaries of the archive lie and to consider the relationship between a text's material form and its place within structures of archival classification. Traditionally, the role of archives has been to hold in perpetuity official records, whereas the role of museums, galleries, libraries, and other heritage locations has been to preserve items judged to be of aesthetic quality or cultural worth. This classification implies assumptions about authority, value, and evidential status, such as the higher levels of financial support attracted by national 'treasures' over non-canonical materials. The examples mentioned in this chapter include texts held in state archives, national libraries, special collections, and in private ownership. Their locations in these institutional and collection contexts is a defining dimension of their materiality and has a direct bearing on their access, treatment, use, and interpretation.

The function of a text is shaped by and profoundly invested in its material boundaries, which can include not only analogue but also digital forms. Writing can be born analogue or born digital, and it can be carried across media between analogue and digital, in either direction, any number of times. Each move involves a transformation in material form, such as when an analogue textual object is photographed and the image is stored to be used as a surrogate. An archive might hold a collection of paper-and-ink newspapers printed in the eighteenth century, as well as, of those same newspapers, microfilm scans made in the 1970s; black-and-white digital scans of these microfilms held as a jpg files made in the 1990s; colour digital images held as a tiff file made in the 2000s; and, subsequently derived from the digital scan of the microfilm, OCR-generated machine-tagged text held as xml files.[5] Each of these (the analogue paper-and-ink newspapers, the microfilms, and the digital tiff, jpg, and xml files) is a textual artefact with its own distinctive material form, media archaeology, and production and reception history. To describe these forms and the transitions between analogue and digital, we must interrogate a textual object according to a layered conceptualization of analogue and digital materiality. To put it another way, to unpick the meanings of materiality we must always, on encountering an archival text, ask critical questions about its material form, which apply whether it is an analogue textual source or a digital one. The critical questions that we must ask of a written archival textual object include the following. (1) Where is the text and why is it here at this location? (2) What is it and what are its inherent physical forms and features? (3) Who owns it and who was and is using and presenting it? These are questions about materiality. More specifically, they are questions about *distributed*, *formal*, *forensic*, and *performative* materiality.[6] They have long been asked by historians of analogue sources and more recently of digital ones, and they are questions relevant to all users of archival texts.[7] We must ask them of every archival text we encounter if we are to evaluate its authority, authenticity, and integrity as a source, and if we are to unravel its meanings and its actual and potential uses. The remainder of this chapter unpacks these three sets of critical questions to be asked of the material forms of written texts and argues that they can indicate the needs of users working with archives today.

Distributed Materiality

The first question we must ask on encountering a written archival text is: where is it and why is it here at this location? To consider where a text is located and how it came to be there is to consider its *distributed materiality*, which includes its place within the order and hierarchy of records, its provenance, and its collection context. Digital features of distributed materiality include the co-dependent storage systems upon which a digital artefact is contingent, the interrelated systems of servers, software, hardware, and networked environments that are, by their nature, distributed, and upon which any single digital textual entity is reliant. To consider digital distributed materiality requires access to a transparent record of when a text was added to a digital repository, the parties responsible, and, in the case of digitized (rather than born-digital) texts, why an analogue text was selected for digitization. The placement and provenance of an archival text determines its authority, authenticity, and how we interpret its meaning. Archive users have been intensely interested in a text's creation circumstances, provenance, preservation, and publication histories; that is, in the metadata (the collection context, catalogue data, and material distribution of texts, which is a subject of study in its own right). The fractures that exist between data and metadata remind us that metadata is data itself. To explicate these points, the following case study considers letters as a text-type that is numerous in archives and requires researchers to be especially alert to archival distribution. As the methods established for historical correspondence are often applicable to email and digital messaging, it is a textual form of special relevance today.

A letter's archival placement can be vital to decoding its meaning and function. While we can find examples where a letter was addressed to a person, sent to that person, and then reached that person and only them, such a straightforward line of transmission was as much the exception as it was the norm. There are innumerable examples in archives where the stated and actual destinations of a letter are not one and the same. The instructions for delivery stated on a letter should not be automatically trusted to show where a letter in fact reached or the role it later came to have. There are a multitude of reasons for the gaps that exist between stated and actual reception circumstances as letters were lost, intercepted, stolen, shipwrecked, forgotten, returned, forwarded, displaced, forged, never sent, sent in a contextualizing dossier of materials, or any combination of these scenarios. These were not exceptional circumstances but were part of the everyday operations of letter-writing. For example, during the period 1664–1817, numerous letters around the world were written, addressed, loaded onto ships, and sent out for delivery, but before they could reach their intended destinations were seized by enemy vessels at sea. Today c.160,000 of these seized and confiscated letters constitute the High Court of Admiralty Collection, at The National Archives of England and Wales, Kew (TNA). This vast collection of letters has been held in storage, largely untouched, with many letters still stuffed into mailbags sealed with wax, until in 2018 it became the subject of the Prize Papers Project.[8] Researchers are now cataloguing, transcribing, digitizing, and analysing these letters, sometimes reading them for the first time. The Prize Papers collection uniquely captures in time a global network. The catalogue metadata is already starting to uncover the tracks of international communication pathways, uncovering a global picture of the eighteenth-century world.

Capture by enemy ships is one way a cache of letters might enter an archival collection. Another is as procured intelligence and there is a long history of letters being intentionally gathered to provide information on matters of state security. The illustrations show the front and back of a letter from King James VI of Scotland written on 29 January 1581, sent to his mother Mary Stuart (known as Mary, Queen of Scots) during her captivity in England.

At this point in time, James was fifteen years old and his Catholic mother had already been a prisoner of the Protestant English Queen Elizabeth I for twelve years. In this letter, James VI paid his respects to his mother, asked her for advice, thanked her for a piece of jewellery (a ring) she had sent him, and told her that he had sent one in return. The content of his letter might prompt us to speculate on the political and personal nature of this royal mother–son relationship. But the most important piece of information about this letter is its archival location. The letter is held by the TNA in their collection of English State Papers Domestic and we know it must have entered this collection at an early date because it is endorsed (on the back: 'K[ing] of Scotts to his mother') in the hand of Thomas Phillippes, intelligencer to Elizabeth I. The collection context thus indicates that King James's letter is unlikely ever to have reached its intended stated recipient. If we wish to place this letter within a historical narrative we must envisage it in the hands of Elizabeth I, or her chief minister Lord Burghley, or their expert multilingual coder and intelligencer Thomas Phillippes, rather than in the hands of Mary, Queen of Scots, who never saw it. There are at least another ten intercepted letters from James VI to his imprisoned mother held in the TNA State Papers Domestic.[9] There are several hundred more letters, from a range of European correspondents, allies, and sympathizers, sent to the captive Scottish Queen but which never reached her as they were intercepted. These intercepted letters are now distributed across repositories in the Cecil, Cotton, Yelverton, and Harley collections, which are all sub-collections derived from the personal papers of Elizabeth's ministers and later incorporated into the State Papers. These intercepted letters include endorsements and are often accompanied by duplicate copies and deciphered versions penned in the handwriting of Elizabeth's officers and secretaries—their handwriting can be seen all over these documents. It is the evidence of collecting, gathering, networking, and intercepting documents (that is, the evidence of distributed materiality) that gives us this story of the control of information, more than the semantic content of the letter-texts themselves. To read only the content of the letter from James VI as if it were floating decontextualized from its material networks, would be to miss the main story that it tells, of interception, information control, and surveillance.

In these ways distributed materiality can inform how we map a collection as a whole or how we close-read an individual letter. Aware of these potentials, recent projects have begun to push the possibilities to be achieved through application of digital methods to letter-catalogue metadata. Especially compelling have been the findings of the Tudor Networks of Power Project, which has extracted catalogue

202 ALISON WIGGINS

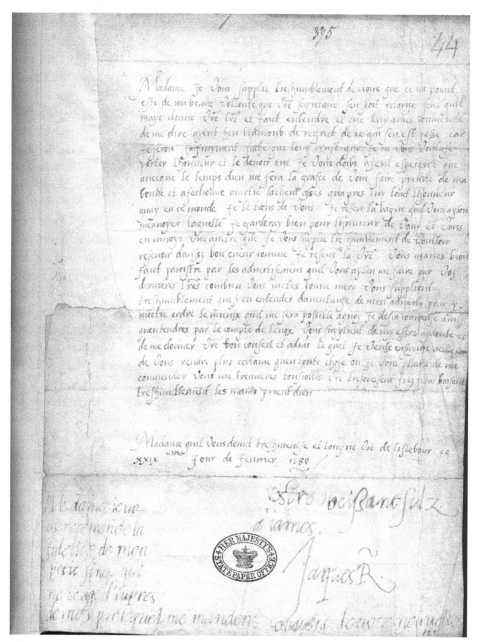

Figure 14.1 King James VI to his mother Mary, Queen of Scots, 29 January 1581. The inside of the letter, The National Archives, SP 53/11 f. 44r (reproduced with permission).

Figure 14.2 King James VI to his mother Mary, Queen of Scots, 29 January 1581. The outside address and endorsement of the letter. The National Archives, SP 53/11 f. 44v (reproduced with permission).

metadata from over c.130,000 Tudor letters from the State Papers 1485–1603, held as xml fields for date, addressee, and stated sender.[10] From quantitative analyses of these metadata fields, the project team have generated visualizations that represent the correspondence networks and collecting strategies of the Tudor State. It is a macro-level digital approach that brings a new perspective to these archival texts, one not apparent from analogue reading alone. Their analyses have enabled behavioural fingerprinting to reveal algorithmically individuals whose lives pattern-match with espionage activities or who were outliers to networks likely to reward deeper historical investigation.[11] Network methodologies represent a major paradigm shift in approaches to archival texts, one especially applicable to collections that are unwieldy or where the data content is unavailable. These include collections containing sensitive data protected by legislation or embargo but where the metadata is openly available and accessible to researchers. To take a well-known example, the contents of the archive of author Sir Salman Rushdie's personal papers and emails are embargoed, but the restrictions do not cover the metadata, such as email header information. As the header fields include persons, places, and the times his emails were sent, both to and from, they can be used to generate visualizations to map his network correspondence patterns over time.[12] As more researchers seek to apply digital methodologies to text corpora, archives may need to give as much consideration to the access, use, and handling of collection metadata as to collection data. The provision of collection data and metadata will give researchers not only the opportunity for close reading via analogue viewing interfaces, but also for distant reading and the application of digital analytics.

Digital methodologies change the scale at which we can analyse an archive's distributed materiality. Digital methods can further be transformative in the context of more traditional search-and-browse interfaces, as they offer opportunities to re-conceive the structure, order, and boundaries of a collection's distribution. The creation and curation of digital meta-collections can make it possible to right some of the gaps carried over by earlier collecting practices without damage to earlier collection structures or loss of the cultural information they carry. Several recent projects have augmented or re-shaped pre-existing archival finding-aids to off-set some of the biases of earlier cataloguing practices. For example, the Seward Family Digital Archive Project has digitally reunited the 'public' and 'private' sides of this archive of American nineteenth-century family papers.[13] The structure of the analogue collection, the paper-and-ink letters and documents and the microfilms, carries over outdated cataloguing practices from the 1950s, whereby documents related to servants and female family members were placed in the category of 'private' or 'family' papers, rendering them less visible to historians in a way that encompassed bias along race and gender lines. One outcome of seamless digital searching across a single interface has been the effect of re-incorporation of these 'private' or 'family' papers into the main body of the archive with the result that wives, daughters, sisters, aunts, and servants are more discoverable. The lives of these often-overlooked individuals (who included household members or

Figure 14.2 King James VI to his mother Mary, Queen of Scots, 29 January 1581. The outside address and endorsement of the letter. The National Archives, SP 53/11 f. 44v (reproduced with permission).

metadata from over c.130,000 Tudor letters from the State Papers 1485–1603, held as xml fields for date, addressee, and stated sender.[10] From quantitative analyses of these metadata fields, the project team have generated visualizations that represent the correspondence networks and collecting strategies of the Tudor State. It is a macro-level digital approach that brings a new perspective to these archival texts, one not apparent from analogue reading alone. Their analyses have enabled behavioural fingerprinting to reveal algorithmically individuals whose lives pattern-match with espionage activities or who were outliers to networks likely to reward deeper historical investigation.[11] Network methodologies represent a major paradigm shift in approaches to archival texts, one especially applicable to collections that are unwieldy or where the data content is unavailable. These include collections containing sensitive data protected by legislation or embargo but where the metadata is openly available and accessible to researchers. To take a well-known example, the contents of the archive of author Sir Salman Rushdie's personal papers and emails are embargoed, but the restrictions do not cover the metadata, such as email header information. As the header fields include persons, places, and the times his emails were sent, both to and from, they can be used to generate visualizations to map his network correspondence patterns over time.[12] As more researchers seek to apply digital methodologies to text corpora, archives may need to give as much consideration to the access, use, and handling of collection metadata as to collection data. The provision of collection data and metadata will give researchers not only the opportunity for close reading via analogue viewing interfaces, but also for distant reading and the application of digital analytics.

Digital methodologies change the scale at which we can analyse an archive's distributed materiality. Digital methods can further be transformative in the context of more traditional search-and-browse interfaces, as they offer opportunities to re-conceive the structure, order, and boundaries of a collection's distribution. The creation and curation of digital meta-collections can make it possible to right some of the gaps carried over by earlier collecting practices without damage to earlier collection structures or loss of the cultural information they carry. Several recent projects have augmented or re-shaped pre-existing archival finding-aids to off-set some of the biases of earlier cataloguing practices. For example, the Seward Family Digital Archive Project has digitally reunited the 'public' and 'private' sides of this archive of American nineteenth-century family papers.[13] The structure of the analogue collection, the paper-and-ink letters and documents and the microfilms, carries over outdated cataloguing practices from the 1950s, whereby documents related to servants and female family members were placed in the category of 'private' or 'family' papers, rendering them less visible to historians in a way that encompassed bias along race and gender lines. One outcome of seamless digital searching across a single interface has been the effect of re-incorporation of these 'private' or 'family' papers into the main body of the archive with the result that wives, daughters, sisters, aunts, and servants are more discoverable. The lives of these often-overlooked individuals (who included household members or associates who were female, African American, or former slaves, and those directly engaged with the abolitionist cause) can now be re-inserted into the historical narrative of the political life and abolitionist campaigning of this family.

Formal and Forensic Materiality

The second question we must ask on encountering a written archival text is: what is it and what are its integral physical forms and visual features? This is the question historians and literary scholars have most often been asking when they mention 'materiality'. That is, they are referring to an item's incontrovertible substantive properties and intrinsic physical make-up and appearance, which can more precisely be referred to as its *formal* and *forensic materiality*. Formal and forensic materiality can include a textual object's visual features, such as its style of script and decoration, and its physical properties, such as its type of writing surface, glue, binding boards, folding patterns, shape, and dimensions. Digital features of formal and forensic materiality would include a text's encoding conventions and the architecture of its data standards, and whether a textual object has been transformed from an analogue source.[14] Visual, physical, and formal features have communicative functions that extend well beyond a text's linguistic or informational content. Choice of font, handwriting style, layout, paper type, the colour of silk ribbon ties, or the design of an official stamp or wax seal: these forms and features can shape negotiations, function as markers of authenticity, politeness, deference, or social superiority, they can signal affinity with a movement or a tradition, display gravitas and official formality, build interpersonal connections, encourage community bonds, or say one thing whilst insinuating something else. Formal and visual features such as these can draw upon culturally specific etiquettes, procedural conventions, and traditions of textual communication.[15] To them we can add the stories embedded within a text's physicality that tell us about its production economics and life cycle. To undertake formal and forensic analysis is to decode these layers. The nature of the evidence means that this research has been transformed in recent years by technology. Our awareness of the physical and visual features of archival texts has burgeoned with the explosion of availability of images. The following discussion considers how advances in textual science and imaging techniques change what we can see and the data we can extract from a written textual object.

A photograph never shows us all of a written textual artefact. But a photograph can encourage us to look more closely at its visual features and offer us the opportunity for a slower and more sustained viewing experience.[16] Access to images encourages us to attend to visual features and affords comparison between the appearance of texts held in different repositories. The results have been especially rewarding for handwriting analysis. For example, in 2006 Linne Mooney published her claim that she had discovered the identity of the scribe who had, six centuries earlier, c. 1400, copied the earliest texts of Chaucer's *Canterbury Tales*; a scribe named Adam Pinkhurst. The groundwork for this discovery was over a decade of sustained comparison of digital images of handwritten copies of Chaucer's poetry, made available via The Canterbury Tales Project.[17] Every flourish, dot, curve, and turn of the quill was taken as evidence and used to track down and eventually discover Pinkhurst's name and biographical trace. The discovery has changed our view of medieval London's textual cultures and re-engaged questions around the labour of textual production, the connections between administrative and political writing, and the operations of government and bureaucracy. While the semantic content of the poetry tells us one story (Chaucer's), the visual appearance of the handwriting in which that poetry was copied tells us another (Pinkhurst's). That is, the text carries information about not only the thoughts of the author but also the identity and labour of its scribe and the politicised motivations behind its production. Pinkhurst's identity continues to be debated despite the extensive scrutiny of these texts, which is no surprise given that palaeographic and forensic handwriting analysis are notoriously controversial, and that digital photographs, while they enhance the evidential base, tend to raise rather than resolve questions.

Going well beyond what we can see with the naked human eye, the application of photographic techniques from the fields of medicine and forensic science gives us radically alternate views of the same archival text. Light shone through (rather than onto) hand-made paper allows us to see watermarks indicative of the date and origins of a text. Raking light has revealed previously unnoticed drypoint inscriptions scratched into vellum by lost early medieval readers. CT (computerized tomography) scanning has made it possible to look inside sealed bundles of documents and read them without causing invasive damage by opening. Forensic fingerprint analysis has identified the finger and palm impressions pressed into the still-warm wax of medieval seals, from which we have learnt how these communities came together to ratify documents.[18] Among the most important archival applications of photographic technology has been the use of multispectral imaging to recover illegible texts, such as palimpsests, erasures, and texts burned by fire or damaged by water. The numbers of such texts are huge: for the Western medieval period alone, we know of at least 60,000 unreadable European manuscripts.[19] Texts that have been brought back from near or total invisibility include those worn over time, such as the 1871 field diaries of David Livingstone bearing his eye-witness account of a slave-trade massacre in central Africa written on unstable decaying makeshift paper and inks. And they include texts in situations of jeopardy and precarity as a result of war, such as the c.300,000 African manuscripts smuggled out of Timbuktu. The Timbuktu manuscripts are listed under UNESCO's Memory of the World Register and are of such high cultural value that UN peacekeepers were assigned the rare charge of guarding them following the 2012–2013 Al Qaida attacks and occupation, where books were being burned. Having been taken away from one threat of destruction, the move from the dry climate of Northern Mali to the Southern capital of Bamako subjected them to the adverse effects of the humid environment at their new location. The ongoing international project in Bamako to conserve them has included digitization and multispectral imaging.[20] It is a use of technology contiguous with a centuries-long scholarly archival tradition of buying, collecting, copying, studying, and storing handwritten texts by the people of Timbuktu.[21] While digitization alone is not the answer, it can be part of the picture in response to threats to cultural heritage.

Going beyond visual reproductions, textual science takes us into the very fabric of an artefact, right down to the molecular level. The Covid-19 Pandemic made us acutely aware that substrates can carry not only writing but also particles, parasites, and genetic material, as libraries and archives quarantined books and papers as potential vectors of the SARS-CoV-2 virus.[22] And the TNA recently withdrew the Migrated Archives FCO 141 became of the evidence of pesticides on them.[23] But the biology and chemistry of archival texts can take us back into a long history. DNA analysis of the skin used for parchment pages and the beeswax used for seals, combined with chemical analysis of paint pigments, is now uncovering the trans-national trade routes and gendered labour behind medieval book production. EVA analysis of writing substrates has been used to extract 'invisible data' to trace drugs, pathogens, infections, and medicines, which tell hidden stories latent in historical textual objects.[24] One of the most compelling applications of technology in recent years has been from heritage scientists at the TNA, who applied X-ray fluorescence (XRF) spectroscopy to volumes of Victorian wallpaper samples in order to detect the presence of arsenic-containing compounds in paints, inks, and dyes. Fashionable vivid-green pigments such as 'Paris Green' and 'Emerald Green' were the subject of controversy in the nineteenth century, as questions raged over whether their metallic particles were poisonous. Only today has the truth been confirmed that these dyes were deadly to those who lived and worked around them. Solving this Victorian mystery has uncovered a hidden history of childhood illness and toxic living and working conditions, as poisonous pigments were used in numerous everyday items that ranged from playing cards, product packaging, labels, fabrics, lick-and-stick postage stamps, and book bindings.[25] Some of these archival items are regarded still to be dangerous and a risk for today's readers and archivists, given that the toxicity of arsenic does not diminish over time. Certain arsenic-laden artefacts have therefore been separated, boxed, or stored in ventilated cabinets, labelled as poisonous books, had their pages encapsulated in plastic, or been entirely digitized by workers wearing hazard suits.[26]

Performative Materiality

The third question we must ask on encountering a written archival text is: who owns this text, who is using and presenting it, and who were its earlier owners and readers (whether human, machine, or a combination)? To situate a document socially and culturally, is to consider its *performative materiality*. Performative materiality emphasizes texts as events and focuses upon moments of reading and of use, changing reception contexts, and the human and community interactions that determined what a textual object meant at certain points in time. Digital features of performative materiality include how an encoded textual object is processed, visualized, and displayed at any moment, which include the performances of algorithmic searching and the realities of which textual sources are retrieved when we perform a search, versus which are not. The constellation of problems with search algorithms and interfaces include their proven amplification of biases and inequalities along intersectional lines of class, race, and gender. These are among the most urgent issues of our time and we are learning, from scholars who include Ruha Benjamin, Catherine D'Ignazio, Lauren F. Klein, and Safiya Umoja Noble, how the performances of search and browse are shaping and structuring our everyday lives.[27] To consider what happens when we search, is to consider the gaps that can exist between the text itself, the text that is searched, and the text that is retrieved and displayed on screen following a search. These gaps tell us about the roles and responsibilities of editors, archivists, developers, computer scientists, resource providers, and users. To consider these points, the following discussion reflects upon the case of how scholarly digital editions and search-and-browse interfaces for historical texts function as instances of performative materiality.

The role of the scholarly editor is, by definition, to produce an accurate text of a document within a contextualizing interface or set of annotations that render it more intellectually accessible. One of the ways editors make texts more comprehensible is by creating indexes of lemmatized forms, modernized and normalized spelling versions, and lists of terms and topics to inform search and browse functionalities. To take the example of The Washington Papers, a multi-part scholarly project to create documentary editions of c.135,000 family papers associated with the life of America's first president George Washington (1732–1799).[28] Washington's letters and diaries are searchable via The Papers of George Washington Digital Edition interface, which provides options for language-specific searching (French or English), and for lemmatized, normalized, and thematic searching. These editorial indices are designed to assist researchers attempting to navigate the peculiarities of these historically and culturally distant texts. If we perform a keyword search for the word 'slavery' it yields only a handful of results from Washington's letters and diaries, as the word itself was rarely used in these texts. Yet as it is a major topic of enduring interest to researchers, the editorial index includes the word 'slavery' as an index item with links to over 500 documents relevant thematically. Thus the editorially constructed index generates results that are truer to the source than would be a free-text search.

Another set of editorial challenges are presented by Washington's financial accounts, searchable through The George Washington Financial Papers Project. For each financial account text, the digital resource provides two different transcriptions: a literal transcription and a regularized clear-text transcription, known within the project as the 'Document Text' and 'Data Text'. The 'Document

Text' represents character-for-character the text as it appears in the analogue archival document, whereas the 'Data Text' incorporates editorially expanded abbreviations and shorthand forms. The many instances of the word 'ditto' in the financial records are transcribed as 'ditto' in the Document Text, but, in the Data Text, are expanded to give the reference to the person or item indicated, such as to improve the effectiveness and accuracy of keyword searching. Users have the option to search the Document Text, or the Data Text, or both, or, alternatively, to browse thematic topic-based metadata from controlled vocabulary lists. They may also download the textual data themselves for off-line processing. The digital edition enables users to perform calculations based on the sums of money recorded in the financial accounts and to generate on-the-fly results. This digital edition therefore goes beyond the affordances of print: it is built around functionalities that are not possible in print and that require the user to interact with the encoded text.

The situation changes once we move beyond the careful attentions of the scholarly textual editor. Existing mass editions of written texts (driven by the private and commercial sectors, with very little input from universities or academic historians) have been labelled 'garbage dumps and train wrecks' of metadata that flatten and abstract texts that are decoupled from their contexts and structures of meaning.[29] Historians and digital scholars, who include Tim Hitchcock, Laura Mandell, Andrew Prescott, and Jane Winters, have pointed out the data gaps, design deficiencies, misleading search methods, and outright inaccuracies that pervade digitized collections of historical texts. The problems these present for historians include the fissures between the text that is actually searched (the imperfect, uncorrected, raw OCR) and the text that is displayed and returned to the user following a search (an image of the original archival document).[30] Such occlusions and misalignments have been persistently overlooked by uncritical users, resulting in examples of history written with a startling naivety about the source materials on which it is based. Users must keep continually in view the distortions and imbalances inevitable in sources and be aware that search results never give us straightforwardly realistic, statistically meaningful, or transparent social or historical truths. We have a responsibility to be aware of and to take account of the structures and interfaces of textual data, whether a meticulously prepared scholarly edition, an unedited corpus, or a rapidly scanned machine-read commercial resource, as these determine the methodologies that are appropriate to the data.

We perform roles when we work with archives, as do the digital interfaces (human- or machine-created) we work when we access archives online. The roles we perform, or that are coded into archival resources, create different output results from the same collection of texts. The knowledge carried by texts can be re-formed to produce new meanings and to take account of different perspectives, a view that has prompted creative digital archival projects that centre subjectivity. For example, The John Latham Archive since 2011 has offered three different interfaces to the same set of archival materials, each named and modelled after a Karamazov

Brother: Mitya, Ivan, and Alyosah. Whereas Mitya gives a random selection of documents as a slideshow, Ivan provides a structured index from controlled vocabularies, and Alyosha offers users an 'intuitive' tool that uses sound loops: it is a form of creative archiving modelled on contrasting modes of perceiving the world.[31] Another example is the War Child Archive, which presents mixed-media materials from the Second World War Evacuee Archive at the Museum of English Rural Life (MERL). The materials are curated through a series of conversations with Martin Parsons, the historian who gathered the collection, and with his friends and family, who speak about how the archive continues to shape their lives. At the centre is Martin's relationship to the archive, as his responses and attachment to items guide us through the archive's fluid boundaries, and ask us to locate emotion in the archive.[32] These curated archives give us ways to connect with archival texts beyond the binaries of search and results-based questioning. They offer models that lean towards centring the human, their own memories, discomforts, forms of empathy, personality, wishes, sense of connection with the past, and current needs. As we look to archival futures, the humanities will have an important role not only in the arenas of big data and textual science, but also in how we shape interfaces that encourage creativity, nuance, subjectivity, multiple perspectives, intuition, fictionality, and individual expression as frames for interpretation. The humanities show us how archives are layered, give rise to ambiguities, embed multiple perspectives, are polyvocal, and can connect us emotionally to the past.

Attending to Materiality

Written archival texts are not static blocks of information, they are animate sites of evolving knowledge. They are not containers of abstracted information and their meanings are not bounded by their syntax and grammar. Written texts carry meanings in their collection structures, linguistic forms and scripts, physical and visual features, and in the responses and appropriations of their readers and users. Written texts can be subjected to a wide range of material processes: they can be selected, collected, ordered, stored, tagged, edited, visualized, photographed, tested for pathogens and contaminants, quarantined, lit up, folded up, indexed, annotated, searched, displayed, narrated, and re-contextualized. Without attending to these material contexts, we have a boundless and formless cauldron of words that can be re-hashed and re-mixed for any number of meanings or purposes. If archives are to shift away from being storehouses towards being processing hubs, it will be the material boundaries, contexts, and interfaces that structure knowledge and make written archival texts meaningful and usable. The way that a society views the materiality of the archive is a marker of its human values around privacy, identity, rights, and representations. The decisions we make require a grounding in traditional scholarly and archival methods combined with current critical and ethical frameworks.

FURTHER READING

Paul Dornish, *The Stuff of Bits: An Essay on the Materialities of Information* (Cambridge, MA, and London: MIT Press, 2017)

Julia Flanders and Fotis Jannidis, eds, *The Shape of Data in the Digital Humanities: Modelling Texts and Text-Based Resources*, Digital Research in the Arts and Humanities (London and New York: Routledge, 2019)

Michael Suarez and H. R. Woudhuysen, eds, *The Book: A Global History* (Oxford: Oxford University Press, 2013)

Jennifer Wemigwans, *A Digital Bundle: Protecting and Promoting Indigenous Knowledge Online* (Regina: University of Regina Press, 2018)

NOTES

1. S. McRanor, 'Maintaining the Reliability of Aboriginal Oral Records and Their Material Manifestations: Implications for Archival Practice', *Archivaria* 43 (1997), 64–88; and B. Granville Miller, *Oral History on Trial: Recognizing Aboriginal Narratives in the Courts* (Vancouver, British Columbia: UBC Press, 2011). A linguistic account and conceptualization of writing is provided by T. Lillis, *The Sociolinguistics of Writing*, Edinburgh Sociolinguistics (Edinburgh: Edinburgh University Press, 2013).

2. These figures are from the project poster for *TAAL: Text Annotation for African Languages* by E. Ngué Um, F. K. Ameka, F. Menuta, M. Setaka, R. Ajah, R. Mabuya, S. Petrollino, and V. Nyst, presented at the workshop *Digital Humanities—The Perspective of Africa*, Lorentz Centre, Leiden, and at the international Alliance of Digital Humanities Organizations conference for the Digital Humanities in Utrecht, 1–5 and 9–12 July 2019, available online at https://dhafrica.blog/outcomes/. Further information can be found via the Network for the Digital Humanities in Africa https://dhafrica.blog/. A discussion of full stack language support is provided by S. R. Loomis, A. Pandey, and I. Zaugg https://srl295.github.io/2017/06/06/full-stack-enablement/.

3. Calls to decolonize typography are discussed at the Columbia University blog https://languagejustice.wordpress.com and by the Berkeley Script Encoding Initiative, http://linguistics.berkeley.edu/sei/.

4. An account of Text as a conceptual category, and its material conditions, is provided by E. Treharne and C. William, *Text Technologies: A History*, Stanford Text Technologies (Stanford: Stanford University Press, 2020), 1–7.

5. An illustrative discussion that considers the interpretative implications of changes in material form is provided by A. Prescott, 'Searching for Dr. Johnson: The Digitisation of the Burney Newspaper Collection', in S. G. Brandtzæg, P. Goring, and C. Watson, eds, *Travelling Chronicles: News and Newspapers from the Early Modern Period to the Eighteenth Century* (Leiden: Brill, 2018), 49–71; doi:10.1163/9789004362871_004.

6. J. Drucker, 'Performative Materiality and Theoretical Approaches to Interface', *Digital Humanities Quarterly*, 7.1 (2013), www.digitalhumanities.org/dhq/vol/7/1/000143/000143.html; P. M. Leonardi, 'Digital Materiality? How Artefacts without Matter, Matter', *First Monday*, 15.6–7 (2010), http://journals.uic.edu/ojs/index.php/fm/article/view/3036/2567; and S. J. Shep, 'Digital Materiality', in S. Schreibman, R. Siemens, and J. Unsworth, eds, *A New Companion to Digital Humanities* (Chichester: John Wiley, 2016), 322–330.

7. Digital Source Criticism, The Luxembourg Centre for Contemporary Digital History, University of Luxembourg, https://ranke2.uni.lu/.

8. The Prize Papers Project (www.prizepapers.de) is discussed in the report 'All at Sea: The Prize Papers as a Source for Global Microhistory', *German Historical Institute London Bulletin* 37.1 (2015), 124–135. A comparable example is discussed in Chapter 23 by N. Akkerman and P. Langman.

9. King James VI to his mother Queen Mary, 29 January 1581, TNA SP 53/11, f.44, accessed from *State Papers Online*, Gale, Cengage Learning 2019, Gale Document Number: MC4307883668. Analyses of the practice of running the Elizabethan state archives are provided by: N. Popper, 'From Abbey to Archive: Managing Texts and Records in Early Modern England', *Archival Science* 10.3 (2010), 249–266; and E. Williamson, 'Archival Practice and the Production of Political Knowledge in the Office of Sir Francis Walsingham', in A. Brendecke, ed., *Praktiken der Frühen Neuzeit: Akteure, Handlungen, Artefakte*, Frühneuzeit-Impulse 3 (Köln, Weimar, Wien: Böhlau Verlag, 2015), 473–484; doi:10.5282/ubm/epub.49319.

10. The project and its results are reported by R. Ahnert and S. E. Ahnert, 'Metadata, Surveillance and the Tudor State', *History Workshop Journal* 87 (2019), 27–51; doi:10.1093/hwj/dby033.

11. Further discussion is provided in Chapter 10 by R. and S. Ahnert.

12. This example is suggested and discussed by archivist E. R. Roke, 'Collections as Data', 16 July 2019, blog post for bloggERS, the Society of American Archivists [SAA] Electronic Records Section, https://saaers.wordpress.com/2019/07/16/collections-as-data/.

13. The Seward Family Digital Archive (https://sewardproject.org); the structure and content of the analogue archive is described at https://rbscp.lib.rochester.edu/william-henry-seward-papers.

14. Further explication can be found for example in Shep 'Digital Materiality'.

15. For example, M. A. Dias Paes, 'Legal Files and Empires: Form and Materiality of the Benguela District Court Documents', *Towards A History of Files, Administory, Zeitschrift für Verwaltungsgeschichte* 4 (2019), 53–70; J. Daybell, *The Material Letter in Early Modern England: Manuscript Letters and the Culture and Practices of Letter-Writing, 1512–1635*, Early Modern Literature in History (Basingstoke and New York: Palgrave Macmillan, 2012); L. Gitelman, *Paper Knowledge: Towards a Media History of Documents* (Durham and London: Duke University Press, 2014).

16. A discussion in favour of an iterative, considered, slower-paced approach to digitization, and that includes the Pinkhurst example, is provided by A. Prescott and L. Hughes, 'Why Do We Digitize? The Case for Slow Digitization', *Archive Journal*, Special Issue: Digital Medieval Manuscript Cultures, M. Hanrahan, and B. Whearty, eds (2018), www.archivejournal.net/essays/why-do-we-digitize-the-case-for-slow-digitization/.

17. L. R. Mooney, 'Chaucer's Scribe', *Speculum* 81 (2006), 97–138. Details of The Canterbury Tales Project are at www.dhi.ac.uk/projects/canterbury-tales/. The attribution to Pinkhurst is discussed and refuted by L. Warner, *Chaucer's Scribes: London Textual Production, 1384–1432*, Cambridge Studies in Medieval Literature (Cambridge: Cambridge University Press, 2018).

18. Historical watermarks are the subject of the Memory of Paper Project www.memoryofpaper.eu. The potentials of multi-directional imaging are discussed by B. Endres, *Digitizing Medieval Manuscripts: The St Chad Gospels, Materiality, Recoveries, and Representation in 2D and 3D* (Leeds: ARC Humanities Press, 2019). Video

demonstration of the use of RTI imaging are provided by B. Endres at https://lichfield.ou.edu. X-Ray scanning of locked documents has been applied successfully to ancient papyri scrolls and early modern letters and court rolls, for example by D. Mills and L. Fikkers in their analyses of the sealed Ward-16 Collection. The technology involved is documented in the 2016 and 2018 scientific reports published in *Nature*; doi:10.1038/srep27227 and doi:10.1038/s41598-018-33,685-4. The Imprint Project brings techniques and equipment from forensic science to bear upon thousands of wax seals from England c.1150–1350 wwwimprintseals.org.

19. These figures and examples are from The Lazarus Project (www.lazarusprojectimaging. com/) and Livingstone Online (www.livingstoneonline.org/spectral-imaging). One of the early multispectral imaging recovery projects was the Electronic Beowulf 4.1, ed. by K. S. Kiernan, British Library and University of Kentucky: ebeowulf.uky.edu/ (version 4 was published in 2015 but the project dates back to the early 1990s).

20. Details of the research centre at Bamako and the collaborative project Safeguarding the Manuscripts from Timbuktu are available at www.manuscript-cultures.uni-hamburg. de/timbuktu/ and www.tombouctoumanuscripts.org/.

21. A detailed account is by S. Jeppie, 'Making Book History in Timbuktu', in C. Davis and D. Johnson, eds, *The Book in Africa: Critical Debates* (Basingstoke: Palgrave Macmillan, 2015), 83–102.

22. Research to establish the detectability of the SARS-CoV-2 virus over time in circulated library materials is the subject of the REALM Project www.webjunction.org/explore-topics/COVID-19-research-project.html; I am grateful to Louisa Coles and Robert MacLean from Glasgow University Library Special Collections for this reference.

23. The Migrated Archives FCO 141 are discussed in the Introduction to this volume and a statement from the TNA is available at https://cdn.nationalarchives.gov.uk/documents/background-temporary-withdrawal-fco-141.pdf.

24. The ERC-funded Beasts2Craft project concerns biocodicology as an approach to book history, https://sites.google.com/palaeome.org/ercb2c; S. Zhang, 'Why a Medieval Woman Had Lapis Lazuli in Her Teeth: An Analysis of Dental Plaque Illuminates the Forgotten History of Female Scribes', *The Atlantic*, 9 January 2019; A. D'Amato, G. Zilberstein, S. Zilberstein, B. L. Compagnoni, and P. G. Righetti, 'Of Mice and Men: Traces of Life in the Death Registries of the 1630 Plague in Milano', *Journal of Proteomics* 180 (2018), 128–137; doi:10.1016/j.jprot.2017.11.028.

25. L. Hawksley, *Bitten by Witch Fever: Wallpaper & Arsenic in the Nineteenth-Century Home* (London: Thames & Hudson and The National Archives, 2016). H. Wilson, 'X-rays and Wallpapers: The Hunt for Arsenic', TNA blog post, 23 February 2017, https://blog.nationalarchives.gov.uk/x-rays-wallpapers-hunt-arsenic/. Victorian bindings of medieval and Renaissance books have been found to contain arsenic-laden pigments that were applied as a preservation practice, their noxious properties acting as a pesticide to keep away insects and vermin. I am grateful to those at the two-day workshop 'Materialities of digitizing in the heritage and archive sector', The National Archives / University of Glasgow, 28–29 June 2018, part of the TNA's *Digital Experimentation* series.

26. R. C. Kedzie, *Shadows From the Walls of Death: Facts and Inferences Prefacing a Book of Specimens of Arsenical Wall Papers*, Michigan State Board of Health (Lansing: W. S. George, 1874) is now digitized and available at the US National Library of Medicine, http://resource.nlm.nih.gov/0234555. Further examples are discussed by A. C. Meier,

'Some Books Can Kill', *JSTOR Daily*, 3 September 2018, https://daily.jstor.org/some-books-can-kill/.

27. R. Benjamin, *Race after Technology: Abolitionist Tools for the New Jim Code* (Cambridge: Polity, 2019); C. D'Ignazio and L. F. Klein, *Data Feminism* (Cambridge, MA: MIT Press, 2020); S. U. Noble, *The Intersectional Internet: Race, Sex, Class, and Culture Online*, 105 Digital Formations (New York: Peter Lang, 2016).

28. The Washington Papers (http://gwpapers.virginia.edu/), which includes: The Papers of George Washington Digital Edition (Rotunda, University of Virginia Press, 2008–2019) https://rotunda.upress.virginia.edu/founders/GEWN.html; and the George Washington Financial Papers Project, ed. by J. E. Stertzer, et al. (Charlottesville: Washington Papers 2017), http://financial.gwpapers.org/. The *Papers* digital edition version mirrors the content of and index in the print edition (there is no difference in their content, the screen-based version only providing an alternative to the inconvenience of physically handling the seventy volumes in the print series).

29. P. Gooding, 'Mass Digitization and the Garbage Dump: The Conflicting Needs of Quantitative and Qualitative Methods', *Literary and Linguistic Computing* 28.3 (2013), 425–431.

30. J. Winters and A. Prescott, 'Negotiating the Born-Digital: A Problem of Search', *Archives and Manuscripts* 47.3 (2019), 391–403; doi:10.1080/01576895.2019.1640753. A. Prescott, 'Searching for Dr. Johnson' (2018), from 67. T. Hitchcock, 'Confronting the Digital. Or How Academic History Writing Lost the Plot', *Cultural Studies and Social History* 10.1 (2013), 9–23. L. Mandell, 'Brave New World: A Look at 18thConnect', *Age of Johnson* 21 (2012), available at https://earlymodernonlinebib.files.wordpress.com/2012/10/mandell-fixed-final-oct-2012.pdf. 'Gender and Big Data: Finding or Making Stereotypes?', Keynote Lecture, 'Text Mining Across the Disciplines Conference', University of Michigan, 1 February 2016, available at https://deepblue.lib.umich.edu/handle/2027.42/117493. While in the case of Eighteenth-Century Collections Online (ECCO) the resource provider, Gale, is willing to work with researchers to provide raw versions of the data and to respond openly to queries about the data content and structure, there has nevertheless been a tendency for researchers to interrogate this and other resources uncritically.

31. Ligatus: John Latham Archive, University of the Arts, London, funded by the AHRC (2011) www.ligatus.org.uk/jla/node/74. A discussion is provided by A. Velios, 'Creative Archiving: A Case Study from the John Latham Archive', *Journal of the Society of Archivists* 32.2 (2011), 255–271; doi:10.1080/00379816.2011.619705.

32. War Child: Meditating on an Archive, T. Murjas and J. Rattee (2016), funded by the Arts Council of England with MERL and Reading Museum, https://war-child-archive.com.

CHAPTER 15

SOUND AND VISION

The Audio-Visual Archive

SIMON POPPLE

Much must survive, and much must be forgot

Bertolt Brecht (1955)[1]

Over the course of the past two decades the increasing digitization and online accessibility of archival materials, coupled with the digital nature of the archive itself has provoked something of an ontological crisis. What we have historically regarded as an archive is being questioned. The tradition of the material space in which we encounter material objects is changing, and as a consequence we have to adapt our understanding of what an archive was, is, and can be. We need to be open to new archival possibilities and practices. This entails reframing technologies of conservation and dissemination, changing curatorial responsibilities, and embracing the potential of shared ownership and new copyright arrangements. Above all else though, we need to address the shifting materialities of the archive and the archival object. Indeed, we are faced with some serious challenges in seeking to redefine the nature of the archival as we stand at 'the intersection of material and immaterial, the institutional and the independent, and most importantly, the theoretical and the practical'.[2]

In starting to deal with the question of apparent archival de-materialization in an unfolding digital landscape we can perhaps imagine an archival rebirth in a form of digital 'projection'—something emergent from traditional material repositories. In trying to make sense of such a concept we can use our experiences of the audio-visual archive to reframe and interpret post-material content and new sensorial affordances. At the heart of this approach is the unique nature of the audio-visual archive—a form that historically and materially stood apart from the mainstream.

As a disruptive and often immaterial form of archive it is not perhaps burdened with the same sense of material expectation. Its reliance on projection, performance, or broadcast technologies to fully explore its content means that it is often remote from the historicized experience we might expect. Consequently, its sense of difference might allow us to think experimentally about a range of pressing questions. For instance, how can we build on what has already been achieved in terms of the digital liberation of content, its creative potential, educational value and harness the sensory? What can the audio-visual archive teach us about the very nature of what an archive might be and how we can treat other types of material once a digital process has taken place? And what about the born digital that increasingly constitutes archival content? In the digital, where the predominant haptic experience is perceived as with the keyboard or the screen, can we think about our experience in different sensory contexts? Not just in terms of the archival space, but in the projection space and even our own remote embodied contexts? What types of new experience can we envisage? As David Toop wrote in relation to the digitization of the music archive, 'as the world has moved towards becoming an information ocean, so music has become immersive. Listeners float in that ocean...'[3]

This chapter will draw on current research and creative practice to model the future potential of the audio-visual archive and explore how the idea of the text as something fixed can be remade within a range of contexts. Drawing on examples of creative partnerships, experimental forms, and contested spaces, it will sketch a new vision of the archive as a self-mediated, sensual, and immersive experience increasingly integrated into social and cultural practice. It will try and answer the call issued by Elizabeth Edwards to make the archive 'a dynamic social object'.[4]

Ashes to Ashes: Authentic Dust 4.0

Arlette Farge, in common with many other authors has documented the sensory experiences of the archival encounter.[5] In so doing, she grounded them in a tactile co-present built around a direct contact with the past via the text within a defined archival space. The archive is thus a portal and a necessary condition of historical and intellectual telekinesis. Such a focus on the authentic physical and sensory archival encounter with books, manuscripts, and objects—their heft, smell, texture, and even taste—suggest a richly entropic sensual relationship with history through the object and its attendant accretions and palimpsests. The whole notion of the authentic grounds the veracity of interpretation and cements the attachment between researcher and their sources. As Walter Benjamin noted, what is vital is the, 'here and now of the original'.[6] What seems especially affecting is the sense of co-presence, the pairing of reader and written, often anchored in discomfort, isolation, and archival protocol. As Peter Lester notes, the archive is, 'a holistic experience, in which cognitive and physical reactions shape one another'.[7] The experiential is foremost to such an extent that it can forge a direct, spectral attachment to the archive through a realization that we are breathing in the skin of former scribes, archivists, and readers that constitute 90 per cent of the composition of archival dust. Unlike ordinary citizens who are only made of star dust, denizens of the archive are made of the DNA of the archive itself. In short, our traditional relationships are built on a process of 'deep hanging-out' within a materially bounded insular environment.[8]

These are very personal and heartfelt reflections that say a lot about the research experience and the 'historiographic'—but often veer too much towards the confessional and a therapeutic introspection that has become a common default position—which at worst becomes an act of narcissism. More a 'What I felt in the Archive' than a 'What I found there'. This though perfectly illustrates our traditional need to authenticate the experience of the archival space and ground the nature of the encounter in the physical—but it increasingly seems an irreconcilable antithesis in the current digital age. For some it is even a heresy. The archive is thus as a protective caul, a cocooning meta-text. What I want to suggest is that we set it and its content free.

Self-writing into the archive and a lesser focus on knowledge can have a tendency to privilege the author's own materiality in relation to meaning and make the embodied author the central focus.[9] We become seduced by a fetishization of space, environment, and content in an inexorably sensorial fix. As I think about this, I can't help falling into the same traps of contemplating and enjoying the privileged space of the historical private subscription library which is my own retreat into a form of archival reverie and faux nostalgia. I feel I need to stake a claim in the authentic space of the archive if I am to write about archival futures. I am comforted by its boundaries, peculiarities, and rituals. But just who is an archive for anyway? Surely not just archival crawlers alone? Accepting that we have a tendency to fetishize the archive and the archival encounter is an important first step to thinking beyond the archival encounter as an embodied experience. It shows us the traps we may have fallen into, and the potential of thinking outside the archive by holding our autobiographic tendencies in check. In confronting a love of the archive and the quest for authenticity that lurks everywhere, the Catalan photographer and theorist Joan Fontcuberta explored the idea of an archival imaginary in his 1987 project FAUNA. He created a 'lost' archive of strange creatures based on a discovery of the entire papers of an unknown scientist. As the exhibition catalogue states, this was a major find and the 'archive' very intriguing.

> In the summer of 1980, Joan Fontcuberta and his friend Pere Formiguera were staying in a gloomy old mansion being run as a B&B at Cape Wrath, in the far north of Scotland. During an afternoon exploring the damp basement of their accommodation, they discovered the archive of the work of Professor Peter Ameisenhaufen. The archive meticulously documented zoological discoveries made by Ameisenhaufen during his expeditions to different parts of the world, in search of 'exceptions' to Darwin's theory of evolution.[10]

Through the comprehensive manufacture of documents, medical notes, specimens, x-rays, film, and photographs Fontcuberta playfully dissembled and reassembled the notion of an archive through a creative process wholly grounded in a respect for the claims of authenticity. Using time-bound protocol and convention he constructed something that was both preposterous and compelling to reveal what is a problematic fetishization of our understanding of the archive. He did this to simulate a deeply rooted sense of historical authenticity complete with 'everything you expect' from a natural history display.[11] In a survey conducted at one of the exhibitions at the Barcelona Museum of Natural Science in 1989 '30% of the visitors aged 20 to 30, with university training, believed that some of our animals could have existed'.[12] Knowing exactly which triggers to push lies at the heart of Fontcuberta's practice and an innate acknowledgement of our need for the material experience. Other of his projects have similarly relied on the presentation of such material evidence as fossilized mermaid bones planted on the seabed and in mountainside fossil deposits in his *Sirens* (2000) project. Whilst his work is consciously playful it has serious intent—but does not cause offence and the deceptions are entertaining and fantastical. They are akin to the Victorian sideshow where we are desperate to suspend disbelief, finding ourselves in need of a new 'cultural logic of realism'.[13]

Fontcuberta's works are grounded in the tangible and as such enjoy a different status to this next example of the manufactured archive—one which was digitally constructed online. Artist Whaled Raad and a group of associates formed The Atlas Group (TAG) in 1999—a fictitious foundation that wanted to explore representations of the Lebanese Civil War.[14] Working with found and constructed documents the group established an online archive of the war which includes work attributed to fictional historians and witnesses. Responses to this archive were extremely hostile—not just because of the serious subject matter but because the 'hoax' was taken seriously. The intent was to provoke a response to a largely underreported war and to think about the orthodoxies associated with the archive as a site of historical instruction and collective consciousness. Raad described the archive as a propagation of 'cultural fantasies erected from the material of collective memories'.[15] The performative nature of the archive and associated screenings, exhibitions, and publications further added layers of authenticity until the real nature of the archive was uncovered.

The bitter response to their act of constructive deception reveals a perception of the archive as a sacred and historically grounded institution. An institution perhaps only guaranteed by a tangible, physical repository and place of documentary certainty. Ultimately this is what both faux-archives lack (although ironically, they are now themselves archived). Recent events illustrate the strong association we make between the archaeon, the place of archival arrest, and the archive and the sense that the two are synonymous in their promise of authenticity. The deep historical trauma of the loss of the great Library at Alexandria in 48 BC, and the painfully recent destruction of Brazil's 200-year-old Museu Nacional in September 2018 remind us

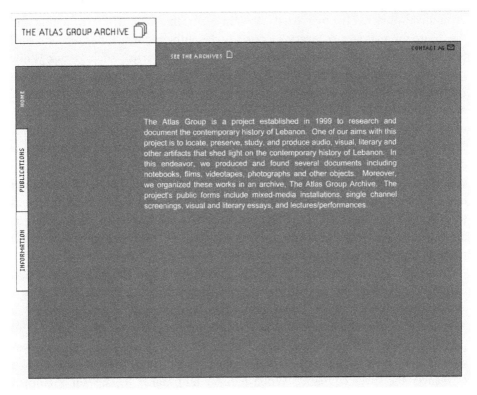

Figure 15.1 Title page of the Atlas Group Archive from https://commons.wikimedia.org/wiki/File:Online_archive_of_The_Atlas_Group.png accessed 14 February 2022. CC BY-SA 4.0.

of talismanic value of the archaeon. The shock and awe of the building, its historical and cultural status and reputation which is imbricated in the fabric of national identity. Marina Silva, a former Brazilian minister likening the event to 'a lobotomy of the Brazilian memory'.[16]

Sound and Vision: Archival Newbies and the Slippery Text

In common with the 'digital' the Audio Visual (AV) archive perhaps lacks an authenticity granted by traditions of emplacement and material acts of encounter. They are archives populated by 'slippery texts' and increasingly distributed through streaming platforms and consumed on portable devices. They are slippery as they have no real physical materiality themselves and the attachment to memory is devoid of the historical contexts of the framing archival space. The server rack lacks the romanticism of the wood panelled reliquary, the artefact 'no longer bound to any given physical context'.[17] They are also a cause of an enhanced anxiety in terms of their ephemerality and lack the auratic and physical presence of the manuscript or archival object. This may partly explain a current vogue for retro-mania and the desire for analogue recovery—a crisis of the authentic which has seen a return to analogue film and sound recording and some music artists such as Jack White recording on shellac and Neil Young regressing to the wax cylinder. Another material return in the form of cassette culture marks the retrofitting of the haptic and an act of archival consubstantiation. We have also seen the rise of analogue simulation apps for film and photography on mobile devices—with built in 'archival' filters. Hipstamatic and Instagram both possess these superpowers. 3D printing is another resurrection technology. Fears over longevity and stability in the digital are creating a desire for a more heightened sense of materiality. The digital revolution has occasioned a closer focus on the materiality of the archival text and threatens to eviscerate the presence of the archive itself. This feeds a return to analogue as a reaction to the dematerialization of knowledge and culture as embodied in the physical text and physical archival space.

Similarly, cinema has seen the resurgence of thirty-five and seventy mm film making driven often by aesthetic recoveries and preservation strategies amongst archives and major studios.[18] The special nature of the audio-visual marks out a different type of archival territory in terms of format, process, engagement, and perhaps, intellectual status and historical value. Historically film archiving was seen as an inconvenient practice and for many years nitrate film was melted down to recover the silver content.[19] When pioneer film-maker R. W. Paul attempted to establish the world's first film archive in the British Museum in 1897 he was sent away with a flea in his ear, the press commenting that

> ... the ordinary work of the print-room at the British Museum is quite disorganised by the collection of animated photographs that have been pouring in upon the bewildered officials .... Seriously, does not the collection of rubbish become a trifle absurd?[20]

It was widely seen, like recorded sound—as a commercial sideshow—something to amuse but not as a matter of historical record. Film was late to the archival game—too ephemeral, too recent, too disruptive, and too transitory to be seriously considered. Indeed, AV sources—film in particular—are still often seen by historians and programme makers as forms of illustrative content within their own disciplinary frames often wildly distorting the nature of the material to fit a particular narrative. We have only recently, in archival terms, come to validate these texts as legitimate archival sources that have found their place within the broader dimensions of accepted scholarship and cultural value.[21]

AV archives are the same but different. They have always had a different type of presence, different materialities based on the varied technologies that reveal their very essence. Akin to the scorched papyri of Herculaneum they need special tools for reading. They demand to be taken out of their archival sarcophagi and projected back into the world. Their exceptionalism is valuable and the fact that their trans-materiality often holds them apart from corporeal, embodied archival texts and traditions means that they are ripe for experimentation. Central to this notion of exceptionalism is the inbuilt quality of the need to project them beyond their original textual state to make them intelligible. A projection being seen as something thrown 'out' or an emanation from a physical or metaphysical source via intermediate technology/gies to become simultaneously tangible and intangible. Projection is used here as a unifying concept that can point the way towards new archival futures that combine seemingly contradictory contexts, forms, and materialities. The specificities of the audio visual can be used to frame this.

Trying to pin down the illusive presence of the projection and its tangibility is a slippery process itself. In 1978 artist and photographer Hiroshi Sugimoto began to produce a series of photographs under the title *Theatres* which used extreme long exposure techniques to capture the duration of a projected movie on a range of cinema screen across the USA. What is revealed in the trace of the movie is two hours-worth of projected images condensed into an iridescent glow of light on the screen. The text once projected defies re-capture. The artist Idris Khan deployed a different approach to recording the nature and duration of sound when he photographed the entirety of a musical score in one multiple exposure image. Khan's *Mozart ... Requiem* (Venice 2005) captures the complexities and temporality of sound in terms of the static blur of accreted notes and patterns but is at the same time unintelligible in terms of the underlying musical score. Both artists pose, in their different strategic approaches, the following question—what exactly is the AV archival text? Is it the transport that carries the text, is it the various technologies that can unlock it—or is it only constituted in the presence of a performer and an audience?

In answer we can claim that all form part of a complex system of factors and archival elements. Unlike a book, which is complex enough, the process of reading a film or listening to a shellac disc or to a series of ones and zeroes has more that is fallible or impenetrable if one element is missing or corrupted. There is also an element of variation and mutation in each encounter so that the re-playing of the text or projection is never the same. What kind of experience—what kind of exchange is lost in the transaction? And what is gained? One recent project has taken some of these problems in relation to recorded sound and addressed them through unifying tangible and intangible elements—technologies, archival files, and performativity or projection. *Citizen Bravo* (aka Matt Brennan) uses a specially constructed sculpture composed of historical playback devices to mix and remix elements though a piece of musical sculpture.

SCI★FI★HI★FI is what its name suggests: a science-fiction inspired hi-fi system that can play seven of the most historically significant recording formats (Edison wax cylinder, 78 rpm disc, vinyl LP, cassette tape, compact disc, mp3 on hard drive, and streaming remotely from the cloud). It explores how playback technology changed the parameters of musical work at different moments in history: from two minutes of lo-fidelity mono sound on wax cylinder, to a streamed algorithmic remix that is unstoreable and infinite in length.[22]

From the finite to the infinite in duration—defying a fixed archival process—it produces ongoing performance and revels in an ongoing sonic mutability. The coding-music nexus in which created sound is potentially endless poses again questions about what constitutes the nature of the underlying text and what if anything should or can be archived. The algorithm itself, a formless code is the obvious though intangible answer. However, if one must, one can locate the materiality of digital music in the energy and infrastructure used to power its online existence.[23] The experimentation and exposure of multiple elements and factors really does suggest the future potentialities of the AV archive and also the open nature of the experience and the co-production of distributed knowledge as the archive is performed, circulated online, and unbound in a never-ending range of *loci*.

Always Crashing in the Same Car: The Archive Unbound

> If the archive can serve as no more than a tomb of remnants and traces, where is the place for that which does not survive or which by virtue of the archive, is forgotten?[24]

Pioneer internet archivist Rick Prelinger recently asked a critical question in relation to the materiality of film as he considered the fate of large bodies of nitrate prints in an increasingly digital landscape. Recounting a visit to a large storage facility and the complexities of dealing with volatile nitrate prints he provocatively asks whether we can dispense with the physical artefact once it has been digitized.[25] And perhaps by implication—what and when are we allowed to forget? Do we have to keep everything or are some things allowed to pass from material to immaterial but still remain innately tangible like cinema. The prosthetic qualities of the archive, technologies like the gramophone record and the film camera, as Freud pointed out, are extensions of natural memory—a portable archive that can reboot the subconscious.[26]

So, are sets of new archival practice like digitization and digital dissemination, a creeping reliance on software and algorithmic structures—really so problematic—so existential? Or should we accept change and the promise of new experiences, new traditions, and new cultural memories which entail forgetting or loss? The sensory nature of decay and transformation is akin to the mushroomed rot of an old house or of an elderly relative slowly letting go. They are with us in another form. Similarly, can we eventually mourn the loss or corruption of noughts and zeroes—or the failure of digital infrastructure in the same way? Perhaps at the present, the best thing to do is to accept a plurality of practices and explore the dialogues and affordances that exist in the diminishing gulf between them. Even to inhabit the archival space digitally—at a remove—is to at least understand and picture the origins of the text or artefact and make a connection between the host institutions, the objects, and their place in a collection. Being able to virtually glimpse the organizing structures of the institution is better than no experience of it at all.

Breaking Glass: Translation and New Modes of Archival Projection

We live cinematic and electronic lives ... a radical alteration to the forms of our culture's previous temporal and spatial consciousness and our bodily sense of existential 'presence' to the world, to ourselves and to others.[27]

The same applies to the archive and our task is, as Elizabeth Edwards has noted, to 'translate the material saliency of the archive into the digital environment' through the careful exploration of what can be preserved in the digital that does not eviscerate past tradition.[28] However we must guard against the sense that the digital is simply a proxy for the authentic, ice to the fire of the real thing. To ensure that we are not trapped in a series of oppositional and countervailing debates about the relative values of the archive as either one thing or the other we would do well to think about the potential of dealing with different concepts of materiality and presence, and look at recent moves within the AV sphere to celebrate experimentation. And in so doing can we reconcile these practices, respect their distinctive nature, and harvest their continually intersecting bounty?

The underlying proposition is thus to take the 'archive out of the archive' and through so doing stage an intervention in this debate through forms of creative and re-creative practice.

Perhaps one of the earliest and most affecting interventions in the materiality of the archive and an attempt to make it, through appropriation and excavation, relevant to the moment was Bertolt Brecht's *War Primer* (1955). Published a decade after the end of World War Two and at the height of the Cold War it was a series of archival images of conflict culled from magazines, books, and archives given new contextual meaning through the addition of Brecht's own strongly pacifist poetry. It is a complex and layered polemic constructed of the seemingly ephemeral image. Seen by some as a betrayal of the archive at the time it has come to represent how images and meaning can be taken outside their original contexts and frames of reference. In 2011 Adam Broomberg and Oliver Chanarin's *War Primer 2* (2011), winner of the Deutsche Börse Prize in 2013, appeared as an update of Brecht's assemblage, and this time its focus was the so-called war on terror.[29] The original work was superimposed by a series of new images—largely digital in nature taken from online sources to reflect the nuances of the current conflict, the originals still visible beneath these new texts. The result is clearly not a desecration of a

Figure 15.2 Michael C. Coldwell, Cross Templar Street, 1901–2017. From *The Remote Viewer* exhibition at the Brotherton Gallery, Leeds, 5 October 2018. Reproduced courtesy of the author. Created using archival materials courtesy of University of Leeds Special Collections (photographs of properties situated in the Quarry Hill unhealthy area, taken December 1900 and January 1901).

desecration—but an ongoing dialogue through the archive and historical condition. A layering of meaning and context that looks to the past and future, combining the analogue and the digital.

Both versions of the *War Primer* illustrate the potential of different approaches to the use and reuse of the archive and the ways in which artistic intervention opens up new insights into what is possible. Those who use the archive as a central feature of their practice and as a reflexive tool to engage with its ontology are particularly illuminating. One such artist Michael C. Coldwell explores the boundaries between the material and immaterial archive through re-photography, hauntological filmmaking, and electronic sound and music. Coldwell has been working with a series of historical photographic archives in his home city of Leeds as the basis for filmmaking and the re-photography of the changing landscapes of the city and its environs. Drawing on recent works using the Godfrey Bingley Archive at the University of Leeds Special Collections his work certainly fulfils the promise of the archive outside the archival context. We discussed the potential of the different material constructions of the digital archive and the consequences of its altered states.[30]

Popple: Can you envisage a different type of living digital archive, one that is co-produced, distributed, and constantly projected and re-projected, flipped, remixed, and made vital?

Coldwell: As soon as the archive becomes digital it shifts into a different networked reality, transformed and infinitely transformable by other nodes. Digitization grants historical assets and artefacts a new audience and a new extended afterlife, but the resulting traces are then extremely malleable—any user can copy and potentially edit the data. Therefore, while digitization increases the chances of survival it cannot guarantee precise preservation and may in fact accelerate its opposite. While digital artefacts do not crumble and decay like physical ones and seem to be frozen in time at the point of capture, they can be eroded in other ways.

This first question certainly drew out the benefits of digital access and the potential to develop new audiences and new forms of association—but also a note of caution in terms of the vulnerabilities of the digital file as a form of preservation and guarantor of longevity—meaning that the digital protection of material alone was not enough. This pushed our discussion onto what is realistically achievable in the digital; and what this does to the material traditions of the archive. We were both interested in the potential of the digital and digital practices to unbind the orthodoxies around archival texts whilst respecting the value of the material.

Popple: What about the idea of the text as something fixed that can be digitally remade within a range of contexts—could this be part of the longer-term future potential of the audio-visual archive?

Coldwell: The archive can so easily be cited and appropriated in online popular culture that this not only changes the nature of archives but culture itself. This increasing cultural engagement with the digitized past has now been with us for some time, and we have seen a retrospective turn alongside new forms of music, art, and cultural exchange that depend entirely on the digital appropriation of past media. Projecting the archive into different locations, and in different ways to conventional museum exhibits, has the potential to create temporary spaces in which people can engage with memory socially in places with direct links to the memories being revisited.

Here the strategy of taking the 'archive out of the archive' and into new contexts, creative and historical practices really resonated, and we acknowledged the concept of projection as a central practice and metaphor for the process of digital experimentation.

Popple: Could the archive be a self-mediated, sensuous and immersive experience?

Coldwell: Projection installation works can create immersive and sensuous experiences of the archive which are easily shared in a physical space—the technology can be invisible, and therefore doesn't pull focus or form a barrier between participants.

The projection of Coldwell's archival films in situ within the changed city space makes perfect sense and the experience of seeing the archive liberated from the album or server could help resolve many of the anxieties that surround digitization and the perceived loss of the material encounter for anxious archivists and purists alike. These extra-archival encounters allow archival materials back into meaningful contexts and into the sites and places from which their content was first 'removed'. As Sontag said, to photograph is to take something away, in extremis it is an act of violence/violation.[31] To archive feels like something similar but to de-archive is perhaps restorative. Of course, to do it digitally rather than materially keeps everyone happy and protects the essential sanctity of the 'original'. Whilst Coldwell seeks to take the archive back to its former sites and reconstitute an emplaced and mutable series of projection other strategies also increasingly exist whereby the archival space itself emerges from the depths of an institution and becomes a public space in which archival and library begin to become one entity.

Archives+ in Manchester is a core example of this new tendency to seek to make the archive a place of un-arrested knowledge and to provide open access to material, immaterial, and creative expressions of the archive. Founded in 2014 and funded by the Heritage Lottery Fund it is an amalgamation of several archives and collections within the public space of Manchester Central Library where all services are accessible physically and digitally in a purpose designed atrium that allows users to

Figure 15.3 Archives+ at Manchester Central Library front entrance; image reproduced by permission.

mix a broad range of sources and experience performances as well as take refreshments.[32] This is a long way away from the reserved silence of most archives. The different nature of the Archives+ whose central collection encompasses the North West Regional Film Archive similarly suggests a different way of experiencing the archive as a concept and the release of the archive into the public sphere.

Its Director, Marion Hewitt provided answers to a series of questions that point to the impact this has had on the conceptualization of the AV archive and a possible model for others to explore in respect to the presentation and use of film materials.[33]

Popple: Does the space the archival space effect the way in which people experience or respond to film?
Hewitt: The online experience is totally different to a cinema screening, and different again to something like the NWFA Pods which are to be found in Archives+. All are satisfying to people in their different ways, providing a communal and shared experience, or a more private, intimate experience.

Archives+ offers a range of means to engage with film and also the ability to contextualize materials hosting access to its own regional collection and the National Film Archive through a regional BFI Mediatheque. The different materialities of their own collection—in both print and digitized form are integrated and are co-actively presented.

Popple: Are films intrinsically different from other forms of archival texts such as book and manuscripts in the ways in which they can be experienced?
Hewitt: Yes—they require more interpretation probably; and being time-based material, they need more time and focused attention than words or pictures, and of course the essential playback equipment.
Popple: Are digital files an effective substitute for the projection of film?
Hewitt: The ubiquity of digital file copies of cine film has made an enormous difference to the accessibility of moving images. Pragmatically, they are a perfectly acceptable substitute since they provide access where there may be none via cine film. The original cine film requires careful conservation and storage to ensure its survival—especially when it is the only one known (particularly true of e.g. amateur film and regional TV news). There are purists who tend to fetishize projection of cine film, and in its place, this is an atmospheric experience—however to ensure access to the widest range of material this is impossible. It's akin to the revival of vinyl records and VHS cassettes perhaps—niche, but not sufficiently inclusive.

The concluding reflection on inclusivity and the pluralistic nature of the archive as represented by Archives+ powerfully illustrates the changing nature of the AV archive and by implication, the nature of all archives over time.

The New Age: Conclusions

From the archive as a repository of documents to the archive as a dynamic and generative production tool.[34]

Music and audio archives give me more pleasure than just about anything else. I have my own unique and idiosyncratic archive that begins with a collection of several Edison Wax cylinders selected due to their pristine condition, the vivid packaging, and the legend that 'Edison Records Echo All Over the World'. I have and have never had any intention of listening to these artefacts. I am secure in the knowledge that they exist as examples of the first form of recordable sound and fulfil a personal fascination with recording technologies and the birth of mass audio-visual media. They are also very decorative objects. Similarly, I have collection of self-recorded cassettes of John Peel sessions from the 1980s with no means of playing them. Both are an innate and precious object within my personal music archive. I can access and recover their contents through a variety of online digital sources—some archival such as the National Sound Archive—some enthusiast's blogs and some commercial streaming platforms such as Spotify and YouTube where many old Peel sessions reside.

But what reconciles them and allows me to make these emotional, cultural, and historic connections is the projection of those sounds via whatever source or technology that facilitates them. It grounds them in my presence and for a brief moment—the duration of a song or a brief snatch of dialogue—I am co-present with text. I am having an embodied experience in a range of sensory contexts of my own choosing and opening up the potential to create a new experience on every occasion dependent of where I am, what I am engaging with and my current emotional state. I might be in my former teenage bedroom at my parent's house wallowing in nostalgia, driving my car, walking through woodland at dusk. Whatever the projection of the archive is with me—it is not fixed and determining its specific framing of the text—seducing me with its own particular allure and materiality. I have the material evidence of the text at hand if I need it for re-assurance—through technological forms of recording format or through the presence of a playback device so I am materially in contact. My understanding is uniquely situated and resituated with every encounter, every archival playback. There are constant dilemmas and rejections also—sets of negotiations between points of memory, reference, and source. And I can always look back to the artefactual. For instance, the download code offers access whilst the vinyl artefact is a guarantor of the authenticity and pedigree of the text that is too precious or valuable to violate. Its meaning extricated and digitized, made spectral.

The spectral is hard-wired into the audio-visual. You can hold and smell nitrate film cans—or appreciate the cold feel of shellac and vinyl but cannot get beyond the essence of meaning and experience of the support technology or virtual presence.

Figure 15.4 'Comforting' archival media supports © Simon Popple 2022.

You can fetishize the support material and technologies in these cases (and some people really do—buying albums that they never intend to play) but what about code or the projected text itself once freed from its support via the appropriate technology? What about the creative/expressive substrate that is its raison d'être in the first place? To embrace all forms of the archival we must then be open to a range of potentially transgressive practices that are part a consequence of their ontology but increasingly products of a newer spirit of exploration and experimentation. As Prelinger has advocated in his recent manifesto, we should see AV archives 'as places of possibility, as places where we might seek to perform struggle, expose presentism, make theories actionable, refuse dominant narratives of inevitability, and imagine and stage a broad spectrum of futures'.[35] The AV archive has much to suggest here and fuses more traditional outlooks and practices with boundary pushing activities—acting as a core point of confluence—being on its own terms a composite of the material and immaterial, the ephemeral and the grounded, the projected and embedded. To borrow Tom Gunning's cinema of attractions model of the competitive nature of early film—we should now prescribe an archive of attractions.[36] One that luxuriates in the endless possibilities of a deeply phantasmagoric experience bounded only by perceptual constraint, allowing us to float in our own archival oceans.

FURTHER READING

Ernst van Alphen, *Staging the Archive: Art and Photography in the Age of New Media* (London: Reaktion Books, 2014)

Elizabeth Edwards and Janice Hart, eds, *Photographs Objects Histories: On the Materiality of Images* (London: Routledge, 2004)

Penelope Houston, *Keepers of the Frame: Film Archives* (London: BFI, 1994)

Nicola Liberati, *The Creation of Digital Materiality: A Phenomenological Investigation of Augmented Reality and Its Effects on Society* (Milan: Mimesis International, 2022)

Simone Osthoff, *Performing the Archive: The Transformation of the Archive in Contemporary Art from Repository of Documents to Art Medium* (New York, Dresden: Atropos Press, 2009)

Simon Reynolds, *Retromania: Pop Culture's Addiction to Its Own Past* (London: Faber and Faber, 2012)

Roger Smither and Catherine A. Surowiec, eds, *This Film Is Dangerous: A Celebration of Nitrate Film* (Bloomington: Indiana University Press, 2002)

NOTES

1. B. Brecht, *War Primer* (London: Verso Press, 2017), 71.
2. A. Lison, 'Contesting "The Archive", Archives, and Thanatarchy', in A. Lison, M. Mars, T. Medak, and R. Prelinger, *Archives* (Minneapolis: University of Minnesota Press, 2019), viii.
3. D. Toop, *Ocean of Sound* (London: Serpent's Tail Press, 2018), 3.
4. E. Edwards, 'Photographs: Material Form and Dynamic Archive', in C. Caraffa, ed., *Photo Archives and the Photographic Memory of Art History* (Berlin: Deutscher Kunstverlag, 2011), 54.
5. A. Farge, *The Allure of the Archives* (New Haven: Yale University Press, 2013).
6. W. Benjamin, 'The Work of Art in the Age of Mechanical Reproduction', in H. Arendt, ed., *Illuminations*, trans by H. Zohn from the 1935 essay (New York: Schocken Books, 1969), 214.
7. P. Lester, 'Of Mind and Matter: The Archive as Object', *Archives and Records* 39.1 (2018), 73–87; doi:10.1080/23257962.2017.1407748.

8. C. Geerz, 'Deep Hanging Out', *New York Review of Books*, 2 October 1998; www.nybooks.com/articles/1998/10/22/deep-hanging-out/.

9. N. Moore, A. Salter, L. Stanley, and M. Tamboukou, *The Archive Project: Archival Research in the Social Sciences* (London: Routledge, 2016).

10. National Media Museum exhibition notes www.scienceandmediamuseum.org.uk/what-was-on/joan-fontcuberta-stranger-fiction.

11. National Media Museum exhibition notes.

12. Joan Fontcuberta interview with Diane Neumaier [1991]. D. Campany, *Art and Photography* (London: Phaidon, 2003), 285.

13. V. Sobchak, 'The Scene of the Screen: Envisioning Photographic, Cinematic, and Electronic "Presence"', in S. Denson and J. Leyda, eds, *Post-Cinema: Theorizing 21st-Century Film* (Falmer: Reframe Books, 2016), 8.

14. N. Lambouris, 'Fabricating: Facts and Fiction in the Work of the Atlas Group', *photographies*, special issue on photography, artists, and museums, 7.2 (2014), 163–180; doi:10.1080/17540763.2014.943022.

15. The Atlas Group, 'Let's Be Honest, The Rain Helped'. C. Merewether, *The Archive: Documents of Contemporary Art* (London: Whitechapel Gallery, 2006), 180.

16. A. Horton, '"A Lobotomy of the Brazilian memory": Devastating fire destroys Rio's National Museum', *The Washington Post*, 3 September 2018: www.washingtonpost.com/world/2018/09/03/lobotomy-brazilian-memory-devastating-fire-destroys-rios-national-museum/.

17. M. P. Schofield, *Aura and Trace: The Hauntology of the Rephotographic Image* (PhD thesis, University of Leeds, 2018), 180.

18. See for example Quentin Tarantino's use of 70 mm film.

19. P. Houston, *Keepers of the Frame: Film Archives* (London: BFI, 1994).

20. *The Westminster Gazette*, 20 February 1897.

21. J. Baron, 'Contemporary Documentary Film and "Archive Fever"': History, the Fragment, the Joke', *The Velvet Light Trap* 60.1 (2007), 13–24.

22. M. Brennan, *Citizen Bravo: A Music + Research Experiment* www.citizenbravo.com/research.html, accessed 20 August 2019.

23. K. Devine, *Decomposed: The Political Ecology of Music* (Cambridge, MA: MIT Press, 2019).

24. Merewether, *The Archive*, 12.

25. Prelinger, 'Archives of Inconvenience', in Lison et al., eds, *Archives*, 9.

26. S. Freud, 'Notiz über den "Wunderblok"', Internationale Zeitschrift für Psychoanalyse 11 (1925a [1924]), 1–5; A note upon the mystic writing pad. SE, 19, 227–232.

27. Sobchak, 'The Scene of the Screen', 2.

28. Edwards, 'Photographs', 48.

29. https://mackbooks.co.uk/products/war-primer-2-paperback-br-adam-broomberg-oliver-chanarin.

30. M. C. Coldwell. Interview with the author 12 August 2019.

31. S. Sontag, *On Photography* (London: Penguin Books, 2002), 4.

32. Further information about Archives+ is available from their Facebook site (www.facebook.com/archivesplus), Twitter feed (https://twitter.com/archivesplus), and blog (https://manchesterarchiveplus.wordpress.com/).

33. M. Hewitt. Interview with the author, 9 August 2019.

34. S. Ostoff, *Performing the Archive: The Transformation of the Archive in Contemporary Art from Repository of Documents to Art Medium* (New York, U.S.A. and Dresden, Germany: Atropos Press, 2009), 11.
35. Prelinger, 'Archives of Inconvenience', in Lison et al., eds, *Archives*, 4.
36. T. Gunning, 'Cinema of Attraction[s]: Early Film, Its Spectator, and the Avant-Garde', *Wide Angle* 8.3–4 (1986), 63–70.

CHAPTER 16

DOORS INTO THE ARCHIVES

Material Objects and Document Collections

CATHERINE RICHARDSON

This chapter explores the history of the sometimes uncomfortable and anomalous place that material objects occupy within contemporary archives. It investigates some of the ways in which they enter the archive in the first place, their relationship with other parts of the collections, and the challenges and opportunities which they present for a deeper engagement with those collections. All archives are, in one way or another, miscellaneous collections, and our sense of how material and textual deposits relate to one another has changed over time. Focussing on the non-textual objects makes it possible to understand the distinction-making process that has in many cases led to their removal to other places over time, and in doing so to explore from this angle the changing nature of our conception of archives as collections. The focus is upon two case-study groups of objects and texts which have not been so dispersed, one in Canterbury Cathedral Archives and the other in The National Archives, and I aim to use these examples to think through the relationship between things and the wider textual archive to which they relate—the documents kept within and written about them and their owners and compilers.

The first is the Bargrave Collection, three cabinets of curiosities, with drawers of different sizes enclosed by outer doors, put together by Dr John Bargrave (c.1610–1680), canon of Canterbury Cathedral, during his travels around Europe and North Africa. The second object is two doors with an inscription, a rather unusual item in The National Archives collection that once provided the way into one or more cupboards in the Exchequer of Receipt, within which some of its documents were kept. Both sets of objects will be related, not only to their associated documentary holdings, but to other similar things (cabinets of curiosity and administrative archival furniture) with different histories of preservation.

Taking these two starting points, the chapter will then briefly explore issues around the boundaries between archives and museums. It will investigate questions of animation—how things and documents can bring one another to life. Thematically, my interest here is in working practices, so at the end, reference will be made to other things that allude to spaces and their related practices, such as artists' studios and writers' huts—creative spaces which can be shut off from surrounding environments. Inadvertently, the main focus is therefore on things with doors—things that open and close, contain and reveal other objects and practices within. This coincidence is in the main, of course, a contingent feature of the objects chosen as case studies for thinking about the material in an archival context. It does, however, speak to the way documents can become implicated and entangled in the spaces that produce and house them, and I would therefore like to use it as a metaphor for how these things might function for archives and their users. Welcome inside …

Bargrave's Cabinets

The illustration shows one of three cabinets that house the collections of Dr John Bargrave, 'Church of England clergyman and collector of curiosities', as his *Oxford Dictionary of National Biography* entry describes him. He apparently had it specially made for him in the 1660s, based on the model of his fellow Canterbury cleric Meric Casaubon's coin cabinet, c.1630, itself built to house a collection with which Bargrave's own was merged when Casaubon bequeathed it to him.[1] These cabinets

Figure 16.1 Dr John Bargrave's cabinet of curiosities, Canterbury Cathedral Archives and Library (reproduced with permission).

bear a striking resemblance to some of the woodwork in the Cathedral Library, so may have been made within the precincts, where we know that immigrant joiners plied their trade in the seventeenth century.[2]

Bargrave was born in 1610 in Bridge, just outside Canterbury. His father was a soldier in the wars with Spain, and an investor in the Virginia Company, activities providing a context of travel and exploration for his son. Bargrave senior was also the elder brother of Isaac Bargrave, Dean of Canterbury Cathedral, which gives a further focus to the younger man's career trajectory. His mother was the daughter of a London haberdasher, an advantageous match which helped to secure the family's social position—a year after his second son's birth, John senior applied for a grant of arms and retired from soldiering to build a country house at Patrixbourne. As a second son, John junior was intended for the church, and educated at The King's School, Canterbury, and Peterhouse, Cambridge.

Both John and his uncle Isaac held to their political and religious loyalties at the Civil War, the one being ejected from his Cambridge fellowship and the other sent to the Fleet as a consequence. It was due to this inhospitable political climate that, between 1645 and 1660, Bargrave travelled the continent. He began in the Low Countries, then in 1645 he toured France, keeping a travel diary. In 1646–1647 he went to Italy, making four journeys to Rome as a kind of chaperone/tutor to elite young men, and publishing a guidebook, the *Mercurio Italico*, under the name of his nephew, John Raymond. Resuming his ecclesiastical career at the Restoration as canon at Canterbury, Bargrave went on a royal mission to ransom Christian slaves from Algiers in 1662.

During these travels he collected his 'curiosities', arranging and documenting his collection with labels and a manuscript catalogue up to his death in 1680, at which point he bequeathed it to the Dean and Chapter of the Cathedral. His widow deposited it there in 1685. The collection was much broader than the cabinets alone, including 'All my Large and lesser Mapps of Italy, Ould Roome and New, in sheets at large very fayre' and a selection of optical instruments,[3] both of which are now lost, two portraits and a large octagonal marble table, apparently also acquired on Bargrave's travels.

Bargrave's collection came into what was then Canterbury Cathedral Library, where the books stayed, the cabinets and their supporting documents being transferred to the archive after its establishment in 1954. Since its initial deposit, a marble table almost identical to Bargrave's own, belonging originally to his travelling companion Lord Stanhope but in use in the archdeaconry for many years, was given by Dr George Stanhope, Dean in the eighteenth century. Then, several catalogues of the coin collection have been made: the most complete (CCA DCc Lit. Mss. E16c) describes the contents of the three cabinets tray by tray, shelf by shelf, commenting on the descriptions originally given by Bargrave in his own documentation. Made by Samuel Shuckford (1693/4–1754), eighteenth-century prebend of the Cathedral, it continues the link between clerical identity, antiquarian tendencies, and an interest in order and spatial relationship. Bargrave's travel diary came into the collection via the local Irby family in 1957. A brief initial guide to the collection, *The Gentle Traveller* was published in 1983 and is now archived as part of the ephemera surrounding it.

In recent times, the collection has been described in rather pejorative terms. The great collections of elite patrons on grand tours form an unflattering context for Bargrave's objects, which are characterized by their small size, all essentially portable for a man on the move, and including the bags in which they were originally kept as he travelled. Despite the fact that John Evelyn, visiting Bargrave at Canterbury in 1672, refers to him as 'my old fellow Travelor in Italy & greate Virtuoso',[4] the scale of the objects weighs against the collection. One of the most celebrated items, the mummified finger of a Frenchman, was actually a substitute, an afterthought, by the Franciscans of Toulouse, who first offered Bargrave a mummified baby. Unable to take it because he was not yet homeward-bound, he took the finger instead. Stephen Bann suggests Bargrave's more pragmatic, non-aristocratic ambition: 'Where the great Earl of Arundel, paragon of English collectors in the seventeenth century, purchased a notable obelisk lying in a Roman circus, Bargrave's strategy was to break off a piece "of the butt end" of the same monument and have it shaped and polished.' Although the finger and the butt end are unusual in the collection as a whole, the sense they give of a collection of metonyms—of parts that stand for a whole to be completed in the memory of the traveller and the tales he tells of them—makes them apt symbols of the way Bargrave thinks about the archiving of his objects.

Although in relation to aristocratic collecting policies it seems rather small, in the context of Bargrave's original intentions the collection's size makes perfect sense. It was originally kept in the study at his house in the cathedral precincts. As he says of the genesis of his coin collection, 'My often seeing of them [coins] put me likewise into a humour of curiosity, and making this collection insuing, which I have now, in 1676, in a cabinet in my study at my canonical house, at the metropolitical church of Christ, Canterbury.'[5] Bann suggests that we are to imagine the cabinet Bargrave had made 'as the centerpiece of a study that also possessed numerous shelves for the display of the statuettes and freestanding pieces',[6] and Sturdy and Henig state that the objects were 'to be taken down and handed round', the small portraits designed 'To hang upon my cabinet', as Bargrave suggests in the catalogue, presumably from the drawer knobs, with many of the medals 'suspended on ribbons from the shelves'.[7] This is the space within which the collection came alive, and in which he made sense of it for visitors like Evelyn.

In other words, Bargrave's collection as originally conceived created a performative space that facilitated the reconstruction of his travels through the objects and stories which he told of them. In the catalogue he prepared, some of these stories come through—for instance the crystal bought in the Alps: 'I remember that the Montecolian man that sold it to me told me that he ventured his life to clamber the rocks to gett it.' His original label records the exact mountain 'now Caled mount

Figure 16.2 A page from Bargrave's travel journal, CCA-U11/8, showing the town of Sancerre (reproduced with permission).

Samplon'. The texts, generated from and generating oral recount, speak to both the original moment at which the object entered the collection, and the moment of display back in Canterbury.[8] Putting together a collection, then, means generating a narrative patchwork that is itself an uber-story of travel and articulation of the world witnessed through that travel. Objects and texts are mutually dependent for meaning.

The long, drawn-out series of acquisitions that form the wider Bargrave collection, stretching to the present day, is partly a feature of the particular kind of archive that Canterbury represents. As its archivist Cressida Williams explains, 'Canterbury Cathedral is the oldest collecting institution in the country, because it has been on this site since 597.' Its site specificity is key to Bargrave's initial deposit—he was giving the objects back to the community within which he lived—but also to the way the Cathedral has cared for them. As Cressida tells the story, while we sit in her office within the archive, 'Bargrave was an East Kent man, his house is 100 yards away, he is buried 100 yards away, his uncle was Dean, and he's in the archive as a working man as well as a collector, so we have his signature and handwriting on lots of the documents.' These particularities also indicate a different connection between archives, libraries and museums to one that might pertain in other places, she suggests: 'If the Cathedral had a separate museum or displays suitable for the collection, we'd think about it slightly differently. Cathedrals' objects connections are complicated because many of the objects remain working ... collections are still live and a Cathedral's not a museum per se.' This archive's close links to place ensure the continuity of the collection's stories.

This particularity has also affected the way the archive has treated the cabinets: 'Our decision has been to keep the objects in the cabinets, and I think that's part of their charm, because other collections have been dislocated or dispersed.' At the end of our conversation, Cressida gives the cabinets a central position in the Cathedral's story: 'Working with the interests of the collection at our heart, you can't just fish out loads of items from it, it's keeping it in the belly of the Cathedral that matters.' The unity of Bargrave's cabinet, objects, and documents, is guaranteed partly by its location, suggesting it is best seen as part of the identity of the archive.

Other 'mixed' collections at Canterbury raise issues that shed a different light on the place of objects in archives. The St Augustine's College Collection (a nineteenth-century collection from a missionary college close to the archives' site) shares with

Figure 16.3 John Evelyn's cabinet on a stand, 1652, John Hammond / Museum of the Home: 46/1979.

Bargrave's the local dimension, being a part of the history of the site on which the archive itself is based. Although its balance is documentary, it too has objects slipped in, such as an academic hood, a portable communion set, and the left ulna of Archbishop Justus (d. 627). As a part of the deposit, these things needed to be retained, but have no intrinsic value—they only make sense as part of that archive. These 'interleaved' objects, suspended between documents in ways that enrich one another's meanings, provide a tangible link with practice, and with the human context within which documents were produced and consumed.

The parity of historical interest in object and documents is relevant in both cases. In relation to other such cabinets held in museums, as in relation to narratives of the Grand Tour, Bargrave's appear less showy, with their practical construction and workmanlike doors. Comparing them with the finer pieces of furniture familiar from museum visits is of limited value—the reasons for opening the doors are different, as aesthetic function overrides contextual curiosity. The contents of John Evelyn's stately, Paris-made version, with its engraved veneered ebony doors, and internal doors and cupboards with fruitwood and ivory marquetry, has long since been dispersed, leaving his cabinet denuded—turned from a vibrant display of its owner's curious mind into a fine but silent piece of furniture that no longer gives up secrets, and remains unperformed.

The varied nature of the cabinets and content represents a challenge that is common to other intimately connected deposits of documents and objects. The Cathedral Archive also has a large collection of medieval charters, some of which have tally sticks or seals (sometimes with their own elaborate fabric bag) attached, some both.[9] These different materials have differing needs in terms of packaging and handling for the archive, making their preservation complex both individually and in relation to one another. The literal interdependence of material and textual evidence demands specialist attention, and the appeal of separating out cabinets and objects is obvious.

The Bargrave cabinets cannot be brought out of the strong rooms, but despite the problems with access the Cathedral are well aware of the collection's potential. 'The public who walk through our front door [in the Cathedral precincts] know what a museum is and a library, but not what an archive is.' Cressida points out that we archive our emails, but this popular usage doesn't offer the public a very intuitive way into the collections, and it makes them seem less vibrant. Represented digitally perhaps, objects like the Bargrave cabinets could bring people in, forming a tangible portal into a wider collection. They intend to continue to use it in this way, to open up the archive thematically, to think about the nature of collecting, Canterbury's connections with the wider world, and the Cathedral's. In the context of their multi-million-pound 'Canterbury Journey' project, Bargrave's peripatetic experience in a period of religious and political turmoil helps them to think through concepts of exile: 'they engage with current issues of refuge: individual objects won't tell you about that, but the complete archive does'. Objects at rest in archives still open up their periods of movement; they were and can again be hard-working.

The Exchequer Doors

The records of the Exchequer, the main financial department of the medieval and early modern English state, responsible for the accounting and audit of Crown revenue, are complex and extensive. They include the 'feet of fines', identified as 'the inaugural set of records made strictly for archival reasons',[10] produced by the late-twelfth-century Archbishop of Canterbury Hubert Walter, and their series numbers at The National Archive contain, in the main, documents in runs from the thirteenth to the nineteenth or twentieth centuries. In this sense, they transcend the particularity of individual organizational and curatorial practice that Bargrave's cabinets suggest and resist the particular events that generate stories. An exception, however, is E 409, containing only 'A pair of wooden doors with a painted inscription, which once enclosed a cupboard in the Exchequer of Receipt in which were kept the receipt and issue rolls and other procedural documents'.[11] The doors, which although similar are not a pair, measure approximately seven feet by two feet each. They still retain their original ironwork—hinges and a lock—and the inscription, with an ornate painted border around the panel on which it is painted.

The inscription reads, 'Annis regnorum Philippi et Marie 2 & 3, this place and the rest of the office were stablyshed by the righte honorable W. Marques of Wynchester and Highe Treasurer of England, for keepynge of all Pelles of Receipts and Exitus of the Court of Receipts called inferius scacarrium, and of all warrants and wrytynges belongyng to the same and accordynge to the aincyent ordre thereof. And also of certayne orders and rules of late yeres neglected and now agayne renewed from henesforthe to be observed of all and every officer of the said courte contayned in the redde booke of this said office made for the same intent.' It is 'signed', Edmonde Cockerell, gent. 'then the said Lord Treasourers clerk wryter and keeper of the Pells, warrants and writynges aforsaid. Anno Domini 1555'. Some of the working documents are signed by Cockerell too, giving a direct connection of authorship and practice between objects and texts.[12] He was one of a large family of Guernsey merchants, who moved to London and was admitted to the freedom in 1531, as a grocer, and later joined there by his brother Thomas. Edmund had only been appointed clerk of the pells late in 1555, having become MP for Portsmouth in 1554, thanks to the patronage of William Paulet.[13] The inscription points to a period of great change within the institution, one to which the doors themselves are inextricably linked.

Hamilton Bryson charts the development of the Exchequer as a court at this time. He points to the development of the office under William Paulet as Lord Treasurer, who revived it 'as the major financial institution of the kingdom'. By 1550, the king's privy chamber was no longer being used as a treasury to handle royal revenue, and in 1554, the year before the inscription was written on the doors, the revenue courts of First Fruits and Tenths were amalgamated with the Exchequer.[14] In addition, the jurisdiction of the court expanded, from the receipt of money due to the crown, to aiding 'the king's debtors to recover from their debtors', allowing the court's officers

DOORS INTO THE ARCHIVES 241

Figure 16.4 Cupboard doors from the Exchequer of Receipt, TNA E 409 (reproduced with permission).

to sue and be sued solely in the Exchequer, and the grant of privilege to collectors of the royal revenue.[15] Cockerell was a new man in a new office when he caused the inscription to be painted, giving clarity to a rapidly changing situation.

The inscription, then, marks a new function for the doors themselves, as witnesses to and guarantors of the probity of a considerably increased level of business. They enclose part of the written records of that business, but also guard the Red Book of the Exchequer, one of the tools through which the Exchequer exercised its influence.[16] In cases of conflict between two courts, this book, which dated from the early thirteenth century, was used to determine the Exchequer's priority of suit in a most performative way: the cursitor baron took it to the other court, and asserted that 'the defendant was an officer or accountant in the Exchequer and could be sued only there. The cursitor baron showed the copy of the writ of privilege which was in the Red Book, an official record, at folio 36.'[17]

The historiography of the Exchequer is, like the documents it created, both key to our understanding of the functioning of early modern society and impenetrable and alienating to the point of frustration. Bryson, one of the main writers on the institution, stated in the abstract to his 1972 doctoral thesis on the topic that he was motivated by the obscurity of the equity side of the Exchequer, aiming 'to shed some light upon this court and to explore its jurisdiction', staff, procedure, and records, but recognizing that institutional history 'has an unfortunate tendency to dryness and remoteness, which coupled with the author's literary short-comings portends a tedious undertaking for the reader of this work'.[18] Subsequent work has been dominated by the need to untangle procedure and faction, both labyrinthine topics to which there is rarely a straightforward answer that holds true across principle and practice.

So, can the doors offer a way into this archive once more? The inscription refers to both 'this place', presumably the cupboard, or small room, which lay behind the doors, and 'the rest of the office'—both a physical place and the processes and procedures by which it operated. As objects, then, the doors point us in similar directions to Bargrave's cabinets—they invite us to think through both the physical environment within which they were experienced before they entered the archive, and the way they, as key objects within that environment, shaped its practice. They demand that we pay attention to the lived experience of archival material.

Attending to the sensory experience of the Receipt as space, Zoe Hudson has unearthed repeated references to the glass windows that indicate the importance of light for daytime working, plus details of payments for a lantern 'provided to serche the receipte in the night season'.[19] The year after the inscription on the doors, she notes a payment of 3s 6d for 'strewing herbes' and 18d for 'p[er]fumes' used in the Lord Treasurer's office within the Exchequer, payments which continue with more detail (in autumn 1582, e.g., 'three ounces of cloves, rosewater & other perfumes') throughout the Elizabethan period. Moving between object and working practice makes it possible to reconstruct the environment within which the different types of archived material were produced.

Like Bargrave's collection in the cathedral, the organization of Exchequer space itself has left an early modern record beyond the initial objects. Order generates writing about order. Taking the inscription on the doors as a starting point, we can also expand our sense of the mindset that they aim to enshrine. In 1610, Arthur Agarde Esq. compiled a 'Compendium of the Records in the Treasury'. This valuable contribution to the ordering of the nation's records has been identified as notable as the result of his multiple interest in them as lawyer, scholar, and archivist.[20] These qualities are demonstrated partly in the painstaking inventories of the office's four treasuries he drew up, and partly in the working practices that his document reveals. Although it was written long after the doors took up their message, he is thought to have begun it in the 1570s, if not before, when they were still in place.[21]

Agarde begins by suggesting that those who come after him in his job may 'have a speciall regard to observe some instructions (I presume soe to call them, because by longe experience I have learned and noted them)'.[22] His list of the 'fower fould hurte that by necligence may bringe wracke to recordes' gives a clear sense of the responsibilities he felt as guardian of the Exchequer archive: 'Fier, Water, Rates 't mice, Misplacinge' plus, 'plaine takinge of them away' (314). His fear of 'misplacinge' in particular is palpable, and it lies behind the rigid material and administrative cultures of the Receipt: 'it is an enemye to all good ordre, and the bringer in of all horror and inconvenience amonge records. For if theere bee not had regard for every record to be placed in its right or knowne chest ... but one thrust into an others bagge or misplaced in its Kinge's time ... it is impossible to find any thinge certaine'.

The theme of time and practice is extended in Agarde's asides about the length of the jobs which various types of filing took him. Records sorted into two chests, A and B, were 'put into order by me, in a summer spent onely therein'. Time also passes feelingly with 'Robert Catesby the treator's evidence, selected out of twoe great hampers delivered in to me by my late Lord Threasaurer th Earle of Dorset, by the commaundement of Sir Henry Hubbard Attorney Generall, which cost me a quarter of a yeare's worke'. This is the extension of the culture that the sign on the doors inaugurated, and it helps us to understand what is at stake in the organization of the archive.

The ability to divide and close off, seen already with Bargrave's cabinets, is very clearly apparent in Exchequer practice. Order is maintained in these spaces through the use of a wide variety of containers—there are chests, presses, bags, great bags, and baskets. Spatial systems, akin to memory theatres, form environments of order and interrelation in the Exchequer, as they did for category and find-type in Bargrave's study. Under 5, Agarde lists 'a little rome adjoyninge to the same Court, wherin are three chestes in which are records placed, vizt ... The first next to the dore, conteyneth pleadinges of *Quo Warranto coram Justic itinerantibuz* ... in Kinge Ed. the firstes time onely: put by me, some two shires in a bagge, and some one shire, for the more easy findinge and preservacon where before they lay confused togeither'. In the margin against this entry is a later addition, showing the same accretive tendency that the Bargrave cabinets displayed: 'These are put into a presses for yt purpose on the left hand of ye dore, 1633—And divided into ye proper Countys.' And once again, objects and writing form a mutually supporting system, for instance, 'Item a bagg of canvas of speciall recordes, abbreviated in a sheete of paper in the bagge', and, in a suggestive example for the doors' function: 'In the Third Threasuary, beinge in the ould Chappter House of the Abbay of Westminster under a dore with three lockes, are contayned these recordes; put very faire into chestes with lockes and written upon with parchment, as followeth.'[23] Objects need writing, and writing objects, to order Agarde's national archive.

The TNA doors must have belonged to one of the spaces Agarde describes. Perhaps one of the smaller spaces-within-spaces, where 'Mr Gidiok Warder keepth the two Pelles, the one of Redditus called Introit and the other of Exitus, whereof both sorts in a parrticuler office in a rome appoynted for that use nerre the Court of Receipt', or perhaps one of the presse within these: 'on the further side this rancke goinge forward, marked thus G'.[24] If the latter, then we might look at the Exchequer doors in relation to an oak cupboard made to store the Stratford Corporation records in 1594, its plank-built carcase fronted by a pair of eight-panel doors, its interior fitted with twelve drawers of nailed construction and with iron ring handles.

Figure 16.5 Corporation cupboard of boxes, Shakespeare Birthplace Trust, STRST: SBT L513 (1594 002). CC-BY-NC-ND © Shakespeare Birthplace Trust.

Restored and added to over the years like all the objects considered here, we have the sense of an item in use over a long period of time, adapted and mended to keep it functioning, and thereby becoming an integral part of the order and visual impression of the things it housed for its users. Its protective function comes with it into the archive, ordering spaces nestled inside one another.

These organizing objects, then, draw evidence of the spaces and practices which shaped their textual record with them when they are archived. They preserve valuable traces of the practices of labour and the spaces of production and consumption—a working environment or ecology that explains the form and content of the objects they house.

Working Environments

The objects and documents so far considered form a bedrock of archival practice, indicating the significance of storage objects at the particular moment when both personal and administrative archives increased in size and complexity. They are important markers of the history of archives in England. But the urge to connect writing and things has a wider significance, one that moves beyond storage and order to connect us to more modern concerns about the way in which things might keep in themselves evidence for the environments that enable creative practice.

In 2012 Outside Studios rebuilt Roald Dahl's writing hut—the space in which he worked daily for over thirty years and in which all his books were written—for the Roald Dahl Museum and Story Centre. The company, 'developer, designer and deliverer of the unexpected in museum galleries', state their 'firm belief' in an attraction's ability to 'offer something unique, something different to life at home

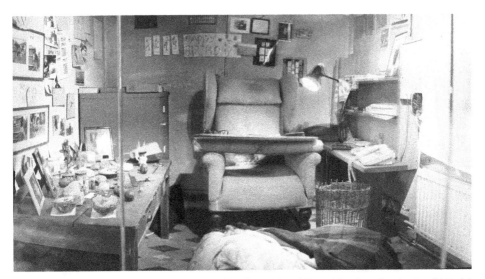

Figure 16.6 Outside Studios' 2012 rebuild of Roald Dahl's writing hut for the Roald Dahl Museum and Story Centre, Great Missenden; image reproduced by permission.

or at school'. Here, their practice was painstaking: 'we built a millimetre-perfect replica of the inner writing room and hinged a whole section of the structure; when the Museum is quiet, the hut can be closed for maximum, spine-tingling impact'. In order to fill the replica, 'The hut's contents were moved forensically, right down to the dirt on the floor and the tobacco-stained polystyrene wall insulation.' Each object was 'carefully recorded, checked and conserved before the display was recreated in its new, museum-grade enclosure'. The exhibit was then explained in writing, 'covered with illustrated roses setting out, in the words of one of his daughters, Roald Dahl's writing process'.

Rachel White, Archive Manager at the Museum, says that 'Stepping inside is always a special experience. Immediately you notice the smell of tobacco, clinging to the polystyrene sheets which line the walls. There is also the scent of paper, dust and old furniture, all carefully preserved so that you get the sense that Roald Dahl has only just walked out.' She details the modifications he made to the interior to set it up perfectly for his practice—the particularities that turned everyday things into his perfect working environment: 'In here, Roald placed an armchair that used to belong to his mother, an Anglepoise lamp carefully weighted with a golf-ball to shine at just the right angle and an old suitcase filled with logs to rest his feet on', and 'his homemade desk (a board with green felt propped up on a roll of corrugated cardboard)'. Gradually the small table in the room was filled with strange and wonderful objects which held personal meaning for him—a model Hurricane plane, like those he had flown in World War Two; his own hipbone, removed during an operation; a fragment of ancient stone with Cuneiform script, picked up during his time in Babylon in 1940; a heavy metal ball, made from the silver wrappings of chocolate bars; an opal, sent to Roald by a boy in Australia as a present.

It seems that Dahl got the idea for his shed from another writer's practice—Dylan Thomas. Thomas lived in Laugharne, Wales, from 1944 until his death in 1953 and wrote in a shed overlooking the Taf Estuary. But the museum may also have got the idea for both the power of such a space and the importance of its meticulous removal (the millimetre accuracy) from the way in which the studio of the artist Francis Bacon was moved from its original home in Reece Mews in London to the Dublin City Gallery. The studio was acquired in 1998, and found to contain over 7,000 objects. Each of these was logged in an online database which, the Studio Museums website claims, 'forms the first computerized record of the entire contents of an artist's studio'. The team that undertook the work was led by a conservator, but also comprised archaeologists who 'made the survey and elevation drawings of the small studio, mapping out the spaces and locations of the objects and conservators and curators who tagged and packed each of the items, including the dust. The walls, doors, floor and ceiling were also removed'. They describe the resulting database as 'the first computerized archive of the entire contents of a world ranking artist's studio', and list the types of entry as 'approximately 570 books and catalogues, 1,500 photographs, 100 slashed canvases, 1,300 leaves torn from books, 2,000 artist's

Figure 16.7 Photograph of Francis Bacon's Studio by Perry Ogden. Collection & image © Hugh Lane Gallery, Dublin © The Estate of Francis Bacon. All rights reserved/DACS 2023.

materials and 70 drawings. Other categories include the artist's correspondence, magazines, newspapers and vinyl records'.

The logic of these wholesale relocations of creative environments seems to be that the genius of the resulting outputs is seen to be located in the precise interrelations between the objects in space—replicating them in their exact relationship both guarantees authenticity and permits the discovery of the practices that led to the artists' remarkable outputs. The Studio Museums website describes 'fascinating environments in which great art has been created', and places 'filled with the spirit and atmosphere that inspired their former occupants to produce some of the world's best-loved art'. It also characterizes the particularity of Bacon's studio in the caption to its image, describing it as 'chaotic and energetic', the opposite of our early modern examples.

Perhaps we might ask, 'why bother'—the treatment of dust in both descriptions is striking—or more positively, what does that bothering tell us about our cabinets and doors? Dublin City Gallery illuminates the evidence of practice that can be found within the objects and spaces of work. They draw attention to one object in particular: 'The door of Bacon's Reece Mews studio is probably the best-known image of the artist's studio.' No artist's palette was found there, and they suggest that he used many different pragmatic substitutes. One of them was the door, and the way he used it offers fascinating insights into his practice: 'The fact that both the front and back of the door have paint accretions would indicate that Bacon sometimes painted with the door open and also with it closed.' Another surprising material find within the studio-archive was a number of scraps of thick corduroy trousers, and these allow a series of material connections to be made: 'Imprints from corduroy are also evident on the door of the Reece Mews studio suggesting that Bacon applied paint to the door, printed the corduroy and then applied it to the canvas.' The corduroy imprint 'is evident in many of his paintings'—in other words a direct connection can be traced from the pieces of fabric, to the door, to the face of the canvas, and therefore from the way the space and objects of the studio were configured to Bacon's artistic practice, to his painterly technique, and to the finished work of art as hung in gallery or private collection. The museum's bold claim that their cataloguing and display practices have 'changed the shape and focus of exhibitions of Francis Bacon's work ever since' indicates the explicatory power of these tiny archived details in relation to the particular nature of their subject's creativity.

It might, then, be helpful to think about archives as repositories of productive environments of the past. What connections can we make from the objects that epitomize the lived experience of production to the things that were produced there, and how can we begin to excite new audiences about recordkeeping through those connections? How can we enrich our description of those practices through the stories of space and making that archives contain? Archives are records of work done, of time spent, and the laying down of the layers of practice in ways that encourage us to think about continuity and a change managed by the physical forms of both documents and objects. As we work longer and longer hours, but face a future defined partly by the challenges of mechanization of repetitive tasks, perhaps now is a good moment to pause and think about what archived objects can tell us about a creative environment—does it include the spaces of prosaic writing as well as the spinning out of fantasy yarns; how can we curate it, to explicate the changing relationships between spaces and what is produced in them for new generations? Using our imagination, and the readily-available evidence for sensory and emotional engagement with archived spaces, we can perhaps allow men like Agarde to open the doors to the archive and shine a lantern to search inside.

FURTHER READING

Stephen Bann, *Under the Sign: John Bargrave as Collector, Traveller, and Witness* (Ann Arbor: University of Michigan Press, 1994)

Alison Booth, *Homes and Haunts: Touring Writers' Shrines and Countries* (Oxford: Oxford University Press, 2016)

W. Hamilton Bryson, 'The Court of Exchequer Comes of Age', in DeLloyd J. Guth and John W. McKenna, eds, *Tudor Rule and Revolution: Essays for G. R. Elton from his American Friends*, (Cambridge: Cambridge University Press, 1982), 149–158

John D Cantwell, *The Public Record Office 1959–1969* (London: Public Record Office, 2000)

Wanda M. Corn, ed., '"Artists" Homes and Studios: A Special Kind of Archive', *American Art* 19.1 (2005), 2–31

Elizabeth M. Hallam, 'Nine Centuries of Keeping the Public Records', *The Records of the Nation: The Public Record Office 1838–1988; the British Record Society 1888–1988*, ed. G. H. Martin and P. Spufford (Woodbridge: Boydell, 1990), 23–42

Maggie Yax, 'Arthur Agarde, Elizabethan Archivist: His Contributions to the Evolution of Archival Practice', *The American Archivist* 61 (1998), 56–69

NOTES

1. D. Sturdy and M. Henig, *The Gentle Traveller* (Abingdon: Abbey Press, 1983), 16.
2. T. Hamling and C. Richardson, *A Day at Home in Early Modern England: Material Culture and Domestic Life, 1500–1700* (New Haven: Yale University Press, 2017), 168.
3. See S. Bann, *Under the Sign: John Bargrave as Collector, Traveller, and Witness* (Ann Arbor: University of Michigan Press, 1994), 73; Sturdy and Henig, *The Gentle Traveller*, 16.
4. Quoted in Bann, *Under the Sign*, 1.
5. C. Robertson, ed., *Pope Alexander the Seventh... With a catalogue of Dr. Bargrave's Museum* (London: Camden Society, 1867), 115–116.
6. Bann, *Under the Sign*, 93.
7. Sturdy and Henig, *The Gentle Traveller*, 16.
8. Bann points out 'the singular status of the curiosity and its capacity to generate a narrative'; *Under the Sign*, 76.
9. See, e.g., CCA-DCd-ChAnt/G/138/a, which has a notched tally stick and seal.
10. M. T. Clanchy, *From Memory to Written Record: England 1066–1307* (Oxford: Blackwells 1993; 2nd edn), 68–69; M. Yax, 'Arthur Agarde, Elizabethan Archivist: His Contributions to the Evolution of Archival Practice', *The American Archivist* 61 (1998), 56–69, 58. Feet of fines are currently held in the records of the Court of Common Pleas (CP 25). The archive also includes Domesday Book, the oldest public record in continuous custody, and the oldest surviving English record series, the Pipe Rolls.
11. Other exceptions include medieval chests in the Treasury of Receipt, and the red dispatch box used by the Chancellor of the Exchequer for budgets: https://discovery.nationalarchives.gov.uk/details/r/C640145.
12. Zoe Hudson states that, This was the same Edmund Cockerell who signed off a document about the distribution of stationery, noting that it was "Examyned by me" (TNA: E407/68), Z. Hudson, *Locations, Networks and Cycles: Studying the Everyday Life of Richard Stonley (1520–1600)* (PhD thesis, University of Kent, 2017), 108.
13. P. Hyde, 'COCKERELL, Edmund (by 1510-59/60), of London', in S. Bindoff, ed., *The History of Parliament: the House of Commons 1509–58*: www.historyofparliamentonline.org/volume/1509-1558/member/cockerell-edmund-1510-5960.

14. W. H. Bryson, 'The Court of Exchequer Comes of Age', in D. J. Guth and J. W. McKenna, eds, *Tudor Rule and Revolution: Essays for G. R. Elton from his American Friends* (Cambridge: Cambridge University Press, 1982), 149–158 (151).
15. Bryson, 'The Court of Exchequer', 153–154.
16. E 164/2; the Red Book was regarded as second only to Domesday Book as an authoritative record, and kept in an iron chest.
17. Bryson, 'The Court of Exchequer', 156.
18. The thesis eventually became Bryson, *Equity Side of the Exchequer* (Cambridge: Cambridge University Press, 1975).
19. Hudson, *Locations*, 105.
20. Yax, 'Arthur Agarde, Elizabethan Archivist', 68.
21. 'By the time the inventories were completed in 1610, Agard had been at work on the records for at least forty years'; G. H. Martin, *ODNB*, doi-org.chain.kent.ac.uk/10.1093/ref:odnb/206, accessed 1 April 2019. While there is no specific explanation for the doors' deposit, the entry for the Exchequer records as a whole states: 'Most of these records were kept in the Pell Office on the eastern side of Westminster Hall until the beginning of the nineteenth century (with some early ones in the Chapter House), in damp conditions, where the wooden partitions of the storage and the many hearths in the office laid them at risk from fire.... They were probably transferred to the attic storage in Somerset House in 1822, and "heaped in some places up to the ceiling and in an exceedingly dirty state". Retrieved in 1840 to undergo cleaning and bundling at the Comptroller of the Exchequer's Office in Whitehall Yard, they were removed to racks in Rolls House in 1841 to await listing and labelling prior to their transfer to the new Public Record Office in Chancery Lane, which opened in 1858.'
22. F. Palgrave, ed., *The Antient Kalendars and Inventories of the Treasury of His Majesty's Exchequer Vol II* (Commissioners on Public Records, 1836), 313.
23. Palgrave, *The Antient Kalendars*, 329.
24. Palgrave, *The Antient Kalendars*, 215, 325.

CHAPTER 17

ARCHIVES, ART, AND THE PERFORMATIVITY OF PRACTICE

JANE BIRKIN

Work that takes place inside archives and work that is designated as art are often perceived as distinct practices—one bureaucratic and the other creative—yet it is quite possible for the two to share common concepts and techniques. Archival labour follows a controlled methodology, through predetermined approaches to arrangement, cataloguing, and systems of storage; a similarly programmed approach can be taken to the production of artworks, frequently with broad links to archival thinking. Artistic practice—whether image-based, text-based, or a combination of both—can be produced using rules that are defined by the artist, and this opens up an interesting theoretical debate that is pertinent to archives and yet lies outside of conventional archive theory. As an artist who has worked a 'day job' in an archive, the procedural link between the two practices is a critical factor in my own research. I do not wish to elaborate on specific artworks of my own in this fairly limited space, the one exception being my 2014 film *El Rastro*: screenshots from this film punctuate this chapter and I briefly mention the piece later. Rather, I want to consider in more general terms how specific parallels to archival practices present in my own work, and in that of other artists.

With regard to my own practice, I want to discuss the ways in which my appropriation of the regulated methods of image description in the archive has resulted in a writing—and subsequent reading—of the photographic image that contrasts with traditional models of image analysis. The visual content-based image description techniques that underpin my work are familiar in the archive, but they appear idiosyncratic when taken outside, into a milieu where images abound and description therefore seems unnecessary. Mine is a practice that does not oppose archival standards, but instead uses them and builds upon them. This is a methodology that runs through the various practices of other artists referred to in this essay, as their work is to some degree positioned within, and constrained by, the established archival fields of recordkeeping, indexing and classification. It is also important to note that while my work and that of others mentioned here tap into the formalities and the structures of the archive, they are still able to make space for complex and abstract thinking around images and image sets, and around the language that might interact with these images. My own work lies between what may be thought of as affective image and dry text, and it represents an attempt to restructure the perceived differences between the two forms, as the text must stand in for—and have parity with—the image. Although archive professionals may not be the expected audience for the *practices* discussed, this concept alone would certainly be a familiar one to them. My hope is that there may be an opportunity for the reverse flow of 'work experience' here; that an unpicking of the methods and thinking of a certain type of art research could be useful and constructive when taken back into the archive. The examples of art practice and conceptual writing that are highlighted here traverse notions of instructional practices, material culture, cultural theory, and media archaeology, which are, after all, as pertinent to archives as they are to art.

Media archaeology, in particular, has clear connections to the archive. It offers an understanding of digital cultures through physical examination and theoretical critique of past media forms, and archival methods of organization and storage can certainly be explored in a media-archaeological way, as a prototype for network storage systems. The paper catalogue (or stand-alone database) might be thought of, at a time of networked archival systems, as a past media form, except that it is still in widespread use. Technically speaking, the object-level image description of the visual content of an image originated before the images themselves were easily reproduced and shared. In media-archaeological terms, object-level description is one of many archive cataloguing and organizational techniques that influence and question network call-up and storage behaviours. The word 'archive' has itself been incorporated into our digital vocabulary and the structure of the archive has firm ties to the organization of *digital* media of all kinds. Media theorist Cornelia Vismann, in her book *Files: Law, Media and Technology*, emphasizes the *physicality* of these ties, as she explains how in 'highly unmetaphorical fashion, files and their techniques organize the very architecture of digital machines'.[1] But there is a danger that the use of archival terms in digital systems can obscure the vast differences between the physical and the digital handling of information. Media archaeologist Wolfgang Ernst perceives shared language, such as the word 'archive', as distinctly metaphorical. He argues, 'If we disregard the metaphorical use of the word archive for all possible forms of memory and cultural memory and use it to mean the specific agency of memory technology, the Internet is not an archive.'[2]

In his essay, 'The Body and the Archive', artist and theorist Allan Sekula emphasizes the archival traits of early physiognomic applications of photography: 'The central artifact of this system is not the camera but the filing cabinet'; it becomes 'a merger between optics and statistics'.[3] My working relationship with collections began with a five-year stint as slide curator in a London art school. With one foot in the technical medium of analogue photography and one foot in collection management, I occupied a curious and very material space between camera, image, typewriter, and filing cabinet. As a practising artist I was already an advocate of image sets, where notions of interdependencies and interrelationships between objects take precedence over the assets of the single image. Techniques of image organization began to overflow from my day job and become important and dynamic considerations in my own visual practice. Until recently, and for nearly two decades, I worked within a large, mixed-media archive inside a university library, and since this time my practice has taken a distinct 'archival' turn. The relationship between art practice and archival structures has become central in terms of my own theoretical and practical explorations, of image description in particular, with the rules and methodologies of cataloguing and recordkeeping *becoming* the practice.

In his correspondence with Ruth Maclennan, London-based artist Uriel Orlow—whose work frequently intersects with archives—argues that when one is not involved in specific research one can focus on the procedural aspects of archives, 'the sheer materiality of the collections, beyond the specific information its documents contain'. He goes on to ask how we can comprehend 'the meaning and status of the archive as a whole, operating as it does like a memorial behind closed doors'.[4] By spending time behind these closed doors, I have developed an understanding of the overtly material nature of the archive. I have been able to observe the spaces, systems and practices from the inside: the corridors, offices, and strongrooms, the documents, files, boxes, and shelves, the extensive human labour involved, and the media materiality and the operational importance of the catalogue.

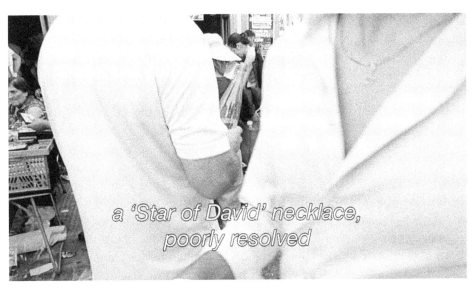

Figure 17.1 Still from *El Rastro* at 0'25" © Jane Birkin 2014.

A spatiotemporal understanding of the archive emerges: how papers, files, boxes, and shelves all function together in physical hierarchies, echoing those recorded in the catalogue. Once lived, worked, and understood in this way, the archive, its structure, and the position of the single object relative to it, start to acquire tangibility. From October 2001 to July 2002, McLennan herself worked as artist in residence in the Archives of the British Library of Political and Economic Science, at the London School of Economics. This was the first time that an artist had been a resident in a UK academic archive and, importantly, McLennan was treated as a member of the staff and enjoyed unlimited 'behind the scenes' access.

From the inside, one begins to understand the performative nature of archival practices; they are carried out to prescribed standards, laid down by bodies such as The International Council on Archives, which, through its International Standard Archival Description (General) or ISAD-G, puts forward clear principles. I use the term 'performative' here in a specific way, one that is carefully and clearly set out by Margaret Iversen in her 2010 essay on artist Ed Ruscha, 'Auto-Maticity: Ruscha and Performative Photography'.[5] Iversen sees performative practice as one that 'begins with an instruction or rule which is followed through with a performance'. It is Iversen's definition that is significant to the comparison of performativity in art and archive that I am presenting here. Her specification of two distinct actions, the second dependent on the first, differentiate this use of the word 'performative' from the earlier designation by J. L. Austin in *How to Do Things with Words*, where the 'saying' and the 'doing' are one and the same thing (famously, the performative utterance of 'I do' in the course of the marriage ceremony).[6] Iversen also argues that the term performative is often wrongly used to define work that has an element of theatricality, whereas it should be about the repetition and iteration that follows from instruction. In her discourse on gender performativity, Judith Butler draws on theatrical and phenomenological aspects of performance that are often associated with performance art (and are somewhat alien to the rationale of the archive), but, interestingly, she too sees repetition as critical and emphasizes the greyness of the activity itself: 'This repetition is a reenactment and reexperiencing of a set of meanings already socially established; it is the mundane and ritualized form of their legitimation.'[7]

Within Iversen's definition of performativity then, the *implementation* of work, such as the production of Ruscha's seminal *Twentysix Gasoline Stations* (1963), which she highlights, is critical; the work may be conceptual—or proto-conceptual in the case of Ruscha—but the concept by itself does not constitute the artwork. Iversen sees the instructional element within her definition of performativity as a relinquishment of authorial control, and she acknowledges and accepts the possibility of chance or accidental occurrences that might produce unexpected results. In performative art practice authorial control is clearly present, but it is established early on in the work, in the design of the workflow rather than in the implementation. Archivists, working to established conventions, likewise produce work to instruction, and where their authorship is also largely unrecognized. In this setting too, unexpected results can materialize. Differences in language use between cataloguers persist, even though arrangements are put in play to manage and minimize them. What is important here is that cataloguing is directed by nature of the objects being catalogued—the hierarchical model put forward in the ISAD-G shows only a *typical* case—and the time available to catalogue them; there is no unconditional 'one size fits all' scheme for arrangement and description. So, an interesting hybridity between human and system can be seen in all aspects of archival labour, as well as in information management systems more generally.

Aside from the structures and the non-human aspects that intervene, description and classification of images remains a task best performed by humans, even though there has been great progress in the field of computer image recognition. Research into artificial neural networks has thrown up exciting results in the field, but the scope of machine learning of real-world situations required for practical application is extensive and therefore not cost efficient for cash-strapped archives, or even for large corporations. Compared to the high cost of research into artificial intelligence, digital labour schemes that use *human* intelligence, such as Amazon Mechanical Turk, are low-cost. There are also well-subscribed schemes that offer no financial reward at all, with large institutions such as the British Library and the Library of Congress uploading images to Flickr groups for users to tag, relying on the participants' wish to be collaborative individuals, part of a large group of like-minded people performing socially useful tasks. The tag itself has become a byword in the discourse on socialization and connectivity, as it works across social media to bind things, ideas, *and people* together.

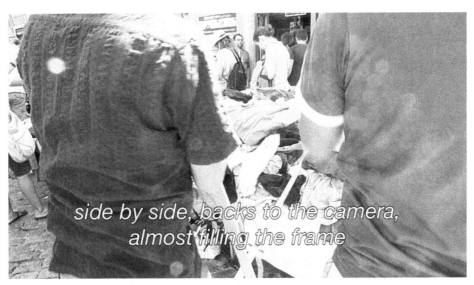

Figure 17.2 Still from *El Rastro* at 2'27" © Jane Birkin 2014.

Sekula argues in relation to the photography and related textual documentation of Alphonse Bertillon and Francis Galton, as they attempted to identify 'criminal types' for the Paris Police Archive in the latter half of the nineteenth century, 'Photography was to be both an *object* and *means* of bibliographic rationalization.'[8] Distinct from the description or cataloguing *of* photographs, photography has been used as a cataloguing and classification *technique* from the start. Early photography was quickly assigned to scientific enquiry, and the new technology produced new images, new classifications, and new knowledge. Most importantly, it allowed certain types of scientific investigation to take place that had previously been impossible. Similarly, modern scientific imaging techniques, including ultrasound, magnetic resonance imaging (MRI), and advanced microscopy (all now largely focusing on emerging 3D imaging technologies) have in more recent times afforded important new research possibilities in the field of biomedical sciences. Artistic practice around photographic classification and collection—similarly offering an object and a means of typological investigation—has been demonstrated and defined over time by artists and photographers such as (and this is a very limited sample) August Sander, Berndt and Hilla Becher, Ed Ruscha, and Taryn Simon, all working to varying degrees of self-initiated instruction. Georgio Magnani[9] cites the Bechers' industrial typologies (water towers, gas tanks, and pitheads, for example) as drawing on strategies that can be traced back to Sander's vast opus *People of the Twentieth Century* (1892–1854), a photographic project that, like Bertillon's, can be positioned within the pseudo-science of physiognomy. Magnani argues:

> Meaning undergoes a circular series of displacements that transfer significance from a single image, to a comparison between similar images, to the overall project that brings the images together, to the conditions that produced the project as they are instanced in the individual images. It is only through their participation in a system of presentation, under the model of the archive, that the single images gain a significance which is larger than their particular instances.

So, the image set, 'the model of the archive', becomes more important than any one single image, whose significance wanes. The notion of 'part-to-whole relationship' that is critical to understanding an archive persists through the work of all the artists mentioned above.

In her 2009 piece Contraband, artist Taryn Simon photographs items illegally imported into the United States and seized by the authorities. Contraband meets Iversen's definition of performativity: it is performed to strict instruction. The project is carried out in a pre-set manner and over a pre-set time span (five days at JFK airport, New York). The 1,075 contraband items are each photographed and presented in the same way: simply, clearly, and stripped of context, as though the project were a documentation of museum objects. The images are presented to us in simple groups, such as FITNESS DVD'S (PIRATED); POTATOES (PROHIBITED); U.S. CURRENCY (INCIDENTAL TO ARREST). As Hans Ulrich Obrist[10] argues in his 'Ever Airport: Notes on Taryn Simon's *Contraband*', a foreword to Simon's subsequent book of the project, the photographs are 'something approaching the approximately impersonal and administrative form of the list'. He continues, 'The photographs and texts of Simon's Contraband reveal disorder and chance within the strictures of a system determined by absolute order and control ... Simon's images and lists embrace both order and disorder, and open up a third space within the cracks of these forms of control.'

Obrist's 'administrative form of the list' leads us directly to the idea of archival practices, and his 'order and disorder' to the 'third space' of original order. Archival order, guided as it is by the collection and use of objects prior to their arrival into the archive, contrasts with the ordering systems of libraries, where, as Judith Ellis points out in *Keeping Archives*—published in 1993 and still an immensely useful resource for anyone setting up a small archive—they are dealing with 'consciously authored information products', and not with the rich, complex, and variously kept records of a life or an organization.[11] Michel Foucault famously and succinctly defines the archive as 'that which determines that all these things do not accumulate endlessly in an amorphous mass, nor are they inscribed in an unbroken linearity'.[12] The notion of original order—with its unexpected connections, relationships, and insights—has clear confluence with modern historical analysis and thinking around seriality and time, most notably by Foucault, where objects are seen sometimes as 'temporally neutral', sometimes as implying 'a particular temporal direction'.[13] In relation to this theoretical framework, the archival catalogue list is of great practical importance. It is not only significant as a finding aid, but as an insurance policy against the misfiling of objects, against the loss of evidence of the time-critical mechanisms of collection and use.

Archives are built upon the structure of the list: they are organized by list and populated by many objects that fall into the broad category of list. Rolls, registers, accounts, and inventories, many of them government and legal documents, are commonplace. Vismann, who traces the list back to the Babylonian Empire, uses the term 'second writing scene' to describe listing, whilst at the same time recognizing the power of this simple form to control and regulate.[14] Whilst Simon's and others' classificatory photographs form a *visual* list, other artists have chosen to engage the power of the list in its more familiar written form. Conceptual artist Dan Graham's *Schema* (1966) is a list-based invitation to inventorize the grammatical structure of the publication in which it exists, as defined by the editor of the publication, so there are as many versions of *Schema* as there are publications. A generic version of *Schema* is published in volume one, number one of the journal *Art-Language* (May 1969), along with some instruction on how to implement the piece, to *perform* it. It could be argued that this work falls into J. L. Austin's definition of the performative—that the instruction itself is the work—but the implementation is implicit *in* the work. And, completely in line with Iversen's definition of performativity, Alexander Alberro argues that *Schema* 'effects the total depersonalization of the work—the artist virtually disappears behind the structure's self-generation.[15] *Art-Language* was the journal of the Art & Language group; a collective first conceived by British conceptual artists Terry Atkinson and Michael Baldwin, around 1966. Their language-based work provided a challenging riposte to both the modernist and the minimalist art mainstream that operated at that time. In fact, the first issue of *Art-Language* puts forward three different text works in list form: Sol Lewitt's *Sentences on Conceptual Art*, Graham's *Schema*, and Lawrence Weiner's *Statements*. Conceptual Art's relationship with early computing and cybernetics is evident. Number 29 of LeWitt's *Sentences* reads, 'The process is mechanical and should not be tampered with' and in his 1967 piece, *Paragraphs on Conceptual Art*, he states, 'The idea becomes a machine that makes the art.' Iversen, in her definition of performativity set out above, uses words and phrases such as 'putting into play', 'repetition', and the 'iterative character of the instruction', all similarly indicative of computational methods.

In conceptual writer and poet Kenneth Goldsmith's two pieces *Day* (2003) and *Seven American Deaths and Disasters* (2013), rules for making are set and the resulting texts are indeed not tampered with. In their co-authored *Against Expression: An Anthology of Conceptual Writing*, Craig Dworkin and Goldsmith describe the methodology for *Day*:

> *Day* (Great Barrington, Mass.: The Figures, 2003) is a complete transcription of the entire edition of the *New York Times* from Friday, September 1, 2000. Kenneth Goldsmith predicated his procedure on the constraint of uncreativity, which he refers to as 'the hardest constraint a writer can muster'. He systematically worked through each page, moving from one article to the next. Anywhere in the newspaper where there was a word, letter, or number, he transcribed it. He made no distinction between editorial and advertizement. Finally, when published, everything was set in the same font, without the use of styling such as bold or italic. The result is a leveling of information to text, which is stripped of hierarchy and design.[16]

In *Seven American Deaths and Disasters*, Goldsmith similarly transcribes radio reports (jingles included) of catastrophic events such as the Kennedy assassinations and the Challenger space shuttle disaster. In March 2015, Goldsmith's techniques caused major controversy, particularly in the US, as he performed *The Body of Michael Brown*, a reading of the autopsy report of Brown, an eighteen-year-old black man who was fatally shot by a white police officer. Goldsmith, a white male poet, was accused of racist exploitation, but he passionately defended his work, for example in an article in *The Guardian* newspaper arguing that it was in the tradition of *Seven American Deaths and Disasters*:

> I took a publicly available document from an American tragedy that was witnessed first-hand (in this case by the doctor performing the autopsy) and simply read it. Like *Seven American Deaths and Disasters*, I did not editorialize; I simply read it without commentary or additional editorializing.... The document I read from is powerful. My reading

of it was powerful. How could it be otherwise? Such is my long-standing practice of conceptual writing: like *Seven American Deaths and Disasters*, the document speaks for itself in ways that an interpretation cannot. It is a horrific American document, but then again it was a horrific American death.[17]

Both transcription and description are commonplace in the archive, and are undertaken without interpretation or gloss. Like the archivist, Goldsmith is presenting what already exists, and what already exists may unfortunately be unpalatable. The phrase conceptual writing was coined by Dworkin as a way to include the practices of conceptual artists and those of language poets, such as the *Oulipo* group, who used restricted writing techniques such as—but not confined to—'lipograms', systematic compositions that omit a certain letter throughout. For Dworkin the term conceptual writing offered 'a way both to signal literary writing that could function comfortably as conceptual art and to indicate the use of text in conceptual art practices'.[18] The restricted writing technique that I employ through my descriptions of photographs is a conceptualization of an already restricted institutional writing practice. It therefore comes under Dworkin's 'conceptual writing' umbrella, and shares many qualities—greyness, uncreativity—with today's conceptual writers, such as Goldsmith. Unlike Goldsmith, I do not directly appropriate text, but instead I appropriate an existing system of generating text and managing images. As I take my writing off the page and into film, installation, and lecture-performance, it demands of the viewer a combination of both direct reading and conceptual thought. In this, it is no different to how the researcher approaches the archive catalogue.

Figure 17.3 Still from *El Rastro* at 4'41" © Jane Birkin 2014.

The visual content-based description that I use is embedded within the hierarchical cataloguing arrangement of the archive. Levels of description move from the general to the specific, and the temporal configuration follows this structure, as it too moves from general to specific time: units of description proceed downwards through general descriptions of *events* in time, through to discrete *situations*—in the case of photographs, to technical images that inhabit extremely short moments in time. Contextual information tends to lie at higher levels, leaving the object-level image description largely without context. My descriptions push this disconnect and de-contextualization, emphasizing the synchrony of the moment of capture and the duration embodied in the image. Photographs are always already technically de-contextualized objects, breaks in time. This specific technique of writing the image is readily distinguishable from hermeneutical analysis, as it is placed outside of the system of signs that is most often considered in discussions of photographic representation, and this is key to the epistemological positioning of my own performative practice around archives. The cataloguing process is framed not *only* as documentation, but also as a complex, albeit standardized, form of knowledge production in itself, one that takes place even before any reconfigurations and realizations by researchers. The histories and practicalities of photography—not just in terms of photographic media and production but also through cataloguing, storage, and access—are extremely relevant to the study of digital photographic practices today and are consistent with the recent material and post-representational turn in photographic studies, where we are encouraged to look *at* photographs, rather than *through* them.

Description is often perceived as a low form of writing, but classical scholar D. P. Fowler[19] celebrates it as an example of 'narrative pause'—and he calls for the freeing of description from the 'poor relation status' to which it is attached. He cites the French experimental writers of the 1950s and '60s—known as the *Nouveaux Romanciers* (new novelists)—as champions for the cause of description. (Amongst these writers, Georges Perec is particularly revered in conceptual writing circles.) Images are *technical* pauses in the narrative and image sets in the archive can be viewed through something other than a narrative gaze, as the juxtapositions within them, and the lists that describe them, expose what is often a non-chronological advancement, because of the adherence to original order. In my work, as in the archive, the image is frequently hidden, but its visual content is described in detail, given the 'true autonomy' that Fowler demands.

The visual content-based methodology constitutes a writing of the image that is commonplace in the archive, but may seem alien when presented outside of the institutional setting; the language could be perceived as quirky and unfamiliar in today's image-saturated world, where visual content description is rendered unnecessary, practically speaking. Inside the archive however, the description is often the researcher's primary point of contact with the image, and the image's primary way of communicating with the outside world. The description writer needs to present a neutral view that is open enough to allow different research directions, yet which presents and supports the position of the archive image as information and evidence. As such, it is a text form that must be very carefully managed. The description does not set out to assign meaning to the image in question, because meaning that is based on intuition and uncorroborated by content is regarded as extraneous and problematic in the archive. Similarly, I do not attempt to direct meaning or flag up visual signifiers that might encourage the completion of a narrative outside of the discrete and limited time of the image. Whilst it is impossible to accurately anticipate the mind of the reader—and it is even arguable that the grey, uncreative language used in description actually encourages imaginative interpretations—the visual content-centred approach asks for consideration of the image *and* the description as discrete but not autonomous objects, as units in a bigger organizational scheme that take their cultural and spatiotemporal context from their surrounding objects and from their recorded place. In this way, the structure of the archive becomes the sign system for the archived photograph.

Of course, many photographic practices actively demand completion by the viewer. For example, British conceptual artist and theorist Victor Burgin uses the idea of audience completion to take his photographic practice into a desired cultural and political framework. Throughout his career, Burgin has worked across a variety of forms of visual representation, and with a strong linguistic presence. Using language in a typically restrained and carefully constructed way, he alludes to notions that lie outside of the image itself. Burgin recognizes the effect of completion: he begins his book, *The Remembered Film*, with a Wittgenstein quote, which concludes, 'If you complete it you falsify it.'[20] This is fitting advice for archivists writing descriptions *and* for researchers looking at images.

As with Simon's temporally regulated and restricted *Contraband* project, time has become a fundamental preoccupation in my own archive-related work. This should come as no surprise, as time is central to the archive, through the historical nature of collections as well as aspects of material decay and degradation that document the passing of time—and of course the time-intensive labour of cataloguing, storage, and preservation. My work with description utilizes the time-based media of film and scripted performance, always with text present—written or spoken—and is tightly controlling of the time of the viewer. In common with objects and descriptions inside archive institution, the photographs that I use and the descriptions that I make are presentations of discrete situations that are unaffected by outside time. They are rendered time-critical and yet timeless through processes of documentation, preservation, and storage. The images reproduced throughout this chapter are screen shots from my film *El Rastro* (2014), where single frames are made visible by description. Film theorist Laura Mulvey[21] argues that the moment in time that each frame in a film is exposed to light behind the lens—she terms this the 'process of inscription'—is an index, 'the source of the image's place in time'. She is concerned for the visibility of the 'index' in the moving image, where the narrative of the film

Figure 17.4 Still from *El Rastro* at 5'08" © Jane Birkin 2014.

overrides the time of inscription. The original index remains hidden, 'masked by the story-telling function of cinema'. This is core to the understanding of the technical and the textual narrative pause, the image *and* the image description.

Over the past decade or more, public interest and artistic practice in response to the archive has proliferated. We have become obsessed with the ideas of the archive as memory institution, with the past mostly being objectified by degradation and decay. Over the years, much archive-related art practice has centred around human issues of memory and nostalgia, often materializing in the use of visibly degraded archive images. Certainly, such practice can be a valid way of exploring issues of memory and trace, as seen in the work of artists such as Christian Boltanski, whose photo-installation *Menschlich (Humanity)* (1994–1995) evoked the fading memories of the atrocities of the twentieth century through the use of imperfect images from a variety of archival sources. But, in some circumstances, degraded archive media could be seen to embody a 'glitch aesthetic' of the past, fitting in with the obsession for vintage-inspired filters that can be seamlessly applied to images, through popular software applications that twist the temporalities of old and new images alike.

Image appropriation, and associated tactics of reordering and re-contextualization have become mainstream artistic strategies, and they are easily accessible strategies in the age of the networked image. Both archive and network are spaces of storage and retrieval, and archive objects—physical ones—are dynamic entities that can be rearranged and re-contextualized endlessly through the work of researchers, but they are always returned to their designated place in the strongroom. Systems such as user registers and carbon-copied paper slips maintain the integrity of the archive, preventing material from being lost through misfiling. In contrast, the digitized archive object, once released to the outside, into network space, loses any special status as document and behaves like any other digital object; it can be called up, copied, altered, discarded, or rearranged—by artists and others. In effect, when removed from its context in this way, it ceases to be a 'document' in the way that Lisa Gitelman[22] defines it, using librarian and 'documentalist' Suzanne Briet's 1951 example of the antelope: if it were running wild, it would not be a document, whereas if it were to be put in a zoo, it would; it would be framed as evidence. Undoubtedly, the networking and movement of archival images represents a democratization of the archival object, a freeing from its institutional chains; but although appropriating images from any source can be productive and meaningful, loss of context means a loss of cultural significance that we may not be able to regain. Gitelman points out that the word 'document' comes from the Latin root *docere*, to show or teach; the document *exists* in order to document. In an archive setting, this is the photograph's primary function; it is fully accepted, catalogued and described *as* a document, along with all the many other forms of document that can be found there.

The tensions that exist between framing the photograph as art or as document—as art object or as archive object—surface interestingly in a debate over Julia van Haaften's reorganization of the New York Public Library. Douglas Crimp describes this act as one of reclassifying images according to their newly acquired value—that of art; where 'World War II becomes Robert Capa.' This is an exercise that Crimp[23] traces back to John Szarkowski (director of MOMA's Department of Photography from 1962 to 1991) and his modernist vision of photography as an art form, a medium of subjectivity. Crimp describes the image as 'ghettoized' through its journey from archive to museum, arguing, 'It will no longer primarily be useful within other discursive practices; it will no longer serve the purposes of information, documentation, evidence, illustration, reportage. The formerly plural field of photography will henceforth be reduced to the single, all-encompassing *aesthetic.*'

Of course, ghettoization is a strong and emotive term, but Crimp uses the word precisely: to ghettoize is to segregate, to confine to a particular area or category, and, in doing so, to strip of any cultural and political power. In 'Reading an Archive: Photography between Labour and Capital', artist and writer Allan Sekula reiterates Crimp's point as he discusses at length the question of information, politics, and aesthetics of the photographic image through his case study of images taken from the Shedden archive for the production of a book. He states, 'The very removal of these photographs from their initial contexts invites aestheticism.'[24] This idea is also debated in Sekula's essay 'On the Invention of Photographic Meaning', where he argues against the photograph as an autonomous object and labels the much-peddled notion of the 'universal language of photography' as 'bourgeois folklore'. To support his argument he attempts to lay bare the Lewis Hine photograph *Immigrants Going Down Gangplank, New York* (1905) and Alfred Steiglitz' *The Steerage*

(1907), interestingly, by describing them in a naive manner, 'divesting both images of context, as though I and the photographs fell from the sky'.[25] The arguments that Crimp and Sekula make are even more pertinent in terms of the networked image: digital objects can be moved, reassigned, and re-valued in a click, and often with no reference to their provenance; indeed, 'as if they fell from the sky'.

Description is a cultural technique that is universally familiar, but inside the archive institution it is a form of labour that is fast becoming too time consuming and so too expensive for many archives to carry out. However, it can be readily accepted as part and parcel of the production of art, which is, after all, expected to be time and labour intensive, and frequently comes up for criticism when it is not. With this, an adversarial relationship between 'work' and 'art' is generated, one that is particularly interesting from my dual position of artist and archive worker. My own art practice, relying as it does on the time management of two separate but connected activities, does not fit either of what Maurizio Lazzarato[26] perceives to be Jacques Rancière's 'two politics of aesthetics': the first of which is 'the becoming life of art', where there is no separation between the two; the second, 'resistant art', is one that actively seeks separation, so as to maintain art as a commodity. Perhaps, as Lazzarato argues in the case of the readymade, this relationship between work and art has more to do with the *dispositif*, the performing or the positioning of the piece on a public stage, outside of its original private location, so transforming both the 'ordinariness' of the activity and the 'ordinariness' of the product. My practice indeed lies in a transitional and transformational space between two activities of work, and the transformation itself is critical to its functioning. This notion of the transformation of the ordinary underpins the perceived idiosyncrasy

Figure 17.5 Still from *El Rastro* at 9'17" © Jane Birkin 2014.

of archival description in the outside world that I identify at the beginning of this chapter.

ACKNOWLEDGEMENTS

This chapter is a reworking and an updating of my article 'Art, Work, and Archives: Performativity and the Techniques of Production', first published in November 2015 in *Archive Journal*, in the special issue: *Radical Archives*, edited by Lisa Darms and Kate Eichhorn. I would like to thank the editors and the anonymous reviewers for their help with that article, and I can recommend looking at the whole of this very interesting special issue.

FURTHER READING

Liz Kotz, *Words to be Looked At: Language in 1960s Art* (Cambridge, MA: MIT Press, 2007)

Kari Kraus, 'Picture Criticism: Textual Studies and the Image', in N. Fraistat and J. Flanders, eds, *The Cambridge Companion to Textual Scholarship* (Cambridge: Cambridge University Press, 2013), 236–256

Sharon Marcus, Heather Love, and Stephen Best, 'Building a Better Description', *Representations* 135 (2016), 1–21

Jussi Parikka, *What Is Media Archaeology?* (Cambridge: Polity Press, 2012)

Sven Spieker, *The Big Archive: Art from Bureaucracy* (Cambridge, MA: MIT Press, 2008)

NOTES

1. C. Vismann, *Files: Law, Media and Technology*, trans by G. Winthrop-Young, 1st ed. (Stanford, California: Stanford University Press, 2008), 164.
2. W. Ernst, *Digital Memory and the Archive*, ed. J. Parikka (Minneapolis: University of Minnesota, 2013), 84.
3. A. Sekula, 'The Body and the Archive', *October* 39 (1986), 3–64, 16–18.
4. U. Orlow and R. Maclennan, *Re: The Archive, the Image, and the Very Dead Sheep* (London: School of Advanced Study/The National Archives/Double Agents, 2004), 79.
5. M. Iversen, 'Auto-Maticity: Ruscha and Performative Photography', in D. Costello and M. E. Iversen, eds, *Photography after Conceptual Art* (Chichester: Wiley-Blackwell, 2010), 15–16.
6. J. L. Austin, *How to Do Things with Words* (Oxford: Clarendon Press, 1962), 5.
7. J. Butler, 'Performative Acts and Gender Constitution: An Essay in Phenomenology and Feminist Theory', in A. Jones, ed., *The Feminism and Visual Culture Reader* (London: Routledge, 2003), 397.
8. Sekula, 'The Body and the Archive', 57 (original emphasis).
9. G. Magnani 'Ordering Procedures: Photography in Recent German Art', *Arts Magazine*, 64 (1990), 78–83, 81–82.

10. H. U. Obrist, 'Ever Airport: Notes on Taryn Simon's Contraband', in T. Simon, *Contraband* (Göttingen: Steidl, 2010), 9.
11. J. Ellis, *Keeping Archives* (Port Melbourne, Australia: D. W. Thorpe in association with The Australian Society of Archivists, 1993), 11.
12. M. Foucault, *The Archaeology of Knowledge*, trans. A. M. Sheridan Smith, Routledge Classics (London: Routledge, 2002; originally published in English 1972), 145.
13. Foucault, *The Archaeology of Knowledge*, 186.
14. Vismann, *Files*, 6.
15. A. Alberro, 'Structure as Content: Dan Graham's *Schema (March 1966)* and the Emergence of Conceptual Art', in G. Moure, ed., *Dan Graham* (Barcelona and Santiago de Compostela: Fundació Antoni Tàpies, Barcelona y Centro Galego de Arte Contemporánea, Santiago de Compostela, 1998), 27.
16. C. Dworkin and K. Goldsmith, eds, *Against Expression: An Anthology of Conceptual Writing* (Evanston: Northwestern University Press, 2011), 249.
17. www.theguardian.com/books/2015/mar/17/michael-brown-autopsy-report-poem-kenneth-goldsmith.
18. Dworkin and Goldsmith, *Against Expression*, p. xxiii.
19. D. P. Fowler, 'Narrate and Describe: The Problem of Ekphrasis', *Journal of Roman Studies* 81 (1991), 25–35, 25.
20. V. Burgin, *The Remembered Film* (London: Reaktion Books, 2004), 7.
21. L. Mulvey, 'The "Pensive Spectator" Revisited: Time and its Passing in the Still and Moving Image', in D. Green, ed., *Where Is the Photograph?* (Maidstone and Brighton: Photoforum and Photoworks, 2003), 116–117.
22. L. Gitelman, *Paper Knowledge: Towards a Media History of Documents* (Durham and London: Duke University Press, 2014), 1–3.
23. D. Crimp, 'The Museum's Old / the Library's New', in R. Bolton, ed., *The Contest of Meaning: Critical Histories of Photography* (Cambridge, MA: MIT Press, 1989), 6–7.
24. A. Sekula, 'Reading an Archive: Photography between Labour and Capital', in L. Wells, ed., *The Photography Reader* (London: Routledge, 2003), 448.
25. A. Sekula, 'On the Invention of Photographic Meaning', in V. Burgin, ed., *Thinking Photography* (Basingstoke: Macmillan, 1982), 86–88.
26. M. Lazzarato, 'Art, Work and Politics in Disciplinary Societies and Societies of Security', *Radical Philosophy* 149 (2008), 26–32.

CHAPTER 18

DIGITAL INNOVATION AND ARCHIVAL THINKING

EIRINI GOUDAROULI

Drawing examples from the history of natural sciences, the American philosopher of science Thomas Samuel Kuhn (1922–1996) introduced the concept of the *paradigm shift* to describe a fundamental theoretical and epistemological change that may occur in a scientific discipline.[1] According to Kuhn, after a period of instability and intellectual crisis, a thorough transformation of the scientific framework occurs leading to the reshaping of basic well-established concepts, theories, methods, and practices of the discipline in crisis. This eventually leads to *incommensurability* between the old, pre-revolutionary, science and the new, post-revolutionary, science and makes the communication between the scientists of the new paradigm and those of the old one hard, if not impossible. Kuhn's ideas were published in his book *The Structure of Scientific Revolutions* (1962), and since its publication they have influenced the theoretical, methodological, and conceptual foundations of disciplines beyond the natural sciences.

Terry Cook was one of the first archivists and archival theorists to bring the concept of the *paradigm shift* to the context of archival science, and used it repeatedly to describe the evolution of various fields of archival science.[2] Writing in 2012, Cook studies the evolution of archival theory and practice through the lens of Kuhn's theory and argues that archival practice 'has moved from evidence to memory to identity and community', which, consequently, pushed the boundaries of the role, identity and skillset of archivists beyond the traditional limits of their own discipline.[3]

Over the past century, archival science moved from the Hilary Jenkinson's era to a new age of Artificial Intelligence (AI)-assisted recordkeeping. Archivists have gradually become 'active shapers of the archival heritage',[4] rethinking the well-established archival framework whilst they experience the emergence of new technologies and actively seek ways to embed these new technologies in their theories and practices. Today, as archives and archivists witness a radical revolution that the adoption of digital and technological innovation brings to the record and recordkeeping practices, the paradigm is rapidly shifting. However, this time, archival science is not moving from the relatively steady principles of the discipline to the shaping of a new state of normality. Instead, archival science is moving from a relative stability to a continual, digitally and technologically advanced, change.[5]

This chapter aims to open up the discussion about the theoretical and methodological challenges that the complex digital environments and archival systems, and their evolving nature, bring to the Archive. Although the emergence and adoption of advanced technologies impacts the ethical, legal, economic, and financial decisions, policies, and frameworks of the Archive, these issues need to be discussed separately to receive the thorough consideration they require. Therefore, this chapter will mainly focus on the complexities that digital brings at a technological and practical level and how these complexities transform the record and reshape archival thinking and practice.

To do so, I will focus on the variety of complexities that the increasing volume of digital (both digitized and born-digital) records brings to the archival framework, requiring new capabilities and approaches on how best to curate (that is, to collect, capture, preserve, contextualize, present, and provide access to) the increasingly digital records. I will briefly reflect on some of the biggest challenges that we, at The National Archives, are facing as we seek to become a second-generation digital archive, that is digital by instinct and design.[6] At the end of the chapter, I will also explore the benefits and opportunities that derive from the integrations of archival and computational thinking and practice; and how computational archival science can help us approach these pressing challenges, as well as the new exciting opportunities, in new ways.

The Evolving Nature of Archival Artefacts: Moving from Paper to Digitized to Born-Digital

Over the past decades, rapid and continuous digital and technological development and innovation have radically reshaped the archival landscape. The nature of archival objects has fundamentally altered in the light of digital, leading to their radical transformation and, consequently, their reconceptualization. Traditionally, an archival object or artefact is considered to be a physical item that is tangible, is defined by its material characteristics (i.e. paper, textile, wax) and can be preserved as a record based on its aesthetic and physical qualities as well as its information value. However, during the last few decades, archival practice and theory have moved from the paper realm to a (brave) new digital world, which consists of new archival objects that reside in increasingly complex systems and rapidly evolving environments.

This move is also evidenced by the transformation of traditional archival terminology. For example, according to The Society of American Archivists' first glossary, apart from its traditional definition, an archival object may be 'a collection of data with defined boundaries that is treated as a single entity; a resource; a digital object', or 'an instantiation of a class or entity that forms a component of a system'. It may also refer to 'an anomaly in data that results from the methodology used to capture or analyse the data, or that was introduced or produced during a procedure'.[7] The uncertain and unbounded nature of these new types of archival objects contests not only the traditional terminology, but also the well-established archival framework and, as a result, raises ethical and legal questions on how to work more openly, accountably, and transparently when we curate these new types of digital records.

The large volumes of these new types of records, that come in a variety of new formats (Microsoft Word documents, emails, high-definition video, snapshots of websites and social media pages, executable code, structured datasets, and records derived from machine learning systems to name just a few) and with little or no structure, makes the traditional archival painstaking manual processes impossible for tasks such as appraisal, selection, and sensitivity review. They require new complex digital infrastructures and archiving systems that effectively deal with their increasing influx and can enable digital recordkeeping at scale. They also require new capabilities and approaches to develop these new generation infrastructures and systems and quickly adapt to new emergent technologies to ensure their maintenance and sustainability in a constantly evolving digital environment.

However, the adoption of new technologies continuously alters the traditional archival landscape, requiring new skills and capabilities to manage vast volumes of complex digital records that reside in complex digital infrastructures and systems. For decades, archivists have been using long-standing practices to curate records that traditionally addressed paper records and other physical objects and artefacts. Although today's archivist has started adapting to the use of new emergent technologies (Google Docs, hashing algorithms, blockchain technology, and the cloud to name just a few), the majority of these new technologies are still applied to and within a long-established body of archival practices devised for physical records. Nevertheless, as the archival world is moving rapidly towards an increasingly complex, continuously changing digital future, archival and recordkeeping institutions must find ways successfully to disrupt and adapt entrenched practice,[8] and push the boundaries of the role, identity, and skillset of today's archivist beyond the limits of the existing archival framework.

Therefore, the need to rethink the record has never been more profound. Undoubtedly, by moving from the physical to digitized to born digital records, new opportunities are opening up (such as ways of presenting, accessing, and analysing complex large-scale collections as data for research, exploration, and experimentation), leading to a more open and inclusive archive.[9] However, the need to rethink our practices in the light of digital requires approaching the record as something broader and less rigidly defined, fundamentally changing the archival landscape.

Moving into the (Archival) Future: The Disruptive Archive

Complexities that Change the World

The National Archives is the official archive and publisher for the UK Government,[10] and for England and Wales, and a cultural heritage institution. In 2015, The National Archives stated its new strategic vision, *Archives Inspire* (2015–2019). This new strategy identified *digital* as The National Archives' biggest challenge and set an ambitious plan to think and organize the archives differently.

To achieve our goals, at The National Archives, we have been exploring different ways of using our knowledge and expertise. We have also been learning from outside the heritage sector and have been adopting new approaches from other domains in order to provide strong leadership on how best to address the various challenges the archival sector is facing in the light of digital.[11] Over the four years since *Archives Inspire*, we have embarked on a strategic transformation to become a second-generation archive that is digital by instinct and design.[12] As part of this transformation, we have learned an enormous amount about the nature of the challenges we face, our capabilities, and the best way to rethink our practice. As we seek to become a second-generation digital archive our ambition is to transcend the legacy of our paper collections and our traditional recordkeeping practices, by being disruptive.[13]

The disruptive archive brings an end to the archival world as we know it. Being disruptive means to be able to constantly adapt and evolve accordingly to the digital and technological landscape in which the disruptive archive operates. It also means to have the capacity proactively to recognize how that digital and technological landscape will change and act by making informed decisions on how best to rethink and reshape its practices to meet future challenges. In addition, it means to have the ability to understand when and how to develop new skills, by adopting new approaches from other domains and disciplines, in order to reaffirm and transform its historic mission for the digital age.[14]

There are three main pillars upon which the disruptive archive is conceptualized and shaped. Firstly, the new types of digital records that archives curate; secondly, the need to develop technologically advanced infrastructures and archiving systems that are able to deal with the ever-increasing volume of these new types of digital records; and, thirdly, the need to adopt new and emerging technologies to our every-day recordkeeping thinking and practice, to enable the management of complex digital records at scale. In what follows, I will briefly explore these three points separately through the lens of The National Archives.

Digital Records

The National Archives has a long-established legacy as a trusted guardian of the physical collections it holds, approximately 200 kilometres of paper documents documenting 1000 years of human history and culture, stored and preserved in its repositories in Kew and Cheshire.[15]

However, in the last few decades, The National Archives added to their holdings millions of pages of digitized records and an ever-increasing volume of all sorts of formats and types of born-digital records. Focusing on the preservation, contextualization, presentation, and provision of secure and constant access to these new types of digital records that are deposited in vast volumes, The National Archives' remit is to maintain its long-established standing in assuring the legitimacy of the evidence it holds, ensuring it remains available to future generations whilst taking into consideration issues relating to data protection and appropriate levels of openness. In brief, as it stated at our website, there are three broad categories of digital records preserved by The National Archive:

> Born-digital records. A born digital record refers to records that originally produced in digital form such as spreadsheets, emails, websites, databases, images, and video.
> Digitized records. A digitized record is a scanned copy of paper or parchment record that is accessioned in place of the paper record.
> Digital surrogates. A digital surrogate is the digital image that is used as an access copy of a paper or parchment original which is retained as the record.[16]

These new types of records include records that are data that depend on code. Therefore, these particular types of records may bring a variety of new dependencies, relating to the way that these records have been created as well as their provenance, that archivists need to understand, explore, and manage at scale, over time and through generations of technological change.[17]

Digital Infrastructures (Cloud Computing)

In 2011, the Information Technology Laboratory at The National Institute of Standards and Technology in the US published a report exploring cloud computing as an evolving paradigm and providing recommendations on what it is and how to best use it. According to the report, cloud computing 'is a model for enabling ubiquitous, convenient, on-demand network access to a shared pool of configurable computing resources (e.g. networks, servers, storage, applications, and services) that can be rapidly provisioned and released with minimal management effort or service provider interaction.'[18] Its main characteristics include on-demand self-service, broad network access, resource pooling, rapid elasticity, and measured service.[19]

The arrival of cloud computing services at the archive brings a variety of new technologies that today's archivists need to explore, understand, adapt, and use which consequently brings both new challenges and benefits to the forefront.[20]

In the two years since the Digital Strategy, we, at The National Archives, have been investigating the benefits that we can gain from the use of cloud-based services. As a result of this investigation, we are already beginning to use these services not only for storage and management of digital content over time, but also for hosting our public facing digital services, such as The National Archives' website, Discovery (our digital catalogue), legislation.gov.uk and the UK Government Web Archive.[21]

AI and Automating the Archive

In 'Computing Machinery and Intelligence' published in *Mind* in 1950, Alan Turing explored a question, that it is still relevant today: *Can Machines Think?* Almost seven decades after Turing's influential study we have not properly answered this question. But we have followed his suggestion that machines can learn from experience when they are trained to do so. Based on this particular idea, AI has developed as a field and among many other applications is broadly used for the analysis of large-scale data. Statistical models and algorithms become powerful tools for automating tasks that have traditionally been done manually, allowing the exploration and analysis of large-scale data in a fast and consistent way.

AI offers new exciting possibilities to the archive in approaching such challenges as appraisal, selection, and sensitivity review of complex large-scale digital records. Machine learning, that is algorithms that can automatically improve with experience to produce better probabilistic outputs, can offer new innovative approaches of exploring, analysing, and managing large volumes of complex digital records that come to the archive in a variety of new formats and with little or no structure. Using AI and machine learning technologies can revolutionize the traditional archival processes for everyday tasks and enable digital recordkeeping at scale.

At The National Archives, we see a future where AI and emergent technologies become part of our daily practice, whilst we explore, understand, and consider thoroughly the ethical, theoretical, and epistemological implications relating to digital archival preservation, description, presentation, and use. For example, we are particularly interested in exploring ways of automating the accessioning (registration, transfer, and ingest) of new digital records that we receive from government departments. We are also interested in using AI (such as neural networks, natural language processing, statistical machine learning, and deep learning) to automate the creation of metadata not only to improve the findability of our content but also to create faster and more consistent descriptions of our digital records.[22] However, implementing automatic generation of item-level metadata around our born-digital records requires us to understand the implications of shifting from the manually generated descriptive layer over our holdings to automatically generated metadata. Therefore, we aim to focus on questions of authority and quality assurance around AI-assisted practices in the broader context of evolving standards for archival description and related schemas and ontologies, that will help us to explore new ways of helping our users to engage with and interrogate uncertain descriptions.[23]

Facing New Challenges

The disruptive archive revolutionizes archival thinking and practice.[24] New types of records are explored, processed, and managed with the use and adaptation of AI to recordkeeping practices and within technologically advanced infrastructures. However, this brings a variety of new types of challenges to the archival landscape, as well as ethical, theoretical, and epistemological implications, to the archival landscape that archivists and archives are now actively seeking to address. The most crucial challenges are linked to two core long-standing archival concepts, that is, trust and risk. Although the concepts of trust and risk are interconnected, in what follows I will briefly discuss them separately to highlight how they may have been affected by the digital shift and how this new dynamic makes the archive a complex digital environment.

Trust

Trust has always been central to archives. However, the digital contests long-established archival practices, spotlighting questions relating to trust. The National Archives is actively seeking to maintain the long-established legitimacy they historically confer and to ensure that the public records it holds are trustworthy and accessible in what we assume will be a further digitally advanced future.

In 'Trust in Digital Records: An Increasingly Cloudy Legal Area' (2012), Luciana Duranti and Corrine Rogers argue that, by developing and adopting new computer technologies, modern society changed the way that people trust the records. According to the authors, traditionally 'trust in records depends on four types of knowledge about the creator or custodian of the records: reputation, past performance, competence, and the assurance of confidence in future performance.'[25] These fundamental criteria cannot play their role in the digital world: being in a state of continuous technological change radically alters the way of documenting evidence.

In an era of increasing dependence on AI, remaining trusted custodians today and in the future, means that cultural and recordkeeping institutions need to invest time and resources to explore the conceptual, epistemological, and practical challenges that the application of AI and machine-learning technologies bring to the way we approach, understand, and manage the intangible record. It also involves understanding and tackling the challenges relating to records' integrity and continuity derived from the use of cloud computing, whilst ensuring that our recordkeeping theories and practices correspond to the current and future landscapes.

As we at The National Archives see a future where AI and emergent technologies become part of our everyday recordkeeping practices, ethical implications also need to be considered thoroughly. For example, AI requires us to rethink entirely how we preserve evidence of both the system and the decisions we make, as increasing societal dependency on decision-making by algorithms fundamentally impacts the evidential landscape. AI and machine-learning technologies use records that are data, and depend on code to create and train algorithms, which are then applied to new data. This is becoming more widespread and multifarious. At the more complex end of the spectrum, where neural networks operate in a dynamically evolving and interactive environment, it becomes challenging to be transparent about the basis on which outcomes are determined.[26] Therefore, becoming more accountable and transparent about the practices and the decisions we make are fundamental to us, for the current and future benefit of government and citizens, whilst questions around trust and openness become more profound as we move towards to an AI-assisted recordkeeping future.

Risk

Archives have always carefully planned the best ways to deal with potential risks and threats. Identifying and understanding those risks and threats and developing innovative risk management methodologies have historically been among the core interests of archival and recordkeeping institutions. Traditionally, institutions focused on building management and developing risk methodologies and regular assessments for physical disasters of threats related to physical causes. Fire, earthquakes, floods, or gas explosions rank high in the risk-management planning and strategies of archival institutions, shaping policies, monitoring, and assessment strategies.

What's more, risk and threats relating to the holdings and collections are part of the risk-management policies at archival institutions. Risks linked to the environmental conditions in the repositories, the handling of physical collections in the reading room, and the conditions of the collections themselves, such as mould growth, shape the development of preservation strategies and policies and set the framework for dealing with physical threats, enabling monitoring of the relative changes in stewardship of the collection over time.

Over the past few decades, technological developments and innovation have expanded the discussion from physical threats and disasters, to the buildings' redevelopment and systems' maintenance, to digital-related risks in areas such as security, digital preservation, loss of data, and contravention of General Data Protection Regulation (GDPR). In the age of complex digital infrastructures and archival systems (such as cloud computing), as well as of increasing dependency on AI, archivists and recordkeeping institutions are continuously seeking to ensure and maintain their trusted, both digital and physical, repositories.

For example, using cloud-based services may benefit archival and recordkeeping institutions technologically, economically, and strategically. However, using cloud computing for storage and management of complex digital records over time brings challenges not only at organizational level, but also at a practical and methodological level. Shifting to technologically advanced infrastructures and archiving systems requires a change in our approaches to measuring and managing potential risks. Therefore, there are two main categories of risk that come to the forefront: (i) risks relating to long-term digital preservation including issues around the security, integrity, authenticity, and authentication, and reliability of digital records that may be fragile due to the risk of loss, corruption, and obsolescence and (ii) risks relating to accuracy, accountability, and transparency of digital infrastructures.

Recognizing and exploring the risks that the digital record and these technologically advanced archival environments bring to recordkeeping theories and practices can help us understand where our digital vulnerabilities reside and, as a result, develop policies and frameworks on how to best manage digital risks, to communicate these risks effectively, and address the legal and ethical challenges raised during this process.[27] Therefore, archival and recordkeeping institutions are seeking to adopt more risk-based approaches that combine practical considerations about new digital technologies and information resources with critical business processes to ensure continuity and maintain a good prospect of longevity. By identifying and tackling the risks that the digital brings, archival and recordkeeping institutions will continue to work towards good governance, political openness, accountability, and transparency, serve the public interest, and remain trusted custodians of the future archive.

Unlocking New Opportunities: Towards the Integration of Archival and Computational Thinking

In the previous section, I outlined three fundamental ways that the archive alters in the digital age, that is, through the evolution of the record; the technological upgrade of archival systems and infrastructures; and use of AI technologies in recordkeeping practices. The aim was to highlight the ways in which the archive changes due to the challenges raised by the new digital and technological developments, and to explore why being disruptive can help archival and recordkeeping institutions not only to be proactively prepared to address current and upcoming challenges, but also recognize the possibilities offered and benefit from them.

As discussed in the previous section, digital is shaping what types of records are created and captured, transforming the ways that they are accessed and used but also the systems in which they are stored, preserved, and managed. Due to the profound impact that the digital and technological development and innovation brings to both the record and the recordkeeping framework, it is currently recognized as one of the biggest challenges for archival and recordkeeping institutions worldwide. However, it is also recognized that it unlocks new potentials that can lead archival and recordkeeping institutions around the world strategically to invest time and resources to explore both the challenges, as well as the new possibilities, that the digital brings.

The new possibilities that the digital unlocks include the use of computational methods and tools within archives. For example, one of the areas in which the technological development opens new opportunities is linked to the accessibility and findability of the archival content, unlocking it for exploration, research, and experimentation. Using AI technologies to approach and extract archival content as data for exploration and analysis, enables the creation of aggregated, large-scale datasets. It also enables archival and recordkeeping institutions to rethink the ways of providing access to archival collections through innovation in digital catalogues and other digital services but also create new opportunities in collection, analysis, preservation, contextualization, use, and reuse of their content.

Computational Archival Science: New Possibilities, New Approaches

The National Archives is recognized as an Independent Research Organization (IRO) by the UK's Arts and Humanities Research Council (AHRC), which means that we are eligible to lead research proposals submitted to any of the UK's seven research councils for funding. Therefore, The National Archives has a dedicated research team that actively seeks to develop new research collaborations to explore and address the major questions and challenges that are fundamental to us as a national and digital archive.

One of our latest funded research activities brings together experts from Archival and Higher Education institutions from the US and the UK. In February 2019, King's College London's Department of Digital Humanities partnered with The National Archives, the Digital Curation Innovation Center at the University of Maryland iSchool, and the Maryland State Archives in the US to explore the application of computational methods and tools to large-scale digital heritage collections. This collaboration was awarded an International Research Networking grant for UK–US Collaborations in Digital Scholarship in Cultural Institutions by the AHRC.[28]

The one-year AHRC-funded CAS Network highlights the important role that computational thinking and practice can play in archival science in the digital age and draws expertise from previous work in the field. In brief, we are investigating the potential and exploring new ways to address the challenges that the digital brings to the archive. This work is led by a group of researchers who have identified a new field of study: Computational Archival Science (CAS).[29] The CAS initiative aims at creating an interdisciplinary space that brings computation and archival theories and practice together and welcomes a two-way exchange of knowledge between its foundational disciplines. As a result, its definition may evolve as the disciplines involved (that is, computer science, data science, digital humanities, and archival science) contribute to the shaping of theoretical and methodological foundations of the new computational archival science. According to the group, CAS is:

> A transdisciplinary field concerned with the application of computational methods and resources to large-scale records/archives processing, analysis, storage, long-term preservation, and access, with the aim of improving efficiency, productivity, and precision in support of appraisal, arrangement and description, preservation and access decisions.
>
> The intent is to engage and undertake research with archival materials as well as apply the collective knowledge of computer and archival science to understand the ways that new technologies change the generation, use, storage, and preservation of records and the implications of these changes for archival functions and the societal and organizational use and preservation of authentic digital records.
>
> This suggests that computational archival science is a blend of computational and archival thinking.[30]

The AHRC-funded CAS Network derived from a workshop organized at The UK National Archives in collaboration with King's College London in September 2017. The focus of the workshop was on automating the archive, exploring how computational approaches can be used to support archival practice in the creation and preservation of reliable and authentic records and archives. The network takes into consideration the ideas generated in the workshop and draws expertise from the previous work done within the context of CAS initiative. In brief, it focuses on the ways that the digital and technological innovation impacts the nature of both the record and traditional recordkeeping practices, with a special interest on contextualizing the record. The network's scope is to investigate the potential of a broad range of computational methods and tools to meet challenges in the archival problem space, with a specific focus on contextualizing digital records, both digitized and born-digital. The context of a record is key for understanding its value as historical evidence, and the ability to map out and provide access to that context is key for conferring value on what would otherwise may be disconnected pieces of information, enabling them to be used (i.e. found, understood, and re-purposed) effectively by researchers drawing on the archival evidence base.

The CAS Network's scope is also linked to the broader objectives of the CAS initiative which focus on seeking to (i) contribute to the development of the theoretical foundations of a new trans-discipline of computational archival science; (ii) design the educational foundations and deliver training in the field in support of industries relating to archives and archival science; (iii) to develop a virtual and physical laboratory to test and apply scientific advances in a collaborative environment.[31]

Most important, the CAS Network is broadly interested in contributing to the integration of 'computational thinking' and 'archival thinking', as recordkeeping innovation and technological development can only go hand in hand. However, there is a need to create opportunities for knowledge exchange and interdisciplinary synergies that will enable the infusion of archival concepts, principles, theories, and methods with the computational and vice versa.[32]

Training and education are crucial in integrating computational and archival thinking.[33] However in this phase the CAS Network is primarily concerned with building research communities to enable knowledge exchange and interdisciplinary synergies, and bringing together computational and archival experts. Creating an environment where information and archives professionals can effectively interact with each other and the data will contribute to exploration of the major questions and challenges that archival and recordkeeping institutions around the world are facing in the age of AI-assisted recordkeeping.

The Intangible Record

The intangible record changes the way that heritage and recordkeeping institutions around the world take decisions and develop their strategic visions, whilst they rethink their long-standing archival, technological, ethical, legal, economic, and financial policies and frameworks. It also fundamentally changes the role of archivists, requiring new capabilities and approaches on how to develop and sustain new digital archiving systems and infrastructures and to manage complex digital records, in different formats with little or no structure and in vast volumes, through digital recordkeeping at scale. These changes inevitably bring a variety of theoretical and practical complexities to the archival thinking and practice that needs our close attention, thorough consideration and prompt action.

The urgent need for establishing a framework that enables digital recordkeeping at scale requires the rethinking of our existing capabilities and urges us not only to embrace but also actively to seek to merge emergent technologies and computational methods with archival practices. Integrating archival thinking with computational thinking means that new knowledge acquired from outside the archival domain will embed or reshape archival theories and practices, whilst archival knowledge and expertise will contribute to the rethinking of the existing computational practices. Breaking the disciplinary silos and shifting to a more interdisciplinary and collaborative mentality will enable us to unite our skills to address jointly the challenges that digital and technological development and innovation bring, and to take advantage of the opportunities emerged.

In the age of large-scale data analytics and AI-assisted recordkeeping, we recognize that bridging the gap between computational and archival thinking is the best, if not the only, way to move forward as we seek to address the existing and future challenges that are fundamental to us as heritage and recordkeeping institutions.

FURTHER READING

Paul Feyerabend, *Against Method. Outline of an Anarchistic Theory of Knowledge* (London, New York: New Left Books, 1975)

Hans Hofman, 'Rethinking the Archival Function in the Digital Era', *Comma: International Journal on Archives* 2 (2012), 25–34

Laura A. Millar, 'On the Crest of a Wave: Transforming the Archival Future', *Archives and Manuscripts* 45.2 (2017), 59–76

Laura A. Millar, *Matter of Facts: The Value of Evidence in an Information Age* (Chicago: American Library Association, 2019)

Eric Oberheim and Paul Hoyningen-Huene, 'The Incommensurability of Scientific Theories', Edward N. Zalta, ed., *The Stanford Encyclopedia of Philosophy*, Fall 2018 edn., https://plato.stanford.edu/archives/fall2018/entries/incommensurability

Nanna Bonde Thylstrup, *The Politics of Mass Digitization* (Cambridge, MA: MIT Press, 2019)

NOTES

1. Dr Erini Goudarouli is Head of Digital Research Programmes, The National Archives, UK. This chapter is © Crown copyright (2021). Licensed under the Open Government Licence v 3.0.
2. T. Cook, 'What is Past is Prologue: A History of Archival Ideas Since 1898, and the Future Paradigm Shift', *Archivaria* 43 (1997), 17–63; H. MacNeil, 'Archival Theory and Practice: Between Two Paradigms', *Archivaria* 37 (1994), 17. Luciana Duranti mentions that in 1987 Hugh Taylor discussed the concept of paradigm shift in archives in the keynote speech entitled 'Transformation in the Archives: Technological Adjustment or Paradigm Shift?' at the Association of Canadian Archivists annual meeting: 'Archival Science in the Cloud Environment: Continuity or Transformation?', *Atlanti: Special Issue in Honour of Charles Kecskeméti* 23 (2013), 45–52.
3. T. Cook, 'Evidence, Memory, Identity, and Community: Four Shifting Archival Paradigms', *Archival Science*, 13 (2013), 95–120, in particular 102; doi:10.1007/s10502-012-9180-7.
4. Cook, 'Evidence, Memory, Identity, and Community', 102.
5. The National Archives, *Archives Unlocked* (2017), 6; www.nationalarchives.gov.uk/documents/archives/Archives-Unlocked-Brochure.pdf; E. Goudarouli, A. Sexton, and J. Sheridan, 'The Challenge of the Digital and the Future Archive: Through the Lens of the National Archives UK', *Philosophy and Technology* 32 (2019), 173–183.
6. The National Archives, *Digital Strategy* 2017; www.nationalarchives.gov.uk/documents/the-national-archives-digital-strategy-2017-19.pdf.
7. Society of American Archivists Glossary, www2.archivists.org/glossary/terms/a.
8. The National Archives, *Archives Unlocked*, 6.

9. The National Archives' New strategy, *Archives for Everyone* 2019,www.nationalarchives.gov.uk/about/our-role/plans-policies-performance-and-projects/our-plans/archives-for-everyone/.

10. All central government departments are required to identify records of historical value and transfer them for permanent preservation to The National Archives by the time they are thirty years old, under the Public Records Act. The Government is reducing this timeframe from thirty to twenty years. For more information about the twenty-year rule, see: www.nationalarchives.gov.uk/about/our-role/transparency/20-year-rule/.

11. The National Archives, *Archives Inspire* 2015, http://nationalarchives.gov.uk/about/our-role/plans-policies-performance-and-projects/our-plans/archives-inspire/.

12. The National Archives, *Digital Strategy*.

13. The National Archives, *Archives for Everyone*.

14. The National Archives, *Archives for Everyone*.

15. The main repository of The National Archives is located in Kew, south west London. The second repository, a former salt mine, is called the 'Deep Store' and is located in Cheshire.

16. For more information, please have a look at: www.nationalarchives.gov.uk/information-management/manage-information/preserving-digital-records/our-role/.

17. The National Archives, *Digital Strategy*, 4.

18. P. Mell, Timothy Grance, *Recommendations of the National Institute of Standards and Technology* (Gaithersburg: The NIST Definition of Cloud Computing, 2011), 2;https://nvlpubs.nist.gov/nistpubs/Legacy/SP/nistspecialpublication800-145.pdf.

19. Digital Preservation Coalition, *Digital Preservation Handbook*, www.dpconline.org/handbook/technical-solutions-and-tools/cloud-services accessed on 30 July 2019.

20. G. Michetti, 'Provenance in the Archives: The Challenge of the Digital Environment Archives in Liquid Times', in F. Smit, A. Glaudemans, and R. Jonker, eds, *Archives in Liquid Times* (The Hague: Stichting Archiefpublicaties, 2017), 228–237.

21. The National Archives, *Guidance on Cloud Storage and Digital Preservation* (2nd edn.), www.nationalarchives.gov.uk/documents/CloudStorage-Guidance_March-2015.pdf.

22. The National Archives, *Digital Strategy*.

23. The National Archives, *Digital Cataloguing Practices* 2017, www.nationalarchives.gov.uk/documents/digital-cataloguing-practices-march-2017.pdf; Goudarouli et al., 'The Challenge of the Digital and the Future Archive', 7.

24. The National Archives, *Archives for Everyone*.

25. L. Duranti, and C. Rogers, 'Trust in Records and Data Online', in J. Lowry and J. Wamukoya, eds, *Integrity in Government through Records Management: Essays in Honour of Anne Thurston* (Farnham: Ashgate, 2014), 203–216.

26. Goudarouli et al., 'The Challenge of the Digital and the Future Archive', 4.

27. Goudarouli et al., 'The Challenge of the Digital and the Future Archive', 5–6.

28. For more details on the project, see the network's website: https://computationalarchives.net/.

29. For more on Computational Archival Science (CAS) initiative, see the CAS portal at https://dcicblog.umd.edu/cas/.

30. R. Marciano, V. Lemieux, M. Hedges, M. Esteva, W. Underwood, M. Kurtz, and M. Conrad, 'Archival Records and Training in the Age of Big Data', in J. Percell, L. C. Sarin, P. T. Jaeger, and J. C. Bertot, eds, *Re-Envisioning the MLS: Perspectives on the Future of*

Library and Information Science Education, Advances in Librarianship, 44B (Bingley: Emeral Publishing, 2018), 179–199, in particular 2.

31. The objectives of the CAS group can be found at the CAS portal's *About* page: https://dcicblog.umd.edu/cas/about-us/.

32. Marciano et al., 'Archival Records and Training in the Age of Big Data', 4.

33. Although, the author recognises the importance of education and training to the integration of computational and archival thinking, this chapter will not focus on this area. For more on this, see work done within the context of the CAS initiative. For example: W. Underwood, D. Weintrop, M. Kurtz, and R. Marciano, 'Introducing Computational Thinking into Archival Science Education', *2018 IEEE International Conference on Big Data* (2018), 2761–2765.

CHAPTER 19

RESPONSE TO 'MATERIALITIES'

LAURA MANDELL

Eirini Goudarouli powerfully describes the radical 'disruption' to traditional archival practices created by a shift in focus from 'a physical item that is tangible' to 'new archival objects that reside in increasingly complex [digital] systems and rapidly evolving environments'. Digitized recordings, documents, and records are often seen as 'ephemeral', 'immaterial', or 'intangible' (Popple, Goudarouli). However, the chapters in this section of *Archives: Power, Truth, and Fiction*, on 'Materalities', discuss archival systems using the language of media archaeology, the sociology of texts, network theory, and the new materialism productively problematize the notion of digital *im*materiality.

In *The Panizzi Lectures* of 1985, D. F. McKenzie infamously redefined 'text' to include 'verbal, visual, oral, and numeric data ... everything in fact from epigraphy to the latest forms of discography'[1] which invites us to extend Alison Wiggins's description of the kind of information preserved by 'archival texts' to archival objects of any kind (substituting, of course, the relevant material format for ink and paper). According to Wiggins, '[a]rchival texts ... have value for the information carried in the forms of their collection contexts, reception histories, formal features, and in their paper, ink, and bindings, about the economics of labour, knowledge networks, intelligence exchange, and patterns of trade'. In the words of new materialist Timothy Morton, archival objects are 'hypermaterial', that is, generated by and generating complex, intersecting cultural systems of the past and present.[2] Catherine Richardson examines 'chests, presses, bags, great bags ... baskets', and, of course doors, paying attention to the practices they organized as 'key to our understanding of the functioning of early modern society'. Archives, she argues, are 'repositories of productive environments of the past', which is to say infrastructures for producing knowledge in and about 'the medieval and early modern state'. Digital infrastructures are our current productive and hypermaterial environments for producing knowledge, meaning, significance. And while at first glance, it may seem that Jane Birkin's statement about 'the vast differences between the physical and digital handling of information' subscribes to the idea of digital intangibility, the key word in her statement is '*hand*ling'.

Palpably physical especially when they break down, digital infrastructures are, as we all know, comprised of material digits, the 0s and 1s that are registered on and forensically retrievable from 'hard' drives. But infrastructures are also hyper-material because of the digits, the human hands, that create and use them in order to participate in ambient cultural systems. Digital objects, like Richardson's Exchequer doors, 'become implicated and entangled in the spaces that produce and house them' (Richardson), as is especially visible in recent work on the bias produced by Machine Learning algorithms (Wiggins). While Cathy O'Neil is right to argue in *Weapons of Math Destruction* that an algorithm is 'an opinion formalized in code',[3] we now know from Safiya Umoja Noble, Ruha Benjamin, Timnit Gebru, and others that the bias problem also resides in the data from which machines learn: AI bots pay most attention to, and unfortunately reiterate, racist 0s and 1s because a preponderance of them exist in data that has been created by human fingers typing on keyboards. Whose digits? Why? 'Data', Yanni Alexander Loukissas argues in *All Data Are Local*, 'is always curated ... [i]n ways that are often invisible' but materially (over)determining:

> Data ... are not simply facts. They are cultural artifacts, manufactured and presented within contexts that matter. ... [Y]ou must learn to look *at data*, to investigate how they are made and embedded in the world. ... [T]hinking locally is thinking critically.[4]

There is a real danger in imagining data as immaterial insofar as it disconnects data from the specific human digits that produced them.

I wish to end this discussion with theoretical considerations made possible by Alan Liu's interrogation of historical materiality found particularly in *Local Transcendence*.[5] The archival work so beautifully described in these chapters demonstrates that objects 'have no intrinsic value—they only make sense as part of [an] archive' (Richardson). Archival activity makes objects, and the past, *graspable* in the metaphorical sense: conceivable through reduction, abstraction, and location (using any kind of conceptual scheme, from 'box 452' to 'Harrison, Alabama' to 'slavery'). When one cannot grasp a historical object through any of these methods, it is then only physically grabbable. A lost archival object can be experienced as *purely* material (*only* grabbable), not at all thought, because we cannot lay hands on it. (Phenomenologically, when people rifle through papers to find a missing document, their minds grasp something about each piece of paper—something that indicates whether it is the missing document or not; the missing document, however, is an inert, un-(re)cognized piece of paper until digits grab it and it is seen or felt *as* the missing thing.)

The notion that materiality only exists for humans as an absence is more than a postmodern old saw. When the comedian pulls the chair away just as the straight man is sitting down in it, it is stripped of all the human ideas surrounding chairness and is now experienced as a thing precisely because it is not there. When a digital object 'disappears into the ether', as we say, we run up against its materiality as the thing needed which is lost. I would argue that such vanishing acts are produced by too many human digits inaugurating too many computational processes at once. The comedian is the sysadmin who typed 'Update' at the very moment that I, as straight man, typed Ctrl-s to save. And the point here is that, as archivists experience what Goudarouli calls the 'radical transformation' of archival practices enabled by digital environments, we need to focus on the undeniably hypermaterial part of any archive, digital or otherwise: human hands.

NOTES

1. D. F. McKenzie, *Bibliography and the Sociology of Texts: Panizzi Lectures, 1985* (The British Library, 1986), 29.
2. T. Morton, *Hyperobjects: Philosophy and Ecology after the End of the World*, Posthumanities 27 (Minneapolis and London: University of Minnesota Press, 2013).
3. C. O'Neil, *Weapons of Math Destruction: How Big Data Increases Inequality and Threatens Democracy* (New York: Crown Publishers, 2016), 53.
4. Y. A. Loukissas, *All Data Are Local: Thinking Critically in a Data-Driven Society* (Cambridge, MA, and London: MIT Press, 2019), xv–xvi.
5. Alan Liu, *Local Transcendence: Essays on Postmodern Historicism and the Database* (Chicago: University of Chicago Press, 2008).

PART IV

ENCOUNTERS AND EVOLUTION

CHAPTER 20

THE AGENCY OF ARCHIVERS

ERIC KETELAAR

Archivers

New concepts of 'the archive' have been embraced during the past twenty-five years, by anthropologists, sociologists, psychologists, philosophers, cultural and literary theorists, and artists.[1] Most users of the archive are aware of the fact that it reflects a reality as perceived or constructed by its creator. For example, judicial archives present the world as seen by each of the parties in a lawsuit, financial records serve to make reality calculable, government records on people serve to make people legible as citizen, taxpayer, etc. When using archives, one has to know the why, who, what, and how of archiving in order to assess which reality may be reflected in the archives. This entails acknowledging the people who were involved in the archive: the record subjects, authors, clerks, registrars, antiquarians, genealogists, and other users. Listening to their voices reveals cultural practices of creation, classification, filing, arrangement, appraisal, use and abuse, selection, and destruction of archives. Each 'archiver' participates in the recursive production and mediation of the archive. The mediation involves not only definition, selection, organization, interpretation, representation, and presentation, but also concealment, displacement, and destruction.

The Constructed Archive

One specific archiver has not yet been mentioned: the archivist. Very seldom users reflect on the agency of the archivist when they simply describe their encounter with the archive without any mention of the archivist. As Elizabeth Yakel observed, many users are

> largely unaware of the invisible archival role and responsibility behind the data they are using, particularly in a networked environment. Thus, they may see the role of the archivist as essentially preserving the data or perhaps managing the information, but not as having anything to do with knowledge creation.[2]

Until recently, archivists themselves assumed that their work consists of innocent, technical, and neutral processing of archives. However, 'archivists preside over what ultimately forms the archive'.[3] The historical record is re-created in the mediation by the archivist, through appraisal and selection, arrangement and description, providing access and reference service, preservation, and digitization. Scrutinizing the central position of the archivist in these practices has led to several propositions to 'decentring the archivist' and empowering other archivers. This raises the final question what the archivist distinguishes from other participants. Let me first discuss practices of archival mediation and the people involved.

Appraisal and Selection

Archiving entails appraisal. Appraisal is the basis for selection, that is identifying materials to be preserved because of their enduring value. However, appraisal is broader because evaluation (making a value judgement) happens at every stage in the life of a record. Appraisal supports decisions such as: which actions are documented and how are they documented to provide sufficient representation of the action. What is 'sufficient' depends on the archiver who makes a conscious or unconscious choice (determined by social and cultural factors) to consider something worth documenting and archiving. These factors, in turn, are controlled by different societal powers: institutions like the State, Business (that also control the technologies of archiving), the Church, the Press, but also by ideologies and socialized norms based on class, gender, race, etc.

Social and cultural factors also determine which archives are deemed worthy of transfer to Archives (with a capital A). For example, in 1982 the UK Public Record Office (now The National Archives) refused to take over the recently discovered Migrated Archives, being about 20,000 records removed from British colonies upon independence.[4] The PRO maintained that they were not UK public records, and refused to have them transferred and made accessible. That value judgement caused the records to remain in a limbo. That they were not destroyed subsequently was not due to active intervention, but rather to administrative inertia which, by the way, has so often caused the survival of documents in the past.[5]

The issue in this case was how far the mandate of the archival institution stretched and to what extent the archivist could influence this. These are important questions for archival institutions, not only for those that work with government (public) archives, but also and acutely for those that collect archives from the private sector. The creator, donor, and depositor of these private archives are the first to judge whether their documentary heritage is worthy of keeping for eternity. They are agents in appraisal in conjunction with the archivist who is coaching them.

Archival institutions collecting private papers include community archives. In the UK these have proliferated recently (www.communityarchives.org.uk). Many if not most community archives are separate from mainstream archives. They are managed by community members, who are not necessarily professional archivists. Deciding which archives to keep and what to refuse is principally a community decision. 'The very existence of an archive has come to be viewed as constitutive of a community's claim to identity', John Tagg reminds us, the questions 'what should be in the archive, who should adjudicate it, and who should have access to it, have become questions of urgent social and political significance'.[6]

Some people assume that appraisal of records (what to keep, what to destroy) is no longer necessary in the digital age because of the unlimited storage capacity and searchability of digital media. That is, however, a myth. Permanent storage and permanent access require enormous resources: buildings, staff, energy, constant upgrading and migration of software and hardware, etc. Every terabyte less as a result of appraisal, is a saving in these annually recurring costs. In fact the appraisal process begins with the design of the recordkeeping system when one determines which documents are captured, that is: accepted by the system and thus becoming records. Moreover, digital records cannot be left on the shelves for years, waiting to be appraised. Therefore at the front-end one has to decide which records have to kept in the system, and which records can be disposed of later, either through destruction or by transferring them to another system. 'Archiving by design' means that when designing the information systems that support work processes, one has to take into account the sustainability of the information from the work processes. Organizational and societal requirements play a role in assessing the function and value of records for accountability, evidence, and memory. This situation applies equally to paper and digital records.

Appraisal in the stricter sense (distinguishing records of continuing value from those of no further value so that the latter may be eliminated) is one of those interventions which co-determine the meaning of the archive, because the archive after appraisal is not the same as the archive before appraisal. Appraisal has been deemed the fine art of destruction. Since the 1980s archivists have been debating how to perform this art. The terms of that debate about selecting archives have generally been the needs and concerns of archivists. In many countries the general public is invited to comment on draft appraisal schedules (in the UK: operational selection policies), but rarely are non-archivists involved in earlier stages of the appraisal process. Two of the exceptions are Spain and the Netherlands. In Spain architects, anthropologists, geographers, historians, and other specialists are involved in the *evaluación*. In the Netherlands historians, sociologists, political scientists, and others are involved by the National Archives in identifying the 'hot spots' in recent history: events and issues which have led to a remarkable or intensive interaction between government and citizen, which should be documented in the records. Moreover, each working group that is to draft an appraisal schedule has to include an outsider with expertise regarding the relationship between citizen and government and the importance of public records for that relationship. Every draft schedule is put up for public notice, and comments from the public are invited.

Arrangement and Description

Processing archives begins with the seemingly neutral operation of packing and repackaging, often removing the documents from their original containers and putting them in acid-free archival boxes, reformatting the 'stuff' from the muniment room, basement, or attic. No longer can the archive be read in its original state. Reading the archive involves, inter alia, reading the materiality: deciphering what the little holes in documents, the folds or the pink tape, the binding and rebinding, etc., reveal about the history of the file and its archiving. Alas, often these traces have been removed by ordinary housekeeping procedures.

Archival arrangement is not primarily physical ordering of an archive, it is identifying relationships in order to identify the original order and the context in which the documents were created and used for their primary purpose. The same applies to description, that is: creating a representation of a document. However, arrangement is more than mechanically identifying and restoring original order and a representation of a document is more than just recording the reflection of the document. Both are interpretive and creative acts, making a finding aid a political statement, which effectively shapes the archive. 'These processes', Jennifer Meehan writes, 'are not neutral or objective; rather they are situated within specific sociocultural, professional, institutional, and individual contexts'.[7] Every representation is biased 'because it reflects a particular world-view and is constructed to meet specific purposes'.[8]

Access and Reference Service

I have explained how the archive is constructed through appraisal, arrangement, and description. Another form of mediation is providing access and reference service to users. Both are constrained by legal, political, cultural, and professional norms. Archivists cannot change the legal access rules, but they have a certain leeway in applying the rules. A 2007 study on restrictions on access to national archives in Europe found that in enabling access to restricted material, some archives differentiate between researchers. For example, in Liechtenstein, Norway, Finland, Poland, Germany, and Hungary the director of the archives is allowed to grant access to archives which have been transferred under special conditions, but only to professional researchers or scientists, and not to members of the general public.[9]

There are still archival institutions where access to the finding aids is restricted or where access is only granted if the user complies to certain conditions, including paying a fee. The Principles of Access to Archives promulgated by the International Council on Archives in 2012, state 'The equal right to access archival records is not simply equal treatment but also includes the equal right to benefit from the archives'.[10] However, the Declaration in recommending to minimize operational constraints on access, implicitly acknowledges that such constraints exist.

Many archivists are reconceptualizing reference service as an interaction among various participants and systems. However, basically it remains understanding the research question as formulated by the user and translating that question into one that can be matched with the archival holdings. Most users lack the ability to perform these steps effectively. It therefore is the archivist who in a negotiating process frames the research question to make it commensurable with the institutional knowledge system. In doing so, the archivist applies his or her expertise embedded in a particular world-view. This implies that the archivist largely remains in control of the retrieval of the right information in a meaningful form.

Preservation and Digitization

Reconstruction of the archive also happens through preservation and digitization. These seem to be mere technical processes, but they involve appraisal and mediation. Not only appraising which documents are restored or digitized and which not. Archivers must also take decisions on mediation, because they choose the technologies to be used. Any restoration of a document changes its current 'look and feel' and risks obliterating material traces from the past. In the digital world, one has to decide on the preservation mode even before documents are created. Migration or conversion replaces a digital record by a new record which, however, will not have exactly the same features and functionalities (lay-out, colours, embedded links, etc.) as its predecessor. Deciding on the degree of divergence is in fact a form of appraisal: we must choose what to lose.

When digitizing a document, archivers have to decide on the image capture technology and settings, on image manipulation with editing software, on image export to printers, websites, etc. Each of these decisions is constrained by financial limits and managerial considerations. Digitization creates various layers of mediation between the original and the user or viewer of the digital representation. The decisions taken at each of these layers have to be documented so that we can answer questions like: 'What are the effects of decoupling a text from its physical carrier? What does it mean for a work, a text or a book to be digital, and how are users to make sense of the many different kinds of digital offerings available?'[11]

New Roles for the User

Never was the user an outsider, because using the archive means participating in the production and mediation of the archive. Users' interactions, interventions, interrogations, and interpretations are activations which co-constitute the archive and determine the archive's meaning. Any use of the archive retrospectively affects all earlier instances of use, or to put it differently: we can no longer read a text as our predecessors have read it. Recently, however, new roles for the user have been made possible. Textual agency plays an important role in the creation of user-generated content in what is called Web 2.0: an umbrella term covering different features and occurrences on the web in which the difference between providers and users of information is diminishing or even disappearing. The boundaries of documents, websites, and databases created by government and the private sector are becoming interfaces with co-creators outside the organization. Legislation allows citizens in the EU and the UK to use 'public sector information', to enrich that information, giving new uses and meaning to that information. It is significant that the motor of this development in the UK is the Office of Public Information, which operates from The National Archives.

A step further will make people into co-creators of public archives. Such a role is gradually acknowledged for 'record subjects': adopted children, patients, clients, prisoners, and all other people who are subject of institutional recordkeeping and thereby co-creators of the archives of governmental and care institutions. Such co-creatorship entitles the record subject to various rights, as spelled out in recent legislation on data protection. My doctor's file is also my file, part of what is called a participatory archive. Participation in the archive is not limited to a conversation *about* a medical (or other) file, but instead uses the file 'as a conversation and an arena for participation'.[12]

The emerging model of a participatory archive will change the role of what is still called the user of archives in each of the archival processes discussed before. In appraisal the participation of users may move from being consulted on a schedule prepared by experts towards actively taking part in its preparation and monitoring its implementation. This would open up the process of appraisal, but not necessarily lead to a less constructed archive than the one for which only the archivist is responsible. Any outcome of appraisal is constructed because its value is not intrinsic, but assigned, constructed.

Arrangement and description have already been opened to users in Archives 2.0, an approach in which archivists use technology to become more user-centred, by inviting user contributions and participation in describing, commenting, and reusing collections. As the website of the UK National Archives explained, some of this approach may lead to refresh and modernize some of the language of the descriptions, making them relevant to today's users. Examples would be replacing certain terms in descriptions of colonial archives by less offensive ones, and enhancing descriptions by adding users' comments and transcriptions. Many archival institutions organize crowdsourcing: enlisting users (online or offline) to make or to correct finding aids or to index series of records. Users' participation is still choreographed by the archivist, but may lead to some degree of democratization and decolonization of the archival endeavour. Arrangement and description by users will certainly shift the power of defining the archive from the archivist to a joint venture of archivist and user. However, this shift will not necessarily lead to a less constructed archive, but merely to an archive constructed by multiple voices and interventions.

As with the other archival functions, Archives 2.0 is changing our notions of access. Archival temples guarded by archontic power are being replaced by virtual spaces of memory maintained by communities of archivers. Access to archives is provided through access to the internet and thus governed by the rules (or rather the absence of rules) of the internet, and its search and retrieval practices. Archival documents are downloaded from the internet to be copied, used, reformatted, abridged, photoshopped, etc., resulting in a (re)constructed archive. The archivist risks to become decentred or even removed from interaction with users. Social media, including chat services, have come to fill the gap left by the physical disappearance of the archivist behind the reference desk.

New Roles for the Archivist

Archivers are acting in practices of creation, classification, filing, arrangement, appraisal, use and abuse, selection, and destruction of archives. In what way differ archivists from the other archivers? This question raises another question: what is a professional archivist?

A profession is, according to the Oxford English Dictionary, 'an occupation in which a professed knowledge of some subject, field, or science is applied; a vocation or career, especially one that involves prolonged training and a formal qualification'. Sociologists distinguish four partly overlapping phases in professionalization: differentiation, specialization, institutionalization, and legitimization. By differentiation a certain activity is branched off from the whole of the division of labour. The professional develops expert knowledge and skills providing him or her with a monopoly in a given domain. Fixed structures and patterns arise, such as an education of one's own, jargon, work methods, knowledge, and skills. This institutionalization protects the individual professional and ensures continuity in professional practice. Professional associations play a major role in this institutionalization. A fourth process in the development of a profession is legitimization by society of the profession and its share in the division of labour. The profession is formed when these four processes have taken place.

As regards the archival profession, these processes were accomplished in different countries at different times. On the European continent the archival specialist emerged in the eighteenth century. In the nineteenth century special institutes for the education of archivists were founded in France, Italy, Austria, and Germany. A diploma of such a school became a condition for entering the service of the State Archives. Professional associations of archivists were founded, the oldest one in the Netherlands in 1891. In several countries the archival profession became regulated by archival legislation in the nineteenth and early-twentieth centuries, thus closing the sequence of differentiation, specialization, institutionalization, and legitimization.

What distinguishes the professional archivist from other archivers is his or her loyalty to the archive. No one else cares for the archive as an end, which is different from using archives as a means as most if not all other archivers do. No one else is the advocate ensuring the integrity of the archive. Archives are unique because of their 'contextual envelope' and what archivists call provenance, that is their embeddedness in the contexts in which the archive is created and recreated over time. It is the archivists' calling to preserve that uniqueness. Identities of individuals and communities are rooted in memories and these memories need inscription and need a space. Both inscription and space will increasingly be 'located' 'in the cloud' and maintained (in distributed custody) by individuals, communities, and memory institutions. Together they are actors in an ecology which comprises archives and other memory texts in a societal context. For archivists this context is significant, leading to partnerships with communities and with professionals in other memory institutions; contributing to new forms of Archives 2.0, archival activism, and participatory archiving; and becoming relevant actors in our society's communities.

A profession is not static, it adapts itself to changing circumstances in society. This is what is happening right now in a society where people are striving for 'archival autonomy', a concept recently proposed by Australian scholars: 'the ability for individuals and communities to participate in societal memory, with their own voice, becoming participatory agents in recordkeeping and archiving'.[13] In these circumstances responsibilities are shared by archivists and other archivers. They include 'citizen archivists': people trained by professional archivists how to preserve, manage, and use digital personal, family, and community archives. However, do these non-professional archivists also share the authority—traditionally vested in the archivist and the archival institution—which endows the archive with trustworthiness, reliability, and authenticity? As Elisabeth Yakel writes, authority 'is a major issue that is both at the center of and challenged by Archives 2.0'.[14] She envisions archives developing into 'a social structure characterized by a shared approach to governance, authority, and concern for sustainability of the communities' forming around the records.[15] I would argue that these social structures will still need some form of shepherding, coaching, and even control by the archivist, not the archivist having *empire* over the archiving process, but the archivist as an *umpire* participating in the game and guarding the integrity of the archive.

FURTHER READING

Francis X. Blouin, and William G. Rosenberg, *Processing the Past: Contesting Authority in History and the Archives* (Oxford: Oxford University Press, 2011)

Paul Delsalle and Margaret Procter, *A History of Archival Practice* (London and New York: Routledge, 2017)

Heather MacNeil and Terry Eastwood, eds, *Currents of Archival Thinking*, 2nd ed. (Santa Barbara, Denver: Libraries Unlimited, 2017)

Kate Theimer, ed., *A Different Kind of Web: New Connections between Archives and Our Users* (Chicago: Society of American Archivists, 2011)

NOTES

1. Parts of this chapter have been published in my 'A dualidade do arquivar', trans. J. Carvalho do Amaral, in: R. Medeiros Pimenta, L. Klebia Rodrigues da Silva, and T. Rodrigues Rangel, eds, *Informação e memória: perspectivas em movimento* (Rio de Janeiro: Instituto Brasileiro de Informação em Ciência e Tecnologia [IBICT], 2021), 163–185.
2. E. Yakel, 'Thinking Inside and Outside the Boxes: Archival Reference Services at the Turn of the Century', *Archivaria* 49.1 (2000), 140–160 (152).
3. F. X. Blouin and W. G. Rosenberg, *Processing the Past: Contesting Authority in History and the Archives* (Oxford: Oxford University Press, 2011), 143.
4. M. Banton, 'Displaced Archives in The National Archives of the United Kingdom', in J. Lowry, ed., *Displaced Archives* (London and New York: Routledge, 2017), 41–59.
5. A. Prescott, 'The Textuality of the Archive', in L. Craven, ed., *What are Archives? Cultural and Theoretical Perspectives: A Reader* (Aldershot: Ashgate, 2008), 31–52 (48).
6. J. Tagg, 'The Archiving Machine; or, The Camera and the Filing Cabinet', *Grey Room* 47 (2012), 24–37 (33).
7. J. Meehan, 'Arrangement and Description: Between Theory and Practice', in C. Brown, ed., *Archives and Recordkeeping: Theory into Practice* (London: Facet, 2014), 63–100 (81).
8. W. M. Duff and V. Harris, 'Stories and Names: Archival Description as Narrating Records and Constructing Meanings', *Archival Science* 2.3–4 (2002), 263–285 (275).
9. J. Valge and B. Kibal, 'Restrictions on Access to Archives and Records in Europe: A History and the Current Situation', *Journal of the Society of Archivists* 28 (2007), 193–214.
10. www.ica.org/sites/default/files/ICA_Access-principles_EN.pdf.
11. M. Deegan and K. Sutherland, *Transferred Illusions: Digital Technology and the Forms of Print* (Abingdon: Routledge, 2016), 145.
12. I. Huvila, 'Participatory Archive: Towards Decentralised Curation, Radical User Orientation, and Broader Contextualisation of Records Management', *Archival Science* 8.1 (2008), 15–36 (27).
13. J. Evans, S. McKemmish, E. Daniels, and G. McCarthy, 'Self-determination and Archival Autonomy: Advocating Activism', *Archival Science* 15.4 (2015), 337–368 (347).
14. E. Yakel, 'Balancing Archival Authority with Encouraging Authentic Voices to Engage with Records', in K. Theimer, ed., *A Different Kind of Web: New Connections Between Archives and Our Users* (Chicago: Society of American Archivists, 2011), 78.
15. Yakel, 'Balancing', 95; E. Ketelaar, 'Archives as Spaces of Memory', *Journal of the Society of Archivists* 29 (2008), 9–27.

CHAPTER 21

STATE POWER AND THE SHAPING OF ARCHIVES IN MALAWI

PAUL LIHOMA

In 'The Power of the Archive and its Limits', Achille Mbembe points out the paradoxical relationship of the State and the archive, stating that on one hand, there is no State without its archives and on the other hand, the very existence of the archive constitutes a constant threat to the State. As a result of the perceived threat posed by archives, Mbembe goes on to argue that 'some states have thought that they could do without archives and have therefore attempted, either to reduce them to silence, or, in an even more radical manner, to destroy them.'[1] From Mbembe's perspective, it follows that where States have created silences in the archive or destroyed the archives for whatever reasons and under what circumstances, the historical record has been, consequently, shaped by the State—political powers. This situation, however, is in sharp contrast to such foundational texts of archival literature as the Dutch manual, and the manuals by Jenkinson and Schellenberg that benignly assume that public servants, and not the State political powers, are the ones that shape the historical record.

Perhaps one explanation why some States get threatened by the archive, if Mbembe's position is to be sustained, is that the archive itself has the power to enlighten anyone who engages it in any inquiry. It is the enlightenment that enables archive enquirers to take the State or individual office-bearers to task on any matters that anyone or society might feel aggrieved.

This chapter describes a number of case studies that demonstrate the power of the archives and discusses how, on several occasions, the State has created silences in the archive and even destroyed the archive itself, thereby shaping the historical record in Malawi. Firstly, treaty documents that early European planters prepared and gave illiterate native chiefs to sign by printing their thumb nails to formalize land sales, are discussed. These documents have remained a source of land-ownership struggles between tea-estate owners and the 'real owners of the land'. Secondly, tax receipts, which were issued to local tax-payers during the colonial period, are discussed to demonstrate the power of the tax document because mere possession of a tax receipt exempted the bearer from harsh punishment for tax non-payment. Similarly, the power of a party card to exempt its bearer from atrocities inflicted by the dictatorial rule for non-possession of a seemingly ordinary document is discussed. Fourthly, the power of the archive to enlighten researchers is discussed in light of access to the archive by researchers. The chapter goes on to consider how, over the years, the State has controlled the archive thereby creating silences and gone even to the extent of destroying the archive. Finally, the chapter celebrates the return to an order where the consumption of the archive becomes, as Mbembe puts it, 'a communal tool of the state and of society'.[2]

Treaty Documents as a Source of Land Conflicts in Southern Malawi

A survey by the University of Malawi on estate land utilization and the Malawi Presidential Commission of Enquiry on Land Policy Reform among others, found that 'all land that the colonialists claim to be their own under freehold title in Thyolo and Mulanje, was fraudulently acquired and that this remains a cause of legitimate land grievances in southern Malawi'. The source of these grievances can be traced to treaty documents, which early European planters signed with illiterate local chiefs in the 1880s. The planters who had arrived before the proclamation of the Protectorate 'had already acquired large amounts of land' from the native chiefs.[3] Such planters, in the words of A. J. Hanna, 'arrived in Nyasaland rich only in aspirations and with a small stock of calico and powder and a few cheap guns' to pay the native chiefs for the vast amounts of land, made treaties with the chiefs by inducing the latter 'to put [their] mark on a paper conferring vast territories and sovereign rights on the needy pioneer'.[4] The land treaty documents were, however, limited to the custodians of the native lands, the chiefs. While the documents involved two parties, they served the interests of one party, the authors of the documents, more than the other.

This situation was common particularly in the tea-growing Mulanje and Thyolo districts. When traditional chiefs sold vast plots of prime land, they in return obtained material possessions, which benefitted themselves personally and not their subjects. While the estate owners have valid claims to ownership of their vast estates as evidenced by their centuries-old treaty documents, communities around the estates also claim ownership of the same land so much that conflicts over land have remained unresolved.

The struggle by local communities to repossess estate land from the estate owners climaxed in 2009 when the Peoples Land Organization (PLO), an indigenous legal grouping of concerned people in Thyolo and Mulanje was established in order to resolve 'this land injustice'.[5] Since 2009, the PLO has engaged the estate owners, government and other stakeholders in order to have their grievances resolved. In February 2015, the PLO officially wrote both the estate owners and government in which it 'resolved to clear these past mistakes by asking the current colonial estate owners to pay the descendants of the real owners of the land some fee for the use of their land on rent starting from 1914 to the present at a rate of £65 per acre per year'.[6] The letter also demanded that any further expansion of colonial estate infrastructure into the 25,000 hectares of idle colonial estate land should be stopped immediately because the owners of the land needed it for cultivation and settlement.

Observing that neither the government nor the estate owners complied with its demands, the PLO appealed to the UN Secretary General in July 2015 requesting for the United Nations to intervene in the land struggle by ordering the government of Malawi to rule that all companies owning tea estates in the districts got them illegally and that tea estates which are not being used should be shared to the local communities who apparently lack land to cultivate. The PLO further requested the UN that should the Malawi government not implement the UN order, the UN should 'preside over a REFERENDUM on the political independence of Thyolo and Mulanje Districts from the republic of Malawi so that this unique land issue should be resolved by the affected people of Thyolo and Mulanje alone in their own sovereign State, under the United Nations, in the interest of self-determination'.[7]

Frustrated with the UN's non response to the matter, in 2017 the PLO announced plans for the cessation of Mulanje and Thyolo districts from the republic of Malawi. The two districts were to be inaugurated as an independent State known as the African Traditionalist Republic of the United States of Thyolo and Mulanje (MUST) at a ceremony that was to be held on 26 October 2017 in Thyolo. During the ceremony a new nation, flag, coat of arms, passports, identity cards, and currency and national anthem were to be introduced.[8] Heavy police presence prior to and on the scheduled inauguration day, however, foiled the ceremony and the local people are still agitating for their ancestral land.

Power of the Hut Tax Receipt

The introduction of hut tax in 1891 as a major source of revenue for running the Nyasaland Protectorate resulted from lack of a direct grant-in-aid from the British Treasury and insufficient funds provided by Cecil Rhodes.[9] When currency (coins) was introduced in the country, it circulated in a few areas in southern Nyasaland owing to its limited supply, and because not everyone could afford to pay the tax in cash, the government devised appropriate mechanisms for receiving the tax at the district offices in the form of grain, fruit, eggs, and other produce, and livestock.

After paying his annual hut tax, the tax payer was issued with a hut tax receipt. The receipts, simple as they might have looked, proved so valuable that people, despite their lack of familiarity with any principles of recordkeeping, adopted elaborate security measures for keeping them, so that they were readily available.

The government adopted different methods of punishing tax defaulters, such as burning huts and holding hostage wives and children of tax defaulters.[10] However, the common method of punishment was compelling the defaulters to work for the government (in Blantyre) for a period of one month, at the rate of three shillings, which was also the annual hut tax, per adult male from the age of fourteen, later increased to sixteen.[11] Observing the maltreatment of the tax defaulters by the government, Dr. William H. Murray the then head of the Dutch Reformed Church Mission stationed at Mvera, in November 1900 remarked that:

> Things have lately taken place that might shame any Savage, if committed by him, and that in the name and by the instruments of the Govt. Because men refuse to pay their taxes (on account of the hardships entailed in going to work 200 miles away from their homes, where there is a great scarcity of food) women and little children have been ruthlessly shot down by native policemen, and we've still to see what's going to become of it.[12]

Upon their return from the forced migrant labour in Blantyre, the tax defaulters were a sorry sight, for they looked like 'walking skeletons' (Rev. T. C. B. Vlok).[13] Not wishing to suffer these traumatic consequences, the natives became 'well aware that the possession of a hut tax receipt exempted them from requisition as defaulters'.[14] The value of paying tax and keeping the tax receipts safely became so priceless to the natives that one District Officer at the beginning of the twentieth century observed that:

> the number of those who could be legitimately compelled to work, even for the space of a single month in the year, grew smaller and smaller, until at last Collectors of districts found themselves placed between Scylla and Charybdis—between a European community clamouring for labour, and a native population who did not wish to work, and who knew themselves to be under no obligation to do so.[15]

Power of a Party Card

What a tax receipt was to natives of Nyasaland during the early colonial period was a party card to Malawian citizens between 1964 and 1994. Soon after independence in July 1964 and following a revolt by some cabinet ministers against Dr Banda between August and September the same year, the President grew more autocratic and was restrictive of any form of dissent. As the Malawi Congress Party (MCP) was the only political party allowed in the country, everyone was supposed to be a member of and demonstrate loyalty to the party by, among others, buying a party membership card every year. The combination of the party and Young Pioneers, the party's para-military wing, served as an effective intelligence network at every level of society. Strict measures were in place and enforced to ensure that everybody purchased a party card such that one of the duties of government ministers was to promote sale of party cards. To be seen to carry out this duty faithfully, one cabinet minister was quoted in 1967 as saying:

> There are still people who have not yet bought Malawi Congress Party cards. It is the duty of party officials, chiefs and village headmen, members of the Youth League and members of the Women's League to see that everyone buys cards.[16]

As Africa Watch (1990:14) observes, 'at a more basic level a party card [was] a requirement to obtain the basic necessities of life'. The cards had to be carried at all times and presented at random to police and party inspections in order to enter a market, board a bus, or obtain health care. Those, like the Jehovah's Witnesses sect, who refused on principle to buy party cards, were subjected to severe persecution. The sect was banned and its members were detained, harassed, driven into exile, and, in hundreds of cases, killed by Young Pioneers or MCP gangs.[17] For three decades Malawians viewed a party card not merely as evidence of their allegiance to the party. Rather, it was largely a symbol of personal liberty in a repressive one-party dictatorship since non-production of the seemingly ordinary document was interpreted as a revolt against the regime and any perceived indifference to party activities attracted the wrath of the regime.

Archives as a Tool for Research

Official government records were first generated in 1891 following the establishment of the colonial administration in Malawi. Operating under the sixty-year rule, public access to government records started in 1951. Until January 1959 when the new fifty-year access to public records rule was introduced, the records of the Nyasaland government that could be accessed by researchers were those from 1891 to 1898.

Access to public records was either ordinary or special. Through ordinary access to public records, researchers could consult public records that were more than sixty years old. From 1959, the period was reduced by ten years, which meant that people could have access to public records, which were fifty years old or more. All records that had passed the closure period of either sixty or fifty years were freely made accessible to researchers. After 1951 when government records were opened for public access, the Nyasaland Government granted access to all who had applied for access to the archives. This type of public access to government records was normally straightforward, such that once an application was submitted to the Secretariat, within a short period of time the application was approved and permission to consult the records was granted to the applicant.

The second type, special access to government records, involved access to records that were within the closure period of fifty years. The process of accessing this type of record was a long one. A researcher had to submit an application specifying the records to be accessed and the reasons for accessing those records. The application was submitted to the Records Committee, which scrutinized it. In turn, the Committee forwarded the application to the Chief Secretary together with its recommendations. If he so wished, the Chief Secretary would then obtain the permission of the Colonial Office, following instructions of the Secretary of State for the Colonies to the Governor in Nyasaland in 1958.

Once special access was granted, and before the material was consulted, the Colonial Office instructed that the researcher was to sign an undertaking to obtain official approval before publishing, at any time in the future, any information derived from his privileged access. Staff of the Archives assisting the researcher was to ensure that only the approved material was consulted.

Although only two requests for access to government records that were less than fifty years old were turned down,[18] all ordinary and other requests for special access were granted between 1951 and 1963.

Archives as a Tool for Creating Silences

Following the departure of Governor-General, Sir Glyn Jones on 5 July 1966, records from the Secretary to the Governor-General were transferred to the National Archives of Malawi on 9 July 1966. The Government Archivist at the time noted that

> Many more files (such as Executive Council Minutes, correspondence concerning Dr. Banda, etc.) were sent to England, in spite of representations by myself to the Governor-General's Secretary, as it was felt that their contents were of an embarrassing nature and should not be seen by the Malawi Government.[19]

Exportation to England of these records before the transfer of power was calculated deliberately in order to create a particular silence in the records, convenient to the out-going administration. If such records had been returned, it would interest researchers to learn about the Colonial rulers' views of Dr Banda and other nationalist leaders during the agitation for independence.

While researching for his book in the National Archives of Malawi and National Archives of Zambia, Rotberg (1965) noted that whereas many categories of records from the Secretariat and other offices had been brought into the Archives for administrative and security reasons, the post-World War Two sensitive files, a large proportion of the more important secret and confidential files, were not deposited in the Archives and had unfortunately been lost. Additionally, 'a number of unclassified files [had] been destroyed and/or removed from their repositories in Lusaka and Zomba by the retreating colonial authorities'.[20] Rotberg goes on to state that:

In the period before the emergence of Northern Rhodesia and Nyasaland as Zambia and Malawi, British officials apparently denied to posterity the records of the 1959 emergency and, in large measure, the secret and confidential accounts that depicted the early growth of modern nationalist movement in both countries. Police Special Branch reports have, for the most part, also disappeared.[21]

On the removal and exportation of records from the African colonies by the Colonial Administrators, John Thomson, the Foreign and Commonwealth Office Sensitive Reviewer confirms that approximately 2,300 boxes of records were sent to the UK during the independence period from different territories and that out of this number, nineteen contain Nyasaland files.[22]

During the transfer of power, the Secretariat instructed District Commissioners to destroy all sensitive records as testified by a former DC who was stationed at Port Herald between 1963 and 1964, who says

> We received instructions from the Secretariat in Zomba that we should destroy all the sensitive files to avoid the new government seeing them. You should have seen the bonfire behind the DC's office at the *Boma*—the files were up in flames. I was personally there, the Police was there and other people gathered to see what was happening.[23]

Destruction of district records during the transfer of power created a permanent gap in the country's documentary sources for understanding Malawi's pre-independence history. It is likely that many people who played some part in the struggle for independence or who were thought to be informers of the Colonial Administration from all parts of the country will remain forgotten by history since official records that identified them perished in fires at the DC's offices throughout the country.

History repeated itself in 1994 when the out-going one party government ordered selective destruction of public records with a view to creating silences in the records. Since the government had committed a number of atrocities and indulged in malpractices during its thirty-year rule, in order to conceal any documentary evidence against it, Kachala says that 'the government decided to consign to hell any information that was deemed politically sensitive'.[24] To this effect, the government ordered heads of departments to undertake wholesale destruction of classified documents in their departments from the month of January 1994. This order was also extended to the Malawi Police.

From the perspective of the regime this unfortunate incident saved the former ruling elite from prosecution after losing power. When a new government came into power after the May 1994 general elections, many serious cases were levelled against the past rulers and senior public servants. However, since the public records had earlier been purged of any evidence of wrong doing by the ruling elite and some senior public servants, it was difficult to commence criminal litigation against those concerned because of lack of evidence. One prominent criminal case that was brought up before the court of law, in which the President, his closest minister, the Inspector-General of Police, and other police officers were accused of murdering three cabinet ministers and a Member of Parliament in an alleged car accident in 1983, was later dismissed and all the accused persons were released because of a lack of evidence.

Archives as a Tool for Consolidating Political Power and Creating More Silences

In August 1964 barely a month after independence, the situation in the National Archives was 'a pity [... because the] Archives [was] no longer the quiet backwater it used to be.'[25] The Home Affairs Minister imposed some strict conditions for accessing public records such that all records that were within the fifty-year rule were now precluded from special access by researchers. This was contrary to the advice of the Secretary of State for the Colonies to the Governor of Nyasaland in 1951 and the practice during the colonial period. Instead, only those records that were more than fifty years old could be accessed. Although this was the case, the government adopted a much stricter line about the inspection and publication of even these records.[26]

As Dr Banda and his government grew more autocratic and intolerant to any criticism, more control over the Archives was exerted than ever before. Between 1964 and 1966, applicants wishing to access public archives were supposed to appear before the Minister for interviews and from 1966, research applicants were required to appear before the President himself and only a very small number was allowed to access the archives between 1966 and 1980.

Working in this political environment, the national archivist was forced to please his masters by spying on a few researchers who were accepted to access the archives. For this reason, a number of researchers whom he reported to the authorities as seemingly having different political views from those of the government, were banned from using the archives and deported.

Between 1965 to 1993, the National Archives was ordered to close on a number of occasions each of varying duration, for different reasons as the President saw fit. For instance, the institution was closed to all research workers on the following dates: between May and July 1965;[27] between July and October 1966;[28] between April and September 1972[29]; a period of twenty months between 1967 and 1968; and between June and December 1993. These closures affected researchers and other interested users of the National Archives in different ways.

The government further controlled access to the archives by banning all foreign researchers from 1968 after a researcher had published an article, which was critical to the Malawi government. This being so, only 'persons of Malawian origin, a few expatriates (only heads of departments) of the University of Malawi and persons doing research on behalf of the Malawi Government' were permitted access to the Archives.[30] Access to the public records was accorded to these categories of people simply because they were all resident in the country and could be traced easily and dealt with if they wrote anything considered subversive.

Another way in which the government controlled access to archives was restrictions on research topics. From 1968 no researcher was allowed access to archival material unless he or she proved that his or her research would make a palpable and significant contribution to the development of the country.[31] Only research where the government could make immediate use of the results was permitted. For this reason, research of a purely historical nature was not allowed. To ensure that this condition was complied with, all researchers were required to send lists of all files they wanted to consult for presidential scrutiny and approval.

By exerting control over the archives, the government was actually hiding the archival resources from public access and scrutiny. As long as the limitations were in force, the largest proportion of the archives that should have been available for public access remained virtually closed and grossly underutilized. No wonder Tony Woods argues that 'the National Archives of Malawi were for all intents and purposes closed from the late 1960s until the early 1980s.'[32]

Archives as a Tool for Re-writing the Country's History

Up to 1993, several State and political apparatuses were used to exercise total control over the Malawian society. One important aspect over which the government exercised strict control was information, a factor which prompted Article 19 to label Malawi as having 'one of the most elaborate systems of formal censorship in Africa' and a country 'whose history was based on concealment'.[33] The new constitutional provision for the freedom of access to information held by the State removed most of the barriers that had been built during the one-party regime that prevented the public from accessing information held by the State. In 1994, following removal of such barriers, the Robert F. Kennedy Memorial Centre for Human Rights, which sought to document the extent of human rights abuses during the one-party rule in Malawi, was able to review government documents from different departments. The review indicated that official information about systematic abuses existed that had not been previously reported. Access to such documentation would not have been possible prior to 1993.

The political transition period brought about the freedom of the press that was recognized by and mandated in the 1994 Constitution. Due to this freedom, by the end of 1993 there were over thirty independent newspapers.[34] The emergence of press freedom opened up widely the once-closed archives and enormous volumes of historical records generated from 1891 were made open and widely accessible to the general public.

Through unhindered access to public records, a number of academicians and other researchers have used the records to rewrite Malawi's history by publishing books, journal articles, and other publications to present a diverse range of views and interpretations that differs from or corrects that which the one-party regime officially sanctioned. *The Monitor*, one of the new independent newspapers, for instance, began a series on the history of Malawi in 1993 that was enthusiastically received by many of its readers. In 1994 Article 19 had noted that academic historical research on the Banda period was beginning that would in the long term change the generally accepted interpretation that Malawi was an orderly, well-run society at that time.

Archives as a Tool for Accountability for Atrocities and Restitution

In order to account retrospectively for the atrocities committed during the one-party era, the 1994 Constitution provided for the establishment of the National Compensation Tribunal (NCT) whose objective was to entertain claims with respect to alleged criminal and civil liability of the Government of Malawi which was in power before 18 May 1994. The NCT had a number of options for making reparations to valid claimants. These were in form of medical care, formal acknowledgement and apology, establishment of memorials, pensions, job retraining, restitution of property, bonds and shares, and monetary compensation.

To achieve its objective, the NCT was given all powers of investigation necessary to establish the facts of any case before it. Between January 1995, when it started receiving claims against the government, and July 2003, when it stopped receiving new claims, the NCT registered 24,363 claimants.[35] Out of this number, 8 per cent received full payments, 40.8 per cent received interim payments, 23 per cent required additional information from the claimants, 1.3 per cent were rejected for lack of documentary evidence, and 22.7 per cent were yet to be assessed.

Validation of the claims brought before the NCT hinged on availability of supporting documentary evidence; 45.7 per cent of the valid registered claimants suffered detention, while 5.6 per cent had their property confiscated.

In order to reduce the NCT's burden of handling additional claims from hundreds of civil servants who were dismissed between 1964 and 1993 on political grounds, the Office of the President and Cabinet (OPC) took up this responsibility. To this effect, the government made a public announcement and directed all Principal Secretaries and Heads of Departments that all civil servants who were dismissed or had their appointment terminated on political grounds should be deemed to have retired either on attaining the age of fifty-five years or on 21 May 1994, if they had reached the mandatory retiring age (then) of fifty-five years.[36] Claimants were given a period of ten years within which to lodge their claims against the government.

A few public servants were handed dismissal letters, but most had their employment terminated verbally. Documentary evidence to validate claims of this nature was either a dismissal letter or claimant's departmental personal file. It is worth mentioning that some former civil servants who were victimized by the Banda regime and qualified for compensation had passed away before 1995, while others could not manage to register their claims in person. In both cases, the government allowed relatives of the victims to lodge claims on their behalf.

When the OPC handled the claims between 1995 and 1996, claimants who did not have—most of them did not have—dismissal letters to support their claims against the government were issued with certificate letters. In turn, the claimants presented the letters to the National Archives asking the Department to release personal files of bearers of the certificate letters for compensation purposes. The claimants presented the files to the OPC, and after the cases had been concluded, the OPC returned the files to the Archives. Similarly, when the Ombudsman took over from the OPC the settlement of claims of former public servants, the Archives was required to make available personal files to certified claimants.

In its Circular of 21 April 2005, the government made a public announcement of its decision to stop entertaining any further claims by former public servants who were dismissed on political grounds, observing that the concerned people had been given sufficient time (ten years) to take up their claims with the government.[37] Between 1995 and 2005, the National Archives assisted hundreds of victims of the former oppressive regime, most of whom had never had any dealings with the Department before. For these people, the Archives were their only hope of ever being able to receive compensation for their suffering. In this way, the National Archives contributed towards the healing process of many people who had been victimized by the government through summary dismissal from the public service.

The analysis of how the archive in Malawi has been used by the society over the decades, demonstrates the inherent power of the archive and how the archive is not a quiet place per se, but a place that is close to the heart of political power. It is at the archive where the society prior to independence, tapped the archival power to equip themselves with research data, information, and knowledge for different purposes. It is also the same archive, which was used by the emerging autocratic one party as a tool for stifling access to information by the majority of the society. Furthermore, when it became apparent to the regime that it would lose power and in order to avoid prosecution, it ordered destruction of the records as a way of uprooting the evential power of the archive. Ironically, after the minority ruling elite had lost the power resulting from introduction of the democratic rule, the archive was freed up and a majority of local masses that had suffered from various atrocities during the dictatorial regime, relied on the archive for evidence in order to hold their oppressors accountable and, eventually, get compensation from the State.

FURTHER READING

Colin Baker, 'Tax Collection in Malawi: An Administrative History, 1891–1972', *The International Journal of African Historical Studies* 8.1 (1975), 40–62

Mandy Banton, *Administering the Empire, 1801–1968: A Guide to the Records of the Colonial Office in the National Archives of the UK* (London: Institute of Historical Research, The National Archives of the UK, 2008)

Davide Chinigò, 'Rural Radicalism and the Historical Land Conflict in the Malawian Tea Economy', *Journal of Southern African Studies* 42.2 (2016), 283–297

Paul Lihoma, *Impact of Administrative Change on Recordkeeping in Malawi* (PhD thesis, University of Glasgow, 2012)

Stephanie Regalia, 'Malawi: The Road to the 2019 Tripartite Elections: Reflections on Corruption, Land and Multiparty Politics', *Notes de l'Ifri* (2019) www.ifri.org/sites/default/files/atoms/files/regalia_malawi_2019.pdf

Tony Woods, 'Capitaos and Chiefs: Oral Tradition and Colonial Society in Malawi', *International Journal of African Historical Studies* 23.2 (1990), 259–268

NOTES

1. A. Mbembe, 'The Power of the Archive and its Limits', in C. Hamilton, V. Harris, M. Pickover, G. Reid, J. Taylor, and R. Saleh, eds, *Refiguring the Archive* (Cape Town / Dordrecht: David Phillip / Kluwer, 2002), 19–26 (23).
2. Mbembe, 'The Power of the Archive and its Limits', 24.
3. B. S. Krishnamurthy, ' Economic Policy, Land and Labour in Nyasaland, 1890–1914', in B. Pachai, ed., *The Early History of Malawi* (London: Longman Group Limited 1972), 384–404.
4. A. J. Hanna, *The Beginnings of Nyasaland and North-Eastern Rhodesia, 1859–95* (Oxford: Clarendon Press, 1956), 230, 384.
5. Peoples Land Organization letter to the United Nations Secretary General, 14 July 2015.
6. Peoples Land Organization letter.
7. Peoples Land Organization letter.
8. *Malawi24*, 'Malawi Losing Two Districts Today', 26 October 2017.
9. C. Baker, 'Tax Collection in Malawi: An Administrative History, 1891–1972', *The International Journal of African Historical Studies*, 8.1 (1975), 40–62.
10. R. H. Palmer, 'Johnston and Jameson: A Comparative Study in the Imposition of Colonial Rule', in B. Pachai, ed., *The Early History of Malawi* (London: Longman, 1972), 293–322 (306).
11. H. L. Duff, *Nyasaland Under the Foreign Office* (London: George Bell and Sons, 1903); J. L. Pretorius, 'An Introduction to the History of the Dutch Reformed Church Mission in Malawi 1889–1914', in Pachai, *The Early History of Malawi*, 365–383.
12. Pretorius, 'An Introduction', 370–371.
13. Pretorious, 'An Introduction', 371.
14. Duff, *Nyasaland Under the Foreign Office*, 355.
15. Duff, *Nyasaland Under the Foreign Office*, 355.
16. *The Times*, Blantyre, 30 November 1967.

17. *WRITENET, Malawi: Between the Referendum and the Elections*, 1 May 1994, available at www.refworld.org/docid/3ae6a6be8.html (accessed 3 January 2020).

18. National Archives of Malawi (NAM), 1/5, Access to Public Archives (Communication from the Deputy Archivist to R. A. Hamilton, 10 January 1951, and communication from the Chief Secretary to G. Shepperson, 31 July 1952). In 1951 R. A. Hamilton's application to consult records that were less than fifty years old in 1951 was rejected by the Chief Secretary, while in 1952, G. Shepperson's application was also turned down for the same reason as that of R. A. Hamilton.

19. NAM, NA/1/3/90A, State House Transmittal List.

20. R. I. Rotberg, *The Rise of Nationalism in Central Africa: The Making of Malawi and Zambia, 1873–1964* (London: Oxford University Press, 1965), 325–326.

21. Rotberg, *The Rise of Nationalism*, 325–326.

22. On 18 April 2012, more than 1,200 files of the migrated archives 'were released at the National Archives in Kew, west London, the first of six tranches in a process which was due to be completed in November 2013'. See *The Independent*, 18 April 2012. See also the discussions, in this volume, in the Introduction and in the chapter by Eric Ketelaar.

23. Oral Testimony: I. Strachan, Perth, Scotland, 13 March 2010.

24. F. C. Kachala, 'Unfolding Events Leading to Political Pluralism in Malawi: Drawing Lessons From the Archives', Paper presented at the XVII ESARBICA General Conference, Maputo, Mozambique, 22–26 July 2003.

25. NAM, 18-5-2R/14,801, Access to Public Records. Correspondence from the Archivist for Malawi to a researcher Dr J. van Velsen, 4 August 1964.

26. NAM, 18-5-2R/14,801, Access to Public Records. Correspondence from the Archivist for Malawi to a researcher Dr. J. van Velsen, 2 September 1964.

27. NAM, 1/5, Access to Public Archives. Letter from the K. M. Mtapiko, the Deputy National Archivist to Dr B. S. Krishnamurthy, concerning the closure of the Archives, 31 May 1965.

28. NAM, 1/5, Access to Public Archives. Letter from the Archivist for Malawi to J. McCracken, informing the latter that the Archives would be closed from 1 July to October while the former was away, 4 April 1966.

29. NAM, 1/5, Access to Public Archives. Memo from the Government Archivist to the Prof. B. Pachai, head of the History Department at Chancellor College, informing members of the History Department and any other interested persons about the closure of the Archives, 7 April 1972.

30. NAM, 1/5, Access to Public Archives. Memo from the Local Government Secretary to the Vice-Chancellor of the University of Malawi on the access conditions to the National Archives, 17 July 1968.

31. NAM, 1/5, Access to Public Records. J. D. C. Drew (Government Archivist) to H. W. MacMillan, 7 May 1968.

32. T. Woods, 'Capitaos and Chiefs: Oral Tradition and Colonial Society in Malawi', *The International Journal of African Historical Studies* 23.2 (1990), 259–268 (259).

33. ARTICLE 19, '"Who Wants to Forget?": Truth and Access to Information about Past Human Rights Violations' (London, December 2000), unpaginated; available at www.article19.org/data/files/pdfs/publications/freedom-of-information-truth-commissions.pdf.

34. Kachala, 'Unfolding Events'; J. L. Lwanda, *Kamuzu Banda of Malawi, 1961–1993: A Study in Promise, Power and Paralysis* (Glasgow: Dudu Nsomba Publications, 1993).

35. This number excludes that of hundreds of civil servants who were dismissed from the service between 1964 and 1993 on political grounds.
36. OPC Ref. No. 5/06/4, Circular from the Chief Secretary to all Principal Secretaries and Heads of Departments, 28 July 1995.
37. OPC Ref. 5/06/4, Circular from the Chief Secretary for Public Service, to all Principal Secretaries and Heads of Departments and advertised in the press, 21 April 2005.

CHAPTER 22

ARCHIVAL IMPULSES AND THE GUNPOWDER PLOT

PAUL STROHM

The modern researcher of historical events relies on predecessors who enacted what might be called 'archival impulses'—acts of preservation, whether formal or informal, idiosyncratic or systematic, springing from laudable or sinister motives or no expressed motives at all. Pursuing some questions about the Gunpowder Plot, and turning to the remarkable array of Gunpowder documents now preserved in the National Archives at Kew, I have had occasion to reflect on the mixture of deliberate choice and sheer accident involved in the creation of such a collection. Whatever fortunate and unfortunate accidents may have occurred along the way, the collection's final or 'archival' form becomes influential in its own right. The preserved documents not only enjoy added prestige resulting from the simple fact of their survival, but also, bolstered by their archival status, gain the authority to regulate the terms of their own study.

A 'Paper' Archive

The new king James I was a great respecter of written records, and, perhaps more important, their uses. One of his many points of indignation at the Gunpowder plotters is that, had their plans to blow up Parliament succeeded, they would have destroyed so many valued records. 'A Discourse of the Manner of Discovery of the Gunpowder Plot', written on the king's behalf, possibly by Francis Bacon, laments that one of its effects would have been the destruction of the halls of Justice, and that 'All the records, as well of Parliament as of every particular man's right, with a great number of Charters and such like should all have been comprehended under that fearful Chaos.'[1] For seventeenth-century England already possessed a fully documentary culture. All participants in apprehending the Gunpowder plotters and bringing them to trial (as well as succeeding in the more nebulous court of public

ARCHIVAL IMPULSES AND THE GUNPOWDER PLOT 311

opinion) understood the foundational importance of obtaining and securing the right kinds of records.

Authorities already knew a good deal about the conspiracy on that early morning of 5 November 1605 when they seized Guy Fawkes upon his exit from the powder-laden cellar, bound him head and foot, and delivered him to hasty interrogation. Examinations were conducted according to protocols and interrogatives proposed by the king himself, and submitted to the Lords Commissioners in his own hand-writing.[2] In addition to the other persuasions, torture was brought to bear in order to obtain the necessary results. (In his instructions to the Commissioners, the king adds of Fawkes that 'If he will not otherwise Confess, the gentler Tortures are to be first used upon him, until gradually he is stretched to the extremest' ['et sic per gradus ad ima tenditur'].)[3] And if, at first, the 'necessary results' involved simple information-gathering about the identities and intentions of the plotters, the inter-rogations quickly moved on to a second objective: obtaining persuasive *written* proofs of matters already known. Records—examinations, depositions, testimonies, and confessions—were generated and revised and re-revised until judged fit for purpose.

Crafting a Document

Production of Gunpowder records was overseen by a formidable team including Edward Coke (Solicitor General and already a renowned prosecutor, conspicuous for his conduct of the Raleigh treason trial), William Waad (Keeper of the Tower), and other government agents, under the specific and efficient co-ordination of Robert Cecil, the newly created lord Salisbury. Salisbury and the others understood that written, rather than merely oral, testimony was necessary to their purposes, both prosecutorial and propagandistic. In addition to having relevant points in writing, other goals were sought as well. Best of all was to have the record in the defendant's *own* handwriting; failing in that, it should at least be signed by the defen-dant. Additionally, it should not simply be an 'examination' or random record of testimony; it would be more valued in the form of a narration, not only enumerat-ing the facts of the conspiracy but setting names, dates, places, and other details in a persuasive causal order. On 8 November 1605, three days after Fawkes' detention, Keeper William Waad wrote to Salisbury to announce that these purposes appeared to have been achieved, only to fail at the last instance:

> Yesternight I had persuaded him to set down a clear *narration* of all his wicked plottes from the first entering on the same to the end they pretended with the discourses and projects that were thought upon amongst them which he undertooke and craved tyme this night to bethinke him the bet[ter.] But this morning he hathe changed his mind, and is [so] sullen and obstinate as there is no dealing with him.[4]

With Fawkes's compliance or without it, the full-throttle attempt to narratize the conspiracy was already well underway. A first account of the plot's discovery was attempted (probably on 7 November) written out by Salisbury's secretary Levinas Munck and with corrections in Salisbury's own hand, commencing with the Mounteagle letter that initially brought the conspiracy to public attention and carrying on to the Fawkes interrogations.[5] Then on 8 November, the very day of Fawkes's obstinacy, the examiners produced a document modestly headed 'Examination of G Fawkes', which sets the crucial events of the conspiracy in narrative order, spanning the major highlights of the scheme, its reverses, and ultimate failure.[6] Yet even this new document falls short in several ways. It is transcribed in a secretarial hand, rather than in Fawkes's own. It also, crucially, fails the test of specificity, not yet 'naming names', but simply identifying the key conspirators as 'gentlemen of name and blood'. (Fawkes says that he first met with an 'English layman', but does not name him.) The document also remains impersonal; as is conventional in such records, Fawkes is treated in the third person ('He confesseth')—confessing, indeed, but in the impersonal person of an 'examinand', rather than a free and uncoerced subject. A final shortcoming is that, although yielding the information contained in this document, Fawkes seems still to have refused to set his name to it.

Then, on 9–10 November, a further breakthrough. William Waad predicts it in a note to Salisbury: Fawkes will relate his story, orally though not in writing, to Salisbury. But they will have the prize of his signature:

> I have prevayled so much at the length with my prisoner by plying him with the best perswasions [that is: more torture] I could use as he hath faythfully promised me by narration to discover to your lordship all the secrets of his hart, but not to be set down in writing. Your lordship will not mislyke the exception; for when he hathe confessed himself to your lordship ... he will not make dainty to set his hand unto it.[7]

All would be fulfilled. This time we have a 'Declaration', taken 9 November and signed 10 November, with the faint and tremulous 'Guido' that has seemed to commentators to confirm personal infirmity resulting from torture, even to the extent of his inability to write his full name.[8] It launches in by naming the 'English layman' of the day before: 'Thomas Winter came over into the Low Countries unto this examinate ..., expressly to break with him about some course to be taken for the advancement of the Catholic religion'. Other names are soon introduced: 'this examinate came into England in the company of the said Winter, by whose means he was acquainted with Thomas Percy, Robert Catesby, and John Wright'. This account represents a milestone, and is proudly endorsed by the key parties: 'Taken before us and subscribed by the examinate before us. Sir Edw Coke, W. G. Waad, Edward Forsett'.

One more step remained to be taken, issuing in a narrative document of uncertain—though later November—date, headed 'The declaration of Guy Fawkes, prisoner in the Tower of London, taken the 27 of November 1605 acknowledged before the lords commissioners.'[9] This might be considered the culminating document of the series, signed (and now more firmly) by Guido Fawkes, and bearing a list of 'principal persons' involved in 'this horrible conspiracy.'[10] Two additional ambitions are achieved. First, its previous heading was 'The deposition of Guy Fawkes', treating it as a court document. In this new document, the term 'deposition' is struck through, and the term 'declaration' subbed in for it. Am I wrong in suggesting that this latter term suggests a more volitional statement, an utterance volunteered by a subject who wishes to assert a view? So completely did most 'declarations' generated under such circumstances serve the interests of the eventual prosecution, rather than those of the accused party, that the very idea of a freely composed statement was something of a joke among contemporary observers. (A whimsical commentator on the just-completed treason trial of Sir Walter Raleigh observed of such carefully-curated records that the accused plotters 'were all condemned upon their own confessions, which were set down under their hands as Declarations and compiled with such labour and care ... as if they had feared they should not say enough to hang themselves.'[11])

The idea of Fawkes as an unconstrained subject is of course absurd, but not the idea of presenting him in that guise. In keeping with this adjustment, the document recasts Fawkes, not as a third-person 'examinand' ('He confesseth') but rather into the volitional first-person ('*I confess* that a practice ... was first broken *unto me*'). This embrace of personal responsibility was undoubtedly the idea of the interrogators rather than Fawkes himself, but it may also be read as a proud claim, sorting well with his customary attitude of personal defiance.[12] In any case, Fawkes's document gains considerable force, when seen not as the coerced production of an imprisoned 'examinand', but as the willing testimony of an autonomous participant in the conspiracy.

This motivated recrafting marks the special importance of the Fawkes documents to the prosecution of the case, but similar interventions are found elsewhere within the Gunpowder records. Dozens of these papers show signs of selective editing and reworking—for recopying and circulation among heads of State and influential citizens, and then, even more consequentially, for purposes of oral recital in the January 1606 show trial. One of them, headed 'The Examination of Guy Fawkes London the 8th of November 1605' is especially conspicuous in its displays of markings and excisions, in Salisbury's hand, of materials considered inessential for prosecutorial/propaganda purposes.[13] Another—a copy of Thomas Wintour's 23 November Declaration—contains a marginal editorial notation ('uncleare phrase') in the king's own hand.[14] Also active in the marking and selective indexing of the Gunpowder papers was Edward Coke who, with prosecutorial responsibility for the Gunpowder trial, was heavily engaged in excerpting and reframing the collected Gunpowder materials for persuasive oral presentation.

But here arises a paradox which must be explored. All the care taken to obtain and frame these documents would seem to be aimed at their opportune display, whereas in fact their most pressing and immediate use then turns out to be their radical re-editing and re-framing for piecemeal use in a new script designed for other purposes altogether. As Holger Schott Syme has argued in his investigation of Edward Coke's use of similar written materials gathered for the 1603 Essex trial, these avidly-curated documents were then treated with considerable disrespect in the runup to trial, scrawled upon, encoded, radically abstracted, refashioned for courtroom presentation in what would be an effectively oral performance.[15] A consequence is that, once strip-mined for purposes of oral use in the trial situation, these arduously compiled source-documents might be seen as having fulfilled their primary function—thus finding themselves subject to sudden devaluation. And so here, then, is the paradox: rather than casting the Gunpowder documents aside once they had served their prosecutorial purpose, Edward Coke—who had played an active role in selectively disassembling and reassembling them—would turn out to be the person indispensable to their ultimate archival presentation.

Coke's Buckroom Bagg

Waad and others were responsible for seeing that matters concerning the Gunpowder Plot got written down; Salisbury and even the king were their avid readers and sometime editors; but Solicitor General and zealous prosecutor Edward Coke was their first curator. Records of the trial itself would have gone to the charmingly designated *Baga de Secretis*, behind the door of a triple-locked cabinet, along with other records of treason trials occurring between 1477 and the end of the seventeenth century.[16] But the now-superceded records utilized by the Crown and prosecution were another matter. They had their own long sojourn, but in a surprising place: in yet another bag, the buckram bag of Edward Coke, who, having mobilized them in the trial, now retained them for his own purposes—not necessarily for purposes we would now call 'archival', but through some indeterminate mixture of enjoyment, curatorship, or potential for future political use.

Certainly, the emphasis of the Gunpowder papers on matters of treasonous conduct would have commended them to Coke in all three respects. Treason is a prominent subject of his voluminous writings and commentaries on matters of the common law, and is treated in one entire book, *The Third Part of the Institutes of the Laws of England* (printed in numerous editions). Coke does indeed make some practical (though rather glancing) use of Gunpowder precedents in this work, as when he references the Gunpowder-related trial of Henry Garnet, the Jesuit Superior in England at the time of the conspiracy.[17] But other pleasures of possession and enjoyment must be allowed as well; Syme comments keenly on Coke's 'fetishistic' enjoyment of court documents and written records.[18]

Coke's papers would be relinquished only upon royal demand—demand, ultimately, of Charles I—when they were called in for inspection at the end of Coke's life. One such canvass of Coke's records had already occurred, during a period of disfavour in 1620–1621, when his study was ransacked by Keeper of Records Thomas Wilson, in the company of Robert Cotton. But the searchers either weren't interested in Gunpowder records or came up empty-handed at this time.[19] Then, in 1631, pressing the recovery of State Papers in the possession of Edward Coke, including papers of the Gunpowder Plot, Charles I ordered another search, this time of Coke's residence, with a particular emphasis on papers, in the hope that 'use may be made of them ... for his majesties service and some suppressed that may disserve him'.[20]

Other searches would follow. Most crucially, in 1634, as Coke lay dying, the Privy Council issued a Commission to one Francis Windebank, noting the presence of 'papers and Manuscripts of great consideration and weight yet remaining in the possession of Sir Edward Coke', authorized him 'to repaire to the house ... of Sir Edward Coke, and there to seize and take into your charge, and bring away all such papers and Manuscripts as yow shall think fitt'.[21] Their search resulted in some recordkeeping in its own right: an inventory of Windebank's findings, now preserved at Lambeth Palace Library.[22] This inventory is headed, 'A catalogue of Sr Edward Cookes papers, that by warrant from the Councell were brought to Whitehall; whereupon his Ma[jes]ties pleasure is to be knowen, which of them shall remain there.' This inventory is accompanied by a supplementary document, described by Windebank as 'A note of such things as were found in a Trunk taken from S[i]r Edw[ard] Cokes seruant at London. This trunk I was commanded by his M[ajesty] to bring to Bagshot, w[hi]ch I did: 9 September 1634: and there his M[ajesty] brak it open.'[23]

Coke's modalities of preservation and storage, as revealed in these inventories, were typical of his day. The inventories refer to black boxes, numerous larger and smaller bundles of letters and papers, two little 'pacquetts', an old purse, 'one lidd of an old painted boxe', 'one greate book of Statutes called the buckskin book' together with other books, 'a great canvas bagg', a 'black lether bagg', 'a Table booke, embroidered with gold and silk', and similar items. The workhorses of the collection are three buckram bags, including, most crucially, 'A great buckrom bagg of the pouder treason'. This bag is, in turn, supplemented by 'A blacke buckrom Bagg of the procedings against Sr Walter Raweley', as well as 'A great canvas bagg containing diverse matters about the treasons and other offences' of multiple others, including Gunpowder conspirators Percy and Catesby. These bags were brought to Whitehall, inspected by the King or his minions, and—since the Gunpowder papers were evidently not among those he was wondering about—there remained, an important augmentation of the nascent Paper Office.

In the useful formulation of Alexandra Walsham, a collection of 'records' becomes an 'archive' when it no longer exists solely for immediate utility but is stored for 'the use of others than those who originally created them'.[24] By this standard, Coke's buckram bag began functioning as a rudimentary archive when persons other than those for whom the records were created began to consult its contents for emergent or latterday purposes. One such person was Robert Abbott, Professor of Theology at Oxford and afterwards Bishop of Salisbury. An arch anti-Catholic and, especially anti-Jesuit, he composed a vehement tract *Antilogia* (London, 1613) aimed at proving beyond all doubt that Henry Garnett, SJ, Superior of the English Jesuits (executed, 1606) had been a principal architect of the Gunpowder Plot. In his exposition, Abbott displays an impressive knowledge of the Gunpowder records, and there is no doubt that he was enjoying privileged access to the contents of Coke's buckram bag.

Most of these records seem to have been consulted in situ or returned, but some went missing. Abbott was particularly interested in those records containing overheard and incriminating conversations (or 'interlocutions') between Garnett and a confederate during his pretrial incarceration. One such record, an Interlocution between Garnet and Oldcorne dated 25 February, never made it back to the buckram bag. Once unmoored, it resurfaced in other hands—as part of a private collection of anti-Catholic records assembled by William Sancroft, Archbishop of Canterbury (appointed 1677), and a notorious anti-Catholic. His term of office coincided with the upheavals attending Titus Oates' accusations of a 'Popish Plot' in 1678. Sancroft was a staunch adversary of the Catholic James II in 1685–1688, and an opponent of the Declaration of Indulgence in 1688. As a component of his argument against Catholics, he prepared his own transcription of the 25 February Interlocution, probably along with other anti-Catholic materials, and his original, now missing, was never returned to the archive. The circle was finally closed when a copy of his copy was restored to the State Papers, in the first half of the nineteenth century.[25]

Within Whitehall

In March 1609–1610, a Patent of James I created a notionally more secure location for state papers, a Paper Office within a 'library' housed in several smallish rooms and turrets within Whitehall.[26] This library was bolstered by Salisbury's own papers, and the Keepers were Salisbury's own secretary Levinas Munck as well as faithful Salisbury protégée Thomas Wilson, who for some years previously (since 1606 and probably earlier than that) had acted as overseer of the twenty or so 'chests' containing state papers.

Now, with the addition of materials seized from Coke, including the contents of his 'buckroom bagg', the nascent Paper Office was gaining a rather formidable Gunpowder collection. Some documents were already there when the Coke papers arrived. They appear in an early listing of the contents and categories of the Office, surviving in an eighteenth-century copy of Wilson's own notes, 'A General Account of the State-Papers Preserved in the Royal Repository called the Paper-Office.'[27]

Wilson's plan for the Office, as preserved in his notes, include eight subsections or 'stages', encompassing Regalia, Legalia, Ecclestica, Militaria, Politica, Criminalia, Mechania, and Britania. A special interest was in preserving treaties between Britain and other European nations. But, under Criminalia, various treason-related papers were preserved. These include 'Touching the Gunpowder plot a Relation of its discovery under the parliament house together with the Letters of the Lord Salisbury to our ambassador then beyond the Sea relating to its discovery' and pamphlets prepared for the use of the English ambassador to Spain bearing on 'the execution of [Henry] Garrett'. Other similar materials include 'Papers touching the Treasons and attainder of Sir Walter Rawleigh'.[28]

In the course of the seventeenth century, there in the Whitehall archive, some Gunpowder papers—presumably including those preserved by Coke and screened by Charles I—were gathered under their own rubric, 'Gunpowder Treason Papers, Jac. I'. But, although now better housed, these papers could not be considered secure by anything like modern archival standards. Wilson himself complains that even in its first decade the Paper Office has lost materials 'which Diverse Privy Counsellors [have borrowed] about the recovering whereof I am now very much busyed', adding that one of his largest problems is recovering papers from the estates of peers now dead.[29] Nor was the new library proof against less official incursions. In a letter attached to the third volume[30] of the Gunpowder papers, the nineteenth-century historian David Jardine—who suspected that 'those fellows, the Jesuits' may have removed some records incriminating Garnet 'in the time of the Powder Plot'— reports subsequent Jesuitical activities during the reigns of Charles II and James II 'when Jesuits and "Jesuited persons" had free access to the State Paper Office'. Other vicissitudes included a great fire in Whitehall in 1619 when papers were 'hastily cast in blankets' and general neglect in the eighteenth century when they were assailed by 'vermin and wet'.[31] Nor were its travels over; it was moved to several intermediate locations—including one that had previously housed Scotland Yard, and another building in Great George Street, and then (in 1833) to St James Park, and then, following upon an Act of 1838 aimed at consolidating the various Public Records scattered among a half dozen locations, a century-long sojourn in a vastly improved situation in the Public Record Office in Chancery Lane, into which the Rolls and other documents were installed beginning in 1856.[32] Then, since 1997, they have been held at The National Archives in Kew.

An Archive within an Archive

Various persons had flirted with the idea of creating a separate archive of select Gunpower papers. In the course of the seventeenth century, for example, an Irish historian and antiquarian—Sir James Ware—took advantage of visits to London to prepare a collection of extracts (in various hands and with personal commentary) of some 130 Gunpowder items.[33] Likewise, a substantial collection of eighteenth-century transcripts, mostly pertaining to the Gunpowder Plot, had been prepared by Dr Adee, a physician of Guildford, for the use of a Mr Bray.[34]

These early devotees left the papers where they found them. Their separation as an archive-within-an-archive would await the activities of the redoubtable Robert Lemon, who joined the State Paper Office in 1795 as Second Clerk, was promoted to Deputy Keeper in 1818, and served until his death in 1835.[35] Lemon was clearly a man of ambition—at once a longtime servitor, a hard worker, and something of a self-promoter. (He gained considerable notoriety for his 1823 discovery amidst the rubble of the State Papers Office of a unique copy of Milton's *De Doctrina Christiana*.) He decided early on that among his self-appointed tasks would be the creation of a separate Gunpowder Archive. A preliminary effort, probably commenced in the years prior to his promotion, was a *Calendar of the Supplementary Papers relative to the Gunpowder Treason, 1605. Recently discovered in the State Paper office by Mr Lemon*. This document identifies an initial gathering of 130 items.[36] It has the character of a working draft, with excisions, provisional interpretations, and annotations like 'important', 'curious', and 'interesting' throughout.[37] Lemon's claim of 'discovery' may be taken with something of a grain of salt, given the previous explorations by antiquarians like Ware and Adee,[38] and the prior separation of some records under the previously-mentioned rubric 'Gunpowder Treason Papers, Jac. I'. But Lemon may not have known of efforts like Ware's and Adee's, and there is no question of his dedication to his task. He stayed with it and, shortly after his 1819 appointment as Deputy Keeper, he went public with a considerably expanded version, chosen to illustrate the course of the conspiracy through its most vivid documents, arranged in cumulative sequence, commencing with the rental of a property adjacent to Parliament and concluding after the trials of the crucial participants. This time the claim of 'discovery' is omitted from its title; the new calendar is more modestly entitled *Original Documents in His Majesty's State Paper Office relative to the Gunpowder Treason, 1605, compiled by Robert Lemon, Deputy of Keeper of State Papers, 1819*. These documents, now conclusively separated from the general archive, were bound in two volumes as State Papers vols 216/1 and 216/2, and joined by a third volume, 216/3, including Lemon's expanded calendar.

Lemon considered himself a defender of the newly constituted collection. Bound into the *Gunpowder Plot Book* is an 1857 letter from David Jardine to Robert Lemon's son, regretting the latter's distress at any implication that records had been removed from the collection: 'Nothing could be further from my thoughts than to suggest the possibility of the abstraction of records from the State Paper Office in modern times.'

There can be no doubt that the existence of three bound volumes containing Lemon's calendar and 246 selected items related to the Gunpowder Plot has facilitated research into its subject-area—the more so, since they can now be conveniently viewed in State Papers Online. But a question might also be raised: as to whether the segregation of approximately half the items concerning the Gunpowder Plot does not represent a form of 'document tourism'—the segregation of a select category of items likely to reward cursory curiosity, rather than to provide a wider conspectus of all known materials as a basis for more thorough historical inquiry. Certainly, the Gunpowder papers had always had what might be called 'star power'. This was recognized upon the move to the Public Record Office (PRO) on Chancery Lane when a PRO 'Museum' offered a continuing display of selected papers of 'historical or artistic interest' in rooms adjacent to the Round Room collections. There, amidst formidable rivals for public attention like the Domesday Book, displayed on a central pedestal, were Jonson's letter to Salisbury (8 November 1605), the notorious Monteagle letter exposing the plot to public attention (26 October 1605), the two Declarations of Guy Fawkes (17 November and 10 November 1605), and the Interrogations of 6 November 1605 in which James I proposes that *tortours* be applied to the newly captured and recalcitrant Fawkes. (Although a conspirator and valued informant, Fawkes was not one of the conspiracy's leaders; that title must be reserved for Robert Catesby or Thomas Wintour, or any of several others. But the centrality and prominent display of the Fawkes documents have had their own role to play in establishing him as the 'face' of the Plot.)

Meanwhile, questions about the segregation of 246 papers from among the general run of diverse Gunpowder-related materials remain. Of course, nothing prohibits a researcher from making his or her way through the full Calendar of State Papers, and all papers may now be summoned electronically with the touch (or several touches) of a key.

Certainly, subsequent to Lemon's segregation of the Gunpowder Plot papers, the larger body of State Papers for November 1605–March 1606 still contain hundreds of frequently-neglected items that he, based on subjective considerations, passed over or rejected. These items have since been calendared along with other State Papers from 1603–1610 (*Calendar of State Papers Domestic: James I, 1603–10*, Her Majesty's Stationery Office, 1857), without any segregation—either of Gunpowder records from each other, or of Gunpowder records from other, more routine matters of business. The 1857 Calendar thus represents a more neutral *listing* of varied records, in which Gunpowder papers sit alongside entries on other matters, better serving an idea of historical objectivity.

What are some of the records left behind? Many concern the interrogations of small-fry associated with the conspiracy: wives worried about husbands leaving home bearing arms; non-fervent servants compelled to reluctant co-operation with Catesby and the other plotters; nervous country gentry explaining the presence of disused armour in their barns; procurers of arms and horses for the anticipated rebellion in Staffordshire and surrounding areas; carters dragooned to carry rusted arms from place to place; lukewarm loyalists who tentatively joined the plotters in a tentative state of mind and then deserted them as their prospects declined. Although the more spectacular confessions and more sweeping narrations of Fawkes and

Wintour command and reward the highest degree of attention, a case may be made that the real history of the Catholic predicament in Jacobean England, and the failure of insurrectionary resolve following the Plot's disclosure, may be written from these secondary records and from the revealed lives of these lesser players.

In any case, matters of vivid human and historical interest are to the found amongst the larger body of State Papers. There we encounter Ben Jonson's letter to Salisbury, seeking to clear himself of past incriminating association with some of the plotters, offering his services as informant and predicting that 500 Catholic gentlemen remain to be apprehended.[39] There we encounter moments of human interest and apologetics, as when the Earl of Northumberland, ruined by the Conspiracy, writes pleadingly to Salisbury of his self-restriction to 'privat dometicall pleasures', urging that any examination take note of his devotion to 'buildings, gardening, theas two years past'.[40] Or craven self-promotions like that of Lord Dunfermling, who writes to Salisbury in a letter larded with classical allusion, with suggestions for the best means of applying torture to arrested persons: 'when occasioun sall serve of Torture, the slawlier it be used, at dyvers tymes, and be intervallis, the mair is gotten be it'.[41] Or homely details, like Sir William Waad, Warden of the Tower, worrying about procuring additional bedding and hiring additional guards for new prisoners in the Tower, and reporting on the demeanour and mood-swings of persons in his charge (including pensiveness on the part of aptly named Lord Mordaunt).[42] Mainly ignored by Lemon were records concerning Henry Garnet, the Jesuit superior, and his remarkable intimacy with Mrs Vaux. Not to mention other critical aspects of the texture of the conspiracy and its disclosure: printed proclamations and bills, accounts of unfounded rumours, and the like. All materials of history, if not from 'below', at least from a side aisle, and no less interesting for that.

ACKNOWLEDGEMENT

With grateful thanks to Andrew Prescott for his assistance with this chapter.

FURTHER READING

Siân Echard, 'House Arrest: Modern Archives, Medieval Manuscripts', *Journal of Medieval and Early Modern Studies* 30 (2000), 185–210

Nick Popper, 'From Abbey to Archive: Managing Texts and Records in Early Modern England', *Archival Science* 10 (2010), 249–266

State Papers Online: Early Modern Government in Britain and Europe (Detroit: Gale Cengage, 2008–13) [Letters and Papers containing Gunpowder papers alongside other miscellaneous state papers chronologically arranged for May 1605–February 1616 are accessed as SP 14, vols 14–16. The Gunpowder Plot, 1604–6—a thematically-restricted collection of correspondence, depositions, and papers bearing exclusively on the Gunpowder Plot—is separately gathered as SP 14, vol. 216, parts 1–3.]

Elizabeth Williamson, 'Archival Practice and the Production of Political Knowledge in the Office of Sir Francis Walsingham', Arndt Brendecke, ed., *Praktiken der Frühen Neuzeit: Akteure, Handlungen, Artefakte*, Frühneuzeit-Impulse 3 (Köln, Weimar, Wien: Böhlau Verlag, 2015); doi:10.5282/ubm/epub.49319

NOTES

1. Published with *King James His Speech ... on Occasion of the Gunpowder-Treason* (London: His Majesties Printers, 1679).
2. TNA, SP 14/216/1, no. 17, f. 34.
3. TNA, SP 14/216/1, no. 18, f. 34.
4. TNA, SP 14/216/1, no. 48B, f. 82.
5. TNA, SP 14/216/2, no. 129, f. 34.
6. TNA, SP 14/216/1, no. 49, f. 82.
7. TNA, SP 14/216/1, no. 53, f. 89.
8. TNA, SP 14/216/1, no. 54, f. 90.
9. TNA, SP 14/216/1, no. 101, f. 152.
10. The chronology of this document, and its predecessor, has been routinely mistaken, based on the reasonable assumption that the tremulous 'Guido' represents a further deterioration in Fawkes's condition under torture; in fact, the tremulous 'Guido' precedes this document, and its firmer signature may suggest improved treatment of the now-compliant Fawkes.
11. Jardine, *Criminal Trials* [London, 1847], vol. 1, 465.
12. The general turn in the seventeenth century towards the superior authority of the first-person witness is documented by A. Frisch, *The Invention of the Eyewitness: Witnessing and Testimony in Early Modern France* (Chapel Hill: University of North Carolina Press, 2004).
13. TNA, SP 14/216/1, no. 49–50, ff. 82–3.
14. TNA, SP 14/216/2, no. 114, ff. 6–11.
15. H. S. Syme, *Theatrical Testimony in Shakepeare's England* (Cambridge: Cambridge University Press, 2012), especially 72–82, 102–110.
16. For a pre-1934 description of the bags of secrets, prior to their removal by the PRO to more modern storage, see L. W. Vernon Harcourt, 'The Baga de Secretis', *EHR* 23 (1908), 508–529.
17. *Institutes*, part three, 6th ed. (London, 1658), 27.
18. Syme, *Theatrical Testimony*, 101.
19. *Acts of the Privy Council*, 1621–23, 106–7. Dated 27 December is a Warrant to Sir Thomas Wilson 'requiring him to make immediate repair to Sir Edward Coke's house in Broad Street, London, in search of anie writeings or papers' found there. Then, dated 30 December, is a Privy Council warrant to Wilson and others 'to make dilligent search for all such papers and writeings as doe anie way concerne his Majestie's service and the same to seale up and bringe forthwith unto us'.
20. TNA, SP 16/183/18, f. 29. Cited by J. H. Baker, 'Coke's Note-Books and the Sources of His Reports', *Cambridge Law Journal* 30 (1972), 59–86.
21. TNA, SP 16/272 no. 62a, f. 125.
22. London, Lambeth Palace Miscellaneous Papers MS 943, ff. 371–372.

23. The note is at ff. 369–370. The preservation of these inventories itself provides a glimpse into the circuitous avenues by which documents find their way into an archive. First carefully preserved among the papers of Archbishop Laud, they were gathered into a volume which passed into the possession of Archbishop Tenison at the end of the seventeenth century, and then came within a whisker of destruction in the mid-eighteenth century administration of Archbishop Thomas Herring. A note accompanying the volume observes that the manuscripts were 'in a Box which A[rchbishop] Tenison directed his Executors to burn without opening: but the Box bursting in that fire ... this Book whiche they supposed was forgot by the A[rchbishop] was taken out & preserved'. Eventually, together with other of Archbishop Tenison's papers, this book passed to the collections of the Lambeth Palace Library.

24. A. Walsham, 'The Social History of the Archive: Record-Keeping in Early Modern Europe', *Past and Present* Supplement 11 (2016), 1–48

25. For this re-re-transcription see TNA, SP 14/18, no. 117, f. 176, with the note in the Deputy Keeper's hand: 'Taken from a collection of papers relating to the Gunpowder Plot mostly in the hand-writing of Archbiship Sancroft amongst the *Tanner MSS in the Bodleian Library*, vol. 75. p. 292'.

26. F. S. Thomas, *A History of the State Paper Office* (London, 1849).

27. Preserved as London, British Library Stowe MS 548.

28. Respectively at fols 17v, 21v, 78v, and 77v.

29. In Stowe MS 548.

30. TNA, SP 14/216/3.

31. Thomas, *A History of the State Paper Office*.

32. *Catalogue of the Manuscripts and Other Objects in the Museum of the Public Record Office*, 4th ed. (London, 1907).

33. It is preserved as Oxford, Bodleian Library, Bodleian MS Tanner 75, fols. 140–221.

34. Surviving as London, British Library, Additional MS 6178.

35. His obituary appears in the *Annual Register*, 1835.

36. Preserved in the Bodleian Library as MS Add D. 91.

37. Curiously, despite its preliminary character, it is cross-referenced at several points to already existing *volumes* of 'Gunpowder Treason Papers'—perhaps referring to the existing category of 'Gunpowder Treason Papers, Jac. I'.

38. Lemon may not have known Adee's efforts until 1837, when he mentioned the existence of his transcripts in a note added to the third volume of his *Gunpowder Plot Book*.

39. TNA, SP 14/16, no. 30, f. 54a. Curiously, no image of this letter is included in the Gale State Papers database and only the very summary calendar entry is given. An image and full transcript of Jonson's letter is however available on the British Library website: www.bl.uk/collection-items/autograph-letter-by-ben-jonson-concerning-the-gunpowder-plot.

40. TNA, SP 14/16, no. 77, f. 146.

41. TNA, SP 14/16, no. 81, f. 150.

42. TNA, SP 14/16, no. 82, f. 152.

CHAPTER 23

ACCIDENTALLY ON PURPOSE

Denying Any Responsibility for the Accidental Archive

NADINE AKKERMAN AND PETE LANGMAN

It is, perhaps, an irony worth noting that the term 'accidental archive' came into being accidentally. It first appeared as the title of an article discussing the Library of Congress Collection: 'The Accidental Archive' (1966), by the film scholar Harvey Deneroff.[1] Since then, the term has popped up in anthropology, history, feminist literary theory, and new media studies, for example in Amy Tector's 'The Almost Accidental Archive' (2006), Rebekah Ahrendt and David van der Linden's 'The Postmasters' Piggy Bank: Experiencing the Accidental Archive' (2017), Carol Pal's 'The Accidental Archive' (2018), and Michael Moss and David Thomas's 'The Accidental Archive' (2018), to name but four.[2] Certainly, the term's survival appears to be entirely accidental as three of these pieces manage to have the term in the title but not in the body text, which is perhaps why the only one that uses the phrase points out (rather astutely, it appears) that the term is under-theorized, before actually giving the reader a definition (albeit almost *en passant*):

> We need a new archival methodology, one that relies not just on the formal archives consciously created by people interested in keeping a record of the past but also on what we call the 'accidental archive': a set of sources handed down to us not by an institution but by people who never dreamed of creating a formal record of the past.[3]

Ahrendt and Van der Linden almost, therefore, define the accidental archive, but do so primarily in terms of what it is not. Rather than professing a new methodology, they then carry out a process they term 'the archaeology of the archive', essentially an object biography, a scholarly uncovering of the history of the Brienne Collection, the archive at the heart of their study. And they carry this out very well indeed, though they continually both assert and deny that there is any moment during the process at which one may point and say '*This* is the archive' (accidental or otherwise). In essence, for them, the archive can never be settled or stable: it resists such interpretations.

What we would like to suggest is that not only *can* an archive be considered settled and stable, it *must* be in order for us to consider it an archive, even if such stability is never, in fact, possible. In our *assumption* of stability we can, in the end, make use of its fluidity.

When Is an Archive: The Brienne Collection

The Brienne Collection is, depending on your viewpoint, a trunk full of letters, a lot of letters and a trunk, or a lot of letters. As two of the international team of scholars assembled to make some sense of this 're-discovery', Ahrendt and Van der Linden unravel the travails of this collection, now held in the media museum Sound and Vision The Hague, the Netherlands (formerly Museum voor Communicatie in The Hague), describing the life of these letters first amassed by the Briennes, a highly respected seventeenth-century Postmaster and Postmistress, and explore the rationale behind their collection.

In 1676, Simon de Brienne (né Veillaume) was appointed Postmaster to deliver international mail, letters to and from the Southern Netherlands and France, in The Hague, the capital of the Dutch Republic. He shared the position with Christoffel Tromer, who was replaced ten years later by Marie Germain, Brienne's wife. She was appointed as Postmistress, one of the few offices to which a woman could officially be appointed in the seventeenth century (in The Hague, she was preceded by Postmistress Cornelia Borrebach,[4] and the Briennes also employed a '*bestelster*', a woman called Geertruy Lus, responsible for delivery of letters to a home address).[5] In 1689, a year after the Glorious Revolution, the pair decamped to England for eleven years to serve the Stadtholder-turned-king of England William III and Queen Mary at Kensington Palace as 'housekeeper and wardrobe-keeper'.[6] In this time one of their employees began to put aside so-called 'dead' letters: letters that could either not be delivered or that were refused. Whether this was done under orders or on the employee's own initiative is not known, but the motivation was clearly financial: in the early modern period it was the recipient who paid for delivery, so each dead letter represented a coin unreceived. This is why the letters all bear a mark in red crayon: the price of redemption.

The undelivered letters remained set aside until someone chose to redeem one by paying the postage owed, and the monies collected thereby were split annually between Brienne and his 'deputy-cum-successor, Willem Gerrit Dedel, who had been appointed in 1703 to replace Brienne's [recently] deceased wife'.[7] This process was actually illegal, however, as 'Dutch postmasters were obliged to return such "dead letters" to France within a fortnight, so that the French could be reimbursed for their costs to the Dutch border.[8] Illegal or not, a note made by Brienne's accountant Hugo van der Meer following Brienne's death in 1707 refers to the profits made from the undelivered letters as a *spaarpotje*, or 'piggy bank'.[9] Brienne and Dedel were at best withholding and at worst cozening money from foreign authorities. So far, so good: but how do we go from here to the Brienne Collection being an archive (whether accidental or otherwise)? Perhaps the simplest way possible is worth a try.

In 1620, the politician, essayist, and philosopher of science Francis Bacon made a series of observations on the most appropriate manner in which natural historical observations ought to be noted down:

> make sure that everything which is adopted is set down briefly and concisely, so that they are not exceeded by the words that report them. For no one collecting and storing materials for shipbuilding or the like bothers (as shops do) about arranging them nicely and displaying them attractively; rather his sole concern is that they be serviceable and good, and take up as little space as possible in the warehouse.[10]

What Bacon is talking about is, in effect, a data storage facility—and such a facility is not far off from becoming an archive. In fact, one might even suggest that every archive was once such a facility, no matter how informal—any potentially finite mode of storage might suffice. But the question at hand is whether we can produce a working definition of the 'accidental archive' that is of some actual use. Naturally, deciding on what each word means gives us a head start, so let's return to the very term 'archive', and see what new methodologies become apparent from a re-appraisal.

Eric Ketelaar finds common ground 'between traditional and current archivistics':

> archives consist of documents holding 'information created, received, and maintained as evidence and/or as an asset by an organization or person, in pursuance of legal obligations or in the transaction of business or for its purposes, regardless of medium, form or format'.[11]

In these terms, namely *ISO 30300*, the Brienne Collection is most definitely an archive, because its constituent parts (the undelivered letters), were being 'maintained as an asset' in a specifically delineated collection 'in pursuance of business'. Ketelaar further notes that:

> Within the archival profession many distinguish between records (created and used in the course of business and kept as long as that business requires) and archives (records to be kept beyond their primary purpose). Many more, however, understand that this distinction has little relevance, especially in the digital age.[12]

Ignoring this distinction between records and archives not only leads us down a rabbit hole in which the only thing of importance is data, but also privileges certain data-bearing units over others—letters over material objects, for example. Accordingly, we would like to propose another definition of archive, one which is not only of some use in its own right (digital age notwithstanding), but which also allows for the further theorization of sub-categories such as 'accidental'.

In order to do so, we must grasp the nettle and dare to designate the actual point at which an archive comes into being: the 'archival moment', if you like. This 'moment' we define as follows:

> when a collection of data-bearing units that coheres under a certain designation has been stored (either literally or conceptually) in a manner that suggests or expects stability and finality.

By stability or finality, we mean the moment of their Derridean domiciliation, their institutionalization or 'house arrest'.[13] The period before this *terminus ante quem*, that is, before the data-bearing units were deemed to be an archive (a moment which might also coincide with the naming of the archive), allows the scholar to distinguish what *flavour* of archive it is—the manner of its coming-into-being can supply us with clues as to how best to approach its study or *use*. An archival type functions as a caveat against contextual errors.

The archive is to data what the invention of moveable type was to religion: finally we could all be sure that each of us was singing from the same hymn-sheet. Of course, the idea of absolute consistency in books is as impossible as it is in archives, but life is like that. Sometimes we just have to accept that change is inevitable, and that becoming overly concerned with these possible changes is counterproductive.

Archives are often (and rightly) accused of reproducing or representing contemporary power structures, and to read them without awareness of this tendency is liable to lead to disaster. Were we, for example, to read the papers of William Cecil, Lord Burghley, Secretary of State to Elizabeth I, as an impartial and complete account of activities within his office we would produce distorted history: the documents he saved were partial, highly curated, and retained for his own purposes. An equally foolish move, however, might be to treat an archive as if it were accumulated along Cecil's lines when the only real connecting strands are that, for the sake of argument, the documents were all in the same postal sack when their 'moment' came about. Assuming relationships that do not exist is just as damaging as ignoring those that do.

As with many attempts to delineate the form of something that is continually changing (that is, as methods of reading data evolve, for example), it is perhaps foolhardy to suggest that there is only a fixed number of types. More possible and useful is to formulate a definition of an accidental archive alongside definitions of those other types of archives with which it might easily be confused. We propose four basic types of archive: the asserted, the unintentional, the incidental and, last but not least, the accidental. Each of these types has its own distinctive features, and thus comes with its own caveats.

The Asserted Archive

asserted archive: an archive which consists of a collection of data-bearing units gathered together under a certain designation with the intention that they remain a coherent whole: an individual's papers; receipts, etc. This collection's archival moment comes about when a particular action asserts it as being finite, fixed, and stable. Such a moment might obtain in the death of the collector, its donation to a museum, and so forth. While from this moment the archive may not *actually* remain stable, it is asserted as being such.

Exemplar

Between 1697 and 1700, John Somers, Baron Somers, then in office as Lord High Chancellor of England, had arranged the papers of John Thurloe to 'be bound up in sixty seven volumes in folio'.[14] At that moment the papers of Thurloe, Oliver Cromwell's most memorable spymaster, became an Asserted Archive (and, conveniently, pertained to the *ISO 30300* guidelines as 'records to be kept beyond their primary purpose'). Somers had bought them from a clergyman, a friend of a certain Mr Tomlinson, who had discovered them in a 'false ceiling in the garret' of the third floor of no. 13 of the Dial Court at Lincoln's Inn, long since pulled down. Thurloe had moved there in 1659, having been forced to leave the somewhat grander apartments of no. 24, on the left hand of the ground floor of the Gatehouse Court (now the Old Buildings) which he had occupied since 1647, following complaints that he was too rarely in residence. A Mr William Battin, an Utter barrister, was generous enough to share his chamber and garret, the second and third floors of no. 13, with Thurloe for the reasonable fee of £10. It is in these more humble chambers originally adjoined the west end of the chapel that Thurloe died in 1668.[15] Thurloe had kept the papers he collected during his time as Cromwell's Secretary of State, chief intelligence officer, and Postmaster General, hiding them from the reinstated royalist regime. They mostly comprised intercepted documents: officers in his so-called Black Chamber, an intelligence unit that systematically spied on the post, would carefully open letters, copy their contents and refold, reseal (and where necessary repair paper tears with glue made from isenglass) in the hope that the recipient would not realize the information he or she was about to receive and possibly take action upon had been compromised. Thurloe kept these copies, but also other original letters and interrogation reports. At the Restoration, Charles II initially let him be, but Thurloe was arrested on suspicion of plotting the return to power of Richard Cromwell. His subsequent release came, however, when he blackmailed the government, saying he was in possession of 'a black book which should hang half them that went for Cavaliers'.[16] The black book in question has never been found, if it ever existed, but since the administration of Lincoln's Inn has always been referred to as 'black books', he could well have had in mind the papers hidden in his chambers.

These papers eventually passed from Somers's hands to those of Richard Rawlinson, the antiquary and nonjuror, who bequeathed his manuscripts to the Bodleian Libraries. Thurloe's papers were a database when he was alive: he never committed them to the ashes but kept them to retrieve information with which he might prosecute and/or blackmail individuals and their families; on his death they were transformed into an archive by those who scooped them up and bound them into a specific set of volumes. Unfortunately, they lacked souls poetic enough to have them bound into black volumes, but perhaps to expect a metaphorical black book to have its archival moment at the hands of a bookbinder with black boards is asking too much of history.

The caveat in this case is that the documents were held on account of the data within each one, allowing the historian to justifiably analyse and cross-reference this information in an attempt to extract what, exactly, Thurloe had wished to hold close.

If, however, it turns out that Thurloe kept these papers fully intending to disperse them, destroy them or otherwise, then it becomes what we call an *Unintentional Archive*.

The Unintentional Archive

unintentional archive: an archive which consists of a collection of data-bearing units gathered together under a certain designation with the specific intention that they do not remain a coherent whole: a bookseller's stock; a collection of undelivered letters, intended for exchange for profit. This collection's archival moment is the same as for an asserted archive. The difference is that its archival moment is indicative of its failure as a collection—it ought, by rights, to have been dissipated. Its moment thus also obtains in the death of the collector, its donation to a museum, and so forth. And similarly, while from this moment the archive may not *actually* remain stable, it is asserted as being such.

Exemplar

On 10 April 1926, the Ministry of Finance in The Hague donated the Brienne Collection, which they had owned since 1860 when the papers of the Orphanage of Delft were transferred to the ministry, to a collector intend upon opening a museum (which would open in November 1930). Queen Wilhelmina enacted a law in 1929 which '*retroactively empowered*' ministries to donate state goods to private foundations: governmental intervention now allowed for a particular article to be legally transferred from state ownership to a new museum. In this case what we now call the Brienne Collection became property of Het Nederlandsche Postmuseum in The Hague, soon to be renamed the Museum voor Communicatie, a privately funded foundation.[17] It was at this moment the collection was 'arrested'.

As the collection itself was intended for dissolution—that is, the letters swapped for ready cash—the Brienne Collection is an *unintentional archive*. The letters were initially collected on account of their being undelivered, so one might be led into making a category error at this juncture, and suggest that the only thing the letters have in common is that they were undelivered. If this was the case, and they had simply remained in the possession of the Briennes, we might be tempted to put this collection into a different category. But the letters were collected *because* they were undelivered, and this collection was a purposeful act—and one, as previously pointed out, that was actively illegal. This one purposeful act, along with the intent of later sale, is enough to allow the collection's archival moment to place it within the category of *unintentional archive*, but if this is not convincing, there are two extra pieces of evidence that support the case.

In his will, the devout Brienne signed over the undelivered letters to the Directors of the Orphanage of Delft, not wanting his Catholic brothers to lay claim to 'their share of the inheritance'. They could only do so on the condition that they converted to Protestantism, as he had done himself in the 1660s:

> The Testator declared that he did not to want or desire that these his heirs, or any one of them [individually] should have full disposition of their share of the inheritance; but that the capital will be administered by the Directors of the Orphanage of the City of Delft, who shall annually send or distribute to each of them and their descendants their portion of the interest on the said sum, for so long as they will be and remain within the community of the Roman Church.[18]

This indicates that after Brienne's death, the collection was still treated as a potential source of revenue—it was regarded as a monetary asset forming part of his estate—and this cannot have been because the letters were valuable to the recipients, as they would, like Brienne, either be deceased or nearly deceased. One item from the collection may serve to demonstrate the nature of many of these letters, as well as explain why they could be worth their weight in gold. The letter is dated November 1689 and from one lawyer to another:

> I feel by yours She [i.e. Lady Francesca Belmont] has not made you understand cleare enough the stat[e] of her concern in Holland which stands thus. Prince Rupert by vertu of a transaction made the year 1680 betwixt the Palatine [i.e. his brother] and him was to receave yearly a certain somme which the States [of Holland or General] payed yearly to the Palatine by way of pension, of this monyes after the Princes and the Palatines death a considerable somme of arrieres was lying in Mr de la Grottes hands a man known and easely to be found out in the place where you are. The Duk[e] of Orleans at the Palatines death fallowing out the pretensions of his Dutchesse laid claim to all he thought did belong to him and haveing hard of this monys lying in de la Grotts hands after the death of the Palatine of Prince Rupert and of Captaine [Dudley] Rupert [as he was titled] his son at Buda [i.e. Dudley Bard, the son Rupert had begotten by Francesca and who died at the siege of Buda in 1686] non[e] then appearing that had any right to that monyes, the Intindent of the Duk[e] d'Orleans traitted with de la Grotte and

as its thoughts quitted him a shar[e] and receaved the reste for his Maister. My lady Bellemont who after her sons death had been for a year in a great distemper become better produces Prince Ruperts will to her son ... by which she is made his universall legataire lays claim to this monye receaved by Mr dOrleans as beqeathed to her by her son and to him by his Father.[19]

These letters often include, or are even dominated by, reports regarding legal matters, children, or death notices. In this case, it is a document asserting that Prince Rupert of the Rhine wrote a bastard son into his will and that the family of the child's mother could lay claim to the inheritance.[20] The letters were not mere items of sentimentality: they were legal evidence. Brienne assumed that the descendants of the authors would at some point wish to avail themselves of the evidence within so that they might prove their connection to the addressees ... and thus, perhaps, legitimate their claim to an inheritance, as Lady Francesca would later assert with success.[21] It is even possible to imagine that interested parties might be required to pay more than the postage to lay claim to an undelivered letter, were the contents to prove interesting enough. For Brienne it was not an innocent assemblage of letters written by various correspondents on a vast variety of topics; for him, their unifying principle was that they were documents with which he might exploit the precarious nature of human existence and displacement. Brienne must have known that these letters contained information without which some people might not be able to lay claim to what was rightfully theirs. There might also, of course, be the potential to blackmail, hold to ransom or generally make individuals pay handsomely to keep this same information secret.

If one were to assume that the Brienne letters were kept purely to be redeemed for postage, then it is likely that you would miss this second, rather more sinister, layer of data. Of the 2,600 letters that comprise the collection, some 600 are unopened. If just one of the other 2,600 was opened by Brienne, then it could only be to appraise himself of what was inside, and it is difficult to see any other reason to do so than to view the data to ascertain if it is worth money.

If, however, upon reading the letters, only a handful appear to fit a particular dataset of this sub-type, then these letters form what we call an *Incidental Archive*.

The Incidental Archive

incidental archive: the incidental archive is a collection of data-bearing units that form a part of a larger archive but that also has its own, internal coherence: letters to people in prison distributed in amongst a larger group of items; letters to women 'scientists', etc. This internal coherence may or may not have been intentional on the part of the original collector, it may simply become visible as research continues and new methods of capturing data are conceived and tested, or it may simply be recognized by a historian.

Exemplar

The possibilities for the discovery of incidental archives are almost boundless, and care must be taken in their analysis, as it is particularly easy to move from 'the Brienne collection is formed of letters which were undelivered but kept in order to realise their monetary value at a later date, and a handful of these concern musicians' to 'in amassing the collection of letters the Briennes hoped, at some point, might be realizable into ready cash, they included amongst the letter types they held back those to or from musicians'. The letters concerning musicians form an *incidental archive*, and this information must be treated as such (as it always has been). Another example of an incidental archive, albeit one that is rather more sketchy, can be found in amongst the items recovered from a shipwreck, in this case, a series of bookbindings, some of which were stamped with the crest of the Royal House of Stuart, the royal line who had governed England from the death of Elizabeth Tudor in 1603 to the accession of William and Mary in 1688 (barring a little republican hiccough in the 1650s).[22]

In this latter case, these bookbindings, the *incidental archive*, are to be found in an *Accidental Archive*.

The Accidental Archive

accidental archive: a collection of data-bearing units for which the unifying principle behind their coherence is their archival moment: where this moment leads to a suggestion or expectation of stability and finitude. The contents of a trunk or a sack full of letters that have been placed together simply for the sake of their storage and transport become an accidental archive if the ship that is carrying the trunk or sack sinks, for example. While from this moment the archive may not *actually* remain stable, it appears as such.

Just as a theoretical (and waterproof) sack of letters on board a sinking ship may comprise an accidental archive, so might the entire contents of said ship. The possibility of multiple, overlapping archives can lead to things getting rather tricky, and it is here where devices of containment assume a certain importance—how can the scholar differentiate between items contained within discrete containers of their own (a trunk, for example) when the trauma of sinking and lying on the seabed for four hundred years has mixed everything up? Further to that, how can one be sure that a certain group of items did not come from another shipwreck, or were not thrown overboard from a perfectly serviceable vessel as it passed overhead? Again, this is where power structures return to haunt us—a scholar seeking a grant to study an 'archive' needs it to be discrete, not disparate.

Exemplar

Between 1645 and 1660, a ship that was built in *c.* 1645 foundered and sank off the coast of Texel, one of the Dutch Wadden Islands. In 2009, its wreck was discovered by Dutch amateur divers, and by 2010 it was officially registered with the Rijksdienst voor het Cultureel Erfgoed (RCE) as BZN17[23]—meaning this was the seventeenth wreck found on Burgzand, part of the Rede van Texel.[24] When the divers brought up a dress, or the remains thereof, in August 2014, having begun to bring up textiles in order to save them, interest in the wreck suddenly increased. The news was made public in April 2016. The 1,000–1,200 items recovered, including the silk dress of unknown origin and a selection of bookbindings whose paper contents had long since disintegrated, were recorded into a database as a discrete collection.[25] At this point, it may seem as though it was an archive waiting to happen—that is, when there is nothing left to bring up, or it is impossible to bring up anything more, the collection becomes an archive, and accidentally so. It is therefore an accidental archive. If we consider that the archival moment is at this point, then this is plainly correct. There is another possibility, however.

Once the decision has been taken to investigate the wreck and preserve whatever can be safely extracted, is it not then an archive, merely an *Invisible Archive*?

The Invisible Archive

invisible archive: a collection of data-bearing units whose existence has been postulated in such a way as to be contained within a finite boundary that is more or less clearly definable at the archival moment. Items yet to be removed from the invisible archive are merely data sets whose immanence is yet to be asserted through extraction. Such an archive may include items from a wreck yet to be preserved.

This final category, which we suggest with tongues only mildly contained (or archived) within cheeks, brings us neatly to the problem that besets all archives, namely, what are the boundaries or limits? In the case of the Brienne Collection, this boundary is supplied quite conveniently in the form of the trunk with which it has been, and will forever be, associated. Because the trunk is an object, it is particularly easy to fetishize, as Ahrendt and Van der Linden demonstrate at the outset of 'The Postmasters' Piggy Bank':

> Hidden away in the vaults of the Museum ... lies a most extraordinary trunk.... Although it appears inconspicuous, the wooden trunk was once a priceless object, its valuable contents protected from water damage by a layer of sealskin and from prying eyes by a heavy iron hasp lock. Glistening red wax seals bespeak the well-traveled nature of the trunk across the centuries. On opening the vaulted lid, a linen-lined interior is revealed. And the trunk is full, brimming with some twenty-six hundred undelivered letters.[26]

And herein lies the real problem. The trunk simply is not full of letters. It may once have been, but it most certainly is not now, and if it ever was, the point until which it remained so is unknown.

Certainly, when Nadine first saw it, in 2014, it was empty, the letters having been taken out and stored individually. Of course, when she recently visited the museum to film part of a documentary, the museum suggested that a layer of letters be placed in the trunk so that it *appeared* full. We readily agreed. That is what it is *meant* to look like. That is how it was intended, right? More to the point, our post-Romantic sensibilities demand that the Brienne Trunk house the letters 'it was designed to hold'. Well, there is no evidence that it is anything other than a rather common-or-garden trunk (other than, perhaps, the sealskin exterior, or even its wax seals, were we to identify to whom they must be attributed), in which this collection of letters was, at some point in its life, either stored, transported, or simply placed. The fact is that we do not know. The more interesting point is that the trunk itself *has no bearing on the status of the collection as an archive whatsoever*. And that holds even if you consider collection and trunk together to form the archive in question.

Ahrendt and Van der Linden illustrate here the problem with all archives, a problem they probe and manipulate throughout their piece, as they repeatedly reinforce and undermine any sense that an archive is ever, or can ever be seen to be, in any way stable:

> The trunk and its contents acceded into the collection of a museum, and at that moment they were transformed into a unified entity, an archive subjected to rules and organisation.[27]

Our post-Romantic sensibilities, as we have determined, demand that the trunk arrive at the museum 'full of letters', even though it is unclear when the trunk and the letters joined forces. The trunk does have a note attached describing it as containing the collection (*'Ongeopende brieven/Boedel De Brienne/Weeskamer Delft'*), but at the time of writing the date of the note is unknown—was it written in 1707, the 1850s, or, perhaps 1928?[28] There are even question marks over whether it is physically possible to fit the letters into the trunk.[29] More to the point, perhaps, is the note that accompanied the collection on its arrival at the museum in 1928: '*1 koffertje en 2 pakketten van honderden brieven uit de nalatenschap "de Brienne"*'.[30] Ahrendt and Van der Linden translate this as a 'chest and two packets of letters' but a better translation is perhaps 'a briefcase and two packets of letters', a briefcase such as someone working in government would carry—the collection was, after all, delivered *by* the ministry of finance. Perhaps there never was a trunk? Did a museum employee, confronted with a pile of old letters, spot an empty trunk in the museum stores, think to themselves '*I* know what'll look good in there!' and fool a group of serious academics almost a century later? Perhaps dendrochronology must come to our aid.

In this chapter, we have considered what an archive contains and what contains an archive. During this process we have hopefully been able to think harder about the problems that we face in archival studies, namely reading the archive such that we avoid catastrophic errors of contextual misplacement. It is not about 'allowing the documents to speak with their own voice', because that is simply not feasible. It is about trying to avoid stifling documents such that their data becomes stored in aspic. To return to the words of Francis Bacon:

> we should always remind ourselves that what is being prepared is a granary and store-house of things, not comfortable accommodation for staying or living in, but a place we go down to when we need to fetch out something useful for the work of the *Interpreter*, which comes next.[31]

Yes, Bacon was talking of natural history, but the same is true for all manner of archival studies.

Ahrendt and Van der Linden suggest that an archive is:

> A repository of information, a container in which historical truths might be sought and constructed, and whose component parts beg to be further contained through the processes of ordering, cataloging, and interpreting.[32]

This is both correct and incorrect. An archive *is* an historical truth. It is made up of units of *fact* which need interpretation. Its container is conceptual, though in certain circumstances, this container's boundaries may accord perfectly with a physical container—and in other circumstances, these two containers, literal and metaphorical, may accord closely but not perfectly. What is at stake in all this is, of course, our ability to read *through* the power structures that have led to items coalescing into archives, and thus reading these items as existing in relation to, and possibly even because of, each other.

ACKNOWLEDGEMENT

This research has been made possible by a grant from the Netherlands Organisation for Scientific Research (NWO) for the project 'Maritime Archaeology Meets Cultural History: The Texel Shipwreck BZN17 in Context'. Project no. 342-69-001.

FURTHER READING

S. D. Goitein, *A Mediterranean Society: The Jewish Communities of the Arab World as Portrayed in the Documents of the Cairo Geniza*, 5 vols (Berkeley: University of California Press, 1967–1993)

The Prize Papers www.prizepapers.de

Signed, Sealed and Undelivered [the Brienne Collection] http://brienne.org

Alan Stewart, 'Familiar Letters and State Papers. The Afterlives of Early Modern Correspondence', in James Daybell and Andrew Gordon, eds, *Cultures of Correspondence in Early Modern Britain* (Philadelphia: University of Pennsylvania Press, 2016), 237–252

Alexandra Walsham, 'The Social History of the Archive: Record-Keeping in Early Modern Europe', *Past and Present*, Supplement 11 (2016), 9–48

NOTES

1. H. Deneroff, 'The Accidental Archive', *Film Society Review* 2 (1966), 20–31. We thank Eileen Clancy for pointing this out.
2. A. Tector, 'The Almost Accidental Archive and Its Impact on Literary Subjects and Canonicity', *Journal of Canadian Studies* 40.2 (2006), 96–108; R. Ahrendt and D. van der Linden, 'The Postmasters' Piggy Bank: Experiencing the Accidental Archive', *French Historical Studies* 40.2 (2017), 189–213; C. Pal, 'Accidental Archive: Samuel Hartlib and the Afterlife of Female Scholars', in V. Keller, A. M. Roos, and E. Yale, eds, *Archival Afterlives: Life, Death, and Knowledge-Making in Early Modern British Scientific and Medical Archives* (Leiden: Brill, 2018), 120–149; and M. Moss and D. Thomas, 'The Accidental Archive', in C. Brown, ed., *Archival Futures* (Edinburgh: Facet, 2018), 117–135.
3. Ahrendt and Van der Linden, 'The Postmasters' Piggy Bank', 191.
4. K. Zandvliet, *De 250 rijksten van de Gouden Eeuw: kapitaal, macht, familie en levensstijl* (Amsterdam: Rijksmuseum, 2006), 338–339 ('Simon de Brienne', no. 203).
5. W. J. M. Benschop, *Het postwezen van 's Gravenhage in derdehalve eeuw* (The Hague: Staatsbedrijf der Posterijen, Telegrafie en Telefonie, 1951), 86.
6. 'Letters patent of King William III, and Queen Mary, appointing Simon de Brienne and Mary his wife, housekeeper and wardrobe-keeper at their house at Kensington', 12 October [1689], as printed in *Catalogue of Additions to the Manuscripts in the British Museum* (London: Trustees of the British Museum, 1850), i.102.
7. Ahrendt and Van der Linden, 'The Postmasters' Piggy Bank', 202.
8. Ahrendt and Van der Linden, 'The Postmasters' Piggy Bank', 201.
9. Ahrendt and Van der Linden, 'The Postmasters' Piggy Bank', 202.
10. Francis Bacon, *Parasceve* in *The Oxford Francis Bacon*, vol XI, *The Instauratio Magna: part II. Novum organum and associated texts*, ed. Graham Rees (Oxford, New York: Clarendon Press, 2000), 457.
11. E. Ketelaar, 'Foreword', in L. Corens, K. Peters, and A. Walsham, eds, *Archives & Information in the Early Modern World* (Oxford: Oxford University Press, 2018), p. xv, quoting *ISO 30300: Information and Documentation: Records Management—Part 2: Guidelines* (Geneva: International Standards Organization, 2011), 3.1.7. *ISO 30300* is due to be replaced by *ISO/DIS 30300*, but no information is yet available on what this might comprise (source: www.iso.org/standard/74291.html accessed 5 October 2019).
12. Ketelaar, 'Foreword', p. xv.
13. See Ahrendt and Van der Linden, 'The Postmasters' Piggy Bank', 204–205.
14. T. Birch, ed., *A Collection of the State Papers of John Thurloe, Esq.*, 7 vols (London: Thomas Woodward, 1742), i, 'Preface', v.
15. C. W. Heckethorn, *Lincoln's Inn Fields and the Localities Adjacent: Their Historical and Topographical Associations* (London: Elliot Stock, 1896), 17.

16. T. Venning, 'Thurloe, John', *ODNB*, quoting *Fifth Report of the Royal Commission on Historical Manuscripts. Part I: Report and Appendix* (Historical Manuscripts Commission, 1876), 208.

17. Ahrendt and Van der Linden, 'The Postmasters' Piggy Bank', 197, 203.

18. Gemeentearchief Delft, Weeskamer no. 11867: 'Testament of Simon de Brienne, The Hague, Jan. 13, 1707', as identified and translated in Ahrendt and Van der Linden, 'The Postmasters' Piggy Bank', 199.

19. MvC, Brienne Collection, DB-1910: unknown to Monsieur Carney, 3 November 1689.

20. This assertion was correct. See Rupert's will, signed 27 November 1682, proved 1 December 1682, TNA, PROB 1/46, in which Rupert assigns the palace of Rhenen in the province of Utrecht to Dudley Bard, as well as everything owed to him by those 'not naturall borne subjects of the King of England'. Dudley Bard's illegitimacy is open to question, however; while the *ODNB* suggests that Rupert never acknowledged the marriage contract with Lady Francesca, in his will he terms Dudley 'my Naturall Sonne'.

21. Regardless of the legitimacy of the marriage, Lady Francesca would, in 1695, receive 20,000 crowns from Emperor Leopold I in settlement of her claim, see J. F. Chance, 'A Jacobite at the Court of Hanover', *The English Historical Review* 11.43 (1896), 527–530.

22. See J. Dickinson, 'Een Unieke Collectie Verdronken Boeken', in Birgit van den Hoven, Iris Toussaint, and Arent Vos, eds, *Wereldvondsten uit een Hollands schip: Basisrapportage BZN17/Palmhoutwrak* (Province Noord-Holland, 2019), *passim*. See also J. Dickinson, 'Drowned Books and Ghost Books: Making Sense of the Finds from a Seventeenth-Century Shipwreck off the Dutch Island of Texel', *The Seventeenth Century* 38.1 (2023), 49–85.

23. Arent Vos, 'Inleiding', in van den Hoven, Toussaint, and Vos, eds, *Wereldvondsten*, 19.

24. Arent Vos, 'Achtergronden en vondstgeschiedenis', in van den Hoven, Toussaint, and Vos, eds, *Wereldvondsten*, 32.

25. R. van Eerden, 'Proloog', in van den Hoven, Toussaint, and Vos, eds, *Wereldvondsten*, 11.

26. Ahrendt and Van der Linden, 'The Postmasters' Piggy Bank', 189.

27. Ahrendt and Van der Linden, 'The Postmasters' Piggy Bank', 193.

28. See Ahrendt and Van der Linden, 'The Postmasters' Piggy Bank', 202.

29. While fitting over 3,000 letters into the Brienne trunk would itself be quite a feat, to do so in such a manner that an individual letter would be retrievable easily enough to claim the few coins its redemption may warrant is another matter entirely.

30. Ahrendt and Van der Linden, 'The Postmasters' Piggy Bank', 198.

31. Bacon, *Parasceve*, 459.

32. Ahrendt and Van der Linden, 'The Postmasters' Piggy Bank', 193.

CHAPTER 24

RESPONSE TO 'ENCOUNTERS AND EVOLUTION'

JULIE A. FISHER

It is striking that the word repository does not appear, even once, across the four chapters that comprise the 'Encounter and Evolution' section of *Archives: Power, Truth, and Fiction*. This is for good reason, because the authors' concerns extend well beyond the physical space of collections. Repository's other meaning, as a place of repose, is equally inapplicable because it is the antithesis of what these scholars are highlighting: archives do not rest, they are sites of creation and recreation, as they have always been. These chapters capture the awareness that an archive evolves through encounters between people and materials. It is a site of activity, a place where people make and remake meaning.

Taken together, these four chapters speak to a variety of actors and how their encounters with materials, predominantly textual material, can create or destroy archives. This range, of course, cannot be divorced from degrees of authority and power. On one end of the spectrum is State power, as in Paul Lihoma's investigation into the power of the State government to control Malawi's narrative by denying access and even destroying parts of Malawi's National Archives in the twentieth century. Though separated by centuries, Paul Strohm interrogates a similar process in early modern England, where high-ranking politicians crafted the crown's account of the infamous Gunpowder Plot. In both cases, men in power leveraged archival materials, either by selecting or destroying them, to privilege a single story.

In contrast, Eric Ketelaar illustrates that one need not wear a crown to exert authority. The number of those with the power to shape and even create archives expands, as Ketelaar points out, if we consider the 'host of archivers who shape the archives' across time and space. This assortment includes those who may have historically fallen outside of the definition of archivists—'authors, clerks, registrars, antiquarians, record managers, keepers, website builders, genealogists, and other users'—who have shaped archives all the same. Continuing along that line, Nadine

Akkerman and Pete Langman remind us that humans have even granted the forces of nature (such as a storm that sinks a ship), or inanimate objects (such as a storage trunk), the power to create archives. In sketching out the range of agents with influence in relation to archives, these authors collectively help historicize the changes in the nature of archives and their creators.

Does an evolving sense of who creates an archive in turn impact our concept of what an archive is? Absolutely, and the world of archives is richer for it. In particular, the theoretical framings these authors propose are needed to meet the new opportunities and challenges that are emerging as people and communities, many whom the State and other institutions have traditionally excluded from the archival process and even the repositories themselves, are expanding the work. For example, consider the efforts in a growing number of First Nations and tribal communities. While the work concerning the repatriation of sacred items, including human remains, is important and on-going for many Indigenous communities the world over, there is an equally pressing archival reimagining happening simultaneously.

A rising number of First Nations are collecting and transforming material collected from a wide range of places—personal collections, tribal organizations, recovered material from State and federal archives—into community accessible archives. These repositories are extensions of long held recordkeeping practices that include, but have never been limited to, physical collections and extend back time out of mind. Figures like tribal knowledge keepers and cultural memory keepers pose an interesting counterpoint to Ketelaar's discussion about what makes someone 'loyal' to an archive—professional training or a vested interest in its contents? These are not mutually exclusive propositions. There is an increasing amount of community archival work done by Indigenous archivists and supporting organizations, such as the Association of Tribal Archives, Libraries, and Museums.

As the contributors here know, access to and creating archives is a powerful act and one that has long been reserved by the State. This is precisely why many tribal communities, as self-governing bodies, have long been involved in their own archive-building efforts.[1] Unsurprisingly, the expansion of many tribal archives has been government to government relations with colonial and then later federal and State powers. This includes, but is not limited to, ongoing legal cases ranging from the enforcement of treaty rights to federal tribal recognition. To wage these legal battles, tribes often face many archival struggles: chief among them, they are infrequently afforded the luxury of a single repository that contains all the materials. For federal recognition cases, in which the United States Government asks the applicant group to demonstrate its continued existence as a political and social entity, tribes must locate documents that stretch across multiple repositories, many centuries, and even the rise and fall of empires.

To meet these challenges, tribes build archives as intentional as Strohm describes when Edward Coke selected documents 'for persuasive oral presentation'. It is not just court cases, however, that offer the 'archival moments' that Akkerman and

Langman propose. The on-going work of language revitalization projects is another example of an 'archival moment' that First Nations are responding to by exploring new ways to expand tribal archives. One example is the emergence and adoption of digital collections. Digital platforms like Mukurtu are specifically designed to meet the needs of First Nations by allowing greater community control over access while also offering ways for the community to gather and apply their own knowledge and organizing priorities. Digital access is not only a way to bridge the distance between a community and the repository that houses the material, but digital access also can connect tribal members that live at a distance from ancestral homelands as well as tribal communities who State or federal governments forced off their ancestral lands.

In their own way, each author captures the possibilities born of the understanding that the archive is a site of creation, a place where people continue to make and remake meaning as a direct result of their encounters with the material. These frameworks are especially welcomed because they offer helpful perspectives for on-going archival work and welcome the increasing number of people who are joining that process or moving the process in new directions.

NOTE

1. For more on the history and ongoing archival work by First Nations and the role of that archival work in tribal sovereignty, see Rose Miron's work, *Indigenous Archival Activism: Recovering Native History in the Mohican Tribal Archive and Beyond* (forthcoming).

PART V

NARRATORS

CHAPTER 25

FROM REPOSITORIES OF FAILURE TO ARCHIVES OF ABOLITION

KARINA BERAS AND JARRETT MARTIN DRAKE

Archives constitute a critical component for repressive governments to exercise their dominion and violence against peoples within and seeking to enter their borders. The contemporary political landscape within the United States, for example, demonstrates the myriad ways that undocumented migrants within the country endure hardships and hurdles in their pursuit to maintain both kinship and citizenship ties. The United States federal government has responded to this pursuit in ways that state governments responded to the presence of Black populations in the antebellum period: mass criminalization. Fundamentally, both the criminalization of Black people and migrants serves to establish bounds of belonging as well as constrict claims to citizenship. These processes rely heavily on an archival apparatus capable of executing the legibility practices of state authority.[1] These practices are inconceivable without archives and, as was the case during the antebellum era of the United States, contemporary law enforcement agencies at the federal, state, and local levels rely on archives to criminalize, surveil, and expel migrants. At the same time, people in contestation with the dominion and violence of States rely on archives as modes of resistance. This produces a paradox. How, on one hand, do governments construct archives to constrict populations and how, on the other, do those same populations construct counter-archives to subvert the means of their constriction? Where and how do archives—the processes and the technologies—matter in the landscape of the punishment paradigm in the United States? How do archivists factor into this dynamic?

Archivists obsess over obsolescence. If one accepts that the English word obsolete originates from the Latin verb *obsolescere*, meaning to 'fall into disuse, be forgotten about', then one might see archives as an exercise in mitigating or managing the obsolescence of people, places, and ideas. In addition to the standard processes of archives such as appraisal and description, archivists engage in a series of subsequent actions—they digitize collections and curate exhibits, for example—to encourage the public to use archival records in their custody so that particular narratives escape obsolescence. Concretely, archivists express this obsession in response to the growing concerns for the technological obsolescence of software applications and the requisite hardware to ensure long-term preservation and access of born-digital files. Evidence of this obsession exists in the pages of professional literature on the subject of digital forensics as well as the establishment of an inter-institutional and international collaborative consortium that offers solutions and services for archivists to ameliorate if not avoid the impacts wrought by obsolescence.[2] Obsolescence, then, is deeply embedded into the past, present, and future of archives.

The philosopher Angela Davis shares an obsession with obsolescence, albeit in a radically different context and with a radically different conclusion. She posits in her book *Are Prisons Obsolete?* that:

> Many people have already reached the conclusion that the death penalty is an out-moded form of punishment that violates basic principles of human rights. It is time, I believe, to encourage similar conversations about the prison.... The question of whether the prison has become an obsolete institution has become especially urgent in light of the fact that more than two million people (out of a world total of nine million) now inhabit U.S. prisons, jails, youth facilities, and immigrant detention centers.[3]

Whereas archivists engage obsolescence as a warning, Davis engages obsolescence as a welcome. For Davis, the obsolescence of the prison—the anchor of America's punishment paradigm—beckons justice advocates to consider the prison's *abolition* and not merely its *amendment*. Moreover, Davis couches her claims for prison abolition with the caveat that no single system can serve as its substitute. Instead, prison abolition must be accompanied by the construction of a 'constellation of alternatives', including emergent institutions that will subsume the social and physical landscape in which prisons presently predominate. Accordingly, Davis asserts the centrality of education to this goal by stating that, 'Schools can therefore be seen as the most powerful alternative to jails and prisons.'[4]

This chapter builds on the writings of Davis and other theorists to argue that abolitionist archives constitute a critical component to the constellation of alternatives to imagine a societal landscape free from our present punishment paradigm. It will begin by characterizing the scope and the origins of the punishment paradigm in the United States as well as its lasting linkages between prisons and police. Next, the chapter will connect this legacy with the contemporary criminalization of immigrants before concluding with an exploration of how abolitionist archives might come into formation and assist in the sustenance of a society that relies on new sets of relationships to promote justice and reduce violence.

The Punishment Paradigm

The punishment paradigm might be characterized as a perspective *and* an administration of justice that responds to social discords, disruptions, and disturbances by authorizing armed agents of the State to enact arbitrary amounts of violence—including but not limited to incarceration, surveillance, and forced labour—upon those peoples in a society deemed to be its deserving delinquents. More than a mere view of justice, the punishment paradigm entails an active administration of violence that agents are authorized to exact in traditional sites of punishment, such as local jails and state/federal prisons, as well as nontraditional sites of punishment, such as schools, psychiatric hospitals, libraries, and, increasingly, airports and borderlands. The variety of venues in which State agents exact this violence demonstrates that its authors are found not only in obvious roles of police or correctional officers but also in more conspicuous roles of school resource officers, doctors, librarians, and customs agents. The irrational and inconsistent logic of the paradigm posits that control and capitalization of incorrigible bodies supersedes any concerns for actual safety and security, as safety and security are pro forma considerations for a paradigm empowered for the prima facie purpose to encumber and enslave (in)discriminately.

The origins of this peculiarly American punishment paradigm extend before the experiment of the United States existed. In colonial America, jails outnumbered public schools and hospitals.[5] While much of the rhetoric following the Revolutionary War rejected executive tyranny at the still-forming federal level, the nascent nation encouraged such tyranny at local levels to mitigate the problem that 'too much liberty was fatal to citizens and patriarchal political power was needed to defend citizens and their liberty'.[6] Of particular concern were the existential threats that designated delinquents posed to the order of a government disguised as democracy. In examining the establishment of jails and almshouses in early Philadelphia, Simon P. Newman and Billy G. Smith explain that:

> it was only in the later eighteenth century that civic authorities in American cities began to regard symptoms of poverty as evidence of personal moral degeneracy and criminality rather than as a result of larger social circumstances. The rising number of impoverished immigrants from Europe, especially Ireland, as well as of black migrants ... contributed to an increasing sense that a rapidly growing class of masterless men and women threatened property, proper social order, and good republican government.[7]

Thus, the punishment paradigm in America germinates from a societal and political contract to control and coerce Black, poor, feminine, and immigrant bodies. Only after recognizing the primary purpose of the punishment paradigm can one trace its path. With the birth of a new nation, that path deviated from the methods of punishment perfected in Western Europe and imported to colonial America. These methods ranged to include everything from banishment and branding to torture and executions. Moreover, the public presentation of punishment underscored its intent to foment fear into potential lawbreakers. But a new republic ushered in a new method to prescribe punishment: science in secret. Prominent physicians, most notably Benjamin Rush of Philadelphia, viewed punishment as a science that states could calculate and administer like drugs to sick patients.[8]

Time became the prescription that penal reformers advocated for most vociferously, and authorities proportioned it out to prisoners based on the offender's background and crime. Their collective rationale argued that prolonged separation from family, community, and society provided the safest and swiftest means through which to return 'healthy' citizens back into the world. But this rationale fails to explain the conspicuous rise of the early nineteenth century's pro-prison movement alongside anti-slavery campaigns in northern states such as New York and Pennsylvania, nor go along with present day practice of detaining and incarcerating both legal and illegal immigrants in the United States. In fact, the first director of Newgate Prison located in New York, Thomas Eddy, also lobbied for passage of the state's 1817 gradual emancipation law.[9] Whereas Pennsylvania reformers emphasized rehabilitation through solitary confinement and penitence—hence, the creation of the world's first penitentiary in Philadelphia—the New York prison administration style that emerged in the early 1800s at the state's prison in Auburn emphasized strict obedience, complete silence, and forced labour. This mode of prison administration, the Auburn system, influenced the direction of the state's Sing Sing maximum-security prison, itself constructed with labour of Auburn's prisoners in 1826. Because of its focus on forced labour, within a few years after its establishment Sing Sing became the first prison in the United States to produce a profit rather than incur a debt.[10]

The Auburn system of prison administration gained the most currency with anti-slavery and pro-prison activists elsewhere in the United States and it dominated the direction of further prison construction across the country. The apparent contradiction between advocating freedom for slaves but advocating incarceration for convicts is reconciled with the reality that enslavement itself was a form of incarceration and likewise incarceration was a form of enslavement. In both instances, bodies were confined, controlled, and made to toil against their will for the production of wealth. Resistance resulted in severe punishment, although in both spaces slaves and prisoners shared vital information used to plot escapes and increase their prospects at survival.[11] As such, it is not the case that enslavement and incarceration suddenly converged after the Civil War, a common misconception due to the Thirteenth Amendment's provision allowing slavery as punishment for convicted criminals. Rather, these institutions nurtured one another. The punishment paradigm holds, then, that incarceration is not a *descendant* of slavery but in fact a *surviving sibling*. The right of individuals to control Black bodies and capitalize from their forced labour, a pillar of Southern economy and society, evaporated while the right of states to do the same, a pillar of Northern economy and society, elevated.

The peculiarities of the American punishment paradigm leads Scott Christianson to conclude: 'Prisons are repositories of failure that remind us of problems which would prove unsettling if put in open view'.[12] But it is incumbent to recognize this failure's function and comprehend the very point of incarceration, which Michel Foucault asserts is not to eradicate violence and crime but rather to distinguish them, to distribute them, or to use them [... to provide] them with a general 'economy'.[13] A society can only actualize this utility of violence and crime if it is able to isolate them, surveil them, and transform them into a 'useful delinquency', a transformation Foucault argues is unthinkable without 'the development of police'.[14] It follows that the project of the punishment paradigm is incomplete without the police, as the paradigm relies on the institution to exact its violence onto delinquents no longer or not yet in the grip of imprisonment. Testimonies of those currently or formerly ensnared within that grip illuminate the ingredients to the punishment paradigm's persistence.

Twin Mechanism

Prisons and police are complementary purveyors of punishment. To silo discussion of one institution at the exclusion of the other obscures the intimate link between them, a link that also traces its root back to enslavement. Lawmakers of the Carolina colony created the first slave patrols in 1704 to address the dual threat of slave revolts and foreign invasion from the nearby Spanish settlements in Florida, establishing an enduring link between policing Blackness and policing 'outsiders'.[15] The historical present of the criminalization of immigration demonstrates that the punishment paradigm is systematically incapable of holding its most public-facing institutions—the law enforcement entities of police, sheriffs, border patrol, and customs agents—accountable for abuses against society's designated delinquents. In fact, these abuses and subsequent absence of accountability serve to further entrench the paradigm's presence, and the paradigm persists in part precisely *because* the institution of policing commits routine and spectacular acts of violence against people living at the intersections of poverty, gender nonconformity, race, and, increasingly, immigration status.

Heightened policing of immigrant communities became especially acute following the attacks of 11 September 2011. Using the guise of national security, policing in the United States shifted from its decades-long agenda of the War on Drugs to a newly proclaimed War on Terror. This new focus fed off the prevailing political sentiment that the country had entered a new stage of vulnerability and was susceptible to attack by foreigners, thereby establishing a pretext to prioritize the safety and security of the American public. The punishment apparatus thus began to occupy an ever-expansive element of the quotidian life of marginalized and poor communities. Though the attacks of 9/11 most directly affected peoples of Arabic nations and Islamic religious traditions by way of increased racial profiling, particularly at airports and in other public spheres, another group of non-White persons also experienced increased racial profiling and criminalization: immigrants from Central and South America.

Laws and policies surrounding the immigrant experience in the United States date as far back as the nineteenth century with the Anti-Coolie Act of 1862, which restricted the immigration of and employment opportunities for Chinese persons.[16] Another similar policy restricting employment opportunities for undocumented immigrants was the Immigration Reform and Control Act of 1986 (IRCA).[17] The IRCA criminalized the hiring of undocumented workers as such creating a larger cycle of poverty and linking immigrant status to policies that, if broken, result in criminality. At the same time, there was an increase in resources for border patrolling to further monitor the movement of persons across the US–Mexican border, specifically.[18]

In a span of a decade, the United States government would come to create new legislation to further categorize, capture, and criminalize immigrant persons of colour. Most notable in contributing to the detention and deportability of undocumented immigrants was the Illegal Immigration Reform and Immigration Responsibility Act of 1986 (IIRIRA).[19] The IIRIRA expanded the number of actions classified as criminal offences and excluded immigrants from being eligible for due process or legal representation.[20] Matters of immigration are deemed civil and administrative in nature, thus concealed from the general public and subjected to arbitrary regulations and violence enacted by the Immigration and Customs Enforcement (ICE) and Customs Border Protection (CBP). Immigrant imprisonment has been masked as detention, a 'simple' hold over time prior to court hearings, though given the punishment of a criminal defendant and lacking in constitutional protections.[21]

The dehumanization of immigrants has reached new heights over the past twenty years. Unwarranted suspicion and intensified scrutiny have shaped the immigrant experience in both the public and private spheres of life. Federal enforcement entities have fabricated a landscape of institutionalized racial violence and policing as part of the immigration system agenda.[22] The work of immigration and other law enforcement agents is to accuse, criminalize, dehumanize, and dispose of racialized immigrant bodies. Family separation, travel bans, physical border expansions, overcrowded immigrant detention centers, and detainee deaths are but a few of the recurring news inundating media outlets. In those cases, it is worth noting that the targeted immigrant groups are people from Mexico and Central America, and of Islamic faith-based nations. However global immigration to the United States may be, the same pressures and accusations are not imposed on all who travel to the United States as refugees and asylum seekers, who come for economic opportunities or family reunification, who overstay their visas, or who exist in the country as permanent residents with minor criminal records. The otherizing of and trauma inflicted upon immigrants has been of minimal concern to the American public as immigrants have been unjustly generalized and labelled as 'illegal aliens' and 'criminals'. Hyperbolized stories of Latin American immigrants, such as Donald Trump's infamous statement referring to them as 'drug dealers, criminals, and rapists', has aided and fuelled growing anti-immigrant sentiments in the United States.

It is within this context of the punishment paradigm that the New York Immigration Coalition (NYIC) was founded in 1987, by a group of legal service providers, in response to the Immigration Reform and Control Act of 1986. Since its founding it has expanded to become the umbrella policy and advocacy organization in New York, representing over 200 immigrant and refugee rights groups in the state. More recently, in 2017, the NYIC launched their 'This Is Our New York' initiative to combat President Donald Trump's propaganda about immigrant communities. The initiative aimed to highlight the contributions of immigrants across the state of New York. Also in 2017, the NYIC launched Blueprint for Immigrant New York, a comprehensive policy agenda with goals targeted towards the full inclusion of immigrants and immigrant rights in New York by 2030. On Monday, 17 June 2019 the state of New York passed the 'Green Light NY' bill into law allowing undocumented immigrants to hold driver's licences. The new law, going into effect in December 2019, is an example of progressive legislature giving access and returning a sense of liberty to a community living under shadows and in fear.

Despite organizations like NYIC, both documented and undocumented immigrants face increased scrutiny, violence, and loss of life at the hands of the American government. In December 2018 two children died within three weeks of each other after being taken into US Customs and Border Protection custody. The death of the first child, seven-year old Jakelin Caal Maquin from Guatemala, made national news headlines. The tragedy has been highly condemned as a consequence of extreme immigration enforcement policies under the Trump administration. However, the American government did not take responsibility for Jakelin's death and instead placed blame on the father for choosing to migrate across countries with a young child. The vilification of and violence towards immigrants have reached the point of senseless loss of life at the hands or under the watch of immigration enforcement agencies without any recognition of human need and the systemic economic and political turmoil, in part caused by United States imperialism, that has driven large waves of immigrants attempting to cross the southern border.

Immigrant detention has gone beyond the scope of border cities and states. In May 2019 the US Immigration and Customs Enforcement (ICE) announced the creation of a new programme, Warrant Service Officer (WSO), in collaboration with local law-enforcement. WSO is intended to give local law-enforcement groups the ability to arrest and detain immigrant persons; superseding any local jurisdiction that has prohibited the detaining of persons on the basis of (perceived) immigration status. The programme reinforces and makes possible the partnership that exists between ICE and local police forces to further expose, extort, and export immigrant bodies. It serves to promote a fraudulent idea of creating safer communities but lacks sufficient evidence of acts of violence or crimes committed by immigrant persons. Hence, checks and balances when deciding to arrest and incarcerate immigrants are nearly nonexistent. ICE has effectually bypassed and disregarded local policies infringing upon citizen rights and governmental power.

The absence of accountability in these instances highlights the functional malfunction in a punishment paradigm intent on its self-perpetuation. The paucity of accountability for excessive police violence serves to communicate to State agents that no amount of force is unjustifiable in the subjugation of poor, genderqueer, Black, immigrant, and/or disabled citizens because a system can never harm those for whom it was never intended to protect. It is at this juncture of rationalization that the prison meets police in the punishment paradigm and the two unite to create what Foucault calls a 'twin mechanism' to secure 'the differentiation, isolation, and use of delinquency'.[23] The punishment paradigm's roots in racism and other forms of structural inequality as well as its incapability of holding itself accountable require a re-envisioning of justice and accountability that lay beyond the bounds of punishment, and abolitionist archives offer a means to that end.

Abolitionist Archives

The abject absence of accountability that pervades the punishment paradigm has led generations of advocates to advance reform as an answer to the inhumanity and indignities of America's prison paradox, but Angela Davis argues that reform, necessary as it may be, predictably emphasizes 'generating the changes that will produce a *better* prison system' and reinforces 'the stultifying idea that nothing lies beyond the prison'.[24] Davis's analysis that the framework of reform buttresses the presence of the punishment paradigm corroborates Foucault's claim that the repetition of a 'reform'—which he terms the 'element of utopian duplication'—is the fourth and final element to the carceral system.[25] Amidst this tension of 'reformist reform' and 'non-reformist reform', abolition emerges as praxis of the latter, with the goal to 'end systemic violence, including the interpersonal vulnerabilities and displacements that keep the system going'.[26] The late lawyer and organizer Rose Braz characterizes it as:

> Abolition defines both the end goal we seek and the way we do our work today. Abolition means a world where we do not use prisons, policing, and the larger system of the prison industrial complex as an 'answer' to what are social, political, and economic problems. Abolition is not just an end goal but a strategy today.[27]

Braz's characterization highlights a point crucial to comprehending abolition as an ongoing struggle and not a static outcome. Ethnic studies scholar Dylan Rodriguez's assertion that abolition 'is a perpetual practice, not a definitive end' amplifies the educator and organizer Mariame Kaba's claim that the process of abolition requires 'imagining, strategizing, and practicing other futures' through the construction of community spaces that shift attention to 'harms that our current systems of policing and punishment ignore, neglect, or are unable to resolve'.[28] To that end, abolition does not concern itself with polishing or promoting a new, sleeker model of an already-oppressive punishment regime. Instead, whereas the punishment paradigm foregrounds control of bodies and capitalization from their labour, abolition imagines a society past the paradigm that affirms the humanity of those who survive violence as well as those who commit it, while working to upend the 'set of relationships [comprising] the prison industrial complex' that ensure the perpetuity of violence sanctioned, sponsored, and supported by the State.

Archives, records, and the people who manage them also assist in the perpetuation of this violence, as demonstrated by different cases spanning multiple decades and multiple continents. In her coverage of the 1950s Mau Mau Uprising in colonial Kenya, the historian Caroline Elkins notes that 'the British colonial archive is derivative and reflective of the colonial state itself, and a means by which the state—both at the time of empire and thereafter—exercised its power and affirmed its fictions'.[29] After outlining the diligent destruction of archival records by British officials during the waning days of rule in Kenya, Elkins poses a question that by its very inquiry implicates the supporting role of archives and archivists with State violence: 'In what ways is the orchestration of systematic violence to personhood and documents connected to the morphing of individuals such as Terence Gavaghan from chief torturer to decorated archivist?'[30] Whereas Elkins's analysis centres on the British government's destruction of assumedly accurate records, the anthropologist Christine Folch narrates how police agencies under the dictatorship of Alfredo Stroessner in Paraguay systematically created fictitious records during the construction of the Itaipú Hydroelectric Dam in the 1970s and 1980s. These records, part of the 'The Archive of Terror', did not merely chronicle activities of the State and its violence. Rather, 'what happened to documents within Paraguayan bureaucracies produced the Paraguayan state', and as such the production of knowingly false records still 'created reality and thus served as the ultimate proof of the Stroessner state's power'.[31] Kirsten Weld's coverage of the Guatemala Nation Police Archive illuminates a similar dynamic.[32] These examples, though separated by distance, time, and context from the contemporary United States and its punishment paradigm, serve to show that repressive regimes rely on records and archives to rationalize their reign and protect it from potential prosecution, forming the 'ignoble archives' which Foucault describes as 'where the modern play of coercion over bodies, gestures and behaviour has its beginnings'.[33]

Taken together, the sum of these cases suggests that archives, at their best, *sustain* State violence and at their worst *silence* it. The duality of sustenance and silencing of State violence signals that archives play a pivotal part in the maintenance of the punishment paradigm in the United States and, for that same reason, they must play a pivotal part in its abolition. Yet the role of archives in abolition requires a reoriented relationship with the punishment paradigm, lest they further entrench the systemic violence and inequality that the carceral State cultivates.[34] That reoriented relationship between archives and the punishment paradigm is actualized through an array of projects, which we term abolitionist archives, across the United States that create, collect, and provide access to documents featuring first-person narratives and voices of people whose lives have been marked by the impact of the punishment paradigm. Collectively, these projects serve abolitionist functions through multiple methods, but two in particular merit explication: limitation and resistance.

The first function is, as Angela Davis and other abolitionists advocate, to limit the number of people who come into contact with police and prisons to begin with, thereby slowly dislodging the necessity of those institutions. The StoryTelling and Organizing Project (STOP), for instance, publishes to its website audio stories in which people narrate everyday actions they have taken or might take to intervene safely to prevent or stop interpersonal violence without calling police.[35] The purpose of STOP, a project of the Oakland-based advocacy organization Creative Interventions, is to provide users with practical, actionable steps that they can use in the future if and when they are a witness to interpersonal violence, an issue that disproportionately impacts women and people whose gender identities exist outside the socially constructed gender binary. STOP's provision of access to tips and techniques that can markedly enhance the lives of marginalized communities aligns with the vision set out by the Living Bridges Project, which gathers anonymous audio stories of people responding to child sexual abuse. It, like STOP, seeks to centre voices of the full range of individuals impacted by the issue, from people who have survived child sexual abuse, committed it, observed it, stopped it, and of course the many people who have done a combination of those actions. The ultimate goal of the Living Bridges Project, created by the organizer and educator Mia Mingus, is to emphasize both smaller and larger interventions people—not Title IX coordinators, school resource officers, or other punitive state-based officials—can make to work towards a society without *structural, intergenerational* sexual abuse against children.[36]

This fight for the eradication of intergenerational structural harm is one also being waged by the Texas After Violence Project, which puts abolition into practice by confronting Texas's violent history with forced removal of Indigenous communities and lynchings while also fighting for a future with reduced violence and more justice.[37] TAVP's dual focus on addressing both state and interpersonal violence stems from the project's assertion that state policies focused on retribution extend violence and trauma onto individuals who themselves may be grappling with their own separate experience with or commission of violence. This transfer of violence translates into a cycle of unaddressed and reinforced harm, thereby systematically reproducing violence and trauma. To face these interpersonal and systemic levels of violence, TAVP organizes storytelling circles, peace-building dialogues with youth, and oral history interviews with a range of individuals, families, and communities directly impacted or implicated by the punishment paradigm. These measures and their voluntary, non-punitive nature create new spaces that challenge the punishment paradigm by centring survivors and crowding out incarceration as an alternative, two goals that abolition stress as necessary to imagining a new landscape for safety and security.[38]

In a similar manner, the Immigration Defense Project (IDP) aims to abolish a racially biased legal system and immigration policies that violate human rights and separates immigrants from their families and communities.[39] IDP fights to end mass deportation and inhumane treatment of immigrants who are taken under custody by ICE and other immigration law enforcement agencies. On a more legally involved front, they provide criminal-immigration advice and challenge unfair laws through impact litigation. IDP also has a bilingual set of Know Your Rights infographics to equip undocumented immigrants with the knowledge of what to do when confronted with a violation of their rights when encountered by ICE. Through their free Deportation 101 training tool, IDP has helped train immigrant leaders and community organizers on the history and work of the deportation system, addressing the needs of someone facing deportation, and developing strategies to build case campaigns and respond to abuse in detention. IDP has expanded their services beyond the state of New York and modified their training to address problematic policies across different states.

While STOP, TAVP, and IDP offer a few examples of projects that work to limit the number of people who engage directly with the punishment paradigm, other grassroots efforts work towards abolitionist futures by using archival approaches to organize resistance and facilitate survival among from people currently, formerly, and not-yet ensnared in the institutions of jails and prisons. The Transgender, Gender Variant, and Intersex Justice Project (TGIJP) achieves this aim by publishing on its website survival guides, video testimonials, and newsletters explicitly serves the needs and interests of genderqueer people incarcerated throughout the nation's jails and prisons. This information campaign fits within the group's larger organizing mission to 'forge a culture of resistance and resilience to strengthen us for the fight against human rights abuses, imprisonment, police violence, racism, poverty, and societal pressures'.[40] Similarly, Beyondmedia Education launched its project *Women and Prison: A Site for Resistance* to reach formerly incarcerated people, activists, and learners of all ages who are concerned about the decades-long exploding crisis of women's incarceration.[41] Through a collection of interviews, poetry, artwork, and other media produced by women who have been or are currently incarcerated, the project serves resources for resistance that invite coalitions to form against the circumstances and conditions that exacerbate the injustices women face amidst the punishment paradigm. The project Amplify Voices, led by the Inside-Outside Alliance in Durham, North Carolina, extends a similar invitation but does so by publishing on its website letters and artwork (with consent) of people incarcerated at the county jail for people on the outside who wish to stand and act in solidarity with their struggles.[42] Additionally, Amplify Voices periodically curates a newsletter that it then circulates back inside to foster communication, community, and learning among people incarcerated in conditions explicitly aimed at suppressing all three.

These digital, grassroots projects and dozens of others reorient the traditional relationship between archives and the punishment paradigm by deploying creative instances of the former to destabilize the latter. Thus, these projects constitute the essence of an abolitionist archive, which might be defined as memory, information, and documentary projects, networks, or efforts that strive towards the construction of a society in which all bodies and minds enjoy an equal opportunity to be free of coercion, cages, and control by state and individual actors alike. Abolitionist archives align themselves explicitly or implicitly to the larger abolition movement, and in that sense are concerned less with destruction of existing institutions—a focus that would limit the range of alternatives—than with (re)constructions of new ways of relating to people that do not rely on coercive power or violence.

While abolitionists would recognize and embrace these projects as emblematic of abolitionist praxis, archivists may be less inclined to do so regarding archival praxis. After all, almost none of the projects outlined above identify themselves as archives or mention the word explicitly within their websites. Yet, abolitionist archives both converge and diverge with traditional archival practice. As these projects show, they converge by compiling primary source information and records of human activity and subsequently provisioning public access to general as well as specific designated communities. This is the bare essence of the archival endeavour. Yet, abolitionist archives diverge from traditional archival practice in several significant ways. First, they exist independently from larger memory institutions organizations or state agencies, opting instead to remain embedded within existing grassroots organizations or efforts that are explicitly or implicitly doing the work of prison abolition, which is a cornerstone for these archives' accountability to the movement as it enables a freedom to engage in transformative work that the geographer Ruth Wilson Gilmore might label as 'non-reformist reform' due to its attack at the very root of the punishment paradigm.[43] Second, abolitionist archives do not, as traditional archives do, emphasize the acquisition and long-term preservation concerns so much as they focus on the activation of materials already in its custody. Put another way, for abolitionist archives, the 'stuff' and the containers are secondary to societal change. Finally, and perhaps most strikingly, abolitionist archives do not necessarily allow for the meticulous, individual-based biographical research done in traditional archives but instead allow for more ethnographical work to take place. In this sense, the point is not to verify names, places, or events, as customarily done by the historical guild and its associated scholarly communities. Abolitionist archives articulate truths that complicate temporality, spatiality, and veracity.

Moreover, the projects described also demonstrate two aspects which are centred by abolitionist archives centre: reparation and restoration. Regarding reparation, abolitionist archives serve as loci to facilitate radical truth-telling about the damage done by the multi-century impacts of the punishment paradigm, a plea the anti-lynching advocate Ida B. Wells-Barnett made in her publication *The Red Record* in which she preempted questions about how readers can get involved by stating simply and succinctly, 'The answer always is: "Tell the world the facts."[44] This repara-tory justice manifests itself through tribunals, truth commissions, or trials but also encompasses modes of memorializing in public spaces and educational curricula. Regarding restoration, abolitionist archives learn from experts in restorative jus-tice and heed their call by 'investing in the social service infrastructure that reduces the likelihood of violence in the first place, including schools.'[45] In practice, this entails abolitionist archives advocating for complete divestment from the punish-ment paradigm of police and prison and the redirection of those funds, in part, to the operation of more libraries and archives. The decision to employ more police and correctional officers than librarians and archivists is a political one, but the punishment paradigm precludes the thought that this decision is an immoral one. It also obscures the reality that the safest communities have more computers than cops, more broadband than badges, and more books than body cameras.

Archives, abolitionist or other, comprise more than just documents, buildings, and the organizations responsible for their management. At their essence, archives articulate theories about power; its concentration, its control, and its codification. Archives, then, do not merely reflect ambitions of larger political projects but rather actively participate in the construction of those ambitions by rendering time and space as dimensions that can be captured, circumscribed, and inscribed. As such, abolitionist archives do not constitute a sudden departure from the archive as a political project. Instead they demonstrate that the so-called traditional archives of nations, states, and corporations stand as the most political of them all. Abolitionist archives recognize the indispensability of records and documents to the capture, confinement, and caging of human beings, processes that neither begin nor end with the prison as a discrete site but extend towards state, national, and international borders. The map might well become the ultimate documentary battleground of belonging, lending legitimacy to supranational efforts that aim to contain particular persons to particular localities and thereby bound them to spaces, increasingly poi-soned by capitalism's spear of environmental destruction, in ways not too dissimilar from incarceration. Abolitionist archives illustrate these connections, build resilient solidarities, and forge paths forward that make freedom, justice, and liberation as irresistible as they are attainable.

In a rush to remain neutral and removed from struggles for justice, what is most at risk for obsolescence will not be the born-digital records maintained by the archive, but the archive itself. To develop values that extend beyond evidential and histori-cal, such as transformational and liberational ones, might well be a requirement for the viability of the archivist's craft. Yet the homogeneity of the profession's demo-graphics suggests that this adaptation is further away than it is close, perhaps from a misguided mindset that the issues of the punishment paradigm matter only to those communities most directly impacted. In that case, the words of Fred Moten and Stefano Harney resound:

> coalition isn't something that emerges so that you can come help me, a maneuver that always gets traced back to your own interests. The coalition emerges out of your recognition that it's fucked up for you, in the same way that we've already recognized that it's fucked up for us. I don't need your help. I just need you to recognize that this shit is killing you, too, however much more softly[46]

FURTHER READING

David Brotherton and Philip Kretsedemas, eds, *Keeping out the Other: A Critical Introduction to Immigration Enforcement Today* (New York: Columbia University Press, 2008)

Simone Browne, *Dark Matters: On the Surveillance of Blackness* (Durham: Duke University Press, 2015)

Aviva Chomsky, *Undocumented: How Immigration Became Illegal* (Boston: Beacon Press, 2014)

Marisa J. Fuentes, *Dispossessed Lives: Enslaved Women, Violence, and the Archive*, Early American Studies (Philadelphia: University of Pennsylvania Press, 2016)

Patrisia Macias-Rojas, *From Deportation to Prison: The Politics of Immigration Enforcement in Post-Civil Rights America* (New York: New York University Press, 2016)

Jennifer Osorio, 'Proof of a Life Lived: The Plight of the Braceros and What It Says about How We Treat Records', *Archival Issues* 29.2 (2005), 95–103

Emily S. Rosenberg and Shanon Fitzpatrick, eds, *Body and Nation: The Global Realm of U.S. Body Politics in the Twentieth Century*, American Encounters/Global Interactions (Durham: Duke University Press, 2014)

John Torpey, *The Invention of the Passport: Surveillance, Citizenship, and the State*, Cambridge Studies in Law and Society (Cambridge, New York: Cambridge University Press, 2000)

NOTES

1. J. C. Scott, *Seeing Like a State: How Certain Schemes to Improve the Human Condition Have Failed* (New Haven: Yale University Press, 1998).
2. M. G. Kirschenbaum, R. Ovenden, and G. Redwine, 'Digital Forensics and Born-Digital Content in Cultural Heritage Collections' (Washington, D.C.: Council on Library and Information Resources, December 2010), www.clir.org/wp-content/uploads/sites/6/pub149.pdf; C. A. Lee et al., ' From Bitstreams to Heritage: Putting Digital Forensics into Practice in Collecting Institutions Christopher' (College Park, MD: Maryland Institute for Technology in the Humanities, September 2013), http://hdl.handle.net/1903/14736.
3. A. Y. Davis, *Are Prisons Obsolete?* (New York: Seven Stories Press, 2003), 10.
4. Davis, *Are Prisons Obsolete?*, 107–108.

5. S. Christianson, *With Liberty for Some: 500 Years of Imprisonment in America* (Boston, MA: Northeastern University Press, 1998), 60.
6. M. E. Kann, *Punishment, Prisons, and Patriarchy: Liberty and Power in the Early American Republic* (New York: New York University Press, 2005), 44.
7. S. P. Newman and B. G. Smith, 'Incarcerated Innocents: Inmates, Conditions, and Survival Strategies in Philadelphia's Almshouse and Jail', in M. L. Tarter and R. Bell, eds, *Buried Lives: Incarcerated in Early America* (Athens: University of Georgia Press, 2012), 67.
8. Kann, *Punishment, Prisons, and Patriarchy*, 225.
9. Christianson, *With Liberty for Some*, 155.
10. J. Graber, *The Furnace of Affliction: Prisons & Religion in Antebellum America* (Chapel Hill, NC: University of North Carolina Press, 2011), 104.
11. S. E. O'Donovan, 'Universities of Social and Political Change: Slaves in Jail in Antebellum America', in *Buried Lives*, 124–148.
12. Christianson, *With Liberty for Some*, p. xv.
13. M. Foucault, *Discipline and Punish: The Birth of the Prison* (New York: Vintage, 1995), 272.
14. Foucault, *Discipline and Punish*, 280.
15. S. E. Hadden, *Slave Patrols: Law and Violence in Virginia and the Carolinas* (Cambridge, MA: Harvard University Press, 2001), 19–20.
16. K. L. Hernández, 'Amnesty or Abolition? Felons, Illegals, and the Case for a New Abolition Movement', *Boom: A Journal of California* 1.4 (2011), 54–68; doi:10.1525/boom.2011.1.4.54.
17. L. Abrego et al., 'Making Immigrants into Criminals: Legal Processes of Criminalization in the Post-IIRIRA Era', *Journal on Migration and Human Security* 5.3 (2017), 694–715; doi:10.1177/233150241700500308.
18. J. X. Inda, 'Subject to Deportation: IRCA, "Criminal Aliens", and the Policing of Immigration', *Migration Studies* 1.3 (2013), 292–310; doi:10.1093/migration/mns003.
19. Abrego et al., 'Making Immigrants into Criminals'.
20. S. Ahmed, A. Appelbaum, and R. Jordan, 'The Human Cost of IIRIRA—Stories from Individuals Impacted by the Immigration Detention System', *Journal on Migration and Human Security* 5.1 (2017), 194–216; doi:10.1177/233150241700500110.
21. P. Pope and T. Garrett, 'America's Homo Sacer: Examining U.S. Deportation Hearings and the Criminalization of Illegal Immigration', *Administration & Society* 45.2 (2013), 167–186; doi:10.1177/0095399712451888.
22. D. M. Provine and R. L. Doty, 'The Criminalization of Immigrants as a Racial Project', *Journal of Contemporary Criminal Justice* 27.3 (2011), 261–277; doi:10. 1177/1043986211412559.
23. Foucault, *Discipline and Punish*, 282.
24. Davis, *Are Prisons Obsolete?*, 20.
25. Foucault, *Discipline and Punish*, 271.
26. R. W. Gilmore, 'Foreword', in D. Berger, *Struggle Within: Prisons, Political Prisoners, and Mass Movements in the United States* (Oakland, CA: PM Press, 2014), viii.
27. L. Samuels and D. Stein, 'Perspectives on Critical Resistance', in CR10 Publications Collective, ed., *Abolition Now!: Ten Years of Strategy and Struggle against the Prison Industrial Complex* (Oakland, CA: AK Press, 2008), 11.

28. D. Rodriguez, 'Dylan Rodríguez on Abolition', *Abolition Journal* (blog), 17 July 2015, https://abolitionjournal.org/dylan-rodriguez-abolition-statement/; M. Kaba, 'Working Toward Abolition...', *Prison Culture* (blog), 5 October 2015, www.usprisonculture.com/blog/2015/10/05/working-toward-abolition.
29. C. Elkins, 'Looking beyond Mau Mau: Archiving Violence in the Era of Decolonization', *The American Historical Review* 120.3 (2015), 855; doi:10.1093/ahr/120.3.852.
30. Elkins, 'Looking beyond Mau Mau', 866.
31. C. Folch, 'Surveillance and State Violence in Stroessner's Paraguay: Itaipú Hydroelectric Dam, Archive of Terror', *American Anthropologist* 115.1 (2013), 52; doi:10.1111/j.1548-1433.2012.01534.x.
32. K. Weld, *Paper Cadavers: The Archives of Dictatorship in Guatemala* (Durham: Duke University Press, 2014).
33. Foucault, *Discipline and Punish*, 191.
34. J. M. Drake, 'Liberatory Archives: Towards Belonging and Believing' (Co-keynote address, 21 October 2016), https://medium.com/on-archivy/liberatory-archives-towards-belonging-and-believing-part-1-d26aaeb0edd1.
35. 'Stop Violence Everyday', StoryTelling & Organizing Project, www.stopviolenceeveryday.org.
36. 'Living Bridges Project', Living Bridges Project, http://livingbridgesproject.com
37. 'Texas After Violence', Texas After Violence Project, http://texasafterviolence.org.
38. G. D. Solis, 'Documenting State Violence: (Symbolic) Annihilation & Archives of Survival', *KULA: Knowledge Creation, Dissemination, and Preservation Studies* 2.1 (2018), 7; doi:10.5334/kula.28.
39. 'Immigrant Defense Project—Fighting for Justice & Human Rights for ALL', Immigrant Defense Project, www.immigrantdefenseproject.org.
40. 'About—TGI Justice', TGI Justice Project, www.tgijp.org/about.html.
41. 'About the Project—Women and Prison: A Site for Resistance', Women + Prison, http://womenandprison.org/about/.
42. 'Amplify Voices Inside | Amplifying the Voices of Durham's Incarcerated Population and Their Loved Ones', Amplify Voices Inside, https://amplifyvoices.com.
43. R. W. Gilmore, *Golden Gulag: Prisons, Surplus, Crisis, and Opposition in Globalizing California* (Berkeley: University of California Press, 2007), 242.
44. I. B. Wells-Barnett, *A Red Record: Tabulated Statistics and Alleged Causes of Lynchings in the United States, 1892–1893–1894* (Chicago: Donohue & Henneberry, 1895).
45. D. Sered, ' Accounting for Violence: How to Increase Safety and Break Our Failed Reliance on Mass Incarceration' (New York: Vera Institute of Justice, February 2017), 30; www.vera.org/publications/accounting-for-violence.
46. S. Harney and F. Moten, *The Undercommons: Fugitive Planning & Black Study* (New York: Minor Compositions, 2013), 140–141.

CHAPTER 26

WRITER–EDITORS MAKING THE HAITIAN AND CARIBBEAN ARCHIVES TALK

RACHEL DOUGLAS

How do we make archives talk? One answer is: through an editor. This chapter examines how the editor especially in the Caribbean context challenges archival gaps and silences in official records. As explored here, the editor can be thought of as epitomizing Derrida's notion of 'archive fever'.[1] Who is the editor? Can it sometimes be the writer themself who tries to preserve everything of their own work in the face of possible annihilation? To answer these questions, this chapter considers the postcolonial archives in book form produced by numerous Caribbean writers. Their work, this chapter argues, constitutes a form of archive in the face of constant threats from natural hazards including earthquakes, hurricanes, landslides, and flooding; the impact of which is magnified by manmade disasters including deforestation, dictatorship, gang violence, climate change, and human waste. Editing can be a decolonial strategy, which comes most clearly into view when we set side-by-side two triangular paradigms. There is a three-way relationship linking editor, author, and text as a triangle, following Susan Greenberg:

Figure 26.1 Triangulation: Working Definition. After Susan Greenberg, *A Poetics of Editing* (London: Palgrave Macmillan, 2018), 19.

Here, the third point on this triangle represents the editor as a midwife—an active participant in editing practice who brings forth the text to the world. Yet, this chapter makes the case that self-editing of writers' own work is a widespread and important phenomenon, particularly in the contexts of Haitian and Caribbean twentieth and twenty-first century literature. Triangles are particularly loaded paradigms in the Caribbean context where they represent the transatlantic triangular trade of slaves, raw materials, and manufactured goods peopled these islands:

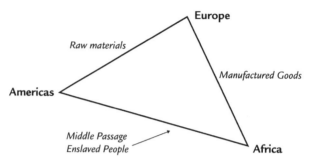

Figure 26.2 The triangle of the transatlantic slave trade.

Self-editing, the chapter argues, helps Caribbean writers to short-circuit the old triangular slave trade symbol and decolonize that other traditional triangle involving the editing of the printed book. Here, responsibility for acts of editing has often fallen to the author, while moving away from the intermediary third-party editor. Editing has also often been a rather invisible activity, but many Caribbean writers attempt to bring their own editing roles more clearly into view. What, this chapter asks, are the consequences of this shift towards the author clearly revising their own text instead of someone else's work? Before moving on to this question, the discussion, in the next section, considers the broader context of how editors have engaged with archives. The long tradition of scholarly editing is implicit in the privileging of certain categories of archival materials, yet, at the same time, the approaches developed by scholarly, and particularly by authorial editors offer opportunities for those seeking to recover marginalized or silenced voices from the archive.

Editing and Archives

Scholarly editions offer mediations between archives and their users or readers. They bridge the gap that often exists between the reader and materials that may be obscure, unknown, or present obstacles to understanding because of their difficult handwriting, culturally specific references, ambiguities, language, material damage, inaccessibility, loss, or because there are multiple versions to choose between. Scholarly editors use a range of methods to make texts more accessible and understandable to readers, as well as to point out texts of interest and to highlight their potential value.[2] Editions indicate why the text might be worth reading, and they provide frames of reference for analysis, whether for analogue reading (for example, indices, explanatory notes, cross references) or for digital use (for example, extractable corpora, and the means to sort, search, and visualize).

In order to achieve these aims, editors have drawn on different approaches and methods, which are selected depending on the nature of the text, the intended readers, the mode of access, and the medium and scope of the publication. It is worth pointing out some of the benefits and limitations inherent in different editorial methods, as a broader framing context for the case studies in the next section. First and foremost in scholarly editing, a distinction exists between non-critical and critical editions, in addition to which we can consider the implications of digital versions of each of these.

Non-critical editions seek to represent the document and tend to prioritize faithful capture of a single textual source. Perhaps most relevant for literary works have been facsimile editions of rare or unique books, typically codices, often handmade, where visual features are especially important to the interpretation of the textual component. For example, facsimile editions have been produced for the poetry of William Blake and for illuminated medieval manuscripts. For feminist editors dealing with women writers who did not participate in print culture, facsimile editions hold an important place, such as the photographic facsimiles of Emily Dickinson's handwritten envelope poems.[3] For historical records, the most extreme form of documentary editing is the calendar, which assumes that an abstract is sufficient and detailed transcripts are not necessary. In one of the most influential handbooks on editing historical records, R. F. Hunnisett even argued that all post-1200 records should be calendared, an approach that remains influential to this day.[4] Digital calendaring can make it possible to find in the archives particular social groups, depending on the markup structures. With the development of online resources we find older calendars being combined with digital scans of documents, sometimes subsequently linked to curated resources, so that the distinctions between catalogue, calendar, facsimile, and edition are narrowed as hybrid digital forms of resource emerge.

Critical editions, by contrast with non-critical or documentary editions, seek to recover the authorial text, typically through a process of selecting between variants where there are multiple witnesses of a work. How the 'authorial text' is conceptualized has been extensively debated within the field of scholarly editing, as have been the methods to determine how to select the best witnesses and choose between textual variants. Debates in critical editing have tended to focus on the codex, on print, and on single-authored canonical texts. The methods developed have been strongly influenced by Biblical textual scholarship, the classics, and editing of canonical writers such as Shakespeare: these are the texts that around which the major debates in the field have been shaped. Therefore, the main role of the editor has come to be defined as that of selecting between variants, while other textual problems, which are numerous and complex, have received less attention and tend to be regarded as a less serious concerns for scholarly editors. The focus on a single recoverable authorial text, and authorial 'voice', that can be discovered through analysis and comparison of variants, has been the central concern of debates for many years. For editors concerned with recovery of lost or undervalued cultures from the archive, critical editing therefore has much to offer. For example, the concept of an authorial text and style has been important to editors of letters and literature by women writers where the aim is to seek to recover a 'voice' and for the edition to preserve and draw out that voice above other concerns. It is particularly authorial self-editing that 'makes the archives speak' in the archive-like Caribbean books I will now examine. In my case, in the discussion below, I look at how the voice of the author can be drawn out from a mass of archival materials which have tended to be regarded as the dead textual ruins.

Digital editing is not an editorial approach in itself and we can find digital editions that are both critical and non-critical. They tend to be wide ranging and, as we have seen already, bring in new hybrid models and social editions to contextual texts cultural and socially.[5] Digital editing present opportunities for the writers who are the focuses of this chapter. These Caribbean writer–editors weave particularly polyvocal, community-minded, open-ended, and mobile texts and archival materials together. For this Caribbean group, models of social editing have been fundamental, as in 'Our Collective Notebook': a collaborative and decolonial retranslation of Aimé Césaire's foundational poem.[6] As the name suggests, this new digital edition in English was an experiment in collective annotation and digital translational dialogue in an open forum with multiple participants. To take another example of the opportunities presented by digital methods, the developments in textual markup, that go beyond hierarchical models for structuring text, are highly relevant for presenting such avant-garde Caribbean literary works. These include the ability to transcribe texts using spatial and material concepts including zones and surfaces, instead of each nested textual unit. Such innovations can help to provide an encoding framework for transcribing complex documents, such as Marcel Proust's messy notebooks.[7] These approaches come closest to overcoming the two-dimensional 'page paradigm', and help to reproduce the narrative sequences, layout, spacing of the draft page by moving the transcription *within* the facsimile, and by using some interactivity from computer games.[8]

Despite all the technological advances from pre-digital to digital-era cultures, it is important to point out that not everyone across the world has equal access to the digital, especially in the context of a country like Haiti, which will be one of my case studies below. Haiti is one of the lowest income countries in the world and has an illiteracy rate of more than fifty per cent. Yet where digital and technological access are concerned, the situation can change fast also in poor countries such as Haiti. Laura Wagner, project archivist for the Radio Haïti-Inter Archives at Duke University, has carried out some informal qualitative research in Haiti. While telecommunication companies certainly exploit and make money off poor Haitians, Wagner suggests that even in somewhere like Haiti, people are more connected to the internet, digital media, and technology than might be expected, with people accessing the web via smartphones and by purchasing data daily for the equivalent of a few cents.[9] How to get information out of the hands of rich foreign and Haitian (digital) elites is a challenge.

Editing as *Rasanblaj* (Gathering or Reassembling)

This case study explores the literary creation of three prominent twentieth- and twenty-first-century Caribbean writers: Franківtienne and Dany Laferrière from Haiti, and the late Kamau Brathwaite from Barbados. It focuses on the strong tendency in the Caribbean context of self-publishing/self-editing particularly in texts relating to Haiti; a place where issues facing the Caribbean region as a whole are particularly acute. The primary materials examined here are multiple versions of the same text by these serial rewriters. In connection with Franківtienne's work, I have had access to a limited number of manuscripts or typescripts, particularly relating to his play *Melovivi or The Trap*, which are currently in the author's collection at his house in Port-au-Prince. Franківtienne, Laferrière and Brathwaite's own private archives and manuscripts are not currently available to be consulted. Due to this lack of access to pre-publication materials, the multiple different published versions of these writers' works—and especially the variants which only emerge when these editions are compared and contrasted—form the corpus analysed by this chapter. In order to compare and contrast these multiple published versions, the Juxta Commons and CollateX collation and comparison digital tools would have been useful. Unfortunately, without a maintenance budget, Juxta Commons was shut down in 2020.[10] Particularly Franківtienne's editions self-published in Haiti— especially during the 1960s to 80s of the notorious dictatorship of François 'Papa Doc' and Jean-Claude 'Baby Doc' Duvalier—are published on poor-quality paper so fragile and brittle that it can turn to dust when handled. These books include Franківtienne's *Mûr à crêver* (1968) and *Dézafi* (1975), which were printed in short print runs by Haitian printing presses. Consequently, such books are today rare and fragile with libraries holding few copies. Sometimes even the authors themselves do not have their own copy of these hard-to-find texts. Our focus is on Franківtienne's first graphic novel, published for the first time in Haiti in 1993, and then in Paris by publisher Jean-Michel Place in 1998. In the Haitian edition, the flimsy paper is so thin that text on the other side is visible. In the French edition, the use of thicker paper solved this problem with transparency. To this day, Franківtienne often continues to self-publish the first edition in Haiti of new books. Subsequently, the book will then be published in France or Montreal.

Brathwaite's self-publication trajectory is different in some respects. At the start of his literary career, his first collections of his poems were published in the 1970s by traditional publisher Oxford University Press. Brathwaite was one of the founders of *Savacou*, the journal of the Caribbean Artists' Movement. Its first issue was published in June 1970 and there would be fifteen issues between 1970 and

1979.[11] After that in the 1980s, Brathwaite would retain the name 'Savacou' for his own publishing imprint in the Caribbean. Later still, from the 1990s onwards, he would use the name 'Savacou North' to label his self-edited publishing ventures in New York, the United States. Like Franketienne, Brathwaite's decision to self-publish enabled him to have fuller control over every edition. Caribbean writers are confronted with a challenge: the tough publishing context and lack of commercial publishers and resources across the region. This has forced successful writers including Haitian writer Franketienne and Barbadian writer Brathwaite, among others, to self-publish their own work as it increases in innovation.[12] The form and content of their recent (analogue) printed books often reaches out to the digital as a means of freeing themselves from the tight grip of those called by Brathwaite 'Prospero' publishers—who dictate limits concerning the format, size constraints, and who refuse to reproduce the author's draft layout.[13] Here, he oversaw the printing and layout of each book in printing/photocopy stores. Brathwaite did in later life have productive editorial relationships with New Directions, Wesleyan University Press, and with kindred collaborative editors including Nathaniel Mackey. Such collaborations helped to develop further Braithwaite's own editorial poetics.[14]

One major issue concerning all these authorial Caribbean self-made books is that they are not housed in archival collections, as might be expected. Instead, the archives of the work's making are published inside the different low print-run physical copies of editions of the actual books themselves. Across the world, there are very few copies of these self-published books. For example, the self-made pamphlet *Dream Haiti* (New York: Savacou North, 1995) is only available at major libraries including the British Library and University of Warwick in the UK; New York University, State University of New York at Buffalo, Harvard University, Michigan State University, University of Texas in the US; the University of the Virgin Islands, and University of Antwerp in Belgium. My own image from *Dream Haiti* in this chapter is from this self-published pamphlet, which I bought from the author's wife Beverly Brathwaite in April 2009 from the writer's then-residence beside New York University. This edition is particularly noteworthy as it is the only 'book' with this title. Otherwise, 'Dream Haiti' has been published in the format of a (long) short story. As Brathwaite, like Franketienne, is a serial rewriter, several revised versions of 'Dream Haiti' have been published, including in: *Dreamstories* (1994), *The Oxford Book of Caribbean Short Stories* (1999), *ConVERSations with Nathaniel Mackey* (1999), and *DS (2): Dreamstories* (2007).[15] Some of these versions are self-published, while others have been edited by publishers and journals. There is also a significant French translation of Brathwaite's story *RêvHaïti*, translated by Christine Pagnoulle, and published by the Haitian-owned publishing house Mémoire d'encrier based in Montreal, Canada; an important centre of the Haitian diaspora.[16] With constant rewriters like Kamau Brathwaite and Franketienne, archiving and editing became authorial practices and processes. Rewriting continues across Brathwaite's entire œuvre but is particularly concentrated in his Haiti-focused experimentations. Here, we concentrate on the multiple versions of his long poem 'Dream Haiti' about the plight of Haitian boatpeople.

Figure 26.3 Frankétienne, *L'Oiseau schizophone* (Paris: Jean-Michel Place, 1998), 386.

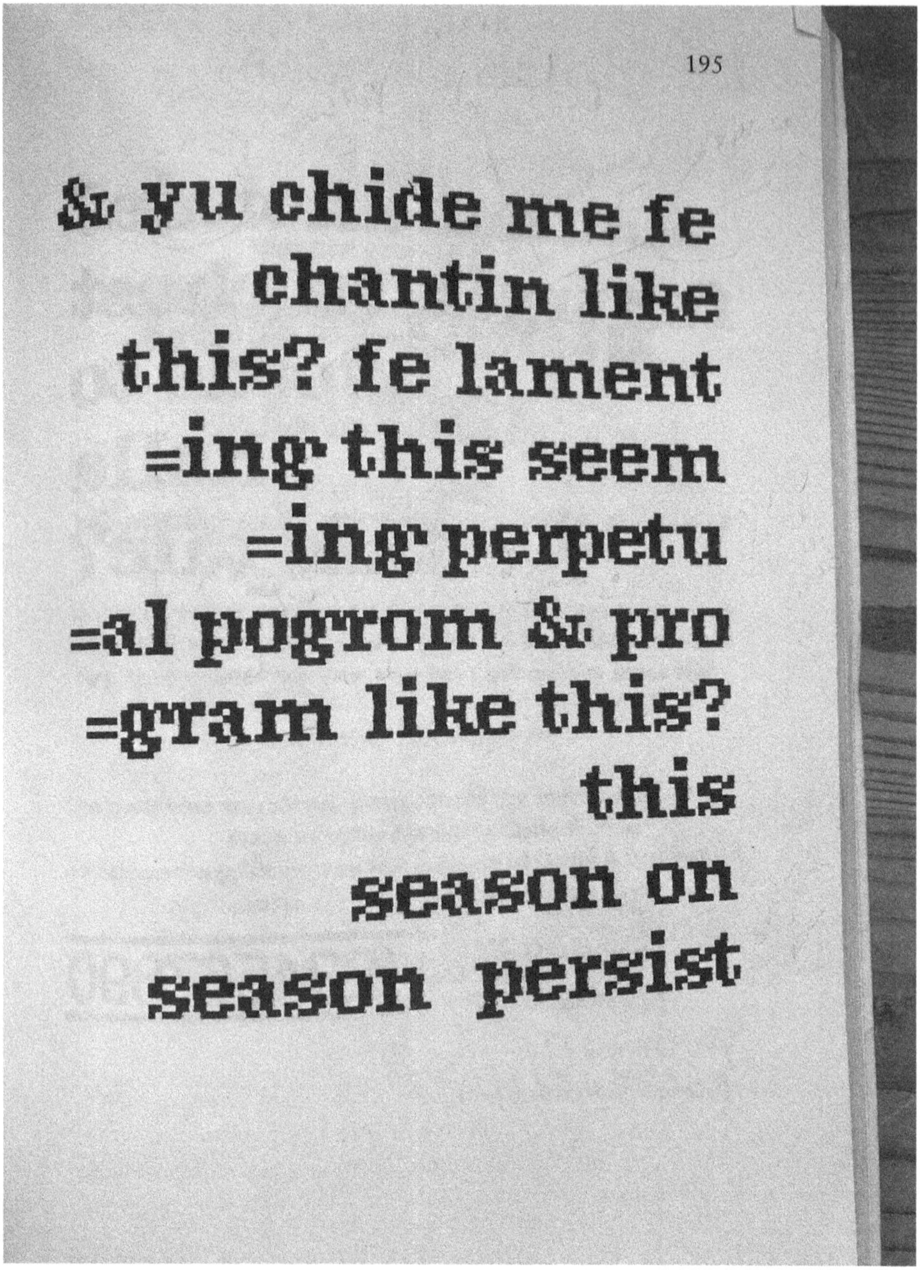

Figure 26.4 Kamau Brathwaite, 'Dream Haiti', in *DS (2): dreamstories* (New York: New Directions, 2007), 195.

This chapter argues that we can view the pages of the multiple editions as a *rasanblaj*: this word means gathering or reassembling in Haitian Kreyòl and refers to Haitians doing and making things piece-by-piece like a hybrid multipart mosaic.[17] There is often a visual *rasanblaj* collage-type dimension which incorporate visual images, headlines, and striking fonts.

Caribbean writers often try to decolonize the book and technologies through, for example, what Brathwaite calls 'Sycorax video style'—his distinctive own-design fonts that reach to the digital and reclaim Caliban's absent mother for the Caribbean. According to Brathwaite, 'we have to have a presentation of ourselves', become 'visible in our own image', and bring 'self into focus' by creating 'fonts with our faces on':[18]

Such books try to look visibly different, outwit usual book confines, and create formats using more fluid, non-hierarchical, and multimodal forms of representation. Recent Caribbean writing is highly changeable and fluid. Self-publishing has increasingly led Caribbean writers to become self-editors who treat their own changeable works editorially themselves. Like Greenberg, Bryant conceptualizes the normally three-sided editing process with the writer normally being the first reader when writing, and then the second reader when reading back his or her own work, while the third reader is often the editor—the third party to whom the author submits their writing, initiating the collaboration of the editorial revision process. To decolonize the book and regular editing processes, these Caribbean writers attempt to short-circuit the usual triangular editorial model by self-editing, while also trying to escape from, and fend off, the old triangular model of the transatlantic slave trade.

One clear trend in late-twentieth and early-twenty-first century Caribbean writing has seen the roles played by author, editor, and autofictional narrator become the main ones as writers such as Laferrière and Brathwaite prominently repeatedly insert these personas inside their own literary texts themselves. As self-editors, these writers tell the story of how their works came to be in versions of the works themselves. Before the reader's eyes as he or she reads are the layers upon layers of the narrative as the writers self-fashion the self-genesis of their own textuality as they draw parallels between authorial revision and editing. The triangle of author-text-editor is short-circuited as the author performs the editing process.

Sometimes, the ever-prominent editor is a separate person who is showcased in the book itself; particularly in the case of Laferrière's novels set in Montreal. There, writer and editor have a difficult relationship as narrativized in the pages of many of his books that tell of the editor's anxious wait for the writer's next instalment. The editor and the author's direct interventions are a prominent use of *mise en abyme* mirroring strategies with the mirror inside the narrative presenting miniature versions of the editor and the author-narrator actually in the acts of writing and editing within the book itself. Such deliberate inscription of the editing and editing process within the books, the editor clearly acts as a double for the writer figure, and we can see him in the act of carefully selecting the work alongside the author.

Even in books which do not feature an intradiegetic editor *en abyme* within the narrative itself, there is in much recent Haitian literature a clear focus on the act of editing, and the active work of making the narrative through careful assembly from the writers' larger archives of notebooks, rough and more polished drafts, as well as interviews. This practice of rewriting is rife in Haitian literature and often entails multi-layered acts of self-editing by the writers themselves. Increasingly, despite being in the so-called digital age, numerous living and dead Caribbean writers continue to write by hand—including Frankétienne and Yanick Lahens—and, in the cases of Laferrière (2018, 2019, 2020) and Frankétienne (2002, 2003)—are even inscribing the handwritten trace and publishing the final book in handwritten format.[19] They are seeking permanence of the printed text for the handwritten literary archives and producing these literary archives (notes and drafts) in the physical book-form of every copy of the book. Here archive and edition merge and blur.

Making so many copies of these book-archives can help to maximize their chances of survival, stopping natural or manmade disasters, such as earthquakes, hurricanes, or dictatorships from destroying every copy. Reproducing the book-archives in print means that of the many copies of them, at least some of them should live on, as in the LOCKSS programme at Stanford University whose acronym stands for 'Lots of Copies Keep Stuff Safe'. Digital iterations of significant Caribbean texts could offer new possibilities for multiplication and preservation, as seen in archival initiatives led by Digital Library of the Caribbean (dLOC) to digitize and thereby protect endangered Caribbean patrimony. Currently, these initiatives do not stretch to literary archives, which are at particular risk as they are often in private hands and do not have any official institutional repository. These multiple print copies of Caribbean book-archives store, capture, and format textual information almost like a Portable Document Format/PDF or a facsimile. Such analogue printed copies which reach out to digital transformation would benefit from complete remediation to become interactive digital editions.

Can such complex books only be edited by the authors themselves? On narration, Gérard Genette, French narratologist whose theory of narrative discourse is fundamentally important, offers detailed typologies of narrators and levels of narration. Yet, Genette says little about the *editor* per se who is, according to James Parr, the supernarrator.[20] The far-seeing intratextual editor—supernarrator is present everywhere inside of Caribbean literature and can also be described as a *superarchivist*. I use this term in the superlative sense of the archivist to the highest degree possible, to the power of all the archivist's archives themselves. Caribbean writers, in other words, are often self-editors and self-editors of their own constantly changing texts. Here Caribbean self-editors keep a self-fashioning record of all changes, preserving not just some final text, but in fact presenting all the evolutionary stages of the process of their literary creation. Here, 'edition' merges with literary archives and self-editing. If the 'normal' editor who is not the author can be described as the third reader to whom writers submit their writing, then the second reader begins to emerge when the writer himself or herself starts to revise their own work.

Self-editors have been viewed as unusual cases by editorial theorists. Bryant's outline of 'fluid texts' emphasizes the category of the writer that is the self-editor.[21] Relegated to a footnote is Gabler's observation that the self-editor 'is a culturally fascinating strand in the traditions of editing' about which he says little as '[a]uthor's self-editions ... are not generally scholarly editions'.[22]

Yet, self-editors—particularly pervasive in Caribbean contexts—should not be relegated to the footnotes. Many of Bryant's 'fluid texts' are authored by self-editors.[23] McGann conceives of 'autopoiesis': a recursive process of self-collaborative feedback loops in the creative process 'that cannot be separated from those who manipulate and use them'.[24] As for narratologist Genette's 'hypertextuality' typology—referring to the relationship between a hypotext (earlier text) and a hypertext (later text)—this includes the interesting category of autotextuality or rewriting oneself, about which he has little to say.[25] Genette also has nothing to say about interventions by self-editors who edit their own works. For Caribbean writers, writing is an act of self-genesis revealing the layers upon layers in the archaeology of their own texts where text and apparatus form an integrated whole.[26] Caribbean literature self-editors create works-in-progress, about which we could echo Beckett's statement about the same notion in Joyce: 'Here form *is* content, content *is* form.... His writing is not *about* something; *it is that something itself*.'[27] Caribbean writers' own notes, intermediary drafts, and marginalia are turned inside-out and put prominently and permanently on display.

Here the Haitian phenomenon of *rasanblaj* is fundamental. Significantly, *rasanblaj* can be both a verb (something you do), and a noun (something in itself). In the aftermath of the 2010 Haitian earthquake, Haitian anthropologist–artist Gina Athena Ulysse has called for new non-stereotypical narratives about Haiti and this chapter builds on her reflections about *rasanblaj* and new narratives for Haiti further in this context of self-editing.[28] Vital for (re)constructing any new narratives about Haiti is *rasanblaj*—which can be collective end-product and also fluid collective processes of (re)assembly, collage or montage of found objects—created like the multilayered self-edited Haitian narratives themselves. *Rasanblaj* is also a regrouping (of ideas, things, people), a Vodou ceremony, and a protest where factors such poverty and class can be involved, and where people can come together and participate in times of need. But *rasanblaj* can also be a methodology for self-editing and disaster risk reduction linked to effective preservation, restoration, and digitization. In constructing their *rasanblaj* with each textual version, Haitian writers are constantly and extensively changing their own narratives even as multiple print versions of the same text.

There is in Haitian literature therefore a constant process of *rasanblaj*, of recreating new narratives about Haiti self-edited by Haitian writers themselves. Why? In Caribbean and especially Haitian contexts, there is a perceived lack of archival records and gaps/silences in the official archives. Relevant to Haitian book–archives is a deconstructionist type of postcolonial historiography associated with the process of silencing the past. Michel-Rolph Trouillot has written compellingly of the silencing of the Haitian Revolution, drawing attention to uneven power in the production of sources, archives, narratives, and history. Archives are, Trouillot argues, 'products/symbols of neo-colonial domination'.[29] Silencing is an active and transitive process—something that is actively done to someone or something else. Sources and archives about the Haitian Revolution were primarily from the point of view of literate French planters or French army generals—people with vested interests in keeping the Caribbean plantation slavery system going and preventing Haitian independence. Most Haitian Revolutionaries including leaders were illiterate, leaving few written records of their own. Beyond the Haitian Revolution silences noted by Trouillot, other gaps include: the US occupation of Haiti (1915–1934), the dictatorial regimes of François 'Papa Doc' Duvalier (1957–1971) and Jean-Claude 'Baby Doc' Duvalier (1971–1986), the coups d'état of the 1990s, the Haitian earthquake (2010), Hurricane Matthew (2016), and current tensions relating to the whereabouts and spending of Venezuelan aid–development money from Petro-karibe.

With all these gaping silences and absences in the official archives and records, what to do? Derrida's *Archive Fever* talks about being 'en mal d'archive', as being in *need* of archives—this expression sums up some of the archival silences in official Haitian records. The archive is often conceived as power and law. Michel Foucault sums up the archive as 'the law of what can be said, the system that governs the appearance of statements as unique events'.[30] For Derrida, the archive is the *place* where 'men and gods *command, there* where authority, social order are exercised'.[31] Archives have been viewed therefore as a storage place, an institution, as things, and as the law. Regarding place and space, colonialism was always archive-driven scramble to occupy as much place and space as possible.[32]

Disasters such as earthquakes and hurricanes have led to archival materials being lost or destroyed. In the face of all the silences in the official records, there is a need for deconstructive perspectives of the archive, after the philosopher of deconstruction and archive fever Derrida himself. In the postcolonial Caribbean context, we need to go beyond the idea of archives as physical official records with an architectural, institutional dimension. During the almost thirty-year rule (1957–1986) of the Duvalierist regime, Papa Doc and his son Baby Doc institutionalized, controlled, and destroyed records and archives to sponsor and support their state power. Not only did François Duvalier control the official Haitian archives, his own so-called *Œuvres essentielles* were presented as the only 'essential reading'. As Derrida reminds us, there is no political power without control of the archive.

Self-editing Haitian writers create alternative unofficial Haitian archives which are materially constituted in the form of their own books and circulated as multiple copies of these books themselves. Haitian writer–editors give voice in these alternative archives to those who are voiceless. Following the 2010 Haitian earthquake, one relief initiative called 'voices of the voiceless' aimed to give as many of the 1.5 million displaced people in Haiti as possible a voice. How can we record lost voices and decolonize the archives? One strategy has been to read colonial archives against the grain from bottom-up perspectives. Ann Laura Stoler and Marisa Fuentes advocate reading not crossways, but instead along the bias of the archival grain by stretching the historical fragments of official records.[33] In seismic disaster-prone Haiti, writer–archivists write along the fault lines of the archives when constituting their own narratives about Haiti.

Through their editorial *rasanblaj*, Caribbean writer–editors read against or along the grain, using the resources of the literary imagination to fill in the gaps in official records creatively. They reassemble archival fragments and their resulting book–archives are montages of fragments, putting scraps and debris back together, remaking the archive and forming something new that is more open-ended and multi-layered than the archives in official state repositories. Here in-the-making *rasanblaj* and archiving is a never-ending process—an alternative production of subaltern historical and cultural knowledge. These book–archives expand the historical documents of traditional archive sources by adding new voices of whom there is little official archival trace. These writer–editors give voice to the voiceless by piecing together multi-layered *rasanblaj* collages of alternative archival traces, which together resemble Haitian-style postcolonial Noah's arks.

These *rasanblaj* sketch out the basis for unfinished Caribbean community identity formation and cultural survival in the present and the future, as the self-editors constitute their own archives preserving community narratives. Today the Haitian Devoir de Mémoire Foundation serves to recall and commemorate atrocities committed by the Duvalierist dictatorship.[34] Caribbean writer–editors stretch out any archival fragments in order actively and transitively to un-silence the past. They have a 'devoir de mémoire'—a duty to remember and to represent the 'unrepresentable': the suffering of slavery, dictatorship, the earthquake, cholera, hunger, and food and supply shortages. This tension between remembering and forgetting recalls the Haitian Kreyòl proverb used frequently to remember especially the Duvaliers' victims: 'Bay kou bliye, pote mak sonje' [The one who strikes the blow easily forgets, but the one who carries the scars must remember]. These self-editors actively and transitively give voice to those silenced in the official archives. We and they—as editors/readers of their own work—need to read along the fault lines and the scars of unofficial archives too.

FURTHER READING

Jeanette Bastian, John A. Aarons, and Stanley H. Griffen, *Decolonizing the Caribbean Record: An Archives Reader* (Sacramento: Library Juice Press, 2018)

Laurent Dubois, 'Maroons in the Archives: The Uses of the Past in the French Caribbean', in Francis X. Blouin and William G. Rosenberg, eds, *Archives, Documentation, and Institutions of Social Memory: Essays from the Sawyer Seminar* (Ann Arbor: University of Michigan, 2005), 291–300

Carolyn Hamilton, Verne Harris, Michèle Pickover, Graeme Reid, Jane Taylor, and Razia Saleh, eds, *Refiguring the Archive* (Dordrecht: Kluwer, 2002)

P. D. A. Harvey, *Editing Historical Records* (London: British Library, 2001)

Jenny Sharpe, *Immaterial Archives: An African Diaspora Poetics of Loss* (Evanston: Northwestern University Press, 2020)

James L. W. West, *Making the Archives Talk* (University Park: Pennsylvania State University Press, 2011)

NOTES

1. J. Derrida, *Archive Fever: A Freudian Impression* (Chicago: University of Chicago Press, 1995).
2. For an overview of editorial approaches such as stemmatics, copy-text theory, genetic criticism, and other key methods, see: D. C. Greetham, *Textual Scholarship: An Introduction* (New York: Garland, 1992); M. J. Driscoll and E. Pierazzo, *Digital Scholarly Editing: Theories and Practices* (Open Book Publishers, 2016) available at www.openbookpublishers.com/product/483/digital-scholarly-editing—theories-and-practices; *Literature Compass*, special issue on 'Scholarly Editing in the Twenty-First Century' 7.2 (2010).
3. E. Dickinson, M. Werner, and J. Bervin, with a preface by S. Howe, *The Gorgeous Nothings* (New York: Christine Burgin/New Directions in association with Granary Books, 2013).
4. R. F. Hunnisett, *Editing Records for Publication* (London: British Records Association 1977).
5. An overview is provided by E. Pierazzo, *Digital Scholarly Editing: Theories, Models and Methods* (Farnham: Ashgate, 2015); *The Rossetti Archive*, general editor J. McGann (IATH, University of Virginia, 2000–2007) rossettiarchive.org; *A Social Edition of the Devonshire MS (BL Add. MS 17,492)*, general editor R. Siemens (Iter; Medieval and Renaissance Texts and Studies; A. Matthew Digital) https://en.m.wikibooks.org/wiki/The_Devonshire_Manuscript.
6. See https://via.hypothes.is/https://cahier1939ms.github.io/texts/translation/ and http://caribbeandigitalnyc.net/2020/cahier/.
7. E. Pierazzo and J. André, 'Le Codage en TEI des brouillons de Proust: vers une édition numérique', *Genesis* 36 (2013), 155–161; E. Pierazzo, 'Unpacking the Draft Page: A New Framework for Digital Editions of Draft Manuscripts', *Variants* 11 (2014), 29–46.
8. See Pierazzo, 'Unpacking the Draft Page', 36, 43.
9. See L. Wagner, 'Forgetting Is Not Democratic: The Digital Archive of Radio Haïti-Inter, A Case Study', in J. Bastian, J. A. Aarons, and S. H. Griffin, *Decolonizing the Caribbean Record: An Archives Reader* (Sacramento CA: Library Juice Press, 2018), 629–630.
10. Correspondence with Nicholas Laiacona, creator of Juxta Commons, and Alex Gil, Digital Scholarship Librarian at Columbia University Libraries.
11. See K. B. Josephs, 'Where Do Journals Go? *Savacou*, Fifty Years Later', sx salon 35 (October 2020), http://smallaxe.net/sxsalon/discussions/where-do-journals-go-savacou-fifty-years-later.

12. The actual manuscripts or pre-publication literary archives largely remain both unedited and inaccessible. They are generally still with the authors' families. The self-edited works are generally rare books, which are available in limited numbers at major national and university libraries. This chapter is based on analysis of differences across published versions.

13. On 'Prospero' publishers, see Kamau Brathwaite, *Golokwati 2000* (New York: Savacou North, 2002), 216.

14. See A. Foley, '*Hambone*'s Call: Nathaniel Mackey and Editorial Poeticism', *Textual Practice* 34.6 (2020), 881–901.

15. Kamau Brathwaite, 'Dream Haiti', in *Dreamstories* (Harlow: Longman, 1994), 94–111; Kamau Brathwaite, 'Dream Haiti', *Hambone* 12 (1995), 123–185; Kamau Brathwaite, 'Dream Haiti', in S. Brown and J. Wickham, eds, *The Oxford Book of Caribbean Short Stories* (Oxford: Oxford University Press, 1999), 169–186; Kamau Brathwaite, *ConVERSations with Nathaniel Mackey* (New York: We Press, 1999); Kamau Brathwaite, 'Dream Haiti', in *DS (2): dreamstories* (New York: New Directions, 2007), 155–202.

16. Kamau Brathwaite, *RêvHaïti*, trans C. Pagnoulle (Montreal: Mémoire d'encrier, 2013).

17. On this concept/process, see G. A. Ulysse, 'Seven Keywords for This Rasanblaj', *Anthropology Now* 8.3 (2016), 122–125.

18. Kamau Brathwaite, 'The New Aesthetics and the Nature of Culture in the Caribbean: "The Dream Coming in with the Rain"', *Carifesta* 5 (1992), 149; Kamau Brathwaite, *Cultural Diversity and Integration in the Caribbean* (Mona: University of the West Indies, 1973), 53; Kamau Brathwaite, *MR/Magical Realism* (New York: Savacou North, 2002), 39.

19. D. Laferrière, *Autoportrait de Paris avec chat* (Paris: Grasset, 2018); Dany Laferrière, *Vers d'autres rives* (La Tour d'Aigues [France]: Éditions de l'Aube, 2019); *L'Exil vaut le voyage* (Paris: Grasset, 2020); Frankétienne, *H'éros-chimères* (Port-au-Prince: Spirale, 2002); Frankétienne, *Miraculeuse* (Port-au-Prince: Spirale, 2003).

20. J. Parr, 'Don Quixote: The Quest for a Supernarrator and Supernarratee', www.lehman.cuny.edu/ciberletras/v04/Parr.html. Superarchivist is my own term being used here. I am following Roland Barthes's distinction between 'work' and 'text'. Here, the 'work' is a concrete, definite and complete object that can be handled; 'a fragment of a substance occupying a part of the space of books'. In contrast, the 'text' is plural, incomplete, open-ended; an activity of production and not the definite object. Instead, the 'text' is like a 'woven fabric' that can be assembled differently when the reader interacts with it and takes meaning from it. See R. Barthes, 'From Work to Text', in *Image, Music, Text* (London: Fontana, 1977), 155–164.

21. J. Bryant, *The Fluid Text: A Theory of Revision and Editing for Book and Screen* (Ann Arbor MI: University of Michigan Press, 2002).

22. H. W. Gabler, 'Theorizing the Digital Scholarly Edition', *Literature Compass* 7.2 (2010), 55n2.

23. Bryant, *The Fluid Text*, 99.

24. J. McGann, *The Textual Condition* (Princeton, NJ: Princeton: University Press, 1991), 15.

25. G. Genette, *Palimpsestes. La littérature au second degré* (Paris: Seuil, 1982).

26. On the notion of self-genesis, see Bryant, *The Fluid Text*, 14.

27. S. Beckett, *Disjecta* (New York: Grove Press, 1984), 27 (original emphasis). See also D. Van Hulle, 'Exogenetic Digital Editing and Enactive Cognition', in Driscoll and Pierazzo, *Digital Scholarly Editing*, 113.
28. G. A. Ulysse, *Why Haiti Needs New Narratives: A Post-quake Chronicle* (Middletown CT: Wesleyan University Press, 2015); and 'Seven Keywords for This Rasanblaj', *Anthropology Now* 8.3 (2016), 122–125.
29. M.-R. Trouillot, *Silencing the Past: Power and the Production of History* (Boston: Beacon Press, 1995), 105
30. M. Foucault, *The Archaeology of Knowledge* (New York: Pantheon Books, 1972), 129.
31. Derrida, *Archive Fever*, 9.
32. M. Kurtz, 'A Postcolonial Archive? On the Paradox of Practice in a Northwest Alaska Project', *Archivaria* 61 (2006), 63–90 (at 75–76).
33. A. L. Stoler, *Along the Archival Grain: Epistemic Anxieties and Colonial Common Sense* (Princeton, NJ: Princeton University Press, 2009); M. Fuentes, *Dispossessed Lives: Enslaved Women, Violence, and the Archive* (Philadelphia: University of Pennsylvania Press, 2016).
34. See www.devoirdememoire.ht.

CHAPTER 27

FINDING WOMEN IN THE ARCHIVES OF 1381

SYLVIA FEDERICO

Dear Sylvia (if I may),
   I would of course be delighted to meet you and hear more about your project. Please do come round to my rooms for sherry at five o'clock once you are settled. The porter will show you in.
   Yours with best wishes,
   Barrie

In the spring of 1996, I was awarded a doctoral research grant to study women's participation in the 'Great Rising of 1381', also known as the 'Peasants' Revolt'. Before I left for England, I had written to R. B. Dobson, Professor and Chair of Medieval History at Cambridge, and esteemed author of *The Peasants' Revolt of 1381*, which is still the crucial collection and examination of contemporary narratives of the Great Rising.[1] This episode in English history witnessed scores of thousands of people in urban and rural localities across the country rising in apparently coordinated violent protests concentrated over the course of several days in June of 1381. The causes of the revolt are still debated, though some consensus exists around a confluence of factors including increased expectations for economic agency on the part of labouring and mercantile classes in the wake of the population crash caused by the Black Death, coupled with increasingly onerous taxation and uncustomary and obnoxious collection methods, along with an underlying xenophobia and suspicion of foreigners. The aims and objectives of the rebels are understood to be multiple and sometimes conflicting, ranging from calls to an end to serfdom to more diffuse reformist energies such as fairer wage structures or more advantageous market regulations for specific constituencies. Some of the hallmark methods or signs of the rebellion included the burning of legal documents pertaining to labour and tenancy, the murdering of royal and clerical agents deemed enemies to the 'true commons', the carrying of banners of St George, and the breaking of prisons. While local outbreaks of the rebellion occurred in towns as far flung as

Beverley and York, much of the attention of contemporary chroniclers and modern scholars turns on the large assemblies of rebels especially from Kent and Essex who marched to London and, while in the city, killed scores of Flemings in the streets, killed the Archbishop of Canterbury, and held a series of dramatic parlays with the young Richard II. Declaring themselves his 'true men', these groups demanded measures of reform in the king's government along with charters of manumission for themselves. Under duress, the king granted these charters, causing most of the rebels to disperse and return to their homes; the rebellion was vigorously squashed in its aftermath as royal agents pursued and held accountable the ringleaders and local juries were sworn to determine guilt and exact justice. As this brief summary has reflected, the revolt swept up people from all walks of life, from chief justices, royal ministers, and the king himself through landless serfs and itinerant preachers, merchants, knights, labourers, and monks—everyone at every level of society was affected. The interpretive crisis engendered by the revolt was similarly multivocal: chroniclers and poets weighed in, and sometimes revised existing work, to make sense of what happened, and the bureaucratic legal machine recorded hundreds of thousands of pages of accusation and retribution.

Surprisingly, while its complex social component had been extensively analysed, largely in two main phases of critical attention in the 1890s and the 1980s, in 1996 no one had yet analysed the rebellion through the lens of gender: even large demographic studies neglected to consider the roles of women in 1381.[2] Surely, I reasoned, if every single type of person was involved, women should have been part of that demographic sample—it seemed shocking to me that such an oversight had persisted in the scholarship for so long. My grant, which was funded by Indiana University's Research University and Graduate School, covered my residency in London for eight weeks, affording me time to examine the judicial records of the rising housed at the Public Record Office then located in Chancery Lane. I was also to consult the local documents housed at Cambridge University Library, which has significant holdings of manorial records. My hope was to find documentation proving the widespread participation of women in the revolt. Certain hints in the secondary reading supported my hypothesis, including symbolic representations of female rebels in works by Chaucer and Gower along with the mention of a handful of women's names in some of the published records. Indeed, one of the most iconic acts of the revolt, cited in most every major study from Edgar Powell's in 1896 through Steven Justice's in 1994, is that attributed to a woman named Margery Starre, who—during the disturbances in Cambridge—tossed the ashes of burnt documents to the winds, shouting 'away with the learning of clerks! away with it!'.[3] In my mind's eye, Margery was a feminist beacon, her anti-authoritarianism inspiring me to challenge those modern 'clerks' (contemporary academics) who had failed to account for her presence in history.

I didn't really expect a reply from Dobson and was floored to receive back the invitation from 'Barrie' to speak in person. I was also slightly flummoxed (sherry?—I mean of course I'd heard of it—but rooms? porter?). As well versed as I was in all the usual subject positions of a doctoral student in the US, nothing prepared me for the customs and attitudes I would encounter in the various micro climates of UK academia and affiliated research enterprises. In many respects, I now see in hindsight, it was only because I was so radically outside of this habitus, and was myself such a pre-interpreted phenomenon in relation to its modes of analysis, that I was able to stumble around within it with any degree of success. My palaeographical training thus far had been limited to work with facsimiles and the occasional examination of the deluxe manuscripts held at the Lilly Library in Bloomington, where the books allowed for inspection were precious and the rules about touching were strict. This would be my first trip to England and the first time I would confront a set of medieval working documents.

My first day on the case was a complete disaster: the 'EDC7/17' CUL classmarks I had identified in my secondary reading as possibly containing useful descriptions of the rising in Lakenheath turned out to be a set of shoeboxes (boot sized) stuffed with unruly rolls of double-sided vellum court records. I had no idea how to begin. Each roll was tied with a knotted string, with no index or other identifying scheme I could find. The only way in was to randomly select and unroll each little bundle and see what was there, a noisy and messy manoeuvre accompanied by some anxiety: the rolls felt very brittle—was I doing it the right way? what if they tore or snapped? The reading room was deathly quiet. Once I'd gingerly wrestled a roll into submission on my table, I could make out a good number of men's names and some town names, but everything seemed to be listed haphazardly, without even a chronological order to the entries on a given roll. More disturbingly, even when I found listings from June 1381, nothing looked like the revolt: no banners or burnt documents. Instead, these seemingly haphazard local records described petty crimes such as breaking the assize of ale, selling goods on the wrong day, stealing sheep or gowns, and something I couldn't make out having to do with rabbits (were they stealing them or hiding them?—it was a ridiculous situation, and I felt as conspicuously idiotic with my translation skills as I felt unpractised with the rolls themselves). I committed my first archival foul on this day: setting out to find women, and finding none, I did not bother to record what I was finding. This stubborn blindness—a kind of annoyance with the records for not giving me what I sought, resulting in my not crediting them with what they were offering—as I came to know months later, was not dissimilar to the kinds of wilful myopia that had ignored the evidence of women's participation for so long.

Things were not improved that afternoon by the college porter, who affected to not understand my accent and then squinted at 'Barrie's' signature on the blue aerogram as if I had forged it. The impertinence of myself in even appearing in such a place was palpably beyond his toleration. After a few silent minutes, during which he fumed in his lodge and I stood around pretending to be polite, he eventually declared 'this way, then' and led me through the gate and into the building. We eventually arrived at the great man's 'rooms', an oasis of cushiony chairs, with carpets and piles of books all over the floor and, miraculous at the end of such a day, a little tray with delicate glasses for wine.

I dwell on such minutiae to underscore the difficulties of access to this type of research for scholars who not only do not live nearby the holdings, but for whom other types of soft barriers are an enormous factor. My own experience, even with the privileges attending my class (glossed only in American terms, of course) and race, was often negatively inflected by my age, sex, and nationality. To be a young American woman in this context was to continually present a walking surprise—if not a challenge—to the forms of authority that governed the enterprise; and it was also to attract assumptions and forms of attention specific to those categories. I was never a neutral presence, but rather was often an object of curiosity, and sometimes undisguised hostility—leading to a number of distracting situations that required my management or negotiation of others' expectations before I could be admitted into the space I sought. Archival practice is accustomed to a certain type of scholar; it is a cultural phenomenon, even when experienced as benign, that is 'overdetermined by facts of class, race, gender, sexuality and above all power'.[4]

Dobson and I met for about an hour, during which I told him about my quest to find women in the records. We reviewed the notion, well established in social histories by scholars such as Barron, Bennett, and Hanawalt, that women in the middle ages may seem invisible thanks to their legal identities typically being occluded by their relationships to their fathers or husbands.[5] I would do well to scan for 'uxor' and 'filia', he suggested, when women's proper names were not apparent. We reviewed the classes of documents I intended to search, including the private writs of trespass as well as the royal litigation, and he called to mind not just Margery Starre but in fact several other women whose presence in the rebellion was documented by contemporary narratives, including Katherine Gamen, who prevented Chief Justice John Cavendish's escape from a mob in Lakenheath. While I did not find reference to Gamen on that chaotic first day, I subsequently found her (and two female accomplices) in the King's Bench records in Chancery Lane.[6] Dobson's encouragement was very generous but also very measured: while he agreed that those scholars who had so carefully counted the numbers of smiths and carters who rose up from each town probably did not see the wives and daughters of those men, he was unconvinced that the rising was the women's movement of my imagination. 'Well', he said it very quietly, 'there just might not be anything there.' But then he brightened: 'Doesn't mean it's not worth a look!'

This advice, that one might go and have 'a look' at what is in the archive, as opposed to setting out to find a specific thing, struck me as slightly crazy at the time; precisely because my days were so specially counted (funded and limited), how could I possibly approach the matter so casually? But that's not at all what Dobson meant: he was not advocating a breezy attitude; he was reflecting the most rigorous best practice. One must approach the archive open to seeing what it will yield, reading all of its possibility rather than hunting for elusive prey.

That April and May were especially raw and chilly. I was always on the verge of coming down with a cold, and my rented flat involved pulling the bed down out of the wall each night. I felt in those first couple of sleep-deprived weeks that I would never find what I was looking for. But as I grew more comfortable with what I was doing, and was able not to relax exactly, but to let the records speak (instead of demanding from them the answer to my question), I eventually came to a new understanding about the revolt. The archive may have thwarted my naive intention of finding evidence of an early feminist revolution but granted me an unexpected insight into what 1381 was all about. In 90 per cent of the records I saw, whether involving women or men, the revolt was defined by its concern with small things: sheep and gowns mattered as much as an end to serfdom.

As Andrew Prescott recently writes, archives are both 'intimately linked to the exercise of power' and have the power to 'tell us a great deal about the life of ordinary people'.[7] Truly multivalent in this way, the records have equal potential to uphold the status quo or to utterly subvert it. One way that the archive disappoints is insofar that the judicial records, relentlessly enumerating with great thoroughness of everyday complaints, flatten experience into the formulaic language for criminal cases. But this archival tedium reflects the fact that the revolt itself was often centred on petty violations. Neighbours took advantage of the general unrest to act on long-standing grievances and grudges typically involving the matter of daily routines counted in terms of household goods or livestock. Most people involved in the rising of 1381 were participant via seemingly minor local and domestic actions. While the chronicle accounts paint dramatic pictures of the large theatricality of events in London, most people took the opportunity of the revolt to steal from their neighbours. I couldn't know then that I would not find overwhelming numbers of women rebels in the record. Dobson was right: they simply were not there in the numbers I expected (those scholars weren't that sexist in their historiographical practice). But once I was able to see what was in front of me, I found that the record of the revolt consisted mainly of men and some women behaving badly in ways apparently unrelated to big political ideas. This largely prosaic criminality, I would come to understand, was the nature of the rising of 1381.

If the revolt itself sometimes seemed like the accumulation of thousands of coincidental misdeeds of little political consequence, so also its records often felt like so many pounds of dirty junk. The employees from whom I fetched my documents on Chancery Lane each morning were utterly bored as they thwacked the gigantic rolls down on the counter—just another big load to carry. The King's Bench records have an aesthetic I have since come to prefer to pretty manuscripts: they are yellowed, brittle, and marred by dark spots and holes created by repeated handling, damp, and fire. They are also filthy, conveying hundreds of years of dusty debris, and—as it turned out—extremely irritating to the skin. The undersides of my wrists and fore-arms flushed pink as I crackled the vellum, irritated by them as I contributed to their decay, applying impatient pressure to smooth their curled edges and striping the reading snakes in artful poses all over their bubbled surfaces. No one patrolled the reading room to check if I tore them (I didn't) or if my nose dripped on them. The security guard who made a terrific show of pawing through my pony print purse on the first day—weaponized with lipstick, tampons, and mechanical pencils—smiled me along my way, unsearched, every time after that, his gatekeeping skills having been transferred to his daily request that I 'come have a drink wiff us'. Unlike a museum, the archive is determinedly anti-glamour and anti-precious.

The archive is also hypnotic. KB 9/166/1, for instance, goes on forever, with-out a narrative, drowning in legal formulae abbreviated for efficiency by officials recording the presentments of juries in local hundreds. I spent hours skimming over a hand that at first glance looked to me exactly like a block of uncooked ramen noodles, and equally legible, but which eventually came to resolve itself into utterly predictable patterns. Counting out minims, my Latin just good enough to expand the shorthand common in formulaic legal language, my eye made out a lot of Agneses, Johannas, Margerys, and Phillipas, all of them tagged as either 'uxor' or 'filia'. Some of them were up to no good—stealing, helping to steal, harbouring, or otherwise being part of the rebellion of the commons. They were also frequently described as victims of theft: documents were stolen from wealthy women, pots and pans from the poor. As the weeks went by, and I filled my notebooks with tran-scriptions of repetitive legalese, I committed another archival mistake: when you are bored by your findings you are not reading the right way. Or, to put it another way, the records are boring for a reason.

One of the most common forms in which I witnessed women's names in the royal litigation was as the object of the verbal clause 'rapuit et abduxit': 'raped and abducted'. As I transcribed these many incidents of rape and abduction, I was very aware of the controversy, recently reawakened by Chris Cannon's discovery of a new Chaucer life record, over the meaning of the term 'raptus' in late-fourteenth-century legal history.[8] As several scholars did before him, Cannon reviews the argument that forms of the verb 'rapere' in the later Middle Ages did not refer to rape as we understand it. Instead, 'rape' could mean anything ranging from sexual assault to kidnapping, not to mention the peculiar phenomenon of so-called 'heiress rape' or 'consensual rape', which may have been a strategy for young people to avoid undesir-able matches. While it did often seem that scholars were working very hard to avoid the idea of rape, perhaps to be able to more easily dismiss the idea that Chaucer committed that crime, I must admit I became inured to it myself: such a routinized practice of sexual violence would be in keeping with the 'local grievances' model I had come to appreciate as defining the revolt. It made perfect(ly demented) sense that rape was a common weapon for theft during the breakdown of social order that was the rising of 1381: part of depriving your neighbour of his livelihood, part of exacting revenge for his insult, is to steal and insult in turn. Through the commodified sexuality of a woman's body, one man could take value from another man.[9] Reading the way modern men assumed that medieval men would read, I dully noted 'raped and abducted' over and over again in my notebook, the occurrence so common that it threatened to become normal, equivalent in meaning to the other recurring small crimes that characterized the revolt.

But rape was not a form of commerce, even in the middle ages. Rape then, as now, was an assertion of power—physical, psychological, and social—and was perceived as such in the late 1300s. In fact, according to one of the major chroniclers, one of the causes of the rising of 1381 was the ritual sexual humiliation of young women in the countryside by tax collectors seeking to address the widespread evasion of the third poll tax. Henry Knighton, whose account is valued by historians for the inclusion of many details not found in other of the contemporary narratives, claimed in his Chronicle that the royal commissioner John Leg would

> shamelessly raise young girls' skirts, to discover whether they were corrupted by intercourse with men, and thus ... compel their friends and parents to pay the tax for them, for many would rather choose to pay than to see their daughters so shamefully mistreated.[10]

Such a systematic and public process was perceived by the community as a strategic and invasive disempowerment, and was grievously felt. Why did Knighton include this anecdote? and why did he assert it as a cause of the revolt? surely it was not out of sympathy for the women involved? Prescott articulates the difficulty of answering such questions when he notes that the 'archives are full of the marginalized, excluded and forgotten, but we meet them only through the agency of the officials who write and guard the archive'.[11] In this case, Knighton's account accords with the 'boring' jurors' returns in suggesting that sexually based offenses were part of the fabric of life for women before and during the rebellion—tactics deployed both by the authority figures and those who resisted such figures.

But while John Leg's violation of the young women in the countryside is stated as a cause of the revolt by Knighton, this point has not been taken up in the modern scholarship with any degree of seriousness.[12] It is as if such an accusation does not merit critical attention precisely because of its sexualized, thus wild or aberrant, nature. Women constitute a category that on the one hand is a calculated component of masculine schemes of authority and which on the other hand transcend and terrify those schemes. Or, to put this as Lacan did, '"Woman" is a symptom, a symptom of a man—a construct that fits into the psychic order only as fantasy object'.[13] If the rising of 1381 was not an event in which equal numbers of men and women took violent action, it was one in which women's bodies were understood as contested space through which to assert meaning—however phantasmatic. Chaucer's infamously singular mention of the revolt features women shrilly shrieking, wielding large knives, on the chase; Gower's vision includes a gigantic chicken, pecking her husband on to evil deeds.[14] Women's status in the fantasy life of the late medieval imagination shows them functioning as powerful symbols through which to interpret the social order—whether as outrageous threats to that order, or as sanctified/idealized order itself disrupted by internal or external threats.

Where existing scholarship had neglected to count the actual women who rose up in 1381, it had also dismissed as unimportant the signalling of women's roles in the interpretation of the revolt in its aftermath. Take for example another freakish mention of women's outsized participation, this one recorded by the Westminster chronicler (who, like Knighton, is especially valued because some of his details are not recorded elsewhere). According to this account, the surviving Flemings in London were granted the extraordinary privilege of exacting revenge on the rebels who had murdered their family members:

> The friends of those Flemish dwellers along Thames-side who had been put to death at the hands of the peasant mob were, at their own request, permitted to carry out the punishment of those who had slaughtered their dear ones; and indeed the wives of victims were given authority to behead their husbands' murderers.[15]

The spectacle of Flemish widows beheading Englishmen is the stuff of nightmares—or at least of fiction; this episode seems to have been just too weird, too much to take on board, for scholars trying to make sense of 1381. But, really, how much stranger is it than Chaucer's and Gower's imaginings, or the notion that women were routinely subjected to rape or something hardly to be distinguished from rape?[16]

The results of my study, which were published as 'The Imaginary Society: Women in 1381', *Journal of British Studies* 40.2 (2001), 159–183, concluded very simply that real life historical women played in roles every bit as significant and varied as those played by men. I had set out to find insurrectionists by the thousands; what I found instead were scores of women who participated as rebels and as victims of the rebellion. In this regard, Shannon McSheffrey is right: fewer than one per cent of the rebels on the pardon roll were women.[17] But it is not correct to say that women were absent. Or that the rising of 1381 was a 'men's rebellion'. Where Judith Bennett cautions us to not take individuals as universals, my analysis suggested a collapse of the tidy borders between the symbolic and the historical.[18] Perhaps the relationship between 'weird' or 'strange' imaginative utterances in chronicles and poems and the formulaic peculiarities of the archive is best considered as connective tissue rather than as a mirror, however distorting; one does not reflect reality any more than the other. Women constituted an overdetermined signifier in 1381, as a means of addressing interpretive crisis, as a mechanism through which to think about the theory and practice of order.

Several of the central questions arising from my study still remain: how did women's participation in 1381 change or surprise how we see the revolt? How can we productively gloss the idea of women in the revolt, in relation to the archival traces of that reality and the fantasy of women's roles? How can we productively gloss the themes of concealment, obfuscation, and silence that attend the search for women in the archives?—and how, indeed, to navigate the resistance of archival documents to interpretation? We might correspondingly re-gloss the very terms 'failure' and 'success' insofar as they apply to archival research, given that our findings almost never look like what we set out to seek. As we reach twenty years into the twenty-first century, the academic field has shifted: more women than ever participate as research scholars in the academy (both in the US and the UK), and yet scholarship on the lives of women in the Middle Ages has not correspondingly increased—in part, perhaps, thanks to the shift in contemporary emphasis away from exclusionary definitions of feminism.[19] While such discussions are crucial—including the movement away from longstanding restrictions on identity that have been harmful to many individuals—let us hope that we will not have to wait for agreement on who can be a woman to resume feminist historicist practice.[20] For many people, non-inclusive archival structures and other academic and non-academic barriers constitute insurmountable barriers: it should be the shared mission of experienced researchers not only to demystify the workings of our field but to work to dismantle the notion of its 'mystique' in the first place. If any junior scholar has time to get together a grant proposal, the manorial court records still represent a largely untapped source for research on the revolt in general and for evidence of men's and women's lives during the period. It's certainly worth a look and I'd be happy to help.

FURTHER READING

Jenny Adams and Nancy Mason Bradbury, eds, *Medieval Women and Their Objects* (Ann Arbor: University of Michigan Press, 2017)

Susan Crane, 'The Writing Lesson of 1381', in Barbara Hanawalt, ed., *Chaucer's England* (Minneapolis: University of Minnesota Press, 1992), 201–221

Justine Firnhaber-Baker and Dirk Schoenaers, eds, *The Routledge History Handbook of Medieval Revolt* (London: Routledge, 2016)

Alice Raw, 'Gender and Protest in Late Medieval England, c.1400–c.1532', *English Historical Review* 136 (2021), 1148–1163

Joel Rosenthal, *Social Memory in Late Medieval England: Village Life and Proofs of Age* (New York: Palgrave, 2017)

Hilda L. Smith and Melinda S. Zook, eds, *Generations of Women Historians: Within and Beyond the Academy* (New York: Palgrave, 2018)

NOTES

1. R. B. Dobson, ed., *The Peasants' Revolt of 1381* (London: Macmillan, 1970) and *The Peasants' Revolt of 1381* (London: Macmillan, 1983; 2nd edn).
2. Major studies of the revolt include A. F. Butcher, 'English Urban Society and the Revolt of 1381', in R. H. Hilton and T. H. Aston, eds, *The English Rising of 1381* (Cambridge:

Cambridge University Press, 1984), 84–111; C. Dyer, 'The Social and Economic Background to the Rural Revolt of 1381', in Hilton and Aston, *English Rising of 1381*, 9–42; A. Harding, 'The Revolt Against the Justices', in Hilton and Aston, *English Rising of 1381*, 165–193; R. H. Hilton, *Bond Men Made Free* (London: Routledge, 1973); S. Justice, *Writing and Rebellion* (Berkeley: University of California, 1996); E. A. Powell, *The Rising in East Anglia in 1381* (Cambridge: University of Cambridge, 1896). H. Eiden, 'Joint Action against "Bad" Lordship: The Peasants' Revolt in Essex and Norfolk', *History* 83.269 (1998), 5–30; W. E. Flaherty, 'The Great Rebellion in Kent of 1381 Illustrated from the Public Records', *Archaeologia Cantiana* 3 (1860), 65–96; A. Réville, *Le Soulèvement des travailleurs d'Angleterre en 1381* (Paris: A. Picard, 1898); Dobson, *Peasants' Revolt*. The most significant study to date remains A. Prescott, 'The Judicial Records of the Rising of 1381' (PhD thesis, University of London, 1984), available at https://uk.bl.ethos.319371.

3. London, British Library, Arundel MS 350, fol. 17v.

4. N. Proctor, 'Feminism, Participation and Matrixial Encounters: Towards a Radical, Sustainable Museum (Practice)', in A. Dimitrakaki and L. Perry, eds, *Politics in a Glass Case: Feminism, Exhibition Cultures and Curatorial Transgressions* (Liverpool: Liverpool University, 2003), 53; cited in A. Prescott, 'Tall Tales from the Archive', in J. Jahner, E. Steiner, and E. Tyler, eds, *Medieval Historical Writing: Britain and Ireland, 500–1500* (Cambridge: Cambridge University, 2019), 356–369.

5. C. M. Barron and A. F. Sutton, eds, *Medieval London Widows, 1300–1500* (London: Hambledon, 1994); J. M. Bennett, *Ale, Beer, and Brewsters in England: Women's Work in a Changing World, 1300–1600* (Oxford: Oxford University, 1996) and *Women in the Medieval English Countryside* (New York: Oxford University, 1987); P. J. P. Goldberg, *Women, Work, and Life Cycle in a Medieval Economy* (Oxford: Clarendon, 1992); B. Hanawalt, *Crime and Conflict in English Communities, 1300–1348* (Cambridge, MA: Harvard University Press, 1979); and D. L. Boyd and R. M. Karras, 'The Interrogation of a Male Transvestite Prostitute in Fourteenth Century London', *The GLQ Archive: A Journal of Gay and Lesbian Studies* 1.4 (1995), 459–465.

6. KB 9/166/1 m. 2. Gamen saw Cavendish making for a small boat and craftily set it loose before he could reach it; he was subsequently beheaded by the mob.

7. Prescott, 'Tall Tales'.

8. C. Cannon, '"Raptus" in the Chaumpaigne Release and a Newly Discovered Document Concerning the Life of Geoffrey Chaucer', *Speculum* 68.1 (1993), 74–94.

9. Readers of Chaucer will readily understand this perverse logic from the evidence of the 'Reeve's Tale', in which a student decides to rape a miller's daughter as payback for the miller having stolen his grain. Indeed, while Lee Patterson famously read the 'Miller's Tale' as a possible commentary on the political ethos of 1381, the 'Reeve's Tale' offers itself as a more accurate reflection of the kinds of local violence that characterized most of the revolt. See L. Patterson, *Chaucer and the Subject of History* (Madison: University of Wisconsin, 1991), 244–279; H. Crocker, 'Affective Politics in Chaucer's Reeve's Tale: "Cherl" Masculinity after 1381', *Studies in the Age of Chaucer* 29 (2008 for 2007), 225–258.

10. G. H. Martin, ed. and trans., *Knighton's Chronicle* (Oxford: Clarendon, 1995), 209.

11. Prescott, 'Tall Tales', 356–369.

12. S. Rigby, *English Society in the Later Middle Ages: Class, Status and Gender* (London: Palgrave, 1995), 121, comes closest in noting that a central aspect of

the revolt was its protest against 'the growing intrusion in the life of the local community'.

13. J. Lacan, 'Seminar of 21 January 1975', *Ornicar?*, 3 (1975), 104–110; cited in E. Zakin, 'Psychoanalytic Feminism', in E. N. Zalta, ed., *The Stanford Encyclopedia of Philosophy* (Summer 2011), https://plato.stanford.edu/archives/sum2011/entries/feminism-psychoanalysis.

14. 'Nun's Priest's Tale' (ll. 3375–97) in L. D. Benson, ed., *The Riverside Chaucer* (Boston: Houghton Mifflin, 1987), 260; *Vox Clamantis* (Book I, l. 545), in E. W. Stockton, ed. and trans., *The Major Latin Works of John Gower* (Seattle: University of Washington, 1962), 62.

15. L. C. Hector and B. F. Harvey, ed. and trans., *Westminster Chronicle, 1381–94* (Oxford: Clarendon, 1982), 16–17. For discussion of Flemings in London, see M. Hanrahan, 'Flemings', in P. Brown, *A New Companion to Chaucer* (Hoboken: Wiley Blackwell, 2019), 151–165.

16. As Cannon, '"Raptus"', 88, notes, 'abduction in practice may easily shade over into something that is hardly to be distinguished from sexual assault: both wrongs involve physical coercion, and this coercion even if it involves no overt sexual component may be implicitly threatening in clearly sexual terms'.

17. S. McSheffrey, 'Gendering Popular Medieval Politics: Medieval Riot, State Formation, and the Absence of Women', *History Workshop Journal* 88 (Fall 2019), www.historyworkshop.org.uk/gendering-popular-politics-medieval-riot-state-formation-and-the-absence-of-women.

18. J. M. Bennett, *A Medieval Life: Cecilia Penifader of Brigstock, c. 1295–1344* (New York: McGraw Hill, 1998), 11, notes that Cecilia's life 'is best read as a case study, not a universal example'.

19. Recent scholarship on women's roles in the legal life of late medieval England include the profile of Margery Tawney at www.1381.online/people_and_places/?story_id=10, plus S. Sagui, 'The Hue and Cry in Medieval English Towns', *Historical Research* 87.236 (2014), 179–193, and S. Bardsley, *Venomous Tongues: Speech and Gender in Late Medieval England* (Philadelphia: University of Pennsylvania, 2006). These studies were prefaced by H. Leyser, *Medieval Women: A Social History of Women in England, 450–1500* (London: Phoenix, 1995).

20. See N. Chaddock and B. Hinderliter, eds, *Antagonizing White Feminism: Intersectionality's Critique of Women's Studies and the Academy* (Lanham, Maryland: Lexington Books, 2019), p. xiv, whose contributors seek to 'disrupt the exclusionary basis of monolithic understandings of the feminine'. It is interesting in this context to note that Karras, had she to do it again, would have understood Rykener as a transgender person rather than as 'transvestite male'; see R. M. Karras and T. Linkinen, 'John / Eleanor Rykener Revisited', in L. E. Doggett and D. E. O'Sullivan, eds, *Founding Feminisms in Medieval Studies: Essays in Honor of E. Jane Burns* (Suffolk: Boydell, 2016), 111–122.

CHAPTER 28

ON FAMILY HISTORY
AND ARCHIVES

NORMA CLARKE

It was as a scholar outside the academy that I began research on what was to become my first book, *Ambitious Heights: Writing, Friendship, Love. The Jewsbury Sisters, Felicia Hemans and Jane Welsh Carlyle* (1990).[1] My subjects were a little-known Manchester novelist, Geraldine Jewsbury; her even less well-known sister, Maria Jane Jewsbury; Maria-Jane's friend, the poet Felicia Hemans who lived in Wales; and Jane Carlyle, wife of Thomas Carlyle, both Scottish, who settled in London in the 1830s. These four women were connected by family and friendship links, but they didn't constitute a group and certainly not a literary 'movement'. They had each, separately, attracted a modest amount of academic interest; paradoxically, the best-known was Jane Carlyle, the only one of the four who did not publish in her lifetime but whose letters were so highly valued they appeared in multiple editions after her death. For each of them there were printed sources. It would have been possible to write about them without consulting any archival materials—and in the book that emerged I make no claims to having made discoveries in the archives. However, it seemed to me essential to view surviving documents gathered in local collections and I travelled to Manchester, Liverpool, Edinburgh, the Lake District, and Cardiff for that purpose, as well as checking out manuscripts in the British Museum. The act of travelling lent a purpose to the endeavour; and sitting with a box of miscellaneous, sometimes uncatalogued, papers raised me in my own estimation as a scholar.

Travel was important for another purpose. Richard Holmes made the classic case for following in the footsteps of a literary subject in his 1985 *Footsteps*, a work which blended personal memoir with travel writing and biographical research.[2] Holmes began by tracking Robert Louis Stevenson's journey in the Cevennes, sleeping rough and dealing with donkeys, using his own experiences to enter imaginatively into Stevenson's. Reaching Paris at the time of the 1968 student riots Holmes similarly built on his own observations and feelings to think about William Wordsworth and Mary Wollstonecraft, Romantic-era writers who were in Paris at the time of the French Revolution. Like Holmes, although not intending to put myself in the picture, I needed to see the relevant landscapes. I stood in front of Comely Bank, the Carlyles' first house in Edinburgh, which still survives, and made several tours of the more famous London residence, now a museum, in Cheyne Row; I also took a bus twelve miles east of Edinburgh to Jane Carlyle's childhood home at Haddington and stayed a night at the George Inn, as Mrs Carlyle herself did in middle-age, arriving unannounced and writing about it in her diary. (I re-read the diary as I ate my solitary dinner.) I went to Craigenputtock, the remote farm where the Carlyles lived for six years and where Thomas Carlyle wrote *Sartor Resartus* and his wife compared her bread-making endeavours to Benvenuto Cellini's description of his Perseus. I followed Felicia Hemans from north Wales to Wavertree, just outside Liverpool, and even to Dublin, where she died and was buried in St Ann's church. I had no address in Manchester for the Jewsbury sisters but I did go to Leamington Spa where Maria-Jane Jewsbury spent some time convalescing after illness, and to Tamworth where Geraldine was at school, and where, filed away in the public library, I chanced on a portrait engraving of Maria-Jane which the librarian—astonishingly—let me take away with me on the promise that I would return it. (I did.)

I did not intend to put myself into the book I was writing, but what Holmes so brilliantly exposed was the fantasy of academic distance. The impulse to come closer that drove the travel was much the same impulse that led to the hallowed precincts of the local archive. When I began research on *Ambitious Heights* I did not know what kind of book I wanted to write, nor how to link together the seemingly disparate lives and works of four remarkable women whose literary endeavours encompassed a wide range of genres: Felicia Hemans was a noted poet, Maria Jane Jewsbury an essayist, poet, and novelist, Geraldine Jewsbury a novelist and publisher's reader, and Jane Carlyle a letter writer. The finished product, with its cumbrous title betraying all the uncertainty I felt about how to present it, was an amalgam of the different kinds of research and thinking that had gone into it. I had pursued my quarry through countless books and articles, via boxes of hand-written manuscripts in local and national collections—and conversations with archivists—and also through meditative hours on trains and buses, in hotel rooms, and stalking across countryside, map in hand. The me that did all this is as present in the book, when I re-read it now, as Holmes is in his *Footsteps*.

In the ten years it took me to research and write *Ambitious Heights* I worked as a part-time tutor for the WEA (Workers Educational Association) and as a part-time lecturer in further education colleges; I was a wife and mother; I had an MA, not a PhD, and no university position, and therefore could not lean on a professional identity as an academic. Even though it was an era of burgeoning feminist scholarship, and one in which 'kitchen-table historians' like myself could find support in organizations like History Workshop and Women's History Network, participating in conferences and accepting editorial posts on journals, I felt a pressure to be doing work that was sufficiently mainstream to be academically respectable. Putting myself in after the fashion of Holmes in *Footsteps* was not an option. Nor (horror!) was the idea of writing a family memoir. In the archives I visited in the 1980s I occasionally saw a person or persons (often a middle-aged couple) poring over the registers of births and deaths, following a trail leading to knowledge of the ancestors—a name, a place, a grandfather's occupation. I remember being pleased with myself when I spotted or chatted to any of these family historians: they were strictly amateur; I was a professional doing 'real' research—research that had nothing to do with me. The distinction between professional and amateur was absolute and comforting, like the distinction between public and private, or male and female.

Almost four decades and several books later, I began to assemble notes and old diary entries for what I planned would be a family memoir. In the intervening years definitional boundaries and absolute categories such as public and private had to a large extent dissolved. Feminist-led literary studies had re-shaped the curriculum so that women writers like those I wrote about in *Ambitious Heights* were being studied in depth and accorded academic respectability. In some cases the secondary sources on their lives and works, scant when I started, were becoming voluminous. The marginal had entered the mainstream. Entrenched assumptions about what mattered in literature, history and life, and what one might, therefore, seek to discover in the archives, and what exactly those archives were, and where they were to be found, no longer held.

Something analogous had happened to family history. 'Everybody does family history now', Alison Light wrote in the preface to her 2014 *Common People: The History of an English Family*.[3] She pointed out that while genealogy used to belong only to the wealthy, now 'everyone who can use a computer or go to a local records office has a stake in the past'. Those record offices, she noted, had become welcoming places, 'they embrace family history'; and they helped feed information to magazines and television programmes, and the proliferating variety of websites like ancestry.co.uk. However, when Light began investigating her family's past, she quickly discovered that where her family was concerned there was 'scant evidence' of the sort that might have ended up in a record office. The archives contained no letters, diaries, or memoirs, no school reports, shop accounts, character references, mortgage documents, or deeds to land. At home there were no possessions passed down through the generations, no portraits, no family Bible, no heirlooms. Why that should be so was not a hard question to answer—her family was poor; but *that* it was so, that the 'ego-documents' and the objects, the 'relics of our past', did not exist had profound implications for how one thought about that past. The lack of material evidence should not mean that the lived lives of her ancestors were absent from history. And yet, how did one access that history without objects and evidence? And, to turn the question around, what did it mean that history was made up from the records of people who were not poor, and who owned houses and land, or had the leisure and education to write letters and diaries?

Common People is a meditation on all aspects of family history as well as a remarkable, and dogged, act of historical recovery. In the absence of ego-documents with which to construct a narrative of her family's past, Light builds a picture of that past and puts them in it. There is a constant see-saw between public and private: archival records illuminate economic and social movements that may account for some of the scraps of family lore available: for example, the movement of an ancestor from one place to another in search of work. Memory is untrustworthy but not wholly to be disregarded. Light is able to know better than her father how his father came to be in Birmingham: there were opportunities for a bricklayer. And she can guess why he left: the building work dried up. By taking herself to Birmingham and viewing the still-standing house her father remembered, she discovers that she was wrong to doubt his sunny memories of his birthplace; the few details he gave her were indeed as he had remembered them. Bit by bit a texture is created out of documents, objects, memories, conversations, contextual reading, and a certain amount of legwork.

Light's book gave me courage to reach back and honour my childhood resolution to write about my family. I didn't conceive of what I wanted to do as history. I didn't think it had anything to do with books or records let alone archives. Archives and libraries belonged in my professional life. Nor was I interested in genealogy. I was interested in stories, mostly the stories I'd been told by the aunts and uncles who lived close by and who liked to entertain us and each other by recalling their childhood in the slums of Blackfriars and their determination to resist Hitler during the war that ended in 1945, a few years before I was born. I was captivated by their stories and at the same time confounded by my own non-existence at that time. I had thought what I wanted to do was fix these stories in print, and I had, on various occasions over the years, made notes of conversations, kept records of key moments, and sometimes added description that verged on the novelistic: 'Aunt Vi was tall and lean and smoked Senior Service cigarettes while reading the Daily Mirror in the armchair by her gas fire.'

The sense that stories belonged in a place that I didn't—because I hadn't been born—was generalized for me when I studied English literature. Chaucer and Shakespeare were associated with Southwark in South London where I grew up, but they were distanced in time; and none of the modern writers I read portrayed the people and settings I knew. Still, fiction was my daily diet. I wrote my own stories, drawing directly on lived experience, imagining myself a detached observer rather than an involved participant in the family drama that was my invariable subject-matter. It was only once I started seriously writing what was to become the memoir *Not Speaking* that I thought more deeply about questions of genre and my assumptions about the materials I was drawing on.[4] More bluntly: when I asked myself how on earth I thought I was qualified to write about a working-class childhood in South London having read nothing to amplify my own experience on the subject. It was a searching and important question because it made me realise that no such book existed: there was no book to help me write about my South London childhood. If I wanted to read about my own experience I had to write the book myself. Research and reading would help me frame questions and provide context but at the heart of any such work was memory, imagination, observation and—inevitably—personal subjectivity. There was no authority against which to measure whatever I produced, no essential and demonstrable truth in which it could be firmly rooted. Had I been a middle-class child, with a wealth of books recording the experiences of middle-class families by those who belonged in them, I might have taken longer to reach this understanding.

In *Not Speaking* I quote Tolstoy's opening lines of *Anna Karenina*, that happy families are the same while unhappy families are unhappy in different ways. But of course all families, happy or unhappy, are unique in the sense that all individuals are unique. The particularities of most lived lives have been culturally unavailable: fiction filled the gap, universalizing the human condition. I describe mine as a post-war, working-class, South London childhood in order to situate it in a recognizable temporal, geographic, and sociological space; and each of those descriptors has a specific set of meanings and associations for me, some of which I can be sure other readers will share; they can all be sub-divided into categories and researched. But until I reveal the one glaring particular that gave its character to *my* post-war, working class, South London family no reader will guess it from those descriptors.

My mother was among a small number of Greek women who married British servicemen and came, as war-brides, immigrants, to live in Britain. Ours was a household in which at least two distinct cultures prevailed and two languages could be heard, one of them foreign and understood only by the person who spoke it. My father, Bill, a dockside labourer's son, had been in a unit of the British army posted to Athens early in 1945. He spoke no Greek. My mother, Rena, was in her teens when the Germans, Italians, and Austrians occupied Greece after the Germans invaded in 1941; she spoke a little German and Italian, but no English. By 1945 when civil war broke out and, as she put it, 'the Greeks started shooting each other', she feared there would be no men left to marry. After a short courtship, aided by the translation skills of her elder sister Toni who did speak some English, Rena agreed to marry Bill. He was handsome in his uniform, tanned and confident. She thought he was an officer, which he wasn't—he was a sergeant-major by then; but he had authority, and he'd had a good war. Or, the war had been good for him in the way it was good for some working-class boys who responded well to the camaraderie, physical fitness, sense of hierarchy and order in the army, and who appreciated the chance to travel. Bill, who had joined up shortly before the war, had been in France, at Dunkirk, in Egypt, Italy, and Greece.

Bill's five siblings and their spouses, all living within walking distance of each other, meeting regularly in local pubs, were a clannish and self-mythologizing bunch. They were sharp, smart, resourceful Londoners; they'd endured the Blitz and, except for Vi's husband Joe, had survived the war. They knew who they were and where they belonged and what belonged to them. They liked to have a good time, singing songs like 'Maybe it's because I'm a Londoner', and laughing a lot. The men worked in low-skilled jobs, the women in factories or cafes, or they went out cleaning. None had more than the most elementary education. They supported the post-war Labour government but they were not politically active. They knew little of any country beyond their own and their travels in England hardly amounted to much. What they made of Rena when she came amongst them is almost impossible to say.

I never asked. It was far too delicate a question. I could put together evidence of various kinds and draw tentative conclusions, but what kind of research methods could one trust to convey the complexity of these encounters?

For the first year of their married life Rena and Bill lived with the widowed Vi and her baby, Robert, sharing a small two-bedroomed flat with an outside lavatory and no bathroom. Vi, according to Rena, complained that Rena 'spoiled' Robert by hugging and kissing him. (Rena loved babies.) Rena and Bill moved into a flat next door and Rena started having her own babies, several of whom Vi helped to deliver. There were to be six altogether and Vi, according to Rena, echoed Bill's despair at the announcement of each pregnancy, and blamed Rena: 'Are you trying to break my brother's back?' Rena felt herself to be superior to Bill's family and neighbours. She was beautiful; she dressed well, making many of her own clothes; she was accustomed to a certain kind of male attention that had never been in short supply given the German, Austrian, and Italian soldiers filling the streets of Athens during her young womanhood. How to convey Vi's deadpan Cockney understatement when she told the adult me, without apparent rancour, 'Well, dear, Rena always expected to be first'? How to account for the absolute silence about what was undeniably well-known to the family and the rest of the street: that Rena in her forties took a lover, a younger man, a Cypriot who drove a flash car, and who habitually waited with the engine running while she put on an extra dab of lipstick before running out to meet him?

In *Not Speaking* I wrote about secrets and silences as aspects of family life that most people would understand from their own experience. Deborah Cohen's *Family Secrets: The Things We Tried to Hide* has as its epigraph a quote from J. R. Ackerley's *My Father and Myself*: 'Of my father, my mother, myself, I know in the end practically nothing.'[5] Cohen tells many stories about what families tried to hide in the past and why. Her book is alert to change: what is shocking and shameful in one era, some places, is openly spoken in others: illegitimacy, adoption, disability, domestic violence, incest, homosexuality. These changes can be tracked and written about as part of social history. Ackerley's observation that in the end he knew nothing points us to the more nebulous sphere of entwined personal histories where the hunt for truth is always qualified. My truth is not my sisters' truth and certainly not that of my brothers, nor of the wider family. What astonishes me now is the opposite of secrecy: Rena conducted her liaison openly and the 'normal' structures of domestic life were stretched to accommodate it. But nothing was said, and in that sense it was secret.

I had my own memories to draw on and in her old age Rena enjoyed recalling this period of her life which extended for over twenty years and ended when she was in her sixties and re-discovered God and the Greek Orthodox church. (She had been a pious child.) After Bill died in 2006 I spent more time with her and systematically set out to gather information, able to hear her story as she wanted to tell it without feeling the need to protect my father, and realizing in the process how much the impulse to protect him had governed not only my responses but also those of my siblings, creating in all of us a powerful desire not to know. Unlike Ackerley, I did feel I knew quite a lot about my mother at the end of it, and of myself; and I was struck by how very little I had known before, and how uncurious I'd been. For me, 'family' had always meant Dad's family, the English aunts and uncles and cousins; I didn't think my Greek relatives had anything to do with who I was. Family history, likewise, meant British history. While I retained a residual prejudice against 'family history', I nevertheless viewed history as part of the enterprise. I knew about Charles Booth's survey of the poor in London (my father's grandparents lived in streets marked 'very poor'); and had read *Round about a Pound a Week*, Maud Pember Reeves's study of housewives in Lambeth, adjacent to where my father grew up.[6] I had seen photographs of London slums.

What did I know about modern Greece? It had not been part of the curriculum for me at school or at university and my mother's formal knowledge was extremely limited. I didn't speak or read Greek but that was no excuse: philhellenism was a significant strand in English (middle-class and highbrow) culture. In truth I was wary of precisely that enthusiasm which had always seemed to me to have little to do with the Greek culture I imbibed at second hand. Nevertheless, writers like Patrick Leigh Fermor helped me situate my mother in a history and amongst a set of general characteristics that gave me a perspective other than that of my childhood self; and Mark Mazower's researches on Greece under the Nazis were invaluable.[7] Following trails begun by conversations with my mother I found myself researching less predictable strands: the vicissitudes of the Greek royal family, laws against gambling, prisons (her father was briefly imprisoned for breaking a law against gambling) the fate of Greek Jews under the Nazis, the singers Maria Callas and Sophia Bempo, the film *Never on Sunday*, and the actress Melina Mercouri. I also researched the crisis in Cyprus in the early 1970s which led to a wave of Cypriot emigration to England and especially London. Many Cypriot men like my mother's lover Louki worked as waiters and there was a flourishing gambling culture among them in the back rooms of cafes in Camden Town and Finsbury Park (it was illegal but Rena assured me the police were paid to take no notice). Cypriot men, Louki among them, were also in the forefront of the taxi wars that broke out when unlicensed mini-cab companies started up.

For a decade and a half Rena spent most of her evenings and much of the night at the mini-cab company in Fitrovia that Louki established with his cousin. They ate at Greek restaurants like *Anemos* in Charlotte St and danced in Greek clubs. As grown daughters, my sister and I were sometimes invited along. When I came to write about these years I could describe some aspects of my mother's world from my own observation but the challenge of understanding it—sociologically, intellectually, emotionally, psychologically, historically, culturally—was considerable, and not only because of the language barrier. I constantly thought I should write it up as fiction so as to screen uncomfortable facts. But when one day a fact landed that demanded to be investigated in the usual manner, by consulting official records, what I felt was relief.

My mother told me an anecdote I hadn't previously heard. It concerned a rival girlfriend who accosted them one evening in the street. (There were other girlfriends; Rena's boyfriend was, she admitted, 'a womanizer'.) It had been raining and Rena was carrying an umbrella. A fight ensued. Rena used the umbrella. A policeman broke up the fight, took both women's names and addresses and, in due course, my mother received a summons to present herself at Tower Bridge Magistrate's Court at a certain time on a certain day. ('I hid the letter from your father'.) A court summons meant court records. My mother had a secret criminal past and there would be documentation! I hastened to London Metropolitan Archives.

And so it was that I sat for two days in the archive, doing family history, not looking for a grandmother's date of birth or grandfather's occupation, but for my mother's appearance in the records of the magistrates' court. I had to guess the year—somewhere between 1962 and perhaps 1966. I had to work through the books, running my finger down the pages. Eventually I found it, and I was pleased, although the repetitive banality of the entries had numbed me by then—so many incidents of drunkenness, so much affray, so many abusive men whose wives chose not to press charges. Rena and her rival were each charged with common assault. The magistrate was unimpressed and dismissed the case. He considered both women equally at fault and neither was hurt. It was the last of many cases that morning and he was probably keen to get away to have a decent lunch.

A longer lasting consequence of Rena's affair was a pregnancy that produced her sixth and last child. She managed to hide this fact from my father, too, persuading him that the child was his, a fiction he was more than happy to go along with. It was not until after Bill's death that my youngest sister, who had long suspected the truth, arranged for a DNA test. Amidst the swirl of fear and fantasy, memory and muddle, the evidence provided by the result of the test was a rock: it called everything into question.

Amongst the five siblings there was tremendous resistance to the new truth about ourselves as a family. We didn't founder on it but we struggled in different ways to absorb its meaning. Most striking to me was the frequently expressed sentiment that the revelation wasn't important after all. Nobody queried it as a fact: the result itself was not called into question: our sister's father was not our father. But, the reasoning went, since our father was the only father she'd ever known, and loved dearly, and he loved her, and since she had always thought of him as her father, what difference did it make if he wasn't her father?

There was a certain laziness in this refusal to think harder and allow the newly discovered reality to change our perceptions. My sister had no interest in acting on what she now knew—she was not eager to meet her biological father and make acquaintance with a family of half-siblings—and this enabled us to stay comfortably inside old habits of thought. For our mother, however, the DNA test and its result was a liberation. Now that her past was no longer a secret, now that all her children knew the truth about her youngest child, she was free to talk about Louki and her years with him. She embraced the opportunity with gusto.

Much of my research for *Not Speaking* consisted of extended and repeated conversations with my mother; she was the only source for many of the things I wanted to know. I believed that everything she told me was an expression of her truth, even when I knew it was factually inaccurate. I trusted none of it: she was a great story-teller, and for her the word 'story' translated as 'lies'. A natural sceptic, she was always accusing others of lying. 'Stories', she would say, 'it's all stories, take no notice, nothing but lies.' She lacked empathy and was rarely interested in the other person's point of view, so this dismissal was also a way of maintaining a position at the centre. I understood this, and also how it had functioned within the domestic space, the 'other person' whose view was to be disregarded generally being my father. Rena had a phrase that she often used when she was at odds with her children, or an argument was not going her way. 'You're all for your father', she would say, and it was true that—as the English half of our DNA—it was with our father and his values that we English-born children mostly identified. She continued to use this phrase indiscriminately, along with 'You're just like your father', even when the sardonic reply would come back from her youngest daughter, 'Which one is that then?'

Family history is generally conceived vertically, working backwards through parents and grandparents. This is what Alison Light does in *Common People*. It is not usually conducted horizontally because siblings have their own stories of family, with themselves at the centre; and for the most part adult siblings, no matter how close, do not want their inner lives and private affairs known and disclosed by the writer in their midst. Parents are fair game and grandparents probably safely dead. That siblings have feelings and can answer back exerts a powerful censorship on family memoirists and historians and is another reminder of the inescapable subjectivity of the exercise. What might appear to be common knowledge in common ownership—domestic habits, settings, sayings, experiences—prove to be as singular as the interpretations put on them when written down. My truth is not that of any of my sisters and brothers, although by thinking about our shared past I help them think about their unique experience of it. The act of writing fixes and changes at once; as, even earlier, does the act of questioning, articulating, having conversations.

My experience of researching and writing *Not Speaking* brought home to me very forcibly that when living people are the archive the story cannot be fixed. It may not be the facts that drive the interpretation. Historians know that evidence-gathering involves choices, and not all significant events are documented; they cannot all be reconstructed. Family historians know that memory is partial and selective and responses are subjective. They know, as Deborah Cohen writes, that secrecy is fundamental to family life. But like everything we know, that commonplace, too, must be subject to change. Now that 'Everybody does family history', and everybody has access to information, now that 'everybody' is busy recording their own lives in selfies and Instagrams and Facebook and Twitter (to name the current outlets, which will also change, but the penetration and game-changing qualities of social media will not) the power of secrecy has already diminished. I question whether it ever had more than a limited traction, relevant for certain kinds of families in particular cultures during circumscribed historical periods. Resistance to facts, documented truths, is not the same as a desire for secrecy. It is the manifestation of a desire for something else. In the public realm, recent years have made all of us aware that resistance to well-attested, documented facts extends beyond the family, beyond private life and into the highest spheres of government. This too may not be a new truth but a new understanding of how we shape truths and therefore how we shape history.

FURTHER READING

Family memoirs and 'untold' or 'forgotten' histories have mushroomed in recent years. The following is a selection of some that have most interested me.

Alison Bechdel, *Fun Home: A Family Tragicomic* (London: Jonathan Cape, 2006)
Michael Collins, *The Likes of Us: A Biography of the White Working Class* (London: Granta, 2004)
Robert Elms, *London Made Us: A Memoir of a Shape-Shifting City* (Edinburgh: Canongate, 2019)
Bernadine Evaristo, *Girl, Woman, Other* (London: Penguin, 2019)
Miranda Kauffman, *Black Tudors: The Untold Story* (London: Oneworld, 2018)
Darren McGarvey, *Poverty Safari: Understanding the Anger of Britain's Underclass* (London: Picador, 2018)
David Olusoga, *Black and British: A Forgotten History* (London: Pan, 2016)
Carolyn Steedman, *Landscape for a Good Woman* (London: Virago, 1986)
Barbara Taylor, *The Last Asylum: A Memoir of Madness in Our Times* (London: Penguin, 2014)

NOTES

1. N. Clarke, *Ambitious Heights: Writing, Friendship, Love, The Jewsbury Sisters, Felicia Hemans and Jane Carlyle* (London: Routledge, 1990).
2. R. Holmes, *Footsteps, Adventures of a Romantic Biographer* (London: Hodder & Stoughton, 1985).
3. A. Light, *Common People: The History of an English Family* (London: Fig Tree, 2014).
4. N. Clarke, *Not Speaking* (London: Unbound, 2019).
5. D. Cohen, *Family Secrets: The Things We Tried to Hide* (London: Viking, 2013); J. R. Ackerley, *My Father and Myself* (London: Penguin, 1971).
6. C. Booth, *Life and Labour of the People in London* (booth.lse.ac.uk); M. P. Reeves, *Round about a Pound a Week* (London: Virago, 1979).
7. P. L. Fermor, *Travels in Northern Greece* (London: John Murray, 1966); M. Mazower, *Inside Hitler's Greece: The Experience of Occupation, 1941–44* (New Haven: Yale University Press, 1993).

CHAPTER 29

AN ARTIST UNPACKS THE ARCHIVES

RUTH MACLENNAN

Institutions; Performing Bodies and Documents; Buildings and Other Containers

My first experience of institutional archives was when I was Leverhulme artist-in-residence in the archives of the British Library of Political and Economic Science, at the London School of Economics.[1] LSE was a fascinating place to think about potential roles for artists in society, in a critical relation to powerful institutions. At LSE I wanted to develop a way of working within, yet not as a member of, the institution, and to use LSE as a stage, a film set, and a meeting place. LSE famously influenced Tony Blair's New Labour, in full swing in 2001. I hoped to learn about and reflect on the ideas and systems that animated LSE. The archives were an ideal base, belonging to the institution but able to take a long view, as well as holding collections that contained the seeds of the ideas that LSE and the Blairite vision of Britain encapsulated.

The archivists allowed me to browse the stacks as if I'd been an employee, but without any set tasks. They were trusting and generous and eager to help. I studied and learned about archiving systems, principles and practices, and the archive as an ur-system of memory retrieval, containing other memory retrieval systems. Archives represent an institution but can push against it too, resisting pressure to conform to a corporate message by keeping records of messy truths and awkward beginnings (the meanings of this are addressed expertly in other chapters in this book). Archives quietly give licence to be unruly because we trust the rules that govern their structure and maintenance. I made a poster of an archival mis-en-abîme—*Memory Retrieval Systems*, a Venn diagram of different kinds of memory retrieval system.

In my video, *The Gatekeepers*, the attention for once is on those who make archives accessible, the self-styled 'gatekeepers'. The archivists speak straight to the

Figure 29.1 *Memory Retrieval Systems* poster, designed by Kapitza, 2001 © Ruth Maclennan.

Figure 29.2 *The Gatekeepers*, single channel video, 14'34", 2001 (installation view, Lewis Glucksman Gallery, 2014) © Ruth Maclennan.

camera about their interests and motivations, performing their roles publicly. My questions and their repetitions are removed. The editing is obtrusive, but logical, recollecting their editing of an archive. There are echoes of Andy Warhol's *Screen Tests*. Equally important, is a film tradition documenting people performing overlooked but vital jobs (Michelangelo Antonioni's *Sanitation Department*, 1948, Anne Tallentire's films and others). Here it is invisible intellectual labour, not street cleaning.

I made three other video works in response to the LSE and its archive collections: *Dialogue #3 (That's not for me to say)* (2002), *Calling All Workers* (2004–5), and *Dialogue #4 (What is your culture?)* (2004). The archives for me were a store of images and stories that I could (re)use to speak to the present.

The National Institute of Industrial Psychology was founded after the First World War, funded by among others the confectioners Cadbury and Rowntree. The NIIP conducted studies in ergonomics and productivity through time and motion studies in English factories and South African mines. It also developed the Myers-Briggs psychology test and IQ tests. Its experiments and research are documented in photographs, diagrams, printed, and other materials, all located in the LSE archives. In the 1930s the NIIP conducted perhaps the first successful market research experiment using focus groups to design the Black Magic chocolate box. In order to avoid

Figure 29.3 *Calling all workers*, single channel video, 10'52", 2004, video still © Ruth Maclennan.

conflicts of interest and commercial rivalry between its sponsors, the NIIP abandoned market research after the Black Magic experience, but the black cat was out of the bag. This spelt the downfall of the NIIP.[2] The NIIP archive is evidence of at least one important precursor of the by then (2001) ubiquitous spread of management consultancy, focus groups, and market research, and scientific research models applied to the humanities, arts, and social sciences. The archive also holds early visual materials relating to theories of performance and productivity in the workplace.

The Director's dining room was a wood panelled cage, out of place inside the 1960s block next to the LSE staff canteen. I chose it as the set for *Dialogue #3 (That's not for me to say)*. A man in a suit paces this cage with its shiny table, funereal flower arrangement, and empty wine glasses, rehearsing a speech to an unseen audience. Business euphemisms pile up around an ominous unspecified economic situation. 'Public opinion has reached a crescendo' and other hyperbole reveal the hollowness of the language, and the constraints it puts on those who use it. Somehow emotions still manage to bubble up. The character is the luckless inheritor of the efforts of the NIIP, the Myers-Briggs-testing corporate everyman, who might be a 'leader' or a

Figure 29.4 *Dialogue #3 (That's not for me to say)*, single channel video, 11'58", 2002, video still © Ruth Maclennan.

'team-player', given half a chance. His corrosive self-censorship and performance of efficiency attempt to distract from what Richard Sennett in a lecture called 'the spectre of uselessness' that hangs around so many white-collar workers. I would make two more film 'dialogues' where the camera and future audience are the interlocutor.

The first photograph shows women outside the Rowntree factory in 1933, from the NIIP archive. The second, also from 1933, in the Beatrice and Sydney Webb archive, is from a photo album that was given to the Webbs when they visited Leningrad in 1933. It shows women being led through similar exercises in a shop in Leningrad. These photographs punctured the glossy surfaces of the corporate interiors that LSE's ones mimicked: the Foster library with its open-plan crowd choreography and its new glass atrium. What was happening to workers' bodies now? 1930s capitalist Britain and Stalinist Russia shared the Taylorist ideas about the worker's body as part of the industrial machine. Training healthy bodies would produce productive workers, and it was the bosses' responsibility to enforce this. Now exercise has been privatized, office workers' labour appears dematerialized, and it is the responsibility of workers to exercise at their own expense in their own time.

(a)  (b)

Figure 29.5a and 29.5b Photograph from Beatrice and Sydney Webb Archive and National Institute for Industrial Psychology Archives, London School of Economics (reproduced with permission).

The idea of mechanized bodies at the mercy of or reduced to machines is associated with World War One and the Ford Model T Factory. These ideas found their way into modern dance, in the mechanical gestures of the revolutionary theatre of Meyerhold and Mayakovsky, Fernand Léger's *Ballet Mécanique* and in Charlie Chaplin's 1936 film *Modern Times*. The production line and its imposition on workers' bodies is a founding trope of Modernism in both communist and capitalist countries. Both photographs were promotional: the first documented and promoted the work of the NIIP (for potential clients and stakeholders) and the second, the Stalinist regime of the USSR (to foreign sympathizers). Different politics, almost identical ideologies. In both, women are the subjects, either because they weren't unionized (at Rowntree), or because women in the USSR tended to work in shops.[3]

Calling All Workers transposes these ideas, as they appear in the archival photographs, into the workplace today. The film takes its name from an anthem by Eric Coates played daily on BBC radio in 1940, to galvanize the home front during the war. To make the film, volunteers took part in a group exercise class that I devised with choreographer Susanne Thomas (of Seven Sisters Group). Drawing on references to calisthenics, Busby Berkeley films, army training videos, modern dance, Tai Chi, and movements gleaned from contemporary office life, the video reenacts notions of the 'mass ornament' (Siegfried Kracauer).[4] The soundtrack, composed by Quentin Thomas, uses office and factory sounds, Eric Coates' music, and contemporary hip hop beats. I shot the film with four cameras at LSE, in its new student services reception area, transposing the action into the period of surveillance capitalism. The viewpoints mimic surveillance cameras and point to the constant observation and measuring of workers' performance—in many different lines of work, including the knowledge economy where it is not always immediately apparent. LSE is a social science

Figure 29.6 *Calling all workers*, single channel video, 10'52", 2004 © Ruth Maclennan.

university, just the place to study the history and observe the deployment of social engineering.

The film is another instance of performing the archive. The photographs, and the filmed exercises, could be read as coercive and oppressive, but the film's multiple references and imperfect performances keep the readings open. The viewer witnesses pleasure in the performance, emotion and rebellion, within the confines of the corporate environment.

A few months later I was approached by a curator to propose a new work inspired by the archives of the scientists who discovered the structure of DNA, for an exhibition at the Wellcome Trust, 'Four Plus: Writing DNA'. Despite my efforts with the Rosalind Franklin archive in Cambridge, and Maurice Wilkins speaking at length on the British Library Sound Server, the archives didn't speak to me. What I remembered of genetics I had learned from television. Television connected 1953 when Watson and Crick made the first model of the Double Helix to today's genetic sequencing and cloning. *Tomorrow's World, Horizon*, etc.—I would research the television archive, from early live television preserved on film, up to contemporary digital broadcasts. I would look for forgotten stories, overlooked patterns and obsessions among the grand narratives. I watched programmes on VHS tapes in the

Wellcome archives, and once the BBC had given me permission I transferred and digitized masters on film and tapes of different vintages. This materiality together with my non-linear digital editing reflected the processes being discussed and illustrated in the footage: recombining DNA, editing genes. My film, *We Saw It—Like a Flash*, shows how television and genetics developed and together helped shape popular understandings of science over fifty years.[5] It charts the transformation of visual representations and metaphors of the gene, from the model of the Double Helix to Dolly the sheep and computers sequencing genomes. The film's clips together show how conventional yet powerful tropes of science were polished and performed for television: the Eureka moment, the evil or innocent scientific genius, the positivism of scientific progress, personal stories versus the 'objective' truth, the drama of a race to a discovery. All these and more charted both the evolution of television and of genetics.[6] I did not understand all this at once. It was through endlessly watching, deconstructing, and reassembling material from different times that I came to appreciate the inextricable relations between the craft, ideology, and politics of television making.

The UK National Archives is located across two buildings in Kew. The artist Uriel Orlow and I browsed the catalogue allowing free association to guide our search.

Figure 29.7 *We Saw It—Like a Flash*, single channel video projection, 46'52", 2003–2005 (footage ©BBC).

During that first visit, we were shown the electronic 'telelift' which delivered boxes with documents from the storeroom to the reading rooms.[7] We decided to replace a box with two cameras, pointing forwards and backwards, and to send them along the entire length of the track in a figure of eight. The resulting one-hour long film loop *Satellite Contact* has been exhibited several times on two screens in different configurations.[8]

Satellite Contact was a film that made itself once we'd set it in motion. Mondrian-striped markings on white walls give way to silver space-age tunnels, to copper pipes, to darkened storeroom shelves, to bustling reading rooms, to shadowy in-between spaces with glitches and glimpses of adjacent human worlds. The analogue, mechanical journey taken by documents is a reminder that the digital too always has a material support however disembodied it seems, however much we disavow the processes, and resources, that make data, text, sounds, and images appear and reappear again and again. *Satellite Contact* seems like a precursor to or warning of the many digital archives generated by non-human processes, by algorithms or automated functions, that somewhere somehow have to be accommodated on this planet, for humans to then make sense of, and use. The film methodically navigates the physical, architectural environment of the archives, bringing it to light as a heterogeneous evolving ecosystem. Giving up the camera to the lift system was a way of capturing a non-human perspective.

Figure 29.8 *Satellite Contact*, with Uriel Orlow, synchronized two channel video projection 1h 3'39" © Ruth Maclennan and Uriel Orlow.

Figure 29.9 *Capital*, single channel video, 16'54", 2007 production still © Ruth Maclennan.

The buildings of the National Archive are deliberately approachable. They embody democratic accountability. An image search for national archives brings up classical buildings, symbols of authority and order, and quite a few new statement buildings by famous architects, projecting national pride. In Astana, the capital of Kazakhstan since 1997, temporarily renamed Nur-Sultan after the outgoing president Nursultan Nazarbayev, the archives building is a giant mosaic-inlaid egg. Its shiny impenetrable surface stands out on the city skyline in the desert landscape of my film *Capital*. The archive has few visitors. I was told there was nothing much in the building and that the archives had been sent somewhere outside the city. *Capital* conjures coexisting parallel cities lived in by different sections of the population, who each inhabit their own world. It speaks of the dangers of trying to blot out the city's past. It isn't only about Astana, but could easily stand in for other twenty-first century cities. Wandering through the streets of Astana, filming whatever caught my eye, I captured a vanishing city, and some of the lives vanishing with it.[9]

Leaving Buildings Behind; Bookworks; Archives in the Landscape and City; an Archival Principle

Around the same time as *Satellite Contact*, Uriel and I conceived and wrote the bookwork, *Re: the Archive, the Image, and the Very Dead Sheep*. Both works were a commission from the School of Advanced Study and the National Archives, initiated and enthusiastically supported by Professor Derek Keene of the Institute of Historical Research, and launched at the conference 'Unleashing the Archive' at the School of Advanced Study. After filming in the National Archives, Uriel and I left London to go on holiday and continued our conversation by correspondence. I travelled to Caithness in the Highlands of Scotland. I drew inspiration from the ruins and Pictish remains in the landscape, from local newspapers, and the activities, conversations, and books that animated my days—and most of all from bouncing ideas back and forth with Uriel, honing our idea of the archival principle. The book was the point where we took the idea of the archive out of the institutional frame and tried reading, seeing, interpreting the archival in the familiar urban and rural landscapes of our childhoods.

This silver suitcase was also about seeing what happens when ideas and art travel. In this photograph, the suitcase is a sculpture on a plinth in an exhibition of ambiguous objects, props, and costumes from performances and films. It also performed in my multi-channel film installation, *Dialogue #5 (It's not your problem)*. The protagonist carries it with him, swings it around his head, lies down next to it in the street. I filmed *Dialogue #5* in Archway for my collaborative, site-based art project Archway Polytechnic.[10] I invited many artists, known as visiting professors, to spend time in Archway to develop a performance, live event, or other artwork, for one of the seven departments of Archway Polytechnic. *Dialogue #5* was presented as an installation in the empty office building it was shot in, as well as exhibited on screens carried around Archway by performers, in a 'promenade video performance'.

On the day of the 'Eagle Document' symposium, I removed the silver suitcase from its plinth in the exhibition, and opened it up. I spread its contents on the floor: flyers, publications, local newspapers featuring the Polytechnic, a rubber stamp,

Figure 29.10 *Re: the Archive, the Image, and the Very Dead Sheep*, with Uriel Orlow London: Double Agents, 2004 © Ruth Maclennan and Uriel Orlow.

Figure 29.11 *Archway Polytechnic in a Suitcase*, installation view in the exhibition, *The Eagle Document*, Stephen Lawrence Gallery, University of Greenwich, 2009 © Ruth Maclennan.

invitations, and other bits and pieces. Into the shiny silver back of the open suitcase, I projected films documenting performances and other works made for the departments of Archway Polytechnic. The works had been performed over an afternoon or evening, leaving no physical trace in the streets. The silver suitcase was, still is, an archive of Archway Polytechnic, a container for the stuff the Polytechnic generated, and a vehicle for thinking about how Archway Polytechnic and its ideas might be understood in new contexts. I travelled with *Archway Polytechnic in a Suitcase* to many other places, and opened it up for talks and screenings. The suitcase is a slippery object, secretive and playful, but also suggests something that can't be contained by a website or a book, but which may be taken anywhere, unpacked, and used again.

Hide was a twelve-hour filmed performance for Archway Polytechnic, broadcast live on the internet. I invited seven guests to join me in an urban hide—a student flat—overlooking Archway tube station. A camera filmed the view out the window, and our conversations were recorded and transmitted over the images. Internet audiences could respond online as the day unfolded. At the end of the day the film was taken down. The event was only viewable live online—there was nothing to see

Figure 29.12 *Dialogue #5 (What is your problem?)*, four channel video installation and performance, 23', photo by Rowan Durrant, 2009–2010 © Ruth Maclennan.

Figure 29.13 *Unpacking Archway Polytechnic in a Suitcase*, performance, *The Eagle Document* symposium, Stephen Lawrence Gallery, University of Greenwich, 2009 © Ruth Maclennan.

Figure 29.14 *Hide*, twelve-hour live online video broadcast, production photograph © Anna Hart, 2010 © Ruth Maclennan.

in Archway, where all the other Polytechnic events of the previous years had taken place. We decided, with Anna Hart the director of AIR who worked with me on all Archway Polytechnic projects, to produce a document of the live event. Why document the live artwork? The conversations had reflected deeply on both the lived moments of the day, and the history of Archway Polytechnic. We wanted to document the day and its conversations in a thoughtful, readable form; to make a new art object from the documentary evidence of a live art work. The book, *Hide*, brings together edited transcriptions of the conversations, images from the film and from Archway Polytechnic's extensive archive. It sits on a shelf next to the suitcase, and inside it.[11]

A Potential Archive; Things that Have Disappeared Still Exist

Among my archival forays were those I made in a foreign landscape of epic proportions. I visited the steppes in Kazakhstan near Almaty to make a film about traditional Kazakh hunting with *berkut* golden eagles. The practice had been suppressed during the Soviet period, seen as elitist and nationalist. The film I ended up making follows the making of my film. I am a character trying to find the story, caught up in competing narratives in this post-colonial environment. *Valley of Castles* is the name of a bleaker, smaller, echoing Grand Canyon. The film is shot by me

Figure 29.15 *Valley of Castles*, single channel video, projection, 19'26", 2007 production photograph © Alexander Ugay © Ruth Maclennan.

and my companions, and finally by a camera attached to a Kazakh *berkut*—a living camera after the robotic cameras in *Satellite Contact*. The hunting tradition, nearly lost, is brought to life in a performance with the cracks showing—the haggling over fees, the choice of vehicle and costume, the tensions and conflicts over what to do. The eagle soars above us, and the landscape is sublime.

The landscape of *Valley of Castles* felt familiar, in the way a filmed landscape can. The Kazakh steppes had been used to film Soviet Westerns. I decided to make a Western-inspired film, which ultimately became *Anarcadia*. The film reveals invisible but still tangible archival traces drawn in the landscape: the histories and fantasies of the Silk Road, the Great Game between the Russian and British empires, the recent Soviet and post-Soviet ruins, and backwards to when pre-history began with horses or stories. Two fictional protagonists, an oil prospector and an archaeologist, search the landscape for signs of what lies beneath. The prospector has something of the gunfighter about him—appearing out of the desert from elsewhere, dressed in a dark shirt and broad-brimmed hat, alluding to Moonstone and to a dark past. He is seeking more than hydrocarbons. The archaeologist is from this place, the unnamed steppes, uprooted by history but determined to reconstruct the past from the traces in the landscape. In *Anarcadia*, as in the book *Re: the Archive, The Image, and the Very Dead Sheep*, the archive survives in ruins, rocks, and markings in the landscape, in things that resist destruction or that can

Figure 29.16 *Valley of Castles*, video still from eagle camera © Ruth Maclennan.

still be felt, or conjured from echoes in the language, in memories, habits, stories, and material remains. *Anarcadia* was inspired by a story about a railway station that was built in the steppes to be a new capital city that was abandoned before the railway lines could be laid. I was told conflicting stories about when and why this happened (from Stolypin's time to Khrushchev's). When I finally found someone who could take me to look for the station, the building had recently been destroyed, the brick reclaimed and used to build a spa on the nearby Kapchagay Reservoir. All that was left were the foundations and a pile of rubble. The conflicting stories, my search, my disappointment, and the physical location itself, gave me the fictional characters and scenario of *Anarcadia*. The film pries open and stretches a moment in time where geological, prehistoric, recent historical time, and future time are all layers of rolling, drifting, morphing sediment in a vertical landscape. The film has many conscious and unconscious inspirations—westerns and spaghetti westerns, the Egyptian desert fathers, Alexander Platonov's *Soul*, Yuri Dombrovsky's *The Faculty of Useless Knowledge*, Patrick White's *Voss*....

In Kazakhstan I turned to institutional archives again. I visited the National Film and Photographic Archives in Almaty. I looked for footage of eagles, and used an excerpt from a documentary to make *Capture*, which juxtaposes the capture of a

Figure 29.17 *Anarcadia*, single channel HD video, projection, 35', 2010–2011 video still © Ruth Maclennan.

golden eagle in a net, and scenes of hunting with it, with footage I shot from the *berkut*. Later, I searched for the destroyed railway station with its missing history in the archives. I didn't find it, but found photographs of similar railway stations in the steppes, and a film of prisoners building the Turksib railway in 1930. The image archive was hugely important for inspiring my imaginings and fabulations but also keeping them attached to historical truth. I used the archival photographs and film in the *Anarcadia* exhibitions.[12]

Figure 29.18 *Capture* synchronized two channel video projection, 3'16", 2007 © Ruth Maclennan.

Figure 29.19 *The Railway Workers*, series of framed anonymous photographs from the Documentary Film and Audio Archive of Kazakhstan, 1939–1961 (reproduced with permission).

Data Becoming Story: Documenting Disappearance

In the exhibition, *The Faces They Have Vanished*, four columns of blue vinyl text are stuck on the wall. The columns list all the names of the Crimean Tartar villages that were destroyed and wiped off the map beginning in 1944. Some of them were replaced by Russian villages, while others disappeared as if they'd never existed. *The Faces They Have Vanished* also includes a film, *Theodosia*, a series of framed photographs and a pile of large pebbles on the floor. *Theodosia* opens with a man's voice telling the story of a pilot falling out of a burning plane in 1944 over the Crimean steppe. It is told from the point of view of a Tartar, whose ancestor saved the pilot. The story is based on the artist Joseph Beuys's self-mythologizing tale of having been rescued by Crimean Tartars. I figured out that his alleged plane crash would have taken place two months before the entire Crimean Tartar population was exiled to Central Asia by Stalin, who accused them of collaborating with the Nazi invaders. Half of them died before they arrived. The Tartars were later exonerated by Khrushchev but still not allowed to return until the 1990s. These two stories book-end the film. The film and exhibition show Crimea as a place of desire (for artists, holiday makers, invaders, for the Tartars) and exile (for the poet Ovid). It is a palimpsest of crossed paths and layers of competing histories and cultures with traces in the place names, buildings, and landscapes. I shot the film in 2012.[13]

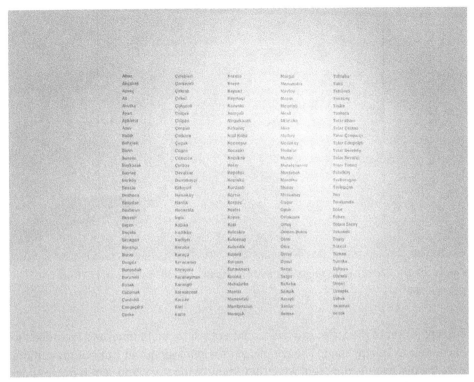

Figure 29.20 *The Faces They Have Vanished*, wall text, installation at Institute of Contemporary Interdisciplinary Arts (ICIA), University of Bath, 2013 © Ruth Maclennan.

I put together the exhibition at the Institute for Contemporary Interdisciplinary Arts in Bath in autumn 2013, a week or so before the Maidan uprising in Kiev, and a few months before Russia's annexation of Crimea. The film now seems prophetic as well as a document of a particular moment.[14]

The Archive as Dungeon: Where Documents Go to Die

In my film *Call of North*, shot near the Arctic Circle in Russian Karelia, a retired couple show me an old photograph they keep in their house in the abandoned village of Keret, where they spend summers tending their vegetable garden. The photo shows a group of men from the village, including the woman's grandfather whom she points out, and a boy. All of them, I am told, except for the child, were shot at Sandermokh, as 'enemies of the people', in 1937. They don't know any of the names except her grandfather's. I asked whether they had contacted or researched the local archives or considered giving the photo to them. They said, 'never! We'd never see the photograph again. Who knows what would happen to it?' The photo was a talisman, all that was left of those people, nearly forgotten, whose village was also on the way to extinction. The archives reflected the couple's experience of the centralized,

Figure 29.21 *Call of North*, single channel HD video, 25', 2015 video still © Ruth Maclennan.

corrupt power of the State, and they couldn't trust them. I filmed and recorded our encounter as it happened. The couple put the photograph in front of my camera, gave it a place in my film, told what they knew of the story, and sent it out to speak in the world. The film here takes the place of an archive. Just as an anthropologist is aware of affecting the places she studies, I am aware and careful of my camera's effect on a situation. I feel the responsibility not to twist someone or somewhere else's story, or experiences, or environment, to suit a pre-existing plot. The possibility of a film prompts me to notice, to listen, to feel the rhythms and movements, to focus faraway, close-up, and aside, to follow the drift, the flow, the conversation, to prompt when necessary, but mostly just to listen and record.

What is the role of the artist vis-à-vis the archive? What is the archive for an artist? Perhaps a role for an artist is to collect or collate, to observe, record, listen to, bear witness to, to intuit and interpret the unarchivable? I have felt this need, and the need to follow an associative principle I call archival which allows the thing—the moment, the image, the encounter—to have multiple meanings, and the potential to speak to future audiences.

Afterword: Messing with Time; Archives and Ecologies

It is almost a truism that the digital messes with chronology, with human time and clock time, with the time it takes to think and do, with copies, originals, and fakes. It messes with our perception and experience of time and place, and labour. You can't touch this text, or see my corrections and drafts. They won't be archived (or not retrievably so). Even though a book seems like a familiar, old technology, when I sign it off I'll not be able to predict or watch the text and images circulate through the digital environments of the world. It is hard not to believe and perpetuate the fiction that the digital is immaterial. When it appears out of nowhere (the Cloud, my computer, my phone) it always appears in some form, typeface, colour, on a liquid crystal display or other flat surface, on a solid or flimsy object. The labour, energy, time, space, and materials that the digital partakes of are of this world, consume this world.[15] Digital communications have rapidly become an essential part of human lives, second nature even. The ecological implications are profound, and hard to grasp. The reluctance to do so is akin to, and part of, the widespread and deep disavowal of the costs of fossil fuel capitalism. I mean ecology as described by Félix Guattari in *The Three Ecologies*: environmental, psychological, and social ecologies.[16] I think archives and the archival can help in approaching the ecologies of the digital. Archives and archivists have a down to earth view of the digital—information is generated and stored somewhere, on some substrate, uses resources, and needs to be retrievable. The future of these structures and the future instability of ecosystems are intimately intertwined.

> Temperatures are rising. Storms are more frequent and deadlier. People and other animals are on the move, forced to flee or seek new homes to adapt to. Crops are drying out before they have matured and can be harvested. This has happened before, but the scale is new. Wilderness is disappearing. The wild still does exist and we need to preserve it—leave it alone—if humans want to know it in the future.[17]

Think for a moment of an ecosystem as a peculiar kind of self-organizing archive— a collection of interconnected things rubbing along together, reliant on each other, connected with other organisms and systems, adapting to changing environmental conditions, or dying. This wild archive (that might well be touched by humans but behaves according to non-human rules) has a history too. Recognizing and appreciating the unruly, unpredictable, historical instances of natural adaptations can help us understand how to thrive in turbulent times. Ironically perhaps, strict protection rules—human laws and treaties—are needed to enable these wild archives to survive. Marine Protected Areas for research and conservation for example. Archiving the wild isn't quite what I mean. The seed vault in Svalbard cannot contain all the conditions that will enable the seeds at some future date to germinate and produce crops and reproduce the ecosystems they came from. It is useful perhaps, but won't save us.

I believe the idea of archives and the experience of archiving are useful, hopeful, full of potential because of the attention they give to individual things, objects, their meanings, conditions of creation, provenance, family, and how they relate to other stuff in the archive. The objects may change, but the principles could still apply. Informal communities will gather and create the archives they need and want (urban potato growers developing their own seed crop to suit their neighbourhood).

At a time of rapid change and threats to humans' survival, it may be useful to cultivate the archivist's respect and care for things, so they can be retrieved and used at some point in the future. There is an ethical imperative to document and attempt to prevent disappearance—loss, destruction—to speak to future audiences, to the world as it will become. We should archive ecosystems (political, social, environmental, technological) for an unpredictable future. We don't know what will be useful. The archivists among us will be able to organize and care for knowledge from a wide range of sources and geographies: from plants, people and other beings, their communities and ecosystems. This will be evidence, a starting point for future stories, future possibilities, and plans.

Acknowledgements

There are many organizations that have supported my art and research, for which I am extremely grateful. Among these are the Wellcome Trust, Arts Council England, the Leverhulme Trust, The British Council, The Lighthouse Foundation, the Arts and Humanities Research Council, London School of Economics, University of the Arts London and the Royal College of Art. I have many people to thank for their support and inspiration and for the pleasures of working together. I am forever grateful to George Jones, Derek Keene, Alister Warman, and Michael Moss who sadly are no longer with us. Thank you especially to Uriel Orlow and Anna Hart, to Sue Donnelly and the archivists at LSE, Nikolas Rose, Anna Harding, Yulia Sorokina, Steven Bode, Stephen Foster, Zinovy Zinik, Ksenia Gavrilova, Joanna Blair, Natacha Nisic, and the artists of the Crown Letter Project. I cannot mention all the friends, family, and colleagues who have been involved but I am grateful to you all.

FURTHER READING

Jane Calow, Daniel Hinchcliffe, and Laura Mansfield, *Speculative Strategies in Interdisciplinary Arts Practice* (Underwing Press, 2014)

Jane Connarty and Josephine Lanyon, *Ghosting: The Role of the Archive within Contemporary Artists' Film and Video* (Bristol: Picture this Moving Image, 2006)

Ruth Maclennan and Julia Lajus, 'Drift, Capture, Break, and Vanish: Sea Ice in the Soviet Museum of the Arctic', in Klaus Dodds and Sverker Sorlin, eds, *Ice Humanities: Living, Thinking and Working with a Melting World* (Manchester: Manchester University Press, 2022), 168–187

Ruth Maclennan and Uriel Orlow, *Re: The Archive, the Image, and the Very Dead Sheep* (London: Double Agents, Central St Martin, School of Advanced Study, and The National Archives, 2004)

Ruth Maclennan, 'Routes and Paths in Arctic Russia', in Bridget Crone, Sam Nightingale, and Polly Stanton, eds, *Fieldwork for Future Ecologies: Radical Practice for Art and Art-Based Research* (Eindhoven: Onomatopee, 2022), 348–375

Ruth Maclennan, 'We Saw It—Like a Flash', *Mute Magazine* 1.27 (2004), 34

Judy Vaknin, Karyn Stuckey, and Victoria Lane, ed., *All This Stuff: Archiving the Artist* (Faringdon: Libri Publishing, 2013)

NOTES

1. Leverhulme artist-in-residence, 2001–2002. George Jones, Professor of Government at LSE introduced me to Ben Eastop, arts coordinator at LSE who introduced me to Sue Donnelly, head archivist.
2. According to Dr. Geoff Bunn, the first curator of a psychology gallery at the Science Museum in London, who was doing research on the NIIP and told me the story.
3. I am grateful to Geoff Bunn for this insight into why women and employees of the NIIP were the subjects of many of the NIIP's photographs in the LSE collections.
4. S. Kracauer, in Frankfurter Zeitung, 9–10 June 1927
5. R. Maclennan, *We Saw It—Like a Flash*, video, 45 minutes, 2003, Wellcome Collection, London.
6. R. Maclennan, 'We saw it—Like a Flash', feature for *Mute* magazine, # 27, winter 2004
7. The telelift has since been removed.
8. U. Orlow/R. Maclennan, *Satellite Contact*, two-channel video projection, 1 hour loop, 2004.
9. I shot the film, *Capital* in Astana (meaning capital city in Kazakh) in September 2006. The archives building features in the film, as a negative space without content that ignores the city itself which is a palimpsest of three different unacknowledged cities where different workers live their ignored and overlooked existences; https://lux.org.uk/work/capital accessed 28 April 2021.
10. Archway Polytechnic, aka Polytechnical Institute for the Study of the Expanding Field of Radical Urban Life, was a site-based, participatory, and collaborative art project based in Archway, developed while I was Cochemé Fellow at Byam Shaw School of Art, produced with Anna Hart in association with AIR, at Byam Shaw (later absorbed by Central Saint Martins College, University of the Arts London). AiRStudio continues to work independently.
11. A. Hart and R. Maclennan, eds, *Hide* (London: AIR, Central Saint Martins, 2009).
12. S. Bode and N. Ernst, eds, *Anarcadia* (London: John Hansard Gallery/FVU 2011).
13. With the support of a Joanna Drew Travel Award.
14. R. Maclennan, 'The Crimea of Russia's Imagination', *BBC Magazine*, 18 March 2014, www.bbc.co.uk/news/magazine-26610276.
15. H.-J. Pochmann, *The Question Concerning the Sustaining Support of Digital Objects* (MPhil Thesis, Royal College of Art, 2015) http://researchonline.rca.ac.uk/1810/1/Hans-Jo%CC%88rg%20Pochmann%20MPhil%20Thesis.pdf.
16. F. Guattari, *Les Trois Ecologies* (Paris: Gallilée, 1989), trans. I. Pindar and P. Sutton, *The Three Ecologies* (London: Athlone Press, 2000).
17. V. Maris, *La Part Sauvage du Monde* (Paris: Seuil, 2018). The author, a French ecological philosopher, defends the need for nature to be left alone to continue to exist in wildernesses; as opposed to the position of some ecologists who say that there isn't any nature left and we have to make the best of it.

CHAPTER 30

RESPONSE TO 'NARRATORS'

ALAN STEWART

In her landmark 2008 essay 'Venus in Two Acts', Saidiya Hartman recounts a dilemma that she faced when researching and writing her then recent book *Lose Your Mother*, a personal 'journey along the Atlantic slave route'.[1] At one point in *Lose Your Mother*, she tells the horrific story of a slave trader, Captain John Kimber, who beat and tortured a young girl of fifteen until she died; another girl, Venus, also perished on that journey. Hartman quotes, from the parliamentary records in Hansard, the speech that William Wilberforce made against Kimber, adding 'He chose not to speak of Venus, the other dead girl. The pet name licensed debauchery and made it sound agreeable'.[2]

Returning to this passage in her essay, Hartman writes 'I wrote two sentences about Venus ... masking my own silence behind Wilberforce's.... I decided not to write about Venus for reasons different from those I attributed to him. Instead I feared what I might invent, and it would have been a romance'.[3] As she explains, she wanted to tell the story of 'two girls':[4]

> If I could have conjured up more than a name in an indictment, if I could have imagined Venus speaking in her own voice, if I could have detailed the small memories banished from the ledger, then it might have been possible for me to represent the friendship that could have blossomed between two frightened and lonely girls. Shipmates. Then Venus could have beheld her dying friend, whispered comfort in her ear, rocked her with promises, soothed her with 'soon, soon' and wished for her a good return.[5]

But, she realized, such a scene would have been impossible, since 'a slave ship made no allowance for grief': 'in the end I was forced to admit that I wanted to console myself and to escape the slave hold with a vision of something other than the bodies of two girls settling on the floor of the Atlantic'.[6]

At first glance, the five chapters in this section of *Archives: Power, Truth, and Fiction*, appear quite distinct. What does a 1990s American doctoral student pursuing the role of women in the 1381 Peasants' Revolt have to do with the ways in which recent Haitian literature might find its superarchivists in its self-aware editors? Where is the common ground between a British historian researching the lives of her living family, an artist working in the LSE library, and two scholars concerned with the racial injustice and violence of the contemporary US penal system? But as I read the five chapters, I was repeatedly reminded of Hartman's essay—since, in various ways, they all centre the narrator or the storyteller, and they all struggle with what we might call, with some understatement, a troubled attitude to the archive.

For some, that struggle exists in the scholar's personal relationship with the archive. For Sylvia Federico as an American doctoral student hoping to find the traces of women's activism in records of the 1381 Peasants' Revolt, the archive is difficult to access—not simply because of the opaque contents of the documents, but because of the opaque protocols of the Cambridge colleges she has to confront. For Norma Clarke, the struggle is more internal. As a professional historian it seemed to Clarke 'essential to view surviving documents gathered in local collections' to do justice to a project (386). But when she started writing about her own family, in what became the memoir *Not Speaking*, she had to submerge her distaste for 'amateur' historians: 'I didn't think it had anything to do with books or records let alone archives. Archives and libraries belonged in my professional life' (389). For Karina Beras and Jarrett Martin Drake, the situation is more dire: 'Archives, records, and the people who manage them also assist in the perpetuation of this [institutional] violence' (351), and 'the so-called traditional archives of nations, states, and corporations stand as the most political of them all' (355)—'archives, at their best, *sustain* state violence and at their worst *silence* it' (351).

And yet these scholars all find ways of using the archives, often working against the grain. For Ruth Maclennan, 'Archives represent an institution but they push against it too, resisting pressure to conform to a corporate message by keeping records of messy truths and awkward beginnings' (397). Or, in Federico's words, 'the records have equal potential to uphold the status quo or to utterly subvert it' (379). Even Beras and Drake admit an opportunity for archivists to 'encourage the public to use archival records in their custody so that particular narratives escape obsolescence' (344), as part of a reparative, restorative project of 'abolitionist archives'. Others find or create their own archives. While Clarke's research eventually led her to the legal archives, the abiding lesson of writing her memoir was that it 'brought home to me very forcibly that when living people are the archive the story cannot be fixed' (395). And for Rachel Douglas, working in Caribbean and especially Haitian contexts where 'there is a perceived lack of archival records and gap/silences in the official archives' (369), she is forced to move beyond traditional archives to examine the roles of author, editor, and autofictional narrator in recent Caribbean writing. Treating this writing as 'literary archives' (368), Douglas sees 'the far-seeing intratextual editor' of this writing as 'a *superarchivist*', as 'Caribbean self-editors keep a self-fashioning record of all changes ... presenting all the evolutionary stages of the process of their literary creation' (368).

Although she dearly wanted to, Saidiya Hartman ultimately 'chose not to tell a story about Venus' because, she argued, 'to do so would have trespassed the boundaries of the archive', and 'History pledges to be faithful to the limits of fact, evidence, and archive'.[7] Over a decade later, the narrators here are finding their own ways, if not to trespass those boundaries, then at least to push at them—to challenge the limits of fact, evidence, and archive in telling new stories.

NOTES

1. Saidiya Hartman, 'Venus in Two Acts', *Small Axe* 26 (2008), 1–14; Hartman, *Lose Your Mother: A Journey along the Atlantic Slave Route* (New York: Farrar, Straus and Giroux, 2007).
2. Hartman, *Lose Your Mother*, 143.
3. Hartman, 'Venus in Two Acts', 8.
4. Hartman, 'Venus in Two Acts', 2.
5. Hartman, 'Venus in Two Acts', 8.
6. Hartman, 'Venus in Two Acts', 8, 9.
7. Hartman, 'Venus in Two Acts', 9.

PART VI

ERASURES AND EXCLUSION

CHAPTER 31

AMERICA'S SCRAPBOOK

A Reckoning in the Archives

LAE'L HUGHES-WATKINS

Searching for America's Scrapbook

I am not superstitious but perhaps intrigued by strange coincidences and an avid believer in the idea of timing and understanding how a sense of timing impacts my existence, my decisions, my movements; we are all bound to time. In 2018 I was invited overseas to Birmingham in the United Kingdom to give one of the opening keynote addresses for the Discovering Collections Discovering Communities fall conference. This would have been my second time travelling across the pond; my first time was earlier that year to support my husband at a presentation in Malaysia.

I was barely packed for my flight out of New York, which was cheaper than flying out of Cleveland and the tolls that were along the way to JFK airport (if I recall correctly). My keynote address was in chunks in several draft stages in various Word files, waiting for me to put everything that made sense into one seamless document. Instead of staying home to work on my speech and finish packing, which I would have typically done in such a situation, I left with my husband to get car repairs and made my way to a Barnes & Noble to work on my address. As I sat at one of the smaller tables, typing away and trying to figure out if I was going to spend another five dollars on another hot coffee with several shots of espresso, I got a call saying my house was on fire. My initial thought process was to think it was a sick and twisted joke, a neighbour with a morbid sense of humour, but it was the truth. I do not enjoy public attention, especially if I am distraught, but I felt tears welling in the corners of my eyes as a feeling of pain began to grip all my senses. I waited for my husband to pick me up from the café. As we hit the corner of our street we could smell the smoke, the lights from the fire trucks flickering on the windows from nearby houses. As we pulled into the driveway, it was nearly gone; in the darkness of the night, I knew the memories we had begun to build in our home, the family mementos, my grandmother's journals, and perhaps all our family scrapbooks were nothing but fiery ash. While neighbours gathered, sharing their well-wishes and attempt to provide optimism that we too did not perish in the fire, part of us did die in that fire. The erasure of moments in time captured by photographs in some of our scrapbooks that had been passed down through generations was now lost. Images of weddings, birthday parties, summer cookouts, holiday gatherings—smoldering in embers.

Despite a desire to try and pull myself together and complete my keynote, I could not make the words make sense; the paragraphs turned into lines of jumbled letters, my thoughts erratic, and my emotions consuming every corner of my being. I sent an email declining the invitation.

The following year I started a new position at the University of Maryland, and I was re-invited to give an opening keynote at DCDC (Discovering Collections, Discovering Communities) conference, organized by the UK National Archives, Research Libraries UK, and JISC. Weirdly, I felt it was something I was able to re-claim from before the fire and gave me a feeling of solace and joy that was beyond what any other invite might have customarily invoked. The published speech in this chapter is the birth of what came from the ashes of my home.

The archive of my family now includes new gaps. The yellow legal pads that belonged to my maternal grandmother, that entailed her feelings towards her children as they moved, or had their own children, reflections of her evolution, engagements that made her flustered, how she saw the world as black woman in the 1960s, questioning her mothering and how she loved, her hopes—evaporated. The re(membering) of those words, her feelings, may fade/change with time, as we grapple to stitch it all mentally back together; after the fire, the erasure now looms large.[1] Trying to see what is salvageable from the soot-covered boxes, some of the remaining photos are marked with curled edges from the heat of the burn, some are unrecognizable. My fear of what would remain was the same fear that spilled out into the streets during the summer of 2020.

The world once again was on fire; it was not quite the Civil Rights Movement of Martin, nor the coalition birthed under Fred Hampton; it wasn't the same force of the Black Power Movement or the rage against the Vietnam War. The summer of 2020 took us somewhere else; the pandemic continued to snatch lives, the deaths from COVID19 further exacerbated the health disparities in marginalized communities, the demands for justice for Breonna Taylor, Ahmad Arbury, and George Floyd re-ignited calls for a racial reckoning with sustained demonstrations that lasted for months as the fire even washed up on foreign shores with protests in China, England, Rome, to Hong Kong. The erasure of futures, fathers, brothers, sisters, mothers, and daughters, the demand to not be forgotten, the re-writing of narratives—peaceful protests versus the violent dismantling of communities filled our social media feeds, daily news, and Google alerts.

I dare not synthesize the summer of 2020, the last four hundred years, the last couple of months, down into a simple task, but I do say as a Black Woman, 'I just want to be seen as a human being', a human being who can go for a run and not be murdered, that can go into her own home and sleep without being killed, a human being who can go to the local bodega and not lose their life in 8 minutes and 46 seconds. I want to be seen as a human being whose bones and spirit can rest in peace and not on the shelves of ivy league institutions.

We are all bound by time, but truth continues to waiver; what will the archive say about this moment? Will the American Scrapbook finally concede to truth and show the full humanity and complexities of Black life, our yearning to be seen as rightfully belonging on the journey to a genuinely democratic state despite the continuous blatant efforts to deny the right of passage? Can the US and other nations stop oppression through legislation, or State violence, the silencing of histories, the attempt to inflict systematic amnesia regarding the contributions of the African Diaspora to the evolution of the United States and beyond. This speech is a call to archivists/memory workers, especially those that work in spaces that suffer from the inequitable distribution of truth-telling about the histories, the afterlives of marginalized communities. May these words compel you to re-build and re-imagine something new, something just, from what remains from the Fire This Time.[2]

A Reckoning in the Archives

I want to begin in metaphor and lay before you a vision of America's scrapbook.[3,4] And before I go further, I would like to concede that this metaphor will ring true when we look at the totality of the aftermath of the African Diaspora and the treatment of these communities across continents.

Imagine being a sibling of a family that continually removes you from photos, tries its best to erase you. At times you make herculean efforts to support the goals, needs, and vision for your family. You stand together with your family in moments of pain, put your life on the line when called upon to prove your commitment to the family. Your roles as the caretaker, innovator, artist, confidant, dream maker, listener, loving, truth-teller, or leader are all questioned. You've been a part of every milestone, you've had fierce arguments, bitter feuds, but you try and hope that there will be this acceptance. As you go through the scrapbook, you see events where you know you were there, where you cried, prayed together, laughed together, but they are missing. You've been a good auntie, cousin, uncle, sister, brother, and have led a life that is no less than those around you, and yet your existence is ignored, stifled, silenced, minimized, bastardized, de-humanized. And yet there you are, gesturing, angling, reinventing yourself for them. You go numb to the blatant disrespect, hatred, vitriol, and still yearn to find yourself reflected somewhere, somehow, to make sure you're even really here? Am I alive? Am I a ghost or something that never was?

But there is a reckoning coming.

James Baldwin wrote, in a letter to his nephew in 1962:

> Try to imagine how you would feel if you woke up one morning to find the sun shivering and all the stars aflame. You would be frightened because it is out of the order of nature. Any upheaval in the universe is terrifying because it so profoundly attacks one's sense of one's own reality[5]

I want to apply this intimate and prophetic prose to what is happening in the intimate spaces of the information fields in digital and analogue areas. There is an upheaval in the universe; there is a reckoning taking place. And for some, it is terrifying. While on the one hand we must acknowledge that the West, more specifically the US, is witnessing a crisis of disinformation, we are also seeing an emergence of a fierce and fantastic interrogation of a reality that has permitted and sanctioned the existence of anti-blackness, homophobic rhetoric, misogynoir, a cultivation of oppressive practices that have silenced communities that have been victims of erasure from that American scrapbook.

We are undergoing a reckoning, and it is the optimist—yes, the activist, the social justice warrior in me that believes everything as it relates to the acquisition, preservation, access—the archival praxis with its traditional colonial, racist, sexist, classist, capitalistic approaches are not only faced but are and continue to change—going through an evolution.

The archival profession is in the midst of its own appraisal process, an interrogation of its development, an analysis of its utility and what is emerging out of this ferocious discourse is a dismissal of neutrality and the slow acknowledgement of racist ideas that have for far too long been allowed to serve as the bastion of truth, and has consciously sanctioned the silencing of oppressed communities, serving as a safe haven for human rights perpetrators where their actions are either glorified and reimagined as triumphs of democracy or completely missing, erased along with the voices of its victims. The profession is being asked to pay its debt; it is being asked to review its violations, asking for reparations for repair!

So how did I get here, what led me to engage in this work?

I spent what I call my formative years in West Philadelphia, Pennsylvania. And I would say it was fifth grade that laid the groundwork for the trajectory of my life. I was introduced to a fantastic fifth-grade teacher that helped me feel seen, which gave me the beginning of a voice. I was introduced to the art of Gwendolyn Brooks, Maya Angelou, Langston Hughes, and Paul Laurence Dunbar. I specifically remember Dunbar's poem, 'We Wear the Mask'. I later understood that contorting, angling, and bending that People of Colour and other underdocumented communities engage in to be part of America's scrapbook.

I didn't have the vocabulary at the time to express my bouts with feeling invisible, from the literature that never had characters that look like me or experiences that seemed vaguely reminiscent of my existence. The overtly Eurocentric approach to my education for the majority of primary and secondary schooling often presented a reality that synthesized the entirety of being black to a few pages on slavery, Harriet Tubman, Martin Luther King, and Rosa Parks. Let alone any significant discussion on the African diaspora and what Blackness was outside the United States. But I did hear of the travels of Ponce De Leon, Magellan, and Christopher Columbus.

It was not until I was working on my first graduate degree that I would have that sense of feeling seen again as I did in fifth grade, a reminder that I was not a ghost. I was working on my thesis, where I decided to investigate the history of the Black Press. I was particularly interested in the role black women had played. Because if it were not for my fifth-grade teacher and the book reports my parents made me do in the summers of my youth, I knew black women had always been part of the revolution for change, of building nations, of working towards democracy, so I knew we were likely critical to the development of the Black Press, as I had only tangential knowledge of Ida B. Wells and Gwen Ifill.

It was an amalgamation of various keywords in a Google search that led me to Fay M. Jackson.[6] Google led me to a small write-up by a Kent State alum Dr Darlene Clark Hines, showing Fay to be a Renaissance woman, born in Dallas, Texas in 1902. Her parents escaped Dallas after a lynching in Waco in 1916 caused massive panic, taking Fay and her siblings to become Angelenos—hoping to leave behind the KKK and mob violence. Fay was the editor and founder of various California-based Black publications reporting on Hailie Selassie, Emperor of Ethiopia, to the Coronation of King George VI, H. G. Wells, and Josephine Baker. Fay frequented the night clubs hoping to catch interviews with the glitterati of Black Hollywood like Jeni Legon. She was one of the earliest women of colour to report on the emergence of Technicolor in film, which would finally show the beauty and hues of African American performers. In those little graphs, I could surmise that Fay was a revolutionary, despite being in a time when strange fruit still hung from southern trees as the indomitable Billie Holiday used to sing.

I learned that the University of Southern California, UCLA, the Huntington Library, the Schomburg in New York held records on Fay in their archives. In 2007, I had never heard of or visited an archive, but the anticipation of seeing what was available left me with heart palpitations. To my heartbreaking dismay, what I found at the time was sparse at best. Unaware of the systemic failures of traditional archives in documenting historically underrepresented lives, I foolishly imagined I would have access to boxes filled with all of Fay's publications, including photographs, letters to lovers, telegrams, newspaper publishers, and scrapbooks. I naively thought every measure had been taken to memorialize her life within these spaces but what I saw instead were a few folders, with a handful of photos, and a couple of browning pages of correspondence. Yes, while each image, newspaper clipping, and note got me closer to Fay's life, she was practically invisible—nearly non-existent within each institution I visited. Indeed, there had to be more considering what she had done. But where was it?

Networking and luck led me to her granddaughter—who was the true custodian of Fay's life. Dale Lya Pierson lived on the Southside of Los Angeles. She had boxes of records on Fay stored in her basement, distributed throughout her home in various containers, plastic bags, and manila folders. Her granddaughter had a significant collection of *Flash* magazine, a publication highlighting the Harlem Renaissance of the West coast, poems, and letters from Langston Hughes and Wallace Thurman. They wrote about colourism in a novel titled *Blacker the Berry*. She had photographs of jazz legends like Alberta Hunter, correspondence from family members who had been slaves promising to bring a loved one home—it was an almost spiritual experience to have this connection to the past. I was personally beginning to feel grounded, an anchor, no longer free-floating, I began to find purpose. I found myself as I was finding Fay through archival research, meeting with her loved ones and friends; I was putting together an image of life, one whose existence needed to be accounted for!

As I got to know the granddaughter further, I found out she had a distrust of institutions—questions of good stewardship, respect of her grandmother's story, issues of access made her suspicious of cultural heritage organizations and the academy. So, I was honoured, humbled, amazed—my soul swelled as I was able to see what Fay accomplished, the path she took, her life's work was a tribute to what was/is possible despite the complexities of a black woman's existence, despite her story all but seeming ephemeral.

I stayed in touch with the granddaughter as I worked to complete my thesis. She had become a distant family member, we had a bond, and at the same time, there was a sense of incompletion or unfinished business. I quickly realized I wanted to be what I thought Dale Lya needed, what I needed, what those who had been disenfranchised, forgotten, made invisible, erased, undermined, under-documented, undervalued, unseen needed; an advocate, a voice, who would be their voice, and demand reparation, elevation, memorialization, decolonization, eradication of traditions, of theories, of a praxis that had historically placed the experiences of those who are privileged over those who are not, where the narratives of the oppressor reign supreme over the silences of the oppressed. I wanted to play my role in making the academy a space where archives document the full breadth of the human experience; I wanted to be a part of that reckoning, to control pages in the scrapbook!

The full breadth of the human existence, however, has now expanded beyond the analogue spaces that I investigated with my work on Fay. Yes, while there are countless narratives in personal archives, in large plastic bins, letters neatly folded in sandwich bags, accordion folders, 11×17 letter envelopes stuffed beyond capacity, or unprocessed materials in Hollinger boxes in ivy leagues, forgotten in the stacks, gathering dust until someone cares to investigate. The lives of minoritized communities are also partially encapsulated in Facebook posts, memes, blogs, tweets, hashtags, Instagram accounts along with an explosion of digital humanities work that is providing access, and new gateways for how we unpack, reconcile and advocate, investigate, critique, and celebrates the lives of these communities.

And as I moved from the researcher to be in a position that decides what comes in the archive, I brought with me a hyper-awareness of the absences. The creation of the reparative archive framework set me on a path of finding a way to have a sense of belonging, a sentiment expressed by Jarrett M. Drake in his Liberatory Archives talk in 2016 along with his co-published piece with Stacie Williams on Building a Community Archive. These helped provide the language and vastness for what damage the traditional archives has created but also motivated me to create space for possible repair.[7]

In 2014, I completed a year serving as the first African American archivist at Kent State University, the home of the Kent State Shootings of 4 May 1970, a tragedy that garnered attention on the international stage when four white students died during a flurry of gunfire by the Ohio National Guard, while wounding nine others during an anti-Vietnam War protest. Responding to, acquiring materials on, doing appraisals of, and engaging in oral histories about the pain experienced after the death of white students was critical to my daily workflows at Kent State University, as was instruction and creating exhibitions. These histories, specifically of the antiwar movement, are well documented within academic and non-academic organizations around the country and can also be found in catalogues across the pond. As a result, they solidify the humanity of those activists in a predominately white movement. But 'I Too, Sing America', in the words of one the most significant literary artists in the United States, Langston Hughes, despite efforts to suggest that I am not an American and that I should be returned to a nation from which my ancestors were stolen and forced to build the very structures and chambers that allow for the free flow of commerce and discourse on democracy when the US was in its infancy.

I became interested in the glaring absence of People of Colour in the narrative surrounding 4 May 1970. It became clear that this history was not interwoven or entrenched within the Kent State Shooting narrative. As I poured through the archival records within our holdings, I began to reach out informally to black alumni. I learned of another movement that was taking place in parallel to the antiwar protests—the Black Campus Movement.[8] Dr Ibram Kendi, *New York Times* best-selling author of *Stamped from the Beginning*, has also published on the Black Campus Movement, the height of this revolution occurring 1965–1972, around the same time as the push began against the Vietnam War.[9] The Black Campus Movement demanded validation of the Black experience through educational development, the creation of cultural centres, diverse student programming, and an increase in black students, faculty, and staff. But these stories were not heavily documented, and I worked to slowly begin an effort to fill in those gaps, to bring that reckoning and reparative framework within our holdings. At the same time I was engaging in this work at Kent State, a resurgence of activism was taking place at campuses around the country. In 2015, *The Atlantic* even published a piece entitled 'The Renaissance of Student Activism', with 160 student protests taking place in the US over the 2014 fall semester alone.

At Kent State University, Black United Students were responding to the death of Michael Brown in Ferguson; they were showing solidarity for the black students and their allies at the University of Missouri, where students of colour were being intimidated with images of swastikas, usage of the n-word. One of the fascinating things about the Mizzou hunger strike was its nearly complete rejection of traditional and corporate media. Signs abounded outside of their encampment, banning media and declaring a 'safe space', while chants of 'back off' usually used against cops were deployed against journalists who were kept out by students and linked arm in arm (and one faculty member reportedly calling for 'muscle'). The Concerned Student 1950 group repeatedly told students not to talk to any media but to email them. 'We will decide if and when we answer any questions', one student who wouldn't give his name said, 'and we will decide the terms'.[10]

As the US was barrelling towards the November elections, Kent State University's Spanish and Latino Student Association (SALSA), while celebrating in the Homecoming parade, faced chants of 'Build the Wall',[11] being yelled by a white fraternity as they walked in the procession. From 2014 to 2016 Kent State was a microcosm for how student organizers were emerging in digital spaces; parts of their lives were unfolding in real time. Social media for many activists serves as a tool for social justice by student organizers from vulnerable populations to post their demands to the administration, to show videos of being harassed, to provide a platform for acts of resistance. Since historically the American scrapbook has failed to tell the stories of black and brown people and other minoritized communities, archivists, memory workers, librarians, and other information professionals who understand the urgency of ethically capturing and understanding digital identities, in minoritized communities must follow the lead of scholars such as Safiya Noble, Meredith Clark, and Bergis Jules, who are giving us the pathways to do this work and tread this new terrain of ensuring these complex and diverse narratives are dealt with utilizing the appropriate tools, and that we're asking the questions we need to ask.[12]

In a report by Deen Freelon, Charlton McIilwain, and Meredith Clark titled 'Beyond the Hashtags: #Ferguson, #Blacklivesmatter, and The Online Struggle, for Offline Justice', they analysed 40.8 million tweets, 100,000 weblinks, and 40 interviews.[13] They surmised that protesters and their supporters were generally able to circulate their narratives on Twitter without relying on mainstream news outlets. What does this suggest for our labour in the information profession? It indicates that we will not be able to rely on previous modes of communication and documentation. Long gone are the days of relying primarily on print newspapers, print photos/negatives, and flyers to document the movements that often change the trajectory of a campus, and leads to creation of LGBT centres, new campus policies, presidential proclamation, task forces, and conversations that are reflective of what is taking place in broader society. As time moves forward, we are less likely to see these documents transferred in folders and boxes or even saved or drives.

How do we work with students to capture weeks/months of conversations in a Meetup app?

In 2016 I founded Project STAND[14] along with co-founder Tamar Chute, the university archivist at Ohio State University. I could not be the only person wondering if and how this resurgence of campus activism was being documented across geographical spaces, specifically activism around anti-blackness, anti-immigration, transphobia, sexual violence, police brutality in traditionally oppressed communities. And how do we engage in documenting these lives, these communities, these contributions of advocacy towards a more democratic society, especially as labour is taking place in digital spaces. The group of nearly seventy colleges and universities have completed close to four hundred collection assessments, which tell us that within the repository holdings of the consortium, the top five decades documented include 2000–present. These findings suggest that academic repositories across the country are working on trying and capturing these fragments. But they are just fragments. As Bergis Jules states:

> the public's use of these social media platforms to document events of historical significance, engage in political conversations, or share and explore personal and cultural experiences, continues to grow even as that same public remains unaware of how their data is being used.[15]

The report by Freelon, McIilwain, and Clark even highlights that the primary goals of social media use among the 40 people they interviewed were education, amplification of marginalized voices, along with it being viewed as a tool to democratize conversations that were previously owned and dominated by pro-corporate, pro-government spaces in the United States.

These communities are conscious of the agency they have in protecting their stories and how they are presented to the world. And as a result, we expressed those concerns when given a platform during the 2017 Documenting the Now event, titled Digital Blackness in the Archive.[16] A Ferguson activist Alexis Templeton mentioned how social media does not provide a complete picture. She said, 'I think they miss people, they miss the interaction, and I think that's super, super important because I'm not just a bunch of retweets and favorites.'[17] The words of Alexis Templeton reinforce the necessity of the whole, the whole individual and all the rich complexities that encompass an individual's life. As the founder of Project STAND, it has been important to find a path forward openly to discuss what it means to document ethically and share the stories of student organizers. Project STAND during the last year has been providing a space at universities and colleges with student organizers asking similar questions around social media, and the sentiments are the same when dealing with vulnerable communities in these spaces. Ginette Rhodes, Ohio State University, mentioned that she thought it was unfair for a tweet to be utilized to define a person. Students should be allowed to explain their full ideas and to provide context and wish archivists would enable them to do so before archiving their tweets. We are still unpacking what it means to archive the NOW.

Project STAND is a reparative archive tool; we are working to assess our gaps and actively working to engage in intentional steps to look at how we do our work moving forwards.[18] The roles of archivists, memory workers, and information professionals are changing. We must finally and completely let go of ideas of neutrality, that concept which was questioned by Howard Zinn in 1970s and Arturo Schomburg the black bibliophile before him—that is simply a way to silence the voices of the oppressed.[19]

But there is an upheaval taking place in the universe, it is challenging the very reality that allowed for the erasure of black and brown people, the discrimination of trans communities, disabled communities; it is questioning what has so long been depicted in America's scrapbook and yes the world's stage as well, with falsehood, half-truths. But as these communities place the stars ablaze with speaking truth to power in analogue and digital spaces, may we all move to a more honest place with who we were, who we have been, and have hope for what we might become.

Further Reading

Jarrett Martin Drake, 'Liberatory Archives', Keynote Address, Community Archives Forum, UCLA, 21 October 2016. Part 1: https://medium.com/on-archivy/liberatory-archives-towards-belonging-and-believing-part-1-d26aaeb0edd1 Part 2: https://medium.com/on-archivy/liberatory-archives-towards-belonging-and-believing-part-2-6f56c754eb17#.4hky7zcjt

Lae'l Hughes-Watkins, 'Moving Toward a Reparative Archive: A Roadmap for a Holistic Approach to Disrupting Homogenous Histories in Academic Repositories and Creating Inclusive Spaces for Marginalized Voices', Journal of Contemporary Archival Studies 5.6 (2018), 1–17

Lae'l Hughes-Watkins, 'Filling in the Gaps: Using Outreach Efforts to Acquire Documentation on the Black Campus Movement, 1965–1972', Archival Issues 36.1 (2014), 27–42

Bergis Jules, 'Confronting our Failure of Care around the Legacies of Marginalized Peoples in Archives', On Archivy (blog), 11 November 2016, https://medium.com/on-archivy/confronting-our-failure-of-care-around-the-legacies-of-marginalized-people-in-the-archives-dc4180397280

Tressie McMillan Cottom, 'Digitized Institutions and Inequalities', in Jessi Daniels, Karen Gregory, and Tressie McMillan Cottom, eds, Digital Sociologies (Bristol, UK/Chicago IL, USA: Policy Press/University of Chicago Press, 2017), 129–146

Miranda Mims, 'Archival Futurism: Archives as Social Justice', InVisible Culture 31: Black Studies Now and the Countercurrents of Hazel Carby, 15 November 2020, https://ivc.lib.rochester.edu/archival-futurism

Notes

1. Here referencing T. Sutherland: 'reconstituting—or (re)membering—is a powerful aspect of bearing witness, of rendering visible what has been made indiscernible or unrecognizable', in 'Making a Killing: On Race, Ritual, and (Re)Membering in Digital Culture', *Preservation, Digital Technology & Culture* 46.1 (2017), 32–40 (35)
2. J. Ward, *The Fire This Time: A New Generation Speaks About Race* (New York: Scribner, 2016).
3. This discussion is based on the plenary lecture delivered on 21 November 2019, DCDC Conference, Birmingham, UK, by Lae'l Hughes-Watkins.
4. America's Scrapbook symbolizes the archive of American history and pushes the boundaries to think on the world.
5. J. Baldwin, *The Fire Next Time* (New York: Dial Press, 1963), 10.
6. L. Hughes-Watkins, 'Fay M. Jackson: The Sociopolitical Narrative of a Pioneering African American Female Journalist' (MA thesis, Youngstown State University, 2008), http://rave.ohiolink.edu/etdc/view?acc_num=ysu1213112337.
7. J. M. Drake, 'Liberatory Archives', Keynote Address, Community Archives Forum, UCLA, 21 October 2016. S. Williams and J. M. Drake, 'Power to the People: Documenting Police Violence in Cleveland', *Journal of Critical Library and Information Science* 1.2 (2017), 1–27.
8. I. H. Rogers [Ibram X. Kendi], *The Black Campus Movement: Black Students and the Racial Reconstitution of Higher Education, 1965–1972*, Contemporary Black History (New York: Palgrave Macmillan, 2012); I. X. Kendi, *Stamped from the Beginning: The Definitive History of Racist Ideas in America* (London: The Bodley Head, 2016).
9. Kendi, *The Black Campus Movement.*
10. S. Thrasher, 'How Racial Justice Advocates Took on Mizzou and Won', *The Guardian*, www.theguardian.com/us-news/2015/nov/10/racial-justice-advocates-university-of-missouri-won, 'The Mizzou campus is about 120 miles from Ferguson, where the Black Lives Matter movement kicked into high gear in August 2014, after the death of Michael Brown. Many students have travelled to Ferguson to take part in the protests, and Ferguson demonstrators have shown up at Mizzou. When explicitly racist trouble happened on campus ... when student body president Payton Head was repeatedly called "n*****" and a swastika made of feces turned up in a bathroom.'
11. M. Corson and E. Keating, 'SALSA Faces Discriminatory Chants During Parade', Daily Kent Stater [Kent State University newspaper] 5 October 2016, available from the Daily Kent Stater Digital Archive, https://dks.library.kent.edu/?a=p&p=home&e=——-en-20-1-txt-txIN——-.
12. S. U. Noble, *Algorithms of Oppression: How Search Engines Reinforce Racism* (New York: New York University Press, 2018). Documenting the Now, www.docnow.io/. Safiya Umoja Noble is an associate professor at UCLA, and is the Co-Founder and Co-Director of the UCLA Center for Critical Internet Inquiry. Bergis Jules is a Senior Consultant, Shift Collective. Meredith Clark is assistant professor of media studies at the University of Virginia.
13. The report is published by the Center for Media and Social Impact and can be downloaded at https://cmsimpact.org/resource/beyond-hashtags-ferguson-blacklivesmatter-online-struggle-offline-justice.
14. Project STAND, https://standarchives.com.

15. B. Jules, E. Summers, and V. Mitchell, 'Ethical Considerations for Archiving Social Media Content Generated by Contemporary Social Movements: Challenges, Opportunities, and Recommendations' (White paper, Documenting the Now, 2018).
16. *Digital Blackness in the Archive*: A Documenting the Now Symposium, https://www.docnow.io/meetings/stl-2017/ (accessed 2019).
17. *Digital Blackness in the Archive.*
18. L. Hughes-Watkins, 'Moving toward a Reparative Archive: A Roadmap for a Holistic Approach to Disrupting Homogenous Histories in Academic Repositories and Creating Inclusive Spaces for Marginalized Voices', *Journal of Contemporary Archival Studies* 5.6 (2018), 1–17; https://elischolar.library.yale.edu/jcas/vol5/iss1/6.
19. H. Zinn, 'Secrecy, Archives, and the Public Interest', *The Midwestern Archivist* 2.2 (1977), 14–26; A. Holton, 'Decolonizing History: Arthur Schomburg Afrodiasporic Archive', *Journal of African American History* 92.2 (2007), 218–238.

CHAPTER 32

IRRECONCILABLE ARCHIVES

Queer Collections and the Truth and Reconciliation Commission

REBECCA KAHN

Few South African politicians have been as divisive as Winnie Madikizela-Mandela. After her death in April 2018, her obituary in the UK-based *The Independent* ran with the headline 'Winnie Mandela, the turbulent life of the woman who went from "Mother of the Nation" to "mugger"'. [1] The *Financial Times* referred to her as 'fallen angel', and the *Guardian*'s obituary described her in the opening paragraph as 'someone who was called to greatness and yet failed that calling decisively ... her reputation irrevocably mired in murder and fraud'.[2] The South African media was much less ambivalent. She was a 'lioness', a 'dignified mother', and an 'icon'. Her misdemeanours—some alleged, some of which she was convicted—were referred to obliquely. Consequently, it is difficult to discuss her role in South African politics with any type of nuance. But through her inadvertent role as a catalyst in the fight for equal rights for gay, lesbian, and transgender South Africans, she also helps to reveal a small, and significant archival sliver which makes up part of an emerging archival paradigm.[3]

This story begins with the kidnapping of four young activists from the Methodist manse in Soweto, Johannesburg and the subsequent murder of one of them, fourteen-year-old Stompie Seipei, whose body was found on a piece of waste ground on 1 January 1990 with his throat cut. A year later, Madikizela-Mandela and others were tried on charges of his kidnapping, assault, and murder. She was convicted of involvement in this episode, but it is not my intention to debate the guilt or innocence of Winnie Madikizela-Mandela in this chapter. Rather, taking a cue from Ann Laura Stoler's impulse to read along the grain of the archive in order to go against the grain of history, this chapter will look closely at two archival collections which document different aspects of the trial and its aftermath and their impact on the burgeoning gay rights movement in South Africa. In this case, the archival grain runs through two important and very different collections—the enormous collection of the Truth and Reconciliation Commission (TRC) and three folders of papers in Gay and Lesbian Memory in Action (known as GALA), a small, queer community archive in Johannesburg.

This juxtaposition frames the central question in this chapter: whether it is possible to read between the lines across two different collections in order to explore the notion of reconciliation between them. This question is particularly resonant in South Africa, where there is a tradition of the law and public opinion being at odds; where different archival collections can tell distinctly different sides of the same story; and where there is a powerful public imagining of the power of the archive as a locus of truth. It will also ask whether it is possible for there to be reconciliation between archives, particularly in cases where their physical boundaries and those of libraries and museums are becoming more porous and less well-defined as they are brought together in digital infrastructures. What 'reconciliation' might mean, and how it may manifest will be examined through the lenses of two archival models—the pluralist archive, and the converged knowledge repository.

This chapter situates the TRC and GALA in the historical context of South Africa in the early to mid-1990s, including the nascent queer liberation movement which emerged alongside the anti-apartheid movement during South African's transition. Building on existing work on community and queer archives as spaces of identity formation, it explores the concept of archival pluralism, and extends this to the reading of the archival collections in question. Focussing on the story of Winnie Madikizela-Mandela's involvement in the kidnapping and murder of Stompie Seipei (a case generally known in South Africa as 'the Stompie trial'), I go on to document the related archival materials in both GALA and the TRC collections and the contrasting narratives they chronicle. The critiques of the TRC presented by prominent scholars form the basis of the final section, which questions the desirability of applying the pluralistic model in this particular context, and makes the case that in order to keep nuanced narrative alive, a degree of disjunction might be required.

Anatomies of the Archives

An attempt to get to grips with the archival context in South Africa is naturally dominated by the TRC. It is the prevailing repository of social memory of the apartheid era, of the forty years of the struggle for liberation, of the ways in which South Africans attempted to make sense of those times, and to refigure their legacy into a viable democratic future. Not only did the TRC set out to document the abuses of individuals in order to facilitate public remembering; it was also charged with investigating any destructions of public records by the State—it was mandated to document public forgetting.[4] At the time, scholars attempted to measure the success of the TRC by conceptualizing the notions of 'truth' and 'reconciliation' and quantifying how much the former could be said to have contributed to the latter and concluded that to some degree, South Africans could be characterized as having 'reconciled' and that this was facilitated by the 'collective memory produced by the process'.[5] Thirteen years later, however, Fanie du Toit argues that a 'discourse of disappointment' at the pace of reconciliation has emerged, as a result of increasing economic inequality and State corruption.[6] This is not simply a result of neo-liberal economic reality, though. Verne Harris points out that the TRC's archival focus on the individual, rather than the collective and community, is one of the reasons why there is significant and growing scepticism about the work and impact of the TRC.[7] He traces a line from this focus on the individual, via the work of Adam Sitze on the historical contexts in which the TRC was located, to argue that the growing economic inequality has, and will continue to, hamper any attempts to come to terms with the past.

In this context of a dominant, and potentially erasing archival narrative, the notion of archival plurality initially presents a compelling and promising possibility for an opening and broadening of the discursive space in South Africa.

GALA was the first gay and lesbian archive to be established in Africa, and was founded in 1997 as an independent project under the auspices of the South African History Archive.[8] It was based on the models of European and North American gay and lesbian archives, and can be read as an attempt to address the 'epistemology of the closet' which emerges when histories are defined by 'gaps, elisions, omissions ... and which render queer histories invisible, missing from official or dominant accounts'.[9] In this respect, GALA is an important source of archival material relating to the varied and complex LGBTQI histories in South Africa. It holds around two hundred collections, ranging from projects which investigated the abuse of gay and lesbian conscripts who served in the South African Defence Force during apartheid, to personal papers, extensive press materials, and ephemera such as t-shirts, posters, and badges. Much of this material was donated by individuals and their families.

The archive also takes its mandate one step further. As an activist archive, GALA has sought to supplement its traditional archival activities with collecting practices that are contextually appropriate, which in some cases forced them to reconsider some of their own archival assumptions. For example, building oral history collections has been an important focus for several years, an approach which recognizes that, for many members of their community, paper-based archives have been exclusionary spaces. In these contexts, vocabularies matter—in a long-running oral history project which aimed to collect stories from individuals over the age of sixty, researchers were initially puzzled by the lack of responses from older, Black South African lesbians. GALA staff soon realized that many of the communities they were interacting with did not have a term to describe same-sex relationships between women, which is why none of their subjects self-identified as such. As soon as archivists 'got rid of their preconceived notions of what a lesbian is, the project took off'.[10] GALA has also worked with activists and collections in other African countries, such as Malawi and Zimbabwe, but maintain that GALA should be a 'repository of last resort, not wanting communities to lose ownership of or access to the original records'.[11] These attitudes, coupled with strong community outreach programmes among LGBTQI youth and a scheme designed to collect stories from LGBTQI migrants and refugees in Johannesburg, has ensured that GALA can be situated between the worlds of 'traditional' community archive (if such a thing can be said to exist), activist community non-profit, and a pluralist archive.

Activist Archival

Grass-roots, activist archives, which collect, preserve, and serve communities which have otherwise been largely left out of archival discourse are, by now, well established entities in the archival landscape. Andrew Flinn, Mary Stevens, and Elizabeth Shepherd position community archives as emerging from within larger movements of groups who have been misrepresented, marginalized, or elided entirely by mainstream institutions, and who initiate these projects as means of constructing and bolstering an archival identity.[12] Flinn has described archival activism as archival work which is associated with a political agenda and which, as part of its objectives, challenges discrimination and actively works towards social justice through an engagement with external activities and groups.[13] As well as articulating and projecting identities outwards, activist and community archives serve important functions for the communities they represent, resulting in the formation of what Michelle Caswell, Marika Cifor, and Mario Ramirez refer to as 'representational belonging', an autonomy and authority which grows out of the archive and enables marginal groups to 'establish, enact, and reflect on their presence' in a variety of symbolic contexts. Writing in the South African context, Harris has argued that activist archivists have a role to play in deconstructing the power hierarchies which result in the silencing of certain groups, narratives, or perspectives in archival collections and collecting.[14] Wakimoto et al., present activist archives and practice as activity which are used to 'challenge injustice and discrimination in order to create a more inclusive and just environment, both in archives and in wider society', and go on to present community archives as the 'embodiment of activism in the archives' precisely because, by the act of collecting materials that might otherwise not have been collected, they challenge the mainstream archival monopoly over history.[15]

Archival plurality is an approach which has been gaining increasing attention from archival theorists who seek a mechanism for realizing the archival multiverse, that plurality of, as Anne Gilliland and Sue McKemmish defined it: 'evidentiary texts, memory-keeping practices and institutions, bureaucratic and personal motivations, community perspectives and needs, and cultural and legal constructs'.[16] Plurality is presented as offering the opportunity for ensuring archival neutrality by encompassing different, and counterbalancing viewpoints through engagement with diversity in memory practices in order to spur activity, driven by dialogue, reflection, and criticism.[17] It is contingent, contextual, and culturally informed; there is no universal path to or plan for pluralism, but rather it must be derived in situ from much effort, reflection, self-evaluation, and iteration. Through this approach, the proponents argue, it becomes possible for archivists to work with records in ways which avoid the archival pitfalls of 'claims of universality, inattention to power structures, the silencing of dissent, and the collapsing of difference'.[18] Archival discourse, like democracies, thrive on conflict and are at their best when citizens and groups disagree with one another, when pluralism prevails.[19]

This chapter aims to extend in this line of thought, and to test the possibility of the pluralistic approach to the reading of archives, as well as the maintenance of it. One of the driving questions behind this is whether it is possible, and desirable, to read across collections and institutions in order to facilitate a re-examination of historical events from a plurality of perspectives. Plurality is presented as a mechanism or opportunity to address the issues that have arisen out of the refiguring of the archive which has taken place since the 1990s.[20] In the literature, these issues are presented as (but not exclusively) the concurrent existence of different memory and evidence paradigms at national, local, or community levels, the notion of parallel provenance and the impact on archival practice of acknowledging communities as co-creators of the records about them.[21]

This is not only an intellectual enquiry, but one with a practical consideration for archivists as well as researchers. Helena Robinson highlights the increasing convergence of museums, libraries, archives, and galleries, under the blanket definition of 'memory institutions' which all hold equal evidential value as sources.[22] There is resonance here with Eric Ketelaar's articulation of the 'archival return' in which understandings of the archive are enriched by seeing them in parallel with developments in other domains.[23] These converged collections may be brought together physically, institutionally, or virtually, and all three potential manifestations have organizational and preservation implications for the institutions. While these convergences are often motivated by the shared goals of preserving the intellectual records of a society and providing access in transparent and flexible ways (as well as the slightly less lofty, but equally critical issue of financial efficiency), Robinson warns that the model is not always conducive to facilitating thorough critical use of the institutions themselves.[24] If we consider the convergence model alongside that of plurality, we see that they share some same essential principles—a recognition of multiple narrative possibilities, diverse ontological approaches to making sense of the world, and the need for transparency in relation to sources and users. However, it is also important to recognize that there is a potential risk to some archival collections from the pluralist and convergent models, which rely on their outlier or outsider status to remain independent and, ironically, to give space to the alternate narratives. This risk is particularly salient when considering community archives, where being separate from mainstream is essential for the survival of the archives.[25]

As well as creating the false impression of universality, in the context of this case study, a pluralistic approach puts important stories at risk of being swamped. One of the questions posed in this chapter is whether some narratives are best left to the preserves of the activist communities who collect and archive them because, despite the constraints these collections might have in terms of resources, their power as loci of community memory are the safest place for such narratives to be embedded.

This question is not a new one for those engaging with community archives in general, and queer archives in particular. One of the risks posed to queer (and other) archives is the 'normativizing' potential of archival practices to the materials and narratives held in queer community archives.[26] In some contexts, there is a risk that normative practices and the politics of respectability can come together to 'discipline' memory, and produce normative narratives about queer pasts. The result is archival spaces and narratives which end up prioritizing 'good citizenship' and respectability over the non-normative, subversive, and radical possibilities of the archives, both in terms of the collections they contain and the archives themselves. In the context of the two collections being examined in this chapter, I hope to show that while a pluralist approach is necessary to challenge the dominance of the TRC's version of a moment in South Africa's history, it should also be deployed with care. The stories held in the collection at GALA are able to persist precisely because they are kept separate from the mainstream versions of certain histories, and in order to further a balanced, and nuanced understanding of that moment, this schism should be preserved.

Thérèse Migraine-George and Ashley Currier highlight the risk of loss of queer African archives, citing both hostile national contexts which are not conducive to the establishment of new archives or the survival of existing ones, as well as preservation concerns, particularly for online collections.[27] In this case, the potential offered by extending the pluralistic multiverse model is compelling. Indeed, some of the digital collections mentioned by Migraine-George and Currier were able to deposit some of their material with GALA before they shut up shop, thereby creating a type of pluralist archive-within-an-archive of materials which exist nowhere else, a type of archive of defunct digitality. One example of this is the Behind the Mask collection (AM 2994), thirty boxes of organizational documents concerned with Behind the Mask, a website and online magazine for LGBTQI communities in Africa, which was a critical source for activists across the sub-Saharan region, including Namibia, Zambia, Kenya, Uganda, Rwanda, Burundi, and Sierra Leone. Actual website content was not preserved and the existing documentation highlights the questions around permanence and loss in African queer archives. Flinn's definition of a community archive as part of an activity of documenting, recording, and exploring community heritage by a group which 'defines itself on the basis of locality, culture, faith, background, or other shared identity or interest' is useful in this context.[28]

These extensions can be read through several, overlapping lenses. The initial question in my mind when starting this research was 'Is it possible to trace the same story, across multiple archives, in order to create a more nuanced picture of difficult and controversial events?' In this enquiry, my approach was to read the materials relating to the Winnie Mandela trial which are in the collection at GALA, alongside a reading of the TRC materials which relate to the same event, but which were presented to the commission several years later, when they conducted their enquiry into the activities of the Mandela United Football Club.

The MUFC, the Stompie Trial, and the Archives

In 1986, Winnie Madikizela-Mandela returned to Johannesburg after several years of banishment and house arrest. She quickly became a central figure in the anti-apartheid community in Soweto, and thus the focus of a great deal of attention from the community, the media, and the South African police force. Her symbolic role as 'mother of the nation' was combined with that of a revolutionary one, and a group of young men soon coalesced around her, calling itself the Mandela United Football Club (MUFC). This group acted as entourage, bodyguards, and adopted family, and was run as if it were a family, including the expectation that MUFC members refer to Madikizela-Mandela as 'mummy'.[29] From 1987 onwards, this group were implicated in an increasing number of violent activities. They acted as an informal militia, accusing anyone who would not join them of being police informers or revolutionary sell-outs, and some members began to disappear. In December 1988, the MUFC carried out the kidnapping, 'interrogation', and assault of Stompie Seipei and three other activists. Seipei's body was found on a piece of scrubland in Soweto in January 1989.

The subsequent trial in 1991 was a massive media event in South Africa and abroad. Madikizela-Mandela and several other members of the MUFC were accused of several counts of kidnapping, assault, and murder. The defence's legal team was led by George Bizos, a veteran human rights lawyer, who had also defended Nelson Mandela. The main line of argument presented was that the young men had been removed from the manse in order to protect them from the attentions of Reverend Paul Verryn, a veteran anti-apartheid activist, liberal Methodist priest, and later a Methodist Bishop. Madikizela-Mandela accused Verryn of being homosexual, and of abusing the young men. By making this claim, Madikizela-Mandela deployed the familiar homophobic trope of conflating homosexuality and child abuse, and throughout the trial she repeatedly said that homosexuality was abnormal and 'un-African'. This line of argument was repeated in the media, with the effect of publicly codifying homosexuality as abusive and homosexual practices as a White colonizing depredation of heterosexual Black culture.[30] A MUFC supporter, protesting outside the court carrying a placard which read 'homosex is not in Black culture' became one of the preeminent images of the trial. Madikizela-Mandela was found guilty of kidnapping, and sentenced to six years of prison, which was suspended on appeal.

Verryn did not take the stand in court, and the accusations against him were later proven to be without merit and unfounded by both the Methodist Church and by a community enquiry, conducted by Soweto residents. While it was clear that the defence team were working hard to deflect attention from Madikizela-Mandela, the strategy also revealed the schisms that were emerging between gay and heterosexual members of the liberation movement, as well as within the gay rights movements, at a time when the rights of gay and lesbian South Africans were beginning to manifest in the public discourse during South Africa's transition from apartheid to democracy.

In 1997 the case was re-opened, when the Truth and Reconciliation Commission launched a special investigation into Madikizela-Mandela and the MUFC. The role of the Club, Madikizela-Mandela and others were investigated in relation to their involvement in the Seipei murder, as well as eight other killings and ten other assaults, abduction, and torture. During the hearings, which were described at the time as 'a South African media event comparable to the release of Nelson Mandela from prison'.[31] The families of the victims, along with former members of the MUFC, leaders of the mass democratic movement, and former police officers were invited to testify at the hearings, as did Madikizela-Mandela herself. Madikizela-Mandela refused to admit to any wrongdoing, and frequently dismissed the allegations as 'ridiculous' and 'ludicrous'.[32] The TRC investigation eventually found her to be 'politically and morally accountable for the gross violations of human rights committed by the Mandela United Football Club and was responsible, by omission for the commission of gross violations of human rights'.[33]

In the early 1990s South Africa was undergoing a transition to democracy from the strictures of the apartheid regime which dictated almost every aspect of people's lives; from where they could live to how they were permitted to learn, work, and move around the country, to who they were allowed to marry, and even with whom they were allowed to have sex. Non-white South Africans bore the brunt of these degrading restrictions, and by the late 1980s and early 1990s, resistance to these regulations was highly politicized, often violent, and in many cases understood as a life-and-death struggle.

Starting in 1990, liberation movements were unbanned and in the following years long and torturous constitutional negotiations took place. The process of transition which took place between the unbannings and the final adoption of the South African Constitution in February 1997 was complicated, delicate, and slow. These processes were designed to avert the risk of a power vacuum in the country, while at the same time encompassing the perspectives of business leaders, religious bodies, traditional leadership structures, trade unions, and over two million ordinary citizens who made submissions to the consultative process. As du Toit also points out, these took place against the backdrop of extreme political unrest. In 1990, an estimated 3699 South Africans died as a result of political violence and these numbers escalated as the years progressed.[34] It was urgent that a clearly articulated and performed solution be found which could convince South Africans that the idea of restoring human and civic dignity was both worthwhile and workable.

Within this context, the role of sexual politics was emergent, but by no means clear-cut. It is practically impossible to describe a 'South African gay experience' of the time, since gay lives were a mirror of the fractured experience of the rest of South African life—divided by political perspectives, gender inequality, and most significantly by racial inequality. Poor, mostly black, South African gay men and lesbians lived in vastly different circumstances to those afforded to their white, middle- and upper-class contemporaries. And while the ideas of sexual freedom and gay subculture were beginning to filter in from Europe and North America, these have to be read alongside the traditions of struggle, resistance, and commitment to social transformation that were entrenched among activist groups and individuals who had developed their consciousness as part of the broader liberation movements. These imperatives did not always (and, many would argue, still do not) sit easily with each other. Attitudes towards homosexuality were coloured by racial politics and statements made by political leaders which equated homosexuality with Western perversion and corruption added to the urgency felt by many gay and lesbian South African involved in the liberation struggle that it was imperative that the rights of gays and lesbians be seen as a specific and essential component of any future dispensation which protected the rights of all South Africans.[35]

While the tensions between the gay-rights movement and the broader liberation movement were influencing the ways in which constitutional democracy was being constructed in the formal context, the trial of Madikizela-Mandela exposed these tensions in a very public and highly charged context. In the ways in which it played out in the courtroom, in the media, and in public opinion, and subsequently, the trial can be seen as 'a barometer of deeply contested ideological ground.'[36] This level of contestation is highlighted by the fact that in the same year, the ANCs Draft Constitutional Committee—a body of legal scholars, activists, politicians, and others—included a clause in the draft Bill of Rights which outlawed discrimination on the basis of sexual orientation. It was against this backdrop of an official policy that the Stompie trial proceeded in a way which disseminated a repudiation of homosexuality, couched in terms of African nationalism, precipitating anxieties among gay and lesbian South Africans about the status of their rights, despite the official, public commitments.[37]

As soon as the defence's intent became clear, gay and lesbian activist groups responded publicly. One of the groups which was vocal in its critique was GLOW (Gay and Lesbian Organization of the Witwatersrand) a multi-racial, leftist group advocating for the rights of gay and lesbian South Africans. One of the founders of GLOW was Simon Nkoli, a veteran of the Delmas Treason Trials, and an out gay man. Nkoli's position was an example of the intersectional tensions faced by many activists. On the one hand, he had been an accused in a high profile treason trial which was seen by many as a watershed moment in South African political history.[38] On the other, as a result of his decision to come out to his fellow defendants, some activists argued that Nkoli's public homosexuality tarnished the reputation and prospects of those involved in the struggle, while others saw it as an important first step for gay and lesbian visibility and activism. Nkoli and many others had to negotiate the delicate balance between their position as struggle stalwarts and representatives of the increasingly visible gay-rights movement. This balancing act can be read very clearly in the GLOW materials in the GALA collection, as well as in other collections at GALA which relate to that period.

The challenge to mainstream archival monopolies presented by activist archives is well illustrated by the materials held by GALA which relate to the Stompie trial and the 1997 TRC investigation. The volume of material on the subject is modest: four collections in particular have relevant materials and there is a degree of duplication across these. The Lesbians and Gays Against Oppression (LAGO)/Organization of Lesbian and Gay Activists (OLGA) Collection (AM 2801), the Simon Nkoli Collection (AM 2623), the National Coalition for Gay and Lesbian Equality (NCGLE) (AM2615), and the Achmat-Lewis Collection (AM 2970) combined provide approximately twenty-five pages of policy papers, correspondence, and newsletters, and two sets of newspaper clippings. Despite these materials only adding up to a few dozen pages, they illustrate a detailed picture of the anxieties and anger in the LGBTQI South African community which were precipitated by the Mandela trial and the TRC investigation.

A reading of these materials reveals a noticeable shift in tone between the initial trial and the later TRC submission. The papers from the early 1990s relate anger and concern, but they are documents which circulated primarily within the community—newsletters, circulars, and a handful of newspaper articles written by prominent gay journalists. By the time of the TRC, the tone of the papers has shifted—the language is emboldened and unapologetic. A more detailed analysis of the discourse may reveal more, but for the purposes of this research, it is possible to observe how the change in the legal recognition of LGBTQI rights in the early 1990s emboldened the activist stance evident in the materials. The documents also reveal the disparities between white and black South Africans within the gay and lesbian population. Most significantly, they provide evidence for the position taken by many LGBTQI South Africans who chose to align themselves with the broader liberation struggle. These groups and individuals viewed this struggle as universal, in which freedom for all South Africans was seen as the ultimate objective, but this was understood to mean that gay liberation would also have a place in the 'new South Africa'.

This alignment is significant, because it reveals how a small group of experienced and well-connected activists (most of the groups, including OLGA, GLOW, and

LAGO never numbered more than a dozen active members) were able to channel these anxieties through the official corridors of power in transition-era South Africa, culminating eventually with the inclusion in the South African Constitution of provisions outlawing discrimination on the grounds of sexual orientation. What is also vividly evident in the materials is the paradox of the period. In the GLOW papers is a transcript of a workshop held in March 1991, at which a prominent activist-lawyer, Edwin Cameron (who later became a Constitutional Court Justice) refers to the inclusion of this provision in the exact same week that, as part of the media furore around the Stompie trial, there were public calls for gay South Africans to be gassed or shot.[39]

In a letter to their members, dated 20 March 1991 (AM 2623—C1.2.6), GLOW stated that they were launching a campaign against the homophobia surrounding the trial, but were also careful to point out their position as supportive of the rights of the accused to a fair trial:

> The purpose of the campaign is not to attack Winnie Mandela. It is important that she receives a fair trial. However, GLOW objects to the homophobic nature of her defence. It confuses sexual abuse and homosexuality and suggest that homosexuality is wrong. The nature of the campaign is an open letter to the Nation Executive Committee of the ANC asking it to clarify the position of the ANC on lesbian and gay rights.

In the subsequent letter to the ANC's National Executive, which is in the same folder, but somewhat confusingly dated 13 March 1991, GLOW state their objections to the ways in which homosexuality was presented in the trial, but position these objections within the framework of the ANC's overall stance on human rights:

> Dear Comrades
> The Gay and Lesbian Organization of the Witwatersrand has always aligned itself with the mass democratic movement and has many ANC members in its ranks. We are writing to you to voice our protest over the way in which some of the issues relating to the trial of comrade Winnie Mandela and others have been handled by the defence ... We wish to stress at the outset that G.L.O.W. has no comment to make on the defendants' guilt or innocence.... The ANCs draft Bill of Rights states in Article 7, paragraph 2, that Discrimination on the grounds of gender, single parenthood, legitimacy of birth or sexual orientation shall be unlawful. In light of this, it is alarming that the NEC has failed to respond to the homophobia that has arisen both within and outside this court as a result of the trial.

The letter then goes on to list three examples of their objections, and concludes:

> This line of defence is irreconcilable with the basic principles of human rights outlined in the ANC's proposed Bill of Rights. The ANC's failure to respond to the above, raises doubts regarding its stated commitment to the recognition of lesbian and gay rights. We therefore demand that the NEC states clearly and unequivocally its position on the rights of lesbians and gay men.

Also in the GALA archives are copies of the 1997 submissions made to the TRC investigation by the National Coalition for Gay and Lesbian Equality and GLOW (AM 2623.- C1.2.8). This submission explicitly focuses on 'homophobia in the conduct and defence of Winnie Madikizela-Mandela' and argues that the ways in which this was articulated had an impact on the human dignity of gay and lesbian South Africans, constituting an abuse of their human rights, and the damage done to reconciliation by the defence in the trial. The submission explicitly makes the point that gay and lesbian South Africans participated in both the liberation struggle and supported the apartheid government, and called for reconciliation within the community between these two groups.

By contrast, the archive of the TRC is massive and inaccessible. Several scholars have examined the problem of access to the archive of the TRC which can be seen as a result of a variety of shortcomings, including logistical difficulties, jurisdictional disagreements, preservation concerns, and political wrangling.[40] At the time of writing, no access to the archive of the TRC is possible. The South African Department of Justice maintains an official website for the TRC, which is divided into ten subdomains, one of which is a set of transcripts from the Special Hearings, and another of which is the Final Report, in seven volumes. The site includes transcripts of the public testimony given to the Special Hearings into the MUFC, which are accessible as plaintext html web pages. Each day of the twelve days of hearings has a separate URL, and contains anywhere between 80 and 260 pages worth of text. There is no index, and as Harris points out, there are 'no linkages between these records and the mass of TRC material from which they are drawn'.[41] None of the transcript pages contain any reference to the submissions made by NCGLE and GLOW. Using simple text searching across the transcripts, I was unable to locate any reference to these organizations either. The final report from the TRC into the MUFC makes for depressing reading. It lists eighteen cases of murder, assault, arson, and torture. It paints a vivid picture of the chaos of Soweto at the time, the atmosphere of distrust, fear, and violence which prevailed, which the apartheid State, in the form of the security forces, actively encouraged. The report repeats the allegations made by Madikizela-Mandela that she was rescuing the kidnapped youths from being sexually abused at the manse, and goes on, in the findings section, to say that these allegations were unfounded. The commission also found that Madikizela-Mandela had slandered Verryn in an effort to divert attention from herself and her household. Nowhere in the report is any mention made of the submissions from gay and lesbian community or activist groups about the impact of the case on their communities.

This lack of access to materials which tell the story of the trial's implications and significance for LGBTQI South Africans creates the conditions for amnesia, secreting and control that Harris refers to when he describes the closing of an archival space for the 'play of remembering, forgetting and imagining'.[42] The narrative, as it emerges from the available TRC archival materials remains that with which most people are familiar—that allegations were made against Revered Verryn, and that alleged homosexual activities were used as a justification for the abductions and a reason for the young men to be subjected to beatings and other assaults. In no part of the transcripts or the final report, was the position of gay and lesbian South Africans articulated, nor were the public statements which described them as 'abnormal' or 'un-African' recorded or examined. Without access to the supporting archival materials it is impossible to know how the Commission considered the submissions made by NCGLE and GLOW, and whether they had any impact on the final findings of the investigation. James Gibson argues that for many South Africans 'reconciliation means nothing more than accepting the Truth and Reconciliation Commission's truth about the past' which assumes, then, by a flawed logic, that some degree of reconciliation in South Africa can be seen as having taken place.[43] In a 2001 survey, Gibson found that the majority of South Africans from all race groups consequently claimed the TRC to be an essential component of the reconciliation process. But in this particular case, an important part of the story is missing. If it were not for the materials held by GALA, it would be extremely difficult for scholars to access the parallel narrative of the struggle for gay and lesbian South Africans to achieve the legal and social acceptance of their rights to self-expression of their identity which was challenged, and some might argue, damaged, by the Madikizela-Mandela trial.

The TRC and Public Memory

The language used to describe Winnie Madikizela-Mandela after her death reveals the extent to which social memory in South Africa is a site of ongoing, complex struggle between remembering and forgetting. Harris, in his analysis of the difficulties of thinking about and working with the TRC archive reminds us that this reshaping of memory is ongoing, and positions 'narrative against narrative, and story against story'.[44] In his formulation the TRC is, among other things, an exercise in formal engagement with history, and not only in terms of remembrance of the past, but also in terms of the TRC as a process, which has generated essential memory resources. In his work, the critiques of the TRC (and there are many) are presented as important debates in part because they force an interrogation of the project which allows space for argument, but also space for healing. However, this is only possible if the space is constituted by the TRC itself, by preserving ongoing access to the records of and about the TRC. In the same piece, he also highlights significant flaws in the ways in which these resources were collected, organized, and processed. These flaws include the loss of some digital and paper-based records through mismanagement and the handing over of others to different State agencies, and which can no longer be located. Harris also describes the difficulties presented to the public in accessing the TRC archive. He concludes that:

> The ultimate test of the TRC as archive is the extent to which it becomes a space for the play of remembering, forgetting and imagining. This play is always underway in an archive whatever the intentions of those who seek to control it. We have seen such

play in and around the TRC archive. However, we also have seen a closing of this space through instincts of amnesia, erasure, secreting and control. These instincts must be resisted.... On all South Africans there is a burden of responsibility to continue giving life to the TRC process, to be always finding the TRC archive, safeguarding, using, promoting and taking it outside the domains of elites.

In his analysis, Brent Harris highlights the contradictory language used to describe the TRC by the members of the Commission themselves. In his view, the TRC is presented as both 'shutting the book' on and 'uncovering' or 'unearthing' the past. Framed as both an exhumation and a reburial, a fixing of knowledge and an end to instability.[45] This desire to fix implies an assumption that the many, many records contained in the TRC have the capacity to speak for themselves, and to reveal an essential truth about what happened in South Africa. But prevailing archival thought holds that it is the tacit narratives in archives that need to be teased out and which may tell another story.[46] Archives, as the current thinking has it, are never closed or complete, which in turn allows every generation to reconstruct the past, using their own interpretation of the archival record.[47]

In the light of these arguments, the materials that are available which refer to the Madikizela-Mandela trial raise the question of whether a pluralistic approach to reading the Winnie Mandela trial actually risks repeating or reinforcing this epistemology of the closet?

There is little reason for concern that the materials at GALA will ever be subsumed into the TRC. Rather, what this chapter has tried to demonstrate is that if a fuller, more nuanced story about the Mandela trial and its effects on South Africa is to be read, or if a history of queer rights in South Africa is to be written, the two collections should be read in parallel. In this regard, reconciliation is desirable, and a pluralistic approach, which enables and encourages reading across archives, is important. But this chapter also shows that the narratives in small, dynamic, activist archives are more than gap-fillers. They are places where queer narratives can be given the space to become fully fledged and multi-faceted, not simply adjuncts to mainstream narratives. The concerns about future scenarios of custody, preservation, and access to the TRC archive which have been raised also put these narratives at risk. The dynamic relationship between remembering, forgetting, and imagining must be given space, and measures that limit the ongoing contestation of meaning must be resisted.

ACKNOWLEDGEMENT

I would like to express my thanks to the staff at GALA, in particular Archives Coordinator Linda Chernis, who welcomed me to the archive in Johannesburg, and whose knowledge of the materials and the subject were invaluable in helping me to plot out the shape of this chapter.

FURTHER READING

Michelle Caswell, 'Toward a Survivor-Centered Approach to Records Documenting Human Rights Abuse: Lessons from Community Archives', *Archival Science* 14 (2014), 307–322

Edwin Cameron and Mark Gevisser, eds, *Defiant Desire: Gay and Lesbian Life in South Africa* (London: Routledge, 1995)

Andrew Flinn, Mary Stevens, and Elizabeth Shepherd, 'Whose Memories, Whose Archives? Independent Community Archives, Autonomy and the Mainstream', *Archival Science* 9 (2009), 71–86

Verne Harris, 'Against the Grain: Psychologies and Politics of Secrecy', *Archival Science* 9.3–4 (2009), 133–142

Eric Ketelaar, 'Archivalisation and Archiving', *Archives and Manuscripts* 26 (1999), 54–61

Sue McKemmish, Shannon Faulkhead, and Lynette Russell, 'Distrust in the Archive: Reconciling Records', *Archival Science* 11.3–4 (2011), 211–239

Rafael Verbuyst, 'History, Historians and the South African Truth and Reconciliation Commission', *New Contree* 66 (2013), 1–26

Wakimoto, Diana K., Christine Bruce, and Helen Partridge, 'Archivist as Activist: Lessons from Three Queer Community Archives in California', *Archival Science* 13 (2013), 293–316

NOTES

1. A. Lusher, 2 April 2018, www.independent.co.uk/news/world/africa/winnie-mandela-dead-madikizela-nelson-wife-life-story-obituary-anc-football-club-soweto-apartheid-a8285581.html.

2. D. Beresford, 'Winnie Madikizela-Mandela Obituary', *The Guardian*, 2 April 2018, www.theguardian.com/world/2018/apr/02/winnie-madikizela-mandela-obituary.

3. V. Harris, 'The Archival Sliver: Power, Memory, and Archives in South Africa', *Archival Science* 2.1–2 (2002), 63–86; doi:10.1007/BF02435631.

4. V. Harris, 'Contesting Remembering and Forgetting: The Archive of South Africa's Truth and Reconciliation Commission', *Innovation* 24.1 (2002),1–9; doi:10.4314/innovation.v24i1.26439.

5. J. L. Gibson, 'Overcoming Apartheid: Can Truth Reconcile a Divided Nation?', *Politikon* 31.2 (2004), 129–155; doi:10.1080/0258934042000280698.

6. F. du Toit, 'A Broken Promise? Evaluating South Africa's Reconciliation Process Twenty Years On', *International Political Science Review* 38.2 (2017), 169–184 (170); doi:10.1177/0192512115594412.

7. V. Harris, 'Antonyms of Our Remembering', *Archival Science* 14.3–4 (2014), 215–229; doi:10.1007/s10502-014-9221-5.

8. A. Manion and R. Morgan, 'The Gay and Lesbian Archives: Documenting Same-Sexuality in an African Context', *Agenda: Empowering Women for Gender Equity* 67 (2006) 29–35.

9. J. A. Boone, 'Creating a Queer Archive in the Public Eye: The Case of Reşad Ekrem Koçu', *GLQ: A Journal of Lesbian and Gay Studies* 23.1 (2017), 51–81; doi:10.1215/10642684-3672303.

10. Manion and Morgan, 'The Gay and Lesbian Archives', 31.

11. T. Migraine-George and A. Currier, 'Querying Queer African Archives: Methods and Movements', *Women's Studies Quarterly* 44.3–4 (2016), 190–207.

12. A. Flinn, M. Stevens, and E. Shepherd, 'Whose Memories, Whose Archives? Independent Community Archives, Autonomy and the Mainstream', *Archival Science* 9 (2009), 71–86.

13. A. Flinn, 'Independent Community Archives and Community-Generated Content: Writing, Saving and Sharing Our Histories', *Convergence: The International Journal of Research into New Media Technologies* 16.1 (2010), 39–51; doi:10.1177/1354856509347707; and 'Archival Activism: Independent and Community-Led Archives, Radical Public History and the Heritage Professions', *InterActions: UCLA Journal of Education and Information Studies* 7.2 (2011) [unpaginated], https://escholarship.org/uc/item/9pt2490x.

14. Harris, 'Contesting Remembering and Forgetting', 1–9.

15. J. A. Bastian and B. Alexander, Community Archives: The Shaping of Memory (London: Facet Publishing, 2009). M. Caswell, A. A. Migoni, N. Geraci, and M. Cifor, '"To Be Able to Imagine Otherwise": Community Archives and the Importance of Representation', *Archives and Records* 38.1 (2017), 5–26; doi:10.1080/23257962.2016.1260445. M. Caswell, M. Cifor, and M. H. Ramirez, '"To Suddenly Discover Yourself Existing": Uncovering the Impact of Community Archives', *The American Archivist* 79.1 (2016), 56–81; doi:10.17723/0360-9081.79.1.56. T. Cook, 'Evidence, Memory, Identity, and Community: Four Shifting Archival Paradigms', *Archival Science* 13.2–3 (2013), 95–120; doi:10.1007/s10502-012-9180-7. D. K. Wakimoto, C. Bruce, and H. Partridge, 'Archivist as Activist: Lessons from Three Queer Community Archives in California', *Archival Science* 13 (2013), 293–316.

16. S. McKemmish, A. J. Gilliland, and A. J. Lau, *Research in the Archival Multiverse* (Clayton: Monash University Press, 2016), oapen.org/search?identifier=628143. See also M. Pugh, 'Educating for the Archival Multiverse', *The American Archivist* 74.1 (2011), 69–101; The Archival Education and Research Institute (AERI), and Pluralizing the Archival Curriculum Group (PACG), 'Educating for the Archival Multiverse', *The American Archivist* 74.1 (2011), 69–101; M. Caswell, 'On Archival Pluralism: What Religious Pluralism (and Its Critics) Can Teach Us about Archives', *Archival Science* 13.4 (2013), 273–292, doi:10.1007/s10502-012-9197-y; F. Upward, S. McKemmish, and B. Reed, 'Archivists and Changing Social and Information Spaces: A Continuum Approach to Recordkeeping and Archiving in Online Cultures', *Archivaria* 72 (2011), 197–237; L. Iacovino, 'Multi-Method Interdisciplinary Research In Archival Science: The Case of Recordkeeping, Ethics And Law', *Archival Science* 4.3–4 (2004) 267–286; doi:10.1007/s10502-005-2595-7.

17. Upward et al., 'Archivists and Changing Social and Information Spaces', 227.

18. Caswell, 'On Archival Pluralism', 273.

19. Gibson, 'Overcoming Apartheid', 151.

20. See: V. Harris, *Archives and Justice: A South African Perspective* (Chicago: Society of American Archivists, 2007); C. Hamilton, V. Harris, M. Pickover, G. Reid, J. Taylor, and R. Saleh, eds, *Refiguring the Archive* (Dordrecht: Kluwer, 2002); A. Gilliland and S. Mckemmish, 'Building an Infrastructure for Archival Research', *Archival Science* 4.3–4 (2004) 149–197; doi:10.1007/s10502-006-6742-6.

21. A. Gilliland, A. Lau, Y. Lu, S. McKemmish, S. Rele, and K. White, 'Pluralizing the Archival Paradigm through Education: Critical Discussions around the Pacific Rim', *Archives and Manuscripts* 35.2 (2007), 10–39.

22. H. Robinson, 'Remembering Things Differently: Museums, Libraries and Archives as Memory Institutions and the Implications for Convergence', *Museum Management and Curatorship* 27.4 (2012), 413–429; doi:10.1080/09647775.2012.720188.

23. E. Ketelaar, 'Archival Turns and Returns: Studies of the Archive', in Gilliland et al., *Research in the Archival Multiverse*, 228–268.

24. H. Robinson, 'Curating Convergence: Interpreting Museum Objects in Integrated Collecting Institutions', *International Journal of Cultural Policy* 24.4 (2016) 1–19; doi:10.1080/10286632.2016.1218859.

25. R. Taavetti, 'A Marshall in Love. Remembering and Forgetting Queer Pasts in the Finnish Archives', *Archival Science* 16.3 (2016), 289–307; doi:10.1007/s10502-015-9251-7.

26. J. A. Lee, 'Beyond Pillars of Evidence: Exploring the Shaky Ground of Queer/ed Archives and their Methodologies', in Gilliland et al., *Research in the Archival Multiverse*, 324–352.

27. Migraine-George and Currier, 'Querying Queer African Archives', 201.

28. A. Flinn, 'Community Histories, Community Archives: Some Opportunities and Challenges', *Journal of the Society of Archivists* 28.2 (2007), 151–176 (153); doi:10.1080/00379810701611936.

29. B. Munro, 'Nelson, Winnie, and the Politics of Gender', in R. Barnard, ed., *The Cambridge Companion to Nelson Mandela* (Cambridge: Cambridge University Press, 2014), 92–112 (102); doi:10.1017/CCO9781139003766.006.

30. R. Holmes, 'Queer Comrades: Winnie Mandela and the Moffies', *Social Text*, 52/53 (1997), 161–180; doi:10.2307/466738.

31. Munro, 'Nelson, Winnie', 106.

32. Munro, 'Nelson, Winnie', 106.

33. Truth and Reconciliation Commission of South Africa Report, Department of Justice and Constitutional Development, Republic of South Africa, www.justice.gov.za/trc/report, 581.

34. Du Toit, 'A Broken Promise?', 173.

35. G. Kraak, 'Homosexuality and the South African Left: The Ambiguities of Exile' in N. Hoad, K. Martin, and G. Reid, eds, *Sex and Politics in South Africa* (Cape Town: Double Storey Books, 2005), 118–135.

36. Holmes, 'White Rapists make coloureds (and homosexuals): The Winnie Mandela Trial and the politics of race and sexuality', in E. Cameron and M. Gevisser, eds, *Defiant Desire: Gay and Lesbian Lives in South Africa* (New York: Routledge, 1995), 284–294.

37. Munro, 'Nelson, Winnie', 104.

38. Reid, 'Fragments from the Archives I', in Hoad et al., *Sex and Politics in South Africa*, 29–32.

39. E. Cameron, 'Archive: Presentation to the GLOW Action Committee and SHOC workshop', in N. Hoad, K. Martin, and G. Reid, *Sex and Politics in South Africa* (Cape Town: Double Storey Books 2005), 178–187.

40. See: A. Verdoolaege, 'Representing Apartheid Trauma: The Archive of the Truth and Reconciliation Commission Victim Hearings', in S. Gibson and S. Mollan, eds, *Representations of Peace and Conflict*, Rethinking Political Violence Series (London: Palgrave Macmillan, 2012), 285–305; doi:10.1057/9781137292254_15; P. Pigou, 'Accessing the Records of the Truth and Reconciliation Commission', in K. Allan, ed., *Paper Wars: Access to Information in South Africa* (Johannesburg: Wits University Press, 2009), 17–39; http://foip.saha.org.za/static/paper-wars-access-to-information-in-south-africa.
41. Harris, 'Contesting Remembering and Forgetting'.
42. Harris, 'Contesting Remembering and Forgetting', 7.
43. Discussed by A. Verdoolaege, 'Representing Apartheid Trauma: The Archive of the Truth and Reconciliation Commission Victim Hearings', in S. Gibson and S. Molan, eds, *Representations of Peace and Conflict, Rethinking Political Violence* (Basingstoke: Palgrave Macmillan, 2016), 285–305.
44. Harris, 'Contesting Remembering and Forgetting', 1.
45. B. Harris, 'The Archive, Public History and the Essential Truth: The TRC Reading the Past', in Hamilton et al., *Refiguring the Archive*, 161–178.
46. E. Ketelaar, 'Archival Temples, Archival Prisons: Modes of Power and Protection', *Archival Science* 2.3–4 (2002), 221–238; doi:10.1007/BF02435623; T. Cook and J. M. Schwartz, 'Archives, Records, and Power: From (Postmodern) Theory to (Archival) Performance', *Archival Science* 2.3–4 (2002), 171–185; doi:10.1007/BF02435620.
47. E. Ketelaar, 'A Living Archive, Shared by Communities of Records', in Bastian and Alexander, *Community Archives*, 109–130.

CHAPTER 33

DESTRUCTION AND DISPLACEMENT

The 2003 War and the Struggle for Iraq's Records

REBECCA ABBY WHITING

Conflict and regime change inevitably and intrinsically reconfigure structures of political and societal power. Within such upheaval, the place of records and archives within the order of things is also inevitably reconstructed. The 2003 allied invasion of Iraq and the subsequent military occupation led to vast amounts of the nation's records and archives being destroyed, damaged, and displaced. In addition to the loss of human life, the ravages of the war left irrecoverable scars on Iraq's cultural heritage and patrimony. While the international community was absorbed with lamenting the extensive damage done to the country's pre-Islamic archaeological assets, domestic Iraqi attention was equally concerned about the loss of Iraq's archives and manuscript and document collections.[1] As archives of immense historic value were left to the mercy of the war's destruction, the invading military forces sought to seize records created by the toppled Ba'th regime. Vast quantities of official Iraqi records were captured and shipped to a military processing centre in Qatar to be searched through for evidence of weapons of mass destruction (WMD) and links to armed groups that might justify the war. In addition to the records de-territorialized to Qatar, which were eventually repatriated in 2013,[2] a further two archival collections were displaced to the United States during the invasion, the Iraqi Jewish Archive (IJA) and the Ba'th Regional Command Collection (BRCC). The histories of these records, their formation into archives in displacement, reflect the politics of the invasion and the power dynamics that have so deeply impacted both Iraqi history and control of the Iraqi historical record.

The treatment of Iraq's records and archives during the 2003 conflict and ensuing occupation demonstrates the ways in which the value of records and archives evolves through conflict. The IJA and the BRCC, which will be the focus of this chapter, hold historical documents vastly different in nature: one primarily consists of records and books created by a minority religious community, one of records generated by the Ba'th Party during its rule. Both were displaced so as to ensure their survival; amid the war and destruction these collections were deemed worthy of preservation. Heritage is a resource, and the extraction of the archives has influenced intellectual control over Iraqi history. While the dislocation of these two collections has ensured their preservation, their removal denotes an epistemological fissure in the documentation of Iraq's past. This dispossession came during a period of political and social turmoil when collective memory was in the process of being reformulated after the fall of a repressive regime.

Throughout history, war has led to the destruction and displacement of records and archives. During conflict, both deliberate and haphazard forces determine what is lost and what survives of the written historical record. In 1992, for example, libraries and archives in Bosnia and Herzegovina were shelled and burned during the conflict. Writing on the attacks, András Riedlmayer described them as an 'attempt to eliminate the material evidence—books, documents, and works of art—that could remind future generations that people of different ethnic and religious traditions once shared a common heritage in Bosnia.'[3] While the destruction of documentary heritage, both in targeted attempts to erase the past or as collateral damage in a war-zone, constitutes an irreversible loss to recorded history, the capture and de-territorialization of materials during conflict also serve to redefine the written record.

Conflict has long resulted in the extensive movement and repeated changing of hands of records and archives. During World War Two, Nazi forces seized books, religious texts, and historical archives from most countries in Europe. At the end of the war, vast quantities of documents looted by the Nazis were captured by Soviet troops and transferred to Moscow where they were held in secret until the early 1990s. The various movements of the documents were determined by historical events, as their imagined uses and perceived value shifted in accordance with the evolving political and social realities. The documents had initially been confiscated by Nazi forces from nations and communities for intelligence and counter-intelligence purposes, for population control, and as part of ideological projects towards Germanization. When the Nazis were defeated, some of these looted materials were seized along with records of German provenance captured by Soviet troops. A considerable portion of the documents were initially valued by Soviet forces for operational analysis and the identification of Soviet citizens who had collaborated with the Nazis. Other materials were seized for their cultural and historical value. Patricia Kennedy Grimsted defines these displaced materials as 'twice plundered' but suggests that they might also be considered as having been 'twice saved', given that they survived the war. However, she concludes, the preservation of the materials is of little worth unless they are identified and returned to the communities that created them.[4]

Considering what documentary heritage survives a war, why it was selected for preservation, by whom, and ultimately for whom, exposes the forces that contribute to defining the historical record in the wake of conflict. The loss of books, manuscripts, archives, and records is grievous, but interventions to preserve the historical record should not be approached as merely benign. Decisions as to what is deemed valuable enough to preserve occur in relation to the newly-emergent social, political, and administrative powers brought into being through the conflict, as evidenced by the fate of Iraq's documentary heritage. After the 2003 invasion, Iraqi records that had administrative functions prior to the war were reimagined as archives of historical interest with social, cultural, or educational value, or as of military and intelligence interest, weaponizable as tools to be deployed against the fallen regime. The seizure of records was indicative of a new order of power that defined what was considered to be of value, who could access it, and how it could be deployed.

In the midst of the widescale destruction brought about by the war, select records and archival materials deemed valuable enough to salvage were shipped to the US. As scholars have argued, debates on the preservation through de-territorialization of Iraq's heritage cannot be had in isolation from recognition of a long history of its patrimony being dislocated by Western nations and held in their cultural and educational institutions.[5] Iraqi scholar Sinan Antoon noted of this trend, 'The narratives that frame the objects and collections and erase the plunder are usually those of "saving" and "recovering".... They are "safe and sound" here and housed in reputable institutions where scholars and experts, who appreciate and understand their value and history, tend to them.... As if the natives, the rightful owners of these objects, do not deserve them.'[6] The displacement of Iraqi archives has instigated an ongoing struggle of conflicting forces vying for control, voices competing over who has legitimate rights to repurpose documents after the fall of a regime. Thus far the actors with the greatest political and economic power have succeeded in delineating the conditions of access to this important documentary heritage and hence dictate who can frame historical questions and write Iraqi history.

Destruction

The 2003 war was a violent agent for radical change to Iraq's sociopolitical topography and within that, the status of its records and archives. The US-led aerial bombing campaign against Baghdad began on 20 March. The next night, precision-guided munitions began to destroy government facilities. On 7 April, air attacks targeted Saddam Hussein and other Iraqi leaders and on 9 April, Baghdad fell to the coalition forces.[7] According to a Human Rights Watch (HRW) report, in the weeks preceding the invasion, Iraqi government officials shredded and burned reams of documents.[8] The aerial bombing campaign then destroyed countless more as the invasion and subsequent military occupation laid waste to much of Iraq's infrastructure. The ephemerality of paper makes documents particularly susceptible to the destructiveness of war, and both contemporary records and historic collections were impacted.

In the days following the invasion, the collapse of the Ba'th regime led to widespread attacks upon and looting of state and cultural institutions, including the Iraq National Library and Archive (INLA) and universities and their libraries. As a result of lootings and two fires on the 10 and 12 April, approximately 25 per cent of the INLA book collections was destroyed, including rare books, and 60 per cent of the archives. Ottoman and Hashemite-era documents were irretrievably damaged, as were the bulk of Ba'th-era records.[9] Saad Eskander, who became the Director General of INLA in December 2003 and remained in this post until 2015, conducted an investigation into the events. He concluded that the fires had been started by regime loyalists intent on torching the archive held within INLA that covered the history of the Ba'th Party since it came to power in 1963 and contained the transcripts of court-martials set up by the regime. Eskander said of the destruction of INLA's collections, 'it was a national disaster on a large scale. These losses cannot be compensated. They formed modern Iraq's historical memory.'[10] US troops stood idly by while museums, archaeological sites, libraries, monuments, and mosques suffered damage and intensive looting activities.[11] The US has been widely condemned for failing to prohibit and prevent the pillaging and misappropriation of cultural property during the invasion, an obligation under Article 4 (3) of the 1954 Hague Convention for the Protection of Cultural Property in the Event of Armed Conflict.[12] The Convention includes archives as cultural property that should be protected during war, subject to the demands of imperative military necessity. Although the US did not ratify the 1954 Hague Convention until March 2009, in 2003 Iraq was a signatory and arguably the law could be applied to all forces acting within its territory. However, even if it were proved that the US had contravened the law in this regard, the international community does not have the power or the inclination to enforce it.[13]

While older archives of great historical value were left unprotected, the invading army also seemingly had no coherent policy towards securing the official records of the regime.[14] HRW had on 9 April 2003 written to US Secretary of State Colin Powell and US Secretary of Defense Donald Rumsfeld urging the allied forces to ensure that Iraqi government offices were not ransacked, so as to ensure the safety of records that could potentially provide key evidence in future war crimes trials.[15] That their missive went unheeded suggests that preserving evidence of human rights abuses was not a priority for the invading forces at the outset of the invasion; records were not initially considered valuable enough to protect for their potential use in pursuing legal accountability for crimes against humanity. In the city of Basra, for example, British officials publicly stated that they allowed the looting of Ba'th Party offices that held important records as a means of demonstrating to the local population that the former regime no longer controlled the city.[16] While the occupying forces permitted these activities in order to symbolize their victory, elements of Iraqi society were also collecting records within the new sociopolitical climate forming after the collapse of the Ba'th regime. Although records were pilfered during the widespread looting of regime institutions, Iraqi opposition groups and civil organizations were also mobilizing to seize vast amounts of state records from government buildings, Ba'th Party headquarters, intelligence and security apparatus offices, and military garrisons across Iraq. Political parties, including the Islamic Da'wa Party and Iraqi Communist Party, secured large numbers of records from the General Security Directorate and the General Intelligence Directorate in Baghdad, hoping to acquire information pertaining to the former regime's violent campaigns against their members. The Iraqi Association of Free Prisoners seized 18 million documents, the majority of which were from the archives of the General Security Directorate. The Association was searching for lists of names of Iraqis that had been executed by the former regime. The lists were pinned on the walls of their premises with photographs found in the files, so as to enable enquiring relatives to identify their missing family members.[17]

As Iraqi political parties and non-governmental organizations appropriated aspects of the Ba'th regime's records and redeployed them within their communities in the wake of its collapse, the invading allied forces were also sweeping through its institutions. Having gained control of Baghdad, military forces scrambled through State and Party buildings looking for evidence of WMD and links to terrorism. The war had been waged on the premise that Iraq was producing WMD and the forces' primary design upon records was seeking evidence that could justify the attack.[18] It is estimated that 100 million pages of documents were seized, a collection far greater than those held by any other body. These were sent to the Combined Media Processing Center in Qatar, which was established by the US Department of Defense in May 2003 for document exploitation in support of the war efforts. In Qatar, personnel sifted through a wide variety of materials gathered by manoeuvre units and mobile collection teams in Iraq looking for documents of intelligence value.[19] The documents were then investigated by the Iraq Survey Group, the team tasked with the elusive mission of determining whether the Iraqi regime had maintained stockpiles of WMD. Despite the intensive drive behind these searches, the invading troops appeared to have a haphazard approach to the treatment of documents. In some instances, official documents were left scattered about for weeks, apparently deemed not to be of value.[20]

As different actors competed over Iraqi records amidst the chaos and destruction of the invasion and occupation, the histories of two very different archival collections stand out. The IJA and the BRCC were shipped to the US in 2003 and 2005, respectively. Unlike the dislocation to Qatar of official records seized by military forces, which could arguably be justified as falling within the international legal parameters of military necessity, both the IJA and BRCC were displaced from Iraq under the primary justification of preserving the materials.

The Iraqi Jewish Archive

The IJA is a collection of manuscripts, documents, and books pertaining to the Iraqi Jewish community, and includes records from synagogues and Jewish organizations in Baghdad. In May 2003, through information provided by a former Iraqi intelligence officer, US troops were informed of the existence of an ancient copy of the Jewish Talmud in the basement of the Iraqi *mukhabarat* (intelligence agency) headquarters in Baghdad. A US mobile exploration team usually tasked with searching for WMD deviated from their hunt for evidence to seek out this valuable cultural artefact.[21] The *mukhabarat* building had been damaged during the aerial bombing campaign, its basement flooded with fetid water due to burst water pipes. The team entered the site accompanied by Dr Harold Rhode, a specialist in Islamic Affairs working with the Coalition Provisional Authority (CPA), the occupation government in Iraq. In the basement, they came across the archives of the *mukhabarat* Israel-Palestine and Jewish Sections. Although they did not find the prized Talmud they were looking for, they discovered over 2,700 published books and tens of thousands of documents including records from Jewish schools and hospitals; correspondence from religious and community leaders, archival documents pertaining to government relations, financial and business records, property information, birth, engagement, marriage, divorce, and death certificates; Rabbinic literature; and fragments of religious parchment scrolls.[22] The presence of these materials in the *mukhabarat* basement tells of the history of persecution and dispossession of Iraqi Jews at the hands of successive regimes.

Iraq is home to the oldest continuously-present Jewish community in the world, although less than ten members of the community reside there today.[23] The once-flourishing community had been of huge economic and cultural importance in Baghdad, particularly in the early twentieth century. In the 1930s, pro-Nazi propaganda seeped into Iraq and anti-Jewish rhetoric became more prevalent. In 1941, a coup overthrew the pro-British regime with funding and support from Nazi Germany. On 1 and 2 June of that year, violent attacks against the Jewish community, who were seen as pro-British, took place in Baghdad. Around 180 Jews were murdered and at least 800 injured. These attacks are known as the *Farhud* (violent dispossession).[24] The 1948 Arab–Israeli war then sparked renewed hostility towards Iraqi Jews and increasingly harsh discriminatory laws were enacted. Many began to attempt to immigrate to Israel, despite not being permitted to do so by Iraqi law. In response to the mass illegal emigration, the Iraqi Parliament passed a law in 1950, effective for one year, that permitted Jews to emigrate if they renounced their Iraqi nationality. Between 1950 and 1951, around 123,000 Jews (of the 135,000 remaining) left Iraq, predominantly to re-settle in Israel. Those who left were permitted to take only a few items of clothing and a small sum of money with them. The property they were forced to leave behind was seized by the Iraqi government. After the Arab–Israeli War of 1967, the situation worsened for those who had remained in Iraq. Under the Ba'th Party, legislation was passed further restricting the rights of Jews and very few chose to stay. In 1969, nine Jewish men and five other Iraqis were publicly hanged on charges of spying for the US and Israel. When Saddam Hussein assumed the presidency in 1979, political violence in attempts to silence dissent surged. Anti-Zionist and anti-imperialist propaganda programmes were regular; the Jewish community increasingly feared for their lives and most of the remaining members attempted to emigrate.[25] As members of the Jewish community were leaving Iraq, they had stored the records and texts they were unable to take with them in the women's section of the last remaining functioning synagogue in Baghdad. Documents from other synagogues were also collected there. The synagogue was later raided by Iraqi security forces and the entire collection of materials was seized, eventually finding their way to the *mukhabarat* basement.[26]

When the US troops found the collection during the 2003 war, some of the items were floating in waste water and many were badly damaged.[27] Rhode, realizing what the materials consisted of, initiated efforts to retrieve them from the flooded basement and brought them out into the sun to dry, where they quickly began to mould. Rhode contacted the US authorities in Iraq to request support in saving the materials, but they showed no interest. In keeping with their wider policies, the preservation of cultural heritage was not a priority. Rhode instead procured a grant from a private individual in the US to pay for initial salvage expenses and reached out to a powerful network of contacts in Israel and the US, requesting that they exert pressure on high-level US officials. This resulted in the US government taking control of the project.[28] At the request of the CPA, a team of conservation specialists from the US National Archives and Records Administration (NARA) in Washington DC came to Baghdad in June 2003 to inspect the materials.[29] They decided that the only way to save the deteriorating collection was to ship it out of Iraq to undergo restoration procedures. The team searched for options to preserve the materials in Iraq, but treatment options were limited,[30] particularly in the wake of the conflict that had so depleted infrastructure and resources, including electricity supply. On 20 August 2003, a contract was signed between NARA and the CPA. Temporary custody of the IJA was granted to NARA so that it could be sent to the US for restoration and it was shipped shortly afterwards. The contract presumed Iraq as the rightful owner and allowed for a two-year loan of the materials after which the collection was to be returned to Iraq.[31] The initial contract was followed by two further loan agreements from the Iraqi government and is currently under renegotiation.

The displacement of the IJA to the US for restoration unleashed a fierce international debate over the ownership of the materials and where the collection should be based. American Jewish groups and the Iraqi Jewish diaspora have argued that as the Iraqi state forcibly confiscated the materials from the community that created it, it is erroneous to consider the collection the legal property of that State. They hold that it should not be returned to Iraq given that the vast majority of the Iraqi Jewish community left the country under persecution.[32] They have received considerable support from the US political elite. On 18 July 2018, a resolution was introduced to the Senate strongly recommending that the US renegotiate the return of the IJA to Iraq. The resolution urged that the materials be 'kept in a place where long-term preservation and care can be guaranteed' and that they 'should be housed in a location that is accessible to scholars and to Iraqi Jews and their descendants who have a personal interest in it', stating that the initial agreement between NARA and the CPA was signed before the complete history of the IJA was known.[33] Iraqi officials and some members of the international archivist community have argued that the collection is important Iraqi patrimony. In 2010, Eskander travelled to the US with a delegation of Iraqi officials to request the return of all displaced Iraqi archives. He argued that it was important that the IJA be repatriated to Iraq and housed at INLA so that future generations of Iraqis can access these materials and understand the contributions made to Iraqi history by the Jewish community and also the repression they faced.[34]

The invading armed forces' deliberate destruction of Iraq's public infrastructure, which came after twelve years of a debilitating United Nations sanctions regime,[35] had rendered the country's economy and resources so eroded that the capacity for conservation treatment of the IJA, or other damaged archival materials, was near non-existent. Eskander, in an attempt to preserve the mildewing remains of the four hundred-year-old Ottoman archive salvaged from the INLA fires, had searched Baghdad for buildings still intact that could house the collection. He eventually stored the materials in an abandoned kitchen freezer and found a generator to power it. He received little help from the CPA.[36] Eskander considered the US' actions in preserving the IJA to be discriminatory, given that considerable efforts were exerted to preserve it while other non-current Iraqi historical records were left to be destroyed or looted.[37] The IJA was the only cultural property that left Iraq for preservation under written contract, de-territorialized after pressure was exerted through the mobilization of a network of powerful individuals. The displacement allowed for an impressive restoration and digitization project which has provided access to the materials to members of the Iraqi Jewish community in the US and to online copies of much of the collection to those with Internet access. However, despite the signed contract that recognized the materials as Iraqi property, full decision-making agency as to the fate of the IJA has been removed from the post-Ba'th Iraqi authorities. With its military, economic, and political might, the US government has posited itself as the arbiter in the struggle over the fate of the collection.

Ba'th Regional Command Collection

The BRCC constitutes records of the Ba'th Party Regional Command headquarters in Baghdad. From 1968 to 2003 the Ba'th Party was the most important of the three pillars of the Iraqi government, alongside the bureaucracy and the military, which its members infiltrated and dominated.[38] The collection includes party membership files, the correspondence and dossiers of the party Regional and National commands, school registers that detail the political affiliations of male school children and the reputations of their family members, and party literature.[39] After the invasion, the materials were found in the basement of the party's headquarters, which due to damage caused by the war had been intermittently flooded. The building was within the militarized Green Zone established by the occupying forces and thus had not been subject to looting activities. It had been searched through by US forces, presumably in the searches for evidence of WMD, but the files had not been seized and sent to Qatar. It is unclear why the collection was passed over by the troops; in Eskander's assessment, they had not considered it to be of pertinent political or security value.[40]

In April 2003, members of the Iraq Memory Foundation were alerted to the existence of the records in the basement of the party's regional command headquarters. The Iraq Memory Foundation was a US-based organization founded by expatriate Iraqi academic Kanan Makiya, a longstanding critic of the Ba'th Party. In 1991 he had been involved in a project that led to Kurdish political parties handing over vast quantities of state records they had captured during a widescale uprising in northern Iraq against the Iraqi central authorities to US forces, who then shipped them to the US.[41] Makiya was a vocal supporter of the 2003 invasion of Iraq, considering it necessary to topple Saddam Hussein's government, and had ties to the US leadership of the occupation. The Memory Foundation had relocated to Baghdad shortly after the invasion began in order to collect and preserve documentation of the Iraqi experience of dictatorship.[42] The organization registered itself in Iraq and Mustafa al-Kadhimi, who was appointed Prime Minister of Iraq in May 2020, took a foundational role. Makiya planned to establish a cultural centre in the capital where the records of the Ba'th regime would be made available to the Iraqi public. He believed this 'memory project' would allow Iraqi society an understanding of the complexities of the nation's recent history and thus contribute towards reconciliation and historical accountability.[43] Through his connections with the CPA, Makiya secured custody of the BRCC for the Memory Foundation by September 2003 and his team began to scan and digitize the collection.

While Makiya defined the project as a civilian one and removed from political activities, his relationship with Bush-administration officials and his public support for the invasion have meant that the Memory Foundation's activities were always intertwined with the politics of the war.[44] On 18 June 2004, Makiya as the director of the Memory Foundation signed a contract with the US military's Defense Contracting Command for $2,100,000. The contract was primarily for the filming of oral histories of 'survivors of Ba'athist atrocities' but also included the collection of 'documentary evidence of atrocities and crimes committed by the former Ba'thist regime'.[45] Although Makiya stated that the US authorities had no involvement in the Memory Foundation's activities after transferring the funds,[46] the contract demonstrates a will on the part of the US to deploy Iraqi records to expose the former regime's crimes to Iraqi and international communities. As the Iraq Survey Group failed to find evidence of an active WMD programme, the US was in need of an alternative strategy with which to retrospectively legitimize its war.[47]

The cultural centre in Baghdad never came into being. As armed opposition to the invasion and occupation grew, the Memory Foundation's team felt that they were unable to complete the digitization process in Baghdad. Email exchanges between Memory Foundation members and US officials in January 2005 show that the team were concerned that the records were endangered amid the ongoing violence and political instability and sought to remove them from Baghdad to ensure their survival.[48] While they had initially hoped to send them to Qatar to be digitized at the US military processing centre there, they eventually agreed to ship them to the US so as to expedite their displacement from Iraq.[49] A memorandum of understanding between the Iraq Memory Foundation and the United States Government (USG) recognized the Foundation as the custodian of the collection and stated that the Foundation would enable USG access to documents of the former Iraqi regime in its custody and 'provide assistance to the USG in extracting, analyzing, and interpreting pertinent information from the Foundation's documents'.[50] After they were digitized by a US government contractor, Makiya formed an agreement with the Hoover Institution in 2008 and both the original records and a digitized version were deposited there. Unredacted digitized copies are made available to researchers upon the signing of a user agreement which forbids all duplication of the materials. The originals were kept in the Hoover Tower under strict security until their repatriation to Iraq on 31 August 2020. The repatriation was conducted discreetly, with neither the US or Iraqi governments announcing the shipment of the materials back to Baghdad.[51] Undoubtedly, the appointment of al-Kadhimi as Iraq's prime minister was instrumental in the return of the archive after years of controversy over its displacement.[52]

Throughout the years of the BRCC's dislocation, debates over its status raged. Although Makiya had always contended that the archive belonged to the Iraqi people and would one day be returned, he had long held that 'Baghdad is just not ready for it'.[53] He was concerned that the Ba'th records, which contain sensitive information, might be used by political parties to exert pressure on their opponents and wanted to see laws passed in Iraq that would protect the privacy of individuals named in them before they were returned. His right to make such a decision over official records has been strongly contested. Eskander in a 2006 interview noted that the Iraq Memory Foundation, 'works without being subjected to Iraqi laws, outside of Iraqi legislative and executive bodies, so they are outside the legal framework of the country'. Like Makiya, he also expressed concerns that the records could be used as political weapons. Eskander, however, wanted to see them in the custody of Iraqi state institutions, not in private hands.[54]

Makiya was positioned to define and represent Iraqi rights regarding the archive through his connections to the political elite of the occupation and the Iraqi Interim Government that replaced the CPA. There are many international precedents for NGOs and other non-state actors archiving and digitizing the records of a former regime. After the wars in Bosnia and Herzegovina between 1992–1995, for example, the deterioration of state-sponsored memory institutions led to alternative institutions increasingly documenting mass atrocities and managing the heritage of the conflict.[55] The Federal Commissioner for the Records of the State Security Service of the former German Democratic Republic, the first institution to make secret police files accessible to the public, had its roots in citizen activism; the public had occupied Stasi records offices after the fall of the Berlin Wall in order to prevent the destruction of records at the hands of Stasi functionaries. When the records were then deployed in processes of political and social transition, legal mechanisms were put in place in attempts to navigate between rights to access information while ensuring the protection of citizens' rights to privacy.[56] In Iraq, although Makiya had initially intended for the BRCC records to be made available to the Iraqi public, his intervention ultimately oversaw the archive's de-territorialization entirely beyond their reach. Any accountability to the Iraqi public to ensure that its rights are upheld was lost. By removing the BRCC from Iraq, Makiya passed control of the archive into the hands of the government that had led the invasion and had vested interest as to how narratives as to Iraq's past would be constructed. When the archive was deposited at the Hoover Institution, decisions as to access were completely in private hands. As visiting the archive while it was in the US was for most Iraqi citizens near impossible, the custody situation enabled the continued dominance of Western scholarship on Iraq in the years after the 2003 war.

The Murder of Cultural Memory

When war reformulates sociopolitical realities, emergent forces inevitably vie to dictate the value and the potential functions of records and archives, the parameters of access to them, and whose rights are considered to be legitimate. The overthrow of Saddam Hussein's regime brought about a new period in Iraq's history, and as Eskander argued, one in which the preservation and provision of access to documents would have contributed greatly to social stability and political progress.[57] The war defined what survived of Iraq's documentary heritage and in whose hands it was held. That there were no mechanisms in place to ensure the protection of historic archives or recent administrative records demonstrates that preserving Iraqi culture as a basis for social unification or securing evidence of human rights abuses were far from primary concerns for the invading forces. Nabil al-Tikriti, writing on the 2003 destruction of Iraqi manuscript collections, archives, and libraries, described the policies towards Iraq's documentary patrimony during the war and occupation as passive and negligent mnemocide—the murder of cultural memory.[58] In the wake of the immense devastation caused by the conflict, the IJA and the BRCC were deemed to be worthy of preservation and deterritorialized. The displacements ensured their survival while redefining the Iraqi historical record by dictating how and by whom these archives could be used. As the 2003 Iraq war shows, the fate of records and archives is determined by the parties with the greatest political and economic power, forces that have outweighed legal and ethical concerns and have served to all but silence the voices within Iraq that have opposed the dislocation and commandeering of the nation's documentary heritage.

FURTHER READING

Nabil al-Tikriti, '"Stuff Happens": A Brief Overview of the 2003 Destruction of Iraqi Manuscript Collections, Archives, and Libraries', *Library Trends* 55.3 (2007), 730–745

Sinan Antoon, 'How the NYT Partook in the Plunder of Iraq', *Al Jazeera*, 24 April 2018, www.aljazeera.com/indepth/opinion/nyt-partook-plunder-iraq-18042 4100839509.html

Raymond W. Baker, Sheeren T. Ismael, and Tareq Y. Ismael, eds, *Cultural Cleansing in Iraq: Why Museums Were Looted, Libraries Burned and Academics Murdered* (London and New York: Pluto Press, 2010)

Arbella Bet-Shlimon, 'Preservation or Plunder? The ISIS Files and a History of Heritage Removal in Iraq | MERIP', *Middle East Report Online*, 2018, https://merip.org/2018/05/preservation-or-plunder-the-isis-files-and-a-history-of-heritage-removal-in-iraq/

Michael P. Brill, 'The Archives of Saddam Hussein's Ba'th Party and the Politics of Remembering and Forgetting the Ba'thist Era in Iraq', *International Journal of Middle East Studies* 55.2 (2023), 336–343. doi:10.1017/S002074382300082X

Michelle Caswell, '"Thank You Very Much, Now Give Them Back": Cultural Property and the Fight over the Iraqi Baath Party Records', *The American Archivist* 74.1 (2011), 211–240

Saad Eskander, 'Minerva Research Initiative: Searching for the Truth or Denying the Iraqis the Rights to Know the Truth?', Social Science Research Council, *The Minerva Controversy* (blog), 29 October 2008, http://essays.ssrc.org/minerva/2008/10/29/eskander

James Lowry, ed., *Displaced Archives* (London and New York: Routledge, 2017)

NOTES

1. N. al-Tikriti, '"Stuff Happens": A Brief Overview of the 2003 Destruction of Iraqi Manuscript Collections, Archives, and Libraries', *Library Trends* 55.3 (2007), 730–745.
2. B. P. Montgomery and M. P. Brill, 'The Ghosts of Past Wars Live on in a Critical Archive', *War on the Rocks* (blog), 11 September 2019, https://warontherocks.com/2019/09/the-ghosts-of-past-wars-live-on-in-a-critical-archive.
3. A. Riedlmayer, 'Erasing the Past: The Destruction of Libraries and Archives in Bosnia-Herzegovina', *Middle East Studies Association Bulletin* 29.1 (1995), 7–11 (8).
4. P. K. Grimsted, 'From Nazi Plunder to Russian Restitution', in P. K. Grimsted, F. J. Hoogewoud, and E. Ketelaar, eds, *Returned from Russia: Nazi Archival Plunder in Western Europe and Recent Restitution Issues* (Builth Wells: Institute of Art and Law, 2007), 3–128 (13, 86); and also by Grimsted, 'Twice Plundered or "Twice Saved"? Identifying Russia's "Trophy" Archives and the Loot of the Reichssicherheitshauptamt', *Holocaust and Genocide Studies* 15.2 (2001), 191–244.
5. A. Bet-Shlimon, 'Preservation or Plunder? The ISIS Files and a History of Heritage Removal in Iraq | MERIP', Middle East Report Online, 2018, https://merip.org/2018/05/preservation-or-plunder-the-isis-files-and-a-history-of-heritage-removal-in-iraq/; M. Saleh, 'Protection or Plunder?: A U.S. Journalist Took Thousands of ISIS Files Out of Iraq, Reigniting a Bitter Dispute Over the Theft of Iraqi History', *The Intercept*, 2018, https://theintercept.com/2018/05/23/isis-files-podcast-new-york-times-iraq/.
6. S. Antoon, 'How the NYT Partook in the Plunder of Iraq', *Al Jazeera*, 24 April 2018 www.aljazeera.com/indepth/opinion/nyt-partook-plunder-iraq-180424100839509.html.
7. Human Rights Watch, 'Off Target: The Conduct of the War and Civilian Casualties in Iraq: II. Conduct of the Air War', 2003, www.hrw.org/reports/2003/usa 1203/4.htm#_ftnref24.
8. Human Rights Watch, 'Iraq: State of the Evidence: III. The Documentary Evidence', 2004, www.hrw.org/reports/2004/iraq1104/3.htm.
9. Al-Tikriti, 'Stuff Happens'.
10. S. Eskander, 'The Tale of Iraq's "Cemetery of Books"', *Information Today*, 2004, www.infotoday.com/IT/dec04/eskander.shtml.
11. R. W. Baker, S. T. Ismael, and T. Y. Ismael, eds, *Cultural Cleansing in Iraq: Why Museums Were Looted, Libraries Burned and Academics Murdered* (London and New York: Pluto Press, 2010).
12. P. Gerstenblith, '1954 Hague Convention on the Protection of Cultural Property', in L. Rothfield, ed., *Antiquities Under Siege: Cultural Heritage Protection After the Iraq War* (Plymouth: AltaMira Press, 2008), 79–89.
13. M. Caswell, '"Thank You Very Much, Now Give Them Back": Cultural Property and the Fight over the Iraqi Baath Party Records', *The American Archivist* 74.1 (2011), 229–230.
14. Human Rights Watch, 'Iraq: State of the Evidence: III. The Documentary Evidence'.
15. Human Rights Watch, 'Iraq: Protect Government Archives from Looting', *Human Rights Watch*, 2003, www.hrw.org/news/2003/04/09/iraq-protect-government-archives-looting.

16. Human Rights Watch, 'Iraq: State of the Evidence: III. The Documentary Evidence'.
17. Human Rights Watch, 'Iraq: State of the Evidence: III. The Documentary Evidence'.
18. J. Battle, 'The Iraq War—Part I: The U.S. Prepares for Conflict, 2001', *The National Security Archive*, 22 September 2010, https://nsarchive2.gwu.edu/NSAEBB/NSAEBB326/index.htm#1.
19. Department of Defense, Combined Media Processing Center-Qatar, Memorandum for all Personnel, 4 February 2006, www.docexblog.com/2012/02/captured-iraqi-document-exploitation.html.
20. Human Rights Watch, 'Iraq: State of the Evidence: III. The Documentary Evidence'.
21. J. Gordon, 'The Savior of Iraqi Jewish Heritage: An Interview with Dr. Harold Rhode', *The New English* Review, December 2013, www.newenglishreview.org/custpage.cfm/frm/160276/sec_id/160276.
22. Iraqi Jewish Archive, *Notes on the Scope of the Iraqi Jewish Archive (IJA)*, https://www.ija.archives.gov/search (accessed 23 June 2018)
23. M. R. Fischbach, 'Claiming Jewish Communal Property in Iraq', *Middle East Report* 248 (2008), 5–7 (5).
24. S. G. Haim, 'Aspects of Jewish Life in Baghdad under the Monarchy', *Middle Eastern Studies* 12.2 (1976), 188–208 (192); H. J. Cohen, 'The Anti -Jewish *Farhūd* in Baghdad, 1941', *Middle Eastern Studies* 3.1 (1966), 2–17 (10–12).
25. C. Basri, 'The Jewish Refugees from Arab Countries: An Examination of Legal Rights— A Case Study of the Human Rights Violations of Iraqi Jews', *Fordham International Law Journal* 26.3 (2002), 680–692; Haim, 'Aspects of Jewish Life in Baghdad under the Monarchy', 195–200; Fischbach, 'Claiming Jewish Communal Property in Iraq', 5.
26. Interview with Harold Rhode, Skype, 28 November 2019.
27. Iraqi Jewish Archive, https://www.ija.archives.gov/search.
28. J. Gordon, 'The Savior of Iraqi Jewish Heritage: An Interview with Dr. Harold Rhode'.
29. The Iraqi Jewish Archive Preservation Report, 2 October 2003, https://www.ija.archives.gov/sites/default/files/page-images/content/1.0/Iraqi%20Jewish%20Archive%20Report.pdf.
30. 'National Archives Unveils Iraqi Jewish Artifacts in Exhibit Opening October 11', *National Archives*, 2016, www.archives.gov/press/press-releases/2013/nr13-96.html (accessed 14 July 2020).
31. Agreement between the Coalition Provisional Authority and the National Archives and Records Administration, effective as of 20 August 2003, https://ija.archives.gov/sites/default/files/MOA_CPA_NARA%201.pdf.
32. C. Basri and D. Dangoor, 'The Iraqi Jewish Archive Is Stolen Property That Should Go Back to Its Original Owners', *The Hill*, 27 April 2018, https://thehill.com/opinion/international/385072-the-iraqi-jewish-archive-is-stolen-property-that-should-go-back-to-its.
33. P. Toomey, 'Text—S.Res.577—115th Congress (2017-2018): A Resolution Strongly Recommending That the United States Renegotiate the Return of the Iraqi Jewish Archive to Iraq', 2018, www.congress.gov/bill/115th-congress/senate-resolution/577/text.
34. A. Kami, 'Iraq Asks U.S. to Return Millions of Archive Documents', *Reuters*, 19 May 2010 www.reuters.com/article/us-iraq-usa-archives-idINTRE64I3J320100519.
35. A. Rohde, *State-Society Relations in Ba'thist Iraq. Facing Dictatorship*, SOAS/Routledge Studies on the Middle East (Abingdon and New York: Routledge, 2010), 65.

36. Z. Bahrani, 'Amnesia in Mesopotamia', *Document Journal* 53 (2013).
37. S. Eskander, 'Minerva Research Initiative: Searching for the Truth or Denying the Iraqis the Rights to Know the Truth? ', Social Science Research Council, *The Minerva Controversy* (blog), 29 October 2008, http://essays.ssrc.org/minerva/2008/10/29/eskander.
38. Joseph Sassoon, *Saddam Hussein's Ba'th Party: Inside an Authoritarian Regime* (Cambridge: Cambridge University Press, 2011), 7.
39. Iraq Documents at Hoover Reference Guide; Dina Rizk Khoury, *Iraq in Wartime: Soldiering, Martyrdom, and Remembrance* (New York: Cambridge University Press, 2013), 180.
40. Eskander, 'Minerva Research Initiative: Searching for the Truth or Denying the Iraqis the Rights to Know the Truth?'.
41. R. A. Whiting, 'The Archive as an Artefact of Conflict: The North Iraq Dataset', *Critical Military Studies* 74.4 (2019), 435–499.
42. Iraq Documents at Hoover Reference Guide.
43. Interview with Kanan Makiya, Cambridge, Massachusetts, 17 April 2018.
44. Khoury, *Iraq in Wartime*, 13.
45. Defense Contracting Command-Washington, contract no. W74V8H-04-P-0393, 18 June 2004, Accession no. 2010C35–11.64/66, Box 104, Hoover Institution Archives.
46. Interview with Kanan Makiya, Cambridge, Massachusetts, 17 April 2018.
47. Wisam Alshaibi, 'Weaponizing Iraq's Archives | MERIP' https://merip.org/2019/09/weaponizing-iraqs-archives/ (accessed 15 October 2019).
48. Correspondence from Kanan Makiya to Dobie McArthur, 14 January 2005, Accession no. 2010C35–11.64/66, Box 104, Hoover Institution Archives.
49. Correspondence from Dobie McArthur to Hassan Mneimneh, 27 January 2005, Accession no. 2010C35–11.64/66, Box 104, Hoover Institution Archives.
50. Memorandum of Understanding between the Iraq Memory Foundation and the United States Government, 31 January 2005, Accession no. 2010C35–11.64/66, Box 104, Hoover Institution Archives.
51. M. Gebeily, 'Return of Saddam-Era Archive to Iraq Opens Debate, Old Wounds', *AFP*, 10 September 2020, https://sports.yahoo.com/return-saddam-era-archive-iraq-015740376.html (accessed 23 December 2020).
52. M. Gordon, 'Baath Party Archives Return to Iraq, With the Secrets They Contain - WSJ', Wall Street Journal, 31 August 2020 https://archive.fo/AQ6yU (accessed 7 September 2020).
53. J. Gravois, 'Disputed Iraqi Archives Find a Home at the Hoover Institution', *The Chronicle of Higher Education*, 23 January 2008, www.chronicle.com/article/Disputed-Iraqi-Archives-Find-a/426.
54. D. Chalabi, 'A Conversation with Dr. Saad Bashir Eskander', *Bidoun* magazine, https://bidoun.org/articles/dr-saad-bashir-eskander (accessed 19 May 2020); Gravois, 'Disputed Iraqi Archives Find a Home at the Hoover Institution'.
55. C. Szilagyi, 'Re-Archiving Mass Atrocity Records by Involving Affected Communities in Postwar Bosnia and Herzegovina', in S. Ristovska and M. Price, eds, *Visual Imagery and Human Rights Practice*, Global Transformations in Media and Communication Research (New York: Palgrave Macmillan, 2018), 131–152 (134).
56. E. Ketelaar, 'Recordkeeping and Societal Power', in S. McKemmish, M. Piggott, B. Reed, and F. Upward, eds, *Archives: Recordkeeping in Society*, Topics in Australasian Library

and Information Studies 24 (Wagga Wagga: Centre for Information Studies, Charles Sturt University, 2005), 277–298 (281); E. Danielson, 'Privacy Rights and the Rights of Political Victims: Implications of the German Experience', *The American Archivist* 67.2 (2004), 176–193.

57. Eskander, 'Minerva Research Initiative: Searching for the Truth or Denying the Iraqis the Rights to Know the Truth?'.

58. Nabil al-Tikriti, 'Negligent Mnemocide and the Shattering of Iraqi Collective Memory', in Baker, Ismael, and Ismale, *Cultural Cleansing in Iraq*, 93–115 (94).

CHAPTER 34

OF BONFIRES, MINDSETS, AND POLICIES

The Multi-Causal Matrix of Silence in Ghanaian Public Archives

EDWINA ASHIE-NIKOI, EMMANUEL ADJEI, AND MUSAH ADAMS

In the aftermath of the coup that overthrew the *Osagyefo* Kwame Nkrumah on 24 February 1966, the former leader's statue that was mounted outside Ghana's Parliament House and declared him the founder of the nation, was toppled and smashed to pieces. This symbolic act of erasure was paralleled by another more destructive and enduring one kilometre away at the presidential palace, Flagstaff House. There, 'rampaging' soldiers 'ransacked' and 'senselessly burned the entire contents of Nkrumah's office', making bonfires of his papers and books.[1] It is difficult, without their documented viewpoints, to speculate about the motivations of these disgruntled soldiers (and, one may imagine, some citizens). Were they driven by disaffection with the 'redeemer' (*Osagyefo*) or were they simply intent on erasing every trace of him? Whatever drove them, these actions created permanent 'vacuums'[2] in the archival record, archival silences that would be recreated and reaffirmed by subsequent coups in Ghana, during which files and records relating to the Nkrumah period were similarly destroyed or disappeared.[3]

Recent interrogations of the archive have shattered the long-held view that archives are neutral sites of knowledge, and archivists passive and unbiased mediators of materials of enduring value. Instead, archives have been identified as 'spaces of power, with the power to include and exclude, to distort, omit and silence voices.'[4] Subsequently, the issue of archival silence—that is, the 'unintentional or purposeful absence or distortion of documentation of enduring value, resulting in gaps and inabilities to represent the past accurately'[5]—has risen to prominence as a subject of enquiry. The conversation around archival silence is a multi-disciplinary one, including among its discussants scholars of Atlantic slavery, for example, to archival theorists of indigenous archives. Of the former, Michel-Rolph Trouillot's elegant reflection of the ways power structures influence history making is often credited with providing the framework within which 'archival silence' could be theorized.[6] Trouillot argued that:

> Silences enter the process of historical production at four crucial moments: the moment of fact creation (the making of *sources*); the moment of fact assembly (the making of *archives*); the moment of fact retrieval (the making of *narratives*); and the moment of introspective significance (the making of *history* in the final instance) [... thus] any historical narrative is a particular bundle of silences, the result of a unique process, and the operation required to deconstruct these silences will vary accordingly[7]

Furthermore, to Trouillot, 'the presences and absences embodied in sources (artifacts and bodies that turn an event into fact) or archives (facts collected, thematized, and processed as documents and monuments) are neither neutral nor natural. They are created'[8], a conclusion with which archival scholars largely concur. Rodney Carter, for example, notes that archives, particularly national ones, are sources of inequity and exclusion by the very act of defining their scope, be it the nation, province, region or State, or the subject area; thus inherent in the very act of archiving is the possibility, the risk, of silence.[9] The archival acts of appraisal and assembly, whereby archivists follow guidelines to select the stories that 'matter', are unquestionably fraught with the possibility of silences as well.

However, beyond these (what we may call) professionally acceptable or sanctioned processes of 'silencing' (whatever the boundaries of acceptability might look like in a given context) are the archival silences that occur deliberately and unwittingly, both at the hands of professionals and non-professionals alike. The kind of pyro destruction described at the beginning of this chapter, of course, is one obvious cause of silence; archival silences can also be created by loss, concealment, or the intentional exclusion of certain narratives, communities' decision to withhold their internal records or archives, or simply because certain materials were never created or preserved.[10]

As archivists, archival theorists, and other scholars have convincingly argued, in the West silence in the archives is a tool used to 'silence the past' of the marginalized, to deny them a participatory voice in the archive and a place in the body politic.[11] There has also been a growing recognition that the archival profession's traditional worldview and practice privileged Western voices and narratives and sidelined others, particularly failing to 'embrace Indigenous frameworks of knowledge, memory, and evidence'.[12] This bias can be reinforced through national archives that exclude certain groups in their conception of the nation and its narratives, thereby concealing, de-legitimizing, or distorting their presence, participation in, and contributions to the nation. Such exclusions were particularly true of African national archives in their initial iteration as colonial archives that supported the project of subjugation. In essence, African public archives were set up to silence the voice of the African populace. As Carter articulates it:

silences are, in part, the manifestation of the actions of the powerful in denying the marginal access to archives and ... this has a significant impact on the ability of the marginal groups to form social memory and history ... the powerful can introduce silences into the archives by denying marginal groups their voice and the opportunity to participate in the archives.[13]

Although there is little disputing the role of power in the establishment, structure, and content of African archives during the colonial period, one may ask whether silence in post-colonial African archives is always the inevitable tool and consequence of power and marginalization? Are there other considerations?

Exploring these questions, and thus determining the intensity of silence in African archives is crucial. In the African context, the notion that 'not every story is told'[14] is of particular concern considering the varied ways in which 'texts'—written, visual, oral, ritual, performative—on the African continent are documented; ways that, strictly observing the theories, philosophies, and conventions of modern archival administration which defines records narrowly as written documents, would mostly render these 'rebel archives'[15] uncapturable. However, beyond the concern for the gaps created by the omission or ignoring of these non-orthodox or alternative archives in African archival work, there yet remains within the conventional practice of archival management on the African continent a simmering mix of factors that create silences.

Silence overshadows African archives. The continent's unfortunate history and, in some cases, continued lived reality of political instability which, as illustrated by the example of the bonfires that destroyed the Nkrumah papers, threaten(ed) the completeness of the archival record. Further amplifying the silence are: the above-mentioned African cultural affinity for 'alternative forms of transmission which are ... susceptible to interruption';[16] the disinclination of most professional archivists and archives, still influenced by conservative frameworks of archival management, to not collect and preserve traditionally documented materials;[17] and other professional missteps such as misunderstanding among African archivists of the concept of confidentiality which then lead to unwarranted closure of records.

Yet, notwithstanding the pervasiveness of silence in African archives and the contributions that African archival explorations about silence could make to the field, archival silence is not a phenomenon generally explored by African archival scholars. It is instructive that when it has been interrogated, archival silence has been a concern of South African theorists examining the issue against the backdrop of apartheid and the struggle for liberation where, as argued by Jacques Derrida, the racial violence of the state is reflected in the archives.[18] Situated in a context absent of such racial and power binaries, this chapter continues the conversation by unravelling some of the strands that cause archival silences in Ghana's public institutions. While conceding that there are other factors that contribute to archival silencing in Ghana (speaking of both conventional and non-conventional 'archives'), we employ examples from the public archives setting to argue that at the core of this matrix of silence that plagues Ghana's archives are three seemingly disparate but interconnected factors which feed into one another and create an environment that promotes archival silences and gaps.

The implications of archival silences, as noted in the literature, are several and severe. However, we maintain that in the African context where archival silence has generally not been explored, an examination of the causes of this silence is necessary and will then provide a better sense of the scope and implications of silence in the African archival environment. Because public archives are the predominant type of archive in Ghana and across the continent, this chapter focuses on that sector.[19]

It is our view that archival loss and silencing in Ghana's public archives cannot be understood fully outside of the legislative context within which they operate. As such, the following section will provide a background on the legislative policies that have shaped the archival environment in Ghana. This chapter then examines the repercussions of these policies' shortcomings using the case of three public multimedia archives. The next section discusses some of the prevailing attitudes towards archives that perpetuate silences in the archival record. Finally, this chapter suggests strategies that could counter archival silence in Ghana's public archives and the wider African archival context.

Creating Silence: Legacies of the 1955 Public Archive Ordinance

The National Archives of Ghana evolved from a 1946 decision by the Gold Coast colonial government to create an archival section under the Colonial Secretary's Office. A British librarian, Marjorie Harris, was tasked with organizing the scattered records of the colonial administration. Harris oversaw the accessioning and classification of these materials 'unbound and dispersed in the record rooms and filing cabinets of the separate government departments'.[20] The transformation of the archives into a professional department continued under the guidance of J. M. Akita, an archivist who had been trained abroad, who was appointed Archivist in 1949. Additionally, the annual number of acquisitions increased, as did government funding. According to Raymond Dumett, transformation was a 'testament to a growing general awareness of the importance of documentary research in the life of emerging African nations on the eve of the independence revolution'.[21] Cognizant of the dangers of loss and destruction of documents vital for an understanding of the foundation of nationalism and constitutional history of the country, archival workers in the 1950s also systematized the search for long forgotten private and family papers. In 1955, the National Archives of Ghana (NAG) was legally established with the passage of the Public Archives Ordinance (PAO).[22]

The PAO gave the NAG a formal structure and authorized it to take custody of, and preserve all public records. As the machinery of government grew, other public records management structures and procedures emerged. For example, the Management Services Division (MSD), established in 1971, took over the registry management and procedures functions of the defunct Organization and Methods Division which had operated in the 1960s.[23] Still, these divisions were all theoretically under the oversight of the NAG, and the PAO empowered the Archivist to examine public records in any government office and provide advice relating to their care, storage and control. In reality, however, the PAO failed as a comprehensive policy for an integrated and holistic approach to the management of the life cycle of public sector records. It only clearly defined the responsibility of the NAG for the third phase of the records life cycle; its responsibility for the second phase (maintenance) was simply implied. As such, and particularly in the period after the Permanent Committee on Public Archives was dissolved, there was no real system in place to handle the appraisal and transfer of archival records; the flow of records from registries into the NAG was effectively stopped.

By the late 1980s, it was clear that the public sector records management system needed to be reorganized. Regional workshops held by the Association of Commonwealth Archivists and Records Managers (ACARM) and the International Records Management Trust (IRMT) alerted the Ghanaian government to the scale of the country's records management problem. A task force was set up to restructure NAG and the government records and information management systems, jettisoning the rigid separation of the records management and archival stages, and unifying the process from record creation to disposal. In 1997, Act 535 replaced the PAO and established the Public Records and Archives Administration Department (PRAAD), formalizing the new integrated structure.[24]

One of the key insights of the reforms was that providing one agency a wider mandate that covers the whole record cycle helps to guarantee the archives of the future.[25] In contrast, the weaknesses of the PAO had led to the inadvertent destruction of archival records. When NAG confined itself to only the archival stage of the records life cycle, it virtually neglected the earlier phases leading to loss of important records from lack of control and deterioration. Without policies for the appraisal of records, the decision to preserve or destroy archival materials was in the hands of public officers who determined the value of the documents based on whether they were useful to them and not based on the professional input and training of records managers or archivists. Besides, after the destruction of documents that occurred after Nkrumah's overthrow, some government offices had not regained their trust in the NAG and were reluctant to entrust them with archival materials.[26] In relation to archival silences, we see then that prior to the reforms which led to the replacement of the NAG with PRAAD, an indeterminate number of civil service and public records that should have been archives were accidentally destroyed because proper records management procedures were not in place.[27] Records were improperly kept, often stored haphazardly on balconies, under stairwells, and in other unfit places exposed to the elements, covered in dust, destroyed in rain, burned by cleaners at the instruction of superiors, and sometimes even sold to street-side food vendors to wrap their products.[28]

Beyond the incalculable number of records that were irretrievably lost in ministry offices and the registries, the volume of Ghana's archival silence created by deficiencies in the PAO is magnified still more when the ordinance's strict interpretation of 'government office' is factored in. Defined as 'a ministry, government department, the Supreme Court of the Gold Coast and the offices of the Legislative Assembly of the Gold Coast', this view left a wide vacuum between government offices on the one hand, and parastatals on the other. The latter did not benefit from the NAG's professional input and were compelled to set up their own systems. Still, had NAG officials desired to go beyond the framework of the ordinance to render such assistance, their ability to do so would have been severely curtailed. Following on from the limitations and failures of the PAO, Ghanaian governments did not see the role archives played and so reduced the level of support to the NAG. Thus the National Archives neither had clout nor resources and, on the eve of the reform that would usher in PRAAD, was on the brink of collapse. The NAG was therefore not in an optimal state to stave off its own decline, much more provide oversight and advice for other State holdings. In such an environment, the disasters that beset Ghana's multimedia heritage kept by three parastatal agencies, discussed below, almost seem inevitable.

Tragic Silences: Ghana's At-Risk Multimedia Heritage

The Ghana Film Industry Corporation (GFIC) was established by Kwame Nkrumah after independence, initially as the Ghana Film Unit. The Ghana Film Unit replaced the Gold Coast Film Unit, a section of the Information Services Department which, during the colonial period, used film as a propaganda and 'civilizing' tool. Like the British colonial government before him, Nkrumah recognized the power of film to influence and he believed that showing Ghanaians good quality locally-produced films would raise the populace's self-esteem and inspire them to buy-in to his development agenda and work for the betterment of the nation.[29] Beyond Ghana, Nkrumah envisioned the GFIC as a critical component of his pan-Africanist development project; the GFIC became a hub of filmmaking in West Africa, training professionals in the sub-region. Nkrumah hired the best and brightest creative minds to oversee the production of films that proceeded from and reflected the African *weltanschauung*. Included among this number was Kofi Awoonor; the celebrated poet was then a young research fellow at the University of Ghana's Institute of African Studies.[30]

In 1997, the GFIC was divested to a Malaysian company, GAMA Media system for $1.23 million, a deal which proved disastrous to Ghana's audiovisual archival heritage. Not interested in cinema, GAMA turned the location into a TV station.

To create space for their television equipment, GIFC's film equipment and the film archives were dumped outside and left to the vagaries of the hot, humid tropical weather.[31] Had the film reels not been sent to a London lab for colour processing, there would be no record of Ghana's post-independence cinema.[32]

The loss of one set of multimedia archives is devastating enough to a nation's heritage-keeping efforts. That these archival silences are repeated in other state institutions, namely the Ghana Broadcasting Corporation (GBC) and the Information Services Department (ISD), is altogether tragic and demonstrates the extent to which the matrix of silence impacts Ghana's audiovisual and multimedia archives.

The Information Services Department, the public relations arm of the government, was established in 1939 with the primary objective of keeping the people of the Gold Coast informed about the progress of the Second World War (1939–1945). The department's cinema vans toured the colony showing war films and distributing a weekly newspaper. The ISD was attached to the Ministry of Information after the overthrow of the Nkrumah regime. The ISD has been the foundation of much of Ghana's current State media apparatus. According to the ISD website, apart from the previously mentioned Gold Coast Film Unit, the ISD's syndicated news activities preceded those of the GBC and the Ghana News Agency (GNA). It is clear, then, that the ISD holds much of the nation's recent memory; however, because of policy issues and a lack of funding and space, its film and photo archives are either in a state of deterioration or at risk of such. In speaking with Beti Ellerson about what inspired her to make *Perished Diamonds*, the documentary about the loss of the GIFC materials, Anita Afonu spoke about her experience researching in the ISD's film archives and remarked: 'it broke my heart to personally discard some of the films because they had gone mouldy, in an almost soup-like state'. P. E. Hormeku concluded that the state of affairs at the ISD means that the department is 'actually losing Ghana's historical heritage and the new generation would have no information about their identity'.[33]

Like the ISD, the GBC held a wealth of Ghanaian multimedia heritage, some from the colonial era. On 24 May 1989, the GBC's Film and Video Library was gutted by a fire that blazed for at least three hours as hapless staff, discovering that none of the three fire extinguishers on site worked, tried to rescue what tapes and equipment they could. Their valiant efforts were not enough; only a handful of the valuable historical visual material dating back to pre-independence days could be salvaged. Tragically, in many cases the destroyed materials were the only existing copies. The irreparable damage created by this gap in the nation's memory cannot be measured.[34]

Beyond being an unfortunate accident, the 1989 fire was the culmination of wider systemic weaknesses relating to policy and preservation practice which, sadly, still persist almost three decades later. Writing about the GBC's Music (Gramophone) Library, Moses Adjetey Adjei bemoaned the poor conservation and preservation, gaps in the records and inadequate policies that plagued the library, described as the 'giant reservoir of African music and more'. Adjei identified the years after the 1979 coup d'état as the beginning of the decline of the Music Library. Problems included a decrease in the purchase of materials, untrained personnel mismanaging the library and its assets, documents supporting the library's activities being burned or discarded, changing management that neglected the library and, among other things, oversaw a reduction in usage of, and donations to the library. To P. A. Atsiatorme, former director of radio, the entire situation left the GBC library 'an orphan to decay'.[35]

Although a digitization project has stemmed the rot in the last few years, the consequences of those 'orphan years' persist. As happened elsewhere, the materials were left exposed to the vagaries of the weather and destructive elements such as dust and pests. Some of what remained was scattered in various offices, others were thrown away to make room for competing office needs.[36] Thus, materials have been lost and silences created.

The implications of archival silence in Ghana's multimedia archives are severe and offer scathing commentary on the lack of foresight displayed by the professionals, management and government who oversee their deterioration. Audiovisual archives are vital elements of institutional and national collective memory as well as are a crucial modern repository of African cultures and history.[37] Films and photographs, for example, capture the evolving contours and dimensions of African societies and values. Audiovisual recordings document multiple aspects of indigenous culture such as oral histories and traditions, songs, dances, and rituals. In other words, multimedia archives are valuable repositories of those alternative African cultural archives that are 'prone to interruption'. Thus, beyond simply preserving the nation's film or music heritage, multimedia archives 'contain materials that reflect the identities and taste of [Africans] over the years concerning changes in religious, generational, economical [sic] and political dispensations, among others'.[38] Adjei's conclusion adds poignant perspective to Awoonor's impassioned response to the sale of the GIFC:

> The sale of the Ghana Film Industry Corporation is a tragedy for Ghanaian culture and African civilisation. It's a betrayal of the Kwame Nkrumah dream [that] we ourselves must be able to tell our own story[39]

One can but only speculate whether these multimedia archives that document(ed) so much of the nation's sociocultural heritage would have been saved or better preserved had there been comprehensive and effective policies governing Ghana's archives. It is likely. Adjei believed that 'good policies, practices and proper funding' would transform GBC's music library into a reliable source of Ghana's history and knowledge.[40]

Still, the general lack of policy backing for Ghana's public archives is also borne out of a related problem alluded to earlier: the lack of recognition and understanding that archival institutions and the professionals that are their custodians suffer. Other attitudes, as destructive as the fires, mould, and dust that caused the damage can be construed from the three cases of silencing in Ghana's audiovisual heritage outlined in the foregoing discussion. To fully appreciate them, these attitudes must be examined from different dimensions: the perspective of the average citizen, public sector workers, and, perhaps most crucially, the government. The following section explores some of these prevailing mindsets that are a potent factor in the matrix of silence that plague Ghana's public archives.

Mind the Gap: Identifying Mindsets of Silence

By burning Nkrumah's archives, the National Liberation Council soldiers unwittingly alluded to the power of archives to include or exclude, to give voice or to silence. What is more likely, however, is that their destructive act was revelatory of an underlying mindset—perhaps borne of ignorance about the work and mandate of archives—that either places little to no value on archives and records, or does not fully appreciate their significance.[41] Otherwise, the soldiers might have considered how the materials could have provided evidentiary justification for their coup. Instead, the documents were set alight, as if they were refuse. Indeed, that is precisely the opinion many still hold of archives.

In informal surveys conducted by two Ghanaian archivists in recent times, archives were variously described by respondents as: 'a place where old things in the house that you no longer use are kept'; 'where we keep old files we can go for at any time'; 'a place where we dump old things'; 'unwanted or useless things'; 'it is like a library, but more archaic than a library. It is a place where we keep historical materials we do not want to destroy or loose quickly.'[42] The findings of empirical investigations into public awareness and attitudes towards archives parallel these opinions expressed in the informal questionnaires administered by Sammy Dzandu and Judith Opoku-Boateng. For example, Bernard Okoampah Otu and Edward Asante's 2015 probe of public awareness and use of the national archives, using evidence from the Volta and Eastern PRAAD regional archives, found that Ghanaians remain 'largely unaware' of archives. Additionally, the archival profession was 'saddled with [an] exceedingly low profile.'[43]

Where respondents had a fair or acceptable understanding of the work of archives—'archives are items you keep for others to have access'; 'initially, I thought it has to do with archaic things that are not relevant, but now a resource center that people go in for books and other relevant materials'; 'an Archive is collection of audio and visual items. It is also, an institution where you keep archival materials'; 'an Archive is a place where materials are stored for people to have access to when they are conducting a research or want to find out about any historical event or happening in the present'—it was glaringly apparent that they did not perceive themselves as possible contributors to the pasts that archives keep. And it is precisely this that is the salient link between the public's perception of archives and the discussion around archival silence.

While exploring the public's attitudes towards archives might, at first glance, seem irrelevant to a discussion of archival silences, it is, in fact, a pertinent aspect of the matrix of silence in Ghanaian archives. How the public perceives archives would directly influence whether they advocate for, or contribute to archival institutions. If the public does not fully appreciate that archives preserve national memory, and that archivists, based on their understanding of historical context, establish and maintain both physical and intellectual control over materials of enduring value, they will not lobby on behalf of, nor support archives, depriving the institutions of potentially significant advocates and partners. Worse still, the average citizen is unaware that they are an integral part of this national narrative public archives are charged to preserve. In Ghana, this is a direct consequence of the erstwhile National Archives operating for the most part with a narrow definition of archives (as non-current records) and thus neither proactively acquiring or promoting the donation of private papers of the citizenry nor educating the public about the potential importance of their letters, photographs, audiocassettes, etc. to the national narrative and how to preserve them. This stance, it must be noted, is at variance both with the NAG/PRAAD's own mandate to acquire 'non-public records' and with similar objectives stated in the National Commission on Culture's *Cultural Policy of Ghana* (Accra, 2004). The cycle of silence thus continues, ostensibly without an end in sight.

As archives are perceived, so the archivists. According to one of the respondents Dzandu interviewed, Ghanaian archivists should not complain about being unemployed because there were many waste management companies that could make use of their particular skill set managing old and unwanted things! On the opposite end of the spectrum was an interviewee who felt that there was no need to hire archivists to take care of 'unwanted things because once something lost its usefulness, the best course of action was to discard it'. If these are the views held by professional people such as accountants and administrators who would be expected to know better, then it is not surprising that archives continue to be inadequately resourced and archivists not valued as professionals whose perspectives and input should be sought during deliberations about what terms ought to have applied to the GFIC materials during the sale, for instance, or how materials rescued from the GBC fire ought to have been (re)stored.

Beyond how the perceptions of archivists and the profession impact on the issue of archival silencing, of significance also is the attitudes that Ghanaian archivists, especially those working in the public sector, have towards their work. A 2002 study of job satisfaction among archival staff, found that although staff affirmed that they were interested in their roles, there were resignations owing to low salaries, lack of job satisfaction, and motivation. Personnel often left for better working and economic conditions elsewhere.[44] Others, while remaining in the profession, are not motivated to develop and keep abreast with advances in the field; when they do pursue further education, they are often driven by the prospect of gaining promotion and earning a higher income.

Lastly, the attitude of government towards archives and the role of its public sector archivists has led to silences in the archives both directly and indirectly. For example, NAG's modest attempts at providing advisory oversight to government departments' and agencies' management of records was constrained by budgetary allocations.[45] Furthermore, the government took the role of archives for granted and failed to provide it with the needed logistical support and resources,[46] eventually leading to a poorer quality of files as 'the ephemeral and the important, the new and the old'[47] were mixed together and became unmanageable, uncontrolled, and ultimately inaccessible, leading to archival loss and silence.

There were gaps created also by the government attitude towards the repositories that held the nation's audiovisual heritage. Immediately clear from the circumstances prior to and in the aftermath of the fire at the GBC Music Library and the sale of the GFIC materials is that the government, contrary to an International Federation of Library Associations (IFLA) statement advising otherwise, regarded audiovisual materials as 'luxury materials' and therefore did not invest in them as required. A new repository was not built, for example, after the fire that destroyed the GBC's film and video archives.[48] Viewing Ghana's multimedia archives as an integral component of the nation's cultural heritage, for example, would have compelled the government to negotiate different terms with GAMA Media System. Several alternatives suggest themselves: the government could have removed the audiovisual materials from the buildings and preserved them elsewhere; the government could have had GAMA preserve or restore the material as part of the agreement; the contract could have stated that the government expected the materials back at end of the term. Instead, Ghana's film archives were considered dispensable and the nation suffered the tragic loss of this heritage.

Notwithstanding the push for legislative reform that led to the PRAAD Act, the general overriding lack of government interest and appreciation for the institution founded by the Act persists. For example, to date PRAAD only has two purpose-built archival repositories, the main one in Accra and the second in Cape Coast. The repository in Kumasi remains uncompleted. Archival records in other regions are inadequately housed in unsuitable offices of the Regional Coordinating Councils. Still, whether in purpose-built or haphazard and temporary facilities, inadequate financial support unfortunately means that equipment such as air-conditioners, a must in humid tropical conditions, and preservation or digitization tools are non-functioning or non-existent. As a result, Ghana's archives perpetually face loss and silencing.

Remedying the Matrix of Silence

We all—or at least I certainly hope we all—now work as professionals in a world in which archives are actively engaged in trying to ensure no new archival silences are created, and that where silences exist in our understanding of the past, we do what we can to help researchers find the voices that survive to fill the void.[49]

To Trouillot, the making of archives involves a number of selective operations—the selection of producers, evidence, themes, procedures—which means, at best, the differential ranking and, at worst, the exclusion of some producers, evidence, themes, and procedures. Consequently, there will always be archival silences. Rather than archivists being paralysed by that fact, Thomas argues, what is crucial is that they ensure 'the silences are appropriate and properly managed ... and that they are recognized for what they are'.[50] Although archival silences may be unavoidable, archivists are to be vigilant, ensuring that silences do not enter the archival record through political manipulation, poor processes or—adding another layer in this digital age—inappropriate use of technology.[51] What is implied by these scholars is that a first step in remedying archival silences would be through an intentional shift in professional attitude.

Thus, beyond legislative—and perhaps even financial—fixes, remedying archival silences hinges on the right perspective and commitment of archival professionals. Indeed, the Ghanaian case explored here has shown that legislative changes have not satisfactorily translated into archival gains. Despite the PRAAD Act's creation of the records class, it is the contention of the authors—all archival studies academics—that the archival profession's earlier poor reputation continues to promote a lukewarm attitude towards the managing of public records and archives in Ghana. Having a vibrant professional association is perhaps key to addressing this. The association must deliberately confront members' professional apathy, holding activities with the aim of reigniting member interest in the work they do. Conversely, based on the experiences and opinions of members, the association could provide input to records management and archival studies programmes that would help shape the academic programme of study. Additionally, the professional association could seek opportunities to co-host activities with student associations and mentor members so as to expose them to the various dimensions of the profession. These steps would hopefully ensure training of people who are both passionate about and effective at preserving documentary heritage. Beyond engaging current and up-and-coming professionals, undertaking a long term campaign aimed at educating the general public about archival work and its significance would not only enable the profession to increase its visibility and image, but would have the added indirect effect of decreasing archival silences as the populace becomes aware of the important documentary materials they may have in their homes that require care and preservation for future generations.

As the national institution with the mandate to provide leadership in the management of records across the public sector, it goes without saying that PRAAD has a role to play in curtailing future loss and minimizing the instances of silence in Ghana's archival record. In most instances this role would not require significant financial outlay but simply the enforcement of the legislative provisions. For example, the PRAAD Act's Section 16 requires the Director to keep a National Register of Archives in which is to be recorded the records in the National Archives and other repositories under the Director's control. Linking this provision to Section 13 which empowers the Director to designate any place other than the National Archives as a place of deposit for specified public records would ensure that PRAAD has absolute control over archives in parastatal agencies and safeguard these materials' preservation and access according to acceptable standards and practices.

The matter of access is especially pertinent to any discussion of archival silence. Inaccessibility amplifies archival silence in two ways—where materials exist but are closed to research or, inversely, where the materials are open for use but poorly described so for all purposes are hidden. To illustrate the latter point, for example, there exists a folder of personal papers among some Nkrumah-related papers at PRAAD that offer a rich window into middle-class lives and marriage relationships in newly independent Ghana.[52] However, the finding aids do not mention it. Poor description is like no access at all, effectively silencing these narratives and leaving them to chance discoveries.

Finally, it is imperative that PRAAD responds to the scholarly conclusions that archives, in their original constructions, excluded the voices of subordinate groups. Consequently, there are but traces of the 'common wo/man' in the colonial and immediate postcolonial era archives and the evidence of him/her in the alternate or 'rebel archives' are disappearing as well, as archivists, trained in the Western traditions of archival administration, do not regard the traditional spaces of documentation nor consider it their responsibility to preserve the accounts stored there. This must change. Certainly if the public archive is to fully represent the collective memory, then all aspects of the national narrative are to be collected. Only then can African national archives truly claim to be the nation's collective memory and only then can the silences be effectively combatted. Otherwise archives fail to be a site of 'representational belonging', a psychical state of things which can negatively impact national development.[53]

What this chapter has sought to do is to unravel the matrix of silence in Ghanaian archives. By so doing it has aimed to demonstrate that exploring archival silence in non-Western postcolonial contexts can be instructive, and open up new vistas for how we think generally about silence in the archives. There is an urgency created by the matrix of silence to compel archivists to reflect on their own role and responsibility, both to give voice and to give access to the under-represented within their archival collections. This professional dissection of the philosophies that undergird practice has yielded projects and policies elsewhere[54] that are worth the consideration of African archivists to ensure the inclusion of narratives that would otherwise be silenced or forgotten, leaving the national story the poorer.

FURTHER READING

Sumayya Ahmed, 'Archives du Maroc? The Official and Alternative National Archives of Morocco', *Archives and Manuscripts* 46 (2018), 255–268; doi:10.1080/01576 895.2018.1558408

Rose Barrowcliffe, 'Closing the Narrative Gap: Social Media as a Tool to Reconcile Institutional Archival Narratives with Indigenous Counter-Narratives', *Archives and Manuscripts* 49 (2021), 151–166; doi:10.1080/01576895.2021.1883074

Ellen Ndeshi Namhila, 'Recordkeeping and Missing "Native Estate" Records in Namibia: An Investigation of Colonial Gaps in a Post-Colonial National Archives', *Informaatiotutkimus* 34.4 (2015), 1–5

Louis-Gilles Pairault, 'Reconstituting "the Archives of Silence": How to "Recreate" Slavery and Slave Trade Archives', *Archives and Manuscripts* 48 (2020), 259–270; doi:10.1080/01576895.2020.1822190

Isabel S. Shellnack-Kelly, 'Decolonising the Archives: Languages as Enablers and Barriers to Accessing Public Archives in South Africa', *Archives and Manuscripts* 48 (2020), 291–299; doi:10.1080/01576895.2020.1815064

NOTES

1. J. Milne, 'Kwame Nkrumah: Life after the Coup and Conakry Years', *New Directions* 14.4 (1987), Article 6, https://dh.howard.edu/newdirections/vol14/iss4/6; and 'The Coup that Disrupted Africa's Forward March', *New African* 448 (February 2006), magazine article start page: 14. Further, according to Samuel Ntewusu, some soldiers also went into the National Archives Ghana and set fire to documents containing information on Nkrumah and his Convention Peoples Party. Thankfully, the soldiers left as soon as they saw the fire had taken hold, but a few individuals put the fire out; 'The Banana and Peanut Archive of Ghana', *History in Africa* 44 (2017), 285–294 (288).

2. S. E. Couper, '"An Embarrassment to the Congresses?": The Silencing of Chief Albert Luthuli and the Production of ANC History', *Journal of Southern African Studies* 35.2 (2009), 331–348; doi:10.1080/03057070902919884.

3. Milne, 'Kwame Nkrumah'. Vincent Dodoo recalls that not long after the coup, some officials from the Ministry of Education visited his school and removed from the stores any book that dealt with the subject of Kwame Nkrumah; 'Kwame Nkrumah's Mission and Vision for Africa and the World', *The Journal of Pan African Studies (Online)* 4.10 (2012), 78–92. Similarly, Moses Adjetey Adjei mentions music valorizing Nkrumah being banned from airwaves although music records were preserved; 'Music Production and Preservation at Ghana Broadcasting Corporation' (MPhil. thesis, University of Ghana Department of Music, 2015), 62.

4. R. G. S. Carter, 'Of Things Said and Unsaid: Power, Archival Silences, and Power in Silence', *Archivaria* 61 (2006), 215–223. See also, D. Thomas, S. Fowler, and V. Johnson, *The Silence of the Archive* (London: Facet Publishing, 2017).
5. Society of American Archivists dictionary https://dictionary.archivists.org/entry/archival-silence.html.
6. M. C. Lingold, 'Peculiar Animations: Listening to Afro-Atlantic Music in Caribbean Travel Narratives', *Early American Literature* 52.3 (2017), 623–650. See also Society of American Archivists dictionary.
7. M.-R. Trouillot, *Silencing the Past: Power and the Production of History* (Boston: Beacon Press, 1995), 26–27.
8. Trouillot, *Silencing the Past*, 48.
9. Carter, 'Of Things Said and Unsaid', 233.
10. E. Doolan, 'Textiles of Change: How Arpilleras Can Expand Traditional Definitions of Records', *InterActions: UCLA Journal of Education and Information Studies* 12.1 (2016) [not paginated]; doi:10.5070/D4121028883. M. Moss and D. Thomas, eds, *Archival Silences: Missing, Lost and Uncreated Archives* (London: Routledge, 2021).
11. See, for example, E. Fishkin Hedges and S. Fisher, *Listening to Silences: New Essays in Feminist Criticism* (New York: Oxford University Press, 1994); Trouillot, *Silencing the Past*; Thomas, Fowler, and Johnson, *Silence of the Archive*. F. Miley and A. Read, 'Entertainment as an Archival Source for Historical Accounting Research', *Accounting History* 26.1 (2021), 146–167; doi:10.1177/1032373220969219.
12. S. McKemmish, S. Faulkhead, and L. Russell, 'Distrust in the Archive: Reconciling Records', *Archival Science* 11.3–4 (2011), 211–239; doi:10.1007/s10502-011-9153-2.
13. Carter, 'Of Things Said and Unsaid', 215, 217.
14. Carter, 'Of Things Said and Unsaid', 216.
15. Here we borrow Kelly Lytle Hernandez's articulation of the 'rebel archives', records created defiantly by those who would otherwise have been erased; *City of Inmates: Conquest, Rebellion and the Rise of Human Caging in Los Angeles, 1771–1965* (Chapel Hill, N.C.: University of North Carolina Press, 2017). Using the term, Genevieve Carpio identifies these archives as documents created by those overlooked by mainstream accounts including family photo albums, school records, popular media, and oral histories; 'Tales from the Rebel Archive: History as Subversive Practice at California's Margins', *Southern California Quarterly* 102.1 (2020), 57–79.
16. Carter, 'Of Things Said and Unsaid', 222.
17. This is not a problem distinct to African archival practice. Carter notes that groups such as indigenous populations of North America and Australia whose own recordkeeping traditions rely on 'speech acts' and not the literary traditions of Euro-American cultures, often find that these documents are not recognized as records. South African archivist Verne Harris states that there is a dire problem of non-responsiveness in the archives to the marginal or 'indigenous' epistemologies; 'The Archival Sliver: A Perspective on the Construction of Social Memory in Archives and the Transition from Apartheid to Democracy', in C. Hamilton, V. Harris, M. Pickover, G. Reid, R. Saleh, and J. Taylor, eds, *Refiguring the Archive* (Dordrecht: Springer, 2002), 150.
18. Jacques Derrida argues in *Archive Fever* that the archive is a site of violence which, because it is extremely selective about what is included as part of its memory, both reflects and provides the source of State power: only those voices that conform to the

ideals of those in power are allowed into the archive; those that do not are silenced. Those marginalized by the State are marginalized by the archive. Archival violence is perpetrated when documents are used to 'enforce and naturalize the State's power and in the active silencing of the disenfranchised' (as quoted in Carter, 'Of Things Said and Unsaid', 219).

19. This attention, however, does not negate the archival silences existent in other types of archives operating on the continent such as university archives, medical archives, etc. Indeed, one of the authors recollects coming up against 'dead silence' when conducting research on traditional council archives. One of the archives was locked up because of chieftaincy litigation and an arson attempt. At another location, the author was shown half burnt record registers which contained minutes and records of judicial sittings, also 'victims' of litigation and arson. The records register was a very important document which spanned many years and several volumes with no other existing copies available. Although the State has, since 1973, staffed the Traditional Councils, these were not trained records or archives personnel nor was there a direct relationship to NAG/PRAAD. Taken in total, with the added factor of attempted and successful arsons, the situation strongly suggests silencing through a loss of valuable archives. Finally, for the purposes of this discussion we include the archives of parastatal units, agencies, and departments under the term 'public archives'.

20. R. E. Dumett, *Survey of Research Materials in the National Archives of Ghana*, Mitteilungen der Basler Afrika Bibliographien 11 (Basel: Basler Afrika Bibliographica, 1974).

21. Dumett, *Survey of Research Materials*, 7.

22. J. M. Akita, 'The National Archives of Ghana', *Ghana Library Journal* 1.1 (1963), 8–12.

23. Also set up in the 1970s was the Permanent Committee on Public Archives (PCPA) which was the final authority on the fate of records in the disposition process and oversaw the transfer of valuable records to the NAG. The PCPA, along with some other boards and committees, was dissolved in 1981 by the Provisional National Defence Council (PNDC) as one of their first directives after staging the coup that brought them to power.

24. Comprising of both the NAG and a newly-created National Records Centre which houses and provides timely access to semi-current records, PRAAD is both a cultural institution and a central agency in the management of administrative records. PRAAD's mandate has three key elements: the effective management of public records through the record life cycle; the acquisition and conservation of archives and the provision of reference services to users; the provision of standards and leadership for the management of records of non-public provenance. P. Akotia, *Records Management: Principles and Practice* (Accra, Ghana: NAB 2015), 83.

25. Akotia, *Records Management*, 79–80.

26. Ntewusu, 'The Banana and Peanut Archive', 288.

27. It is impossible to determine the quantity of materials that were lost in this manner. During the reform project, thousands of boxes from the ministries were boxed into the National Records Centre which can take eighty thousand boxes.

28. Ntewusu suggests that this was the fate of some of the NAG documents rescued from the soldiers' fire; 'The Banana and Peanut Archive', 288. Unfortunately, despite the conventions of records management and the PRAAD and Data Protection acts, this practice continues. In October 2019, a trader in Madina market, Accra was arrested for selling

documents to food vendors and other petty traders at the market. The documents consisted of transfer letters, promotion letters, school certificates, and health records and contained employee bank account and salary information, telephone numbers, social security numbers, and dates of birth. The records originated from the health and education ministries, among others, and private hospitals in the country. The *Daily Graphic's* report of the incident can be found here: www.graphic.com.gh/news/general-news/ghana-news-woman-arrested-for-selling-people-s-personal-data.html.

29. Anita Afonu (director). (2013) Film: *Perished Diamonds*. Length: 40 minutes. Beti Ellerson, 'Anita Afonu: Preserving Ghana's Cinematic Treasures', *African Women in Cinema* (blog), 4 December 2013, http://africanwomenincinema.blogspot.com/2013/12/anita-afonu-preserving-ghanas-cinematic.html?m=1.

30. Ian Mundell, 'We Want to Take Copies', *Cinema is Another Country* (blog), 12 August 2016, https://mundellian.wordpress.com/2016/08/ (accessed November 2020).

31. Ellerson, 'Preserving Ghana's Cinematic Treasures'; Mundell, 'We Want to Take Copies'.

32. However, there still exists another layer of archival silencing here. These copies are stored beyond Ghana's shores and are unknown and largely inaccessible to those to whom the heritage belongs. It must also be noted that the silencing of Ghana's film heritage was not solely a result of the State's poorly thought through sale of the film archives and the neglect the materials experienced post transaction. Decades earlier, portions of this film heritage also suffered the purge Flagstaff House materials did at Nkrumah's fall. The NLC's rationale for the films' confiscation at that instance was that they fed into the Nkrumah personality cult. M. Diawara, 'Sub-Saharan African Film Production Technological Paternalism', *Jump-Cut* 32 (1987), 61–65.

33. P. E. Hormeku, 'Preservation of Multimedia Materials in Ghana: A Case Study of Ministry of Information and Media Relations' (MA dissertation, University of Ghana, 2016).

34. *Daily Graphic*, 'Fire Destroys GBC TV Production Building', 24 May 1989; accounts of the GBC fire can also be found here: https://archive.org/details/GhanaBroadcastingCorporationFire; https://broadwcast.org/index.php/Ghana.

35. Adjei, 'Music Production and Preservation at Ghana Broadcasting Corporation', 46.

36. Adjei, 'Music Production and Preservation at Ghana Broadcasting Corporation', 85.

37. M. Mensah, E. Adjei, and M. Adams, 'Keeping Our Story: Preservation of Audio-visual Archives in Ghana', *Library Philosophy and Practice (e-journal)* 1564 (2017), 1–16. Hormeku, 'Preservation of Multimedia Materials in Ghana'. D. Rakemane and O. Mosweu, 'Challenges of Managing and Preserving Audio-Visual Archives in Archival Institutions in Sub Saharan Africa: A Literature Review', *Collection and Curation* 40.2 (2021), 42–50; doi:10.1108/CC-04-2020-0011.

38. Adjei, 'Music Production and Preservation at Ghana Broadcasting Corporation', 93–94.

39. Kofi Awoonor as quoted in Mundell, 'We Want to Take Copies'.

40. Adjei, 'Music Production and Preservation at Ghana Broadcasting Corporation', 93–94.

41. Speaking of the gaps and omissions sports historians encounter in the archives, Douglas Booth mentions another possible reason for the poor public and political mindset towards archives. While admitting that silences are not always necessarily the result of deliberate political decisions but more likely stem from practical problems associated with limited space and 'the perfectly understandable attitudes of mainly volunteer officials whose priority is day-to-day survival—not preserving the past', he suggests the problem resides in an attitude that dismisses the past. Booth quotes Colin Tatz who

laments, 'we live in an ahistorical age [where] the present and future overwhelm the past to the point where even "last year" conveys a sense of aeons ago'; 'Sites of Truth or Metaphors of Power? Refiguring the Archives', *Sport in History* 26.1 (2006), 91–109.

42. J. Opoku-Boateng, 'Archives and the Public Good: 70 Years of UG's Contribution to Bridging Ghanaian Cultures—the J. H. Kwabena Nketia Archives in Perspective', Department of Information Studies Public Lecture, 11 May 2018, University of Ghana. S. Dzandu, 'Do We Need Archivists in Ghana?' https://www.google.com/.

43. B. Okoampah Otu and E. Asante, 'Awareness and Use of the National Archives: Evidence from the Volta and Eastern Regional Archives, Ghana', *Brazilian Journal of Information Studies: Research Trends* 9.2 (2015), 21–25.

44. E. Agboada, 'A Study of the Work Roles, Job Satisfaction and Career Aspirations of Sub-Professional Archivists of Public Records and Archives Administration Department (PRAAD)' (MA dissertation, University of Ghana, 2002), 69–70.

45. L. Woode, 'Freedom of Information (FOI) and the Management of Public Sector Records in Ghana' (MPhil thesis, University of Ghana, 2008).

46. H. Akussah, 'Preserving Documentary Heritage in Ghana: The National Archives of Ghana in Focus' (PhD thesis, University of Ghana, 2003).

47. P. Akotia, 'The Management of Public Sector Financial Records: The Implications for Good Governance' (PhD thesis, University College London, 1997).

48. According to the Ghanaba Afro-Jazz Gallery, the Radio Section temporarily gave them the use of the current repository. A small room, it is used as an office, archive, and viewing room. Thus, materials are sometimes mis-shelved or lost entirely. The materials that survived the fire are stored in various locations at the GBC studios—the African Heritage Library, and the Tape Library where more recent productions are stored, and the Tape Archive, where earlier inaccessible formats are stored. www.facebook.com/media/set/?set=a.643555995707946.1073741834.131671810229703&type=3.

49. K. Theimer, 'Gaps in the Past and Gaps in the Future: Archival Silences and Social Media', *ArchivesNext* (blog), 17 February 2016, https://perma.cc/8G9R-5TFB (accessed November 2020).

50. D. Thomas, 'Are Things Getting Better or Worse?', in Thomas, Fowler, and Johnson, eds, *The Silence of the Archive*, 163–180.

51. Thomas, 'Are Things Getting Better or Worse?', 167–177.

52. The folder RG 17/1/171 contains correspondence between Amonoo, presumably a Nkrumah staff member or aide, and his wife Agatha, as well as receipts of both a personal and official nature.

53. E. Ashie-Nikoi, 'More Than Songs and Stories: The Nexus between Cultural Records and National Development', *Information Development* 37.1 (2021), 32–44; doi:10.1177/0266666919889105.

54. See, for example, P. V. Dudman, 'Documenting the Undocumented: Archiving and Recording the Refugee Experience', *History@Work* (blog), 24 October 2019, https://repository.uel.ac.uk/item/87w6q; 'Digital Archives of Refugee History: Resources, Challenges and Opportunities', *Refugee History* (blog), 13 May 2017, https://repository.uel.ac.uk/item/87w68.

CHAPTER 35

RESPONSE TO 'ERASURES AND EXCLUSION'

KIRSTEN WELD

One way of describing the perspectival shift occasioned by the 'archival turn' is to say that scholars have moved from analysing what archives contain to interrogating what they omit. Archival absence is now a robust subject of enquiry, as the four chapters in this section on 'Erasures and Exclusion' attest. Its contours are shaped both by accident (war, fire, neglect, dysfunction) and intent (war, fire, neglect, dysfunction), and its effects are unevenly distributed along lines of class, location, race, gender, sexuality, and politics. With it having become a truism to argue simply that archives' contents and lacunae reflect and are shaped by uneven power relations, the task today is to undertake context-specific drilling into how, and why, and with what effects—and, where possible, to engage in the work of archival repair.

What should be the methodology for apprehending what is not there? Theoretical and empirical foundations have been laid to guide us. Michel-Rolph Trouillot shows how silences enter the process of historical production at multiple points, in ways that are functions of the histories themselves. Ann Laura Stoler highlights the necessity of reading both against and along the archival grain. Archivists like Terry Cook and Verne Harris remind us, respectively, that the quotidian work of archival appraisal culls a supermajority of historical documents before they are ever touched by an acid-free box or finding aid, and that the remaining documentary substrate offers but a sliver of a sliver of a sliver of a window onto the past. Rodney Carter notes that for marginalized groups, absence from official archives can be positive, indicating a strategic refusal to conform to institutional notions of the archivable, or to surrender sovereignty over how and for whom their memory materials are kept.[1]

Building on those foundations, the chapters in this section gesture toward additional strategies for approaching archival absence. Edwina Ashie-Nikoi, Emmanuel Adjei, and Musah Adams map out a 'multi-causal matrix of silence' in accounting for the gaps in Ghanaian archives (and in post-colonial African archives more generally), attentive to the layered interplay of purposeful sabotage, myopic archival policy, bureaucratic deficiency, public disengagement, and conservative archival management frameworks' inability or unwillingness to see traditionally documented materials as worthy of preservation. Rebecca Abby Whiting focuses on the phenomenon of extraterritorial archival removal, namely when records seized during wars of occupation are extracted by foreign armies, as in the case of the Ba'th Regional Command Collection and the Iraqi Jewish Archive after the US invasion in 2003. She stresses that in territories formerly under occupation or colonization, what is experienced on the ground as local archival absence can be the result of what might charitably be called archival relocation, often undertaken in the name of 'preservation' but executed in ways that reinscribe stark asymmetries of power and access. Rebecca Kahn compares the silences in two different South African archival collections documenting the 1990 murder of Stompie Seipei, aiming to see if it is possible to 'reconcile', borrowing the language of South Africa's TRC, the distinct versions of history suggested by each. She advocates, following archival theorists, an approach of 'archival plurality' in assessing what is revealed or concealed in each of the two collections, and notes that it can often be positive for material documenting, say, queer life to be preserved in smaller independent collections rather than in dominant institutional repositories like the TRC archives. Finally, Lae'l Hughes-Watkins links a fire that decimated her own family's archive to a broader reflection on how mainstream information science has historically excluded and effaced Black life, but now sits poised to undertake a systemic reckoning with 'its traditional colonial racist, sexist, classist, [and] capitalistic approaches'. How, she asks, can archival praxis be reconceptualized not only to identify past failures and change preservation priorities in the future, but also to pay its debts to the past—to make reparations by dismantling the very systems predicated upon, and responsible for, those modes of silencing?

The work of identifying silences and absences is crucial, but it should not, as new work in archival studies suggests, stop there. Rather, it must serve as the scaffolding for archival projects that liberate, democratize, pluralize, and redistribute the means of documentary knowledge production with reparatory and community-driven goals. These chapters serve in in this way, commendably, by helping further undermine the surprisingly resilient notions of archival impartiality, universality, and neutrality. They make it more possible for all of us to imagine, support, and/or bring into being different and more polyphonous archival worlds.

NOTES

1. M.-R. Trouillot, *Silencing the Past: Power and the Production of History*, 20th anniversary edition (Boston: Beacon Press, 2015); A. L. Stoler, *Along the Archival Grain: Epistemic Anxieties and Colonial Common Sense* (Princeton, NJ: Princeton University Press, 2010); T. Cook, 'Remembering the Future: Appraisal of Records and the Role of Archives in Constructing Social Memory', in F. X. Blouin, Jr. and W. G. Rosenberg, eds,

Archives, Documentation, and Institutions of Social Memory: Essays from the Sawyer Seminar (Ann Arbor, MI: University of Michigan Press, 2011), 169–181; V. Harris, 'The Archival Sliver: A Perspective on the Construction of Social Memory in Archives and the Transition from Apartheid to Democracy', in C. Hamilton et al., *Refiguring the Archive* (New York: Springer, 2002), 135–151; R. G. S. Carter, 'Of Things Said and Unsaid: Power, Archival Silences, and Power in Silence', *Archivaria* 61 (2006), 215–233.

AFTERWORD
VERNE HARRIS

Shortly before I first received the essays which now make up *Archives: Power, Truth, and Fiction,* as part of an unrelated project, I penned the following lines:

> Since when was archive a repository
> Of reliable evidences
> And not a repertoire
> Of interpretive gestures?
> Since people called themselves 'Enlightened'
> And their polities started conquering 'others'

Prescient perhaps, or serendipitous, given the lines of enquiry pursued by many of the chapters' authors, starting with the introductory reflection by Andrew Prescott and Alison Wiggins. Two of these lines stay with me, both bifurcating endlessly. On the one hand the question of performativity; on the other, a call of justice which is also a call to decolonization. Every engagement with archive is a performance, of course. A dance with ghosts, with or without choreography. A dance, by the way, which can become all about a paying of attention to those who are being ghosted by prevailing relations of power, and can become, moreover, even a mobilizing for justice. Archive as performance, as struggle.

While still reading the chapters, in May 2022, I attended the conference *Met Andere Ogen,* hosted by the City Archives of The Hague in the Netherlands. A conversation between archival institutions painfully aware that too many of that country's communities do not feel safe in institutional spaces; do not feel that they belong there. But what can be achieved in conversations *about* such communities? What do conversations *with* and *in* community look like? What to do when communities are made to feel that they don't belong in the society which institutions represent? And what to do when your institutions carry both the imprint and the weight of a modern democracy born in the crucible of imperialism, white supremacy, capitalism, patriarchal positivism, and other intersecting vectors of oppressive power? The call to decolonization is not a meaningless slogan. It is an injunction to continue dismantling these resilient vectors piece by piece, in a movement which must simultaneously reach back to the knowledges from before colonialism—to be found in indigenous pasts and presents—and reach forward to what is unfolding out of the future. These movements promise at least the possibility of turning othering into belonging.

And yet, what does, or can, 'belonging' mean in contexts where the future, in the words of Leonard Cohen, 'is murder'? When Domesday seems to be upon us? Covid has shown us that it could be only a matter of time before a virus gets away from human ingenuity. Russia's invasion of Ukraine has reminded us of those nuclear arsenal buttons close to the hands of the heartless and the deranged. And the impact of climate change is now evident wherever one travels in the world. More and more of the Earth is becoming unliveable for humans.

And so, while still reading the chapters, and again for an unrelated project, I penned the following lines:

> I love a word that describes precisely how I'm feeling
> At the same time as recalling a long-forgotten pubescent whelming
> Solastalgia
> The experience of being an elder
> At the moment the Earth begins ejecting humanity
> The experience of being a teenager
> At the moment home is no longer where you belong

We humans are migrants, just passing through, no matter how much we behave as if places and spaces and lands belong to us. If anything, we belong to them. Ancient knowledges remind us of this, and of the connections between capitalism, colonialism, and brutal deployments of those cudgels 'property' and 'ownership'.

Not unrelated is a (another) line of enquiry which surfaces, and weaves, through *Archives: Power, Truth, and Fiction*—how the same cudgels, property, and ownership, define archival terrains and what goes on in them. And I'm not thinking here exclusively about institutions, legal departments, chief executives, deeds, bequests, and all the other paraphernalia. I'm thinking of the specialists and the professionals, the elders and the anointed ones—the authorized ones. Enough. We humans are all agents of archive, work with and are worked on by archive every day, no matter how often and how insistently we are told by some that it is a space prescribed by authorization. Enough. Archive resists belonging to anyone. If anything, we humans belong to archive.

INDEX

For the benefit of digital users, indexed terms that span two pages (e.g., 52–53) may, on occasion, appear on only one of those pages.

1381 *see* Peasants' Revolt (1381)

abolition 343
abolitionist archives
    abolition and obsolescence in relation 344
    concept and characteristics of 350
    see also obsolescent archives
academic culture 375
access 337, 375
    access enhancement projects, outcomes
        and lessons from 183
    agency, and 290
    control-based definition of finding
        aids 175–176
    crowdsourced transcription and
        tagging 181–184, 186–187
    data reuse 184
    digital finding aids 175
    digitization as access 176
    Early Modern Manuscripts Online
        (EMMO) project 178–181
    Encoded Archival Description (EAD) 175
    finding aids as access tools, emergence
        of 174
    future possibilities for 176–186
    gatekeepers 397
    Google searches as 'research' 174
    new approaches to 174
    user-generated content 177
    volunteer-generated content 177
    volunteer participation 180
accessibility, definition of 3–4
accidental archives
    accidental creation of term '323–324
    asserted archive, the 327

Brienne Collection 324, 328, 331–332
    circumstantial creation of collections 310
    definition of 323, 331
    incidental archive, the 331
    intercepts 323
    invisible archive, the 332
    shipwreck artefacts 332
    Thurloe Collection 327
    unintentional archive, the 328
    when is an archive created? 324
accountability, archives as tool for 10, 275,
    305, 354
activist archive 437
actors *see* agency
aesthetics of archival decay 379–380
African diaspora 425
agency
    access, and 290
    actors generally 337
    appraisal, and 288
    archive construction, and 287
    arrangement, and 290
    description, and 290
    digitization, and 291
    new roles for archivists 293
    new roles for users 291
    participatory archives 40, 42, 43–44,
        79–80, 183, 292
    persons involved in archives, of 287
    preservation, and 291
    reference service provision, and 290
    selection, and 288
appraisal 287, 489
    agency, and 288
    appraisal decisions, difficulties of 114

bad decisions, social impact of 108–118
born-digital records, of 108, 115, 118
continuum of records assessment and
    review 4–5
corporate structures for generation of
    records, of 115–116
definition of 115–116
differences in approaches between
    corporate archives and library special
    collections 116–118
power structures, and 108, 115–118
process of 107–108, 110, 114
theory of 112–113
transparent forms of 115–116
see also original order
archaeology
    media archaeology 252
    shipwreck artefacts as accidental
        archives 332
archival description see description
archival disputes 455
archival education see education and training
archival footage 397
archival legislation 471
archival mediation 287
archival practice
    artistic practice compared 251
    changes in meanings of core concepts 38
    core concepts and principles of 23–27
    creative practice of archiving 233, 251
    emergence of present-day practice 37
    first published manuals of 22
    images description 251
    media archaeology, and 252
    performative nature of 254
    'record' as *the* foundational concept 24–25
    societal influences on 38
archival processing see archiving practice
archival silence see silence
archival studies
    definition of 22
    first published manuals of 22–23
    history of 22
    intellectual contributions of 21
    meaning of 'archives' 21
    non-recognition of professionalism of
        archivists 28
    paths towards reconciliation with
        archives-related humanities
        scholarship 30–32
    shortcomings of humanities scholarship
        on 28
archival theory 37, 100

archival thinking 267
archival turn 1
archive memory see memory
archives
    abolitionist archives 343
        see also abolitionist archives
    access to 174
    accidental archive, the 323
        see also accidental archives
    activist archives 437–440
    aesthetics of archival decay 379–380
    appraisal of 107
    archivists see archivists
    armed conflict, and see Iraq War (2003)
    artists, and 397
        see also art
    asserted archive, the 327
    audio-visual collections 215
    'belonging,' and 492
    boundaries of 37
    Caribbean archives 359
    changed meaning of 'archive' and
        'archives' 38–39
    conceptions of 100
    corporate archives see corporate archives
    creative practice of archiving see archiving
        practice
    culture and see society and culture
    definition of 'archive' 145
    destruction of 489
        see also destruction/erasure of archives
    digital document management 53
        see also digital archives; digital
        management of documents;
        digitization
    disruptive archives 270
    diverse archives 37, 100
    editors, and see writers and editors
    education and professionalism see
        archivists; professionalism
    erasure of see destruction/erasure of
        archives
    evidential value see evidential value
    exclusion from 489
        see also exclusion from archives
    falsehood see authentication
    family history, and 386
        see also family history
    first published manuals of archives
        management 22

496 INDEX

archives (*Continued*)
  forced migration of 53
    see also migration/movement of
      archives
  frameworks for management of 192
  Ghanaian Public Archives 471
  Gunpowder Plot, and 310
  Haitian archives 359
  historian's experience of using
    archives 375
  historians' understanding of meaning of
    'archive' 47
  humanities meaning of 'archives' 21
  incidental archive, the 331
  inclusiveness 437–438
  interdisciplinary approach to study of 22
  invisible archive, the 332
  Iraq War (2003), and 455
  libraries, and 42
  material aspects of 282
    see also materiality
  material objects 233
  meta-archives 154–158
  metadata *see* metadata
  migration/movement of 53
    see also migration/movement of
      archives
  mobile phone (smartphone) archives 62
  museums, and 42
  networks 145
  networks in relation 145
  non-recognition of profession of 28
  obsolescent archives 343
    see also obsolescent archives
  original order of 107
  'part-to-whole relationship' 256
  participatory archive 287
  Peasants' Revolt (1381) 375
  personal (private) archives 65
  photographic archives 62
  plurality 437–438
  participatory archives 40, 42, 43–44,
    79–80, 183, 292
  professionalism *see* archivists
  publishing, and *see* writers and editors
  queer collections 437
  reparative archives 431, 434
  research tools, as 300
  self-publishing writer-editors, and *see*
    writers and editors
  silence creation tool, as 301–303
  smartphone archives 62

  society and culture, and *see* cultural
    memory; society and culture
  special situations and times, in 337
  State policy and power, and *see* Malawi;
    State policy and power
  technological change, and 39, 48
  truthfulness *see* authenticity
  two understandings of 21
  types of 41
  unintentional archive, the 328
  users and uses of researchers (as archive
    users), 420
    see also art; family history; historical
      collections; Peasants' Revolt (1381);
      researchers (as archive users); writers
      and editors
  VHS tape-based records 58–60
  war, and *see* Iraq War (2003)
  women, historical references to 375
    see also Peasants' Revolt (1381)
  writers and editors, and 359
  see also archivists; documents; memory
archives sheriff 100
archivists
  agency of 287
  devaluing of archival work as fallback or
    second-choice career 29
  devaluing of archival work as feminine
    service industry 28
  devaluing of archival work as
    lower-class 29
  education and training of 23, 121, 192
  first published manuals for 22
  new roles for 293
  non-recognition of professionalism of 28
  professionalism of 121
  self-reappraisal as to destruction/erasure
    of archives 428
  shapers of history, new understanding
    as 28–29
  understanding of meaning of 'archive' 44
  see also agency
armed conflict *see* Iraq War (2003)
arrangement 107
  agency and 290
  see also original order
art and artists' practice
  aesthetics of archival decay 379–380
  art *or* archive document/object if 263–264
  artistic practice and archiving practice
    compared 251
  artists' archive-based fieldwork 397
  artist's studio 233

creative practice of archiving, and 251
description as cultural technique 264–265
film, materiality of 222
images description in archives 21, 251
media archaeology 252
'part-to-whole relationship' 256
photographic archives 62
photography as cataloguing and
  classification technique 256
artefacts *see* material objects
Artificial Intelligence (AI)-assisted
  recordkeeping 107, 267–268, 272
artists *see* art and artists' practice
asserted archive, the 327
assessment *see* appraisal
asylum seekers *see* migration/movement of
  archives
audio-visual collections
  authenticity, and 216
  Bosnian War video records 53
  digital de-materialization of 215–216
  digitization, and 215
  document decay and digitization in
    relation 222
  future potential 216
  materiality of 215
  materiality of film 222
  risks from silence 476
  'slippery texts,' and 219
  transition from document repositories
    into new knowledge production
    centres 228
  translation of material saliency of archives
    into digital environment 223
authenticity
  archival fictions 163
  audio-visual collections 216
  blockchain technology, and 48–49
  current issues summarized 9
  definition of 'authenticity' 3–4
  deterioration of record, as sign of
    authenticity 91
  evidential value, and 160
  false information, categories of 160
  false information, inclusion in
    archives 167
  forgeries 167
  imaginal truth 160
  mundane truth 160
  proofs of authenticity 169
  records as commands, and 73, 81
  records whose truth cannot be
    determined 165

scarcity of record, as sign of
    authenticity 92
  selectivity, and 13
  truth and falsehood in relation 160
  truth claims of archives 160
  truth spaces 160
authors (as archive users) *see* destruc-
    tion/erasure of archives, family
    history, historical collections,
    Peasants' Revolt (1381), writers and
    editors
autocratic regimes *see* State policy and power

Bacon, Francis, Reece Mews studio 247–248
Banda, Kamuza 296
Bargrave, Dr John, cabinets of curiosities 234
barriers 420
Ba'th Regional Command Collection
    (BRCC) 455, 463
BBC archives 397
'belonging,' archives and 492
bibliography 282
black people, exclusion from archives 425
blockchain technology 48–49
born-digital records *see* digital management
    of documents
Bosnian refugees
  destruction of archives 40–41
  Flotel Europa (VHS video) 59
  historical background to Bosnian crisis 56
  mobile phone (smartphone) memories 62
  personal (private) archives 65
  photographic memories 62
  reconfigured global archive 55
  'Scorpions' (Serbian Special Police Unit)
    VHS video 60
  Srebrenica massacre on VHS video 60
  VHS tape-based records 58–60
Brathwaite, Kamau 359
BRCC *see* Ba'th Regional Command
    Collection
Brienne, Simon de, letters collection 324,
    328, 332
'buckroom bagg' *see* Coke, Edward
bureaucracy *see* State policy and power

Canterbury Cathedral Archives 233
Caribbean *see* writers and editors; Windrush
    scandal
cataloguing 107, 310
  bias 198, 204–205
  electronic 39
  metadata, and 12–13, 26–27, 137–140
  networks, and 154–155

498 INDEX

cataloguing (*Continued*)
  standards for 3
  see also description; metadata; original
    order
cinema *see* art
civil rights, exclusion of black people from
  archives 489
class (social), devaluing of archival work as
  lower-class 28
classification see cataloguing
cloud computing 271
Coke, Edward, Gunpowder Plot documents
  collection ('buckroom bagg') 314
collaborative document description
  schemes 255
collections
  'archive within an archive' 317
  audio-visual collections *see* audio-visual
    collections
  circumstantial creation of 310
  historical collections *see* historical
    collections
  materiality of 233
colonialism
  Caribbean postcolonial archives in book
    form 359
  colonial records in National Archive
    (UK) 5–6
  decolonization 121, 359
commands
  acts of language as acts of power 69
  data as 78
  impertinent dialectics 79–80, 82
  records as 71, 78
communities 192
complexity 145
computational archival science *see* digital
  management of documents
computerized methods *see* digital
  management of documents;
  technology
conflict *see* Iraq War (2003)
constructed archive 287
content management 177
continuum
  assessment and review, of 4–5
  records continuum model 24–25, 30–31,
    115–116*f*
  time 90–91
controversies *see* dissensus, corporate
  archives
  appraisal and management of 116–118
  original order 116–118

correspondence *see* letters
creative practice *see* archiving practice
Crimea 397
criminal law, criminology *see* abolitionist
  archives, obsolescent archives, United
  States
crowdsourced transcription and
  tagging 181–184, 186–187
cultural memory
  archives as repositories of public
    memory 449
  description, and 262
  description as cultural technique 264–265
  digital data as 'new memory' 87, 97
  drive to record everything 96
  inverted archives 94
  new memory, archives and 87
  physical records, decay and scarcity of 90
  wartime destruction of 465
  see also society and culture
culture
  academic culture 375
  affective attachment to cultural objects
    and documents 64
  description as cultural technique 264–265
  documentary culture 310–311
  indigenous cultures, memory retrieval
    systems 6
  material culture 233
  see also cultural memory; society and
    culture
curriculum, definition and current
  conception of 121–123

Dahl, Roald, writing hut 245–247
data
  biometric datafying of identity 54
  commands, as 78
  'data' and 'facts' in relation 139
  data doubles 69
  datafication 87
  digital data *see* digitization
  drive to record everything 96
  linked data 154–156
  metadata *see* metadata
  reuse of 184
  rhetorical character of 139
debates *see* dissensus
decay *see* preservation
decolonization 121, 359
description 251, 287
Denmark, *Flotel Europa* (VHS video) 59
description

INDEX   499

agency, and 290
appropriation of objects, and 262–263
archivists' role in 27
art *or* archive document/object?
  if 263–264
artistic practice and archiving practice
  compared 251
collaborative digital labour schemes for
  images description 255
computer image recognition 255
core concept, as 26–27
cultural technique, as 264–265
early physiognomic applications of
  photography 252–253
levels of description 260
listing and lists 256–258
material nature of archives 253–254
media archaeology 252
memory, and 262
'narrative pause,' as 260
order and disorder in relation 256–257
original order, and 257
'part-to-whole relationship' 256
performative nature of archival
  practices 251
photography as cataloguing and
  classification technique 256
power, and 258
reordering and recontextualization of
  objects 262–263
time, and 261–262
transcription and description in
  relation 258–259
viewing of object as completion of
  description process 261
writing, and 260–261
see also representation
descriptive metadata *see* metadata
destruction/erasure of archives 107
act of violence, as 427–428
archival profession's self-reappraisal as
  to 428
author's experience of 425
black people's experience of erasure from
  archives 425
crisis of disinformation, as 428
genocide 53
Ghanaian Public Archives 471
Iraq War (2003) 455
observations on 489
wartime destruction of archives 456
wartime survival of archives 457
see also preservation

deterioration *see* preservation
diasporic archives 53, 100
  African diaspora 425
  Bosnian refugees *see* Bosnian refugees
  Jewish archives 455, 460
digital finding aids 175
digital humanities 145
digital identities 425
digital innovation 267
digital management of documents
  Artificial Intelligence (AI)-assisted
    recordkeeping 267–268, 272
  born-digital records 108, 115, 118
  challenges posed by 268, S18S7, S18S11
  collaborative digital labour schemes for
    images description 255
  computational archival science 276
  computer image recognition 255
  digital collaborative document description
    schemes 255
  digital de-materialization of audio-visual
    collections 215–216
  digital infrastructures (cloud
    computing) 271
  digital records 271
  disruptive nature of 270
  force for change, as 270
  forced migration of archives 53
  future possibilities for 270
  innovation in 267
  intangible record, as force for change 278
  integration of archival and computational
    thinking 275
  new opportunities for 275–276
  paradigm shift, concept of 267
  risk, and 273
  transition from paper to digitized to
    born-digital 268
  trust, and 273
digital materiality 197, 282
digital preservation 174
digitization 197, 287
  access, as 176
  agency, and 291
  appraisal, and 108, 115, 118
  Artificial Intelligence, and 267–268
  digital objectivity as to identity 78
  digital verification of identity 78
  drive to record everything 96
  markup languages 136–137
  mass human migration in relation 53–55

500   INDEX

digitization (*Continued*)
  metadata, and 138–139, 141–142
  networks, and 145–147, 155
  'new memory,' digital data as 87, 97
  risk, and 273
  transition from paper to digitized to
    born-digital 268
  translation of material saliency of archives
    into digital environment 223
  trust, and 273
disciplinary writing 69
discovery 174
discrimination
  archives and 'belonging' 492
  exclusion of black people from
    archives 489
displacement *see* migration/movement of
  archives
disruptive archives 267
dissensus
  dissensual archives 80
  records systems as sites of 79
diverse archives 37, 100
Document Type Definition (DTD) 140–142
documents
  archive within an archive 317
  circumstantial creation of collections 310
  digital collaborative document description
    schemes 255
  ethical documentation 425
  historical documents *see* historical
    collections
  materiality of collections of 233
  transition from paper to digitized to
    born-digital 268
  transition of archives from document
    repositories into new knowledge
    production centres 228
Domesday Book 14

early modern administration 233
Early Modern Letters Online (EMLO)
  project 154–157
Early Modern Manuscripts Online (EMMO)
  project 178–181
ecology 397
editors *see* writers and editors
education and training 23, 121, 192
Encoded Archival Description (EAD) 175
English history *see* historical collections
erasure *see* destruction/erasure of archives
ethical documentation 425
evidential value 160, 310

claims for 160
examples of 162–163, 166, 167
integrity, and 162
state of evidence 171
'value' as core concept 26
see also authenticity
Exchequer Doors 240
exclusion from archives, black people 489

facts 139
falsehood, fiction and forgery *see* authenticity
family history 386
feminist scholarship 375
film *see* art and artists' practice
finding aids *see* access
first nations *see* indigenous cultures
Flotel Europa (VHS video) 59
fonds (record groups), preservation of
  structure of (*respect des fonds*) 7,
  22–23, 116–118
forgeries 167
forgetting 87
Frankétienne 359

gatekeepers 397
gathering (*rasanblaj*) 363
gender *see* women
genocide 53
Ghanaian Public Archives
  creation of silences 474
  Kwame Nkrumah papers, destruction
    of 5, 471, 473, 476, 483
  mindsets of silence 479
  multi-causal matrix of silence 471–474
  multimedia heritage, risks from
    silence 476
  Public Archive Ordinance 1955 474
  remedies for archival silence 482
globalization
  migrant peoples archives, of 54–55
    see also Bosnian refugees
  reconfigured global archives 55
Google searches as 'research' 174
Great Revolt *see* Peasants Revolt
  (1381)Greece 386
Gunpowder Plot
  circumstantial creation of documents
    collection 310
  document collection as 'archive within an
    archive' 317
  Edward Coke's papers ('buckroom
    bagg') 314
  State Paper Office document
    collection 316

production of records 311
threat to government records 310–311

Haitian archives 359
handwriting 197
haptic 215
hard copy *see* documents; records
historical collections
    archives as writing tool 304
    circumstantial creation of 310
    documentary culture 310–311
    Domesday Book 14
    Edward Coke's papers ('buckroom
        bagg') 314
    family history 386
    letters *see* letters
    production of records 311
    technological change, and 39
    written records 310–311
    see also family history; Gunpowder Plot;
        humanities scholarship; Peasants'
        Revolt (1381); writers and editors
humanities scholarship
    definition of 'archives' 21
    paths towards reconciliation with archival
        studies 30–32
    shortcomings of scholarship on archives
        profession 28
    understanding of meaning of 'archive' 46
    see also historical collections
Hussein, Sadam *see* Iraq War (2003)
hut tax (Malawi) receipts 298

identity
    affective attachment to cultural objects
        and documents 64
    archivists' own identity 27
    biometric datafying of 54
    collective identity 55–56
    cultural identity 13
    destruction of 65
    digital verification of 78
    documents of 71–73
    document ownership, and 39–40
    group identity 87–88
    identity archives 41
    local identity 56
    memory, and 56–57, 61–62
    political identity 56
    private archives, and 65
    recovery of 65
    social identity 13, 56, 57
    see also appraisal
image description *see* description

imaginal truth 160
impartiality, new approach to teaching
    of 123
impertinent dialectics 79–80, 82
incidental archive, the 331
inclusiveness, archives and 437–438
indigenous cultures 337
    memory retrieval systems 6
information systems as sites of dissensus 79
infrastructures, digital (cloud
    computing) 271
innovation *see* digital management of
    documents
intangible record, as force for change 278
integrity
    blockchain technology, and 48–49
    definition of 3–4
    evidential value, and 162
    see also authenticity
intercepts 323
interdisciplinary studies 22
Internet 69
    Google searches as 'research' 174
    markup languages 136–137
    World Wide Web (WWW), metadata
        and 136–137
inverted archives 94
invisible archive, the 332
Iraq War (2003)
    Ba'th Regional Command Collection
        (BRCC) 455, 463
    destruction of archives 455–457
    destruction of cultural memory 465
    Iraqi Jewish Archive (IJA) 455, 460

Jewish archives 455, 460
justice system *see* abolitionist archives,
        obsolescent archives, United States

language
    acts of language as acts of power 69
    writing distinguished 198
Laferrière, Dany, 359
legal fictions 163
letters
    Brienne collection 324, 328, 332
    Early Modern Letters Online (EMLO)
        project 154–157
literature *see* letters; poetry, writers and
        editors, writing
libraries, archives, and 42
library special collections, appraisal and
        management of 116–118
lies 386

502 INDEX

linked data 154–156
London School of Economics (LSE)
    archives 397

Malawi
    archives as accountability tool 305
    archives as national history writing
        tool 304
    archives as political power tool 303
    archives as research tools 300
    archives as silence creation tool 301–303
    hut tax (1891) receipts 298
    Malawi Congress Party (MCP)
        membership cards 299
    National Compensation Tribunal
        (NCT) 305
    treaty documents as source of land
        conflicts in southern Malawi 297
management *see* records management
Mandela, Winnie Madikizela- *see* South
    Africa
manuals of archives management, first
    published 22
markup languages 136–137, 140
material culture 233
material objects
    anomalous position in archive s233–234
    description of *see* description
    Dr John Bargrave's cabinets of
        curiosities 234
    examples used for study of 233
    Exchequer Doors 240
    Francis Bacon's Reece Mews
        studio 247–248
    Roald Dahl's writing hut 245–247
    shipwreck artefacts as accidental
        archives 332
    textual archives in relation 233
    viewing of object as completion of
        description process 261
    workplaces and working
        environments 240
materiality
    aesthetics of archival decay 379–380
    attention to 210
    audio-visual forms, of 215
    concepts and definitions of 198
    digital de-materialization of audio-visual
        collections 215–216
    distributed materiality 199
    document collections, of 233

    film, of 222
    formal and forensic materiality 205
    material culture 233
    material nature of archives 253–254, 282
    performative materiality 207
    study of 197
    translation of material saliency of archives
        into digital environment 223
    writing and language distinguished 198
    writing and text distinguished 198–199
    written textual forms, of 197
media archaeology 252
membership cards, political party 299
memory
    archives as repositories of public
        memory 449
    cultural memory *see* cultural memory
    identity, and 56–57, 61–62
    memory boom 91, 93, 95
    'new memory', digital data as 87, 97
    social memory *see* cultural memory
memory retrieval systems, indigenous
    cultures, of 6
meta-archives 154–158
metadata
    cataloguing, and 26–27, 137–140
    cataloguing and 12–13
    'data' and 'facts' in relation 139
    definition of 134–136
    definitional function of 140
    digitization, and 138–139, 141–142
    Document Type Definition
        (DTD) 140–142
    Edward Snowden revelations 134
    function of 139–140
    importance 134
    markup languages 136–137, 140
    national security, and 134
    networks, and 154
    power of 138, 141
    rhetorical character of data 139
    types of 135
    use of concept as technical term 134
    World Wide Web (WWW), and 136–137
migration/movement of archives
    Bosnian refugees 53
        see also Bosnian refugees
    digital technology and mass human
        migration in relation 53–55
    globalization of migrant peoples'
        archives 54–55
    part of archives management, as 53
mobile phone (smartphone) archives 62

INDEX 503

moving image (film) *see* art and artists'
    practice
multimedia collections *see* audio-visual
    collections
museums, archives, and 42

'narrative pause,' description as 260
National Archives (UK)
    access and reference service 290
    additional storage 11
    appraisal and selection 288
    arrangement of archives 116–117
    authenticity of documents 169
    buildings 404–406
    colonial records 5–6
    destruction of records 40–41,107–108
    digital archives 268, 270, 271–273, 276
    Gunpowder Plot documents 310, 317
    letters collections 200
    material objects 233
    medieval and early modern
        records 114–115, 148–149,
        164
    metadata taxonomy 146–147
    'Particular Instance Papers'
        (PIPS) 113–114
    Royal Commission papers 111–113
    user interaction and involvement 291
    Windrush scandal, and 110–111
National Compensation Tribunal *see* Malawi
national security
    Edward Snowden revelations 134
    metadata, and 134
national history, archives as writing tool 304
networks
    cataloguing, and 145–146, 154–155
    digitization, and 145–147, 155
    'directed' networks 148
    Early Modern Letters Online (EMLO)
        project 154–157
    linked data 154–156
    meta-archives 154–158
    metadata, and 154
    network science 145–146
    quantitative network analysis 145–154
    tool for analysing archives, as 145–146
    Tudor Networks of Power
        project 148–154
    weighted networks 148
'new memory' *see* memory
Nkrumah, Kwame, destruction of papers
    of 5, 471, 473, 476, 483
not speaking *see* silence

objects *see* material objects
obsolescent archives
    abolition and obsolescence in relation 344
    obsession about obsolescence 343–344
    'obsolete,' meaning of 343–344
    risk of obsolescence 355–356
    value of obsolescence 344
    see also abolitionist archives
original order
    concept of 117
    corporate emphasis on 116–118
    power structures, and 108
    preservation of structure of (*respect des
        fonds*) 7, 22–23, 116–118
    see also appraisal; cataloguing;
        description;
originality, blockchain technology,
    and 48–49

paper-based records *see* documents; records
participatory archives 40, 42, 43–44, 79–80,
    183, 292
Peasants' Revolt (1381)
    advice to author on using
        archives 378–379
    aesthetics of archival decay 379–380
    archives and power in relation 379
    archives as collections of 'junk' 379–380
    author's absorption with archives 380
    author's difficulties with using
        archives 377–378
    author's increased confidence with using
        archives 379
    author's previous experience of
        archives 377
    author's study of 375–376
    author's use of archives 377
    commodified sexuality of woman's
        body 380–381
    Flemish widows beheading of husbands'
        murderers 382
    forms of references to women 380–381
    gender-based study of 376
    publication of results of research 382
    questions arising from results of
        research 382–383
    rape and power in relation 380–382
penology and criminology *see* abolitionist
    archives, obsolescent archives, United
    States
performative nature of archival practices 251
personal (private) archives 65
photography *see* art; images description

plurality, archives and 437–438
poetry 140, 205–206, 224, 353–354, 361
police *see* abolitionist archives, obsolescent
     archives, United States
politics
  archives and *see* Malawi
  party membership cards 299
  political identity 56
postcolonialism *see* colonialism
power
  appraisal and 108, 115–118
  commands as acts of power 69
  metadata, and 138, 141
  see also Malawi; State policy and power
practice of archiving *see* archiving practice
preservation
  aesthetics of archival decay 379–380
  agency, and 291
  decay time 87
  deterioration of record, as sign of
       authenticity 91
  digital preservation 174
  physical records, decay and scarcity of 90
  preservation of structure (*respect des
       fonds*) 7, 22–23, 116–118
  transfer of archives as means of 457
  see also destruction/erasure of archives
prisons *see* abolitionist archives, obsolescent
     archives, United States
professionalism
  archivists, of 121
  'curriculum,' definition and current
       conception of 121–123
  devaluing of archival work as fallback or
       second-choice career 29
  devaluing of archival work as feminine
       service industry 28
  devaluing of archival work as
       lower-class 29
  education and training *see* archivists
  growth of professional training
       programmes 23
  impartiality, new approach to teaching
       of 123
  new approach to education and
       training 129
  non-recognition of archivist profession 28
Project STAND 433–434
provenance, core concept in archival studies,
       as 25–26
public memory *see* cultural memory
publishing *see* writers and editors

punishment, crime and *see* abolitionist
     archives, obsolescent archives,
     United States

queer collections 437

racism
  archives and 'belonging' 492
  exclusion of black people from
       archives 425
Radical Archives 265
rasanblaj (gathering or reassembling),
       writers and editors 363
records
  commands, as 71, 78
  continuum *see* continuum
  deterioration of record, as sign of
       authenticity 91
  digital records 271
  drive to record everything 96
  foundational concept in archival
       studies 24–25
  management *see* records management
  records systems as sites of dissensus 79
  transition from paper to digitized to
       born-digital 268
  transition to data-as-command 78
  whose truth cannot be determined 165
records management
  artificial intelligence, and 4–5
  blockchain technology, and 48–49
  differences in approaches between
       corporate archives and library special
       collections 116–118
  rise of 47–48
  standards for 107–108
  see also digital management of documents
reference service provision, agency and 290
refugees *see* migration/movement of archives
reliability, definition of 3–4
reparative archives 431, 434
representation *see* description
research, Google searches as 'research' 174
researchers (as archive users)
  archives as research tools 300
  self-curation 43–44
  understanding of meaning of 'archive' 43
  see also destruction/erasure of archives;
       family history; historical collections;
       Peasants' Revolt (1381); writers and
       editors
review *see* appraisal
risk

digital management of documents,
and 273
digitization and 274
obsolescence, of 355–356
silence, from 476

scarcity of records, as sign of authenticity 92
'Scorpions' (Serbian Special Police Unit),
VHS video by 60
Seipei, Stompie *see* South Africa; Stompie
Seipei murder
selection *see* appraisal
self-curation 43–44
self-publishing *see* writers and editors
sexual identity, queer collections 437
shipwreck artefacts as accidental
archives 332
signatures, historical 114
silence 471, 489
appraisal, and 472
'archival silence' concept 471–472
archives as creative tool of 301–303
creation of 472, 474
erasure, and 471
Ghanaian Public Archives 471
marginalized peoples' past, of 472
non-neutrality of archives 471–472
silencing as act of State power 473–474
see also Ghanaian Public Archives
'slippery texts' 219
smartphone archives 62
Snowden, Edward 134
social memory *see* cultural memory
society and culture
archives and 'belonging' 492
limitations of archives as agents of social
transformation 438–439
see also cultural memory
South Africa
activist archives 437–440
archival inclusiveness and
plurality 437–438
limitations of TRC archive as agent of
social transformation 438–439
limitations of TRC archive as repository of
public memory 449
Mandela United Football Club
(MUFC) 443
queer collections, establishment of 439
Stompie Seipei, murder of 437–438, 443
Truth and Reconciliation Commission
(TRC) 437–439, 443, 444, 448, 449

Winnie Madikizela-Mandela,
and 437–438, 443–449
special collections *see* library special
collections
Srebrenica massacre *see* Bosnian refugees
State policy and power
abolitionist archives, and 343
bureaucracy as apparatus exercise of State
power 75
control and destruction by 296–297
historical document collections *see*
Gunpowder Plot; historical
collections
obsolescent archives, and 343
paradoxical relationship with archives 296
police and prisons as purveyors of
punishment 347
punishment paradigm of justice
system 345, 347
silence creation as act of *see* Ghanaian
Public Archives; silence
see also criminal law; Ghanaian Public
Archives; Iraq War (2003); Malawi;
South Africa; United States
Stompie Seipei murder 437–438, 443

tax records, hut tax (Malawi) receipts 298
techniques of archiving *see* archival practice
technology
blockchain technology 48–49
cloud computing 271
computer image recognition 255
future technology 48
historical archives and technological
change 39
mobile phone (smartphone) archives 62
VHS tape-based records 58–60
see also digital archives; digital finding
aids; digital management of
documents; digitization; Internet
text
of film 222
materiality of *see* materiality
writing distinguished 198–199
three-dimensional objects *see* material
objects
Thurloe, John, papers collection 327
time, description and 261–262
Tomić, Vladimir, *Flotel Europa* (VHS
video) 59
training and education 23, 121, 192
trust 273

Truth and Reconciliation Commission
(TRC) *see* South Africa
truthfulness *see* authenticity
Tudor Networks of Power project 148–154

unintentional archive, the 328
United Kingdom *see* National Archives (UK)
United States
abolitionist archives 350
black people's experience of erasure from
archives 425
exclusion of black people from
archives 489
obsolescent archives 344
police and prisons as purveyors of
punishment 347
Project STAND 433–434
punishment paradigm of justice
system 345
reparative archives 431, 434
self-curation 43–44
transfer of Iraqi archives to 457
usability, definition of 3–4
user-generated content, access and 177
users
access and 177
agency, and 291
experience of archives 420
experience of erasure from archives 425
new roles for 291
researchers (as archive users) 43
user-generated content 177

value *see* evidential value
VHS tape-based records 58–60
volunteer-generated content 177
volunteer participation 180

war *see* Iraq War (2003)
weeding 113
West Indies *see* writers and editors;
Windrush scandal
Windrush scandal 107
women
devaluing of archival work as feminine
service industry 28
feminist scholarship 375
participation in Peasants' Revolt
(1381) 375
work of archiving *see* archiving practice
workplaces and working environments as
collectable objects 240
World Wide Web (WWW), metadata
and 136–137
writers and editors
Caribbean postcolonial archives in book
form 359
editing and archives in relation 360
editing as *rasanblaj* (gathering or
reassembling) 363
editor as 'midwife' 359–360
editor's role in making archives 'speak' 359
triangular relationship of editor, author,
and text 359–360
triangular slave trade in relation
to editor/author/archive
triangle 359–360
writing
description, and 260–261
disciplinary writing 69
language distinguished 198
Roald Dahl's writing hut 245–247
text distinguished 198–199
written textual forms of materiality 197

www.ingramcontent.com/pod-product-compliance
Lightning Source LLC
Chambersburg PA
CBHW081813290825
31867CB00005B/437